Cooking Light.

ANNUAL RECIPES 2014

Oxmoor House.

A Year at *Cooking Light*®

2013 was a remarkable year for food in America. Millions of Americans continued to embrace the idea that healthy can be delicious and satisfying, and eating healthfully need not keep them from enjoying the food revolution taking place in the country today. American chefs continued to heed the call for healthier restaurant fare, igniting a passionate foodie following. Artisans rose up to show that the food made here in America can be—and is—just as good as the old-world counterparts held so long as the pinnacle in food perfection. Farmers' markets flourished, bringing grower and consumer into an exciting relationship with one another. For our own part, we grew a bounty of fruits and vegetables in our own garden, and featured the produce in our Summer Cookbook recipes. What's fresh, light, and fully delicious is in, and we couldn't be happier.

▲ **Gazpacho with Lemon-Garlic Shrimp** *(page 204)*
The quintessential chilled appetizer soup takes on main-course appeal with a topping of sautéed garlicky shrimp and sliced cucumbers and bell peppers.

Here are some of the year's highlights as we celebrate great food, joyful cooking, and a food-positive, healthy life:

• In January, we vowed to "start your year off light" by devoting our pages to easy recipes, tips, and strategies to make this the healthiest year ever (page 19). And just because we were lightening things up, didn't mean we were going to spare you your favorite indulgence, chocolate, so we shared satisfying, guilt-free 100-calorie chocolate treats. (page 24)

• We paid homage to home cooks in April's "Everything-is-Fast" issue. Our 40 Meals Under 40 Minutes feature (page 75) offered an arsenal of speedy recipes designed to help get a great meal on the table fast. With the same commitment to ease, we loaded the pages of August with simple, super easy, 5-ingredient entrées plus 5-minute sides and salads. (page 185)

• For the first time, our annual Summer Cookbook featured recipes inspired exclusively by our very own garden. We went fully homegrown with our annual ode to the season, developing recipes from local heirloom bounty. We shared our first batch of simple, delicious vegetable-based dishes along with tips for growing, preparing, pairing, and storing. (page 129)

• In October, we populated our pages with a collection of our all-time favorites. We polled readers and editors for their favorite recipes, and then retested, tasted, and narrowed the list to a stellar, enduring Top 25. Our selection ranged from crispy fish, lemonade cake, enchiladas, and dips to pancakes, soups, stuffed jalapeños, and fresh pear cocktails. (page 271)

• We kicked off 2013 by transforming the traditional recipe box into a digital, shareable version with our brand-new "Scan It, Cook It!" app. We know from web traffic reports that more and more of you are cooking from your tablets and phones, so we focused on making our tablet edition more cook-friendly and robust by improving the design to feature bigger recipe displays and larger, more beautiful photos.

• This year's annual Holiday Cookbook, a reader and staff favorite, is geared towards making this the tastiest and easiest holiday ever. We challenged our Test Kitchen to uphold the flavors and traditional foods we cherish *and* make the cook's list of duties fewer. We're sure you'll find our collection of 20 faster, shorter, and make-ahead recipes exactly what you need to enjoy a stress-free and delicious holiday. (page 300)

It is you, our readers, who inspire us to do what we do. You continue to empower us daily through your positive letters, e-mails, and social media comments. Thank you for encouraging us and connecting with us so that we may continue to bring you joy through delicious food.

Scott Mowbray
Editor

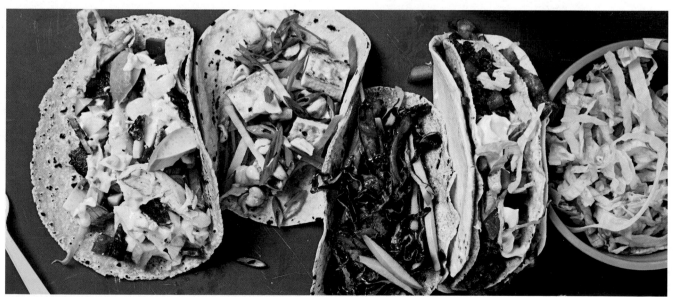

▲ **Cobb Salad Tacos** *(page 110),* **Super Crunch Tofu Tacos** *(page 111),* **Beer-Braised Chicken Tacos with Cabbage Slaw** *(page 111),* **Double-Layer Beef Tacos** *(page 110)*
This recipe turns one of our favorite salads into a taco. From-scratch blue cheese dressing melds with rotisserie chicken, bacon, avocado, lettuce, and tomato to make a quick and delicious meal.

Our Favorite Recipes

Not all recipes are created equal.

At *Cooking Light*, only those that have received a passing grade from our Test Kitchen staff and food editors—a group with very high standards—make it onto the pages of our magazine. We test each recipe rigorously, often two or three times, to ensure that it's healthy, reliable, and tastes as good as it possibly can. So which of our recipes are our favorites? They're the dishes that we can't forget: The ones readers write or call us about, the ones our staff regularly make for their own families and friends.

▶ **Four-Mushroom Pesto Pizza** *(page 82)*
Move over pepperoni and tomato sauce. Pesto and mushrooms are the new darlings in the pizza world. Refrigerated pizza dough speeds up prep, putting dinner on the table quicker.

▼ **Seared Scallop Salad with Prosciutto Crisps** *(page 153)*
With so few ingredients, it's crucial to splurge and buy the best quality scallops for optimum flavor. You won't be disappointed!

Garden Alfredo with Chicken *(page 151)*.
Fresh spring vegetables mingle with tender pasta and chicken in a light, creamy Alfredo sauce.

Cod with Fennel and Orange *(page 106)*
Banish your fear of cooking fish, and let the microwave do its magic for fool-proof results. A zip-top bag traps the steam, cooking the fish gently while keeping it moist and flavorful.

Bulgur with Peaches and Mint
(page 241)
This recipe wowed us with its summertime flavor. Ripe peaches, fresh mint, and hazelnuts add pizzaz to this speedy bulgur side.

Fettuccine with Seared Tomatoes, Spinach, and Burrata *(page 63)* Looking to try a new, but somewhat familiar cheese? Burrata is a fresh cheese made of mozzarella and cream. Once hard to find, it is now available in supermarkets throughout America and makes a great addition to this tomato and spinach pasta.

Banana Bread with Chocolate Glaze *(page 278)*
Banana breads never go out of style and are always a welcome hostess gift. We upped the yum appeal with a chocolate glaze to make it even more irresistible.

Breakfast Quinoa *(page 146)*
Try this whole grain in a new way: breakfast! A serving of fruit on top of high-protein quinoa will kick start any day.

BLT Panzanella Salad *(page 193)*
We took the ingredients of a favorite sandwich and created this riff on the classic Italian bread salad.

Grilled Stuffed Jalapeños *(page 274)*
The rich and creamy combination of bacon, cream cheese, and cheddar nicely contrasts the muted spice of grilled jalapeño peppers. This irresistible appetizer is a healthier alternative to the popular breaded and fried version.

▲ **Butternut-Kale Lasagna** *(page 55)*
Gruyere-spiked Béchamel sauce drapes over the noodles and squash for velvety richness. Hearty, earthy kale perfectly balances the sweet butternut squash, and crunchy, toasted pecans crown the top of this luscious lasagna.

▲ **Shrimp and Grits** *(page 69)*
A Southern favorite, this one-dish dinner combines hearty, quick-cooked grits with shrimp in a spicy cream sauce.

▲ **Creamy, Light Potato Soup** *(page 40)*
The secret ingredient in this recipe is cauliflower—it has two-thirds fewer calories per ounce than starchy potato.

▲ **Great Plains Burger** *(page 161)*
This burger captures the best elements of the Great Plains: corn, bison, grainy mustard, and fresh herbs.

Grilled Chicken with Tomato-Avocado Salad
(page 152)
This quick and easy dinner captures the essence of peak summer produce. A ranch-style buttermilk dressing balances the heat of the chipotle and cumin in the rub on the chicken.

Quick Beef Stroganoff *(page 45)*
This comforting family classic comes in at under 400 calories. The exotic mushroom blend adds a special touch.

Tsukune (Japanese Chicken Meatballs) *(page 252)*
These chicken meatballs are seasoned with ginger, soy sauce, brown sugar, and chile to create the perfect balance of sweet, savory, and spicy.

Tiramisu *(page 65)*
Our recipe makeover of the creamy-coffee-choco classic has less than half the calories. It features decadent espresso-soaked ladyfingers layered in mascarpone and cream cheeses topped with cocoa.

Chocolate Tacos with Ice Cream and Peanuts *(page 107)*
These dessert tacos garnered the highest rating from our food staff. Impress everyone with this show-stopping, make-ahead dessert.

Almond Brittle *(page 105)*
This brittle is foolproof. Steady microwave heat combined with regular stirring cooks it to perfection—no candy-making skills required!

Peach Cobbler Ice Cream with Bourbon-Caramel Sauce *(page 141)*
Here's a delicious ice-cream recipe that has all the flavors of traditional peach cobbler but doesn't require an ice-cream maker. Baked pieces of refrigerated pie dough are stirred in for that top crust crunch.

Avocado Ice Pops *(page 183)*
The popsicle craze has taken the country by storm with some of the most unexpected ingredients and flavors. Avocado's creaminess is perfect for freezing on a stick.

Cantaloupe Sherbet *(page 136)*
Our creamy sherbet captures the essence of fresh, ripe summer melon.

Spiced Apple Two-Bite Tarts *(page 316)*
These little tarts are perfect bite-sized treats. The pastry is reminiscent of pecan shortbread, the apples are graciously spiced, and it all comes together with a dollop of crème fraîche.

Spaghetti with Clams and Slow-Roasted Cherry Tomatoes *(page 52)*
Sweet, slow-roasted tomatoes come together with clams and pasta to create a crowd-pleasing dish.

Key Lime Pie *(page 172)*
There's an addictive quality to Key lime pie's finely tuned balance of the sweet and tart, the creamy and the crunchy, all crowned with fluffy cream.

Blush Mac and Cheese with Tomatoes *(page 85)*
Grape tomatoes add sweetness that pairs well with sharp cheddar cheese and spinach in this contemporary spin on mac and cheese.

Cheddar and Potato Pierogies *(page 331)*
We tried our hand at making pierogies and found out they're easier than we thought! Buttery, cheesy, and all-around good, potato dumplings will make everyone happy, including the kids.

Asparagus and Lemon Risotto *(page 106)*
Surprise! The classic recipe's creamy texture is microwave magic! Because microwave heat hits the Arborio rice from all sides, it cooks more evenly than stovetop risotto and requires less stirring, slashing hands-on time, too!

Classic Crab Cakes *(page 99)*
Crab cake lovers are fierce about the ratio of crab to filler. Our cakes put the crab forward by using just enough mayo and breadcrumbs to hold the mixture together.

Grilled Halibut with Tarragon Beurre Blanc *(page 81)*
Fresh tarragon infuses the white wine–butter sauce to add a touch of elegance to grilled fresh fish.

Corn Bread Stuffing Muffins *(page 305)*
Imagine all the wonderful flavors of Thanksgiving—sausage, celery, sage, and thyme—in a muffin!

Parmesan-Rosemary Flatbread Crackers *(page 247)*
Cheesy, tasty, and crispy—a homemade cracker that's worth the extra effort. Jazz up snack time with these savory bites!

Sunflower Granola Breakfast Parfaits *(page 155)*
For an on-the-go breakfast, make the granola ahead, and then serve with fresh raspberries and Greek yogurt.

Manhattan-Glazed Chicken *(page 76)*
Here we riff off the flavors of a Manhattan cocktail, which is traditionally made with rye whiskey or bourbon, maraschino cherries, and orange rind.

CONTENTS

ISBN-13: 978-0-8487-3989-8
ISBN-10: 0-8487-3989-2

Printed in the United States of America
First Printing 2013

Be sure to check with your health-care provider before making any changes in your diet.

Oxmoor House
Vice President, Brand Publishing: Laura Sappington
Editorial Director: Leah McLaughlin
Creative Director: Felicity Keane
Brand Manager: Michelle Turner Aycock
Senior Editor: Andrea C. Kirkland, M.S., R.D.
Managing Editor: Elizabeth Tyler Austin

Cooking Light Annual Recipes 2014
Editor: Rachel Quinlivan West, R.D.
Art Director: Christopher Rhoads
Production Manager: Tamara Nall Wilder
Assistant Production Manager: Diane Rose Keener

Contributors
Editor: Holley Grainger, M.S., R.D.
Project Editors: Laura Medlin, Julia Sayers
Designer: Carol Damsky
Copy Editor: Jacqueline Giovanelli
Indexer: Mary Ann Laurens
Fellows: Susan Kemp, Elizabeth Laseter, Jeffrey Preis,
    April Smitherman

Time Home Entertainment Inc.
Publisher: Jim Childs
Vice President, Brand & Digital Strategy: Steven Sandonato
Executive Director, Marketing Services: Carol Pittard
Executive Director, Retail & Special Sales: Tom Mifsud
Director, Bookazine Development & Marketing: Laura Adam
Executive Publishing Director: Joy Butts
Associate Publishing Director: Megan Pearlman
Finance Director: Glenn Buonocore
Associate General Counsel: Helen Wan

Cooking Light
Editor: Scott Mowbray
Creative Director: Dimity Jones
Executive Managing Editor: Phillip Rhodes
Executive Editor, Food: Ann Taylor Pittman
Executive Editor, Digital: Allison Long Lowery
Special Publications Editor: Mary Simpson Creel, M.S., R.D.
Senior Food Editor: Timothy Q. Cebula
Senior Editor: Cindy Hatcher
Assistant Editor, Nutrition: Sidney Fry, M.S., R.D.
Assistant Editors: Kimberly Holland, Hannah Klinger
Test Kitchen Manager: Tiffany Vickers Davis
Recipe Testers and Developers: Robin Bashinsky, Adam Hickman,
    Deb Wise
Art Directors: Rachel Cardina Lasserre, Sheri Wilson
Senior Designer: Anna Bird
Designer: Hagen Stegall
Assistant Designer: Nicole Gerrity
Tablet Designer: Daniel Boone
Photo Director: Julie Claire
Assistant Photo Editor: Amy Delaune
Senior Photographer: Randy Mayor
Senior Prop Stylist: Cindy Barr
Assistant Prop Stylist: Lindsey Lower
Chief Food Stylist: Kellie Gerber Kelley
Food Styling Assistant: Blakeslee Wright
Production Director: Liz Rhoades
Production Editor: Hazel R. Eddins
Production Coordinator: Caitlin Murphree Miller
Copy Director: Susan Roberts McWilliams
Copy Editor: Kate Johnson
Research Editor: Michelle Gibson Daniels
Administrative Coordinator: Carol D. Johnson
Editorial Assistant: Alice Summerville
CookingLight.com Editor: Mallory Daughtery Brasseale
CookingLight.com Assistant Editor/Producer: Michelle Klug

To order additional publications, call 1-800-765-6400 or 1-800-491-0551.

For more books to enrich your life, visit **oxmoorhouse.com**

To search, savor, and share thousands of recipes, visit **myrecipes.com**

Cover: *Tomato Ravioli (page 186)*
Back Cover (left to right): *Grilled Sirloin Steak with Mango and Chile Salad (page 203),*
Chicken and Vegetable Stir Fry (page 183),
Pound Cake with Strawberry Glaze (page 112)
Page 1: *Smoky Bell Pepper Soup (page 307)*

START YOUR YEAR OFF LIGHT

Eat better! Lose weight! Put some bounce in your step with recipes and tips for your healthiest year ever.

FLAVOR

Toast Each Day!

The hot, crunchy breakfast standby, now decked out with savory and sweet toppings for 200-calorie (or fewer) meals to keep weekday mornings interesting

Ricotta-Pistachio Toast
Spread 2 tablespoons light ricotta cheese on crusty whole-grain bread. Drizzle 1 teaspoon olive oil over ricotta. Sprinkle with 1 tablespoon crushed dry-roasted salted pistachios.
CALORIES 176; **FAT** 10.9g (sat 2.6g); **SODIUM** 137mg

Garlicky Beans on Toast
Heat 1 teaspoon olive oil, ¼ cup canned white beans, 1 minced garlic clove, and ¼ teaspoon crushed red pepper over medium heat. Spoon over sourdough bread. Sprinkle with fresh rosemary and parsley.
CALORIES 179; **FAT** 5.6g (sat 0.7g); **SODIUM** 168mg

Green Eggs and Ham Toast
Spread 1 teaspoon pesto on a slice of toasted ciabatta. Top with 1 (¾-ounce) slice Canadian bacon and 1 soft-boiled egg (or scrambled, if preferred). Sprinkle with thinly sliced fresh basil.
CALORIES 200; **FAT** 9.1g (sat 2.6g); **SODIUM** 499mg

Cheddar 'n' Apple Cinnamon-Raisin Toast
Melt ¾ ounce shredded sharp cheddar cheese over toasted cinnamon-raisin bread. Top with thinly sliced Granny Smith apple.
CALORIES 180; **FAT** 8.6g (sat 4.5g); **SODIUM** 237mg

Curiously Citrus Toast
Spread 1 tablespoon chocolate-hazelnut spread (such as Nutella) on a slice of crusty French bread. Top with fresh orange segments; sprinkle with sea salt.
CALORIES 191; **FAT** 5.6g (sat 1.8g); **SODIUM** 312mg

Meyer Lemon Panna Cotta

Hands-on: 35 min. Total: 4 hr. 35 min.
Don't pine for dessert ... just make it lighter. This panna cotta has the silky texture of the classic for a blissful, guilt-free hit of sweet and tang. Meyer lemon—a lemon/orange hybrid— is sweeter than conventional lemon. If you don't have access to Meyer lemons, you can use a regular lemon and enjoy a dessert that's a bit more tart.

1 Meyer or regular lemon
11 tablespoons 2% reduced-fat milk, divided
½ cup half-and-half
⅓ cup sugar
¼ teaspoon salt
1¾ teaspoons unflavored gelatin
1½ cups reduced-fat buttermilk
Cooking spray
Mint leaves and lemon rind strips (optional)

1. Remove rind from lemon using a vegetable peeler, avoiding white pith. Squeeze 3 tablespoons juice from lemon. Combine rind, ½ cup milk, half-and-half, sugar, and salt in a small saucepan; bring to a simmer over medium heat (do not boil). Remove pan from heat; cover and let stand 20 minutes. Discard rind. Sprinkle gelatin over remaining 3 tablespoons milk in a small bowl, and let stand at least 10 minutes. Return half-and-half mixture to medium heat; cook 1 minute or until very hot. Add gelatin mixture, stirring with a whisk until dissolved (about 1 minute). Stir in buttermilk and 3 tablespoons juice. Divide mixture among 4 (6-ounce) ramekins or custard cups coated with cooking spray. Cover and refrigerate 4 hours.
2. Run a knife around outside edges of panna cotta. Place a plate upside down on top of each cup; invert onto plate. Garnish with mint and rind, if desired. Serves 4

CALORIES 185; **FAT** 6.3g (sat 3.8g, mono 0.8g, poly 0.1g); **PROTEIN** 7g; **CARB** 26g; **FIBER** 0.1g; **CHOL** 22mg; **IRON** 0.1mg; **SODIUM** 258mg; **CALC** 214mg

Love the Lemon a Lot

Squeeze, zest, and slice this flavor- and mood-lifter. Nothing cheers up food the way lemons do. Keep lots of fat, juicy ones on hand. **Zing No. 1** Stir chopped sections into fruit salsa for an extra pop of flavor; pair with grilled pork or fish. **Zing No. 2** Top pizza with thin slices before baking to add a little zip to cut through the rich, gooey cheese. **Zing No. 3** Perk up snack time by sprinkling freshly grated rind over hot popcorn. **Zing No. 4** Add lightly seared slices to Gruyère or Brie for a bright take on grown-up grilled cheese.

SIX MARINARA USES

Of course you'll want to toss it with pasta right out of the pot. But here are some other great ways to cook with this versatile sauce.

Mussels Marinara

Bring 3 cups marinara to a simmer in a large skillet. Add 4 pounds scrubbed and debearded mussels; cover and cook 5 minutes or until shells open. Serve with crusty bread or over cooked spaghetti. Serves 4

CALORIES 341; **FAT** 9.8g (sat 1.6g); **SODIUM** 623mg

Marinara Poached Eggs

Bring 3 cups marinara and ½ teaspoon crushed red pepper to a simmer in a skillet. Make 4 wells in marinara; crack 1 egg into each. Cook, covered, 6 minutes or until desired degree of doneness. Serve with toast. Serves 4

CALORIES 187; **FAT** 8.4g (sat 1.6g); **SODIUM** 418mg

Italian Tomato Soup

Bring 3 cups marinara and 2 cups unsalted chicken stock to a boil, and stir in 1 cup cooked ditalini pasta. Top the soup with 1 ounce shaved fresh pecorino Romano cheese. Serves 4

CALORIES 232; **FAT** 5.5g (sat 1.2g); **SODIUM** 627mg

Sausage Pizza

Top the pizza dough with ¾ cup marinara; 3 ounces cooked, crumbled hot turkey Italian sausage; and 2 ounces shredded part-skim mozzarella cheese. Bake at 450° for 15 minutes or until the crust is browned. Top the pizza with ⅓ cup torn basil leaves. Serves 6

CALORIES 220; **FAT** 5.5g (sat 1.5g); **SODIUM** 554mg

Shrimp Vindaloo

Bring 2 cups marinara, ½ cup unsalted chicken stock, 2 teaspoons garam masala, 1 teaspoon hot paprika, and 1 pound quartered red potatoes to a boil in a large saucepan. Cover, reduce heat, and simmer 15 minutes. Add 1 pound peeled and deveined shrimp; cover and cook 6 minutes. Serve over rice, and garnish with cilantro. Serves 4

CALORIES 343; **FAT** 4.6g (sat 0.7g); **SODIUM** 485mg

Braised Lamb Shanks

Brown 4 lamb shanks in a Dutch oven; add ½ cup red wine, scraping pan to loosen browned bits. Add 3 cups marinara; bring to a boil. Cover, reduce heat, and simmer 2 hours. Stir in a handful of coarsely chopped pitted kalamata olives in the last 10 minutes. Serves 4

CALORIES 312; **FAT** 17.8g (sat 5.2g); **SODIUM** 507mg

COMFORTS

Make A Big Batch of This Perfect Marinara

This deep, summery-flavored tomato sauce can round out so many dishes. You'll want to keep bags of the stuff in the freezer.

Freezable • Make Ahead
Vegetarian

Slow-Cooker Marinara

Hands-on: 30 min. Total: 9 hr.
Freeze marinara for up to 3 months.

3 tablespoons extra-virgin olive oil
3 cups chopped onion
³/₄ cup diced carrot
¹/₂ cup diced celery
¹/₄ cup minced fresh garlic
3 tablespoons chopped fresh oregano
¹/₄ teaspoon crushed red pepper
2 tablespoons unsalted tomato paste
¹/₂ cup dry red wine (such as cabernet sauvignon)
5¹/₂ pounds plum tomatoes, peeled and chopped
³/₄ cup chopped fresh basil
1¹/₂ teaspoons salt
¹/₂ teaspoon freshly ground black pepper

1. Heat a large skillet over medium-high heat. Add oil; swirl to coat. Add onion and next 5 ingredients (through red pepper); sauté 8 minutes. Add tomato paste; cook 2 minutes, stirring frequently. Add wine; cook 2 minutes or until liquid almost evaporates.
2. Place vegetable mixture and tomatoes in an electric slow cooker. Cover and cook on LOW for 8 hours. Place 3 cups tomato mixture in a blender. Remove center piece of blender lid; secure lid on blender. Place a clean towel over opening in blender lid. Blend until smooth. Return tomato mixture to slow cooker. Add basil, salt, and black pepper. Cook, uncovered, on HIGH 30 minutes. Serves 12 (serving size: about ½ cup)

CALORIES 104; **FAT** 3.9g (sat 0.6g, mono 2.5g, poly 0.6g); **PROTEIN** 2.8g; **CARB** 14.7g; **FIBER** 3.7g; **CHOL** 0mg; **IRON** 1mg; **SODIUM** 319mg; **CALC** 51mg

VEGGIES

Love This Ugly Root Vegetable

Root veggies are healthy, fiber-rich, and in season. With our Cinderella salad, the ugliest one of all—celery root—gets a gorgeous makeover.

Celery Root-Arugula Salad

Hands-on: 12 min. Total: 45 min. It's a good idea to take a sharp knife to the gnarly celery root (also called celeriac), and cut it as finely as possible. If you have a mandoline, use it to make quick, even pieces. Although all celery root will be misshapen and scruffy looking, don't buy roots that are shriveled or that give to the touch.

2 tablespoons extra-virgin olive oil
2 tablespoons fresh lemon juice
¹/₄ teaspoon kosher salt
¹/₄ teaspoon freshly ground black pepper
2 cups matchstick-cut peeled celery root
2 cups thinly diagonally sliced celery
¹/₂ cup very thinly vertically sliced red onion
1¹/₂ cups halved satsuma or other mandarin orange sections
1 cup baby arugula
¹/₂ cup parsley leaves

1. Combine extra-virgin olive oil, lemon juice, salt, and black pepper in a medium bowl, stirring well with a whisk. Add celery root, celery, and onion; toss to coat. Let celery root mixture stand 30 minutes. Add orange sections, arugula, and parsley; toss gently to combine. Serves 6 (serving size: about ⅔ cup)

CALORIES 92; **FAT** 4.9g (sat 0.7g, mono 3.4g, poly 0.6g); **PROTEIN** 1.5g; **CARB** 12.2g; **FIBER** 2.4g; **CHOL** 0mg; **IRON** 0.8mg; **SODIUM** 150mg; **CALC** 61mg

A FOOD LOVER'S RESOLUTION: PLANT SOME HEALTHY GREENS

Gardening gear is likely gathering dust instead of dirt right now, but it's actually prime season for indoor sprouting. Try your hand at growing cut-and-come-again lettuce, a fast and easy crop that can be a mealtime game changer.

Find a sunny windowsill, and get some seeds going; you should be able to snip sizable leaves in about four to six weeks. We like varieties such as arugula, butter-crunch, or (with what is possibly the best varietal name ever) Drunken Woman, all available at southernexposure.com.

NUTRITION

Eat More of The Easiest Whole Grain

Bulgur is wheat that's been parboiled, dried, and cracked into nibbly bits. It cooks fast and tastes good.

Cinnamon-Banana Crunch Bowl

Combine ¼ cup plain nonfat Greek yogurt, 1 teaspoon honey, and a dash of cinnamon in a small bowl. Toss ½ cup cooked bulgur, 1 tablespoon chopped toasted walnuts, and 1 tablespoon brown sugar. Top with ⅓ cup fresh banana slices. Dollop yogurt mixture over bulgur mixture. Sprinkle with additional cinnamon, if desired.

CALORIES 255; FAT 5g (sat 0.4g); FIBER 6.1g; SODIUM 29mg

Chicken-Avocado Salad

Combine 2 teaspoons olive oil, 1 teaspoon orange juice, 1 teaspoon sherry vinegar, and a dash of salt and pepper in a small bowl. Toss ¾ cup cooked bulgur with 2 ounces shredded roasted chicken. Top with ¼ cup sliced avocado and 6 halved cherry tomatoes. Sprinkle with 1 tablespoon feta cheese. Drizzle dressing over bulgur mixture; toss gently to coat. Sprinkle with cilantro.

CALORIES 381; FAT 18.9g (sat 4g); FIBER 9.9g; SODIUM 433mg

Bulgur with Steak and Chickpeas

Combine 1 tablespoon olive oil, 1 teaspoon fresh lemon juice, ¼ teaspoon honey, ¼ teaspoon cumin, and a dash of kosher salt. Combine ¾ cup cooked bulgur, ¼ cup canned chickpeas, ¼ cup minced red bell pepper, and 2 tablespoons sliced red onion. Add dressing; toss. Sprinkle with 2 tablespoons fresh parsley. Top with 2 ounces grilled flank steak.

CALORIES 390; FAT 14g (sat 2.9g); FIBER 9.9g; SODIUM 347mg

A HANDY GUIDE: GRAIN-TO-WATER RATIOS

BARLEY
1 part grain to 2½ parts water

BROWN RICE
Boil like pasta; drain when tender.

FARRO
1 part grain to 2½ parts water

OATS, STEEL-CUT
1 part grain to 3 parts water

QUINOA
1 part grain to 1½ parts water

COOKING & STORING BULGUR

1. Boil a Big Batch
Combine 1½ cups medium-grain bulgur and 3 cups water in a medium saucepan. Bring to a boil. Cover, reduce heat, and simmer for 10 to 12 minutes or until tender. Drain, if necessary. Yield: 5 cups.

2. Store the Extras
Cooked grains should be stored in the refrigerator, where they will keep for up to 1 week. They are easily frozen, too—so cook up a big batch, divvy into manageable portions, freeze, and enjoy later! (As for the uncooked grains, it's best to store them in a cool, dry place, and use within 3 months.)

HOW MUCH WATER AGAIN?

Cooking for too long and in too much water turns grains into a bloated, gummy mess. As a general rule, check 'em early: When the raw taste is cooked out but they're still chewy, they're done. Grains aren't delicate: You can add more water during the cooking process or, if they're done before all liquid is absorbed, drain off the excess.

TECHNIQUE

Master the Omelet

Perhaps the most flexible dish of all, the omelet is perfect for a light breakfast, brunch, lunch, or dinner. Done well, it dazzles and satisfies. Here's what you need to do it with style.

There's much to love about the omelet: It's fast, healthy, and astonishingly satisfying for such a simple dish. Speed is key. Classic French-style omelets cook in about 90 seconds. Yes, they require finesse: Chefs are judged by their omelet skills. But risks are low: You won't ruin it, just overcook it a little. Costs are low, too. You're aiming for an omelet that's smooth outside and gleaming yellow (not browned). It's creamy at the center, like velvety custard. Said French chef Raymond Blanc, "If you do not have two minutes to prepare a proper omelet, then life is not worth living."

Keep other omelet styles in your repertoire. Our Western Omelet delivers the classic diner-style, overstuffed package, and the frittata doesn't even require flipping.

IF YOU DO NOT HAVE TWO MINUTES TO PREPARE A PROPER OMELET, THEN LIFE IS NOT WORTH LIVING.

Classic French Omelet

Hands-on: 3 min. Total: 3 min. *Pull the pan off the heat as needed, while stirring, to control how fast the eggs cook. The finished omelet should be golden outside and un-browned, while still creamy at the very center.*

⅛ **teaspoon kosher salt, divided**
⅛ **teaspoon freshly ground black pepper, divided**
4 large eggs, divided
1 teaspoon butter, divided

1. Combine dash of salt, dash of pepper, and two eggs in a small bowl. Stir with a whisk until just blended (do not overbeat).
2. Heat an 8-inch nonstick skillet over medium heat. Melt ½ teaspoon butter in pan; swirl to coat. Add egg mixture to pan; cook 60 seconds or until eggs are the consistency of very soft scrambled eggs (center will still look wet), stirring constantly with a rubber spatula. Tilt pan while stirring to fill any holes with uncooked egg mixture. Run spatula around edges and under omelet to loosen it from pan. Push one end of omelet up onto front lip of pan. Roll other end of omelet toward lip to close omelet. Turn out onto a plate, seam side down. Repeat with remaining salt, pepper, eggs, and butter. Serves 2 (serving size: 1 omelet)

CALORIES 160; **FAT** 11.4g (sat 4.3g, mono 4.2g, poly 2g); **PROTEIN** 12.6g; **CARB** 0.8g; **FIBER** 0g; **CHOL** 377mg; **IRON** 1.8mg; **SODIUM** 279mg; **CALC** 57mg
NUTRITION NOTE Eggs are naturally high in dietary cholesterol, but these omelets fit well within our fat and calorie guidelines.

FRENCH OMELET, STEP BY STEP

This style of omelet is all about technique. Here, three key steps for turning them out perfectly.

1. Stir egg constantly and briskly to produce the smallest possible curds. Tilt the pan so uncooked egg fills any holes.

2. Once egg is the consistency of very soft scrambled eggs (still wet-looking), push omelet edge onto front lip of pan.

3. Roll other end of omelet toward front to close, and then turn omelet out onto a plate, seam side down.

Western Omelet

(pictured on page 211)

Hands-on: 15 min. Total: 15 min.

1 tablespoon water
⅛ **teaspoon salt**
⅛ **teaspoon freshly ground black pepper**
4 large eggs
1 tablespoon olive oil, divided
½ **cup (1-inch) slices onion**
⅓ **cup (1-inch) slices red bell pepper**
⅓ **cup (1-inch) slices green bell pepper**
¼ **teaspoon chopped fresh thyme**
2 ounces chopped 33%-less-sodium ham
1 ounce shredded Swiss cheese (about ¼ cup), divided

1. Combine first 4 ingredients in a medium bowl, stirring with a whisk.
2. Heat an 8-inch nonstick skillet over medium-high heat. Add 1 teaspoon oil to pan; swirl to coat. Stir in onion, bell peppers, thyme, and ham; sauté 4 minutes or until vegetables are crisp-tender. Remove vegetable mixture from pan; set aside. Clean pan.
3. Return pan to medium-high heat. Add 1 teaspoon oil to pan; swirl to coat. Add half of egg mixture to pan, tilting pan to spread evenly; cook 1 minute or until edges begin to set. Lift edge of omelet with a rubber spatula, tilting pan to roll uncooked egg mixture onto bottom of pan. Repeat procedure on opposite edge of omelet. Cook 1 minute or until center is just set. Sprinkle 2 tablespoons cheese evenly over omelet. Sprinkle half of vegetable mixture over cheese. Run spatula around edges and under omelet to loosen it from pan; fold in half. Slide omelet onto a plate. Repeat procedure with remaining oil, egg mixture, cheese, and vegetable mixture. Serves 2 (serving size: 1 omelet)

CALORIES 331; **FAT** 20.9g (sat 6.5g, mono 10.7g, poly 2.6g); **PROTEIN** 22g; **CARB** 10.7g; **FIBER** 1.7g; **CHOL** 390mg; **IRON** 2.5mg; **SODIUM** 608mg; **CALC** 179mg

Quick & Easy • Vegetarian

Mushroom Frittata

Hands-on: 23 min. Total: 28 min. A frittata is a baked, open-faced omelet with Mediterranean flair.

2 ounces finely grated fresh pecorino Romano cheese (about ½ cup)
¼ teaspoon freshly ground black pepper
8 large eggs
½ teaspoon salt, divided
1 tablespoon extra-virgin olive oil, divided
1 (8-ounce) package sliced mushrooms
¾ cup chopped green onions
⅓ cup chopped fresh basil
2 cups baby arugula
2 teaspoons fresh lemon juice

1. Preheat oven to 350°.
2. Combine first 3 ingredients; add ¼ teaspoon salt, stirring with a whisk. Heat a 10-inch ovenproof skillet over medium-high heat. Add 2 teaspoons oil; swirl to coat. Add mushrooms and remaining ¼ teaspoon salt; sauté 6 minutes or until mushrooms brown and most of liquid evaporates. Stir in onions; sauté 2 minutes. Reduce heat to medium. Add egg mixture and basil to pan, stirring gently to evenly distribute vegetable mixture; cook 5 minutes or until eggs are partially set. Place pan in oven. Bake at 350° for 7 minutes or until eggs are cooked through and top is lightly browned. Remove pan from oven; let stand 5 minutes. Run a spatula around edge and under frittata to loosen from pan; slide frittata onto a plate or cutting board.
3. Combine remaining 1 teaspoon oil, arugula, and lemon juice. Cut frittata into 6 wedges; top with arugula mixture. Serves 6 (serving size: 1 frittata wedge and about ⅓ cup arugula mixture)

CALORIES 145; FAT 8.7g (sat 2.5g, mono 4.2g, poly 1.3g); PROTEIN 10.1g; CARB 4.2g; FIBER 0.4g; CHOL 243mg; IRON 1.6mg; SODIUM 352mg; CALC 87mg

SHOPPING

Plan Some Healthy Food Adventures

Try a new market, neighborhood, or specialty store. Buy foods both fun and new. Shop healthy (lots of grains, beans, veggies, and so on) for a week's menu. Enjoy ... and repeat.

Variety gives new life to New Year's lighter-eating resolutions. A food-focused weekend outing to an Italian, Mexican, Chinese, Lebanese, Southeast Asian, or Greek food store (or neighborhood) is a joy and inspiration that introduces new foods and flavors to your family's diet. (If you have kids, bring 'em along and let them choose some foods; they're more likely to eat what they've helped buy.) Emphasize healthy pantry or freezer staples: lentils, corn tortillas, brown or basmati rice, egg or soba noodles, specialty breads. Choose high-flavor condiments and flavorings, such as salsas, chipotle chiles, deep-green olive oils, and Indian pickles, as well as Asian spice pastes for vegetable or fish curries. Italian shelves groan with interesting shapes and artisanal varieties of pasta. Asian freezers now often offer a profusion of naans and dumplings. Of course, it's easy to pile the basket high with rich treats (cheese, chocolates, cured meats). Buy small portions instead, planning to incorporate these into vegetable- and grain-focused meals.

TREATS

100-Calorie Chocolate Hits

Gooey Turtle Brownie
Drizzle 1 mini brownie bite with ½ teaspoon caramel syrup. Top with 1 toasted pecan half.

Chocolate-Espresso Tartlets
Stir 1 teaspoon brewed espresso (or strong coffee) into 3 tablespoons fat-free chocolate pudding. Divide mixture evenly among 3 mini phyllo cups.

Pistachio-Coated Chocolate-Dipped Apples
Dip 3 apple wedges into 1 (0.375-ounce) melted dark chocolate square (such as Hershey's). Sprinkle with 1 teaspoon crushed salted pistachios.

Chocolate–Peanut Butter Pretzel
Smear the end of 1 pretzel rod with 1 teaspoon creamy peanut butter. Dip into 1 teaspoon melted semisweet chocolate chips.

Deconstructed S'mores
Dip 2 large marshmallows into 1 tablespoon melted semisweet chocolate chips. Roll in 2 teaspoons cinnamon graham cracker crumbs.

Chocolate–Peppermint Patty
Stir 1 finely crushed peppermint candy into 3 tablespoons softened chocolate frozen yogurt. Spoon yogurt between 2 chocolate wafer cookies (such as Nabisco). Press gently to seal.

Crispy Chocolate Snack
Gently stir 2 tablespoons crispy rice cereal, 2 teaspoons chopped dried cherries, and 1 teaspoon toasted chopped almonds into 1 tablespoon melted semisweet chocolate chips. Dollop onto wax paper, and let dry.

Mexican Chocolate Pudding

Stir ½ teaspoon cinnamon, ½ teaspoon vanilla extract, and ⅛ teaspoon ground red pepper into 1 fat-free chocolate pudding cup. Top with 1 tablespoon thawed fat-free whipped topping (such as Cool Whip).

Crunchy Chocolate-Hazelnut Sandwich

Break 1 chocolate graham cracker rectangle in half. Spread ½ tablespoon chocolate-hazelnut spread (such as Nutella) onto one half. Top with remaining half.

CONVENIENCE

Make Your Friday Nights Lighter

If pizza is your no-cook movie-night choice, good news: The latest batch in the frozen-food aisle is healthier and tastier. And they're easy to jazz up with extra toppings.

Newman's Own Thin & Crispy Supreme Pizza

A supreme style pizza, it's complete with roasted peppers, onions, Italian sausage, and uncured pepperoni. We loved the crisp multigrain crust. Also trim and tasty from Newman's Own are their Roasted Vegetable and White Pizza varieties.

⅓ **PIZZA** = **CALORIES** 320; **FAT** 15g (sat 5g); **SODIUM** 750mg

Pizzeria Italiana Organic 4 Cheese Pizza

With a hearty hit of Gouda, provolone, mozzarella, and Parmesan, this pizza is decadently creamy. Our test panel pronounced it too good to be frozen. It offers a perfect base for salt-free toppers like veggies, sliced tomatoes, or a lightly dressed salad.

⅓ **PIZZA** = **CALORIES** 270; **FAT** 10g (sat 7g); **SODIUM** 710 mg

Whole Foods Market Buffalo Mozzarella with Cherry Tomatoes Pizza

This tasty pie keeps its ingredient list fresh, simple, and authentic. Plump cherry tomatoes nestle in a creamy layer of buffalo mozzarella—a scrumptious contrast to the hand-tossed crust. Top it off with fresh basil.

½ **PIZZA** = **CALORIES** 310; **FAT** 11g (sat 7g); **SODIUM** 690mg

Freschetta Simply Inspired Thin-Crust Farmers Market Veggie Pizza

Balsamic-glazed portobello mushrooms, fire-roasted zucchini, and onions make for a sweet-salty balance. A hint of garlic accents the bright tomato sauce. Crust is cracker-crisp.

⅓ **PIZZA** = **CALORIES** 300; **FAT** 15g (sat 7g); **SODIUM** 660mg

JUST HOW BAD CAN DELIVERY BE?

The delivery companies compete for "value" by loading in meat, cheese, and dough. The worst choices serve up a day's worth of sat fat, sodium, and calories.

2 slices Meat Lover's Stuffed Crust Pizza from Pizza Hut

CALORIES 960; **FAT** 52g (sat 22g); **SODIUM** 2,760mg

2 slices Cali Chicken Bacon Ranch Pizza from Domino's

CALORIES 860; **FAT** 50g (sat 18g); **SODIUM** 1,800mg

2 slices John's Favorite Pizza from Papa John's

CALORIES 820; **FAT** 42g (sat 18g); **SODIUM** 2,120mg

STRATEGIES

Simple 100-Calorie Food Swaps

Moves like these can help you lose a pound a month—and that's if you do just one per day.

*Supersized **bagels** can contain more than 300 calories and 400mg sodium.*

Change up the bagel routine.
Swap a 3½-inch **bagel** with 1 tablespoon each cream cheese and fruity jam for a **whole-wheat English muffin** topped with a tablespoon of peanut butter and fresh strawberry slices.

*One cup of **OJ** has 24g of sugar—double the amount in an orange.*

Peel, segment, chew, enjoy.
A 12-ounce bottle of **orange juice** (the size of most to-go bottles) ideally should be split into three 4-ounce servings. Eat a **fresh orange** instead.

*Low-fat **granola** has about 1.5g fat in ¼ cup— that's 75% less than regular granola.*

Flip-flop your breakfast portions.
A generous pour of calorie-dense **granola** is easy to lose in a deep-bottomed bowl of low-fat milk. Instead, portion out a moderate ¼ cup over protein-packed **nonfat Greek yogurt.**

*Bonus benefit to a **wrap:** more room for low-calorie vegetables*

Rebuild the main event at lunch.
Pile sandwich fixings on one (8-inch) 100-calorie **whole-grain wrap,** rather than two slices of hearty multigrain bread.

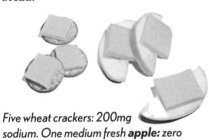

*Five wheat crackers: 200mg sodium. One medium fresh **apple:** zero*

Swap out the crackers for fruit.
Enjoy that savory sharp cheddar cheese with **tart, crisp apple** slices instead of **wheat crackers**—and up your daily fruit count, too!

Corn chips aren't just carbs; skip them, and you'll save 10g fat per ounce.

Lighten up your chili toppers.
Instead of an ounce each of corn chips and sour cream, try **fresh radishes for crunch,** jalapeños for heat, and a small dollop of cool, creamy nonfat Greek yogurt. There's still room for cheese.

Dark chocolate has half the sugar of milk chocolate. Save 8g per ounce.

Flavor strategy #1: darker chocolate
Intense dark chocolate, savored slowly, can last a long time and deliver the satisfaction you want. Try two squares versus a whole candy bar.

Flour tortillas are made with more fat and sodium than their corn kin.

Turn burrito night into fajita night.
Stuff tasty fixings into two (6-inch) whole-grain **corn tortillas** rather than one (10-inch) **flour tortilla.** You'll also save 450mg of sodium.

*There are 400 calories in a half cup of **nuts**—so portion carefully.*

Swap in some whole-grain treats. Two handfuls of nuts are heart-healthy but calorie-heavy. Downsize to one handful (about ¾ ounce), and add a handful of **air-popped popcorn** and whole-grain cereal, such as Chex.

*Be careful: Some specialty **beers** can have up to 10% alcohol—more than wine.*

Flavor strategy #2: darker beer
One glass of full-flavored sipping beer, even with higher alcohol content, can beat two glasses of a light lager.

2013 CHICKEN HOT LIST

25 big-flavor recipes to kick off the new year with our favorite bird.

Kid Friendly • Make Ahead

Classic Chicken Noodle Soup

(pictured on page 209)

Hands-on: 28 min. Total: 55 min.

2 tablespoons canola oil
1 bone-in chicken breast half, skinned
1 pound bone-in chicken thighs, skinned
³/₄ teaspoon kosher salt, divided
¹/₂ teaspoon black pepper, divided
2 cups chopped onion
1 cup chopped carrot
¹/₂ cup (¹/₄-inch-thick) slices celery
1 tablespoon minced fresh garlic
3 parsley sprigs
3 thyme sprigs
1 rosemary sprig
2 bay leaves
1 cup dry white wine
4 cups unsalted chicken stock
1 cup uncooked medium egg noodles
2 tablespoons chopped fresh parsley

1. Heat a Dutch oven over medium-high heat. Add oil to pan; swirl to coat. Sprinkle chicken with ½ teaspoon salt and ¼ teaspoon pepper. Add chicken, flesh side down. Cook 10 minutes; turn thighs after 5 minutes. Cool; shred. Discard bones.
2. Add onion, carrot, and celery to pan; sauté 10 minutes. Add garlic; sauté 1 minute. Place herb sprigs and bay leaves on cheesecloth. Gather edges; tie securely. Add sachet to pan.
3. Add wine; bring to a boil. Cook 4 minutes. Add chicken and stock. Cover; reduce heat. Cook 7 minutes.

4. Add noodles; cook 6 minutes or until al dente. Discard sachet. Stir in chopped parsley, ¼ teaspoon salt, and ¼ teaspoon pepper. Serves 6 (serving size: about 1 cup)

CALORIES 302; FAT 9.2g (sat 1.5g, mono 4.2g, poly 2.1g); PROTEIN 30.6g; CARB 16.2g; FIBER 2.1g; CHOL 103mg; IRON 1.5mg; SODIUM 483mg; CALC 54mg

Make Ahead

If you like peanut butter try: Peanut-Chicken Soup

Prepare Classic Chicken Noodle Soup through step 2, omitting carrot and celery and adding 1 cup thinly sliced leeks and 1 tablespoon grated peeled fresh ginger with onion; omit thyme and rosemary from sachet. Combine ¼ cup creamy peanut butter, ¼ cup water, and 1 (14.5-ounce) can drained diced tomatoes, stirring well. Add peanut butter mixture, 3 cups unsalted chicken stock (such as Swanson), 2 cups water, 2 cups cubed peeled sweet potato, and ¾ teaspoon ground red pepper; bring to a boil. Return chicken to pan. Reduce heat to medium, and simmer 20 minutes, stirring occasionally. Remove from heat; discard sachet. Ladle about 1⅓ cups soup into each of 6 bowls, and top each serving with 2 teaspoons chopped fresh flat-leaf parsley and 1 teaspoon chopped unsalted peanuts. Serves 6

CALORIES 336; FAT 15.2g (sat 2.5g); SODIUM 519mg

Make Ahead

If you like hot peppers try: Spicy Chicken Soup

Prepare Classic Chicken Noodle Soup through step 3, omitting carrot and celery, omitting thyme and rosemary from sachet, and adding 3 cilantro sprigs and 2 halved habanero peppers to sachet. Stir in 2 cups water, 1 cup chopped red-skinned potatoes, 1 cup corn kernels, and 1 tablespoon ground cumin; bring to a boil. Reduce heat to medium, and simmer 15 minutes or until potatoes are tender, stirring occasionally. Remove from heat; discard sachet. Stir in ¼ teaspoon kosher salt and ¼ teaspoon pepper. Garnish servings with 1 cup chopped avocado, ½ cup fresh cilantro leaves, and 1 teaspoon grated lime rind. Serve with lime wedges. Serves 6 (serving size: about 1⅓ cups)

CALORIES 375; FAT 15.1g (sat 2.3g); SODIUM 480mg

Make Ahead

If you like curry try: Curried Chicken Soup

Prepare Classic Chicken Noodle Soup through step 2, omitting celery, omitting thyme and rosemary from sachet, and adding 3 cilantro sprigs, 1 (½-inch) piece peeled fresh ginger, and 1 pierced serrano chile to sachet. Stir in 3 tablespoons Madras curry powder; sauté 20 seconds. Add 3 cups unsalted chicken stock (such as Swanson), 1 cup water, and 1 (14-ounce) can light coconut milk; bring to a boil. Return chicken to pan. Reduce heat to medium, and simmer 15 minutes or until vegetables are tender, stirring occasionally.

continued

Remove from heat; discard sachet. Combine ¼ cup plain 2% reduced-fat Greek-style yogurt, 2 teaspoons chopped fresh cilantro, ¼ teaspoon grated lime rind, and ½ teaspoon fresh lime juice. Serves 6 (serving size: about 1⅓ cups soup and 2 teaspoons yogurt mixture)

CALORIES 302; FAT 13.6g (sat 5g); SODIUM 402mg

Vietnamese Chicken Sandwiches

Hands-on: 38 min. Total: 50 min.

1 (12-ounce) French bread baguette
2 teaspoons canola oil
1 pound chicken cutlets
¼ teaspoon black pepper
2 teaspoons minced fresh garlic, divided
1 tablespoon lower-sodium soy sauce
2 teaspoons dark sesame oil
2 teaspoons hoisin sauce
½ cup sugar
½ cup rice vinegar
1 cup matchstick-cut carrots
1 cup very thinly sliced radishes
2 cups thinly sliced English cucumber
1½ cups thinly sliced romaine lettuce
½ cup cilantro leaves
1 tablespoon Sriracha (hot chile sauce, such as Huy Fong)

1. Cut bread in half horizontally; hollow out, leaving a 1-inch-thick shell.
2. Heat a large skillet over medium-high heat. Add canola oil; swirl to coat. Sprinkle chicken with pepper. Add to pan. Sauté 3 minutes on each side or until done. Let stand 10 minutes. Slice chicken; toss with 1 teaspoon garlic.
3. Combine 1 teaspoon garlic, soy sauce, sesame oil, and hoisin in a bowl; add chicken. Toss. Combine sugar and vinegar in a small saucepan; cook until sugar dissolves. Add carrot and radishes. Cool; drain, reserving 2 tablespoons vinegar mixture.

4. Arrange cucumber and lettuce on bottom half of bread; drizzle with vinegar mixture. Top with chicken, radish mixture, cilantro, Sriracha, and bread top. Cut into 4 equal portions. Serves 4

CALORIES 400; FAT 7.7g (sat 1.1g, mono 3.1g, poly 2.1g); PROTEIN 25g; CARB 59.3g; FIBER 3g; CHOL 54mg; IRON 2.9mg; SODIUM 802mg; CALC 38mg

Quick & Easy

If you like fresh basil try: Tuscan Pesto Chicken Panini

Prepare Vietnamese Chicken Sandwiches through step 2, substituting 8 ounces ciabatta bread for the baguette (do not hollow out bread) and sprinkling ¼ teaspoon kosher salt on chicken with black pepper. Combine 1 cup fresh basil, 1 tablespoon chopped garlic, 1 tablespoon toasted pine nuts, 1 tablespoon olive oil, 1 tablespoon water, ¼ teaspoon black pepper, and ⅛ teaspoon kosher salt in a mini food processor, and pulse until finely chopped. Cut a peeled roasted red bell pepper into quarters; discard seeds and membranes. Arrange pepper quarters on bottom half of bread. Top with 2 (1-ounce) slices provolone cheese and sliced chicken. Spread basil mixture on cut side of top half of bread; place on sandwich. Cut sandwich crosswise into 4 equal portions. Serves 4

CALORIES 391; FAT 15.8g (sat 4g); SODIUM 793mg

FOUR RIFFS ON CHICKEN SANDWICH SATIS-FACTION: SPICY, HERBY, PICKLY, AND AVOCADO-CREAMY

Quick & Easy

If you like pickles try: Pressed Cuban-Style Sandwiches

Prepare Vietnamese Chicken Sandwiches through step 2, substituting 8 ounces Cuban bread for baguette (do not hollow out bread) and sprinkling ¼ teaspoon kosher salt on chicken with pepper. Spread 1 tablespoon spicy brown mustard over bottom half of bread; top with 1 ounce shredded Havarti cheese (about ¼ cup), 1 ounce lower-sodium sliced ham, and chicken. Sprinkle chicken with 2 tablespoons chopped spicy kosher dill pickle; cover with top half of bread. Return pan to medium heat; coat with cooking spray. Add sandwich to pan; top with another heavy skillet to weigh down. Cook 2 minutes on each side or until toasted. Cut sandwich crosswise into 4 equal portions. Serves 4

CALORIES 315; FAT 8.9g (sat 2.5g); SODIUM 761mg

Kid Friendly • Quick & Easy

If you like avocado try: Chicken-Avocado Club Sandwiches

Prepare Vietnamese Chicken Sandwiches through step 2, substituting 12 slices toasted thin wheat bread for baguette (do not hollow out bread), substituting cooking spray for oil, and sprinkling ⅛ teaspoon kosher salt on chicken with pepper. Combine 1 cup mashed avocado, 1 tablespoon fresh lime juice, 2 teaspoons canola mayonnaise, and 2 slices cooked crumbled bacon. Divide avocado mixture evenly among 8 bread slices. Spread ½ teaspoon yellow mustard over 1 side of the remaining 4 bread slices. Top each mustard-topped bread slice with

1 Bibb lettuce leaf and 2 plum tomato slices; sprinkle evenly with ¼ teaspoon black pepper. Divide half of chicken among sandwiches, and top each with 1 avocado-topped bread slice. Repeat layers. Serves 4

CALORIES 404; **FAT** 12.7g (sat 1.8g); **SODIUM** 561mg

Kid Friendly • Make Ahead

Tortilla Chip Casserole

Hands-on: 30 min. Total: 60 min.

1 tablespoon canola oil
½ cup chopped onion
1 tablespoon minced fresh garlic
2 tablespoons all-purpose flour
1 cup 2% reduced-fat milk
½ cup unsalted chicken stock
1 teaspoon ground cumin
½ teaspoon ground coriander
¼ teaspoon kosher salt
¼ teaspoon freshly ground black pepper
4 ounces ⅓-less-fat cream cheese
1 cup organic canned black beans, rinsed and drained
3 cups chopped cooked chicken breast
4 ounces baked tortilla chips, crushed
1 roasted red bell pepper, chopped
8 ounces lower-sodium green chile enchilada sauce (such as Frontera)
2.5 ounces shredded cheddar– Monterey Jack cheese blend (about ⅔ cup)
2 tablespoons chopped green onions

1. Preheat oven to 350°.
2. Heat a saucepan over medium heat. Add oil to pan; swirl to coat. Add onion; cook 6 minutes. Add garlic and flour; cook 2 minutes. Gradually add milk and stock, stirring constantly; bring to a boil. Remove from heat; stir in cumin, coriander, salt, pepper, and cream cheese.
3. Spread ½ cup milk mixture over bottom of a broiler-safe 11 x 7–inch baking dish. Layer beans, 1½ cups chicken,

and 2 ounces chips. Top with ½ cup milk mixture. Layer 1½ cups chicken, bell pepper, and 2 ounces chips; top with 1 cup milk mixture and enchilada sauce. Sprinkle with shredded cheese. Bake at 350° for 30 minutes. Sprinkle with green onions. Serves 6

CALORIES 379; **FAT** 14.6g (sat 6.8g, mono 4.6g, poly 1.4g); **PROTEIN** 28.5g; **CARB** 34.2g; **FIBER** 4.7g; **CHOL** 75mg; **IRON** 1.9mg; **SODIUM** 686mg; **CALC** 215mg

Kid Friendly • Make Ahead

If you like wild rice try: Chicken and Wild Rice Casserole

Prepare Tortilla Chip Casserole through step 2, omitting milk, cumin, and coriander from sauce, and increasing onion to 1 cup and stock to 1½ cups. Cook 2 chopped bacon slices in a skillet over medium heat. Remove bacon; reserve for another use. Add 1 (8-ounce) container sliced button mushrooms to drippings in pan; cook 5 minutes. Add 2 teaspoons canola oil to pan; swirl to coat. Add 1 cup chopped leek, ½ cup chopped celery, and ½ cup chopped carrot; cook 5 minutes, stirring occasionally. Stir in ¼ cup dry sherry; bring to a boil. Cook 3 minutes or until liquid evaporates. Add leek mixture, 4 cups chopped cooked chicken breast, 3 cups cooked brown and wild rice blend, ⅓ cup chopped fresh flat-leaf parsley, ½ teaspoon salt, and ½ teaspoon black pepper to sauce; toss to combine. Scrape mixture into an 11 x 7–inch baking dish. Toss 1¼ cups fresh breadcrumbs with 2 table-spoons melted butter; sprinkle over casserole. Bake at 350° for 25 minutes. Serves 6

CALORIES 475; **FAT** 16.9g (sat 6.6g); **SODIUM** 535mg

Kid Friendly • Make Ahead

If you like poppy seeds try: Poppy Seed Chicken

Prepare Tortilla Chip Casserole through step 2, omitting milk, cream cheese, cumin, and coriander from sauce. Add ¼ cup finely chopped celery to pan with onion. Increase chicken stock to 1 cup, and combine it with ½ cup half-and-half for the sauce. Remove from heat, and stir in 2 cups chopped cooked chicken breast, 1 tablespoon chopped fresh flat-leaf parsley, 1½ teaspoons poppy seeds, 1 teaspoon Worcestershire sauce, ¼ teaspoon kosher salt, and ¼ teaspoon black pepper. Scrape mixture into an 11 x 7–inch glass or ceramic baking dish. Combine 1 cup fresh bread-crumbs, ¼ cup sliced almonds, and 2 tablespoons melted butter in a bowl, and toss to combine. Sprinkle bread-crumb mixture over top of casserole, and bake at 350° for 30 minutes. Serves 6

CALORIES 235; **FAT** 12.7g (sat 4.8g); **SODIUM** 288mg

Chicken in Wine Sauce

Hands-on: 30 min. Total: 1 hr. 15 min.

4 bone-in chicken thighs, skinned
2 bone-in chicken breast halves, halved crosswise and skinned
½ teaspoon kosher salt, divided
½ teaspoon freshly ground black pepper, divided
2 teaspoons canola oil
1 cup chopped onion
½ cup thinly sliced carrot
½ cup thinly sliced celery
1 tablespoon minced fresh garlic
2 cups dry white wine
1 cup unsalted chicken stock (such as Swanson)
2 tablespoons all-purpose flour
3 tablespoons chopped fresh tarragon
3 tablespoons chopped fresh flat-leaf parsley, divided
1 tablespoon whole-grain Dijon mustard
1 bay leaf
1 tablespoon unsalted butter
2 cups cherry tomatoes
Cooking spray
2 applewood-smoked bacon slices, cooked and crumbled

1. Preheat oven to 325°.
2. Heat a Dutch oven over medium heat. Sprinkle chicken evenly with ¼ teaspoon salt and ¼ teaspoon pepper. Add oil to pan; swirl to coat. Add half of chicken to pan, flesh side down. Cook 4 minutes or until browned; remove from pan. Repeat with remaining chicken. Set chicken aside.
3. Add onion, carrot, celery, and garlic to pan; cook 6 minutes, stirring occasionally. Add wine; cook 2 minutes, scraping pan to loosen browned bits. Return chicken to pan, flesh side up. Combine stock and flour in a bowl, stirring with a whisk until smooth. Add stock mixture to pan.

4. Stir in tarragon, 2 tablespoons parsley, mustard, and bay leaf, and bring to a boil. Cover and bake at 325° for 45 minutes or until chicken is done and very tender. Remove pan from oven. Remove chicken from pan, and top with ¼ cup cooking liquid. Keep warm. Heat pan over medium-high heat, and bring to a boil. Boil 5 minutes or until mixture is reduced to 3 cups. Whisk in butter, ¼ teaspoon salt, and ¼ teaspoon pepper. Discard bay leaf.
5. Preheat broiler to high.
6. Arrange tomatoes in a single layer on a jelly-roll pan; lightly coat with cooking spray. Broil 6 minutes or until blistered. Sprinkle chicken with tomatoes, crumbled bacon, and 1 tablespoon parsley. Serve with sauce. Serves 6 (serving size: 2 chicken thighs or ½ chicken breast half and about ½ cup sauce)

CALORIES 339; **FAT** 9.8g (sat 3.2g, mono 3.1g, poly 1.6g); **PROTEIN** 35.8g; **CARB** 11.4g; **FIBER** 1.7g; **CHOL** 116mg; **IRON** 1.9mg; **SODIUM** 435mg; **CALC** 55mg

If you like kalamata olives try: Greek-Style Stewed Chicken

Prepare Chicken in Wine Sauce through step 4, omitting carrot and celery and adding ½ cup chopped, seeded plum tomato and ½ cup thinly sliced green bell pepper instead, decreasing wine to 1¾ cups and adding ¼ cup ouzo (or brandy), and omitting tarragon, parsley, and mustard. Stir in 1½ tablespoons chopped oregano leaves and ½ teaspoon chopped rosemary leaves. Add ¼ cup sliced, pitted kalamata olives and 1 tablespoon fresh lemon juice to sauce mixture when butter is added, stirring until butter melts. Omit steps 5 and 6. Serve with lemon wedges, if desired.

Serves 6 (serving size: 2 chicken thighs or ½ chicken breast half and about ⅓ cup sauce)

CALORIES 349; **FAT** 10.7g (sat 2.9g); **SODIUM** 439mg

If you like saffron try: Moroccan Stewed Chicken

Prepare Chicken in Wine Sauce through step 4, omitting celery and adding ½ cup chopped, seeded plum tomato instead; decreasing wine to 1¾ cups; omitting tarragon, parsley, and mustard; and stirring in ⅓ cup chopped dried apricot halves, ¼ cup sliced pitted green olives, and ¼ teaspoon saffron threads with the bay leaf. Add 1 tablespoon fresh lemon juice to sauce when butter is added, stirring until smooth. Omit steps 5 and 6. Serve with lemon wedges. Serves 6 (serving size: 2 chicken thighs or ½ chicken breast half, about ½ cup sauce, and 1 lemon wedge)

CALORIES 336; **FAT** 9.7g (sat 2.6g); **SODIUM** 454mg

MILKY FRESH MOZZARELLA TAMES THE BITE OF TANGY PEPPERS.

BBQ Chicken Pizza with Fresh Mozzarella and Pickled Jalapeños

(pictured on page 210)

Hands-on: 20 min. Total: 38 min.

3 (4-ounce) chicken breast cutlets
½ teaspoon freshly ground black pepper
⅛ teaspoon kosher salt
2 teaspoons brown sugar
1 teaspoon paprika
1 teaspoon garlic powder
½ teaspoon ground cumin
Cooking spray
12 ounces refrigerated fresh pizza dough
2 tablespoons yellow cornmeal
⅓ cup no-salt-added ketchup
3 tablespoons prepared yellow mustard
1 tablespoon white vinegar
½ cup sliced red onion
¼ cup pickled jalapeño slices
4 ounces fresh mozzarella cheese, thinly sliced
2 tablespoons coarsely chopped fresh cilantro leaves

1. Place a pizza stone or heavy baking sheet in oven. Preheat oven to 450° (keep pizza stone or baking sheet in oven as it preheats).
2. Sprinkle both sides of chicken evenly with black pepper and salt. Combine brown sugar, paprika, garlic powder, and ground cumin in a small bowl, stirring well to combine. Set aside 2 teaspoons spice mixture, and rub remaining spice mixture evenly over all sides of chicken. Heat a grill pan over medium-high heat. Coat pan with cooking spray. Add chicken to pan; sauté 3 minutes on each side or until chicken is done. Let chicken stand 10 minutes, and slice thinly against the grain.
3. Roll dough into a 14 x 9–inch rectangle (or a 14-inch circle) on a lightly floured surface; pierce dough with a fork. Lightly coat dough with cooking spray. Carefully remove pizza stone from oven. Sprinkle cornmeal over pizza stone; place dough on pizza stone.
4. Bake at 450° for 9 minutes. Combine reserved 2 teaspoons spice mixture, ketchup, mustard, and vinegar in a small saucepan over medium heat. Bring mixture to a simmer, and cook 3 minutes or until slightly thick, stirring occasionally. Remove partially cooked crust from oven; spread ketchup mixture evenly over crust, leaving a ½-inch border around the edges. Top with chicken, onion, jalapeños, and cheese. Bake at 450° for 10 minutes or until cheese is browned. Sprinkle with cilantro. Slice. Serves 6 (serving size: 1 slice)

CALORIES 295; FAT 7g (sat 2.8g, mono 0.4g, poly 1.3g); PROTEIN 19g; CARB 39.7g; FIBER 2g; CHOL 40mg; IRON 2.6mg; SODIUM 580mg; CALC 153mg

If you like arugula try: Chicken, Arugula, and Prosciutto Pizza

Prepare BBQ Chicken Pizza through step 3, omitting brown sugar, paprika, garlic powder, and ground cumin. Combine 1 tablespoon extra-virgin olive oil and 2 tablespoons thinly vertically sliced garlic in a skillet over medium-low heat; cook 2 minutes or just until fragrant, stirring constantly (do not brown garlic). Brush uncooked pizza dough with garlic-oil mixture; sprinkle dough evenly with 3 ounces shredded fontina cheese (about ¾ cup) and ½ teaspoon crushed red pepper, leaving a ½-inch border. Bake at 450° for 4 minutes or until cheese melts. Carefully remove partially cooked crust from oven; arrange chicken on crust, leaving a ½-inch border. Bake an additional 5 minutes or until crust is golden and crisp. Place 1½ cups arugula in a medium bowl; drizzle with 1 teaspoon extra-virgin olive oil and 1 teaspoon fresh lemon juice. Sprinkle with ⅛ teaspoon kosher salt. Toss. Arrange 1 ounce thinly sliced prosciutto evenly over pizza; top with arugula mixture. Slice pizza. Serve immediately. Serves 6 (serving size: 1 slice)

CALORIES 307; FAT 12.9g (sat 3.9g); SODIUM 624mg

If you like parmesan try: Three-Cheese Chicken Pizza

Prepare BBQ Chicken Pizza through step 3, omitting spice rub. Combine 1 ounce crumbled blue cheese and 1 tablespoon fat-free milk; spread mixture over uncooked pizza dough, leaving a ½-inch border. Top with chicken, 2 ounces shredded mozzarella, 2 tablespoons grated Parmesan, and ⅛ teaspoon salt. Bake at 450° for 12 minutes. Sprinkle with 1 tablespoon fresh chopped basil and 1 tablespoon fresh chopped oregano. Slice. Serves 6 (serving size: 1 slice)

CALORIES 270; FAT 7.3g (sat 3g); SODIUM 599mg

SECRETS TO COOKING CHICKEN THE LIGHT WAY

BONE-IN BREAST HALVES
White meat chicken cooked on the bone yields tender, juicy, and supremely flavorful results. But the size of bone-in breast halves has ballooned beyond anything reasonable for a single serving, with a random sampling of supermarket specimens yielding a whopping average of 9.75 ounces of cooked meat. In some of the recipes in this story, you'll see that we struck a happy compromise by calling for bone-in chicken breast halves that are halved crosswise into two servings each.

PORTION PATROL
Cooking Light recipes normally call for 1 (6-ounce) skinless, boneless breast half per serving, but the size of chicken breasts can vary widely. If you want to make sure you stick as close to the proper portion size as possible, look for Purdue Perfect Portions; each chicken breast half is trimmed to about 5 ounces, so they're by far the most uniform.

SKIN: ON OR OFF?
You'll notice that we sometimes call for discarding skin, while in other instances we leave the skin on. Leaving the skin on will add about 100 calories and increase the saturated fat by about 3.5 to 4 grams. And when nutrition analysis includes the skin, we reduce portion size for fattier dark meat to a single thigh, versus two skinless thighs.

BIRDS ON A BUDGET
You'll pay for every cut the butcher makes, so for the best value, purchase whole chickens and break them down yourself.

MARINATING DILEMMAS
Marinating lean chicken breasts can be dicey, so as a general rule of thumb—especially with acidic marinades—soak for just 30 minutes. If you soak any longer, the texture of the meat might be compromised.

OPTIMAL CONDITIONS
Because chicken breast is low in fat, the margin of error is small when cooking it. The most fail-safe way to test for doneness is with a meat thermometer. Pull the bird when the temperature registers 165°.

Quick & Easy

Creamy Chicken Pasta

Hands-on: 30 min. Total: 30 min.

9 ounces uncooked orecchiette pasta
Cooking spray
12 ounces skinless, boneless chicken breasts, cut into bite-sized pieces
¾ teaspoon kosher salt, divided
¾ teaspoon black pepper, divided
1 cup unsalted chicken stock, divided
2 tablespoons all-purpose flour
½ cup half-and-half
⅓ cup mascarpone cheese
¼ cup chopped fresh parsley, divided
½ cup chopped onion
1 teaspoon minced fresh garlic
1 teaspoon chopped fresh thyme
8 ounces chopped wild mushroom blend
3 tablespoons red wine vinegar
½ teaspoon Dijon mustard

1. Cook pasta according to package directions, omitting salt and fat; drain.
2. Heat a Dutch oven over medium-high heat; coat with cooking spray. Sprinkle chicken with ¼ teaspoon salt and ¼ teaspoon pepper. Add chicken to pan; sauté 4 minutes. Combine ¼ cup stock and flour. Add flour mixture, ¾ cup stock, and half-and-half to pan; bring to a boil. Cook 2 minutes. Remove from heat; stir in ¼ teaspoon salt, ¼ teaspoon pepper, mascarpone, and 2 tablespoons parsley.
3. Heat a skillet over medium heat; coat with cooking spray. Add onion and garlic; cook 5 minutes. Add thyme and mushrooms; cook 8 minutes. Stir in ¼ teaspoon salt, ¼ teaspoon pepper, vinegar, and mustard; cook 30 seconds. Add pasta and chicken mixture; toss. Sprinkle with 2 tablespoons parsley. Serves 6 (serving size: about 1⅓ cups)

CALORIES 364; FAT 14.3g (sat 7.1g, mono 3.5g, poly 0.5g); PROTEIN 23.2g; CARB 36.3g; FIBER 2.3g; CHOL 67mg; IRON 2.4mg; SODIUM 336mg; CALC 67mg

---

Kid Friendly • Quick & Easy

If you like butternut squash try:

Butternut Squash and Chicken Pasta

Prepare Creamy Chicken Pasta through step 2, substituting 8 ounces cavatappi pasta for orecchiette, and omitting flour and half-and-half. Preheat oven to 450°. Combine 4 cups peeled (1-inch) cubed butternut squash, 1½ cups (1-inch-thick) slices shallots, 3 thinly sliced garlic cloves, and 2 (3.5-ounce) packages shiitake mushroom caps, sliced. Drizzle vegetable mixture with 1 tablespoon olive oil; toss. Transfer squash mixture to a small roasting pan; sprinkle with ¼ teaspoon kosher salt and ¼ teaspoon freshly ground black pepper. Bake at 450° for 20 minutes or until vegetables are just tender. Add vegetable mixture to pasta mixture; cook 1 minute or until thoroughly heated. Sprinkle with 1½ tablespoons chopped fresh chives, ¼ teaspoon kosher salt, and ¼ teaspoon freshly ground black pepper. Serves 6 (serving size: about 1½ cups)

CALORIES 416; FAT 16.2g (sat 7.1g); SODIUM 354mg

Quick & Easy

If you like mascarpone try:

Chicken Caesar Pasta Salad

Prepare Creamy Chicken Pasta through step 2, substituting 6 ounces farfalle for orecchiette, adding 8 cups torn Swiss chard to pasta during last 2 minutes of cooking, omitting half-and-half, and reducing flour to 1½ tablespoons. Preheat oven to 450°. Combine

¾ cup toasted fresh breadcrumbs, 1½ tablespoons chopped fresh parsley, 4 teaspoons minced fresh garlic, ½ teaspoon grated lemon rind, and 3 finely chopped drained canned anchovies. Combine 2 cups halved cherry tomatoes, 1 cup thinly sliced shallots, and 1 tablespoon olive oil. Bake tomato mixture at 450° for 15 minutes. Combine pasta, tomato mixture, and chicken mixture, and cook 1 minute. Spoon about 1 cup pasta into each of 6 bowls, and sprinkle evenly with breadcrumbs. Serves 6

CALORIES 364; **FAT** 15.6g (sat 6.9g); **SODIUM** 446mg

Quick & Easy

Meyer Lemon Chicken

Hands-on: 27 min. Total: 39 min. *If you can't find Meyer lemons, you can use a regular lemon. It will have more of a bitter bite, which you can counter with a pinch of sugar. If you don't like olives, just leave them out; the dish is still tasty.*

2 skin-on, bone-in chicken breast halves, halved crosswise
2 skin-on, bone-in chicken thighs
1 teaspoon kosher salt, divided
³/₄ teaspoon black pepper, divided
Cooking spray
2 tablespoons olive oil, divided
1 pound small red potatoes, quartered
1 Meyer lemon, cut into ¹/₄-inch-thick slices and seeded
¹/₄ cup finely chopped shallots
4 garlic cloves, thinly sliced
¹/₂ cup dry white wine
¹/₂ teaspoon chopped thyme leaves
1 cup unsalted chicken stock (such as Swanson), divided
1 teaspoon cornstarch
2 ounces pitted Castelvetrano olives
2 tablespoons fresh Meyer lemon juice
2 tablespoons butter
1 tablespoon parsley leaves

1. Preheat oven to 400°.
2. Heat a large ovenproof skillet over medium-high heat. Sprinkle chicken with ½ teaspoon salt and ½ teaspoon pepper; coat with cooking spray. Add chicken to pan, skin side down; cook 6 minutes or until skin is golden brown and crisp. Turn chicken over. Place pan in oven. Bake at 400° for 12 minutes or until a thermometer inserted in thickest portion of chicken registers 165°.
3. Remove chicken from pan; keep warm. Discard pan drippings (do not wipe pan clean). Add 1 tablespoon oil to pan; swirl to coat. Add potatoes to pan; sprinkle with ¼ teaspoon salt. Cook potatoes 3 minutes on each side or until browned. Remove potatoes from pan. Add lemon slices to pan; cook 1 minute on each side or until browned. Remove lemon from pan. Add 1 tablespoon oil to pan; swirl to coat. Add shallots and garlic; sauté 2 minutes, stirring occasionally. Add wine and chopped thyme; cook 1 minute or until liquid almost evaporates, scraping pan to loosen browned bits.
4. Return potatoes and lemon slices to pan. Add ⅔ cup stock, ¼ teaspoon salt, and ¼ teaspoon pepper; cook 2 minutes or until potatoes are tender. Combine ⅓ cup stock and cornstarch, stirring with a whisk. Add cornstarch mixture and olives to pan; bring to a boil. Cook 1 minute, stirring occasionally. Stir in lemon juice and butter, stirring until butter melts. Return chicken to pan, turning to coat; sprinkle with parsley. Serves 6 (serving size: 1 breast piece or 1 thigh, about ⅓ cup potato-lemon mixture, and 3 tablespoons sauce)

CALORIES 327; **FAT** 19.4g (sat 5.8g, mono 8.2g, poly 2.7g); **PROTEIN** 18.2g; **CARB** 16.3g; **FIBER** 1.8g; **CHOL** 67mg; **IRON** 1.6mg; **SODIUM** 619mg; **CALC** 33mg

Kid Friendly

If you like red potatoes try:
Skillet Chicken and Vegetables

Prepare Meyer Lemon Chicken through step 3, decreasing potatoes to 12 ounces, omitting lemons and shallots, and substituting 2 cups (½-inch-thick) slices carrot, 2 cups (½-inch-thick) slices celery, and 1 large red onion, cut into 12 wedges. Cook vegetables 10 minutes, stirring occasionally. Substitute 1 tablespoon chopped fresh oregano for thyme. Return potatoes to pan. Combine 1½ cups unsalted chicken stock and 2 teaspoons cornstarch. Add stock mixture, ½ teaspoon kosher salt, and ¼ teaspoon black pepper to pan; bring to a boil. Cook 1 minute. Stir in 2 tablespoons butter and 1 tablespoon fresh lemon juice. Return chicken to pan. Sprinkle with 1 tablespoon chopped fresh parsley. Serves 6 (serving size: 1 breast piece or 1 thigh, about 1 cup vegetable mixture, and about ¼ cup sauce)

CALORIES 399; **FAT** 23.7g (sat 7.2g); **SODIUM** 533mg

Chicken BLT Salad

(pictured on page 211)

Hands-on: 38 min. Total: 50 min.

1 cup fat-free buttermilk, divided
1 large egg white, lightly beaten
³/₄ cup panko (Japanese breadcrumbs)
4 (6-ounce) skinless, boneless chicken
    breast halves
³/₄ teaspoon black pepper,
    divided
¹/₄ teaspoon kosher salt, divided
3 tablespoons canola oil
¹/₃ cup canola mayonnaise
1 tablespoon chopped fresh dill
1 tablespoon chopped fresh chives
2 teaspoons white vinegar
1 teaspoon minced fresh garlic
1 medium head iceberg lettuce, cored
    and cut into 6 wedges
2 cups chopped plum tomato
2 ounces crumbled blue cheese
    (¹/₂ cup)
3 bacon slices, cooked and crumbled

1. Preheat oven to 425°.
2. Combine ½ cup buttermilk and egg white in a shallow dish. Place panko in a shallow dish. Dip chicken in egg white mixture; dredge in panko. Sprinkle with ¼ teaspoon pepper and ⅛ teaspoon salt.
3. Heat an ovenproof skillet over medium heat. Add oil; swirl to coat. Add chicken. Cook 4 minutes; turn over. Bake at 425° for 14 minutes or until done. Let chicken stand 10 minutes; slice crosswise.
4. Combine ½ cup buttermilk, ½ teaspoon pepper, mayonnaise, dill, chives, and vinegar. Place garlic on a cutting board; sprinkle with ⅛ teaspoon salt. Chop until a paste forms, scraping with the flat side of knife to mash. Add garlic to dressing.
5. Place 1 lettuce wedge on each of 6 plates. Top each serving evenly with chicken, ⅓ cup tomato, and 2½ tablespoons dressing. Sprinkle with cheese and crumbled bacon. Serves 6

CALORIES 368; **FAT** 23.5g (sat 4.2g, mono 11.2g, poly 5.2g); **PROTEIN** 26.7g; **CARB** 12.1g; **FIBER** 2.1g; **CHOL** 76mg; **IRON** 1mg; **SODIUM** 538mg; **CALC** 108mg

If you like pita bread try:
Middle Eastern Bread Salad with Chicken

Prepare Chicken BLT Salad through step 3, seasoning chicken with ¼ teaspoon kosher salt and pepper. Combine 4 cups torn whole-wheat pita, 2 cups halved cherry tomatoes, ½ cup torn basil, ⅓ cup thinly vertically sliced red onion, and ¼ cup chopped pitted kalamata olives in a large bowl. Combine ¼ cup red wine vinegar, 2 teaspoons Dijon mustard, ¼ teaspoon kosher salt, and ¼ teaspoon freshly ground black pepper, stirring well with a whisk. Gradually add 2 tablespoons extra-virgin olive oil, stirring constantly with a whisk. Drizzle dressing over pita mixture; toss to coat. Arrange about 1½ cups salad on each of 6 plates; divide sliced chicken evenly among servings. Top each serving with 1 tablespoon crumbled feta cheese. Serves 6

CALORIES 382; **FAT** 18.4g (sat 3.5g); **SODIUM** 603mg

If you like escarole try:
Escarole, White Bean, and Chicken Salad

Prepare Chicken BLT Salad through step 3, adding 1 tablespoon grated lemon rind to buttermilk mixture and 2 teaspoons chopped rosemary to panko, and seasoning chicken with ¼ teaspoon salt and ¼ teaspoon pepper. Combine 5 cups torn escarole, 1 cup parsley leaves, and 1 (15-ounce) can rinsed and drained Great Northern beans in a large bowl; sprinkle with ¼ teaspoon kosher salt and ¼ teaspoon black pepper. Combine ¼ cup fresh lemon juice, 2 tablespoons extra-virgin olive oil, 1 teaspoon minced fresh garlic, and ¼ teaspoon crushed red pepper, stirring well with a whisk. Drizzle over escarole mixture; toss. Place about 1 cup salad on each of 6 plates; divide chicken among servings. Serves 6

CALORIES 296; **FAT** 14.9g (sat 1.9g); **SODIUM** 313mg

MASTER CLASS

TODAY'S LESSON: STIR FRY

This fast, easy, and healthy way to cook involves just two commitments to ensure that your food has wok hay, the hard-to-describe but delicious seared, slightly smoky taste that you've enjoyed in any good Chinese restaurant. First: a wok that's cast iron, stainless steel, or rolled carbon steel (nonsticks can't handle the high heat). Second: a willingness to get that pan really hot. With those two things in place, you can swirl the ingredients briefly, which preserves crunch and heightens natural flavors as the wok hay develops. So find a proper pan, fire up your hottest burner, and get wokking!

Vegetarian

Veggie and Tofu Stir-Fry

Hands-on: 19 min. Total: 49 min.

1 (14-ounce) package water-packed extra-firm tofu, drained
1 tablespoon canola oil, divided
¼ teaspoon black pepper
3½ teaspoons cornstarch, divided
3 green onions, cut into 1-inch pieces
3 garlic cloves, sliced
1 tablespoon julienne-cut peeled fresh ginger
4 small baby bok choy, quartered lengthwise
2 large carrots, peeled and julienne-cut
1 cup snow peas, trimmed
2 tablespoons Shaoxing (Chinese rice wine) or dry sherry
¼ cup organic vegetable broth
2 tablespoons lower-sodium soy sauce
1 tablespoon hoisin sauce
1 teaspoon dark sesame oil

1. Cut tofu lengthwise into 4 equal pieces; cut each piece crosswise into ½-inch squares. Place tofu on several layers of paper towels; cover with additional paper towels. Let stand 30 minutes, pressing down occasionally.
2. Heat a large wok or skillet over high heat. Add 1½ teaspoons canola oil to pan; swirl to coat. Combine tofu, pepper, and 2 teaspoons cornstarch in a medium bowl; toss to coat. Add tofu to pan; stir-fry 8 minutes, turning to brown on all sides. Remove tofu from pan with a slotted spoon; place in a medium bowl. Add onions, garlic, and ginger to pan; stir-fry 1 minute. Remove from pan; add to tofu.
3. Add remaining 1½ teaspoons canola oil to pan; swirl to coat. Add bok choy; stir-fry 3 minutes. Add carrots; stir-fry 2 minutes. Add snow peas; stir-fry 1 minute. Add Shaoxing; cook 30 seconds, stirring constantly. Stir in tofu mixture.
4. Combine 1½ teaspoons cornstarch, broth, and remaining ingredients in a small bowl, stirring with a whisk. Add broth mixture to pan; cook until slightly thickened (about 1 minute). Serves 4 (serving size: about 1½ cups)

CALORIES 233; FAT 11.8g (sat 1.8g, mono 3.9g, poly 5.2g); PROTEIN 12.9g; CARB 17.5g; FIBER 3.2g; CHOL 0mg; IRON 3mg; SODIUM 389mg; CALC 227mg

STIR-FRY SUCCESS

HEAT TILL VERY HOT
Heat a wok over high heat for several minutes. Add oil, preferably canola, peanut, or another oil with a high smoke point.

DON'T OVERCROWD
Add ingredients in stages so each sizzles and "fries." An overcrowded wok will steam the food. In the recipe at left, the tofu is prefried for maximum flavor.

SAUCE IT UP
Make your sauce, and add it to all the ingredients in the wok. This is the finishing touch to most stir-fries—one last toss to complete the dish.

Stir-Fried Lemongrass Chicken

Hands-on: 25 min. Total: 25 min.

1 tablespoon brown sugar
2 tablespoons unsalted chicken stock
   (such as Swanson)
1 tablespoon fish sauce
2 teaspoons lower-sodium soy sauce
1 teaspoon sambal oelek (ground fresh
   chile paste)
2 tablespoons canola oil, divided
1 tablespoon sliced peeled fresh
   lemongrass
2 garlic cloves, sliced
1 cup sliced red bell pepper
1/2 cup sliced shallots
8 ounces haricots verts, trimmed
1 pound skinless, boneless chicken
   thighs, thinly sliced
1/3 cup unsalted cashews
1 Thai chile, thinly sliced

1. Combine first 5 ingredients.
2. Heat a large wok or large skillet over high heat. Add 1 tablespoon oil; swirl to coat. Add lemongrass and garlic; stir-fry 30 seconds. Remove from pan with a slotted spoon; place in a small bowl. Add bell pepper, shallots, and haricots verts to pan; stir-fry 2 minutes. Remove vegetables from pan with a slotted spoon; add to lemongrass mixture. Add 1 tablespoon oil to pan; swirl to coat. Add chicken in a single layer; cook 2 minutes or until browned. Add cashews and chile to pan; stir-fry 2 minutes or until chicken is done. Stir in stock mixture and vegetable mixture. Bring to a boil; cook 1 minute or until sauce begins to thicken. Serve immediately. Serves 4 (serving size: 1 cup)

CALORIES 330; **FAT** 16.9g (sat 2.7g, mono 8.9g, poly 4g); **PROTEIN** 26.7g; **CARB** 19.3g; **FIBER** 2.8g; **CHOL** 94mg; **IRON** 3mg; **SODIUM** 463mg; **CALC** 54mg

EVERYDAY VEGETARIAN

MEATLESS MONDAYS

Kid Friendly • Vegetarian

Butternut Squash Ravioli with Spinach Pesto

Hands-on: 41 min. Total: 1 hr. 15 min.
See our step-by-step ravioli-filling instructions on page 37.

1 butternut squash, halved lengthwise
   and seeded (about 1 1/2 pounds)
Cooking spray
1 tablespoon chopped fresh oregano
2 tablespoons unsalted butter, melted
2.5 ounces fresh Parmesan cheese,
   grated and divided
3/8 teaspoon salt, divided
1/2 teaspoon freshly ground black
   pepper, divided
36 wonton wrappers
1 large egg, lightly beaten
2 garlic cloves
1 1/2 cups fresh baby spinach
1/2 cup fresh basil
1/4 cup walnuts, toasted, chopped,
   and divided
2 tablespoons extra-virgin olive oil
2 tablespoons organic vegetable broth
1 teaspoon fresh lemon juice
6 quarts water

1. Preheat oven to 400°.
2. Place squash halves, cut sides down, on a foil-lined baking sheet coated with cooking spray. Bake at 400° for 30 minutes or until tender. Cool. Scoop out pulp; discard peel. Mash pulp. Combine oregano, squash pulp, and butter in a large bowl. Stir in 2 ounces (about 1/2 cup) cheese, 1/4 teaspoon salt, and 1/4 teaspoon pepper. Working with 1 wonton wrapper at a time (cover remaining wrappers with a damp towel to keep them from drying), spoon about 1 1/2 teaspoons squash mixture into center of each wrapper. Moisten edges of wrapper with beaten egg; bring 2 opposite corners together. Pinch edges together to seal, forming a triangle. Repeat procedure with remaining wrappers, squash mixture, and egg. Cover ravioli loosely with a towel to prevent drying.
3. Place garlic in a food processor, and pulse until finely chopped. Add remaining 1/2 ounce (about 2 tablespoons) cheese, 1/8 teaspoon salt, 1/4 teaspoon pepper, spinach, basil, and 2 tablespoons walnuts. With processor on, slowly pour oil, broth, and juice through food chute. Process until well blended. Place pesto in a large bowl.
4. Bring 6 quarts water to a boil in a large Dutch oven. Add half of ravioli; cook 3 minutes or until thoroughly cooked. Remove ravioli with a slotted spoon. Repeat procedure with remaining ravioli. Add ravioli to pesto; toss gently to coat. Arrange 6 ravioli on each of 6 plates; sprinkle each serving with 1 teaspoon walnuts. Serves 6

CALORIES 344; **FAT** 15.7g (sat 5.2g, mono 5.8g, poly 3.5g); **PROTEIN** 11.1g; **CARB** 41.8g; **FIBER** 3.6g; **CHOL** 57mg; **IRON** 3mg; **SODIUM** 586mg; **CALC** 189mg

SMART SUB: WONTON WRAPPERS

Wonton wrappers, found in most grocery stores near the tofu, are a brilliant sub for fresh pasta when making homemade ravioli. The dough is light and thin, and it cooks to a silky texture and beautiful translucence.

HOW TO MAKE EASY SHORTCUT RAVIOLI

It's so easy—just be sure to seal the edges well so the filling doesn't leak out.

1. Spoon filling in the center of the wrapper.

2. Moisten edges of wrapper with a beaten egg.

3. Fold in half, bringing two corners together.

4. Press edges firmly to seal; then cook in boiling water.

Kid Friendly • Vegetarian

Lemon-Cornmeal Waffles with Raspberry-Rhubarb Compote

Hands-on: 50 min. Total: 65 min. This compote uses frozen fruit, which is as nutritious as fresh and readily available in winter. The honeyed yogurt offers a sweet balance for the tangy compote, which can be made ahead and refrigerated for up to one week. While Greek yogurt offers a thicker base for the topping, plain low-fat yogurt can be substituted, if desired.

Compote:
3/4 cup sugar
1 (16-ounce) package frozen sliced rhubarb, thawed
1 (12-ounce) package frozen unsweetened raspberries, thawed and undrained

Waffles:
3/4 cup medium stone-ground cornmeal (such as Bob's Red Mill)
1 cup boiling water
Cooking spray
2 large eggs, lightly beaten
2 tablespoons unsalted butter, melted
2 teaspoons grated lemon rind
1 tablespoon fresh lemon juice
4.5 ounces all-purpose flour (about 1 cup)
1 tablespoon sugar
2 teaspoons reduced-sodium baking powder (such as Rumford)
1 teaspoon kosher salt
1/2 teaspoon baking soda
3/4 cup plain low-fat yogurt
1/2 cup 2% reduced-fat milk

Topping:
3/4 cup plain fat-free Greek yogurt
2 tablespoons mascarpone cheese
2 tablespoons honey
1/2 teaspoon grated lemon rind

1. To prepare compote, combine first 3 ingredients in a medium saucepan over medium-high heat; bring to a boil. Cover and simmer 25 minutes or until rhubarb is tender and mixture thickens, stirring occasionally. Remove from heat, and keep warm.

2. To prepare waffles, combine cornmeal and 1 cup boiling water in a large bowl. Let stand 20 minutes or until cooled to room temperature.

3. Coat a waffle iron with cooking spray; preheat.

4. Add eggs to cornmeal mixture; stir with a whisk to combine. Stir in butter, 2 teaspoons rind, and juice. Weigh or lightly spoon flour into a dry measuring cup; level with a knife. Combine flour and next 4 ingredients in a bowl; stir to combine. Add flour mixture to cornmeal mixture. Combine low-fat yogurt and milk in a bowl; stir with a whisk until smooth. Add yogurt mixture to cornmeal mixture, stirring just until combined.

5. Spoon about 1/4 cup batter per 4-inch waffle onto hot waffle iron, spreading batter to edges. Cook 3 to 5 minutes or until done; repeat procedure with remaining batter.

6. To prepare topping, combine Greek yogurt and remaining ingredients in a small bowl; stir until smooth. Serve waffles with warm compote and yogurt topping. Serves 8 (serving size: 2 waffles, 1/4 cup compote, and 2 tablespoons topping)

CALORIES 334; FAT 8.7g (sat 4.5g, mono 2.7g, poly 0.9g); PROTEIN 8.9g; CARB 57.8g; FIBER 4.2g; CHOL 72mg; IRON 1.8mg; SODIUM 444mg; CALC 237mg

THE LIFT OF LEMONGRASS

By Naomi Duguid

Most supermarkets now sell this durable, fragrant herb. It's a secret weapon in soups, spice rubs, and more.

With its strong citrusy aroma and light lemon flavor, lemongrass is a cook's friend in dishes beyond the curries with which it's most associated. I like to process it to a paste with garlic, black pepper, and salt or fish sauce, and then rub the paste onto flank steak or chicken before grilling for great flavor.

I find it especially useful in making chicken broth, or even when I have a ready-made soup broth and want to make it more interesting. I use it whole, like a bay leaf, and it's hard to believe what an enlivening difference it makes, adding a sublime fragrance. I've come to think of it as my secret ingredient.

Look for lemongrass that feels firm at the bulb end, even if the upper stalk is dried out. Store it in the refrigerator, loosely wrapped in plastic. It will keep for a week or more, gradually losing flavor as it dries. Keep in mind that the flavor is only in the bulb end—the bottom few inches. Follow the prep instructions in the recipe to release the most flavor.

Kid Friendly • Freezable
Make Ahead

Lemony, Fragrant Chicken Broth

Hands-on: 15 min. Total: 9 hr. 15 min.
Delicious on its own or in recipes that call for broth. For a main-dish soup, pick the chicken meat off the bones, and add it and 1½ cups cooked rice to the broth.

8 cups water
2 pounds skin-on, bone-in chicken leg quarters
3 stalks fresh lemongrass
4 (¼-inch) slices peeled fresh ginger
1 tablespoon chopped garlic
1 teaspoon black peppercorns
½ teaspoon salt
¼ cup cilantro leaves

1. Combine 8 cups water and chicken leg quarters in a Dutch oven. Bring to a boil, skimming and discarding foam as needed. Reduce heat to low.
2. Trim and discard root end of lemongrass stalks; discard toughest outer leaves. Smash stalks with the flat side of a knife. Add lemongrass, ginger, garlic, and peppercorns to pan. Partially cover, and simmer 50 minutes, skimming and discarding foam as needed. Remove chicken from pan using a slotted spoon; reserve for another use.
3. Strain broth through a cheesecloth-lined colander; discard solids. Cool to room temperature. Cover and chill 8 hours or overnight. Skim solid fat from surface; discard.
4. Heat broth in Dutch oven over medium heat, and stir in salt. Sprinkle with cilantro leaves. Serves 6 (serving size: about 1 cup)

CALORIES 19; FAT 0.6g (sat 0.2g, mono 0.2g, poly 0.1g); PROTEIN 3.1g; CARB 0.3g; FIBER 0g; CHOL 12mg; IRON 0.2mg; SODIUM 210mg; CALC 2mg

3 MORE EVERYDAY USES FOR LEMONGRASS

Think of lemongrass as a subtler, more aromatic form of lemon rind.

1. Crush a trimmed stalk, and steep it in a pot of tea.

2. Toss some minced lemongrass in your next batch of steamed mussels or shrimp.

3. Steep a crushed stalk or two in the milk mixture for ice cream.

KID IN THE KITCHEN

KID-SIZED APPLE PIES

Matisse bakes a simple, portable version of the all-American classic.

We asked Matisse Reid, our favorite 11-year-old foodie, to bake some bite-sized pies. Here's her report: "Tonight I made Apple-Toffee Hand Pies, and they were GOOD! I would suggest buying double the ingredients because you are going to want to make these again. If you can't find toffee chips, you can buy toffee candy. Put the candy into a zip-top bag, place the bag on a chopping board, and carefully use a hammer to smash the candy into tiny pieces. This worked great for me in this recipe, and it was pretty fun to do. Rather than mixing it in with the other ingredients, I sprinkled the toffee on the pies right before I sealed them to make sure every pie got some candy. Be sure also to cut the apple into really tiny pieces—you don't want it too big because you can't get as much filling into each pie. You can serve these with vanilla ice cream or whipped cream, but they are delicious by themselves."

Kid Friendly • Make Ahead

Apple-Toffee Hand Pies

(pictured on page 211)

Hands-on: 25 min. Total: 55 min.

2 cups finely chopped Gala or Rome
    apple
2 tablespoons toffee chips
1 tablespoon sugar
1½ teaspoons fresh lemon juice
½ teaspoon ground cinnamon
1 (14.1-ounce) package refrigerated pie
    dough (such as Pillsbury)
Cooking spray
1 large egg, lightly beaten
1 tablespoon unsalted butter, cut into
    12 cubes

1. Preheat oven to 375°.
2. Combine apple, toffee chips, sugar, lemon juice, and cinnamon in a bowl.
3. Roll dough on a lightly floured surface into 2 (12-inch) circles. Using a 3-inch round cookie cutter, cut each dough portion into 12 rounds. Discard any remaining dough scraps. Place 12 dough rounds on a baking sheet coated with cooking spray. Brush half of beaten egg over dough rounds. Spoon about 1 tablespoon apple-toffee mixture onto each round, leaving a ½-inch border around the edges of the dough. Top each round with 1 piece of butter. Top pies with remaining 12 rounds of dough; press edges together with a fork to seal. Brush remaining half of beaten egg over dough rounds. Bake at 375° for 25 minutes or until golden brown. Serves 12 (serving size: 1 pie)

CALORIES 142; **FAT** 8.3g (sat 3.1g, mono 2.4g, poly 1.6g); **PROTEIN** 1g; **CARB** 15.3g; **FIBER** 0.2g; **CHOL** 24mg; **IRON** 0.1mg; **SODIUM** 114mg; **CALC** 4mg

RECIPE MAKEOVER

LESS-LOADED POTATO SOUP

This hearty bowl is made light and velvety-rich with a secret ingredient. No butter, no cream—just good.

The irresistible trifecta of starchy, creamy, and comforting pleasures found in loaded potato soup makes this warming bowl a restaurant and home-cooked favorite, especially on chilly, wintry days. It's comforting all right—and caloric, too, after the humble spud gets lost in loads of butter, cream, bacon, and cheese to the tune of 525 calories and 16 grams of saturated fat.

The challenge with lightening is obtaining that luscious, creamy texture without any cream. You can't just toss potatoes in the blender and puree until smooth. (See tips at right.) Cauliflower, however, has a smooth flavor and less starchy profile. When roasted, it develops a creamy interior that becomes delightfully smooth when blended with reduced-fat milk; this is the light, earthy base for our chunky potato soup. Not an ounce of cream goes into this cozy bowl of goodness, leaving room for some indulgence—the very necessary sprinkle of smoky bacon, sharp cheddar cheese, and bright green onion crunch.

TIPS FOR A PERFECT CREAMY TEXTURE

1. Roasting the cauliflower deepens the flavor and softens the texture. We blend it smooth with reduced-fat milk for a super-creamy base, saving 5g sat fat per bowl over heavy cream.

2. Lightly pulse the potato mixture; do not blend. Overworked potatoes make for gluey, gummy soup. For a fiber (and flavor!) booster, leave the skins on half the potatoes.

3. Fromage blanc (a creamy, tart, fat-free cheese) saves 42 calories and 3g sat fat per ounce over full-fat sour cream. You can sub fat-free sour cream if you can't find fromage blanc.

continued

Creamy, Light Potato Soup

Hands-on: 35 min. Total: 1 hr. 10 min.
Because cauliflower has two-thirds fewer calories per ounce than the starchy potato, swapping some in is both wise and tasty.

1½ tablespoons extra-virgin olive oil, divided
1 cup chopped onion
1 teaspoon chopped fresh thyme
5 garlic cloves, chopped
1 pound cubed peeled baking potato (about 2)
1 pound cubed Yukon gold potato (about 4)
5 cups unsalted chicken stock (such as Swanson)
1 teaspoon kosher salt, divided
1 bay leaf
1 pound cauliflower, cut into florets (about ½ head)
¾ teaspoon freshly ground black pepper, divided
Cooking spray
1½ cups 2% reduced-fat milk
¾ cup chopped green onions, divided
½ cup fat-free fromage blanc (such as Vermont Creamery) or sour cream
2 ounces grated sharp cheddar cheese (about ½ cup)
4 center-cut bacon slices, cooked and crumbled

1. Preheat oven to 450°.
2. Heat a large Dutch oven over medium-high heat. Add 1½ teaspoons oil to pan; swirl to coat. Add onion, thyme, and garlic; sauté 5 minutes or until tender, stirring occasionally. Add potatoes, stock, ½ teaspoon salt, and bay leaf; bring to a boil. Cover, reduce heat, and simmer 35 minutes or until potatoes are very tender, stirring occasionally. Remove from heat; discard bay leaf.
3. While potatoes simmer, combine 1 tablespoon oil, cauliflower, ¼ teaspoon salt, and ¼ teaspoon pepper on a jelly-roll pan coated with cooking spray; toss to coat. Roast at 450° for 30 minutes or until browned, turning once.
4. Place cauliflower mixture and milk in a blender. Remove center piece of blender lid (to allow steam to escape); secure blender lid on blender. Place a clean towel over opening (to avoid splatters). Blend until smooth. Pour cauliflower mixture into a large bowl. Add half of potato mixture to blender; pulse 5 to 6 times or until coarsely chopped. Pour into bowl with cauliflower mixture. Repeat with remaining potato mixture. Place cauliflower-potato mixture in Dutch oven over medium heat. Stir in ¼ teaspoon salt, ½ teaspoon pepper, ½ cup green onions, and fromage blanc; stir until fromage blanc melts. Ladle soup into 8 bowls. Top evenly with green onions, cheese, and bacon. Serves 8 (serving size: about 1¼ cups soup, 1½ teaspoons green onions, 1 tablespoon cheese, and 1½ teaspoons bacon)

CALORIES 223; FAT 6.7g (sat 2.7g, mono 2.8g, poly 0.5g); PROTEIN 12.7g; CARB 29.7g; FIBER 3.5g; CHOL 15mg; IRON 1.8mg; SODIUM 478mg; CALC 185mg

CLASSIC	MAKEOVER
525 calories per bowl	223 calories per bowl
16 grams saturated fat	2.7 grams saturated fat
1,143 milligrams sodium	478 milligrams sodium

WHAT TO COOK RIGHT NOW

A HEALTHY CHILI

Could there be any food more perfect this time of year than meaty, hearty chili—made light for the new year? Here's a new take on the classic, amped up with rich ground bison in place of ground beef (but use beef if you can't find the bison) and chunks of sweet acorn squash.

Freezable • Make Ahead

Bison Chili with Chickpeas and Acorn Squash

Hands-on: 40 min. Total: 1 hr. 50 min.

2 dried ancho chiles
2 cups unsalted beef stock (such as Swanson)
1 (8-ounce) package fresh cremini mushrooms
Cooking spray
1½ pounds 90% lean ground bison or ground sirloin
1 teaspoon kosher salt, divided
¾ teaspoon black pepper, divided
2 cups chopped onion
1 cup chopped green bell pepper
1 tablespoon minced garlic
1 tablespoon unsalted tomato paste
1 tablespoon chili powder
2 teaspoons dried oregano
1 teaspoon ground coriander
¾ teaspoon cumin seeds, toasted
1 (12-ounce) bottle dark Mexican beer
1 (28-ounce) can crushed tomatoes
2 cups (½-inch) cubed peeled acorn squash
1 (14.5-ounce) can unsalted chickpeas, rinsed and drained
½ cup reduced-fat sour cream
½ cup chopped fresh flat-leaf parsley

1. Combine chiles and stock in a microwave-safe bowl; microwave at HIGH 3 minutes. Let stand 10 minutes. Remove stems. Combine chile mixture and mushrooms in a blender; process until smooth.

2. Heat a Dutch oven over high heat. Coat pan with cooking spray. Add bison, ½ teaspoon salt, and ½ teaspoon black pepper; cook 6 minutes or until browned, stirring to crumble. Remove bison from pan. Reduce heat to medium-high. Add onion and bell pepper to pan; sauté 5 minutes. Stir in garlic; sauté 1 minute. Stir in tomato paste; cook 2 minutes, stirring frequently. Add chili powder, oregano, coriander, and cumin; sauté 30 seconds. Return bison to pan. Stir in beer; cook 3 minutes or until liquid is reduced by half. Stir in mushroom mixture and tomatoes; bring to a simmer. Reduce heat, and simmer 25 minutes. Stir in squash and chickpeas; simmer 45 minutes. Stir in ½ teaspoon salt and ¼ teaspoon black pepper. Ladle chili into 8 bowls. Top with sour cream and parsley. Serves 8 (serving size: about 1½ cups chili, 1 tablespoon sour cream, and 1 tablespoon parsley)

CALORIES 295; FAT 9.3g (sat 3.8g, mono 3g, poly 0.8g); PROTEIN 24.3g; CARB 29.4g; FIBER 6.5g; CHOL 53mg; IRON 5.8mg; SODIUM 518mg; CALC 126mg

IF YOU CAN'T FIND BISON, USE LEAN GROUND SIRLOIN INSTEAD.

FEED 4 FOR LESS THAN $10

Pork shoulder becomes meltingly tender in a stew made bright with orange and cranberry. Plus, hearty peas and soup.

$2.15/serving, $8.58 total

Make Ahead

Orange-Cranberry Pork Stew

Hands-on: 36 min. Total: 2 hr. 6 min.

1 medium orange
1½ teaspoons dark sesame oil
1 pound boneless pork shoulder (Boston butt), trimmed and cut into 1-inch pieces
¼ teaspoon kosher salt
½ cup coarsely chopped onion
5 garlic cloves, chopped
1 cup unsalted chicken stock
1 tablespoon dark brown sugar
2 tablespoons lower-sodium soy sauce
1 tablespoon rice vinegar
2 teaspoons sambal oelek (ground fresh chile paste)
1 cup fresh cranberries
4 cups hot cooked long-grain white rice
2 tablespoons diagonally sliced green onions

1. Preheat oven to 325°.
2. Peel and section orange over a bowl; squeeze membranes to extract juice. Set sections aside; reserve juice.
3. Heat a Dutch oven over medium-high heat. Add oil to pan; swirl to coat. Sprinkle pork evenly with salt. Add pork to pan; sauté 5 minutes, turning to brown on all sides. Add ½ cup chopped onion to pan; sauté 2 minutes, stirring occasionally. Add garlic; sauté 1 minute, stirring constantly. Stir in orange sections, orange juice, stock, and next 4 ingredients. Cover; bake at 325° for 1 hour. Stir in cranberries. Bake, covered, at 325° for an additional 30 minutes or until pork is fork-tender. Place 1 cup rice in each of 4 bowls; top each serving with about ¾ cup pork mixture. Sprinkle each serving with 1½ teaspoons green onions. Serves 4

CALORIES 440; FAT 8.8g (sat 2.7g, mono 3.7g, poly 1.6g); PROTEIN 28.2g; CARB 60.4g; FIBER 3.1g; CHOL 68mg; IRON 3.8mg; SODIUM 427mg; CALC 70mg

Kid Friendly

$1.90/serving, $7.58 total

Black-Eyed Peas and Cornmeal Dumplings

Hands-on: 25 min. Total: 55 min. A pot of black-eyed peas on New Year's Day is a Southern tradition said to bring good luck for the year ahead. Make the tradition even better with bacon-y buttermilk dumplings and a dash of your favorite hot sauce. For a quick side of collards, bring ½ cup lower-sodium chicken broth, ½ cup water, and 2 minced garlic cloves to a simmer in a large skillet. Add 1 (16-ounce) bag chopped collard greens; cover and cook 10 minutes or until tender.

2 hickory-smoked bacon slices
1 cup chopped onion
1 tablespoon minced fresh garlic
3 cups unsalted chicken stock (such as Swanson)
1½ cups water
½ teaspoon kosher salt
½ teaspoon freshly ground black pepper
1 (16-ounce) bag frozen black-eyed peas (about 2¾ cups)
3.4 ounces all-purpose flour (about ¾ cup)
⅓ cup finely chopped green onions
¼ cup yellow cornmeal
¼ teaspoon baking soda
2 tablespoons chilled butter, cut into pieces
½ cup buttermilk
Hot sauce (optional)

continued

1. Cook bacon in a Dutch oven over medium heat until crisp. Remove bacon from pan; finely chop. Remove 1 tablespoon drippings from pan; set aside. Increase heat to medium-high. Add 1 cup onion to remaining drippings in pan; sauté 3 minutes, stirring occasionally. Add garlic; sauté 1 minute, stirring constantly. Add stock, 1½ cups water, salt, pepper, and peas to pan; bring to a boil. Partially cover, reduce heat, and simmer 35 minutes or until peas are tender, stirring occasionally.
2. Weigh or lightly spoon flour into a dry measuring cup; level with a knife. Combine flour, green onions, cornmeal, and baking soda, stirring with a whisk. Cut butter into flour mixture with a pastry blender or 2 knives until mixture resembles coarse meal. Add bacon, reserved 1 tablespoon drippings, and buttermilk; stir until a moist dough forms.
3. With moist hands, gently divide mixture into 12 equal portions. Drop dumplings, 1 at a time, into pan; cover and cook 8 minutes or until dumplings are done, stirring occasionally. Serve with hot sauce, if desired. Serves 4 (serving size: about 1 cup pea mixture and 3 dumplings)

CALORIES 405; FAT 8.9g (sat 5.1g, mono 1.6g, poly 0.7g); PROTEIN 20g; CARB 62.3g; FIBER 7.5g; CHOL 23mg; IRON 4.5mg; SODIUM 581mg; CALC 68mg

Make Ahead
$2.49/serving, $9.97 total

Roasted Cauliflower Soup

Hands-on: 20 min. Total: 1 hr. 20 min.
Serve with a salad of parsley leaves and 6 ounces arugula, tossed with a squeeze of fresh lemon juice.

8 cups cauliflower florets (about 1 large head)
2 teaspoons olive oil
½ teaspoon kosher salt, divided
Cooking spray
4 thin slices prosciutto or other cured ham, chopped (about 1½ ounces)

1 tablespoon unsalted butter, divided
¾ cup chopped yellow onion
4 garlic cloves, chopped
4 cups unsalted chicken stock
1 cup water
½ cup half-and-half
1 ounce French bread baguette, torn
¼ cup chopped fresh flat-leaf parsley
3 tablespoons sliced almonds, toasted

1. Preheat oven to 450°.
2. Place cauliflower in a large bowl; drizzle with oil, and sprinkle with ¼ teaspoon salt. Toss to coat. Arrange mixture in a single layer on a jelly-roll pan coated with cooking spray. Bake at 450° for 40 minutes or until tender and browned, stirring once after 30 minutes.
3. Heat a large Dutch oven over medium heat. Coat pan with cooking spray. Add ham; cook 3 minutes or until crisp. Remove ham; drain on paper towels. Melt 1½ teaspoons butter in pan. Add onion and garlic; sauté 5 minutes, stirring occasionally. Add cauliflower, stock, and 1 cup water; bring to a boil. Reduce heat, and simmer 20 minutes, stirring occasionally. Remove from heat; stir in half-and-half. Place half of cauliflower mixture in a blender. Remove center piece of blender lid (to allow steam to escape); secure blender lid on blender. Place a clean towel over opening in blender lid (to avoid splatters). Blend until smooth; pour pureed soup into a bowl. Repeat with remaining cauliflower mixture. Stir in ¼ teaspoon salt.
4. Place torn bread in a food processor; pulse 2 times or until coarsely chopped. Melt 1½ teaspoons butter in a skillet over medium heat; swirl. Add breadcrumbs; sauté 5 minutes or until golden, stirring frequently. Remove from heat. Combine ham, breadcrumbs, parsley, and toasted almonds. Ladle about 1¼ cups soup into each of 4 bowls; top each serving with about 2½ tablespoons toasted breadcrumb mixture. Serves 4

CALORIES 245; FAT 12.6g (sat 5g, mono 4.3g, poly 1.1g); PROTEIN 14.7g; CARB 21.7g; FIBER 5.6g; CHOL 25mg; IRON 2.2mg; SODIUM 646mg; CALC 132mg

DINNER TONIGHT

Fast weeknight menus from the Cooking Light Test Kitchen

READY IN
40
MINUTES

.... *The* ....
SHOPPING LIST

Spicy Shrimp Noodle Soup
Fresh ginger
Garlic
Bean sprouts
Green onions
Fresh cilantro
Fresh basil
Lime (1)
Dried shiitake mushrooms
Cinnamon sticks
Star anise
Unsalted beef stock
8-ounce bottle clam juice
Lower-sodium soy sauce
Fish sauce
Sambal oelek (ground fresh chile paste)
4 ounces flat rice noodles
1 pound peeled and deveined large shrimp

Pickled Vegetables
English cucumber
Red onion (1)
Cauliflower
Garlic
White vinegar
Sugar
Crushed red pepper

The GAME PLAN

Prep pickled vegetables.
While vegetables pickle:
- Simmer stock mixture.
- Cook noodles.
- Finish soup.

Quick & Easy

Spicy Shrimp Noodle Soup

With Pickled Vegetables
(pictured on page 211)

Simple Sub: Use 1 cup sliced fresh shiitake caps instead of dried.
Make-Ahead Tip: Make pickled vegetables a day in advance, and chill.
Flavor Hit: Cinnamon, star anise, and ginger lend the broth enticing, exotic flavor.

3 cups unsalted beef stock (such as Swanson)
1 cup water
1 tablespoon minced garlic
1 tablespoon sambal oelek (ground fresh chile paste) or 1/2 teaspoon crushed red pepper
1 teaspoon fish sauce
1 teaspoon lower-sodium soy sauce
2 (3-inch) cinnamon sticks
1 (8-ounce) bottle clam juice
1 ounce dried shiitake mushroom caps, chopped
1 (1-inch) piece peeled fresh ginger
1 star anise
1 pound large shrimp, peeled and deveined
4 ounces uncooked flat rice noodles
1/2 cup fresh bean sprouts
1/2 cup diagonally cut green onions
1/4 cup cilantro leaves
12 small basil leaves
4 lime wedges

1. Combine first 11 ingredients in a large saucepan. Bring to a boil; reduce heat, and simmer until reduced to 3½ cups (about 12 minutes). Add shrimp; cook 4 minutes or until done. Remove cinnamon, anise, and ginger; discard. Cook rice noodles according to package directions; drain. Place ½ cup noodles in each of 4 bowls, and top each serving with 1 cup stock mixture and about 5 shrimp. Sprinkle evenly with bean sprouts, green onions, cilantro, and basil. Serve with lime wedges. Serves 4

CALORIES 287; **FAT** 2.1g (sat 0.4g, mono 0.3g, poly 0.8g); **PROTEIN** 26.7g; **CARB** 40.3g; **FIBER** 4g; **CHOL** 174mg; **IRON** 11.1mg; **SODIUM** 537mg; **CALC** 96mg

For the Pickled Vegetables:
Combine ½ cup sugar, ¾ cup white vinegar, ¾ teaspoon kosher salt, ½ teaspoon crushed red pepper, ½ teaspoon freshly ground black pepper, and 3 crushed garlic cloves in a small saucepan over medium-high heat; bring to a boil, stirring to dissolve sugar. Remove from heat. Add 2 cups thinly sliced unpeeled English cucumber, 1 cup thinly sliced red onion, and ½ cup cauliflower florets. Let vegetable mixture stand 30 minutes; drain well. Serves 4 (serving size: ½ cup)

CALORIES 123; **FAT** 0.2g (sat 0g); **SODIUM** 127mg

READY IN
40
MINUTES

The SHOPPING LIST

Greek Chicken Bread Salad
Fresh oregano
Lemon (1)
Red bell pepper (1)
Romaine lettuce
Garlic
French bread baguette
15-ounce jar pepperoncini peppers
Olive oil
Red wine vinegar
Crushed red pepper
2 (8-ounce) skinless, boneless chicken breasts halves
Feta cheese

Olive-Almond Green Beans
Green beans
Lemon (1)
Kalamata olives
Sliced toasted almonds
Extra-virgin olive oil

The GAME PLAN

While chicken cooks:
- Make vinaigrette.
- Chop lettuce and slice red bell pepper.
While green beans cook:
- Finish salad.

continued

Quick & Easy

Greek Chicken Bread Salad

With Olive-Almond Green Beans

Shopping Tip: Look for jarred pepperoncini in the olive section.
Prep Pointer: Browning the chicken first speeds up cooking and deepens flavor.
Simple Sub: You can use chopped fresh mozzarella instead of the tangy feta.

3 ounces cubed French bread baguette, crust removed
Cooking spray
1 tablespoon chopped fresh oregano
3 tablespoons olive oil
1½ tablespoons red wine vinegar
2 teaspoons minced fresh garlic
2 teaspoons grated lemon rind
⅛ teaspoon crushed red pepper
1 pound skinless, boneless chicken breast halves
¼ teaspoon freshly ground black pepper
⅛ teaspoon kosher salt
3 cups chopped romaine lettuce
1 cup sliced red bell pepper (about 1 large)
½ cup sliced pepperoncini peppers
1.5 ounces feta cheese, crumbled (about ⅓ cup)

1. Preheat broiler to high.
2. Place baguette cubes on a baking sheet; coat with cooking spray. Broil 2 minutes or until edges are browned, turning once.
3. Reduce oven temperature to 425°.
4. Combine oregano and next 5 ingredients in a large bowl, stirring with a whisk; set aside.
5. Heat a large ovenproof skillet over medium-high heat; coat pan with cooking spray. Sprinkle chicken evenly with black pepper and salt. Place chicken in pan; cook 4 minutes on each side or until browned. Place pan in oven, and bake at 425° for 10 minutes or until chicken is done. Remove

pan from oven. Let chicken stand 5 minutes; slice thinly across the grain.
6. Add bread cubes, lettuce, bell pepper, pepperoncini peppers, and feta to oregano mixture; toss well. Place about 1⅓ cups salad on each of 4 plates. Top each serving with about 3 ounces chicken. Serves 4

CALORIES 325; **FAT** 14.2g (sat 3.4g, mono 8.2g, poly 1.5g); **PROTEIN** 30.5g; **CARB** 18g; **FIBER** 19g; **CHOL** 75mg; **IRON** 2.2mg; **SODIUM** 562mg; **CALC** 88mg

For Olive-Almond Green Beans:
Cook 1 pound trimmed green beans in boiling water in a large saucepan 3 minutes or until crisp-tender; drain well. Heat a large skillet over medium heat. Add 1 tablespoon extra-virgin olive oil to pan; swirl to coat. Add green beans, ¼ cup sliced toasted almonds, 3 tablespoons chopped pitted kalamata olives, 1 tablespoon grated lemon rind, and ⅛ teaspoon salt. Cook bean mixture 2 minutes, tossing well. Serves 4 (serving size: about ½ cup)

CALORIES 129; **FAT** 9.2g (sat 1.1g); **SODIUM** 254mg

READY IN 40 MINUTES

The SHOPPING LIST

Pan-Seared Steak with Chive-Horseradish Butter
Fresh chives
4 (4-ounce) beef tenderloin steaks
Prepared horseradish
Butter

Roasted Sweet Potatoes and Broccolini
Fresh thyme
Sweet potatoes
Broccolini
Extra-virgin olive oil
Crushed red pepper

The GAME PLAN

While oven preheats:
  ■ Prep sweet potatoes and Broccolini.
While vegetables roast:
  ■ Make butter mixture.
  ■ Cook steaks.

Quick & Easy

Pan-Seared Steak with Chive-Horseradish Butter

With Roasted Sweet Potatoes and Broccolini

Kid Tweak: Substitute baby carrots for the Broccolini.
Technique Tip: Snip chives with a pair of kitchen scissors instead of chopping.
Flavor Swap: Substitute 1 minced anchovy filet for the horseradish in the butter mixture.

5 teaspoons butter, softened
1 tablespoon prepared horseradish
1 tablespoon minced fresh chives
4 (4-ounce) beef tenderloin steaks
¼ teaspoon kosher salt
¼ teaspoon freshly ground black pepper
Cooking spray

1. Combine first 3 ingredients in a small bowl. Refrigerate 20 minutes or until firm.
2. Sprinkle steaks evenly with salt and pepper. Heat a large grill pan over medium-high heat. Coat pan with cooking spray. Add steaks to pan; cook 4 minutes on each side or until desired degree of doneness. Remove steaks from pan; let stand 5 minutes. Divide butter mixture among steaks. Serves 4 (serving size: 1 steak and about 1 tablespoon butter mixture)

CALORIES 220; **FAT** 12.4g (sat 5.8g, mono 4.2g, poly 0.5g); **PROTEIN** 25.2g; **CARB** 0.6g; **FIBER** 0.2g; **CHOL** 89mg; **IRON** 1.9mg; **SODIUM** 229mg; **CALC** 32mg

For the Roasted Sweet Potatoes and Broccolini:

Preheat oven to 425°. Combine 1 tablespoon extra-virgin olive oil, 2 teaspoons chopped fresh thyme, ¼ teaspoon kosher salt, ¼ teaspoon freshly ground black pepper, and 1 pound thinly sliced peeled sweet potatoes in a large bowl, tossing to coat sweet potatoes evenly. Place sweet potatoes on a jelly-roll pan, and bake at 425° for 16 minutes. Combine 1 tablespoon extra-virgin olive oil, ¼ teaspoon kosher salt, ¼ teaspoon crushed red pepper, and 6 ounces trimmed Broccolini or broccoli spears in a bowl, tossing to coat Broccolini evenly. Remove sweet potatoes from oven, and stir. Arrange Broccolini on baking sheet with sweet potatoes; bake at 425° for 12 minutes or until Broccolini is crisp-tender and sweet potatoes are fork-tender. Serves 4 (serving size: about ¾ cup sweet potatoes and about 2 Broccolini spears)

CALORIES 138; FAT 6.8g (sat 1g); SODIUM 290mg

READY IN
40
MINUTES

The
SHOPPING LIST

Quick Beef Stroganoff
Onion (1)
Green onions
Fresh flat-leaf parsley
6-ounce package presliced exotic mushroom blend
Lower-sodium beef broth
All-purpose flour
Hot paprika
4 ounces egg noodles
1 (1-pound) flank steak
Fat-free sour cream
Butter

Grainy Mustard Brussels Sprouts
Brussels sprouts
Whole-grain mustard
Butter

The
GAME PLAN

While water for noodles comes to a boil:
- Slice beef.
- Prepare Brussels sprouts.

While beef mixture cooks:
- Cook noodles.
- Cook Brussels sprouts.

Kid Friendly • Quick & Easy
Quick Beef Stroganoff

With Grainy Mustard Brussels Sprouts

Simple Swap: Sub slightly more-tender sirloin for flank steak.
Prep Pointer: Be sure to slice the beef thinly across the grain so it doesn't get tough.
Flavor Hit: Whole-grain mustard adds pungent, tangy notes to the Brussels sprouts.

6½ cups water, divided
4 ounces uncooked egg noodles
1 (1-pound) flank steak, trimmed
Cooking spray
1 cup chopped onion
½ teaspoon freshly ground black pepper
½ teaspoon kosher salt
¼ teaspoon hot paprika
1 (6-ounce) package presliced exotic mushroom blend
1 cup lower-sodium beef broth, divided
5 teaspoons all-purpose flour
⅓ cup fat-free sour cream
3 tablespoons thinly sliced green onions
1 tablespoon butter
2 tablespoons chopped fresh flat-leaf parsley

1. Bring 6 cups water to a boil in a large saucepan. Add noodles; cook 5 minutes or until al dente. Drain.
2. Cut beef across the grain into ¼-inch-wide strips; cut strips into 2-inch pieces.
3. Heat a large skillet over medium-high heat. Coat pan with cooking spray. Add beef to pan; sauté 4 minutes or until browned. Remove beef from pan. Add 1 cup onion, black pepper, salt, paprika, and mushrooms to pan; sauté 4 minutes or until tender. Reduce heat to medium.
4. Combine ¼ cup beef broth and flour in a small bowl, stirring with a whisk. Add broth mixture, beef, ¾ cup broth, and ½ cup water to pan, scraping pan to loosen browned bits. Cover and cook 8 minutes or until sauce thickens. Remove from heat; stir in sour cream, green onions, and butter. Serve beef mixture over egg noodles; sprinkle with parsley. Serves 4 (serving size: 1 cup beef mixture and 1 cup noodles)

CALORIES 357; FAT 11.1g (sat 4.7g, mono 3g, poly 0.4g); PROTEIN 31.9g; CARB 31.9g; FIBER 2.5g; CHOL 80mg; IRON 3.4mg; SODIUM 457mg; CALC 83mg

For the Grainy Mustard Brussels Sprouts:

Halve 16 Brussels sprouts; place in a saucepan with ⅔ cup water. Bring to a boil. Cover, reduce heat, and cook 5 minutes. Stir in 1 tablespoon whole-grain mustard, 1 tablespoon butter, ¼ teaspoon black pepper, and ⅛ teaspoon salt. Serves 4 (serving size: about ¼ cup)

CALORIES 67; FAT 3.3g (sat 1.9g); SODIUM 143mg

SUPERFAST 20-MINUTE COOKING

Bold flavors and fast foods from the supermarket—gnocchi, stir-fry, and more.

Quick & Easy

Seared Scallops with Bacon, Cabbage, and Apple

Quick but hearty. Serve with roasted potatoes.

3 center-cut bacon slices, cut crosswise into ½-inch pieces
6 cups thinly sliced green cabbage
1 tablespoon chopped fresh thyme
½ cup water
1½ cups chopped Fuji apple (1 medium)
3 tablespoons cider vinegar
½ teaspoon freshly ground black pepper, divided
1 tablespoon canola oil
16 large sea scallops (about 1 pound)
¼ teaspoon salt
2 teaspoons chopped fresh dill

1. Cook bacon pieces in a Dutch oven over medium-high heat until crisp. Remove bacon pieces from pan, reserving 1½ tablespoons drippings in pan. Add sliced cabbage and chopped thyme to pan; sauté 2 minutes, stirring cabbage mixture occasionally. Add ½ cup water, scraping pan to loosen browned bits. Bring mixture to a boil. Reduce heat to medium; cover pan. Cook 5 more minutes. Stir in chopped apple and cider vinegar; cover. Cook 5 minutes. Stir in cooked bacon and ¼ teaspoon pepper.
2. Heat a large, heavy skillet over high heat. Add oil to pan; swirl to coat. Sprinkle scallops with ¼ teaspoon salt and ¼ teaspoon black pepper. Add scallops to pan; cook 3 minutes on each side or until scallops are done. Place about 1 cup cabbage mixture on each of 4 plates. Arrange 4 scallops on each serving. Sprinkle each serving with ½ teaspoon dill. Serves 4

CALORIES 201; FAT 6.1g (sat 1.2g, mono 2.3g, poly 1.3g); PROTEIN 22.4g; CARB 15.1g; FIBER 3.9g; CHOL 43mg; IRON 1.2mg; SODIUM 458mg; CALC 86mg

Kid Friendly • Quick & Easy
Vegetarian

Browned Butter Gnocchi with Broccoli and Nuts

Kids like the chewy gnocchi, sweet broccoli, and crunchy nuts. Look for shelf-stable packaged gnocchi with the dried pasta. To cut costs, swap in chopped almonds or pecans for pine nuts.

2 (16-ounce) packages prepared gnocchi (such as Gia Russa)
5 cups chopped broccoli florets
2 tablespoons unsalted butter
2 tablespoons extra-virgin olive oil
¼ teaspoon freshly ground black pepper
3 tablespoons pine nuts, toasted
1.5 ounces shaved fresh pecorino Romano cheese (about ⅓ cup)

1. Cook gnocchi in a large Dutch oven according to package directions. Add broccoli during last minute of cooking; cook 1 minute. Drain.
2. Heat a large skillet over medium heat. Add butter and oil; cook 7 minutes or until butter browns. Add gnocchi mixture and pepper to pan; toss to coat. Spoon about 1½ cups gnocchi mixture into each of 6 shallow bowls. Sprinkle each serving with 1½ teaspoons pine nuts and about 2 teaspoons cheese. Serves 6

CALORIES 368; FAT 12.8g (sat 3.8g, mono 5.1g, poly 2.2g); PROTEIN 7.9g; CARB 56.6g; FIBER 5.7g; CHOL 13mg; IRON 1.2mg; SODIUM 614mg; CALC 104mg

Quick & Easy • Make Ahead
Vegetarian

Chickpea Curry with Basmati Rice

Look for garam masala—an Indian blend—in the spice aisle; Spice Islands and McCormick make it.

1 (3.5-ounce) bag boil-in-bag basmati or brown rice
1 tablespoon canola oil
1 large onion, diced
1½ teaspoons garam masala
2 (15-ounce) cans chickpeas, rinsed and drained
1 (15-ounce) can unsalted crushed tomatoes
1 (6-ounce) package fresh baby spinach
½ cup plain 2% Greek yogurt
½ teaspoon salt
¼ cup chopped fresh cilantro

1. Cook rice according to package directions; drain.
2. While rice cooks, heat a Dutch oven over medium-high heat. Add oil to pan; swirl to coat. Add onion; sauté 5 minutes or until tender, stirring frequently. Stir in garam masala; cook 30 seconds, stirring constantly. Add chickpeas, tomatoes, and spinach; cook 2 minutes or until spinach wilts, stirring occasionally. Remove from heat; stir in yogurt and salt. Sprinkle with cilantro. Serve over rice. Serves 4 (serving size: 1¼ cups chickpea mixture and ½ cup rice)

CALORIES 305; FAT 5.8g (sat 0.7g, mono 2.3g, poly 1g); PROTEIN 12.2g; CARB 52.8g; FIBER 9.5g; CHOL 2mg; IRON 4.7mg; SODIUM 676mg; CALC 118mg

Chocolate-Peanut Butter Pudding

Supereasy. Try bananas on top.

1/3 cup granulated sugar
2 tablespoons cornstarch
2 tablespoons Dutch process cocoa
1 1/2 cups 1% low-fat milk
1/2 cup light cream
2 ounces milk chocolate, finely chopped
1/4 cup creamy peanut butter
1 tablespoon chopped unsalted,
   dry-roasted peanuts

1. Combine sugar, cornstarch, and cocoa in a medium saucepan; stir with a whisk. Whisk in milk and cream. Bring to a boil over medium-high heat. Cook 1 minute or until thick and bubbly. Remove from heat. Add chocolate and peanut butter, stirring until smooth. Spoon about 1/3 cup pudding into each of 6 bowls. Top each serving with 1/2 teaspoon peanuts. Serves 6

CALORIES 245; FAT 13.7g (sat 5.4g, mono 3.8g, poly 1.9g); PROTEIN 6g; CARB 26.6g; FIBER 1.3g; CHOL 12mg; IRON 0.8mg; SODIUM 104mg; CALC 123mg

Lemon-Garlic Swiss Chard

This dish pairs nicely with steak or seared scallops.

1 tablespoon extra-virgin olive oil
1 tablespoon minced fresh garlic
12 cups Swiss chard, chopped
   (about 10 ounces)
2 tablespoons water
1 1/2 teaspoons fresh lemon juice
1/8 teaspoon freshly ground black
   pepper
4 teaspoons shaved fresh Parmesan
   cheese

1. Heat a large skillet over medium-high heat. Add oil to pan; swirl to coat. Add garlic; sauté 2 minutes or until garlic begins to brown. Add Swiss chard and 2 tablespoons water to pan; cook 3 minutes or until chard wilts. Stir in lemon juice and pepper. Sprinkle with cheese. Serves 4 (serving size: about 1/2 cup)

CALORIES 61; FAT 4.1g (sat 0.8g, mono 2.7g, poly 0.5g); PROTEIN 2.7g; CARB 5g; FIBER 1.8g; CHOL 1mg; IRON 2mg; SODIUM 256mg; CALC 78mg

Variation 1: Quick Caramelized Onions

Heat a large nonstick skillet over medium heat. Add 1 teaspoon olive oil; swirl to coat. Add 2 cups sliced yellow onion and a dash of baking soda; cook 10 minutes or until browned. Add 12 cups chopped Swiss chard and 2 tablespoons water to pan; cook 3 minutes or until chard wilts. Stir in 2 teaspoons sherry vinegar and 1/4 teaspoon freshly ground black pepper. Serves 4 (serving size: about 1/2 cup)

CALORIES 64; FAT 1.4g (sat 0.2g); SODIUM 253mg

Variation 2: Golden Raisins and Pine Nuts

Heat a large nonstick skillet over medium heat. Add 3 tablespoons pine nuts to pan; cook 3 minutes or until browned, stirring frequently. Remove nuts from pan. Add 1/4 cup golden raisins and 1/4 cup water to pan; cook 1 minute. Add 12 cups chopped Swiss chard; cook 3 minutes or until chard wilts. Stir in 2 teaspoons white wine vinegar. Sprinkle with pine nuts. Serves 4 (serving size: about 1/2 cup)

CALORIES 90; FAT 4.6g (sat 0.4g); SODIUM 231mg

Variation 3: Warm Bacon Vinaigrette

Heat a medium nonstick skillet over medium heat. Add 2 applewood-smoked bacon slices to pan; cook until crisp. Remove bacon from pan; reserve for another use. Remove pan from heat. Add 2 teaspoons cider vinegar and 1/4 teaspoon freshly ground black pepper to pan, stirring with a whisk.

Pour vinegar mixture over 6 cups chopped Swiss chard; toss. Serves 4 (serving size: about 1/2 cup)

CALORIES 39; FAT 2.4g (sat 0.9g); SODIUM 225mg

Spicy Thai Basil Chicken

Lettuce wraps make for a fresh burst of crunch and flavor, or spoon the stir-fry over rice. Look for fish sauce in your grocery store's Asian foods section.

4 teaspoons canola oil, divided
1/2 cup minced shallots
1/2 cup thinly sliced red bell pepper
4 teaspoons minced fresh garlic
1 pound ground chicken
2 Thai or serrano chiles, minced
1 tablespoon fish sauce
2 teaspoons dark brown sugar
2 teaspoons lower-sodium soy sauce
1/4 teaspoon freshly ground black
   pepper
1 cup basil leaves
1 tablespoon fresh lime juice
4 lime wedges

1. Heat a large nonstick skillet over medium-high heat. Add 2 teaspoons oil to pan; swirl to coat. Add shallots; sauté 2 minutes. Add bell pepper; sauté 1 minute. Add garlic; sauté 30 seconds. Remove shallot mixture from pan.
2. Add 2 teaspoons oil to pan; swirl to coat. Add chicken; cook 5 minutes or until browned, stirring to crumble. Drain well. Return chicken to pan over medium heat. Add chiles; cook 1 minute. Add shallot mixture to pan. Stir in fish sauce and next 3 ingredients; cook 1 minute or until thoroughly heated. Remove pan from heat; stir in basil and juice. Serve with lime wedges. Serves 4 (serving size: about 3/4 cup and 1 lime wedge)

CALORIES 250; FAT 14.1g (sat 3g, mono 7.1g, poly 3.1g); PROTEIN 21.6g; CARB 10.7g; FIBER 1.2g; CHOL 98mg; IRON 1.9mg; SODIUM 486mg; CALC 51mg

LOVE THE WHOLE VEGGIE

A Manhattan chef reveals tricks for giving familiar vegetables exciting new flavors and textures. It's easy—and it's green!

C hef Amanda Cohen approaches vegetables in much the same way that some of the country's best chefs have come to embrace nose-to-tail animal cookery. She looks to use every edible part of the plant. It's a style that reduces waste while being respectful to the produce, and it can be a revelation to someone who tries a dish of carrots that also contains carrot tops: Suddenly, there are new taste dimensions to old-hat ingredients.

She offers beets as an example. "To think that you have this hard root vegetable that you can do so much with—but then there's this extra gift on top! The greens are just as delicious as spinach or chard. But people often just throw them out. It's so sad."

Cohen helms the kitchen at the celebrated, cheekily named little New York restaurant Dirt Candy, which she calls a "vegetable restaurant," as opposed to vegetarian. "At our core, we don't have politics, the environment, or even health as a motivating factor. All I want to do is make delicious food." Her waste-not approach to vegetable cooking is part of her hook. "We realized that if we start to concentrate on other parts of the vegetable, people are going to want to come here. People are looking for the new."

Beyond carrot tops on carrot dishes, she makes celery leaf pesto for Chinese celery-based plates. For her broccoli "carpaccio," she utilizes broccoli stalks, a part that generally ends up in most home cooks' compost bins. Peeled and cut into attractive julienne slices and thin planks, the stalk brings amazing crunch and a green yet nutty flavor to the salad. "People look at broccoli, and all they see are those florets. There's so much more."

Cohen advises home cooks to broaden their thinking when working with produce. "Get the vegetables that look like they're going to be a little more work, if you have the time to bypass the ones in the bag."

Then feel free to experiment with the unfamiliar parts, and don't be nervous. "If it doesn't work out, don't be disappointed. Just try something else. Cooking should be fun, right? You're not trying for world peace with your next dinner, just a tasty meal."

Vegetarian

Broccoli Carpaccio with Broccoli Stalk Salad

Hands-on: 40 min. Total: 40 min. Cohen makes great use of broccoli stalks in a riff on carpaccio, which is traditionally a dish of thinly sliced raw meat. This standout salad won us over at the taste-testing table, earning our highest rating. You can use a mandoline to make easy work of slicing the broccoli thinly and evenly.

Carpaccio:
3 tablespoons chopped fresh Thai basil
1 teaspoon minced peeled fresh ginger
1 teaspoon minced fresh garlic
1 red bird's eye chile pepper, minced (or red serrano chile)
3 large broccoli stalks (about 9 ounces)
3 tablespoons fresh lime juice
1/4 teaspoon kosher salt
2 ripe peeled avocados, cut into 1/8-inch slices

Salad:
- **1 tablespoon extra-virgin olive oil**
- **1 tablespoon fresh lime juice**
- **¼ teaspoon kosher salt**
- **¼ teaspoon freshly ground black pepper**
- **2 cups peeled, matchstick-cut broccoli stalks**
- **2 cups gourmet salad greens**
- **¼ cup thinly sliced red onion**

1. To prepare carpaccio, combine first 4 ingredients. Peel and slice 3 broccoli stalks into 2 x 1 x 1–inch rectangles, squaring off their sides. Slice broccoli lengthwise into ¼-inch planks. Combine broccoli planks, 3 tablespoons juice, and ¼ teaspoon salt. Arrange broccoli planks and avocado slices on 6 plates; sprinkle with basil mixture.

2. To prepare salad, combine olive oil, 1 tablespoon juice, ¼ teaspoon salt, and pepper in a large bowl, stirring with a whisk. Add 2 cups matchstick-cut broccoli stalks, salad greens, and onion; toss to coat. Divide salad evenly among plates. Serves 6 (serving size: about 4 slices broccoli, 4 slices avocado, and ⅔ cup salad)

CALORIES 144; FAT 12.1g (sat 1.7g, mono 8.2g, poly 1.5g); PROTEIN 2.3g; CARB 9.6g; FIBER 5.3g; CHOL 0mg; IRON 0.8mg; SODIUM 176mg; CALC 22mg

OOPS!
YOU SCORCH YOUR ROOT VEGETABLES

In the quest to brown and not burn, size matters most.

A mixed batch of roasted winter vegetables is the perfect healthy side this time of year: hearty, sweet and savory, full of nutrients and fiber. And it seems easy. But what's even easier is turning out vegetables that are pale and soggy from overcrowding, or, worse still, black and dry from overcooking. The problem is that while different veggies can certainly cook in the same pan, they need to be sized and spaced with care. It also helps if you use a good, thick pan, as thin pans conduct heat unevenly and lead to scorching.

The solution: Cut veggies about ½ inch thick. Items that stay whole, like baby carrots, can be your benchmark there. Preheat the oven to between 400° and 450° with a heavy roasting pan inside; the hot pan will jump-start the browning process. Spread oil-coated veggies in the hot pan in a single layer; don't crowd them, because that leads to steaming. Stir after 15 minutes to promote even browning and prevent sticking. Check after another 10 minutes, and then pull when gorgeously browned and fork-tender. If they're well browned but still tough, sprinkle with a couple of tablespoons of water, reduce heat to 350°, and cook until tender.

(sweetly browned)   (blow-torched?)

PERFECT PLEASURES OF PASTA

Nothing satisfies more than these Italian classics—beautiful to serve up as produce markets deliver the first hints of spring.

As you drag long strands of spaghetti through a clingy tomato sauce, or toss twisty-shaped strozzapreti with favas and peas until the vegetables nuzzle into the nooks and crannies of the noodles, the feeling is pure kitchen ahhhhh. There is a precise joy in a pasta perfectly matched to its sauce. Here we've done some matchmaking, mostly with dried pasta, but we've also included a delightful recipe for scratch-made "candy-wrapped" tortelli—a blissful Saturday project.

Quick & Easy • Vegetarian

Linguine with Spinach-Herb Pesto

Hands-on: 19 min. Total: 28 min. Here is a lovely twist on beloved pesto for spring. Baby spinach takes the place of most of the basil to give the sauce an earthy flavor. The thick, emerald sauce beautifully coats the flat noodles and serves up big flavor in every forkful.

4 ounces fresh baby spinach
¼ cup slivered blanched almonds
¼ cup basil leaves
2 teaspoons chopped fresh oregano
1 teaspoon chopped fresh thyme
¼ teaspoon black pepper
1 large garlic clove, chopped
2 tablespoons organic vegetable broth
2 teaspoons fresh lemon juice
¼ teaspoon salt
2 tablespoons extra-virgin olive oil
1 ounce Parmigiano-Reggiano cheese, grated and divided (about ¼ cup)
8 ounces uncooked linguine

1. Place spinach in a microwave-safe bowl; cover bowl with plastic wrap. Microwave at HIGH 2 minutes or until spinach wilts. Remove plastic wrap; cool slightly.
2. Place spinach, almonds, and next 5 ingredients in a food processor. Process until chopped. Add broth, juice, and salt; pulse 5 times. With processor on, slowly pour oil through food chute; process until well blended. Scrape into a bowl; stir in half of cheese. Cover with plastic wrap.
3. Cook pasta according to package directions, omitting salt and fat. Drain. Toss pasta with ½ cup pesto. Arrange about 1½ cups pasta mixture in each of 4 bowls; top each serving with 2 tablespoons pesto and 1½ teaspoons cheese. Serves 4

CALORIES 353; **FAT** 13.2g (sat 2.6g, mono 7.7g, poly 1.8g); **PROTEIN** 12.9g; **CARB** 48.2g; **FIBER** 4.3g; **CHOL** 5mg; **IRON** 3.3mg; **SODIUM** 327mg; **CALC** 145mg

Kid Friendly

Strozzapreti with Favas, Peas, and Prosciutto

Hands-on: 67 min. Total: 67 min.

¾ pound uncooked strozzapreti or other short, twisty pasta
1 tablespoon extra-virgin olive oil
2 teaspoons butter
1 large shallot, thinly sliced
1 cup shelled and peeled fava beans or frozen edamame, thawed
1 cup shelled fresh English peas or frozen peas, thawed
3 tablespoons dry white wine
⅓ cup fat-free, lower-sodium chicken broth
¼ teaspoon freshly ground black pepper
1 ounce prosciutto, chopped
½ teaspoon salt
¼ cup whole-milk ricotta cheese
1 ounce pecorino Romano cheese, grated (about ¼ cup)

1. Cook pasta according to package directions, omitting salt and fat. Drain in a colander over a bowl, reserving ¼ cup liquid; keep warm.
2. Heat a large saucepan over medium heat. Add oil and butter; swirl until butter melts. Add shallots; cook 5 minutes or until shallots are tender

and translucent, stirring occasionally. Stir in beans and peas. Increase heat to medium-high. Add wine; cook 30 seconds. Stir in broth and pepper; cook 5 minutes or until beans and peas are tender. Remove from heat; stir in prosciutto. Stir in pasta, reserved cooking liquid, and salt. Gently stir in ricotta and pecorino. Serve immediately. Serves 6 (serving size: about 1 cup)

CALORIES 319; FAT 6.8g (sat 2.7g, mono 2.6g, poly 0.5g); PROTEIN 13g; CARB 51.3g; FIBER 4.2g; CHOL 13mg; IRON 2.9mg; SODIUM 402mg; CALC 65mg

CANDY-WRAPPED TORTELLI

If you have a hand-rolling pasta machine or a pasta attachment for your stand mixer and haven't used it in ages, here's a recipe to reacquaint you with the pleasures of the homemade noodle. Fresh dough gets twisted around the filling, like a candy wrapper. Cutting and shaping tortelli by hand means each piece is unique—and therein lies the charm.

Kid Friendly • Freezable
Make Ahead

Candy-Wrapped Tortelli

Hands-on: 2 hr. 20 min. Total: 2 hr. 20 min. Follow our step-by-step instructions on page 53 for making hand-shaped tortelli.

Sauce:
1 tablespoon extra-virgin olive oil
3 garlic cloves, lightly crushed
1 (28-ounce) can San Marzano whole plum tomatoes, crushed and undrained
2 tablespoons minced fresh basil
1 tablespoon chopped fresh oregano
¼ teaspoon crushed red pepper
Stuffing:
3 ounces fresh baby spinach, rinsed
2 egg yolks, lightly beaten
1 ounce Parmigiano-Reggiano cheese, grated (about ¼ cup)
1 teaspoon extra-virgin olive oil
1 teaspoon butter
2 tablespoons minced yellow onion
1 garlic clove, finely chopped
6 ounces skinless, boneless chicken thighs, cut into 1-inch pieces
¼ teaspoon salt
¼ teaspoon black pepper
1 tablespoon dry white wine
2 tablespoons fat-free milk
Dash of ground nutmeg
Pasta:
8.5 ounces '00' flour or unbleached all-purpose flour
1 tablespoon semolina
¼ teaspoon salt
Dash of ground nutmeg
3 large eggs, lightly beaten
Topping:
2 ounces Parmigiano-Reggiano cheese, grated (about ½ cup)

1. To prepare sauce, heat a saucepan over medium-low heat. Add 1 tablespoon oil, swirl to coat. Add 3 garlic cloves; cook 2 minutes. Add tomatoes; bring to a boil. Partially cover, reduce heat, and simmer 35 minutes. Add basil, oregano, and red pepper.
2. To prepare stuffing, place spinach in a microwave-safe bowl; cover loosely. Microwave at HIGH 2 minutes or until wilted. Place spinach in a colander; press until barely moist. Finely chop. Combine spinach, 2 yolks, and 1 ounce cheese.
3. Heat a skillet over medium-low heat. Add 1 teaspoon oil and butter. Swirl until butter melts. Add onion and 1 garlic clove; cook 2 minutes. Add chicken. Cover; cook 6 minutes. Add ¼ teaspoon salt and black pepper. Add wine; cook 2 minutes over medium-high heat. Cool slightly. Place in a food processor; pulse 10 times or until finely ground. Add chicken mixture, milk, and dash of nutmeg to spinach mixture. Chill.

4. To prepare pasta, combine flour, semolina, ¼ teaspoon salt, and dash of nutmeg. Arrange mixture in a wide mound with a large well in the center on a work surface. Pour in eggs, keeping within the wall. With a fork, gently begin to whisk flour from the inside wall of the well into the eggs. Continue to whisk gently until mixture is batter-like. When mixture is thick, knead until a rough ball forms. Knead until dough is firm and no longer sticky (about 8 minutes). Form the dough into a ball, and wrap in plastic wrap. Let rest at room temperature 30 minutes.
5. Unwrap dough. Divide into 4 equal portions. Working with 1 portion, pass dough through pasta machine on widest setting (cover remaining dough). Continue moving width gauge to narrower settings; pass dough through rollers once at each setting. Cut into 12 (4 x 3–inch) rectangles. Arrange on a surface well dusted with semolina. Spoon about 1 teaspoon filling in center of each rectangle. Brush long edges of pasta with water. Bring long sides over filling; press to seal. Press short sides to seal filling, and twist in opposite directions (as if twisting a candy wrapper). Place filled pasta on a baking sheet well dusted with semolina. Repeat procedure with remaining dough and filling.
6. Bring a large pot of water to a boil over high heat. Add half of tortelli; cook 7 minutes or until just tender. Remove with a slotted spoon. Repeat procedure with remaining tortelli. Arrange 6 tortelli in each of 8 shallow bowls; top each serving with ⅓ cup sauce and 1 tablespoon cheese. Serves 8

CALORIES 273; FAT 9.3g (sat 3.6g, mono 4g, poly 1.1g); PROTEIN 14.3g; CARB 31.7g; FIBER 2.3g; CHOL 138mg; IRON 3.1mg; SODIUM 581mg; CALC 184mg

SPAGHETTI WITH CLAMS AND SLOW-ROASTED CHERRY TOMATOES

Spaghetti dressed with clams is a Southern Italian classic. The briny liquor released by the clams beautifully coats the noodles, while the little bits of meat get caught up in the tangled strands. Tomatoes are a welcome contemporary addition.

Spaghetti with Clams and Slow-Roasted Cherry Tomatoes
(pictured on page 212)

Hands-on: 42 min. Total: 1 hr. 40 min.

1 pound cherry tomatoes, halved
2 tablespoons extra-virgin olive oil, divided
3 garlic cloves, divided
1/4 teaspoon crushed red pepper
1/2 cup dry white wine
48 littleneck clams, scrubbed
2 tablespoons minced fresh flat-leaf parsley
2 tablespoons minced fresh basil
1/4 teaspoon salt
3/4 pound uncooked spaghetti

1. Preheat oven to 300°.
2. Combine tomatoes and 1 tablespoon olive oil, tossing to coat. Arrange tomatoes, cut sides up, on a jelly-roll pan. Thinly slice 1 garlic clove; sprinkle over tomatoes. Bake tomato mixture at 300° for 1½ hours or until tomatoes are slightly shriveled. Set aside.
3. Mince 2 garlic cloves. Heat a large skillet over medium-low heat. Add 1 tablespoon olive oil; swirl to coat. Add crushed minced garlic and red pepper

to skillet; cook 2 minutes or until garlic and pepper sizzle. Increase heat to medium-high; stir in wine. Add clams; cover and cook 7 minutes or until clams open. Using tongs, remove clams from skillet; reserve liquid. Discard any unopened shells. Strain liquid through a fine-mesh sieve lined with cheesecloth into a bowl; discard solids. Wipe skillet clean; return liquid to skillet. Add tomatoes, parsley, basil, and salt; bring to a simmer over medium heat. Reserve 24 clams in shells. Remove remaining clams from shells; add all clams to skillet.
4. Cook pasta according to package directions, omitting salt and fat. Drain. Combine pasta and clam mixture. Serve immediately. Serves 6 (serving size: 1½ cups)

CALORIES 337; FAT 6.2g (sat 0.9g, mono 3.5g, poly 1g); PROTEIN 18.8g; CARB 48.8g; FIBER 2.8g; CHOL 22mg; IRON 3.4mg; SODIUM 540mg; CALC 55mg

PAPPARDELLE WITH SALMON AND LEEKS

This dish is as elegant as it is easy. Rosy salmon and pale green leeks are tossed with broad ribbons of pappardelle pasta and fresh herbs. If you can't find pappardelle, cut fresh lasagna sheets into wide strips, as we do in Pasta Giardiniera on page 62.

Pappardelle with Salmon and Leeks
(pictured on page 214)

Hands-on: 47 min. Total: 47 min.

3/4 pound uncooked pappardelle pasta
3 tablespoons extra-virgin olive oil, divided
2 large leeks (1 pound), trimmed and thinly sliced
2 teaspoons minced fresh savory or
1 teaspoon minced fresh thyme
   plus 1 teaspoon minced fresh mint

3/4 teaspoon salt, divided
1/4 cup dry white wine
1/2 cup unsalted chicken stock
1 tablespoon minced fresh flat-leaf parsley
1 teaspoon grated lemon rind
1 (1-pound) fresh or frozen sustainable salmon fillet
1/4 teaspoon freshly ground black pepper
2 teaspoons unsalted butter

1. Cook pasta according to package directions, omitting salt and fat. Drain pasta in a colander over a bowl, reserving 1/4 cup cooking liquid; keep pasta and cooking liquid warm.
2. Heat a large saucepan over medium heat. Add 2 tablespoons olive oil; swirl to coat. Add leeks, savory, and ½ teaspoon salt; cook 15 minutes or until leeks are translucent, stirring occasionally. Increase heat to medium-high. Add wine; cook 1 minute. Add stock; bring to a simmer. Remove from heat; stir in pasta, reserved cooking liquid, parsley, and lemon rind.
3. Sprinkle salmon fillet with 1/4 teaspoon salt and pepper. Heat a large skillet over medium-high heat. Add 1 tablespoon olive oil and butter; swirl until butter melts. Add salmon fillet, and cook 5 minutes on each side or until desired degree of doneness. Flake salmon into large chunks. Arrange 1 cup pasta mixture on each of 6 plates, and top evenly with flaked salmon. Serve immediately. Serves 6

CALORIES 415; FAT 13.7g (sat 2.7g, mono 6.9g, poly 2.7g); PROTEIN 23.7g; CARB 47.2g; FIBER 2.6g; CHOL 45mg; IRON 3.3mg; SODIUM 349mg; CALC 50mg

ORZOTTO WITH GREEN AND WHITE ASPARAGUS

Orzo is that small pasta shaped something like melon seeds, and it takes the place of Arborio rice in this risotto-style dish, turning rich and creamy as it is stirred to doneness. Tender asparagus and fresh lemon zest add the welcome flavors of spring.

HAND-SHAPED PASTA IS EASY

The dough is supple and lovely to work with, and the little bundles are a pleasure to form. Try this technique when making Candy-Wrapped Tortelli, page 51.

1. Roll sections of dough through a pasta machine at each setting until very thin.

2. Cut dough into 4 x 3–inch rectangles using a pizza wheel or fluted cutter.

3. Moisten long sides of dough with water, and fold over filling to enclose it.

4. Twist dough edges in opposite directions as if sealing candy in a wrapper.

5. Arrange pasta on a baking sheet dusted with semolina to prevent sticking.

Note: If you plan to cook and serve the tortelli soon after shaping, you can leave them out at room temperature. Otherwise, place the baking sheet, uncovered, in the freezer for 1 hour. Transfer frozen tortelli to a zip-top plastic bag or tightly lidded container, and return to the freezer until it is time to cook them.

Kid Friendly • Quick & Easy

Orzotto with Green and White Asparagus

Hands-on: 33 min. Total: 33 min.

3¹⁄₂ cups unsalted chicken stock
1 tablespoon unsalted butter
2 teaspoons extra-virgin olive oil
1¹⁄₄ cups chopped red scallions or green onions
1¹⁄₂ cups uncooked orzo pasta
1¹⁄₂ teaspoons grated lemon rind
1 tablespoon fresh lemon juice
³⁄₈ teaspoon salt
¹⁄₄ teaspoon black pepper
¹⁄₂ pound green asparagus, trimmed and cut into 1-inch pieces
¹⁄₂ pound white asparagus, trimmed and cut into 1-inch pieces
2 ounces Parmigiano-Reggiano cheese, grated and divided (about ¹⁄₂ cup)
1 tablespoon minced fresh flat-leaf parsley

1. Bring stock to a simmer in a saucepan (do not boil). Keep warm.
2. Heat a saucepan over medium-low heat. Add butter and oil; swirl to coat. Add scallions; cook 7 minutes, stirring occasionally. Add orzo; cook 2 minutes, stirring frequently. Stir in rind, juice, salt, and pepper. Add ¹⁄₂ cup stock to pasta mixture; cook 2¹⁄₂ minutes or until liquid is nearly absorbed, stirring frequently. Reserve 1 cup stock. Add remaining stock, ¹⁄₂ cup at a time, stirring frequently until each portion of stock is absorbed before adding the next (about 13 minutes). Stir in reserved 1 cup stock and asparagus; cook 7 minutes or until asparagus is tender, stirring occasionally. Remove from heat; stir in half of cheese. Sprinkle with remaining cheese and parsley. Serve immediately. Serves 4 (serving size: 1¹⁄₄ cups)

CALORIES 401; FAT 10.1g (sat 4.5g, mono 3.5g, poly 0.5g); PROTEIN 20g; CARB 56.9g; FIBER 6.2g; CHOL 17mg; IRON 3.5mg; SODIUM 580mg; CALC 246mg

---

MORE FAVORITE PASTA SHAPES

1. FARRO CIRIOLE
Whole-grain pasta that is roughly double the thickness of spaghetti. Nutty taste pairs well with hearty meat and mushroom sauces.

2. FUSILLI NAPOLETANI
Twisted rods are ideal for tomato sauce or simple olive oil dressing.

3. FETTUCCINE
Great all-purpose noodle that can handle almost any type of sauce.

4. CAPRICCI
These tight twists are a good match for thick and chunky sauces.

5. WHOLE-WHEAT CHIOCCIOLE
Snail-shaped pasta catches peas and small veggies, plus creamy sauces.

6. PACCHERI
Large tubes are often stuffed with meat or cheese fillings. They also hold creamy sauces.

7. WHOLE-WHEAT RIGATONI
Nice in casseroles and with hearty, chunky sauces; the whole wheat's strong flavor may overwhelm a delicate sauce.

8. WHOLE-WHEAT FARFALLE
Cute bow ties make a great veggie-rich pasta salad.

FIVE LUSCIOUS LASAGNAS

Stack up noodles, cheese, and sauce, and then bake until bubbly. Just add a simple salad, some tasty wine, and good company.

Lasagna is the world's best comfort casserole: layer upon saucy layer, beautifully browned and bubbly on top. With these versions, comfort gets much lighter—our Italian Bolognese Lasagna, for example, cuts about 400 calories and 19 grams of saturated fat per serving. These luscious dishes come together in 40 minutes active time or less and can be assembled and refrigerated a day ahead.

CLASSIC LIGHT BOLOGNESE LASAGNA

We played it straight with this lasagna standard, which retains all its meaty, cheesy, saucy goodness but has less than half the calories.

Kid Friendly • Freezable
Make Ahead

Classic Light Bolognese Lasagna

Hands-on: 40 min. Total: 1 hr. 35 min.
A lighter take on classic Bolognese meat sauce allows for more cheese—always a good thing.

1½ cups coarsely chopped onion
¾ cup coarsely chopped celery
½ cup coarsely chopped carrot
4 garlic cloves
1 tablespoon olive oil
1 tablespoon unsalted tomato paste
1 ounce diced pancetta
1 pound ground turkey breast
¼ cup white wine
¾ teaspoon kosher salt
¾ teaspoon crushed red pepper
½ teaspoon dried oregano
½ teaspoon freshly ground black pepper
1 cup 1% low-fat milk
½ cup chopped fresh basil
1 (28-ounce) can crushed tomatoes, undrained
1½ cups part-skim ricotta cheese
6 ounces shredded part-skim mozzarella cheese, divided (about 1½ cups)
1 large egg, lightly beaten
Cooking spray
6 cooked lasagna noodles

1. Place first 4 ingredients in a food processor; pulse until coarsely ground. Heat a medium saucepan over medium-high heat. Add oil to pan; swirl to coat. Add tomato paste and pancetta; cook 1 minute, stirring constantly. Add turkey, and cook 4 minutes, stirring to crumble. Add wine; cook 2 minutes or until liquid evaporates, scraping pan to loosen browned bits. Add onion mixture, salt, and next 3 ingredients to pan, and cook 3 minutes, stirring occasionally. Add milk and basil; cook 3 minutes, stirring occasionally. Stir in tomatoes; reduce heat, and simmer 20 minutes.
2. Preheat oven to 425°.
3. Combine ricotta, 1 cup mozzarella cheese, and egg in a small bowl.
4. Spread ¾ cup turkey mixture in bottom of a 13 x 9–inch glass or ceramic baking dish coated with cooking spray. Arrange 3 noodles over turkey mixture; top with half of remaining turkey mixture and half of ricotta mixture. Repeat layers once, ending with ricotta mixture. Sprinkle ½ cup mozzarella evenly over top. Bake at 425° for 35 minutes.
5. Preheat broiler to high. (Keep lasagna in oven.)
6. Broil lasagna 2 minutes or until cheese is golden brown and sauce is bubbly. Let stand 10 minutes before serving. Serves 8

CALORIES 364; **FAT** 13.2g (sat 6g, mono 3.7g, poly 0.7g); **PROTEIN** 30.9g; **CARB** 31.4g; **FIBER** 3.8g; **CHOL** 75mg; **IRON** 2.4mg; **SODIUM** 644mg; **CALC** 381mg

THREE-CHEESE LASAGNA

Ricotta, Parmesan, and mozzarella combine to give this lasagna an irresistible gooey factor. Store-bought tomato sauce offers convenience and is perked up with a little fresh basil, garlic, and ground red pepper.

Three-Cheese Lasagna

Hands-on: 30 min. Total: 1 hr. 25 min.

1 cup part-skim ricotta cheese
1/4 cup fresh flat-leaf parsley, divided
1 tablespoon chopped fresh oregano
1 teaspoon chopped fresh thyme
1/2 teaspoon kosher salt
1/2 teaspoon freshly ground black pepper
6 ounces shredded part-skim mozzarella cheese, divided (about 1 1/2 cups)
1 ounce fresh Parmesan cheese, grated and divided (about 1/4 cup)
1 large egg, lightly beaten
1/4 cup torn fresh basil
1/8 teaspoon ground red pepper
4 garlic cloves, minced
1 (24-ounce) jar lower-sodium pasta sauce
9 cooked lasagna noodles
Cooking spray

1. Preheat oven to 375°.
2. Combine ricotta, 2 tablespoons parsley, oregano, thyme, salt, black pepper, 1 cup mozzarella, 1 tablespoon Parmesan cheese, and egg in a small bowl. Combine basil, red pepper, garlic, and pasta sauce in a medium bowl.
3. Cut noodles into 9 (7 x 2–inch) pieces; discard remaining pieces. Spread 1/2 cup pasta sauce mixture in bottom of an 8-inch square glass or ceramic baking dish coated with cooking spray. Arrange 3 noodles over pasta sauce mixture; top with about 2/3 cup ricotta mixture and 3/4 cup pasta sauce mixture. Repeat layers twice, ending with 1/2 cup pasta sauce mixture. Top evenly with the remaining 1/2 cup mozzarella and remaining 3 tablespoons Parmesan cheese. Bake at 375° for 40 minutes.
4. Preheat broiler to high. (Keep lasagna in oven.)

5. Broil lasagna 2 minutes or until cheese is golden brown and sauce is bubbly. Let stand 10 minutes. Sprinkle with remaining 2 tablespoons parsley. Serves 6

CALORIES 339; FAT 11.8g (sat 6g, mono 3g, poly 0.5g); PROTEIN 20.2g; CARB 39.2g; FIBER 2.6g; CHOL 66mg; IRON 2mg; SODIUM 564mg; CALC 424mg

BUTTERNUT-KALE LASAGNA

Gruyère-Spiked Béchamel drapes over the noodles and squash to give this dish velvety richness. Hearty, earthy kale perfectly balances the sweet squash. Crunchy toasted pecans on top? Yes, please!

Butternut-Kale Lasagna

Hands-on: 25 min. Total: 55 min.

1/4 cup water
1 (12-ounce) package prechopped fresh butternut squash
3 cups prechopped kale
1 tablespoon olive oil
1 1/2 tablespoons minced fresh garlic
1.1 ounces all-purpose flour (about 1/4 cup)
2 3/4 cups 1% low-fat milk, divided
2 ounces Gruyère cheese, shredded and divided
1 ounce fresh Parmigiano-Reggiano cheese, grated (about 1/4 cup)
1/2 teaspoon salt
1/4 teaspoon black pepper
Cooking spray
6 no-boil lasagna noodles
3 tablespoons chopped pecans

1. Preheat oven to 450°.
2. Combine 1/4 cup water and squash in an 8-inch square glass or ceramic baking dish. Cover tightly with plastic wrap; pierce plastic wrap 2 to 3 times.

Microwave at HIGH 5 minutes or until tender; drain. Combine squash and kale in a large bowl. Wipe dish dry.
3. Heat a medium saucepan over medium heat. Add oil to pan; swirl to coat. Add garlic; cook 2 minutes or until garlic begins to brown, stirring occasionally. Weigh or lightly spoon flour into a dry measuring cup; level with a knife. Combine flour and 1/2 cup milk in a small bowl, stirring with a whisk until smooth. Add milk mixture and 2 1/4 cups milk to pan; increase heat to medium-high. Bring to a boil; cook 1 minute or until thickened, stirring frequently. Remove from heat. Stir in 1 ounce Gruyère, Parmigiano-Reggiano cheese, salt, and pepper; stir until cheese melts.
4. Coat baking dish with cooking spray. Spread 1/3 cup milk mixture in bottom of dish. Arrange 2 noodles over milk mixture; top with half of squash mixture and 2/3 cup milk mixture. Repeat layers once, ending with remaining noodles and remaining milk mixture. Cover with foil; bake at 450° for 15 minutes. Remove foil; sprinkle Gruyère and pecans over top. Bake, uncovered, at 450° for 10 minutes or until lightly browned and sauce is bubbly. Let stand 5 minutes. Serves 4

CALORIES 420; FAT 16.3g (sat 5.8g, mono 7.3g, poly 2.1g); PROTEIN 20.4g; CARB 51.4g; FIBER 4.5g; CHOL 29mg; IRON 3.1mg; SODIUM 556mg; CALC 557mg

You don't think of lamb when you think of lasagna, but that's one of the reasons you'll love this dish. The meat plays exceptionally well with rosemary and feta.

Freezable • Make Ahead

Greek Lamb and Feta Lasagna

Hands-on: 35 min. Total: 1 hr. 30 min.
We mix the lamb with beef so the lamb flavor doesn't dominate. If assembling ahead, sprinkle with feta cheese just before baking.

2 teaspoons olive oil
1½ cups chopped onion
1½ tablespoons minced garlic
1 tablespoon chopped fresh rosemary
9 ounces lean ground lamb
9 ounces extra-lean ground beef
1¼ cups unsalted chicken stock (such as Swanson)
¾ teaspoon kosher salt
¾ teaspoon freshly ground black pepper
1 (28-ounce) can crushed tomatoes, undrained
1 (14-ounce) can crushed tomatoes, undrained
1¼ cups part-skim ricotta cheese
½ teaspoon grated lemon rind
9 no-boil lasagna noodles
Cooking spray
3 ounces feta cheese, crumbled (about ¾ cup)
3 tablespoons chopped fresh flat-leaf parsley

1. Preheat oven to 375°.
2. Heat a large skillet over medium heat. Add oil to pan; swirl to coat. Add onion and next 4 ingredients; cook 14 minutes or until lamb and beef are browned, stirring to crumble. Add stock to pan; cook 3 minutes. Stir in salt, pepper, and tomatoes. Bring to a boil; reduce heat, and simmer 4 minutes, scraping pan to loosen browned bits.
3. Combine ricotta and rind in a small bowl. Spread 1 tablespoon ricotta mixture over one side of each lasagna noodle.
4. Spread 2 cups tomato mixture in bottom of an 11 x 7–inch glass or ceramic baking dish coated with cooking spray. Arrange 3 lasagna noodles, ricotta side up, over tomato mixture; top with 2 cups tomato mixture. Repeat layers twice, ending with 2 cups tomato mixture. Sprinkle evenly with feta cheese. Cover with foil; bake at 375° for 40 minutes. Remove foil; let stand 10 minutes. Sprinkle with parsley. Serves 9

CALORIES 321; FAT 13.3g (sat 6g, mono 5.1g, poly 0.9g); PROTEIN 23.8g; CARB 28.5g; FIBER 3.8g; CHOL 62mg; IRON 3.7mg; SODIUM 543mg; CALC 206mg

Spicy sausage gives this dish some kick, though you can also go with mild. Three cheeses—ricotta, mozzarella, and Parmesan—make it wonderfully indulgent.

Make Ahead

Turkey Sausage and Spinach Lasagna

Hands-on: 40 min. Total: 1 hr. 35 min.

1.1 ounces all-purpose flour (about ¼ cup)
1 cup 1% low-fat milk
1 cup unsalted chicken stock (such as Swanson)
1 tablespoon canola oil
1 bay leaf
¼ teaspoon kosher salt
½ teaspoon black pepper
Cooking spray
2 tablespoons water
1 (12-ounce) package fresh spinach
2 (4-ounce) links hot turkey Italian sausage
½ cup chopped shallots
1 tablespoon minced fresh garlic
6 no-boil lasagna noodles
1½ cups part-skim ricotta cheese
1 ounce shredded part-skim mozzarella cheese
1 ounce fresh Parmesan cheese, grated (about ¼ cup)

1. Preheat oven to 375°.
2. Weigh or lightly spoon flour into a dry measuring cup; level with a knife. Combine flour and next 4 ingredients in a medium saucepan over medium heat, stirring with a whisk. Cook 8 minutes or until thick and bubbly, stirring frequently. Remove from heat; stir in salt and pepper. Remove bay leaf; discard. Spread 1 cup milk mixture in bottom of an 11 x 7–inch glass or ceramic baking dish coated with cooking spray.
3. Heat a large skillet over medium heat. Add 2 tablespoons water and spinach to pan; cook 2 minutes or until spinach wilts. Drain spinach, pressing until barely moist. Increase heat to medium-high. Remove casings from sausage. Add sausage to pan; cook 4 minutes or until browned, stirring to crumble. Remove sausage from pan. Add shallots and garlic to pan; sauté 2 minutes. Stir in remaining milk mixture, spinach, and cooked sausage. Remove pan from heat.
4. Arrange 2 noodles over milk mixture in baking dish; top with ½ cup ricotta and one-third spinach mixture. Repeat layers twice. Sprinkle with mozzarella and Parmesan cheese. Cover with foil coated with cooking spray. Bake at 375° for 40 minutes. Remove foil.
5. Preheat broiler to high.
6. Broil 4 minutes or until cheese is golden brown. Let stand 10 minutes. Serves 6

CALORIES 332; FAT 14g (sat 5.9g, mono 5.1g, poly 2.1g); PROTEIN 24.3g; CARB 27.8g; FIBER 2.5g; CHOL 61mg; IRON 3.4mg; SODIUM 575mg; CALC 408mg

THE JOY OF THE ASIAN NOODLE BOWL

Every country across the Pacific boasts its own slurpable specialty. Here, we decode some favorites for your surefire success.

As the street-food craze spreads across America, more folks are learning the pure fun of chopsticking into a bowl of noodles. Asian noodles—made from rice, wheat and egg, or buckwheat—are a world apart from Italian pasta, usually chewier, more resilient. Our noodle bowls are based on both street fare and homey comfort classics, with a nutrition tweak. We lowered the sodium (soy, fish, and hoisin sauces pack a lot of salt) while keeping true to the soul of each dish: all those spicy, salty, sweet, sour, and slurptastic thrills.

VIETNAMESE SALT AND PEPPER SHRIMP RICE NOODLE BOWL

An absolute classic, with wonderful contrasts: cold noodles, hot shrimp; chewy noodles, crisp veggies. You can prep the ingredients in advance and bring it all together right before serving. Shrimp is traditionally grilled for this dish, but searing it yields delicious results, too, without as much fuss as firing up the outdoor grill.
–Recipe by Andrea Nguyen

Make Ahead

Vietnamese Salt and Pepper Shrimp Rice Noodle Bowl (Bun Tom Xao)

Hands-on: 45 min. Total: 45 min.

5 ounces uncooked rice vermicelli
  noodles
1/2 cup lukewarm water
3 tablespoons granulated sugar
1/4 cup fresh lime juice
1 tablespoon rice vinegar
5 teaspoons fish sauce
  (such as Three Crabs)
2 serrano chiles, thinly sliced
4 cups (1/4-inch) slices green leaf lettuce
3 cups diagonally cut slices seeded
  Kirby (pickling) cucumber (about 2)
1/4 cup cilantro leaves
1/4 cup torn Thai basil leaves
1/4 cup torn mint leaves
2 teaspoons cornstarch
1 teaspoon dark brown sugar
1/4 teaspoon salt
3/4 teaspoon white pepper
1 pound large shrimp, peeled and
  deveined
2 tablespoons canola oil, divided
1/3 cup (1/4-inch) slices green onions
3 garlic cloves, finely chopped
1/2 cup unsalted, dry-roasted peanuts,
  coarsely chopped

1. Cook rice vermicelli noodles according to package directions. Drain and rinse with cold water; drain.
2. Combine 1/2 cup lukewarm water and granulated sugar in a medium bowl, stirring until sugar dissolves. Add lime juice, vinegar, fish sauce, and chiles; set aside.
3. Combine lettuce, cucumber, and herbs; set aside.
4. Combine cornstarch, brown sugar, salt, and pepper in a large bowl; stir until well combined. Add shrimp; toss to coat. Heat a wok or large skillet over high heat. Add 1½ teaspoons oil, and swirl to coat. Add half of shrimp; cook 1½ minutes on each side or until shrimp are seared. Remove from pan. Add 1½ teaspoons oil to wok; repeat procedure with remaining shrimp. Reduce heat to medium-high. Add 1 tablespoon oil to wok; swirl to coat. Add onions and garlic; stir-fry 30 seconds. Return shrimp to pan; stir-fry 1 minute.
5. Arrange about 1 cup lettuce mixture in each of 4 large bowls, and top each serving with about 1 cup noodles and 2 tablespoons chopped peanuts. Divide shrimp evenly among servings, and serve each with 1/4 cup sauce. Serves 4

CALORIES 462; **FAT** 17.6g (sat 1.9g, mono 9g, poly 5.1g); **PROTEIN** 24.6g; **CARB** 52.9g; **FIBER** 4.4g; **CHOL** 143mg; **IRON** 3.2mg; **SODIUM** 802mg; **CALC** 146mg

Kid Friendly • Quick & Easy

Indonesian Stir-Fried Noodles (Bakmi Goreng)

Hands-on: 28 min. Total: 35 min.

3 tablespoons peanut oil, divided
2 large eggs, lightly beaten
6 ounces dried Chinese egg noodles
6 ounces skinless, boneless chicken
   breast, thinly sliced
4 ounces boneless pork loin chop, sliced
2 garlic cloves, minced
2 cups thinly sliced napa cabbage
3/4 cup sliced green onions
1 celery stalk, thinly sliced
3 tablespoons fat-free, lower-sodium
   chicken broth
1 tablespoon kecap manis (sweet
   soy sauce)
1 tablespoon lower-sodium soy sauce
1/2 cup packaged fried onions

1. Heat a large nonstick skillet over medium-high heat. Add 1 tablespoon oil; swirl to coat. Pour eggs into pan; swirl to form a thin omelet. Cook 1 minute or until cooked on bottom. Carefully turn omelet over; cook 30 seconds. Remove from pan. Roll up omelet; cut roll crosswise into thin strips. Keep warm.
2. Cook noodles according to package directions. Drain and rinse with cold water; drain and set aside.
3. Heat a wok over high heat. Add 2 tablespoons oil; swirl. Add chicken, pork, and garlic; stir-fry 1½ minutes. Add cabbage, green onions, and celery; stir-fry 1 minute. Stir in broth, kecap manis, and soy sauce. Add noodles; stir-fry 3 minutes or until thoroughly heated and noodles begin to lightly brown. Add egg; toss gently. Top with fried onions. Serve immediately. Serves 4 (serving size: 1½ cups)

CALORIES 419; FAT 20.6g (sat 4.7g, mono 9.2g, poly 4.4g); PROTEIN 23.8g; CARB 33g; FIBER 2.3g; CHOL 147mg; IRON 2.7mg; SODIUM 543mg; CALC 86mg

---

INDONESIAN STIR-FRIED NOODLES

This easy dish is an Indonesian street-food noodle classic, and it depends on two things: serving it piping hot, right out of a very hot wok, and finding some *kecap manis* (pronounced KEH-chup MAH-nees), a molasses-thick sweet soy sauce. Most Asian food stores sell it (usually ABC brand). If you can't find dried Chinese egg noodles, spaghetti actually makes a good substitute.

Make Ahead • Vegetarian

Korean Chilled Buckwheat Noodles with Chile Sauce (Bibim Naengmyun)

Hands-on: 40 min. Total: 2 hr. 30 min.

Sauce:
1/4 cup chopped green onions
1 garlic clove, crushed
1/4 cup gochujang (Korean chile paste,
   such as Annie Chun's)
2 tablespoons ground Korean chile
   (gochugaru) or ancho chile powder
1 tablespoon toasted sesame seeds
1 tablespoon rice vinegar
2 teaspoons sugar
1½ teaspoons lower-sodium soy
   sauce
1 teaspoon dark sesame oil
Pickles:
1/2 cup rice vinegar
2 teaspoons sugar
1/4 teaspoon salt
1 cup Korean radish or daikon radish,
   cut into thin 1½ x 1/2-inch slices
Remaining ingredients:
10 ounces uncooked Korean
   naengmyun noodles or soba noodles

24 thin slices Asian pear
1 cup julienne-cut English cucumber
2 hard-cooked large eggs, chilled and
   cut in half lengthwise

1. To prepare sauce, place onions and garlic in a mini food processor; process until minced. Add gochujang and next 6 ingredients; process until smooth. Cover and chill at least 2 hours.
2. To prepare pickles, combine ½ cup vinegar, 2 teaspoons sugar, and ¼ teaspoon salt in a 2-cup glass measuring cup. Microwave at HIGH 2 minutes or until boiling. Place radish in a medium bowl; top with hot vinegar mixture. Cover and chill 2 hours; drain.
3. Cook noodles according to package directions. Drain and rinse with cold water; drain. Arrange about 1 cup noodles in each of 4 bowls; top each with about 2 tablespoons sauce. In each bowl, arrange ¼ cup radish on one side of noodles, 6 pear slices on the other, and ¼ cup cucumber in middle. Top each with 1 egg half. Serves 4

CALORIES 403; FAT 6.3g (sat 1.2g, mono 1.9g, poly 1.7g); PROTEIN 18.1g; CARB 74.8g; FIBER 1.9g; CHOL 93mg; IRON 2.3mg; SODIUM 656mg; CALC 43mg

---

KOREAN CHILLED BUCKWHEAT NOODLES WITH CHILE SAUCE

This dish is most popular in the summer but delicious year-round. Korean naengmyun noodles are made from wheat and buckwheat and are wonderfully chewy; Japanese soba is an adequate substitute but lacks the chewy texture. Because of the noodles' firm texture, the dish comes to the table with scissors, and you are to snip a few times, and then mix everything together after enjoying the initial presentation.

Kid Friendly

Chinese Wide Noodles with Barbecue Pork and Dried Mushrooms

Hands-on: 28 min. Total: 9 hr. 11 min.

Pork:
1 (1-pound) pork tenderloin, trimmed
1/4 cup honey
1/4 cup lower-sodium soy sauce
2 tablespoons hoisin sauce
1 tablespoon dry sherry
1/2 teaspoon five-spice powder
1/8 teaspoon kosher salt
1/8 teaspoon white pepper
Cooking spray
Noodles:
2 cups boiling water
8 dried Chinese mushrooms (such as wood ear mushrooms)
12 ounces dried flat wide wheat noodles (such as wide lo mein noodles)
2 tablespoons lower-sodium soy sauce
1 tablespoon oyster sauce
1 tablespoon hoisin sauce
2 tablespoons canola oil
1 1/2 tablespoons minced peeled fresh ginger
1 garlic clove, minced
1 jalapeño pepper, seeded and minced
1/2 medium onion, thinly vertically sliced
2 cups fresh bean sprouts
3 green onions, cut into 2-inch pieces

1. To prepare pork, slice pork lengthwise, cutting to, but not through, other side. Open halves, laying pork flat. Place plastic wrap over pork; pound to an even thickness using a meat mallet or small heavy skillet. Combine honey and next 6 ingredients in a zip-top plastic bag; add pork. Seal and marinate in refrigerator 8 hours or overnight, turning occasionally.

2. Preheat broiler to high.
3. Remove pork from bag, and discard marinade. Place pork on the rack of a roasting pan coated with cooking spray. Place rack in pan. Pour 2 cups water in bottom of pan. Broil pork 4 minutes on each side or until a thermometer registers 145°. Let stand 30 minutes. Cut pork into thin julienne pieces.
4. To prepare noodles, combine 2 cups boiling water and mushrooms; cover and let stand 30 minutes. Drain in a colander over a bowl; reserve soaking liquid. Cut off and discard any tough, woody stems; thinly slice mushrooms.
5. Cook noodles according to package directions. Drain and rinse with cold water. Drain well; set aside.
6. Combine 2 tablespoons soy sauce, oyster sauce, and 1 tablespoon hoisin sauce; set aside.
7. Heat a large wok over high heat. Add oil to pan; swirl. Add ginger, garlic, and jalapeño; stir-fry 30 seconds. Add sliced onion and pork; stir-fry 30 seconds. Add bean sprouts and green onions; stir-fry 1 minute. Add reserved mushroom liquid, noodles, and soy sauce mixture. Stir in mushrooms. Stir-fry until noodles are thoroughly heated. Serve immediately. Serves 6 (serving size: about 1 1/2 cups)

CALORIES 267; FAT 7.5g (sat 1g, mono 3.7g, poly 1.7g); PROTEIN 20.3g; CARB 29.2g; FIBER 5.3g; CHOL 40mg; IRON 1.4mg; SODIUM 615mg; CALC 28mg

CHINESE WIDE NOODLES WITH BARBECUE PORK AND DRIED MUSHROOMS

Here's a Chinese comfort-food favorite. A quick, healthy version of char siu pork amps up pork tenderloin with a marinade of sweet-salty hoisin sauce and aromatic five-spice powder—slivers of this meat meld with meaty wood ear mushrooms among chewy noodles bathed in a salty-sweet sauce. If you can't find wide lo mein noodles, try fettuccine.

CLASSIC PAD THAI

The national dish of Thailand, simple to make and delicious to eat. You'll find many inauthentic versions in the U.S., some that even use ketchup or are otherwise too sweet. There should be some sweetness to the dish, but it should be balanced by tangy, savory flavors.

Quick & Easy

Classic Pad Thai
(pictured on page 213)

Hands-on: 35 min. Total: 35 min. If you can find salted radish at your local Asian market, do include a bit of it chopped here, as it adds a piquant flavor that's simply irresistible.

6 ounces uncooked flat rice noodles (pad Thai noodles)
1/4 cup rice vinegar
4 teaspoons sugar, divided
2 tablespoons very thinly sliced banana pepper
3 ounces extra-firm tofu, cut into thin strips
1 tablespoon fresh lime juice
1 tablespoon water
1 tablespoon lower-sodium soy sauce
1 tablespoon fish sauce
2 large eggs, lightly beaten
1/8 teaspoon salt
3 tablespoons peanut oil, divided
3 garlic cloves, minced
1 (2-ounce) skinless, boneless chicken thigh, cut into thin strips
4 cups fresh bean sprouts, divided
3 green onions, trimmed, crushed with flat side of a knife, and cut into 1 1/2-inch pieces
1 tablespoon small dried shrimp
1/4 cup unsalted, dry-roasted peanuts, chopped
1/4 cup cilantro leaves

1. Prepare noodles according to package directions; drain.

continued

2. Combine vinegar and 1 tablespoon sugar, stirring until sugar dissolves. Add banana pepper; set aside.

3. Place tofu on several layers of heavy-duty paper towels; cover with additional paper towels. Let stand 20 minutes, pressing down occasionally.

4. Combine remaining 1 teaspoon sugar, lime juice, and next 3 ingredients. Combine eggs and salt, stirring well.

5. Heat a large wok over high heat. Add 1½ tablespoons oil; swirl to coat. Add garlic; stir-fry 15 seconds. Add chicken; stir-fry 2 minutes or until browned. Add pressed tofu; cook 1 minute on each side or until browned. Pour in egg mixture; cook 45 seconds or until egg begins to set around chicken and tofu. Remove from pan; cut into large pieces.

6. Add remaining 1½ tablespoons oil to wok; swirl to coat. Add 2 cups bean sprouts, green onions, and dried shrimp; stir-fry 1 minute. Add noodles and soy sauce mixture; stir-fry 2 minutes, tossing until noodles are lightly browned. Add reserved egg mixture; toss to combine. Arrange remaining 2 cups bean sprouts on a platter; top with noodle mixture. Sprinkle with peanuts and cilantro. Serve with vinegar mixture. Serves 4 (serving size: 1½ cups noodle mixture and 1½ tablespoons vinegar sauce)

CALORIES 432; FAT 19.1g (sat 3.6g, mono 8.3g, poly 6.1g); PROTEIN 14.3g; CARB 52.7g; FIBER 3.6g; CHOL 110mg; IRON 3.3mg; SODIUM 640mg; CALC 80mg

FLAVOR-BUILDING INGREDIENTS

1. RICE VINEGAR
It has a well-balanced tang that isn't as puckery as some vinegars. Buy natural, not seasoned (which has added sugar and salt).

2. FRESH BEAN SPROUTS
You'll usually find mung bean sprouts, which are refreshingly crisp and juicy—great raw or cooked.

3. CILANTRO
The bright, pungent flavor of this herb is a signature of many noodle bowls, where its herbal kick is a fresh finishing touch.

4. DRIED WOOD EAR MUSHROOMS
Mild earthy flavor and, once hydrated, a pleasing chewy-cartilaginous texture.

5. GOCHUGARU
Korean coarse-ground red pepper, found in Asian markets. It's earthy, slightly bitter, and smoky; ancho chile powder is a fine sub.

6. KECAP MANIS
This Indonesian sweet soy sauce is thick as molasses; you'll most often see ABC brand. Don't confuse with *kecap asin,* a salty soy sauce.

7. DRY-ROASTED PEANUTS
Common garnish on Thai and Vietnamese dishes. Crunch is a nice foil to slippery noodles.

8. HOISIN SAUCE
Thick, dark Chinese condiment with a sweet-salty-spiced flavor. It's often used to glaze meats or as a flavor-packed stir-in.

9. DRIED SHRIMP
These crustaceans are sun-dried with a rich, salty flavor. They are used in many Asian dishes for umami depth.

10. FRIED ONIONS
For tasty finishing crunch. Find them in Asian markets, or use French's canned onions—the kind that go on green bean casserole.

11. THAI BASIL
With pointier leaves and a peppery, deeper anise flavor, this basil variety packs more punch than sweet basil.

12. FISH SAUCE
A must for Vietnamese and Thai dishes, with a deeply savory quality that, if used just right, isn't really fishy. We like Three Crabs brand.

13. FRESH GINGER
Knobby root with fantastic peppery-sweet pungent flavor. Store in the freezer and grate it frozen for ginger "snow."

14. GOCHUJANG
Spicy Korean condiment that tastes like a fiery miso. Annie Chun's brand, which we buy at Whole Foods Market, is lower in sodium than most.

15. FIVE-SPICE POWDER
Primarily used in Chinese cooking, this is an aromatic blend of cinnamon, star anise, cloves, Sichuan pepper, and fennel seeds.

SALT IN THE SUPERMARKET

Surprising discoveries about 4 everyday foods. And a few takeout-food findings, too.

Why some shrimp are saltier than others.

When fresh shrimp are frozen (often just minutes after being caught), they are washed in a saline solution to help bring their temperature down faster. Quicker chilling prevents ice crystals from forming inside the shrimp, resulting in better texture when defrosted; it also helps keep them from clumping together as they freeze. "Easy-peel" shrimp are soaked in an additional sodium solution. Pro: They slip out of their shells effortlessly. Con: More salt. How much more?

The test
We steamed and peeled five varieties of shrimp, and then shipped them to the lab for sodium analysis.

The results
(per 4 ounces steamed)
Wild-caught fresh Gulf shrimp (never frozen): 97mg
Farm-raised fresh shrimp (previously frozen): 159mg
Winn-Dixie individually quick-frozen easy-to-peel wild-caught shrimp: 245mg
Whole Foods individually quick-frozen easy-to-peel shrimp: 483mg
Publix fresh frozen easy-to-peel farm-raised shrimp: 730mg

Why some salt labels don't tell the whole story.

Food labels generally tell you what's in the package, not what will be in the food after cooking. Here's a dramatic example of what that can mean for the home cook.

Soba noodle labels list as much as 900mg sodium per serving—which has limited our use of it. But when we boiled five brands of soba, they lost an average of 80% of their sodium, down to about 80mg per serving. The FDA only requires labels to list the nutritional properties of foods as packaged. Food makers may voluntarily present "as prepared" information, but that's an extra step, and calculation, for them. Most foods used in cooking are rarely consumed as packaged—like soba noodles.
Bottom line: Always consider the ingredients added and methods used in preparing foods.

Coarser salt doesn't yield automatic sodium savings.

It's conventional wisdom that big-grained salt contains about 25% less sodium by volume than table salt. The idea: Coarse crystals don't pack tightly and take up more space in a measuring spoon (with lots of air between them), meaning you consume less sodium. Labels on one brand show a 110mg difference between ¼ teaspoon of their table and kosher salts; that's a 19% savings if you use kosher. But our analysis of six salts showed less variation per ¼ teaspoon than you might think.
Bottom line: If you're watching sodium, you can't throw "gourmet" salts around with impunity.

Our fave sauce: a cautionary tale

We've long recommended McCutcheon's bottled marinara sauce because of its great flavor and the low sodium level on its label—only 185mg per half-cup listed. When we tested three batches, though, they came in at more than three times that number. We talked to Vanessa McCutcheon-Smith, and she attributed the difference to a change in the supplier of the canned tomatoes they use as a base (no salt is added during the cooking). It's not routine to test a batch when the tomatoes change, she explained—only to calculate nutrition based on numbers provided by suppliers.

"Knowing what I know about how things change on the supply chain, I don't put a lot of merit in the information on food panels," she added.

Nutrition label numbers are allowed 20% of wiggle room, but the FDA does few random audits. As a general rule: Trust your taste buds; if something tastes salty, it probably is, whatever the label says.

How salty are takeout foods?

Fast-food chains post data on their company websites: Hardee's Monster Thickburger contains almost 3,000mg sodium. But most small, local restaurants don't post nutrition information. We got takeout from three in our town to see how entrées stacked up. They stacked up really, really high.

Trattoria pizza topped with cured meats, sausage, and olives: 3,474mg sodium
Barbecue pulled-pork sandwich with baked beans and slaw: 2,480mg sodium
Bowl of ramen with miso broth: 3,245mg sodium

TEST KITCHEN *CONFIDENTIAL*

Secrets, tips, and recipes from America's healthy cooking experts.

WEEKNIGHT PASTA

FAST, EASY, VEGETABLE-FOCUSED

Brighten the flavor of fresh spring veggies with a quick pickle method.

Impress your family with a weeknight dinner of fresh pasta with mozzarella and gently pickled veggies (called giardiniera) that pack a wonderful tang that's not too puckery. Pickling usually takes days or even weeks as the vegetables soak up the brine, but with our fast method, there's no waiting for the vinegar to imbue them with flavor. Briefly cook the veggies in the vinegar mixture until they soak it up and become crisptender and mildly pickle-y. Toss with pasta, and enjoy!

Vegetarian
Pasta Giardiniera

Hands-on: 29 min. Total: 45 min. Fresh lasagna noodles offer silky texture without the work of making your own pasta. Here we cut the sheets into thick noodles. Sub pappardelle or fettuccine, if necessary.

1 large red bell pepper
10 cups water
10 baby carrots with tops, trimmed (do not peel)
4 ounces red pearl onions
3 ounces sugar snap peas, trimmed
1/4 cup extra-virgin olive oil, divided
3 1/2 ounces shiitake mushroom caps, halved
1 fennel bulb, trimmed and vertically sliced
3/4 teaspoon salt, divided
2 tablespoons champagne vinegar
6 ounces fresh lasagna noodles, cut into 1 1/4 x 5-inch ribbons
1 tablespoon capers, drained
1/2 teaspoon crushed red pepper
3 ounces (1/4-inch) cubed fresh mozzarella cheese (about 3/4 cup)
1 tablespoon thyme leaves

1. Preheat broiler to high.
2. Cut bell pepper in half lengthwise; discard seeds and membranes. Place pepper halves, skin sides up, on a foil-lined baking sheet; flatten with hand. Broil 8 minutes or until blackened. Place in a paper bag; fold to close tightly. Let stand 10 minutes. Peel and cut into strips.
3. While bell pepper broils, bring 10 cups water to a boil in a Dutch oven. Add carrots and onions; cook 2 minutes. Add peas; cook 2 minutes. Drain; rinse with cold water. Drain. Remove carrot skins by rubbing gently with a clean, dry paper towel. Remove stem ends from onions; peel.
4. Heat a large nonstick skillet over medium-high heat. Add 2 tablespoons olive oil, and swirl to coat. Add onions, mushrooms, and fennel; sauté 2 minutes, stirring occasionally. Add 1/4 teaspoon salt; reduce heat to medium, and sauté 3 minutes, stirring occasionally. Add bell pepper, carrots, peas, and vinegar; cook 2 minutes or until liquid almost evaporates.
5. Cook pasta in boiling water 2 minutes; drain. Combine pasta, 2 tablespoons oil, 1/2 teaspoon salt, fennel mixture, capers, and crushed red pepper in a large bowl; toss to combine. Add mozzarella; sprinkle with thyme. Serves 4 (serving size: 1 1/4 cups)

CALORIES 388; FAT 19.8g (sat 5g, mono 10g, poly 1.9g); PROTEIN 10.9g; CARB 43.3g; FIBER 6.6g; CHOL 48mg; IRON 3mg; SODIUM 596mg; CALC 178mg

OFFSET SERRATED KNIFE

I love this odd-shaped offset serrated knife. It cuts even tough veggies easily and is well balanced in the hand, saving your knuckles from hitting the board as you cut. Classic 8" Serrated Offset Handle Deli Knife by Wusthof ($100, swissknifeshop. com)

—Deb Wise, *Cooking Light* recipe tester and developer

Fettuccine with Seared Tomatoes, Spinach, and Burrata

Hands-on: 25 min. Total: 25 min. Don't skimp on the oil: There's a good bit here, but it creates a gorgeous tomato sauce that coats the noodles nicely.

8 ounces uncooked fettuccine
Cooking spray
2/3 cup grape tomatoes, halved (about 10 large)
3 tablespoons extra-virgin olive oil
1/4 teaspoon crushed red pepper
4 garlic cloves, thinly sliced
1 (14.5-ounce) can unsalted diced tomatoes, undrained
3/4 teaspoon salt
3 ounces fresh baby spinach (about 3 cups)
4 ounces burrata cheese
Freshly ground black pepper

1. Cook pasta according to package directions, omitting salt and fat; drain.
2. While pasta cooks, heat a large skillet over medium-high heat. Coat pan with cooking spray. Arrange tomato halves, cut sides down, in pan; cook 1½ minutes or until seared. Stir tomatoes; cook 30 seconds. Remove tomatoes from pan; set aside.
3. Reduce heat to low. Add oil to pan; swirl to coat. Add red pepper and garlic; cook 2 minutes or until fragrant, stirring occasionally. Place canned tomatoes in a mini chopper or food processor; process until almost smooth. Add pureed tomatoes and salt to oil mixture; cook 8 minutes, stirring occasionally.
4. Remove skillet from heat. Add spinach and cooked pasta; toss well until spinach wilts slightly. Arrange about 1⅓ cups pasta mixture in each of 4 shallow bowls. Divide seared grape tomato halves evenly among servings.

Dollop about 2 tablespoons burrata cheese over each serving, and sprinkle with freshly ground black pepper. Serves 4

CALORIES 415; **FAT** 17.1g (sat 5.7g, mono 9.2g, poly 1.3g); **PROTEIN** 13.5g; **CARB** 51.4g; **FIBER** 4.8g; **CHOL** 20mg; **IRON** 3mg; **SODIUM** 593mg; **CALC** 202mg

QUICK TRICKS

BREADCRUMB PASTA TOPPERS

Pulse 2 ounces torn baguette in a food processor for coarse crumbs. Pick a flavor and proceed. Makes plain pasta delicious.

Spicy Sausage:
Heat a skillet over medium heat. Add 1 tablespoon oil; swirl to coat. Add 2 tablespoons Mexican chorizo; cook 1½ minutes, mashing with a fork. Stir in 3 minced garlic cloves; sauté 1 minute. Add breadcrumbs; cook 3 minutes or until toasted. Serves 8 (serving size: about 1½ tablespoons)

CALORIES 54; **FAT** 3.2g (sat 0.8g); **SODIUM** 80 mg

Bacon & Chive:
Cook 2 bacon slices in a skillet over medium heat until crisp, and remove from pan using a slotted spoon. Crumble. Add breadcrumbs to drippings in pan; cook 2 minutes or until toasted, stirring frequently. Remove from heat; stir in bacon and 1 tablespoon chopped chives. Serves 8 (serving size: about 1½ tablespoons)

CALORIES 54; **FAT** 1.3g (sat 0.6g); **SODIUM** 140mg

Spicy Anchovy:
Drain 1 teaspoon oil from a can of anchovy fillets. Heat a skillet over medium heat. Add anchovy oil and 2 teaspoons olive oil to pan; swirl. Add 1 minced anchovy fillet to pan; cook 1 minute. Add 1 minced garlic clove, and cook 30 seconds. Add breadcrumbs and ¼

teaspoon crushed red pepper, and cook 3 minutes or until toasted, stirring occasionally. Serves 8 (serving size: about 1 heaping tablespoon)

CALORIES 37; **FAT** 1.9g (sat 0.6g); **SODIUM** 55mg

Coconut & Chile:
Heat a skillet over medium-high heat. Add 1 tablespoon canola oil; swirl to coat. Add breadcrumbs, and sauté 2 minutes. Stir in ¼ cup toasted flaked unsweetened coconut, 2 teaspoons ground Korean chile (gochugaru) or ancho chile powder, and ⅛ teaspoon salt. Serves 8 (serving size: about 4 teaspoons)

CALORIES 53; **FAT** 3.5g (sat 1.6g); **SODIUM** 67mg

Basil Pesto:
Heat a skillet over medium heat. Add 1 tablespoon olive oil; swirl to coat. Add 2 minced garlic cloves; cook 30 seconds. Add breadcrumbs, 1 tablespoon chopped pine nuts, and 1 ounce grated Parmigiano-Reggiano; cook 2 minutes or until toasted, stirring occasionallly. Remove from heat; stir in ⅓ cup torn fresh basil. Serves 8 (serving size: about 2 tablespoons)

CALORIES 59; **FAT** 3.4g (sat 0.9g); **SODIUM** 91mg

Green Kale:
Place 1 cup chopped kale, 2 teaspoons olive oil, and 1 garlic clove in a food processor; pulse until minced. Heat 1 tablespoon olive oil in a skillet over medium-high heat. Add breadcrumbs, and sauté 1½ minutes. Stir in kale mixture; sauté 30 seconds. Serves 8 (serving size: about 2 tablespoons)

CALORIES 50; **FAT** 3g (sat 0.4g); **SODIUM** 40mg

Cilantro-Peanut:
Heat a skillet over medium heat. Add 1½ tablespoons dark sesame oil; swirl to coat. Add breadcrumbs, 2 tablespoons chopped peanuts, and 1 teaspoon fresh lime juice. Cook 3 minutes or until toasted. Stir in ⅓ cup chopped fresh cilantro. Serves 8 (serving size: about 2 tablespoons)

CALORIES 64; **FAT** 4.5g (sat 0.7g); **SODIUM** 61mg

MEATLESS MONDAYS

Quick & Easy • Freezable
Make Ahead • Vegetarian

Black Bean, Hominy, and Kale Stew

Hands-on: 25 min. Total: 32 min. Roasting the poblano chiles offers a fast route to deep flavor in this hearty bowl.

2 poblano chiles
8 ounces tomatillos, husks removed and halved (about 4)
2 teaspoons olive oil
1½ cups chopped onion
1 jalapeño, seeded and minced
2 garlic cloves, minced
2 teaspoons ground cumin
3 cups organic vegetable broth
¼ teaspoon salt
⅛ teaspoon ground red pepper
2 (15.5-ounce) cans unsalted black beans, rinsed and drained
1 (8-ounce) bunch kale, tough stems removed, leaves chopped (about 4 packed cups)
1 (15-ounce) can hominy, rinsed and drained
6 tablespoons reduced-fat sour cream
2 ounces shredded sharp white cheddar cheese (about ½ cup)
¼ cup chopped fresh cilantro

1. Preheat broiler to high.
2. Place poblano chiles on a foil-lined baking sheet. Broil 7 minutes on each side or until blackened and charred. Place in a paper bag; fold to close tightly. Let stand 15 minutes. Peel chiles; cut in half lengthwise. Discard seeds and membranes; coarsely chop. Set aside.
3. While poblano chiles roast, place tomatillos in a food processor, and process until smooth. Set aside.
4. Heat a Dutch oven over medium heat. Add oil to pan; swirl to coat. Add onion and jalapeño; sauté 5 minutes or until tender, stirring occasionally. Add garlic and cumin; sauté 1 minute, stirring constantly. Add tomatillos, broth, and next 4 ingredients; bring to a boil. Cover, reduce heat, and simmer 10 minutes or until vegetables are tender. Add roasted poblanos and hominy; cook 2 minutes or until heated through. Ladle into each of 6 shallow bowls; top evenly with sour cream and cheese. Sprinkle with cilantro. Serves 6 (serving size: about 1¼ cups)

CALORIES 240; **FAT** 7.7g (sat 3.5g, mono 2.7g, poly 0.8g); **PROTEIN** 10.9g; **CARB** 33.3g; **FIBER** 8g; **CHOL** 16mg; **IRON** 3mg; **SODIUM** 573mg; **CALC** 210mg

RADICALLY SIMPLE

BRING ON SPRING

By Rozanne Gold

By the time March arrives, most of us are ready to move past winter's last gray days into springtime's sunny-fresh flavors. Trouble is, much of the country is still firmly planted in winter, and hearty root vegetables (delicious as they are) dominate the plate. Here's a great way to coax spring flavors out of select year-round ingredients: Combine bright lemons, peppery arugula, and tender green onions for a luscious compote that can be used to accompany salmon. It's a light, fresh dinner that's fantastically easy and fast to make.

Quick & Easy

Sesame Salmon with Green Onions and Lemon

Hands-on: 16 min. Total: 24 min. This dish is simple yet radically sophisticated. If you have access to fresh ramps or baby leeks, use them instead of green onions, and sub pea shoots (or your favorite baby lettuce or microgreens) for the arugula. Black sesame seeds lend lovely contrast to the vibrant red-orange fish, but regular will do the job, too.

4 (6-ounce) sustainable salmon fillets (such as wild Alaskan)
Cooking spray
2 tablespoons sesame seeds
2 tablespoons black sesame seeds
½ teaspoon salt, divided
1 tablespoon butter
1 tablespoon extra-virgin olive oil
2 cups (1-inch) slices green onions
5 thin lemon slices, halved
¼ teaspoon black pepper
1 cup baby arugula

1. Preheat oven to 400°.
2. Arrange salmon in a single layer on a jelly-roll pan coated with cooking spray. Combine sesame seeds and ⅜ teaspoon salt; sprinkle evenly over flesh sides of fillets, pressing gently into fish. Bake at 400° for 14 minutes or until desired degree of doneness.
3. Melt butter in a medium saucepan over medium heat. Add oil to pan; swirl. Add green onions; cook 2 minutes, stirring occasionally. Add lemon slices; cook 2 minutes. Sprinkle green onion mixture with ⅛ teaspoon salt and pepper. Place 1 fillet on each of 4 plates. Place arugula in a medium bowl. Add green onion mixture to bowl with arugula; toss. Divide arugula mixture evenly among servings. Serves 4

CALORIES 312; **FAT** 17.9g (sat 4.4g, mono 7.3g, poly 4.9g); **PROTEIN** 29g; **CARB** 7g; **FIBER** 3.4g; **CHOL** 75mg; **IRON** 2.7mg; **SODIUM** 378mg; **CALC** 152mg

RECIPE MAKEOVER

A TIRAMISU TAKEOVER

We cut fat by 75% and calories by half, but our version of the creamy-coffee-choco classic is still divine.

Chances are good that you've had a moment with the fully loaded version of this elegant, espresso-soaked sponge cake dessert, which is enveloped in rich layers of buttery mascarpone and sweetened whipped cream. And if you haven't, well, we suggest you do … by trying our made-over version.

The classic recipe packs a calorie and fat wallop: a day's worth of sat fat buttressing almost 600 calories. Mascarpone, you see, is Italy's version of a dessert butter: sublime, but you don't need so much to enrich a dessert. To lighten, we sub in ⅓-less-fat cream cheese (leaving a touch of mascarpone for richness) and mix it into a lightly sweetened egg custard. Egg whites are whipped into tall, fluffy peaks that fold beautifully into the mixture, eliminating the need for heavy whipped cream. Crisp, savoiardi-style ladyfingers get dipped into Kahlúa-spiked coffee and are then layered with our creamy, custard-like filling. A final hit of bittersweet chocolate adds one more layer of yum for an indulgent treat that will truly be—for that's what "tiramisu" means—a pick-me-up.

CLASSIC	MAKEOVER
577 calories per serving	234 calories per serving
42 grams total fat	10.6 grams total fat
23 grams saturated	5.2 grams saturated

Make Ahead
Tiramisu

Hands-on: 45 min. Total: 2 hr. 45 min.
We like our coffee überstrong here—you can also substitute 1½ cups strong brewed coffee mixed with a tablespoon of instant espresso.

1½ cups water
½ cup ground dark roast coffee
½ cup sugar, divided
3 large egg yolks
2 tablespoons Kahlúa (coffee-flavored liqueur), divided
5 large egg whites
2 tablespoons water
8 ounces ⅓-less-fat cream cheese, softened
2 ounces mascarpone cheese, softened
24 crisp savoiardi ladyfingers (1 [7-ounce] package)
¾ ounce bittersweet chocolate, finely grated

1. Bring 1½ cups water to a boil, and remove from heat. Add coffee; cover and let stand 10 minutes. Strain through a cheesecloth-lined sieve into a medium bowl; discard solids. Cover and refrigerate until needed.
2. Combine ¼ cup sugar, egg yolks, and 1 tablespoon Kahlúa in the top of a double boiler, stirring well with a whisk. Cook over simmering water, whisking constantly, until thick and candy thermometer registers 160° (about 9 minutes). Remove from heat; refrigerate 10 minutes.
3. Place egg whites in a large bowl; beat with a mixer at high speed until medium peaks form. Combine remaining ¼ cup sugar and 2 tablespoons water in a small saucepan, and bring to a boil. Cook, without stirring, until candy thermometer registers 250°. With mixer on low speed, carefully pour hot syrup over egg whites. Gradually increase speed to high; beat 2 minutes or until stiff peaks form (do not overmix).
4. Combine egg yolk mixture, cream cheese, and mascarpone cheese in a large bowl, and beat with a mixer at medium speed until smooth. Gently stir one-fourth of egg white mixture into cream cheese mixture; gently fold remaining egg white mixture into cream cheese mixture.
5. Add 1 tablespoon Kahlúa to coffee. Quickly dip 12 ladyfingers into coffee mixture; arrange in the bottom of an 11 x 7–inch baking dish. Spread half of cream cheese mixture over ladyfingers. Sprinkle with half of chocolate. Repeat procedure with remaining ladyfingers, coffee mixture, and cream cheese mixture. Sprinkle with remaining chocolate. Cover and chill at least 2 hours. Serves 10

CALORIES 234; FAT 10.6g (sat 5.2g, mono 1.9g, poly 0.5g); PROTEIN 7.1g; CARB 28.4g; FIBER 0.2g; CHOL 101mg; IRON 0.6mg; SODIUM 142mg; CALC 44mg

THE SECRETS TO OUR LIGHTER LAYERS

⅓-LESS-FAT CREAM CHEESE
Mascarpone is a fresh Italian cheese that rivals butter in sat fat. We replace nearly all of it with ⅓-less-fat cream cheese, saving 160 calories and 10g sat fat per serving.

WHIPPED EGG WHITES
Sweetened with a touch of sugar, we fold these light and fluffy fat-free whites into our custard and save 7g of sat fat per serving over heavy whipped cream.

A KICK OF KAHLÚA
We save 23 calories per serving with this full-flavored coffee liqueur. It packs a bittersweet punch that replaces sweet wine and extra sugar in the creamy custard.

DINNER TONIGHT

Fast weeknight menus from the *Cooking Light* Test Kitchen

READY IN
30
MINUTES

················ *The* ················
SHOPPING LIST
··

Haibut with Olive and Bell Pepper Couscous
Red bell pepper (1)
Garlic
Fresh oregano
Lemons (2)
Olive oil
Israeli couscous (½ cup)
Fat-free, lower-sodium chicken broth
Pitted kalamata olives
4 (6-ounce) skinless halibut fillets

Lemon-Garlic Asparagus
Asparagus (1 pound)
Garlic
Lemon (1)
Olive oil

················ *The* ················
GAME PLAN
··

While couscous cooks:
- Sear halibut.
While fish broils:
- Cook asparagus.

Quick & Easy
Halibut with Olive and Bell Pepper Couscous

With Lemon-Garlic Asparagus

Prep Pointer: Snap off the tough ends of the asparagus before sautéing.
Flavor Hit: Briny kalamata olives add a salty punch.
Budget Buy: For a less-expensive option, substitute tilapia or cod for halibut.

2 teaspoons olive oil, divided
½ cup diced red bell pepper
2 garlic cloves, minced
½ cup uncooked Israeli couscous
¾ cup fat-free, lower-sodium chicken broth
2 tablespoons kalamata olives, pitted and quartered
½ teaspoon kosher salt, divided
½ teaspoon freshly ground black pepper, divided
4 (6-ounce) skinless halibut fillets
4 teaspoons torn fresh oregano
2 lemons, cut into ⅛-inch-thick slices

1. Preheat broiler to high.
2. Heat a medium saucepan over medium-high heat. Add 1 teaspoon oil to pan; swirl to coat. Add bell pepper and garlic; cook 1 minute, stirring occasionally. Add couscous; cook 1 minute or until lightly browned. Add broth; bring to a boil. Cover and simmer 7 minutes or until liquid evaporates. Stir in olives, ¼ teaspoon salt, and ¼ teaspoon black pepper.
3. Sprinkle halibut evenly with ¼ teaspoon salt and ¼ teaspoon black pepper. Heat a large ovenproof skillet over medium-high heat. Add 1 teaspoon oil to pan; swirl to coat. Add fillets to pan; cook 3 minutes. Remove pan from heat; turn fillets over. Arrange torn oregano and lemon slices evenly over fillets. Place pan in oven. Broil 5 minutes or until fish flakes easily when tested with a fork. Serve fish with couscous. Serves 4 (serving size: 1 fillet and about ½ cup couscous)

Sustainable Choice | *Look for Pacific halibut.*

CALORIES 308; FAT 6.7g (sat 1g, mono 3.9g, poly 1g); PROTEIN 35.2g; CARB 25.2g; FIBER 2.5g; CHOL 83mg; IRON 0.5mg; SODIUM 557mg; CALC 36mg

For the Lemon-Garlic Asparagus:
Heat a large skillet over medium-high heat. Add 2 teaspoons olive oil to pan; swirl to coat. Add 1 pound trimmed asparagus; sauté 3 minutes or until crisp-tender. Add 1 minced garlic clove; cook 1 minute, stirring occasionally. Remove from heat. Add 1 teaspoon fresh lemon juice, ¼ teaspoon freshly ground black pepper, and ⅛ teaspoon kosher salt; toss to coat. Serves 4 (serving size: about 3 ounces asaparagus)

CALORIES 45; FAT 2.4g (sat 0.4g); SODIUM 63mg

READY IN
30
MINUTES

The
SHOPPING LIST

Pork Chops with Tangy Red Currant Sauce

Onion (1)
Garlic
Lemon (1)
Red wine
Sugar
Red currant fruit spread
Red wine vinegar
4 (6-ounce) bone-in center-cut loin pork chops

Mashed Potatoes

Frozen precut baking potatoes
Extra-virgin olive oil
2% reduced-fat milk

Lemon-Mint Peas

Lemon (1)
Fresh mint
Frozen green peas
Butter

The
GAME PLAN

While sauce cooks:
- Prepare pork.

While pork rests:
- Cook potatoes and peas.

Kid Friendly • Quick & Easy
Pork Chops with Tangy Red Currant Sauce

With Mashed Potatoes and Lemon-Mint Peas

Time-Saver: Look for precut potatoes in the freezer aisle.
Simple Sub: Substitute thyme for mint in the peas.

Cooking spray
$\frac{1}{2}$ cup diced white onion
3 tablespoons minced fresh garlic, divided
$\frac{1}{3}$ cup red wine or unsalted chicken stock
2 tablespoons sugar
2 tablespoons red currant fruit spread
$\frac{1}{4}$ cup red wine vinegar
$1\frac{1}{2}$ tablespoons grated lemon rind
4 (6-ounce) bone-in center-cut loin pork chops, trimmed
$\frac{1}{2}$ teaspoon freshly ground black pepper
$\frac{1}{4}$ teaspoon kosher salt

1. Heat a saucepan over medium heat. Coat pan with cooking spray. Add onion and 1 tablespoon garlic; cook 4 minutes or until onion is tender. Add wine; cook 5 minutes or until liquid almost evaporates. Add sugar and fruit spread; bring to a boil. Cook 1 minute. Add vinegar; return to a boil. Cook until reduced to $\frac{1}{2}$ cup (about 5 minutes).

2. Heat a large grill pan over medium-high heat. Coat with cooking spray. Combine 2 tablespoons garlic and rind; sprinkle evenly over pork, pressing to adhere. Sprinkle evenly with pepper and salt. Add pork to pan; cook 3 minutes on each side or until desired degree of doneness. Remove from pan; let stand 5 minutes. Serves 4 (serving size: 1 pork chop and 2 tablespoons sauce)

CALORIES 300; **FAT** 6.8g (sat 1.9g, mono 2.3g, poly 0.7g); **PROTEIN** 38.1g; **CARB** 17.6g; **FIBER** 0.8g; **CHOL** 117mg; **IRON** 1.4mg; **SODIUM** 222mg; **CALC** 53mg

For the Mashed Potatoes:
Place 2 cups frozen precut baking potatoes (such as Ore Ida Steam n' Mash) in a bowl. Microwave at HIGH 3 minutes, stirring after 2 minutes. Add 2 tablespoons 2% reduced-fat milk, 1 tablespoon extra-virgin olive oil, $\frac{1}{4}$ teaspoon freshly ground black pepper, and $\frac{1}{8}$ teaspoon salt; mash potatoes. Sprinkle with additional pepper, if desired. Serves 4 (serving size: $\frac{1}{2}$ cup)

CALORIES 88; **FAT** 3.5g (sat 0.6g); **SODIUM** 251mg

For the Lemon-Mint Peas:
Place 2 cups frozen green peas and 2 tablespoons water in a bowl; cover. Microwave at HIGH 3 minutes, stirring after 2 minutes. Add 1 tablespoon chopped fresh mint, 1 teaspoon butter, $\frac{1}{2}$ teaspoon grated lemon rind, $\frac{1}{4}$ teaspoon pepper, and $\frac{1}{8}$ teaspoon salt; toss. Serves 4 (serving size: $\frac{1}{2}$ cup)

CALORIES 68; **FAT** 1.3g (sat 0.7g); **SODIUM** 86mg

FLAVOR HIT: GRATED FRESH LEMON RIND HELPS PERK UP ORDINARY PEAS.

READY IN
40
MINUTES

The
SHOPPING LIST

Sausage, Fennel, and Ricotta Pizza
Fennel bulb
Garlic
Red onion (1)
Cornmeal
Extra-virgin olive oil
Part-skim ricotta
Fennel seeds
Crushed red pepper
Italian turkey sausage (4 ounces)
Refrigerated fresh pizza dough (12 ounces)

Arugula and Mushroom Salad
Lemon (1)
Mushrooms (1 cup)
Baby arugula (6 ounces)
White wine vinegar
Extra-virgin olive oil
Parmigiano-Reggiano cheese

The
GAME PLAN

While oven preheats:
- Cook sausage and fennel.
- Roll out dough.
While pizza bakes:
- Make salad.

PREP POINTER:
A PREHEATED
PIZZA STONE
OR BAKING SHEET
ENSURES AN
EXTRA-CRISP CRUST.

Quick & Easy
Sausage, Fennel, and Ricotta Pizza

With Arugula and Mushroom Salad

12 ounces refrigerated fresh pizza dough
1 (4-ounce) link Italian turkey sausage
1 cup thinly sliced fennel bulb
1 tablespoon cornmeal
1 tablespoon extra-virgin olive oil
1/3 cup part-skim ricotta
1 teaspoon minced fresh garlic
1/3 cup thinly sliced red onion
2 teaspoons fennel seeds
1/2 teaspoon crushed red pepper
1/2 teaspoon freshly ground black pepper
1/8 teaspoon kosher salt

1. Place a pizza stone or heavy baking sheet in oven. Preheat oven to 500° (keep pizza stone or baking sheet in oven as it preheats). Let pizza dough stand at room temperature, covered, while oven preheats.
2. Heat a large nonstick skillet over medium-high heat. Remove casing from sausage. Add sausage to pan; cook 4 minutes or until lightly browned, stirring to crumble. Add fennel bulb; cook 4 minutes or until tender.
3. Roll pizza dough into a 16-inch oval on a lightly floured surface. Carefully remove pizza stone from oven. Sprinkle cornmeal over pizza stone; place dough on pizza stone. Brush dough evenly with oil. Sprinkle sausage mixture evenly over dough, leaving a 1-inch border. Combine ricotta and garlic in a small bowl; top pizza with teaspoonfuls of ricotta mixture. Sprinkle red onion and remaining ingredients evenly over pizza. Bake at 500° for 11 minutes or until golden. Cut into 8 slices. Serves 4 (serving size: 2 slices)

CALORIES 344; FAT 9.9g (sat 2.1g, mono 4.7g, poly 1.5g); PROTEIN 15.5g; CARB 46.4g; FIBER 7.6g; CHOL 23mg; IRON 2.2mg; SODIUM 646mg; CALC 84mg

For the Arugula and Mushroom Salad:
Combine 1 tablespoon white wine vinegar, 1 tablespoon fresh lemon juice, 2 teaspoons extra-virgin olive oil, 1/4 teaspoon kosher salt, and 1/4 teaspoon black pepper. Add 1 cup quartered mushrooms and 6 ounces baby arugula; toss gently. Top with 1 tablespoon shaved Parmigiano-Reggiano cheese. Serves 4 (serving size: about 1½ cups)

CALORIES 42; FAT 3g (sat 0.6g); SODIUM 152mg

READY IN
40
MINUTES

The
SHOPPING LIST

Shrimp and Grits
Onion (1)
Garlic
(8-ounce) package presliced mushrooms
Green onions
Quick-cooking grits (3/4 cup)
Crushed red pepper
All-purpose flour
Fat-free, lower-sodium chicken broth
Center-cut bacon (2 slices)
Medium shrimp (1 pound)
Butter
Parmesan cheese (2 ounces)
Half-and-half

Spicy Green Beans
Green beans (1½ pounds)
Garlic
Olive oil
Crushed red pepper
White wine vinegar

The
GAME PLAN

While grits cook:
- Crisp bacon.
- Chop onion and garlic.
While mushrooms cook:
- Sauté haricots verts.

Quick & Easy
Shrimp and Grits

With Spicy Green Beans

Flavor Hit: Parmesan cheese adds nutty depth to the grits.
Shop Smart: Look for bagged, trimmed haricots verts or green beans at the store.
Time-Saver: Have your fishmonger peel and devein the shrimp.

3 cups water
1 tablespoon butter
3/4 cup uncooked quick-cooking grits
2 ounces grated fresh Parmesan cheese (about 1/2 cup)
5/8 teaspoon kosher salt, divided
3/4 teaspoon freshly ground black pepper, divided
2 center-cut bacon slices, chopped
1 cup chopped white onion
1 tablespoon minced fresh garlic
1 (8-ounce) package presliced mushrooms
1 pound medium shrimp, peeled and deveined
1/2 teaspoon crushed red pepper
1/4 cup half-and-half
1 tablespoon all-purpose flour
3/4 cup fat-free, lower-sodium chicken broth
1/3 cup chopped green onions

1. Bring 3 cups water and butter to a boil in a small saucepan. Whisk in grits; cover and cook 5 minutes, stirring frequently. Remove from heat. Stir in cheese, 1/4 teaspoon salt, and 1/2 teaspoon black pepper; cover. Keep warm.

2. Cook bacon in a large nonstick skillet over medium-high heat until crisp. Add white onion, garlic, and mushrooms to pan; cook 8 minutes or until mushrooms begin to brown and give off liquid, stirring frequently. Add shrimp and red pepper; cook 3 minutes. Combine half-and-half and flour in a small bowl, stirring with a whisk until smooth. Add broth, flour mixture, 3/8 teaspoon salt, and 1/4 teaspoon black pepper to pan; bring to a boil. Cook 2 minutes or until slightly thickened. Top with green onions. Serve shrimp mixture with grits. Serves 6 (serving size: 1/2 cup grits and about 1/2 cup shrimp mixture)

 Sustainable Choice Buy Pacific white shrimp farmed in recirculating systems or inland ponds.

CALORIES 236; FAT 7.9g (sat 4.1g, mono 1.4g, poly 0.5g); PROTEIN 18.4g; CARB 22.8g; FIBER 2.1g; CHOL 115mg; IRON 1.3mg; SODIUM 583mg; CALC 173mg

For the Spicy Green Beans:
Heat a large nonstick skillet over medium-high heat. Add 2 teaspoons olive oil; swirl to coat. Add 1½ pounds haricots verts or green beans. Cook 3 minutes or until lightly browned. Add 1 tablespoon minced fresh garlic and 1/4 teaspoon crushed red pepper. Remove from heat; stir in 1½ teaspoons white wine vinegar, 1/4 teaspoon kosher salt, and 1/4 teaspoon freshly ground black pepper. Serves 6 (serving size: about 3/4 cup)

CALORIES 51; FAT 1.7g (sat 0.2g); SODIUM 87mg

FEED 4 FOR LESS THAN $10

Quick & Easy
Spicy Pork Lettuce Cups

$2.18/serving
$8.72 total

Hands-on: 23 min. Total: 23 min. *Serve with long-grain white rice to complete the meal. While the pork mixture stands to allow its flavors to meld, chop the veggies for the lettuce cups and get the rice going.*

1 tablespoon grated peeled fresh ginger
6 garlic cloves, minced
12 ounces lean ground pork
1½ cups diced seeded cucumber
1 cup diced red bell pepper
1/3 cup diced carrot
1/4 cup chopped fresh cilantro
1/4 cup salted, dry-roasted peanuts, chopped
1/2 serrano chile, thinly sliced
3 tablespoons fresh lime juice
1 tablespoon fish sauce
1 teaspoon sugar
16 Boston lettuce leaves

1. Combine first 3 ingredients, mixing gently until just combined; let stand at room temperature 15 minutes.
2. Heat a large nonstick skillet over medium-high heat. Add pork mixture to pan; sauté 5 minutes or until pork is browned, stirring to crumble. Place pork mixture in a large bowl. Add cucumber and next 5 ingredients and stir to combine.
3. Combine lime juice, fish sauce, and sugar in a small bowl, stirring until sugar dissolves. Add juice mixture to pork mixture; toss. Place about 1/3 cup pork mixture in each lettuce leaf. Serves 4 (serving size: 4 lettuce cups)

CALORIES 231; FAT 12.6g (sat 3.4g, mono 5.8g, poly 2.2g); PROTEIN 21.2g; CARB 10.5g; FIBER 2.3g; CHOL 64mg; IRON 0.9mg; SODIUM 385mg; CALC 42mg

Poached Egg and Arugula Salad Bruschetta

$1.32/serving
$5.28 total

Hands-on: 16 min. Total: 16 min. *Top toasts with bacon-y arugula salad, or break the egg and let the golden yolk run over all.*

3 tablespoons finely chopped shallots
2¹/₂ tablespoons extra-virgin olive oil
3 tablespoons white wine vinegar, divided
2 teaspoons Dijon mustard
¹/₄ teaspoon salt
¹/₈ teaspoon freshly ground black pepper
4 ounces French bread baguette, cut into 8 slices
Cooking spray
4 large eggs
1 (5-ounce) package arugula
4 center-cut bacon slices, cooked and crumbled

1. Combine shallots, oil, 1 tablespoon vinegar, mustard, salt, and pepper, stirring with a whisk. Heat a grill pan over medium-high heat. Lightly coat both sides of each bread slice with cooking spray. Add bread to grill pan; cook 3 minutes on each side or until toasted.
2. Add water to a large skillet, filling two-thirds full; bring to a boil. Reduce heat to medium; add 2 tablespoons vinegar to pan. Break eggs into custard cups. When water cools to a simmer, gently pour eggs into pan; cook 3 minutes or until desired degree of doneness. Carefully remove eggs from pan using a slotted spoon.
3. Place 2 toast slices on each of 4 plates. Add arugula to oil mixture; toss. Arrange about 1 cup arugula mixture on each serving; sprinkle evenly with bacon. Top each serving with 1 egg. Serve immediately. Serves 4

CALORIES 270; FAT 15.3g (sat 3.3g, mono 8.2g, poly 2g); PROTEIN 12.4g; CARB 19.1g; FIBER 1.5g; CHOL 183mg; IRON 2.6mg; SODIUM 559mg; CALC 98mg

KID IN THE KITCHEN

MATISSE TACKLES AN ASIAN RICE BOWL

"I love shrimp, so I was excited to make this dish. The recipe was very easy, and I cooked it for my best friend, Sam, who had never eaten shrimp before. If you don't have precooked rice, you can prepare the rice from scratch (like I did) while you're making the rest of the dish. I loved the egg—it added creaminess and complemented the sweetness of the oyster sauce. I could take or leave the shiitake mushrooms, though, so maybe next time I will just use button mushrooms. I loved how the oyster and soy sauces brought this dish together at the end of cooking, and the shrimp were juicy and yummy!"

Kid Friendly • Quick & Easy

Shrimp and Shiitake Rice Bowl

Hands-on: 16 min. Total: 18 min. *If you can't find shiitakes, use button mushrooms.*

1 (8.8-ounce) pouch precooked brown rice (such as Uncle Ben's)
1 tablespoon canola oil, divided
1 large egg, beaten
24 large shrimp, peeled and deveined
1 cup sliced fresh shiitake mushrooms (about 12 medium)
¹/₂ cup chopped white onion
1 tablespoon minced peeled fresh ginger
2 garlic cloves, thinly sliced
4 ounces snow peas, trimmed
¹/₂ large red bell pepper, cut into ¹/₂-inch strips
2 tablespoons lower-sodium soy sauce
2 tablespoons oyster sauce
1 green onion, thinly sliced

1. Heat brown rice according to package directions. Set aside.
2. Heat a large nonstick skillet over medium-high heat. Add 1 teaspoon oil to pan; swirl to coat. Add egg; cook 1 minute or until done, stirring constantly to scramble. Remove egg from pan. Add 1 teaspoon canola oil to pan; swirl to coat. Add shrimp, and cook 2 minutes or until done. Remove shrimp from pan.
3. Add 1 teaspoon oil to pan, and swirl to coat. Add mushrooms and next 3 ingredients; cook 2 minutes, stirring frequently. Stir in peas and bell pepper; cook 1 minute, stirring occasionally. Add egg, shrimp, and rice to pan, and cook 2 minutes or until thoroughly heated. Remove from heat; stir in soy sauce and oyster sauce. Top with sliced green onions. Serves 4 (serving size: 1¼ cups)

CALORIES 206; FAT 6g (sat 0.8g, mono 3g, poly 1.7g); PROTEIN 14.2g; CARB 23g; FIBER 2.9g; CHOL 109mg; IRON 2.5mg; SODIUM 528mg; CALC 63mg

"BEFORE YOU BEAT THE EGG, PRICK THE YOLK. THIS WILL MAKE BEATING IT A LOT EASIER."

THE VERDICT

SAM (AGE 11):
He loved the peppers and how the flavors came together. I was happy he liked it! **10/10**

MATISSE (AGE 12):
This dish smelled delicious, so I was looking forward to the flavors before I even tasted it. **10/10**

FROZEN VEGGIES

In most of the country, longing for spring happens well before spring actually comes along: Light, fresh, fast-cooking veggies are few and far between. But you can get a jump on the season with reliable freezer staples—artichokes and English peas—and turn out a delicious, spring-inspired dish.

Quick & Easy • Vegetarian

Artichoke and Pea Sauté

Hands-on: 12 min. Total: 12 min.

2 teaspoons canola oil
3 cups frozen, quartered artichoke
  hearts, thawed (about 12 ounces)
1¹/₂ tablespoons butter
¹/₄ cup chopped shallots
1 cup frozen peas, thawed
¹/₄ teaspoon kosher salt
¹/₈ teaspoon black pepper
2 tablespoons flat-leaf parsley leaves
1 tablespoon torn fresh mint
6 lemon wedges

1. Heat a large skillet over medium-high heat. Add oil to pan; swirl to coat. Add artichokes; sauté 4 minutes, stirring occasionally. Remove artichokes from pan. Melt butter in pan. Add shallots; sauté 3 minutes or until shallots are tender and butter just begins to brown, stirring occasionally. Stir in artichokes, peas, salt, and pepper; sauté 30 seconds or until thoroughly heated. Remove from heat, and sprinkle with herbs. Serve with lemon wedges. Serves 6 (serving size: about ¹/₂ cup vegetable mixture and 1 lemon wedge)

CALORIES 90; FAT 5.2g (sat 2g, mono 1.7g, poly 0.6g);
PROTEIN 2.8g; CARB 9.4g; FIBER 4.7g; CHOL 8mg;
IRON 0.8mg; SODIUM 168mg; CALC 38mg

SUPERFAST 20-MINUTE COOKING

Flavor-packed solutions for your busy weeknights: Asian-inspired fish, creamy butternut soup, kid-pleasing cheesy pasta, and much more. All ready in 20 minutes.

Quicky & Easy • Make Ahead

Thai Butternut Soup

If you can't find frozen pureed squash, you can cook this soup with 4 cups cubed butternut squash. Just add 5 extra minutes to the cooking time in step 2.

1 teaspoon canola oil
1 cup chopped onion
2¹/₂ teaspoons red curry paste
1¹/₂ teaspoons minced fresh garlic
1 teaspoon minced peeled fresh ginger
1 cup fat-free, lower-sodium chicken
  broth
2 teaspoons brown sugar
2 (12-ounce) packages frozen pureed
  butternut squash
1 (14-ounce) can light coconut milk
1¹/₂ teaspoons fish sauce
¹/₄ teaspoon salt
¹/₂ cup chopped unsalted, dry-roasted
  peanuts
¹/₄ cup cilantro leaves
1 lime, cut into 8 wedges

1. Heat a medium saucepan over medium-high heat. Add oil; swirl to coat. Add onion; sauté 3 minutes. Add curry paste, garlic, and ginger; sauté 45 seconds, stirring constantly.
2. Add broth and next 5 ingredients; cover. Bring to a boil. Reduce heat, and simmer 5 minutes, stirring frequently. Place half of squash mixture in a blender. Remove center piece of blender lid (to allow steam to escape); secure blender lid on blender. Place a clean towel over opening in blender lid (to avoid splatters). Blend until smooth. Pour mixture into a large bowl. Repeat

procedure with remaining squash mixture. Spoon about 1 cup soup into each of 4 bowls; top with 2 tablespoons peanuts and 1 tablespoon cilantro. Serve with lime wedges. Serves 4

CALORIES 302; FAT 15.2g (sat 5.7g, mono 5.3g, poly 3.3g);
PROTEIN 9.5g; CARB 40.7g; FIBER 4.9g; CHOL 0mg;
IRON 2.7mg; SODIUM 591mg; CALC 81mg

Quick & Easy

Hoisin Flounder

1 (3¹/₂-ounce) bag boil-in-bag
  brown rice
2 tablespoons hoisin sauce
1 tablespoon water
2 teaspoons lower-sodium soy sauce
1¹/₂ teaspoons minced peeled fresh
  ginger
1¹/₂ teaspoons dark sesame oil
¹/₂ teaspoon black pepper
3 tablespoons canola oil, divided
4 (6-ounce) flounder fillets
¹/₄ teaspoon kosher salt
1 cup diagonally sliced snow peas
2 green onions, thinly sliced
1 cup sliced shiitake mushroom caps

1. Prepare rice according to package.
2. Combine hoisin and next 5 ingredients in a bowl. Reserve 4 teaspoons.
3. Heat a nonstick skillet over medium-high heat. Add 1 tablespoon canola oil. Sprinkle fillets with salt. Add 2 fillets to pan; cook 4 minutes. Turn; brush each with 1 teaspoon hoisin mixture. Cook 2 minutes. Remove fish from pan. Repeat with 1 tablespoon canola oil, 2 fillets, and 2 teaspoons hoisin mixture.
4. Heat a skillet over high heat. Add 1 tablespoon canola oil. Add peas and onions; sauté 1 minute. Add mushrooms; sauté 2 minutes. Place ¹/₂ cup rice onto each of 4 plates. Top each with 1 fillet and ¹/₂ cup vegetables; drizzle with 1 teaspoon hoisin mixture. Serves 4

CALORIES 360; FAT 17.9g (sat 2g, mono 8.3g, poly 4.4g);
PROTEIN 24.7g; CARB 25g; FIBER 2g; CHOL 77mg;
IRON 1.2mg; SODIUM 462mg; CALC 52mg

Shrimp Linguine with Ricotta, Fennel, and Spinach

Fresh packaged noodles and quick-cooking shrimp make this a snap.

9 ounces fresh linguine
1 tablespoon olive oil
8 ounces medium shrimp, peeled and deveined
1 cup vertically sliced fennel bulb
½ cup thinly sliced shallots
2 garlic cloves, thinly sliced
1 (6-ounce) package fresh baby spinach
1 tablespoon grated lemon rind
2 tablespoons fresh lemon juice
½ teaspoon freshly ground black pepper
¼ teaspoon salt
2 ounces grated fresh Parmesan cheese (about ½ cup)
¼ cup part-skim ricotta cheese

1. Cook pasta according to package directions, omitting salt and fat. Drain in a colander over a bowl, reserving ½ cup cooking liquid.
2. Heat a large skillet over medium-high heat. Add oil; swirl to coat. Add shrimp, fennel, and shallots; sauté 3 minutes. Add garlic; sauté 30 seconds. Add spinach; cook 2 minutes or until spinach wilts.
3. Stir in rind and next 3 ingredients. Stir in reserved cooking liquid; cook 1 minute or until slightly thickened. Add pasta and Parmesan cheese; toss to coat. Top each serving with 1 tablespoon ricotta. Serves 4 (serving size: 1 cup)

CALORIES 377; FAT 10.6g (sat 4.1g, mono 4.6g, poly 0.9g); PROTEIN 23.9g; CARB 43.6g; FIBER 4.8g; CHOL 122mg; IRON 2mg; SODIUM 650mg; CALC 296mg

Beets with Shallot Vinaigrette

You can use red or golden beets.

1½ pounds halved peeled beets
2 tablespoons sliced shallots
1½ tablespoons red wine vinegar
1 tablespoon extra-virgin olive oil
½ teaspoon Dijon mustard
¼ teaspoon freshly ground black pepper
⅛ teaspoon salt

1. Wrap beets in parchment paper. Microwave at HIGH until tender (about 7 minutes). Let stand 5 minutes. Cut into 1-inch pieces.
2. Combine shallots and remaining ingredients in a medium bowl; stir well with a whisk. Add beets; toss gently to coat. Serves 4 (serving size: about ⅔ cup)

CALORIES 110; FAT 3.7g (sat 0.5g, mono 2.5g, poly 0.5g); PROTEIN 2.9g; CARB 17.6g; FIBER 5g; CHOL 0mg; IRON 1.5mg; SODIUM 253mg; CALC 30mg

Variation 1: Blood Orange Salad

Prepare base recipe through step 1. Section 1 blood orange over a bowl; squeeze to juice. Place sections in a bowl. Add 2 tablespoons toasted walnut oil, 2 tablespoons minced shallots, ½ teaspoon Dijon mustard, ¼ teaspoon pepper, and ⅛ teaspoon salt to juice; stir. Add beets, 2 cups greens, and orange sections; toss. Top with ⅓ cup chopped unsalted, dry-roasted pistachios and 2 tablespoons goat cheese. Serves 4 (serving size: about ¾ cup)

CALORIES 229; FAT 12.3g (sat 1.7g); SODIUM 247mg

Variation 2: Couscous, Mint, and Almond

Prepare base recipe through step 1 with 1 pound beets. Bring ⅓ cup plus 2 tablespoons water to a boil. Add ⅓ cup couscous; cover. Remove from heat; let stand 5 minutes. Combine 2 tablespoons minced shallots, 2 tablespoons olive oil, 2 teaspoons fresh lemon juice, ½ teaspoon Dijon, ¼ teaspoon salt, and ¼ teaspoon pepper. Add beets and couscous. Top with ¼ cup sliced almonds and 3 tablespoons fresh mint leaves. Serves 4 (serving size: about ⅔ cup)

CALORIES 201; FAT 9.9g (sat 1.2g); SODIUM 254mg

Variation 3: Toasted Spices

Prepare base recipe through step 1. Heat a saucepan over medium-high heat. Add 2 tablespoons olive oil, 2 tablespoons minced shallots, 1 teaspoon brown mustard seeds, 1 teaspoon minced peeled fresh ginger, ½ teaspoon cumin seeds, and 1 diced carrot; cook 2 minutes. Add 1 tablespoon rice vinegar, ¼ teaspoon black pepper, ⅛ teaspoon salt, and ⅛ teaspoon ground red pepper. Add beets. Sprinkle with 3 tablespoons fresh cilantro leaves. Serves 4 (serving size: about ⅔ cup)

CALORIES 147; FAT 7.3g (sat 1g); SODIUM 218mg

Open-Faced Eggplant Sandwiches

Here's the key to a speedy dinner: While the eggplant broils, toast your bread slices in a toaster oven.

1/2 cup lower-sodium marinara sauce
1/3 cup all-purpose flour
2 large eggs, lightly beaten
1 cup panko (Japanese breadcrumbs)
1 medium eggplant, cut crosswise into 8 (1/2-inch-thick) slices
1/4 teaspoon kosher salt
Cooking spray
4 (1-ounce) slices country wheat bread, toasted
12 large basil leaves
4 ounces fresh mozzarella cheese, shredded

1. Preheat broiler to high.
2. Place marinara in a microwave-safe measuring cup. Microwave at HIGH 2 minutes or until hot; keep warm.
3. Place flour in a shallow dish. Place eggs in another dish. Place panko in another. Sprinkle eggplant evenly with salt. Dredge both sides of eggplant slices in flour; dip in egg, and dredge in panko. Place breaded eggplant slices on a baking sheet coated with cooking spray. Broil eggplant 3 minutes on each side or until lightly browned. Transfer eggplant slices to a plate. Place bread slices on baking sheet; top each slice with 1 basil leaf. Place 1 eggplant slice over each leaf; top eggplant with 1 basil leaf and 1/2 ounce cheese. Top cheese with remaining slices of eggplant; finish with 1/2 ounce of cheese over each eggplant slice. Broil eggplant stacks 3 minutes or until cheese is lightly browned and bubbly. Spoon 2 table-spoons marinara over each serving.

Top with remaining basil leaves. Serves 4 (serving size: 1 sandwich)

CALORIES 326; **FAT** 11.6g (sat 5.5g, mono 2.8g, poly 0.8g); **PROTEIN** 14.3g; **CARB** 40.9g; **FIBER** 5.5g; **CHOL** 118mg; **IRON** 3.4mg; **SODIUM** 415mg; **CALC** 231mg

Homemade Pita Chips with Red Pepper Dip

2 (6-inch) whole-wheat pitas
Cooking spray
1/4 teaspoon salt, divided
1/4 teaspoon paprika
1 cup bottled roasted red bell pepper
1/4 cup Marcona almonds or dry-roasted almonds (about 1 1/4 ounces)
1 tablespoon extra-virgin olive oil
1 1/2 teaspoons red wine vinegar
1 teaspoon minced fresh garlic
1/2 teaspoon ground cumin
1/8 teaspoon ground red pepper
1/8 teaspoon freshly ground black pepper

1. Preheat oven to 400°.
2. Cut each pita into 16 wedges. Carefully peel apart each wedge to make 2 thinner wedges. Arrange wedges in a single layer on a bak-ing sheet coated with cooking spray. Lightly coat wedges with cooking spray; sprinkle with 1/8 teaspoon salt and paprika. Bake at 400° for 6 min-utes or until lightly browned and crisp.
3. While chips bake, place bell pep-per and remaining ingredients in a blender; add 1/8 teaspoon salt. Blend until smooth. Serve with chips. Serves 8 (serving size: 8 chips and about 3 tablespoons dip)

CALORIES 82; **FAT** 3.9g (sat 0.4g, mono 2.6g, poly 0.7g); **PROTEIN** 2.5g; **CARB** 9.9g; **FIBER** 1.4g; **CHOL** 0mg; **IRON** 0.7mg; **SODIUM** 187mg; **CALC** 24mg

Cheesy Penne with Broccoli

Any short pasta can be substituted here—rotini and farfalle are good choices.

8 ounces uncooked mini penne pasta
5 cups broccoli florets (about 1 medium head)
1 1/3 cups fat-free milk
2 tablespoons all-purpose flour
3 tablespoons grated fresh Parmesan cheese, divided
2 tablespoons 1/3-less-fat cream cheese
1 teaspoon Dijon mustard
1/2 teaspoon salt
1/4 teaspoon freshly ground black pepper
1/8 teaspoon freshly grated nutmeg
2.5 ounces cheddar cheese, shredded (about 2/3 cup)

1. Cook pasta according to package directions, omitting salt and fat. During the last 3 minutes of cooking, add broccoli to pan; drain. Place pasta and broccoli in a large bowl.
2. Combine milk and flour in a sauce-pan over medium heat, stirring with a whisk until smooth. Cook 5 minutes or until slightly thickened; remove from heat. Add 2 tablespoons Parme-san and remaining ingredients, stirring with a whisk until smooth. Add cheese mixture to pasta mixture; toss. Sprinkle with 1 tablespoon Parmesan. Serves 4 (serving size: 1 1/3 cups)

CALORIES 381; **FAT** 9.8g (sat 5.6g, mono 2.4g, poly 0.5g); **PROTEIN** 20g; **CARB** 54.9g; **FIBER** 4.6g; **CHOL** 29mg; **IRON** 3mg; **SODIUM** 577mg; **CALC** 331mg

(Mama mia!)

OOPS!
YOUR LASAGNA DRIES OUT

All that work, sad ending. How to keep things gooey.

What exactly happens when a baked dish of noodles, sauce, and gooey cheese comes out withered and pasty, with tough, brittle pasta edges? The problem lies in the layering method itself: If the filling doesn't cover the noodles, lasagna dries out. With light lasagnas, which often contain less filling, it gets trickier.

Solution: Take the time to spread the sauce and filling evenly and all the way to the edges, especially on the top and bottom. Putting plenty of sauce (at least ¼ cup) in the pan first will prevent sticking and, if you're using no-boil noodles, help soften the pasta. If you seem to be running low on sauce, stretch it with about ½ cup unsalted chicken stock or wine (red for red sauce, white for béchamel). Spread another ¼ cup sauce on top to keep the lasagna moist when you brown it under the broiler later. Be aware that no-boil noodles absorb more sauce, so if you use them, keep the pan covered with foil during baking to retain moisture. Even with conventional noodles, if the assembled lasagna looks like it might get dry as it bakes, minimize evaporation by covering it with foil for about two-thirds of the baking time.

(Buono!)

40 MEALS UNDER 40 MINUTES

Here's our second annual speedy menu special, bursting with fast main dishes and easy, healthy sides. Go with the suggested menus, or mix and match.

USE THIS MEAL GUIDE

Nutrition
Our menus contain no more than 800 calories (cut dessert if you want fewer), 9g sat fat, and 920mg sodium.

Print Shopping Lists
and recipes, and share them, at CookingLight.com/40meals.

V indicates a **vegetarian** meal

CHICKEN DINNERS

MEAL NO. 1
Chicken Braised in Wine and Rosemary, p. 77
Quick Chive Mashed Potatoes, p. 92
Asparagus with Lemon and Pecorino, p. 91

MEAL NO. 2
Pan-Grilled Chicken with Chorizo Confetti, p. 78
Green Salad with Simple Vinaigrette, p. 90
Goat Cheese Crostini, p. 92

MEAL NO. 3
Chicken with Quick Chile Verde, p. 77
Grapefruit, Walnut, and Feta Salad, p. 90
Herbed Corn Muffins, p. 92

MEAL NO. 4
Chicken with Quick Chile Verde, p. 77
Rosemary-Garlic Roasted Potatoes, p. 92
Snap Pea and Radish Sauté, p. 91

MEAL NO. 5
Manhattan-Glazed Chicken, p. 76
Glazed Baby Carrots, p. 89
Wilted Spinach with Fresh Chile, p. 91

MEAL NO. 6
Chicken Cutlets with Tarragon-Mushroom Sauce, p. 77
Quinoa with Toasted Pine Nuts, p. 92
Snap Pea and Radish Sauté, p. 91

PIZZA NIGHT

MEAL NO. 7
Pizza Arrabbiata, p. 82
Grapefruit, Walnut, and Feta Salad, p. 90

MEAL NO. 8
Pizza Arrabbiata, p. 82
Asparagus with Lemon and Pecorino, p. 91

MEAL NO. 9
Spring Vegetable Pizza with Gremolata, p. 83
Creamy Tomato Soup, p. 90

MEAL NO. 10
Chicken Tikka Pizzas, p. 82
Green Salad with Simple Vinaigrette, p. 90

MEAL NO. 11 (V)
Four-Mushroom Pesto Pizza, p. 82
Celery and Parsley Salad, p. 91

MEAL NO. 12
Philly Cheesesteak Pizza, p. 83
Smoky Haricots Verts and Mushrooms, p. 93

BEEFY MEALS

MEAL NO. 13
Spice-Rubbed New York Strip with Avocado-Lime Salsa, p. 79
Herbed Corn Muffins, p. 92
Quick Chilled Pea Soup, p. 90

MEAL NO. 14
Hamburger Steak with Onion Gravy, p. 80
Quick Chive Mashed Potatoes, p. 92
Smoky Haricots Verts and Mushrooms, p. 93

MEAL NO. 15
Bistro Steak with Red Wine Sauce, p. 78
Rosemary-Garlic Roasted Potatoes, p. 92
Asparagus with Lemon and Pecorino, p. 91

MEAL NO. 16
Bistro Steak with Red Wine Sauce, p. 78
Quinoa with Toasted Pine Nuts, p. 92
Celery and Parsley Salad, p. 91

MEAL NO. 17
Beef and Mushroom Stroganoff, p. 79
Glazed Baby Carrots, p. 89

MEAL NO. 18
Hoisin-Glazed Steak with Sesame Vegetables, p. 79
Soba Noodle Salad, p. 91

SALAD MENUS

MEAL NO. 19
Tuna Salad Niçoise, p. 87
Goat Cheese Crostini, p. 92

MEAL NO. 20 (V)
Vegetable Pasta Salad with Goat Cheese, p. 86
Quick Chilled Pea Soup, p. 90

EASY CHICKEN ENTRÉES

Impressive slow-cooked flavor in a flash, thanks to great ingredients and smart techniques.

Quick & Easy
Manhattan-Glazed Chicken

Hands-on: 10 min. Total: 17 min.

1¹⁄₂ teaspoons extra-virgin olive oil
4 (6-ounce) skinless, boneless chicken
 breast halves
¹⁄₄ teaspoon salt
¹⁄₄ teaspoon freshly ground black
 pepper
¹⁄₄ cup orange marmalade
¹⁄₄ cup cherry spreadable fruit (such as
 Polaner All Fruit)
1 teaspoon lower-sodium soy sauce
1 teaspoon butter
1 tablespoon bourbon

1. Heat a large heavy skillet over medium-high heat. Add oil to pan; swirl to coat. Sprinkle chicken evenly with salt and pepper. Add chicken to pan; cook 5 minutes on each side or until done. Remove chicken from pan; keep warm.
2. Place marmalade, cherry spreadable fruit, and soy sauce in a small saucepan; bring to a boil. Reduce heat, and simmer 3 minutes or until very thick, stirring frequently. Add butter, stirring to combine. Remove from heat; stir in bourbon. Spoon glaze over chicken. Serves 4 (serving size: 1 chicken breast half and about 1 tablespoon glaze)

CALORIES 316; FAT 7.1g (sat 1.8g, mono 2.8g, poly 0.9g); PROTEIN 36.3g; CARB 23.4g; FIBER 0.2g; CHOL 111mg; IRON 0.7mg; SODIUM 412mg; CALC 17mg

partially covered, 15 minutes or until chicken is done, turning once. Remove bay leaf. Sprinkle with chopped parsley. Serves 4 (serving size: 1 drumstick, 1 thigh, and ¼ cup sauce)

CALORIES 378; **FAT** 14.6g (sat 2.9g, mono 7.6g, poly 2.5g); **PROTEIN** 38.6g; **CARB** 16.5g; **FIBER** 2.1g; **CHOL** 169mg; **IRON** 3.5mg; **SODIUM** 513mg; **CALC** 74mg

---

Quick & Easy
Chicken with Quick Chile Verde

Hands-on: 29 min. Total: 29 min.
If you can't find fresh tomatillos, substitute canned whole tomatillos and use less salt. Grilled lime wedges are a zesty garnish.

4 (6-ounce) skinless, boneless chicken breast halves
¹/₂ teaspoon salt, divided
¹/₂ teaspoon black pepper, divided
1 tablespoon olive oil
¹/₂ cup chopped onion
1 teaspoon sugar
¹/₄ teaspoon ground cumin
¹/₄ teaspoon crushed red pepper
8 ounces tomatillos, coarsely chopped (about 3)
1 large jalapeño pepper, seeded and chopped
1 tablespoon fresh lime juice
¹/₄ cup chopped fresh cilantro

1. Heat a grill pan over medium-high heat. Sprinkle chicken evenly with ¼ teaspoon salt and ¼ teaspoon black pepper. Add chicken to pan; cook 6 minutes on each side or until done.
2. While chicken cooks, heat a small saucepan over medium heat. Add oil to pan; swirl to coat. Add ¼ teaspoon salt, ¼ teaspoon black pepper, onion, and next 5 ingredients; cook 8 minutes or until vegetables are tender, stirring occasionally.
3. Place tomatillo mixture in a blender; add lime juice. Remove center piece of blender lid (to allow steam to escape); secure blender lid on blender. Place a clean towel over opening in blender lid (to avoid splatters). Pulse 10 times or until a chunky salsa forms. Spoon tomatillo mixture over chicken; sprinkle with cilantro. Serves 4 (serving size: 1 breast half and ⅓ cup chile verde)

CALORIES 258; **FAT** 8.4g (sat 1.5g, mono 3.9g, poly 1.3g); **PROTEIN** 37g; **CARB** 7.1g; **FIBER** 1.7g; **CHOL** 109mg; **IRON** 1.1mg; **SODIUM** 494mg; **CALC** 20mg

---

Make Ahead • Quick & Easy
Chicken Braised in Wine and Rosemary

Hands-on: 37 min. Total: 37 min. *This quick braised dish tastes like it has been cooking for hours. We make ¹/₂-inch-deep cuts in the chicken to expedite the cook time.*

4 bone-in chicken drumsticks (about 1 pound), skinned
4 bone-in chicken thighs (about 1¹/₄ pounds), skinned
¹/₂ teaspoon salt, divided
¹/₂ teaspoon freshly ground black pepper, divided
2 tablespoons olive oil
¹/₄ cup all-purpose flour
¹/₂ cup chopped shallots
1 tablespoon chopped garlic
1 teaspoon chopped fresh rosemary
1 cup Chianti or other rich red wine
1 cup unsalted chicken stock (such as Swanson)
1 teaspoon sugar
1 (14.5-ounce) can unsalted whole tomatoes, crushed and undrained
1 bay leaf
2 tablespoons chopped fresh flat-leaf parsley

1. Make 1 (½-inch-deep) cut in each chicken piece; sprinkle evenly with ¼ teaspoon salt and ¼ teaspoon pepper. Heat a large Dutch oven over high heat. Add oil to pan; swirl to coat. Place flour in a shallow dish. Dredge chicken in flour. Add chicken to pan; cook 5 minutes on each side. Remove chicken from pan.
2. Add shallots, garlic, and rosemary to pan; cook 2 minutes or until tender, stirring frequently. Add wine to pan; bring to a boil. Cook 1 minute, scraping pan to loosen browned bits. Add ¼ teaspoon salt, ¼ teaspoon pepper, chicken stock, sugar, tomatoes, and bay leaf. Bring to a boil; return chicken to pan. Reduce heat to medium; cook,

---

Quick & Easy
Chicken Cutlets with Tarragon-Mushroom Sauce

Hands-on: 35 min. Total: 35 min.

2 cups unsalted chicken stock
¹/₂ carrot, cut into 1-inch pieces
¹/₂ celery stalk, cut into 1-inch pieces
¹/₄ onion, halved
1 bay leaf
1 garlic clove, crushed
4 (6-ounce) skinless, boneless chicken breast halves
¹/₂ teaspoon kosher salt, divided
¹/₂ teaspoon black pepper, divided
3 tablespoons all-purpose flour
2 tablespoons olive oil, divided
2 teaspoons butter, divided
1 cup quartered mushrooms
¹/₂ cup frozen pearl onions
1 tablespoon water
2¹/₂ teaspoons cornstarch
1 tablespoon chopped fresh tarragon

1. Place first 6 ingredients in a saucepan; bring to a boil. Cook 6 minutes or until reduced to 1¼ cups. Remove solids with a slotted spoon; discard.
2. Cut chicken breast halves in half horizontally to form 8 cutlets. Sprinkle evenly with ¼ teaspoon salt and ¼ teaspoon pepper. Place flour in a shallow dish; dredge chicken in flour. Heat a large skillet over medium-high heat. Add 1 tablespoon oil and 1 teaspoon butter to pan; swirl until butter melts. Add 4 cutlets to pan; cook 2 minutes
continued

on each side or until golden. Remove from pan; keep warm. Repeat procedure with remaining 1 tablespoon oil, 1 teaspoon butter, and 4 cutlets.
3. Return skillet to medium-high heat. Add mushrooms and onions; cook 5 minutes or until browned, stirring occasionally. Add stock mixture; bring to a boil, scraping pan to loosen browned bits. Combine 1 tablespoon water and cornstarch in a small bowl. Stir cornstarch mixture into stock mixture; cook 1 minute or until sauce thickens. Stir in ¼ teaspoon salt, ¼ teaspoon pepper, and tarragon. Spoon sauce over chicken. Serves 4 (serving size: 2 cutlets and about ½ cup sauce)

CALORIES 322; **FAT** 13.2g (sat 3.1g, mono 6.7g, poly 1.5g); **PROTEIN** 39.9g; **CARB** 8.5g; **FIBER** 0.6g; **CHOL** 114mg; **IRON** 1.2mg; **SODIUM** 523mg; **CALC** 24mg

THESE MEALS ARE DESIGNED TO MAKE YOU LOOK EVEN MORE IMPRESSIVE THAN YOU ALREADY DO: NOT ONLY A MASTER OF THE COMPLICATED ART OF COOKING, BUT ONE WHO IS ABLE TO GET A GREAT MEAL ON THE TABLE FAST.

Quick & Easy

Pan-Grilled Chicken with Chorizo Confetti

Hands-on: 29 min. Total: 29 min.

4 (6-ounce) skinless, boneless chicken breast halves
½ teaspoon kosher salt, divided
¼ teaspoon freshly ground black pepper
Cooking spray
¼ cup Mexican pork chorizo, casings removed
¼ cup sliced onion
2 tablespoons diced carrot
¼ cup diced yellow bell pepper
¼ cup diced red bell pepper
2 tablespoons diced green bell pepper
¼ cup unsalted chicken stock
1 tablespoon chopped fresh cilantro

1. Heat a grill pan over medium-high heat. Sprinkle chicken with ¼ teaspoon salt and pepper. Coat pan with cooking spray. Add chicken to pan; cook 6 minutes on each side or until done.
2. While chicken cooks, heat a large skillet over medium-high heat. Add chorizo; cook 1 minute, stirring to crumble. Add ¼ teaspoon salt, onion, and carrot; cook 2 minutes, stirring occasionally. Add bell peppers; cook 1 minute or until crisp-tender. Add stock; cook 2 minutes or until liquid almost evaporates, scraping pan to loosen browned bits. Spoon chorizo mixture over chicken; top with cilantro. Serves 4 (serving size: 1 breast half and 3 tablespoons confetti)

CALORIES 254; **FAT** 8.2g (sat 2.2g, mono 2.9g, poly 1g); **PROTEIN** 39.2g; **CARB** 3.6g; **FIBER** 1.2g; **CHOL** 133mg; **IRON** 0.8mg; **SODIUM** 586mg; **CALC** 24mg

BEEFY MEALS

We went back to beef basics: big flavor, simple recipes, hunger-beating deliciousness.

Quick & Easy

Bistro Steak with Red Wine Sauce

Hands-on: 26 min. Total: 26 min.

1 tablespoon canola oil
2 (8-ounce) top sirloin steaks, trimmed
⅜ teaspoon salt, divided
⅜ teaspoon black pepper, divided
3 tablespoons minced shallots
2 teaspoons chopped fresh thyme
½ cup full-bodied red wine (such as cabernet sauvignon)
½ cup unsalted beef stock
1½ teaspoons butter
½ teaspoon Dijon mustard
1 tablespoon chopped fresh flat-leaf parsley

1. Heat a large skillet over high heat. Add oil; swirl to coat. Sprinkle steaks evenly with ¼ teaspoon salt and ¼ teaspoon pepper. Add steaks to pan; cook 4 minutes on each side or until desired degree of doneness. Remove steaks from pan. Let stand 5 minutes.
2. Reduce heat to medium-high. Add shallots and thyme to pan; sauté 1 minute or until lightly browned. Add wine; cook 2½ minutes or until liquid almost evaporates. Add stock; cook 3 minutes or until liquid is reduced by half and mixture is slightly thickened. Remove pan from heat. Add ⅛ teaspoon salt, ⅛ teaspoon pepper, butter, and mustard; stir with a whisk.
3. Cut steak across the grain into thin slices; serve with sauce. Sprinkle with chopped parsley. Serves 4 (serving size: 3 ounces steak and 2 tablespoons sauce)

CALORIES 215; **FAT** 9.6g (sat 2.9g, mono 4.5g, poly 1.3g); **PROTEIN** 25.6g; **CARB** 2.3g; **FIBER** 0.4g; **CHOL** 72mg; **IRON** 2.1mg; **SODIUM** 332mg; **CALC** 37mg

Beef and Mushroom Stroganoff

Kid Friendly • Quick & Easy

Hands-on: 29 min. Total: 29 min.

5 ounces uncooked wide egg noodles
1 tablespoon canola oil
1 pound beef tenderloin, trimmed and
   cut into 1-inch pieces
³/₄ teaspoon salt, divided
¹/₂ teaspoon freshly ground black
   pepper, divided
1 cup thinly sliced leek
1 tablespoon chopped fresh thyme
2 teaspoons minced garlic
1 (6-ounce) package presliced shiitake
   mushrooms
1 tablespoon all-purpose flour
¹/₂ teaspoon hot paprika
1 cup unsalted beef stock
¹/₂ cup light sour cream
2 tablespoons chopped fresh parsley

1. Cook noodles according to package
directions; drain.
2. Heat a large skillet over high heat.
Add oil; swirl to coat. Add beef;
sprinkle with ¼ teaspoon salt and ¼
teaspoon pepper. Cook 4 minutes or
until browned, turning to brown on all
sides. Remove beef from pan.
3. Reduce heat to medium-high.
Add leek, thyme, garlic, and mushrooms; sauté 5 minutes or until lightly
browned, stirring occasionally. Sprinkle
mushroom mixture with flour and
paprika; cook 30 seconds, stirring
constantly. Add stock; bring to a boil.
Reduce heat, and simmer 2 minutes or
until sauce is thickened, stirring frequently. Stir in beef, ½ teaspoon salt,
¼ teaspoon pepper, and sour cream.
Serve over noodles; sprinkle with
parsley. Serves 4 (serving size: ½ cup
noodles and ¾ cup beef mixture)

CALORIES 423; **FAT** 15.6g (sat 5.7g, mono 5.2g, poly 1.4g);
PROTEIN 34.7g; **CARB** 34.8g; **FIBER** 2.4g; **CHOL** 115mg;
IRON 4mg; **SODIUM** 583mg; **CALC** 63mg

Spice-Rubbed New York Strip with Avocado-Lime Salsa

Quick & Easy

Hands-on: 26 min. Total: 26 min.

¹/₄ cup finely chopped red onion
2 tablespoons chopped fresh cilantro
1¹/₂ tablespoons fresh lime juice
1 tablespoon extra-virgin olive oil
2 teaspoons finely chopped seeded
   serrano chile
1 avocado, peeled and diced
¹/₂ teaspoon salt, divided
1 teaspoon ground cumin
1 teaspoon paprika
¹/₂ teaspoon garlic powder
¹/₂ teaspoon chipotle chile powder
¹/₄ teaspoon ground cinnamon
2 (8-ounce) New York strip steaks,
   trimmed
Cooking spray

1. Preheat grill to high heat.
2. Place first 6 ingredients in a bowl;
gently stir in ¼ teaspoon salt. Set aside.
3. Combine ¼ teaspoon salt, cumin,
and next 4 ingredients in a bowl; rub
spice mixture over both sides of steaks.
Place steaks on grill rack coated with
cooking spray; grill 3 minutes on each
side or until desired degree of doneness. Let stand 5 minutes; cut across
the grain into thin slices. Serve with
salsa. Serves 4 (serving size: 3 ounces
steak and ¼ cup salsa)

CALORIES 284; **FAT** 17.4g (sat 4.1g, mono 10.1g, poly 1.6g);
PROTEIN 25.8g; **CARB** 6.7g; **FIBER** 4.1g; **CHOL** 68mg;
IRON 2.2mg; **SODIUM** 361mg; **CALC** 34mg

Hoisin-Glazed Steak with Sesame Vegetables

Quick & Easy

Hands-on: 36 min. Total: 36 min.
*A splash of fish sauce adds a rich, savory flavor
to the glaze, but it's OK to omit it if you don't
have it on hand.*

1 teaspoon rice vinegar
1 teaspoon dark sesame oil
1 teaspoon lower-sodium soy sauce
1 cup English cucumber, halved
   lengthwise and diagonally sliced
1 cup sliced radishes, halved
¹/₄ cup torn cilantro leaves
¹/₈ teaspoon salt
3 tablespoons hoisin sauce
1 teaspoon minced garlic
1 teaspoon grated peeled fresh ginger
1 teaspoon fish sauce
¹/₄ teaspoon crushed red pepper
1 (1-pound) flank steak, trimmed
Cooking spray

1. Preheat grill to high heat.
2. Combine vinegar, sesame oil, and
soy sauce in a medium bowl; add
cucumber and radishes. Sprinkle with
cilantro and salt; toss gently to coat.
3. Combine hoisin and next 4 ingredients in a small bowl. Brush half of
hoisin mixture over steak. Place steak
on grill rack coated with cooking spray;
grill 5 minutes. Turn steak over, and
brush with remaining hoisin mixture;
grill 5 minutes or until desired degree
of doneness. Let stand 5 minutes. Cut
steak across the grain into thin slices;
serve with vegetables. Serves 4 (serving
size: 3 ounces steak and ⅓ cup vegetables)

CALORIES 220; **FAT** 10.2g (sat 3.4g, mono 4.8g, poly 0.9g);
PROTEIN 23.3g; **CARB** 7.3g; **FIBER** 0.6g; **CHOL** 65mg;
IRON 1.7mg; **SODIUM** 466mg; **CALC** 26mg

Hamburger Steak with Onion Gravy

Hands-on: 20 min. Total: 20 min.

1 pound ground sirloin
½ teaspoon salt, divided
½ teaspoon freshly ground black pepper, divided
1 tablespoon canola oil, divided
1½ cups vertically sliced onion
2 teaspoons all-purpose flour
1 cup unsalted beef stock
2 tablespoons thinly sliced green onions (optional)

1. Divide beef into 4 equal portions, shaping each into a ½-inch-thick patty. Sprinkle patties evenly with ¼ teaspoon salt and ¼ teaspoon pepper. Heat 2 teaspoons oil in a large skillet over medium-high heat; swirl to coat. Add patties; cook 3 minutes on each side or until browned; remove from pan.
2. Add 1 teaspoon oil to pan; swirl to coat. Add vertically sliced onion; sauté 3 minutes or until lightly browned and tender. Sprinkle onion with flour; cook 30 seconds, stirring constantly. Add stock, ¼ teaspoon salt, and ¼ teaspoon pepper; bring to a boil. Return patties to pan; reduce heat to medium, partially cover, and cook 5 minutes or until gravy is slightly thickened. Sprinkle with green onions, if desired. Serves 4 (serving size: 1 steak and about ¼ cup gravy)

CALORIES 259; FAT 14.9g (sat 4.9g, mono 7.2g, poly 1.4g); PROTEIN 23.8g; CARB 6g; FIBER 1g; CHOL 74mg; IRON 2.8mg; SODIUM 408mg; CALC 28mg

FAST FISH AND SEAFOOD

Salmon, trout, mussels, and more—quick dinners get fancy but stay easy when fish is on the menu.

Quick & Easy

Rainbow Trout with Seared Sugar Snaps

Hands-on: 11 min. Total: 11 min.
U.S.-farmed rainbow trout (pretty much all you'll find at the market) is a sustainable choice.

4 dressed whole rainbow trout
Cooking spray
2½ teaspoons olive oil, divided
2 teaspoons fresh lime juice
½ teaspoon ground cumin
½ teaspoon kosher salt, divided
¼ teaspoon freshly ground black pepper
2 cups sugar snap peas, trimmed and halved diagonally
½ cup vertically sliced shallots
¼ cup pine nuts
2 teaspoons chopped fresh dill

1. Preheat broiler to high.
2. Arrange trout, open with flesh sides up, on a baking sheet coated with cooking spray. Brush flesh evenly with 1½ teaspoons oil. Drizzle juice over flesh. Sprinkle flesh with cumin, ¼ teaspoon salt, and pepper. Broil 5 minutes or until fish flakes easily when tested with a fork.
3. While fish cooks, heat a medium skillet over high heat until very hot. Combine peas, shallots, and pine nuts in a small bowl; add 1 teaspoon oil to bowl, tossing to coat. Add pea mixture to pan; cook 3 minutes or until peas are bright green and blackened in spots and nuts are lightly toasted,

stirring frequently. Stir in remaining ¼ teaspoon salt and dill. Serve over trout. Serves 4 (serving size: 1 trout and ½ cup pea mixture)

CALORIES 321; FAT 16.3g (sat 2.9g, mono 5.9g, poly 5.6g); PROTEIN 33.1g; CARB 10.9g; FIBER 2.4g; CHOL 90mg; IRON 1.7mg; SODIUM 317mg; CALC 151mg

Quick & Easy

Mussels in Smoky Poblano-Cilantro Broth

Hands-on: 20 min. Total: 30 min. All mussels are sustainable stars. They're surprisingly affordable, too.

1 poblano chile
1 cup dry white wine
¼ cup chopped shallots
¼ cup chopped fresh cilantro, divided
¼ teaspoon kosher salt
¼ teaspoon freshly ground black pepper
¼ teaspoon hot smoked paprika
3 garlic cloves, sliced
1 (8-ounce) bottle clam juice
48 mussels (about 2 pounds), scrubbed and debearded
1 tablespoon fresh lime juice
1 tablespoon unsalted butter

1. Preheat broiler to high.
2. Place chile on a foil-lined baking sheet; broil 3 inches from heat 8 minutes or until blackened and charred, turning after 6 minutes. Place in a paper bag; fold to close tightly. Let stand 10 minutes. Peel; discard skins. Chop.
3. Combine chopped chile, wine, shallots, 3 tablespoons cilantro, salt, and next 4 ingredients in a Dutch oven; bring to a boil. Cover, reduce heat, and simmer 8 minutes. Add mussels; cover and cook 3 minutes or until shells open. Remove mussels from pan with a slotted spoon. Discard unopened shells. Keep warm.

4. Bring wine mixture to a boil over high heat; cook until mixture is reduced to 1 cup. Stir in lime juice and butter. Pour liquid over mussels; toss gently. Sprinkle with 1 tablespoon cilantro. Serve immediately. Serves 4 (serving size: about 12 mussels and ¼ cup liquid)

CALORIES 170; FAT 5.6g (sat 2.3g, mono 1.4g, poly 0.9g); PROTEIN 15.2g; CARB 9.1g; FIBER 0.6g; CHOL 43mg; IRON 5.2mg; SODIUM 589mg; CALC 51mg

Kid Friendly • Quick & Easy

Panko-Crusted Cod with Tomato-Basil Relish

Hands-on: 10 min. Total: 20 min. Look for U.S.-caught Alaska cod, gray cod, or true cod.

2 large egg whites, lightly beaten
½ cup panko (Japanese breadcrumbs)
4 (6-ounce) cod fillets
½ teaspoon kosher salt, divided
2 tablespoons canola oil
1 cup grape tomatoes, quartered
½ cup vertically sliced Vidalia or other sweet onion
2 tablespoons basil leaves
2 tablespoons fresh lemon juice
½ teaspoon freshly ground black pepper

1. Preheat oven to 450°.
2. Place egg whites in a shallow dish; place panko in another shallow dish. Dip fish in egg whites; sprinkle fish evenly with ¼ teaspoon salt, and dredge in panko. Heat oil in a large ovenproof skillet over medium-high heat; swirl to coat. Add fish to pan; cook 3 minutes or until browned and very crispy. Turn fish over; place pan in oven. Bake fish at 450° for 7 minutes or until desired degree of doneness.
3. Combine ¼ teaspoon salt, tomatoes, and remaining ingredients in a bowl.

Serve with fish. Serves 4 (serving size: 1 fillet and about ⅓ cup relish)

CALORIES 255; FAT 8.5g (sat 0.8g, mono 4.6g, poly 2.4g); PROTEIN 33.7g; CARB 9.2g; FIBER 1.2g; CHOL 73mg; IRON 0.8mg; SODIUM 383mg; CALC 43mg

Quick & Easy

Roasted Salmon with Soy-Marmalade Glaze

Hands-on: 3 min. Total: 24 min. There are a number of sustainable salmon options available; look for U.S.-caught and U.S.-farmed fish.

¼ cup orange marmalade
1½ teaspoons lower-sodium soy sauce
½ teaspoon kosher salt
½ teaspoon freshly ground black pepper
2 garlic cloves, chopped
4 (6-ounce) skin-on salmon fillets
Cooking spray
2 tablespoons thinly sliced green onions
4 lemon wedges

1. Preheat oven to 450°.
2. Combine marmalade, soy sauce, salt, black pepper, and garlic in a small bowl. Arrange salmon fillets, skin sides down, on a foil-lined baking sheet coated with cooking spray. Brush fish fillets evenly with half of marmalade mixture. Bake fish fillets at 450° for 4 minutes.
3. Heat broiler to high (do not remove fish from oven); broil fish 6 minutes. Spoon remaining marmalade mixture onto center of fillets. Broil fish an additional 3 minutes or until desired degree of doneness. Sprinkle fish evenly with green onions; serve with lemon wedges. Serves 4 (serving size: 1 fillet and 1 lemon wedge)

CALORIES 294; FAT 9.5g (sat 1.6g, mono 3.1g, poly 4.1g); PROTEIN 38.7g; CARB 14.8g; FIBER 0.4g; CHOL 99mg; IRON 1.1mg; SODIUM 423mg; CALC 23mg

Quick & Easy

Grilled Halibut with Tarragon Beurre Blanc

Hands-on: 13 min. Total: 13 min. Choose U.S. wild-caught halibut. The sauce would be tasty with cod or inexpensive tilapia.

⅔ cup dry white wine
¼ cup chopped shallots
½ teaspoon whole black peppercorns
2 large tarragon sprigs
3 tablespoons butter, cut into small pieces
1 teaspoon chopped fresh tarragon
4 (6-ounce) halibut fillets
¼ teaspoon kosher salt
¼ teaspoon freshly ground black pepper
Cooking spray

1. Combine first 4 ingredients in a small heavy saucepan over medium-high heat; bring to a boil. Cook until liquid is reduced to 2 tablespoons (about 9 minutes). Remove from heat; strain through a fine sieve over a measuring cup, pressing mixture to release liquid. Discard solids. Return liquid to pan. Add butter, 1 piece at a time, stirring with a whisk until butter is incorporated. Stir in tarragon.
2. Sprinkle fish evenly with salt and ground pepper. Heat a large grill pan over medium-high heat. Coat pan with cooking spray. Add fish to pan; cook 5 minutes on each side or until desired degree of doneness. Serve with sauce. Serves 4 (serving size: 1 fillet and about 1½ tablespoons sauce)

CALORIES 242; FAT 10.7g (sat 5.9g, mono 3g, poly 0.8g); PROTEIN 29.1g; CARB 2.3g; FIBER 0.4g; CHOL 99mg; IRON 0.4mg; SODIUM 303mg; CALC 21mg

TIME FOR PIZZA!

Ready-to-go dough makes fast, fresh pizzas—from classic Italian spins to fun new pies.

Chicken Tikka Pizzas

Hands-on: 23 min. Total: 23 min.

12 ounces skinless, boneless chicken breast halves
1/4 cup plain low-fat yogurt
2 teaspoons garam masala, divided
Cooking spray
5/8 teaspoon kosher salt, divided
1 (14.5-ounce) can unsalted diced tomatoes, drained
1 tablespoon olive oil
1 teaspoon grated peeled fresh ginger
1/4 teaspoon ground red pepper
3 garlic cloves, minced
2 tablespoons heavy whipping cream
4 (6-inch) whole-wheat pitas
1/3 cup thinly vertically sliced red onion
3 ounces part-skim mozzarella cheese, shredded (about 3/4 cup)
2 tablespoons cilantro leaves

1. Preheat broiler to high.
2. Cut chicken in half horizontally. Combine chicken, yogurt, and 1/2 teaspoon garam masala. Place on a foil-lined baking sheet coated with cooking spray; sprinkle with 1/8 teaspoon salt. Broil 5 minutes on each side.
3. Heat a skillet over medium-high heat. Place tomatoes in a mini chopper; pulse until almost smooth. Add oil to pan. Add 1 1/2 teaspoons garam masala, ginger, red pepper, and garlic; cook 1 minute. Stir in tomatoes; simmer 4 minutes. Stir in 1/2 teaspoon salt and cream; cook 1 minute. Cut chicken into pieces. Add chicken to pan; toss.
4. Place pitas on baking sheet. Broil 1 minute each side. Spoon 1/2 cup chicken onto each. Top with onion and cheese. Broil 2 minutes. Sprinkle with cilantro. Serves 4 (serving size: 1 pizza)

CALORIES 390; FAT 12.9g (sat 5.1g, mono 5g, poly 0.9g); PROTEIN 31.2g; CARB 38g; FIBER 3.8g; CHOL 77mg; IRON 2.6mg; SODIUM 687mg; CALC 240mg

Four-Mushroom Pesto Pizza

Hands-on: 26 min. Total: 36 min.

12 ounces refrigerated fresh pizza dough
Cooking spray
2/3 cup water
1/3 cup dried porcini mushrooms
1 tablespoon olive oil
3 (4-ounce) packages fresh exotic mushroom blend
3 garlic cloves, minced
1/4 teaspoon freshly ground black pepper
1/8 teaspoon salt
1 tablespoon cornmeal
3 tablespoons refrigerated pesto
3 ounces whole-milk mozzarella cheese, shredded (about 3/4 cup)

1. Place a pizza stone or heavy baking sheet in oven. Preheat oven to 500° (keep pizza stone or baking sheet in oven as it preheats).
2. Place dough in a medium microwave-safe bowl coated with cooking spray. Cover and microwave at MEDIUM (50% power) 45 seconds. Let stand 5 minutes.
3. Combine 2/3 cup water and porcini in a 2-cup glass measuring cup. Microwave at HIGH 4 minutes or until tender; drain. Coarsely chop porcini.
4. Heat a large skillet over medium-high heat. Add oil; swirl. Add fresh mushrooms and garlic; sauté 5 minutes. Stir in porcini, pepper, and salt.
5. Roll dough into a 12 x 8–inch rectangle on a floured surface. Carefully remove pizza stone from oven. Sprinkle with cornmeal; arrange dough on pizza stone. Spread pesto over dough, leaving a 1/2-inch border. Sprinkle cheese over pesto; top with mushroom mixture. Bake at 500° for 13 minutes or until crust is browned and crisp. Cut into 8 pieces. Serves 4 (serving size: 2 pieces)

CALORIES 398; FAT 15.2g (sat 4.2g, mono 8.4g, poly 1.5g); PROTEIN 17.3g; CARB 46.5g; FIBER 8.3g; CHOL 21mg; IRON 3.4mg; SODIUM 678mg; CALC 144mg

GO FOR IT! TRY FAVORITE DISHES AS PIZZA TOPPINGS.

Pizza Arrabbiata

Hands-on: 20 min. Total: 30 min.

12 ounces refrigerated fresh pizza dough
Cooking spray
2 ounces prechopped pancetta
1 tablespoon extra-virgin olive oil
2/3 cup chopped onion
1/2 teaspoon crushed red pepper
4 garlic cloves, thinly sliced
1 (14.5-ounce) can unsalted diced tomatoes, drained
2 teaspoons chopped fresh oregano
1/8 teaspoon salt
1 tablespoon cornmeal
3 ounces part-skim mozzarella cheese, shredded (about 3/4 cup)
Oregano leaves (optional)

1. Place a pizza stone or heavy baking sheet in oven. Preheat oven to 500° (keep pizza stone or baking sheet in oven as it preheats).
2. Place pizza dough in a medium microwave-safe bowl coated with cooking spray. Cover and microwave at MEDIUM (50% power) 45 seconds. Let stand 5 minutes.
3. Heat a large skillet over medium

heat. Add pancetta; cook 4 minutes, stirring frequently. Remove pancetta from pan; discard drippings.

4. Add oil to pan; swirl to coat. Add onion, pepper, and garlic; cook 4 minutes, stirring occasionally. Place tomatoes in a mini chopper; pulse 4 times or until almost smooth. Add tomatoes, chopped oregano, and salt to pan; bring to a simmer. Cook 1 minute.

5. Roll dough into a 14-inch circle on a floured surface. Carefully remove pizza stone from oven. Sprinkle stone with cornmeal; arrange dough on stone. Spread tomato mixture over dough, leaving a ½-inch border; sprinkle with cheese and pancetta. Bake at 500° for 10 minutes or until crust is browned. Garnish with oregano leaves, if desired. Cut pizza into 8 wedges. Serves 4 (serving size: 2 wedges)

CALORIES 395; FAT 13.6g (sat 5.1g, mono 4.4g, poly 0.9g); PROTEIN 15.9g; CARB 49.5g; FIBER 7.3g; CHOL 18mg; IRON 2mg; SODIUM 704mg; CALC 181mg

Kid Friendly • Quick & Easy

Philly Cheesesteak Pizza

Hands-on: 30 min. Total: 30 min.

8 ounces flank steak, halved lengthwise
1 teaspoon black pepper, divided
Cooking spray
12 ounces refrigerated fresh pizza dough
1 tablespoon cornmeal
2 teaspoons olive oil
1¹/₃ cups vertically sliced onion
1 green bell pepper, cut into strips
1 orange bell pepper, cut into strips
5 garlic cloves, thinly sliced
1¹/₂ teaspoons lower-sodium soy sauce
¹/₂ cup 1% low-fat milk
1 tablespoon all-purpose flour
2 ounces reduced-fat extra-sharp cheddar cheese, shredded (¹/₂ cup)
¹/₄ teaspoon onion powder
¹/₈ teaspoon salt
¹/₈ teaspoon ground red pepper

1. Place a pizza stone or heavy baking sheet in oven. Preheat oven to 500° (keep stone or baking sheet in oven as it preheats).

2. Heat a large cast-iron skillet over medium-high heat. Sprinkle steak with ½ teaspoon pepper. Coat pan with cooking spray. Add steak to pan; cook 4 minutes on each side or until desired degree of doneness. Remove from pan; let stand 5 minutes. Cut steak across the grain into very thin slices.

3. While steak cooks, place dough in a medium microwave-safe bowl coated with cooking spray. Cover and microwave at MEDIUM (50% power) 45 seconds. Let stand 5 minutes. Roll dough into a 14-inch circle on a floured surface; pierce liberally with a fork. Carefully remove pizza stone from oven, and sprinkle with cornmeal. Arrange dough on pizza stone. Bake at 500° for 10 minutes or until browned and crisp.

4. While crust bakes, return skillet to medium-high heat. Add oil; swirl to coat. Add onion and bell peppers; sauté 3 minutes. Add garlic; sauté 2 minutes. Add steak; sauté 30 seconds or until thoroughly heated. Remove from heat; stir in ½ teaspoon black pepper and soy sauce. Arrange steak mixture over crust.

5. Combine milk and flour in a 4-cup glass measuring cup; stir with a whisk until smooth. Microwave at HIGH 2 minutes or until thickened, stirring every 30 seconds. Stir in cheese and remaining ingredients. Drizzle cheese mixture over pizza. Cut into 8 wedges. Serves 4 (serving size: 2 wedges)

CALORIES 424; FAT 10.3g (sat 3.7g, mono 3.7g, poly 0.8g); PROTEIN 25.9g; CARB 53.6g; FIBER 8.2g; CHOL 44mg; IRON 2.5mg; SODIUM 675mg; CALC 172mg

Quick & Easy • Vegetarian

Spring Vegetable Pizza with Gremolata

Hands-on: 20 min. Total: 30 min.

12 ounces refrigerated fresh pizza dough
Cooking spray
1 large fennel bulb with stalks
1 tablespoon olive oil
¹/₂ cup frozen green peas
1¹/₂ cups (3-inch) pieces asparagus, cut in half lengthwise
5 garlic cloves, thinly sliced
²/₃ cup part-skim ricotta cheese
3¹/₂ tablespoons 2% reduced-fat milk
¹/₂ teaspoon freshly ground black pepper
1.5 ounces pecorino Romano cheese, grated (about ¹/₃ cup)
¹/₄ teaspoon kosher salt
2 tablespoons chopped fresh flat-leaf parsley
1 tablespoon grated lemon rind
1 large garlic clove, minced

1. Place a pizza stone or heavy baking sheet in oven. Preheat oven to 500° (keep pizza stone or baking sheet in oven as it preheats).

2. Place dough in a microwave-safe bowl coated with cooking spray. Cover and microwave at MEDIUM (50% power) 45 seconds. Let stand 5 minutes.

3. Remove stalks from fennel bulb; reserve 1 tablespoon fronds. Cut bulb into thin slices. Heat a large skillet over medium-high heat. Add oil to pan; swirl to coat. Rinse peas in cold water to thaw; drain. Add peas, fennel bulb, asparagus, and sliced garlic to pan; sauté 2 minutes.

continued

4. Roll dough into a 14-inch circle on a lightly floured surface; pierce entire surface liberally with a fork. Carefully remove pizza stone from oven. Sprinkle stone with cornmeal; arrange dough on pizza stone. Combine ricotta, milk, pepper, and pecorino Romano cheese; spread evenly over pizza, leaving a ½-inch border. Bake at 500° for 5 minutes. Carefully remove pizza stone from oven. Top pizza with pea mixture. Bake at 500° for 5 minutes or until crust is browned and crisp. Remove from oven; sprinkle evenly with salt. Combine reserved fennel fronds, parsley, rind, and minced garlic; sprinkle over pizza. Cut into 8 wedges. Serves 4 (serving size: 2 wedges)

CALORIES 372; FAT 9.9g (sat 3.4g, mono 4.4g, poly 0.9g); PROTEIN 16.6g; CARB 52.8g; FIBER 10.1g; CHOL 17mg; IRON 3.3mg; SODIUM 658mg; CALC 221mg

CHEESY MACS

Because some night a bowl of gooey comfort is all that will do. Here are five variations.

Kid Friendly • Quick & Easy

Chimichurri Mac and Cheese

Hands-on: 12 min. Total: 32 min.
Chimichurri—the South American herb sauce typically served with meat—revs up basic mac and cheese with tangy flavors. You can also serve this in individual ramekins or small serving skillets.

8 ounces uncooked ziti rigate
1¼ cups 1% low-fat milk
1 cup unsalted chicken stock (such as Swanson)
3 tablespoons all-purpose flour
¼ teaspoon salt
2.5 ounces extra-sharp cheddar cheese, shredded and divided (about ⅔ cup)

2 ounces light processed cheese (such as Velveeta Light), cubed
1 teaspoon olive oil
1 cup chopped onion
¼ cup oregano leaves
1 tablespoon thyme leaves
¼ teaspoon crushed red pepper
8 garlic cloves, crushed
1 cup chopped fresh flat-leaf parsley stems
¾ cup chopped fresh cilantro stems
2 tablespoons fresh lime juice
Cooking spray
3 tablespoons cilantro leaves

1. Preheat broiler to high.
2. Cook pasta according to package directions, omitting salt and fat; drain.
3. While pasta cooks, combine milk, stock, flour, and salt in a medium saucepan, stirring with a whisk. Bring to a boil over medium heat; cook 1 minute or until thickened. Let stand 5 minutes. Add 2 ounces shredded cheddar and processed cheese, stirring until smooth.
4. Heat a 10-inch cast-iron skillet over medium-high heat. Add oil; swirl to coat. Add onion, oregano, thyme, pepper, and garlic; cook 3 minutes, stirring occasionally. Combine onion mixture, parsley stems, cilantro stems, and lime juice in a food processor; pulse until coarsely chopped.
5. Combine pasta, milk mixture, and parsley mixture. Heat cast-iron skillet over high heat. Coat pan with cooking spray. Add pasta mixture to pan; sprinkle with remaining ½ ounce cheddar cheese. Broil 8 inches from heat for 5 minutes or until cheese is browned. Sprinkle with cilantro leaves. Serves 4 (serving size: about 1½ cups)

CALORIES 419; FAT 10.9g (sat 6.1g, mono 3.1g, poly 0.7g); PROTEIN 20g; CARB 60.9g; FIBER 3.4g; CHOL 28mg; IRON 3.5mg; SODIUM 540mg; CALC 302mg

Quick & Easy

Stout Mac and Cheese

Hands-on: 20 min. Total: 30 min. *Dark beer lovers will appreciate the flavor: cheesy up front and slightly bitter and malty at the end. Garnish with parsley for a pop of color.*

7 ounces uncooked rotini pasta
2 teaspoons canola oil
4 ounces hot turkey Italian sausage
¾ cup diced onion
2½ tablespoons all-purpose flour
½ teaspoon freshly ground black pepper
⅛ teaspoon kosher salt
1 cup Guinness Stout beer
⅓ cup whole milk
2.5 ounces reduced-fat sharp cheddar cheese, shredded
2 ounces light processed cheese, shredded (such as Velveeta Light)
Cooking spray

1. Preheat oven to 450°.
2. Cook pasta according to package directions, omitting salt and fat; drain.
3. While pasta cooks, heat a large saucepan over medium-high heat. Add oil; swirl to coat. Remove casing from sausage. Add sausage and onion to pan; cook 6 minutes, stirring to crumble sausage. Add flour, pepper, and salt; cook 1 minute, stirring frequently. Stir in beer; bring to a boil. Cook 3 minutes or until thick and bubbly, stirring constantly. Remove from heat. Add milk and cheeses, stirring until smooth. Stir in pasta. Divide mixture evenly among 4 ceramic gratin dishes coated with cooking spray. Bake at 450° for 10 minutes or until lightly browned. Serves 4 (serving size: about 1¼ cups)

CALORIES 385; FAT 11.7g (sat 4.3g, mono 4.1g, poly 2g); PROTEIN 15.6g; CARB 48.5g; FIBER 2.3g; CHOL 36mg; IRON 2.4mg; SODIUM 606mg; CALC 43mg

Blush Mac and Cheese with Tomatoes

Hands-on: 29 min. Total: 29 min.

8 ounces uncooked corkscrew pasta
1 (1-pint) container grape tomatoes
1 tablespoon canola oil
¼ cup diced shallots
2 tablespoons minced garlic
1 teaspoon chopped fresh thyme
2 tablespoons unsalted tomato paste
1 tablespoon all-purpose flour
1¼ cups 1% low-fat milk
¾ teaspoon freshly ground black pepper
½ teaspoon kosher salt
4 ounces fresh baby spinach
4 ounces reduced-fat sharp white
   cheddar cheese, shredded

1. Preheat broiler to high.
2. Cook pasta according to package directions, omitting salt and fat; drain.
3. While pasta cooks, place tomatoes on a jelly-roll pan lined with foil. Broil 8 minutes or until tomatoes are beginning to blacken.
4. While tomatoes cook, heat a large saucepan over medium-high heat. Add canola oil to pan; swirl to coat. Add diced shallots, minced garlic, and thyme; sauté 2 minutes or until tender, stirring frequently. Add tomato paste; cook 2 minutes, stirring occasionally. Add flour; cook 1 minute, stirring constantly. Stir in milk, black pepper, and salt; bring to a boil. Cook 4 minutes or until thick and bubbly, stirring frequently. Remove from heat. Add spinach, stirring constantly until spinach starts to wilt. Add shredded cheddar cheese, and stir until smooth. Stir in cooked pasta. Top with the roasted tomatoes. Serves 4 (serving size: 1¼ cups pasta and about 3 tomatoes)

CALORIES 414; FAT 11.2g (sat 4.5g, mono 4g, poly 1.3g);
PROTEIN 12.6g; CARB 59.5g; FIBER 5.1g; CHOL 24mg;
IRON 3.4mg; SODIUM 575mg; CALC 155mg

Poblano Mac and Cheese

Hands-on: 30 min. Total: 30 min.

8 ounces uncooked penne pasta
2 poblano chiles (about 4 ounces)
⅓ cup fresh breadcrumbs
2 teaspoons olive oil
1 teaspoon grated lime rind
⅛ teaspoon ground red pepper
1 cup 1% low-fat milk, divided
1 cup unsalted vegetable stock
3 tablespoons all-purpose flour
1 tablespoon minced garlic
5 ounces queso quesadilla cheese,
   shredded
¼ cup fat-free sour cream
¼ cup chopped fresh cilantro
1 tablespoon fresh lime juice
⅜ teaspoon kosher salt
Cooking spray

1. Preheat broiler to high.
2. Cook pasta according to package directions, omitting salt and fat; drain.
3. While pasta cooks, cut chiles in half lengthwise; discard seeds and membranes. Place chile halves, skin sides up, on a foil-lined baking sheet; flatten with hand. Broil 6 minutes or until blackened. Place in a paper bag; fold to close tightly. Let stand 5 minutes. Peel and cut into bite-sized pieces.
4. Combine breadcrumbs, oil, rind, and red pepper in a bowl. Place ¾ cup milk, stock, flour, and garlic in a saucepan, stirring with a whisk. Bring to a boil; cook 3 minutes or until thick, stirring frequently. Remove from heat. Stir in chiles, ¼ cup milk, cheese, and next 4 ingredients until smooth. Stir in pasta. Spoon mixture into an 8-inch square broiler-safe glass or ceramic baking dish coated with cooking spray. Top with breadcrumb mixture. Broil 1 minute or until browned. Serves 4

CALORIES 424; FAT 11.6g (sat 4.8g, mono 4g, poly 0.9g);
PROTEIN 21.1g; CARB 59.6g; FIBER 2.4g; CHOL 23mg;
IRON 2.3mg; SODIUM 576mg; CALC 375mg

HOMEMADE, FAST: MAC IN ONLY HALF AN HOUR.

Easy Stovetop Mac and Cheese

Hands-on: 30 min. Total: 30 min.

8 ounces uncooked large elbow
   macaroni
2 cups 1% low-fat milk
3 tablespoons all-purpose flour
½ teaspoon freshly ground black
   pepper
Dash of ground red pepper
3 ounces light processed cheese,
   shredded (such as Velveeta Light;
   about ¾ cup)
2.5 ounces extra-sharp cheddar
   cheese, shredded (about ⅔ cup)
¼ teaspoon kosher salt
Cooking spray
¼ cup fresh breadcrumbs

1. Preheat broiler to high.
2. Cook pasta according to package directions; drain.
3. While pasta cooks, combine milk, flour, and peppers in a large saucepan, stirring with a whisk. Bring to a boil; cook 4 minutes or until thick. Remove from heat. Add cheeses and salt; stir until smooth. Add pasta, and stir to coat. Spoon mixture into a 1½-quart glass or ceramic baking dish coated with cooking spray. Sprinkle breadcrumbs evenly over top; broil 2 minutes or until browned. Serves 4 (serving size: about 1¼ cups)

CALORIES 406; FAT 10.2g (sat 5.3g, mono 2.7g, poly 0.8g);
PROTEIN 20.6g; CARB 58.1g; FIBER 2.1g; CHOL 33mg;
IRON 2.3mg; SODIUM 601mg; CALC 300mg

MAIN-COURSE SALADS

Five light, fresh, veggie-packed dishes that are hearty enough for a satisfying meal.

Quick & Easy

Warm Potato and Steak Salad

(pictured on page 215)

Hands-on: 29 min. Total: 29 min.

1 pound new potatoes, quartered
1 tablespoon extra-virgin olive oil
2 (6-ounce) beef tenderloin steaks, trimmed
1/2 teaspoon salt, divided
3/8 teaspoon freshly ground black pepper, divided
3 bacon slices
2 teaspoons all-purpose flour
1/4 cup white wine vinegar
3 tablespoons water
2 teaspoons sugar
1 teaspoon Dijon mustard
1/3 cup shaved celery
2 tablespoons thinly sliced green onions
3 cups baby arugula

1. Place potatoes in a saucepan; cover with water. Bring to a boil. Reduce heat to medium, and simmer 12 minutes or until tender; drain.
2. While potatoes cook, heat a medium skillet over medium-high heat. Add olive oil to pan; swirl to coat. Sprinkle steaks evenly with 1/4 teaspoon salt and 1/4 teaspoon pepper. Add steaks to pan; cook 3 minutes on each side or until desired degree of doneness. Remove steaks from pan; let stand 5 minutes. Cut across the grain into slices.
3. Cook bacon in skillet until crisp; remove bacon from pan, reserving 1 1/2 tablespoons drippings in pan. Crumble bacon, and set aside. Add 1/4 teaspoon salt, 1/8 teaspoon pepper, and flour to pan; cook 30 seconds, stirring constantly. Stir in vinegar, 3 tablespoons water, sugar, and mustard; cook 1 minute or until slightly thickened. Remove from heat; stir in potatoes, steak, bacon, celery, and green onions. Toss with arugula. Serves 4 (serving size: 3 ounces steak and 1 cup salad)

CALORIES 320; **FAT** 16.5g (sat 5.4g, mono 7.3g, poly 1.3g); **PROTEIN** 20.4g; **CARB** 22.3g; **FIBER** 2.4g; **CHOL** 60mg; **IRON** 2.3mg; **SODIUM** 469mg; **CALC** 52mg

Quick & Easy

BLT Salad with Eggs Sunny Side Up

Hands-on: 18 min. Total: 18 min.

3 cups French or ciabatta bread, cut into 1-inch cubes (about 4 ounces)
4 cups torn romaine lettuce
2 teaspoons extra-virgin olive oil
4 bacon slices
12 ounces cherry tomatoes on the vine
4 large eggs
1/4 teaspoon salt
1/4 teaspoon freshly ground black pepper

1. Preheat broiler to high.
2. Arrange bread on a baking sheet. Broil 1 minute or until browned, stirring after 30 seconds. Combine bread, lettuce, and oil; toss well.
3. Cook bacon in a large nonstick skillet over medium heat until crisp. Remove bacon from pan, reserving 1 tablespoon drippings; crumble bacon. Add tomatoes to drippings in pan. Cook 3 minutes or until soft; remove from pan. Gently break eggs into pan; cook 2 minutes. Cover; cook 1 minute or until desired degree of doneness.
4. Arrange 2 cups salad on each of 4 plates; top each with 1 egg. Sprinkle evenly with bacon, salt, and pepper. Serve with tomatoes. Serves 4

CALORIES 253; **FAT** 13.9g (sat 4.3g, mono 5g, poly 1.9g); **PROTEIN** 13g; **CARB** 19.1g; **FIBER** 2g; **CHOL** 197mg; **IRON** 2.6mg; **SODIUM** 536mg; **CALC** 59mg

Make Ahead • Quick & Easy Vegetarian

Vegetable Pasta Salad with Goat Cheese

Hands-on: 22 min. Total: 22 min.

6 ounces uncooked strozzapreti or other short pasta
1 1/2 cups (2-inch) cut asparagus
3 tablespoons white wine vinegar
1 teaspoon sugar
1/2 teaspoon salt
1/4 teaspoon ground red pepper
1/4 cup extra-virgin olive oil
1 cup sliced cremini mushrooms
1/2 cup chopped red bell pepper
1/4 cup sliced green onions
3 tablespoons small basil leaves
2 tablespoons halved pitted kalamata olives
2 tablespoons oregano leaves
2 tablespoons flat-leaf parsley leaves
3 ounces goat or feta cheese, sliced
2 tablespoons coarsely chopped walnuts, toasted

1. Cook pasta according to directions; add asparagus during last minute of cooking. Drain; rinse with cold water.
2. Combine vinegar, sugar, salt, and pepper in a large bowl. Slowly whisk in oil. Add pasta mixture, mushrooms, and next 6 ingredients; toss well. Top with cheese and nuts. Serves 4 (serving size: 1 1/2 cups)

CALORIES 395; **FAT** 22.2g (sat 5.5g, mono 11.9g, poly 3.4g); **PROTEIN** 12.4g; **CARB** 38.4g; **FIBER** 3.6g; **CHOL** 10mg; **IRON** 3.5mg; **SODIUM** 440mg; **CALC** 77mg

Quick & Easy

Spring Garden Salad with Chicken and Champagne Vinaigrette

Hands-on: 24 min. Total: 24 min. *Hit up the farmers' market for the freshest spring veggies. You can also try the dish with shrimp, salmon, or pork in place of chicken.*

7 baby carrots, halved lengthwise
1 cup fresh sugar snap peas
4 cups torn Boston lettuce
1 cup trimmed watercress
1/2 cup thinly sliced radishes
1/2 cup flat-leaf parsley leaves
2 (6-ounce) skinless, boneless chicken breast halves
1/2 teaspoon salt, divided
1/4 teaspoon freshly ground black pepper, divided
8 teaspoons extra-virgin olive oil, divided
2 tablespoons champagne vinegar
2 tablespoons minced shallots
11/2 teaspoons honey
11/2 teaspoons water
1 garlic clove, minced

1. Cook carrots and peas in boiling water 2½ minutes or until crisp-tender. Drain and rinse with cold water; drain. Combine carrot mixture, lettuce, watercress, radishes, and parsley in a large bowl; set aside.
2. Place chicken between 2 sheets of plastic wrap; pound to ¼-inch thickness using a meat mallet or small heavy skillet. Sprinkle chicken with ¼ teaspoon salt and ⅛ teaspoon pepper. Heat a large skillet over medium-high heat. Add 2 teaspoons oil; swirl to coat. Add chicken to pan; cook 4 minutes on each side or until done. Let stand 5 minutes; cut across the grain into slices.

3. Combine 2 tablespoons oil, ¼ teaspoon salt, ⅛ teaspoon pepper, vinegar, and remaining ingredients in a small bowl, stirring with a whisk. Drizzle dressing over lettuce mixture; toss gently. Arrange about 2 cups lettuce mixture on each of 4 plates; divide chicken evenly among servings. Serves 4

CALORIES 230; **FAT** 11.5g (sat 1.8g, mono 7.3g, poly 1.4g); **PROTEIN** 20.4g; **CARB** 12g; **FIBER** 2.9g; **CHOL** 54mg; **IRON** 2.2mg; **SODIUM** 433mg; **CALC** 75mg

Quick & Easy

Tuna Salad Niçoise

Hands-on: 36 min. Total: 36 min.

Salad:
4 ounces haricots verts (French green beans) or green beans, trimmed
1 tablespoon extra-virgin olive oil, divided
12 ounces refrigerated red potato wedges (such as Simply Potatoes)
2½ cups Bibb lettuce leaves (about 1 large head)
1/2 cup basil leaves
1 cup grape tomatoes, halved lengthwise
1/2 cup thinly sliced red onion
1/4 cup pitted kalamata olives, halved lengthwise
2 refrigerated hard-cooked peeled eggs, quartered lengthwise
2 (8-ounce) tuna steaks
1/8 teaspoon salt
1/8 teaspoon freshly ground black pepper
Dressing:
2 tablespoons fresh lemon juice
1 tablespoon water
1/2 teaspoon sugar
1/8 teaspoon salt
1/8 teaspoon freshly ground black pepper
1 garlic clove, minced
3½ tablespoons extra-virgin olive oil
1 tablespoon capers

1. To prepare salad, cook green beans in boiling water 2 minutes or until crisp-tender. Drain and plunge beans into ice water. Drain well.
2. While beans cook, heat a large non-stick skillet over medium-high heat. Add 1 teaspoon oil to pan; swirl to coat. Add potatoes; cook 5 minutes on each side or until browned.
3. While potatoes cook, arrange lettuce and basil evenly on 4 plates. Divide tomatoes, onion, olives, eggs, green beans, and potatoes among plates.
4. Heat skillet over medium-high heat. Add remaining 2 teaspoons oil to pan; swirl to coat. Sprinkle tuna with ⅛ teaspoon salt and ⅛ teaspoon pepper. Add tuna to pan; cook 2 minutes on each side or until desired degree of doneness. Cut thinly across the grain. Arrange tuna on plates.
5. To prepare dressing, combine lemon juice and next 5 ingredients in a small bowl; gradually add 3½ tablespoons oil, stirring constantly with a whisk. Stir in capers. Drizzle evenly over salads. Serves 4

CALORIES 407; **FAT** 21.2g (sat 3.5g, mono 14.3g, poly 2.7g); **PROTEIN** 34.8g; **CARB** 18.5g; **FIBER** 4.1g; **CHOL** 137mg; **IRON** 2.9mg; **SODIUM** 566mg; **CALC** 64mg

OUR RECIPES LEAVE TIME FOR HOMEMADE DRESSING.

HEARTY SANDWICHES

Mushroom, steak, fish, or chicken—and, always, the best bread. These handfuls make a real meal.

Quick & Easy • Vegetarian

Portobello Sandwiches with Red Pepper Sauce
(pictured on page 215)

Hands-on: 30 min. Total: 30 min. *If you don't have almonds on hand, use any nut.*

4 (4-inch) portobello mushroom caps
2 tablespoons extra-virgin olive oil, divided
2 garlic cloves, minced and divided
2 (1/2-inch-thick) slices red onion
1/4 teaspoon kosher salt, divided
8 (1.25-ounce) slices ciabatta bread
1/2 cup bottled roasted red bell peppers, rinsed and drained
1 tablespoon dry-roasted almonds, coarsely chopped
1 teaspoon red wine vinegar
2 ounces goat cheese, crumbled (about 1/2 cup)
1 cup fresh spinach
12 basil leaves

1. Preheat broiler to high.
2. Heat a grill pan over medium-high heat. Remove gills from mushrooms using a spoon; discard gills. Combine 1 1/2 tablespoons oil and half of garlic; brush over mushrooms and onion slices. Place mushrooms and onion slices in pan, and cook 5 minutes on each side or until tender. Remove from heat. Sprinkle mushrooms with 1/8 teaspoon salt. Separate onion slices into rings.
3. Place bread slices on a baking sheet, and broil 1 minute on each side or until toasted.

4. Place 1 1/2 teaspoons oil, garlic, 1/8 teaspoon salt, bell peppers, almonds, and vinegar in a food processor, and process until smooth. Spread red pepper sauce evenly over 1 side of each bread slice; top 4 bread slices evenly with cheese, 1 mushroom, onion rings, spinach, and basil. Top with remaining 4 bread slices, sauce side down. Serves 4 (serving size: 1 sandwich)

CALORIES 357; **FAT** 14.1g (sat 3.5g, mono 8.7g, poly 1.4g); **PROTEIN** 12g; **CARB** 48g; **FIBER** 3.6g; **CHOL** 7mg; **IRON** 3.5mg; **SODIUM** 734mg; **CALC** 49mg

Quick & Easy

Steak Sandwiches with Fresh Herb Topping

Hands-on: 30 min. Total: 30 min.

1 pound flank steak, trimmed
2 tablespoons extra-virgin olive oil, divided
1/4 teaspoon kosher salt
1/4 teaspoon ground black pepper
1 (12-ounce) French bread baguette
1 1/2 cups arugula, divided
1/2 cup chopped fresh flat-leaf parsley
2 tablespoons grated pecorino Romano or Parmesan cheese
1 tablespoon fresh lemon juice
1 teaspoon capers
1 garlic clove, crushed
2 plum tomatoes, thinly sliced

1. Preheat broiler to high.
2. Heat a grill pan over medium-high heat. Rub steak evenly with 1 1/2 teaspoons oil; sprinkle with salt and pepper. Add steak to pan; cook 3 minutes on each side or until desired degree of doneness. Remove from pan; let stand 5 minutes. Cut steak across the grain into thin slices.
3. Cut bread in half lengthwise and crosswise. Hollow tops and bottoms of bread, leaving a 1/2-inch-thick shell. Place bread on a baking sheet, cut sides

up. Broil 1 1/2 minutes or until toasted.
4. Place 1 1/2 tablespoons oil, 1/2 cup arugula, parsley, and next 4 ingredients in a food processor. Process until finely chopped. Spread parsley mixture evenly over cut sides of bread. Layer bottom halves of bread with arugula, steak, and tomato; cover with top halves of bread. Cut sandwiches in half. Serves 4 (serving size: 1 sandwich)

CALORIES 407; **FAT** 14g (sat 4.1g, mono 7.4g, poly 1g); **PROTEIN** 30.5g; **CARB** 40.4g; **FIBER** 1.9g; **CHOL** 69mg; **IRON** 4.2mg; **SODIUM** 656mg; **CALC** 63mg

Kid Friendly • Quick & Easy

Cornmeal-Crusted Tilapia Sandwiches with Jicama Slaw

Hands-on: 21 min. Total: 21 min.

4 (3-ounce) whole-grain sub rolls
1 tablespoon canola mayonnaise
1 tablespoon plain fat-free Greek yogurt
1 tablespoon cider vinegar
1/2 teaspoon kosher salt, divided
2 cups packaged cabbage-and-carrot coleslaw
1/3 cup shredded peeled jicama
1/3 cup shredded peeled Fuji apple
1 jalapeño pepper, thinly sliced
1/3 cup stone-ground yellow cornmeal
1/2 teaspoon freshly ground black pepper
1/3 cup 2% reduced-fat milk
4 (4-ounce) tilapia fillets
2 tablespoons extra-virgin olive oil

1. Preheat broiler to high.
2. Hollow out top and bottom halves of bread, leaving a 1/2-inch-thick shell. Place bread, cut sides up, on a baking sheet, and broil 1 1/2 minutes or until toasted.
3. Place mayonnaise, yogurt, vinegar, and 1/4 teaspoon salt in a medium bowl; stir with a whisk. Add coleslaw, jicama, apple, and jalapeño; toss well to coat.

4. Place cornmeal and black pepper in a dish. Place milk in a dish. Dip fish in milk. Dredge in cornmeal mixture; shake off excess breading. Sprinkle with ¼ teaspoon salt.
5. Heat a skillet over medium-high heat. Add olive oil; swirl to coat. Add fish; cook 3 minutes on each side or until desired degree of doneness. Place 1 fillet in each roll; divide coleslaw among sandwiches. Serves 4 (serving size: 1 sandwich)

CALORIES 392; FAT 12.6g (sat 2.7g, mono 6.3g, poly 1.7g); PROTEIN 30.7g; CARB 42.1g; FIBER 3.9g; CHOL 58mg; IRON 3.3mg; SODIUM 615mg; CALC 104mg

Quick & Easy
Open-Faced Apricot-Chipotle Chicken Club

Hands-on: 15 min. Total: 15 min.

4 (2-ounce) slices country-style wheat bread
8 (½-ounce) slices reduced-fat cheddar cheese
2½ tablespoons apricot preserves
2 tablespoons canola mayonnaise
2¼ teaspoons chopped chipotle chiles, canned in adobo sauce
4 green leaf lettuce leaves
1½ cups shredded skinless, boneless rotisserie chicken breast
2 center-cut bacon slices, cooked and crumbled

1. Preheat broiler to high.
2. Arrange bread in a single layer on a baking sheet. Broil 1 minute on each side or until lightly toasted.
3. Place 2 cheese slices on each bread slice. Broil 1 minute or until cheese melts. Remove from oven.
4. Combine preserves, mayonnaise, and chipotle in a small bowl. Top each bread slice, cheese side up, with about 1 tablespoon preserves mixture, 1

lettuce leaf, and about ⅓ cup chicken. Sprinkle bacon evenly over servings. Serves 4 (serving size: 1 sandwich)

CALORIES 409; FAT 15.7g (sat 5.8g, mono 6.1g, poly 2.5g); PROTEIN 29.6g; CARB 39.1g; FIBER 1.9g; CHOL 75mg; IRON 4.2mg; SODIUM 810mg; CALC 259mg

Quick & Easy
Soy-Marinated Pork Sandwiches

Hands-on: 30 min. Total: 30 min.
Quickly make carrot ribbons with your vegetable peeler.

1½ tablespoons brown sugar
1½ tablespoons lower-sodium soy sauce
2 teaspoons minced fresh garlic
2 teaspoons sambal oelek (ground fresh chile paste) or ½ teaspoon crushed red pepper
¾ teaspoon grated peeled fresh ginger
¾ teaspoon dark sesame oil
12 ounces pork tenderloin, trimmed and thinly sliced
2 tablespoons rice vinegar
2 teaspoons canola oil, divided
¼ teaspoon granulated sugar
1 cup shaved carrot
¼ cup (1-inch) diagonally cut green onions
¼ cup fresh cilantro leaves
4 (1½-ounce) whole-wheat hamburger buns

1. Combine first 6 ingredients in a medium bowl, stirring with a whisk. Add pork to bowl; toss well to coat. Let pork mixture stand at room temperature 15 minutes.
2. Preheat broiler to high.
3. While pork marinates, combine vinegar, 1 teaspoon canola oil, and granulated sugar in a medium bowl; stir with a whisk. Add carrot, onions, and cilantro; toss to coat.
4. Heat a large skillet over medium-high heat. Add remaining 1 teaspoon

canola oil to pan; swirl to coat. Add pork to pan; cook 3 minutes or until done, turning occasionally.
5. While pork cooks, place buns on a baking sheet, cut sides up. Broil 1 minute or until lightly toasted. Top bottom halves of buns evenly with pork. Divide carrot mixture evenly among servings. Cover sandwiches with top halves of buns. Serves 4 (serving size: 1 sandwich)

CALORIES 279; FAT 7.1g (sat 1.3g, mono 3g, poly 2.3g); PROTEIN 22.3g; CARB 32.3g; FIBER 4.4g; CHOL 55mg; IRON 2.2mg; SODIUM 443mg; CALC 73mg

SPEEDY SIDES

This all-star collection of 16 versatile dishes will help you round out your weeknight meals.

Kid Friendly • Quick & Easy
Vegetarian
Glazed Baby Carrots
(pictured on page 216)

Hands-on: 5 min. Total: 10 min. To save time, look for prepeeled real baby carrots in microwavable bags.

1. Combine ¼ cup water, ¼ cup cider vinegar, 2½ tablespoons brown sugar, and 12 ounces peeled baby carrots in a medium skillet over medium-high heat. Cover and bring to a boil. Reduce heat, and simmer 6 minutes or until carrots are crisp-tender. Increase heat to medium-high; cook 2 minutes or until liquid is syrupy. Stir in 1 tablespoon butter, ¼ teaspoon freshly ground black pepper, and ⅛ teaspoon salt. Sprinkle with 1 tablespoon chopped fresh flat-leaf parsley. Serves 4 (serving size: about ⅔ cup)

CALORIES 97; FAT 3.1g (sat 1.9g); SODIUM 161mg

Quick Chilled Pea Soup

(pictured on page 217)

***Hands-on: 18 min. Total: 18 min.** Blending a handful of spinach into the soup enhances the green color and adds subtle earthy notes.*

1. Reserve ½ cup peas from 1 (14.4-ounce) package frozen petite green peas. Place remaining peas and ¼ cup water in a microwave-safe dish. Cover with plastic wrap; pierce once with a knife to vent. Microwave at HIGH 5 minutes. Add 2 cups fresh baby spinach; cover and microwave at HIGH 2 minutes. Drain and rinse well with cold water; drain.
2. While peas cook, heat a small skillet over medium-high heat. Add 1½ teaspoons extra-virgin olive oil to pan; swirl to coat. Add reserved ½ cup peas and 1 minced garlic clove; sauté 4 minutes or until peas begin to brown, stirring frequently. Set aside.
3. Place spinach mixture, 1 tablespoon extra-virgin olive oil, 1 minced garlic clove, 1 cup ice water, 1 tablespoon chopped fresh mint, 1 tablespoon fresh lemon juice, and ¼ teaspoon salt in a blender; blend until smooth (about 4 minutes). Add 2 tablespoons half-and-half; blend until just combined. Pour about ¾ cup soup into each of 4 bowls; sprinkle evenly with sautéed peas and ¼ teaspoon freshly ground black pepper. Serves 4

CALORIES 137; **FAT** 6.2g (sat 1.3g); **SODIUM** 239mg

Creamy Tomato Soup

***Hands-on: 13 min. Total: 30 min.** Smoked paprika and cumin round out the sweetness of San Marzano tomatoes. If you can't find these tomatoes, use a can of regular unsalted tomatoes.*

1. Heat a medium saucepan over medium heat. Add 1 tablespoon canola oil to pan; swirl to coat. Add 1½ cups chopped onion, ½ teaspoon ground cumin, ⅜ teaspoon kosher salt, and ¼ teaspoon hot smoked paprika to pan; cook 8 minutes, stirring occasionally. Increase the heat to medium-high. Add 4 minced garlic cloves; sauté 1 minute, stirring constantly. Stir in 1 (14.28-ounce) can chopped unsalted San Marzano tomatoes, undrained, and 2 cups unsalted chicken stock (such as Swanson); bring to a boil. Reduce heat; simmer 15 minutes, stirring occasionally. Remove from heat; stir in ¼ cup half-and-half.
2. Place half of tomato mixture in a blender. Remove center piece of blender lid (to allow steam to escape); secure blender lid on blender. Place a clean towel over opening in blender lid (to avoid splatters). Blend until smooth. Pour into a large bowl. Repeat procedure with remaining tomato mixture. Top with 2 tablespoons coarsely chopped fresh flat-leaf parsley and ¼ teaspoon freshly ground black pepper. Serves 6 (serving size: about ¾ cup)

CALORIES 74; **FAT** 3.7g (sat 0.9g); **SODIUM** 177mg

Grapefruit, Walnut, and Feta Salad

(pictured on page 217)

***Hands-on: 13 min. Total: 13 min.** You can use oranges or tangerines instead of the grapefruit, and goat cheese in place of feta.*

1. Peel and section 1 small red grapefruit over a bowl; squeeze membranes to extract juice. Set sections aside; reserve 3 tablespoons juice. Discard membranes.
2. Combine juice, 2 tablespoons extra-virgin olive oil, ½ teaspoon sugar, ⅛ teaspoon salt, and ⅛ teaspoon black pepper, stirring with a whisk. Divide 4 cups torn butter lettuce evenly among 4 plates; sprinkle 1 tablespoon crumbled feta cheese and 1 tablespoon toasted walnuts over each salad. Divide grapefruit sections evenly among salads, and drizzle with vinaigrette. Serves 4

CALORIES 145; **FAT** 12.5g (sat 2.4g); **SODIUM** 156mg

Green Salad with Simple Vinaigrette

***Hands-on: 9 min. Total: 9 min.** We love the bright pop of this vinaigrette; for a sweeter version, use balsamic, cider, or rice vinegar.*

1. Combine 4 cups mixed gourmet salad greens, 3 thinly sliced radishes, and ½ cup chopped seeded cucumber in a bowl. Combine 2 tablespoons extra-virgin olive oil, 2 tablespoons white wine vinegar, ⅛ teaspoon salt, and ⅛ teaspoon freshly ground black pepper, stirring with a whisk. Drizzle over salad mixture; toss gently to coat. Serves 4 (serving size: about 1 cup)

CALORIES 72; **FAT** 6.8g (sat 0.9g); **SODIUM** 96mg

LITTLE TOUCHES, BIG FLAVOR DIFFERENCE: ZING OF CITRUS, SPRINKLE OF CHEESE, CASCADE OF HERBS.

Celery and Parsley Salad

Hands-on: 12 min. Total: 12 min.
A crunchy, savory, tangy, wonderful combination.

1. Combine 3 cups thinly diagonally sliced celery, 2 cups baby arugula, ¾ cup packed fresh flat-leaf parsley leaves, and ½ cup coarsely chopped celery leaves in a medium bowl. Combine 2½ tablespoons fresh lemon juice, 2½ tablespoons extra-virgin olive oil, ¾ teaspoon freshly ground black pepper, and ⅛ teaspoon kosher salt in a small bowl, stirring well with a whisk. Drizzle juice mixture over celery mixture, and toss. Top with 1 ounce shaved fresh Parmigiano-Reggiano cheese. Serves 4 (serving size: 1½ cups)

CALORIES 129; FAT 10.8g (sat 2.5g); SODIUM 242mg

Wilted Spinach with Fresh Chile

Quick & Easy • Vegetarian

Hands-on: 8 min. Total: 8 min. You'll often see spinach cooked with dried red pepper flakes; here fresh chile gives that tired treatment a delicious flavor boost.

1. Heat a large Dutch oven over medium-high heat. Add 1 tablespoon extra-virgin olive oil to pan; swirl to coat. Add 4 thinly sliced garlic cloves and 1 thinly sliced small red chile; sauté 1 minute, stirring constantly. Add ⅛ teaspoon kosher salt and 2 (9-ounce) bags fresh spinach; sauté 2 minutes or until spinach wilts. Drizzle with 2 teaspoons fresh lemon juice. Serves 4 (serving size: about ⅔ cup)

CALORIES 92; FAT 3.5g (sat 0.5g); SODIUM 264mg

Asparagus with Lemon and Pecorino

Quick & Easy • Vegetarian

Hands-on: 8 min. Total: 14 min. Spring asparagus shines with just a few flavor enhancements.

1. Bring a large pot of water to a boil. Add 1 pound trimmed asparagus; cook 2 minutes or until crisp-tender. Drain.
2. Heat a large skillet over medium-high heat. Add 2 teaspoons extra-virgin olive oil to pan; swirl to coat. Add asparagus; cook 1 minute. Sprinkle evenly with 2 teaspoons grated lemon rind, ¼ teaspoon freshly ground black pepper, and ⅛ teaspoon salt; toss to coat. Sprinkle asparagus with 1 ounce shaved pecorino Romano cheese. Serves 4

CALORIES 53; FAT 3.1g (sat 0.8g); SODIUM 118mg

Snap Pea and Radish Sauté

Kid Friendly • Quick & Easy Vegetarian

Hands-on: 15 min. Total: 15 min. Cutting half of the peas in half gives the dish a lovely look, but you can skip that step and leave them all whole, if you like.

1. Bring 6 cups water to a boil in a large saucepan. Add 12 ounces trimmed sugar snap peas; cook 30 seconds or until crisp-tender. Drain and rinse with cold water; drain. Cut half of peas in half diagonally.
2. Heat 1 tablespoon butter in a large saucepan over medium-high heat; swirl until butter melts. Stir in 1 teaspoon fresh lemon juice. Add peas and ½ cup thinly sliced radishes; toss to coat. Sprinkle with 1 tablespoon chopped fresh chives, ¼ teaspoon freshly ground black pepper, and ⅛ teaspoon salt. Serves 4 (serving size: about ⅔ cup)

CALORIES 65; FAT 3.1g (sat 1.9g); SODIUM 108mg

Soba Noodle Salad

Make Ahead • Quick & Easy Vegetarian

Hands-on: 10 min. Total: 19 min. Look for soba noodles on the Asian food aisle. If you can't find them, you can sub whole-wheat spaghetti (which takes about 10 minutes longer to cook).

1. Cook 4 ounces uncooked soba (buckwheat noodles) according to package directions, omitting salt and fat; drain and rinse with cold water. Drain well.
2. Combine 1½ tablespoons lower-sodium soy sauce, 1 tablespoon dark sesame oil, 1 teaspoon brown sugar, 1½ teaspoons fresh lemon juice, and ¼ teaspoon crushed red pepper in a medium bowl, stirring well with a whisk. Add noodles, ½ cup (2-inch-long) julienne-cut red bell pepper, ½ cup julienne-cut snow peas, and ¼ cup thinly sliced green onions; toss well. Serves 4 (serving size: ¾ cup)

CALORIES 150; FAT 4.1g (sat 0.5g); SODIUM 221mg

Goat Cheese Crostini

Hands-on: 2 min. Total: 6 min. *Amazing how a little garlicky goat cheese turns toast into something much more special.*

1. Combine 1 tablespoon minced fresh flat-leaf parsley, 2 ounces softened goat cheese, and 1 minced garlic clove, stirring well. Spread evenly over 8 (½-inch-thick) slices toasted French bread baguette. Serves 4 (serving size: 2 slices)

CALORIES 120; **FAT** 3.5g (sat 2.2g); **SODIUM** 198mg

Kid Friendly • Make Ahead
Quick & Easy • Vegetarian

Herbed Corn Muffins

(pictured on page 216)

Hands-on: 12 min. Total: 25 min. *These muffins are tender, moist, and light, with a lovely herbal fragrance from parsley and thyme.*

1. Preheat oven to 400°.
2. Combine 1¼ cups low-fat buttermilk, ¼ cup olive oil, and 1 large egg; stir well with a whisk.
3. Weigh or lightly spoon 4.5 ounces all-purpose flour (about 1 cup) into a dry measuring cup; level with a knife. Combine flour, ¾ cup yellow cornmeal, 1½ teaspoons sugar, 1½ teaspoons baking powder, ½ teaspoon baking soda, ¼ teaspoon salt, ¼ teaspoon freshly ground black pepper, and 2 ounces grated pecorino Romano cheese (about ½ cup) in a medium bowl, stirring well with a whisk. Make a well in center of flour mixture. Add milk mixture, and stir just until moist. Gently stir in ¼ cup thinly sliced green onions, 1 tablespoon minced fresh flat-leaf parsley, and 1 tablespoon minced fresh thyme. Spoon into 12 muffin cups coated with cooking spray. Bake at 400° for 13 minutes or until a wooden pick inserted in center comes out with moist crumbs clinging. Serves 12 (serving size: 1 muffin)

CALORIES 141; **FAT** 5.9g (sat 1.2g); **SODIUM** 226mg

Kid Friendly • Quick & Easy

Quinoa with Toasted Pine Nuts

Hands-on: 15 min. Total: 25 min.

1. Rinse and drain 1 cup uncooked quinoa. Heat a large saucepan over medium-high heat. Add 2 teaspoons extra-virgin olive oil to pan; swirl to coat. Add 2 tablespoons finely chopped shallots; sauté 1 minute or until tender. Add 1 tablespoon minced garlic; cook 1 minute, stirring constantly. Add quinoa; cook 2 minutes, stirring frequently. Add 1¼ cups unsalted chicken stock (such as Swanson) and ¼ teaspoon kosher salt; bring to a boil. Cover, reduce heat, and simmer 13 minutes or until liquid is absorbed and quinoa is tender.
2. While quinoa cooks, heat a large nonstick skillet over medium heat. Add ¼ cup pine nuts to pan; cook 3 minutes or until browned, stirring frequently. Combine quinoa mixture, pine nuts, 1 tablespoon extra-virgin olive oil, ¼ cup chopped fresh parsley, 2 tablespoons chopped fresh chives, and ¼ teaspoon freshly ground black pepper; toss. Serves 6 (serving size: about ½ cup)

CALORIES 187; **FAT** 9.4g (sat 1g); **SODIUM** 111mg

QUINOA IS HOT RIGHT NOW: A FEW PINE NUTS MAKE IT FANTASTIC.

Kid Friendly • Quick & Easy
Vegetarian

Quick Chive Mashed Potatoes

Hands-on: 6 min. Total: 6 min. *Frozen mashed potatoes are a near-instant option, with a better flavor and texture than boxed potato flakes.*

1. Heat 2 cups frozen mashed potatoes (such as Ore Ida Steam 'n' Mash) according to microwave instructions. Stir in 2 tablespoons chopped fresh chives, 2 tablespoons crème fraîche or sour cream, 2 tablespoons fat-free milk, 1 tablespoon butter, and ⅛ teaspoon freshly ground black pepper. Serves 4 (serving size: about ½ cup)

CALORIES 108; **FAT** 5.5g (sat 3.4g); **SODIUM** 204mg

Kid Friendly • Quick & Easy
Vegetarian

Rosemary-Garlic Roasted Potatoes

(pictured on page 217)

Hands-on: 10 min. Total: 36 min.

1. Preheat oven to 450°.
2. Remove white papery skin from 1 garlic head; separate but do not peel cloves. Place garlic, 2 tablespoons extra-virgin olive oil, 20 ounces whole baby potatoes, 3 thyme sprigs, and 3 rosemary sprigs in a large bowl; toss to coat. Arrange potato mixture on a foil-lined jelly-roll pan. Sprinkle evenly with ¼ teaspoon kosher salt and ¼ teaspoon freshly ground black pepper. Bake at 450° for 25 minutes, stirring after 13 minutes. Sprinkle with ⅛ teaspoon kosher salt and 2 tablespoons chopped fresh flat-leaf parsley. Serves 4 (serving size: ⅔ cup)

CALORIES 173; **FAT** 7g (sat 1g); **SODIUM** 208mg

Smoky Haricots Verts and Mushrooms

Kid Friendly • Quick & Easy

(pictured on page 217)

Hands-on: 6 min. Total: 22 min. *Haricots verts are slender green beans; look for them trimmed and ready to cook in microwave-safe bags. If you can't find them, use regular green beans and cook a few minutes longer.*

1. Place a small roasting pan in oven. Preheat oven to 425° (keep pan in the oven as it preheats).
2. While oven preheats, cook 1 applewood-smoked bacon slice in a small skillet over medium heat until crisp. Remove bacon from pan, and crumble. Reserve drippings.
3. Drizzle bacon drippings and 2 teaspoons canola oil into preheated roasting pan; swirl to coat. Add 2 (4-ounce) packages gourmet mushroom blend to pan; stir. Bake mushrooms at 425° for 8 minutes. Add 12 ounces trimmed haricots verts (French green beans), and sprinkle with ¼ teaspoon kosher salt and ⅛ teaspoon freshly ground black pepper; toss. Bake at 425° for 8 minutes or until beans are lightly browned and crisp-tender. Toss with reserved bacon, 2 tablespoons coarsely chopped fresh flat-leaf parsley, and 1 minced garlic clove. Serves 4 (serving size: 1 cup)

CALORIES 75; FAT 3.9g (sat 0.7g); SODIUM 184mg

BACON AND MUSHROOMS BUILD A SAVORY, EARTHY BASE FOR GREEN BEANS.

QUICK DESSERTS

Homemade sweets on a busy weeknight? Yes, with our fast recipes that complement any meal.

Kid Friendly • Quick & Easy
Make Ahead

Granola Cookie Wedges

Hands-on: 13 min. Total: 26 min. *Instead of taking the time to scoop individual cookies, bake a superfast cookie "pie," and then cut it into wedges.*

⅓ cup packed dark brown sugar
2 tablespoons canola oil
1 tablespoon butter, melted
½ teaspoon vanilla extract
¼ teaspoon salt
¼ teaspoon baking soda
1 large egg white
2.25 ounces all-purpose flour (about ½ cup)
½ cup quick-cooking oats
¼ cup chopped pecans, toasted
2 tablespoons semisweet chocolate chips
Cooking spray

1. Preheat oven to 350°.
2. Combine first 7 ingredients in a large bowl; stir until well combined. Weigh or lightly spoon flour into a dry measuring cup; level with a knife. Add flour, oats, nuts, and chocolate chips to sugar mixture; stir until just combined.
3. Scrape dough into a 9-inch glass pie plate coated with cooking spray, and spread to edges using a spatula. Bake at 350° for 13 minutes or until set. Cool slightly on a wire rack. Cut into 8 wedges. Serves 8 (serving size: 1 wedge)

CALORIES 168; FAT 8.6g (sat 1.9g, mono 4.3g, poly 1.8g); PROTEIN 2.5g; CARB 20.9g; FIBER 1.3g; CHOL 4mg; IRON 1mg; SODIUM 136mg; CALC 17mg

Quick & Easy

Dark Cherry Merlot Sauce over Yogurt

Hands-on: 10 min. Total: 20 min. *We love the flavor of a tangy fro-yo with this sweet sauce, but ice cream is also nice.*

2 cups unsweetened frozen pitted dark sweet cherries, thawed
1 cup merlot
2 tablespoons brown sugar
1 teaspoon fresh lemon juice
⅛ teaspoon salt
2 cups vanilla fat-free frozen yogurt

1. Combine cherries, merlot, brown sugar, lemon juice, and salt in a saucepan; bring to a boil. Lightly crush about half of cherries with a potato masher. Reduce heat, and cook until reduced to about 1 cup. Let stand 5 minutes. Spoon warm cherry sauce over yogurt. Serves 4 (serving size: ½ cup yogurt and about ¼ cup sauce)

CALORIES 211; FAT 0g; PROTEIN 4.7g; CARB 39.9g; FIBER 2g; CHOL 10mg; IRON 0.2mg; SODIUM 137mg; CALC 121mg

FAST DESSERTS WITH A TOUCH OF SOPHISTICATION

Quick & Easy

Sparkling Raspberry Parfaits

(pictured on page 215)

Hands-on: 5 min. Total: 5 min. *Raspberry sparkling wine has a pretty pink color and lightly sweet flavor; you can use regular sparkling wine for a less sweet dessert. Or you can skip the alcohol and use raspberry-flavored seltzer water instead.*

2 cups raspberry sorbet
1 cup chilled raspberry sparkling wine (such as Verdi Raspberry Sparkletini) or unflavored sparkling wine
2 tablespoons shaved bittersweet chocolate

1. Scoop ½ cup sorbet into each of 4 wineglasses or small bowls, and drizzle each serving with ¼ cup wine. Top each serving with 1½ teaspoons chocolate. Serve immediately. Serves 4 (serving size: 1 parfait)

CALORIES 180; FAT 1.5g (sat 0.8g, mono 0g, poly 0g); PROTEIN 0.3g; CARB 32.8g; FIBER 2.3g; CHOL 0mg; IRON 0.1mg; SODIUM 0mg; CALC 0mg

Quick & Easy

Balsamic Strawberries over Angel Food Cake

Hands-on: 10 min. Total: 25 min. *Use good aged vinegar for the best flavor.*

¼ cup packed brown sugar
2 tablespoons balsamic vinegar
2 cups halved strawberries
4 (2-inch-thick) slices angel food cake

1. Combine sugar and vinegar in a large bowl; stir until sugar dissolves. Add berries; toss gently to coat. Let stand at room temperature 15 minutes, stirring occasionally. Spoon berries and

sauce over cake slices. Serves 4 (serving size: 1 cake slice and ⅓ cup berry mixture)

CALORIES 157; FAT 0.5g (sat 0.1g, mono 0.1g, poly 0.2g); PROTEIN 2.2g; CARB 37.6g; FIBER 1.9g; CHOL 0mg; IRON 0.6mg; SODIUM 214mg; CALC 63mg

Quick & Easy

Wine-Poached Pears with Raspberries

Hands-on: 12 min. Total: 25 min.

1 cup sweet white wine (such as gewürztraminer)
½ cup water
2 tablespoons sugar
1 tablespoon fresh lemon juice
⅛ teaspoon salt
2 black peppercorns
1 (3-inch) cinnamon stick
4 Bosc pears, peeled, halved lengthwise, and cored
1 cup fresh raspberries

1. Combine first 7 ingredients in a large saucepan, stirring with a whisk. Add pears; cover and bring to a boil. Reduce heat, and simmer 9 minutes or until pears are tender. Remove pears with a slotted spoon. Increase heat to high; bring to a boil. Cook until reduced to ¾ cup (about 5 minutes). Discard cinnamon and peppercorns. **2.** Place 2 pear halves in each of 4 bowls; drizzle with about 3 tablespoons cooking liquid. Top each serving with ¼ cup raspberries. Serves 4

CALORIES 168; FAT 0.4g (sat 0g, mono 0.1g, poly 0.2g); PROTEIN 1.1g; CARB 38.9g; FIBER 3.5g; CHOL 0mg; IRON 0.5mg; SODIUM 76mg; CALC 24mg

SUPERFAST 20-MINUTE COOKING

Bright, fresh dishes for a delicious spring: plump seafood with seasonal vegetables, kid-pleasing barbecue meatballs, and more.

Quick & Easy

Mussels with Peas and Mint

Farmed mussels are a sustainable choice. If you can't find fresh peas, use frozen.

1 tablespoon unsalted butter
1 cup thinly sliced leek (about 1 large)
1 tablespoon thyme leaves
1 tablespoon chopped fresh tarragon
¾ cup organic vegetable broth
¼ cup heavy cream
1 cup fresh shelled green peas
48 mussels (about 2 pounds), scrubbed and debearded
2 tablespoons chopped fresh mint
¼ teaspoon freshly ground black pepper

1. Melt butter in a large saucepan over medium heat. Add leek, thyme, and tarragon to pan; cook 4 minutes or until leek is tender, stirring frequently. Add broth and cream; bring to a simmer. Add peas and mussels; stir well. Reduce heat to medium-low; cover and cook 7 minutes or until mussels open. Remove from heat; discard any unopened shells. Sprinkle evenly with mint and pepper. Serves 4 (serving size: about 12 mussels and about ⅓ cup broth)

CALORIES 228; FAT 11.4g (sat 5.8g, mono 3g, poly 1.2g); PROTEIN 17g; CARB 14.2g; FIBER 2.4g; CHOL 62mg; IRON 5.9mg; SODIUM 459mg; CALC 71mg

Black Pepper Caramel Shrimp

For a milder dish, use only 1 teaspoon black pepper.

1 (3½-ounce) bag boil-in-bag
   brown rice
1 tablespoon water
2 teaspoons cornstarch
1½ tablespoons dark sesame oil
1 pound large shrimp, peeled and
   deveined
2 cups diagonally cut snow peas
2 teaspoons minced fresh garlic
2 teaspoons freshly ground black
   pepper
⅛ teaspoon salt
½ cup fat-free, lower-sodium chicken
   broth
3 tablespoons brown sugar
2 teaspoons fish sauce

1. Cook rice according to package directions, omitting salt and fat. Keep warm.
2. Combine 1 tablespoon water and cornstarch in a small bowl, stirring with a whisk; set aside. Heat a large skillet over medium-high heat. Add oil to pan; swirl to coat. Add shrimp; sauté 2 minutes or until shrimp begin to turn pink. Add peas, garlic, pepper, and salt; cook 1 minute. Remove from heat.
3. Combine broth, sugar, and fish sauce in a small saucepan over high heat. Bring to a boil; stir in cornstarch mixture. Cook 30 seconds or until mixture thickens, stirring constantly. Pour sugar mixture over shrimp. Return shrimp mixture to medium-high heat; cook 2 minutes or until thoroughly heated. Serve over cooked rice. Serves 4 (serving size: 1 cup shrimp mixture and ½ cup rice)
Buy Pacific white shrimp farmed in fully recirculating systems or inland ponds.

CALORIES 280; FAT 7.1g (sat 0.9g, mono 2.4g, poly 2.5g); PROTEIN 19g; CARB 35.2g; FIBER 2.2g; CHOL 143mg; IRON 1.5mg; SODIUM 554mg; CALC 92mg

Barbecue Turkey Meatballs

Serve with simple mashed potatoes on the side to catch the sauce.

2 tablespoons dark brown sugar
2½ tablespoons apple cider vinegar
1 teaspoon ground cumin
¼ teaspoon smoked paprika
⅛ teaspoon ground cloves
1 (14.5-ounce) can diced tomatoes
   with mild green chiles (such as
   Del Monte)
1¼ pounds ground turkey
3 tablespoons Italian-seasoned dried
   breadcrumbs
1 tablespoon chili powder
Cooking spray

1. Place first 6 ingredients in a blender; blend until smooth.
2. Combine turkey, breadcrumbs, and chili powder in a large bowl; using wet hands, shape into 16 meatballs.
3. Heat a large skillet over medium-high heat. Lightly coat pan with cooking spray. Add meatballs; cook 2 minutes, turning to brown on all sides. Add tomato mixture to pan; bring to a simmer. Cover, reduce heat, and simmer 6 minutes or until meatballs are done. Serves 4 (serving size: 4 meatballs and ⅓ cup sauce)

CALORIES 279; FAT 11.4g (sat 3g, mono 3.7g, poly 3.1g); PROTEIN 29.5g; CARB 14.2g; FIBER 2g; CHOL 98mg; IRON 2.4mg; SODIUM 540mg; CALC 61mg

Maple-Pecan Sundaes with Cinnamon Crisps

Vary the nuts to your kids' preferences—walnuts or almonds would be equally tasty.

2 (8-inch) flour tortillas
2 teaspoons butter, melted
2 tablespoons sugar
1 teaspoon ground cinnamon
2 cups vanilla fat-free frozen Greek
   yogurt
2 tablespoons maple syrup
8 teaspoons chopped pecans, toasted
4 mint sprigs (optional)

1. Preheat oven to 400°.
2. Brush both sides of tortillas with butter. Combine sugar and cinnamon in a bowl; sprinkle evenly on both sides of tortillas. Cut each tortilla into 8 wedges. Place tortilla wedges on a large baking sheet. Bake at 400° for 8 minutes or until crisp.
3. Combine yogurt and syrup in a bowl. Spoon ½ cup yogurt mixture into each of 4 bowls; top each with 2 teaspoons pecans. Serve each with 4 crisps. Garnish with mint, if desired. Serves 4

CALORIES 303; FAT 6.7g (sat 1.5g, mono 2.4g, poly 1.1g); PROTEIN 11.5g; CARB 49.7g; FIBER 0.8g; CHOL 10mg; IRON 0.2mg; SODIUM 203mg; CALC 21mg

A BIG BURST OF RADISHES

After a year of happy planting, weeding, and harvesting, we're thrilled to present the first crop from the *Cooking Light* Garden: radishes. And not the plain old variety: These are spring's first treats.

I n the chilly early months of 2012, we decided to get serious about going totally fresh and very local—and start a garden. We wanted to plant a lot of varieties, reflecting the explosion of interest across the country in rare and heirloom vegetables. We sought out Mary Beth and David Shaddix, who have a picture-perfect kitchen garden and nursery, complete with hound and chickens, about 30 minutes from our Birmingham, Alabama, offices. On their counsel— they know what grows best through hot and humid summers, long springs, and occasional frosts—we selected a year's worth of seeds. By early spring, the first thrilling harvest arrived in our Test Kitchen for recipe development. Each month, you'll see the fruits (and vegetables) of our garden project labors. First up: peppery, beautiful, easy-to-grow radishes.

Quick & Easy • Vegetarian

Radish and Arugula Crostini with Brie

Hands-on: 10 min. Total: 10 min. The cheese will spread easily and taste better at room temperature.

16 (1/2-inch-thick) slices diagonally cut French bread baguette (6 ounces)
Cooking spray
1 1/2 cups sliced radishes
1 tablespoon extra-virgin olive oil
1 tablespoon fresh lemon juice
1/4 teaspoon freshly ground black pepper
1/8 teaspoon salt
4 ounces Brie cheese (about 1/2 cup)
2 cups baby arugula leaves

1. Preheat oven to 400°.
2. Arrange bread slices on a baking sheet; coat with cooking spray. Bake at 400° for 5 minutes or until golden brown and toasted; cool.
3. Combine radishes and next 4 ingredients in a medium bowl, and toss to coat.
4. Spread each bread slice with about 2 teaspoons cheese; top with a single layer of arugula and a layer of radish slices. Serves 16 (serving size: 1 crostini)

CALORIES 87; FAT 4.1g (sat 1.9g, mono 1.7g, poly 0.3g); PROTEIN 3.8g; CARB 8.8g; FIBER 0.6g; CHOL 9mg; IRON 0.7mg; SODIUM 163mg; CALC 33mg

Quick & Easy • Vegetarian

Radish Salad with Goat Cheese

Hands-on: 10 min. Total: 10 min. To crumble the goat cheese, freeze for 10 minutes, and then flake with a fork.

4 teaspoons white wine vinegar
1 tablespoon extra-virgin olive oil
1 teaspoon honey
1/4 teaspoon salt
2 cups radishes, cut lengthwise into 1/4-inch wedges, with root and 1/2-inch stem left on
1 tablespoon chopped fresh oregano
4 cups fresh baby spinach
2 ounces goat cheese, crumbled (about 1/2 cup)
1/2 teaspoon freshly ground black pepper

1. Combine first 4 ingredients in a bowl, stirring well. Add radishes and oregano; toss to coat. Place 1 cup spinach on each of 4 plates. Using a slotted spoon, top each plate with 1/2 cup radishes. Sprinkle each serving with 2 tablespoons cheese and 1/8 teaspoon pepper. Drizzle remaining dressing evenly over salads. Serves 4

CALORIES 96; FAT 6.6g (sat 2.6g, mono 3.4g, poly 0.4g); PROTEIN 3.7g; CARB 6.4g; FIBER 2.1g; CHOL 7mg; IRON 1.3mg; SODIUM 259mg; CALC 58mg

STORAGE TIPS

When you bring radishes home from the garden or market, chop off the greens— they'll pull moisture from the root. (The greens can be used raw or cooked.) After rinsing and scrubbing, store the roots in a produce bag in your crisper for up to a week. If they become spongy, crisp them up by placing them in a bowl of ice water for up to an hour.

Purple Plum
Deep purple outside, driven-snow white within. Almost juicy. These came along about two weeks after the Pink Beauties.

Pink Beauty
Perfectly round, mild, and sweet. Our earliest producer—from tiny sprout on March 9 to this golf ball–sized specimen on March 29!

White Hailstone
Looks like a turnip, bites like a radish. Uniformly white all the way through and ready at the same time as the Purple Plums. Even though they're colorless, these had the kickiest flavor.

Chinese Red Meat
Also known as watermelon radish for its white and green skin and rich, magenta interior. These took almost two months to mature (twice as long as other varieties) and prefer the coolness of fall. Early to bolt in spring. Mild flavor.

Seed Pods
Yep, you can eat a radish from root to tip. When our Chinese Red Meats should have been bulbing, warm weather caused them to form blooms, leading to crunchy seed pods. Eat them raw (they taste just like radishes), or toss in a stir-fry.

Quick & Easy • Vegetarian

Radishes in Browned Butter and Lemon

Hands-on: 19 min. Total: 19 min.

3 cups radishes, halved lengthwise, with root and 1-inch stem left on
1 tablespoon butter
1/2 teaspoon grated lemon rind
2 teaspoons fresh lemon juice
1/4 teaspoon salt
1 cup torn radish leaves
1/4 teaspoon freshly ground black pepper

1. Bring a medium pot of water to a boil. Add radishes to pan; cook 4 minutes or until crisp-tender. Drain.
2. Melt butter in a medium skillet over medium-high heat. Add radishes to pan; sauté 3 minutes or until butter is browned and fragrant. Add rind, juice, and salt; cook 1 minute, stirring occasionally. Remove pan from heat; stir in radish leaves and pepper. Serves 4 (serving size: ¾ cup)

CALORIES 42; FAT 3g (sat 1.9g, mono 0.8g, poly 0.2g); PROTEIN 0.8g; CARB 3.5g; FIBER 1.5g; CHOL 8mg; IRON 0.4mg; SODIUM 208mg; CALC 32mg

NUTRITION MADE EASY

NAVIGATING THE MILE-LONG YOGURT AISLE

Sales are way up, and shelves are sagging with choices (Greek-style almond-milk yogurt?). But some are packed with fat. Here, a tour.

Grocery decoder

Artisinal
Small producers favor **fewer preservatives, grass-fed milk.** Prices are higher. Fat runs from none to lots: "Natural" doesn't automatically mean low-fat. Some niche producers are playing up the rich, cream-on-top angle. Read your labels.

Nondairy
A hot category. **Soy, almond, and coconut milks** have less protein and require extra sugars to promote fermentation—as much as 16g. As with some dairy yogurts, plant-derived thickeners (starches, gums, etc.) are added to improve texture.

Greek
Big tang and thick texture kicked off the yogurt boom: **Strained milk,** with less water, has more protein and milk solids. Tangy doesn't mean extra-light, though. We say 11g sat fat in one (6-ounce) version.

Budget
Bigger containers only seem expensive. Unless there's a four-for-$5 deal on the small cups, you can get up to 32 ounces for the same price as three (6-ounce) containers. Bonus: They're usually plain with no added sugars—or calories.

Kefir
Kefir is a more liquid and naturally effervescent dairy product that uses yeast in addition to bacteria for fermentation. It's good for smoothies, and the extra probiotics—as many as 12 strains (versus the 2 required in yogurt)—aid in digestion.

What to look for

Protein: Keeps you full longer
Strained yogurts—like Greek and skyrs—require three to four times more milk to produce than regular, meaning 15g to 20g more protein per 6 ounces **(equivalent to 3 ounces of meat!).**

Healthy bacteria
The FDA requires **at least two strains of bacteria in all yogurt,** *L. bulgaricus* and *S. thermophilus.* Yogurt makers can add more. Look for the National Yogurt Association seal: It ensures 100 million cultures per gram (i.e., lots).

Low-fat, for a calcium boost
When fat is removed, calcium gets concentrated. Lower-fat yogurt contains more—**30% of your recommended daily intake.** Some calcium is lost in the straining process for Greek, but it's still a great source at 20%.

Limited added sugar

Six ounces of plain yogurt have about **12g of naturally occurring sugars** from the milk. Fruit and honey add more. Kid-centric yogurts come in cute 4-ounce containers, but some have more sugar (as much as 17g) than "adult" 6-ouncers.

More calories in the morning

If you're eating yogurt as breakfast, you'll need more oomph to keep you fueled until lunch—about 200 calories, but no more than 4g sat fat. Keep snacks less hefty—about half that.

RECIPE MAKEOVER

NOT-SO-DEVILISH EGGS

Quick pickled onions, creamy Greek yogurt, and fewer yolks make these stuffed eggs more heavenly.

Lord, they do like their deviled eggs down South: a luxe, creamy concoction of mayo, pickles, and mashed yolk piled into a perfect egg-white boat. And, of course, this snack is also favored on Easter and Passover tables, and then bound to pop up at any good backyard summer feast. Only problem: At 150 calories of yum a pop, they're an indulgence, and they tend to be served in large numbers. Our challenge was clear.

First, because this is our fast-recipe issue, we wanted a start-to-finish time of less than 40 minutes. Peeling hard-cooked eggs can be the peskiest task, especially if they're farm-fresh. Our quick trick: Steam them. The result is perfectly cooked eggs with shells that slide right off. For the filling, Greek-style yogurt and canola mayo make a lighter, but no less creamy, stand-in for heavy mayo. We discard two of the yolks to shave a bit of fat, and bump up flavor with quick-pickled red onions, ready-made in the microwave and healthier than sodium-packed relish. Zesty Dijon and a few splashes of Sriracha add a devilish kick. With 50% fewer calories than the original, you can eat more than one ...

Make Ahead • Quick & Easy
Vegetarian

Deviled Eggs with Pickled Onions

Hands-on: 20 min. Total: 35 min.

8 large eggs
¼ cup water
¼ cup cider vinegar
1 tablespoon sugar
¼ cup finely chopped red onion
2 tablespoons plain 2% reduced-fat Greek yogurt
2 tablespoons canola mayonnaise
2 teaspoons Dijon mustard
½ teaspoon Sriracha (hot chile sauce, such as Huy Fong) or hot pepper sauce (such as Tabasco)
¼ teaspoon freshly ground black pepper
⅛ teaspoon kosher salt
2 tablespoons finely chopped fresh chives

1. Add water to a large saucepan to a depth of 1 inch; set a large vegetable steamer in pan. Add eggs to steamer. Bring water to a boil over medium-high heat. Steam eggs, covered, 16 minutes. Remove from heat. Place eggs in a large ice water–filled bowl for 3 minutes.

2. While eggs steam, combine ¼ cup water, vinegar, and sugar in a medium microwave-safe bowl; microwave at HIGH 2 minutes or until boiling. Stir in onion. Let stand at room temperature 15 minutes. Drain.

3. Combine yogurt, mayonnaise, mustard, Sriracha, pepper, and salt in a medium bowl, stirring well to combine.

4. Peel eggs; discard shells. Slice eggs in half lengthwise. Add 6 yolks to yogurt mixture; reserve remaining yolks for another use. Mash with a fork until very smooth. Stir in 2 tablespoons red onion. Spoon mixture into egg white halves (about 1 tablespoon in each half). Garnish egg halves with remaining red onion and chives. Serves 8 (serving size: 2 egg halves)

CALORIES 76; FAT 4.8g (sat 1.2g, mono 2g, poly 1.1g); PROTEIN 6g; CARB 1.6g; FIBER 0.1g; CHOL 140mg; IRON 0.7mg; SODIUM 157mg; CALC 26mg

HOW TO MAKE A BAD EGG GOOD

FEWER EGG YOLKS
The yolk is the source of fat in eggs. It's not much, but it adds up when mixed with other fats, like mayo. We discard two, saving 14 calories and 1g fat per serving.

2% GREEK YOGURT
Equal parts yogurt and heart-healthy canola mayonnaise lighten the filling, saving 53 calories and 6g fat per serving over heavy mayonnaise.

QUICK HOMEMADE PICKLED ONIONS
These zesty onions, made easy in the microwave, replace traditional sweet pickle relish to save 40mg sodium per serving.

CLASSIC	MAKEOVER
150 calories per serving	76 calories per serving
12 grams total fat	4.8 grams total fat
372 miligrams sodium	157 miligrams sodium

TODAY'S LESSON: SEAFOOD CAKES

Fantastic cakes start with the freshest seafood you can find: This isn't a way to hide bland or watery crab or shrimp. In the best cakes, the sweet, clean flavor of the seafood shines. The binder plays a big role. Breadcrumbs and egg should bind the seafood lumps in a nice patty that holds its shape and crisps nicely. Too much binder yields those dry, dense cakes we've all encountered. Too little, and everything falls apart in the pan. Here we've nailed the filler-to-seafood ratio and perfected a shaping method. These cakes are so tasty, they don't even need sauce: A simple squeeze of lemon or lime does the trick.

Kid Friendly • Quick & Easy
Make Ahead

Classic Crab Cakes

Hands-on: 24 min. Total: 24 min.

²/₃ **cup panko (Japanese breadcrumbs), divided**
1 tablespoon minced fresh flat-leaf parsley
2 tablespoons finely chopped green onions
2 tablespoons canola mayonnaise
1 teaspoon fresh lemon juice
1 teaspoon Dijon mustard
¹/₂ teaspoon Old Bay seasoning
¹/₂ teaspoon Worcestershire sauce
¹/₈ teaspoon kosher salt
¹/₈ teaspoon ground red pepper
1 large egg, lightly beaten
8 ounces lump crabmeat, shell pieces removed
1 tablespoon olive oil
1 lemon, quartered

1. Combine ⅓ cup panko and next 10 ingredients in a large bowl, stirring well. Add crab; stir gently just until combined. Place ⅓ cup panko in a shallow dish. Using wet hands, shape crab mixture into 4 equal balls. Coat balls in panko. Gently flatten balls to form 4 (4-inch) patties.
2. Heat a large nonstick skillet over medium-high heat. Add oil to pan; swirl to coat. Add patties; cook 3 minutes on each side or until golden. Serve with lemon wedges. Serves 4 (serving size: 1 crab cake and 1 lemon wedge)

CALORIES 181; FAT 7.8g (sat 0.9g, mono 4.2g, poly 1.4g); **PROTEIN** 16.3g; **CARB** 8.8g; **FIBER** 1g; **CHOL** 107mg; **IRON** 0.9mg; **SODIUM** 482mg; **CALC** 70mg

Kid Friendly • Quick & Easy
Make Ahead
Variation: Salmon Cakes
Prepare Classic Crab Cakes recipe, substituting 8 ounces cooked, flaked salmon for the crab. Serves 4 (serving size: 1 salmon cake and 1 lemon wedge)

CALORIES 210; **FAT** 11g (sat 1.4g); **SODIUM** 307mg

3 STEPS

MIX GENTLY
Combine all ingredients except seafood. Then add seafood, and stir gently just until it's incorporated.

SHAPE THE CAKES
Wet hands with cold water and work quickly to keep the seafood mixture from sticking as you form the balls.

COAT FOR CRUNCH
Spread breading in a shallow dish, and roll each ball in the mixture; flatten balls into cakes. You can do this up to a day ahead.

Thai Shrimp Cakes

Quick & Easy • Make Ahead

Hands-on: 23 min. Total: 23 min.

²/₃ cup panko (Japanese breadcrumbs), divided
¼ cup minced unsweetened dried coconut, divided
2 tablespoons minced green onions
2 tablespoons finely chopped fresh cilantro
2 teaspoons fish sauce
2 teaspoons Sriracha (hot chile sauce)
1½ teaspoons grated peeled fresh ginger
1 teaspoon fresh lime juice
1 large egg, lightly beaten
1 garlic clove, minced
8 ounces peeled and deveined shrimp, chopped
1 tablespoon olive oil
1 lime, quartered

1. Combine ⅓ cup panko, 2 tablespoons coconut, and next 8 ingredients in a large bowl. Add shrimp; stir just until combined. Using wet hands, shape mixture into 4 equal balls. Combine panko and coconut in a shallow dish. Coat balls in panko mixture; press to form 4 (4-inch) patties.
2. Heat a large nonstick skillet over medium-high heat. Add oil; swirl to coat. Add patties; cook 4 minutes on each side or until desired degree of doneness. Serve with lime. Serves 4 (serving size: 1 shrimp cake and 1 lime wedge)

CALORIES 165; **FAT** 8.7g (sat 3.8g, mono 3.1g, poly 0.7g); **PROTEIN** 11.2g; **CARB** 10.3g; **FIBER** 1.3g; **CHOL** 118mg; **IRON** 0.6mg; **SODIUM** 374mg; **CALC** 44mg

---

EVERYDAY VEGETARIAN

MEATLESS MONDAYS

Quick & Easy • Vegetarian

Golden Beet Pasta with Basil-Almond Pesto

Hands-on: 29 min. Total: 29 min.
This bright, earthy springtime dish uses the entire beet—stems, leaves, and all.

8 ounces uncooked whole-wheat penne (tube-shaped pasta)
2 (8-ounce) golden beets with greens
2 tablespoons extra-virgin olive oil, divided
¾ cup water, divided
⅓ cup organic vegetable broth
½ teaspoon kosher salt
½ teaspoon freshly ground black pepper
2 cups loosely packed basil leaves
¼ cup dry-roasted unsalted almonds
3 garlic cloves, chopped
2 ounces fresh Parmigiano-Reggiano cheese, grated (about ½ cup)
1 tablespoon fresh lemon juice

1. Cook pasta according to package directions, omitting salt and fat. Drain.
2. Remove greens and stems from beets; rinse and drain. Coarsely chop greens and stems to measure 4 cups. Peel beets, cut in half vertically, and cut into ⅛-inch slices.
3. Heat a large skillet over medium-high heat. Add 1 tablespoon oil to pan; swirl to coat. Add beets; sauté 3 minutes. Add beet greens and stems, ½ cup water, broth, salt, and pepper; cover. Reduce heat to medium; simmer 8 minutes or until beets are tender.
4. Combine 1 tablespoon oil, basil, almonds, and garlic in a food processor; process until smooth. Add cheese and ¼ cup water; process until blended. Add pasta, pesto, and lemon juice to beet mixture; toss to combine. Serves 4 (serving size: 1½ cups)

CALORIES 419; **FAT** 16g (sat 3.1g, mono 8.6g, poly 2.1g); **PROTEIN** 15.7g; **CARB** 55.7g; **FIBER** 10g; **CHOL** 9mg; **IRON** 4.2mg; **SODIUM** 596mg; **CALC** 254mg

---

BUDGET COOKING

FEED 4 FOR LESS THAN $10

Kid Friendly • Quick & Easy

Quick BBQ Sandwiches with Slaw

$1.60/serving
$6.40 total

Hands-on: 30 min. Total: 30 min.
Serve these sandwiches with smoky grilled corn: Brush 4 ears shucked corn with olive oil, and then grill for 8 minutes. Sprinkle with 1 teaspoon smoked paprika. Serve with lime wedges.

½ cup unsalted ketchup
3 tablespoons cider vinegar
1 tablespoon lower-sodium soy sauce
2 teaspoons Dijon mustard
¾ teaspoon freshly ground black pepper
½ teaspoon onion powder
¼ teaspoon garlic powder
⅛ teaspoon ground ginger
1 (1-pound) pork tenderloin, trimmed and halved lengthwise
Cooking spray
4 (1½-ounce) hamburger buns
1½ cups shredded cabbage
½ cup shredded carrot
3 thinly sliced green onions
2 teaspoons sugar
½ teaspoon kosher salt

1. Preheat grill to high heat.
2. Combine first 8 ingredients in a bowl, stirring well with a whisk. Reserve ¼ cup ketchup mixture; set aside. Add pork to remaining ketchup mixture; turn to coat pork. Place pork on grill rack coated with cooking spray; cover and grill 5 minutes. Turn pork over; grill 6 minutes or until a thermometer inserted in thickest portion registers 150°. Remove pork from grill; let stand 5 minutes. Cut pork diagonally across the grain into thin slices.
3. Arrange buns, cut sides down, in a single layer on grill rack coated with cooking spray; grill 2 minutes or until golden brown and toasted.
4. While pork grills, combine cabbage and remaining ingredients in a medium bowl; toss. Let stand 10 minutes; drain. Place one bottom bun half on each of 4 plates; divide sliced pork evenly among buns. Top each serving with 1 tablespoon reserved sauce and about ½ cup slaw. Place top halves of buns on sandwiches. Serves 4 (serving size: 1 sandwich)

CALORIES 296; FAT 4.3g (sat 1.2g, mono 1.3g, poly 1.1g); PROTEIN 29g; CARB 34.7g; FIBER 2.4g; CHOL 74mg; IRON 3.1mg; SODIUM 695mg; CALC 105mg

PILE THE SLAW ON THE SANDWICH FOR A CRUNCHY CONTRAST TO THE TENDER PORK.

Quick & Easy

$1.97/serving
$7.88 total

Buffalo Chicken Salad

Hands-on: 40 min. Total: 40 min.

1¼ cups all-purpose flour
½ cup 2% reduced-fat milk
1 large egg, lightly beaten
1 pound skinless, boneless chicken breast, cut into 12 strips
³/₈ teaspoon kosher salt
2 tablespoons canola oil
¼ cup hot sauce
5 teaspoons butter, melted
6 cups torn romaine lettuce
¾ cup matchstick-cut carrot
½ cup thinly diagonally sliced celery
3 tablespoons low-fat buttermilk
2 tablespoons canola mayonnaise
½ ounce blue cheese, crumbled (about 2 tablespoons)

1. Place flour in a shallow dish. Combine milk and egg in a shallow dish, stirring well. Sprinkle chicken evenly with salt. Heat a large skillet over medium-high heat. Add oil to pan; swirl to coat. Dredge chicken in flour; dip in egg mixture. Dredge in flour again, shaking off excess. Add chicken to pan; sauté 3 minutes on each side or until done. Remove chicken from pan using a slotted spoon; drain on paper towels. Combine hot sauce and butter in a medium bowl, stirring with a whisk. Add chicken to hot sauce mixture, tossing to coat evenly. Cut chicken into slices.
2. Combine lettuce, carrot, and celery in a large bowl. Combine buttermilk and remaining ingredients, stirring well. Arrange about 1½ cups salad on each of 4 plates; divide chicken strips among salads. Drizzle dressing evenly over salads. Serves 4

CALORIES 438; FAT 22.7g (sat 6g, mono 10.1g, poly 4.5g); PROTEIN 26.8g; CARB 31g; FIBER 3.2g; CHOL 102mg; IRON 2.9mg; SODIUM 584mg; CALC 120mg

Quick & Easy • Vegetarian

$1.57/serving
$6.28 total

Fettuccine with Edamame, Mint, and Pecorino

Hands-on: 27 min. Total: 27 min.

8 ounces uncooked fettuccine
2 tablespoons extra-virgin olive oil
2 medium onions, halved vertically and thinly sliced
5 garlic cloves, thinly sliced
2 cups frozen shelled edamame (green soybeans)
1 cup frozen peas
1 tablespoon grated lemon rind
2 tablespoons fresh lemon juice
1 tablespoon unsalted butter
6 tablespoons grated fresh pecorino Romano cheese
3 tablespoons chopped fresh mint
¼ teaspoon salt
¼ teaspoon freshly ground black pepper

1. Cook pasta according to package directions, omitting salt and fat. Drain in a colander over a bowl, reserving ⅔ cup cooking liquid.
2. Heat a large nonstick skillet over medium-high heat. Add oil; swirl to coat. Add onion; cook 9 minutes or until lightly browned, stirring occasionally. Stir in garlic; cook 2 minutes or until garlic is lightly browned, stirring occasionally. Stir in edamame and peas; cook 2 minutes or until thoroughly heated. Add pasta, rind, juice, and butter; stir until butter melts. Remove pan from heat; stir in pecorino Romano cheese, mint, salt, and pepper. Stir in reserved ⅔ cup cooking liquid. Serve immediately. Serves 4 (serving size: 1¾ cups)

CALORIES 443; FAT 15.7g (sat 4.5g, mono 5.7g, poly 0.9g); PROTEIN 18g; CARB 59.3g; FIBER 7.5g; CHOL 15mg; IRON 3.9mg; SODIUM 329mg; CALC 151mg

COCONUT MILK

By Naomi Duguid

In my house, coconut milk most often goes into Thai curries. If you have some left over after making such a dish, transfer it to a glass jar, seal, and keep in the refrigerator for up to three days. I've found that it's a good substitute for yogurt or cream—great if you're cooking for someone who is lactose intolerant or vegan. It works beautifully in creamy soups such as the one here. I also add some to lean ground beef when making sliders (along with toasted ground cumin and coriander seeds). Similarly, my go-to skillet cake recipe calls for 1 cup yogurt, but I find that an equal volume of coconut milk plus a tablespoon or two of lime juice gives equally good results.

WE'VE USED LUXURIOUS FULL-FAT COCONUT MILK, WHICH YIELDS A DECADENT, SILKY SOUP.

Kid Friendly • Quick & Easy
Make Ahead • Vegetarian

Butternut Soup with Coconut Milk

(pictured on page 215)

Hands-on: 10 min. Total: 29 min. Serve this full-flavored soup as a first course, or as a smooth vegetable stew over rice with a side of cooked greens. You can use light coconut milk instead of full-fat, if you prefer, for a soup with less body (and only 1g saturated fat per serving).

1 tablespoon olive oil
½ cup thinly sliced shallots
1 tablespoon minced garlic
1 tablespoon minced peeled fresh ginger
2 cups water
½ cup canned coconut milk
1 teaspoon salt
¼ teaspoon ground red pepper
2 (12-ounce) packages fresh cubed butternut squash
1 tablespoon fresh lime juice
Ground red pepper (optional)
Cilantro leaves (optional)

1. Heat a large heavy saucepan over medium-high heat. Add oil to pan; swirl to coat. Add shallots; sauté 3 minutes or until softened, stirring occasionally. Add garlic and ginger; sauté 1 minute. Add 2 cups water, coconut milk, salt, red pepper, and squash; bring to a boil. Cover, reduce heat, and simmer 20 minutes or until squash is tender, stirring occasionally.
2. Place squash mixture in a blender. Remove center piece of blender lid (to allow steam to escape); secure blender lid on blender. Place a clean towel over opening in blender lid (to avoid splatters). Blend until smooth. Stir in juice. Garnish with additional pepper and cilantro leaves, if desired. Serves 8 (serving size: about ⅔ cup)

CALORIES 86; **FAT** 4.1g (sat 2.5g, mono 1.2g, poly 0.2g); **PROTEIN** 1.5g; **CARB** 12.7g; **FIBER** 2g; **CHOL** 0mg; **IRON** 0.8mg; **SODIUM** 304mg; **CALC** 47mg

8 GREAT BREADSTICKS

If you have leftover pizza or bread dough, put it to delicious use. Start with 4 ounces dough. Roll into an 8 x 4–inch rectangle, and proceed.

Parm & Pepper

Cook 2 teaspoons olive oil and 2 crushed garlic cloves in a skillet over low heat 5 minutes. Discard garlic. Brush oil over dough; sprinkle with ¼ cup grated Parmigiano-Reggiano cheese and ¼ teaspoon black pepper. Cut dough into 4 (4 x 2–inch) rectangles. Arrange on a baking sheet coated with cooking spray. Bake at 425° for 10 minutes. Serves 4 (serving size: 1 breadstick)

CALORIES 116; **FAT** 4.3g (sat 1.2g); **SODIUM** 198mg

Spicy-Sweet Five-Spice

Brush dough with 1 teaspoon melted butter. Combine ¼ teaspoon sugar, ⅛ teaspoon five-spice powder, a dash of kosher salt, and a dash of ground red pepper. Cut dough into 8 (8 x ½–inch) strips. Arrange dough on a baking sheet coated with cooking spray; bake at 425° for 10 minutes or until golden. Serves 4 (serving size: 2 breadsticks)

CALORIES 81; **FAT** 1.5g (sat 0.6g); **SODIUM** 160mg

Chocolate–Sea Salt

Cut dough into 8 (8 x ½–inch) strips. Arrange dough on a baking sheet coated with cooking spray. Bake at 425° for 8 minutes. Place 1 ounce chopped semisweet chocolate in a zip-top plastic bag; microwave at HIGH 1 minute. Snip a tiny hole in 1 corner of bag; drizzle chocolate over breadsticks. Sprinkle with ⅛ teaspoon fine sea salt; let stand until set. Serves 4 (serving size: 2 breadsticks)

CALORIES 105; **FAT** 2.6g (sat 1.3g); **SODIUM** 192mg

Honey-Almond

Cut dough into 8 (8 x ½–inch) strips. Arrange dough on a baking sheet lined with parchment paper. Bake at 425° for 8 minutes. Combine 1 tablespoon honey and 1 teaspoon melted butter; brush over hot breadsticks. Place ¼ cup toasted sliced almonds in a shallow dish, and roll breadsticks in almonds. Serves 4 (serving size: 2 breadsticks)

CALORIES 128; **FAT** 4.3g (sat 0.8g); **SODIUM** 130mg

Pesto

Cut dough into 4 (8 x 1–inch) strips; twist each strip. Arrange dough on a baking sheet coated with cooking spray. Bake at 425° for 11 minutes. Combine 1 tablespoon melted butter, 1½ tablespoons thinly sliced fresh basil, and 4 minced garlic cloves. Brush butter mixture over breadsticks. Serves 4 (serving size: 1 breadstick)

CALORIES 102; **FAT** 3.6g (sat 1.8g); **SODIUM** 147mg

Caraway

Brush dough with 1 lightly beaten egg; sprinkle with 1½ teaspoons caraway seeds and ⅛ teaspoon kosher salt. Cut dough into 4 (8 x 1–inch) strips; arrange strips on a baking sheet coated with cooking spray. Bake at 425° for 10 minutes or until golden. Serves 4 (serving size: 1 breadstick)

CALORIES 93; **FAT** 2g (sat 0.4g); **SODIUM** 199mg

Herbed

Sprinkle 1 tablespoon chopped fresh oregano and 1 tablespoon chopped fresh thyme over dough. Fold dough over twice; knead 4 times. Roll into an 8 x 4–inch rectangle. Cut into 4 (4 x 2–inch) rectangles; twist. Arrange on a baking sheet coated with cooking spray. Bake at 425° for 10 minutes. Brush with 1 teaspoon olive oil; sprinkle with ⅛ teaspoon each kosher salt and black pepper. Serves 4 (serving size: 1 breadstick)

CALORIES 84; **FAT** 1.8g (sat 0.2g); **SODIUM** 182mg

Orange-Honey

Combine 2 tablespoons honey, 1 teaspoon melted butter, and ½ teaspoon grated orange rind in a small bowl; brush honey mixture over dough. Starting at short end, roll up dough, jelly-roll fashion. Cut roll crosswise into 4 equal rounds. Arrange rounds on a baking sheet coated with cooking spray, and bake at 425° for 11 minutes. Serves 4 (serving size: 1 breadstick)

CALORIES 112; **FAT** 1.5g (sat 0.6g); **SODIUM** 130mg

WHAT TO COOK RIGHT NOW

A GORGEOUS SALAD

Jazz up basic fresh veggies with a shave and a lemony dressing. Shaving carrots and zucchini into thin ribbons with a simple peeler or, if you have one, a mandoline transforms ho-hum texture and turns the plate into a bright gift of color. Fresh mint adds fragrance, and the dressing ties it all together with a zing.

Quick & Easy • Vegetarian

Shaved Carrot and Zucchini Salad

Hands-on: 10 min. Total: 10 min. *Use a mandoline or Y-shaped vegetable peeler to make veggie shavings. This salad comes together in a flash.*

2 tablespoons extra-virgin olive oil
2 tablespoons fresh lemon juice
1 teaspoon Dijon mustard
¼ teaspoon sugar
2 cups thinly shaved carrot
2 cups thinly shaved zucchini
¼ cup thinly sliced red onion
¼ cup loosely packed fresh flat-leaf parsley
2 tablespoons torn mint leaves
¼ teaspoon kosher salt
¼ teaspoon freshly ground black pepper

1. Combine first 4 ingredients in a medium bowl, stirring well with a whisk. Add carrot, zucchini, and onion; toss. Sprinkle with herbs, salt, and pepper; toss. Serves 6 (serving size: ⅔ cup)

CALORIES 68; **FAT** 4.8g (sat 0.7g, mono 3.3g, poly 0.6g); **PROTEIN** 1g; **CARB** 6.2g; **FIBER** 1.6g; **CHOL** 0mg; **IRON** 0.5mg; **SODIUM** 131mg; **CALC** 25mg

OOPS!

YOUR PORK IS DRY AND GRAY

Here's how to heed the new safe-temperature rules.

(145 Degrees)

(160 Degrees)

The USDA rules about pork changed more than two years ago—the safe internal temperature dropped from 160° to 145°—which makes all the difference in getting juicy results from a lean, go-to cut like tenderloin. But fess up: It's taken a little psychological adjustment to serve pork that's gently pink. There's still a slight inclination to let it cook just a little longer, a hesitation that can shoot fast-cooking cuts past the right temperature before you know it.

Solution: Insert a thermometer into the thickest portion of the tenderloin after the minimum cook time recommended by the recipe. Even better, insert a remote-probe thermometer at the beginning of cooking. Watch for 140° to 145°, and then remove the pork from the oven. If it reaches the desired temperature in the oven, it will overcook as it rests. Check once more before cutting, and then carve.

MICROWAVE MAGIC

In most kitchens, the microwave is a reheater and a defroster. But there are ways to coax out delicious flavors and textures that you'd swear came from an old-fashioned, slow-cook oven.

We had a thousand-watt mission to demonstrate that cooks who use microwave ovens only to reheat coffee or to thaw and heat frozen foods are missing a fundamental point: The microwave can actually cook food. By "cook" we mean deliver crisp textures and complex flavors associated with the dry heat of the much slower regular oven. We wanted a quick, moist meat loaf, for example, or a genuinely creamy risotto that takes half the stovetop time and requires half the amount of stirring. Some of our early experiments wandered the zone between disappointment and disaster.

If there is a way to nuke whole chicken pieces to an appetizing color and consistency—neither pallid nor rubbery—we didn't find it. Microwave steak? Just … don't. But we did cook delectable fish in a gorgeous dish that pops with color and bursts with flavor. We produced a supremely juicy meat loaf. We even found ways to deliver big, surprising crunch: fat-free, supercrisp veggie chips for a great snack, and the simplest almond brittle—with a fabulous light texture—for a sweet ending to a meal.

Kid Friendly • Make Ahead

Almond Brittle

Hands-on: 15 min. Total: 45 min.
Substitute pecans, walnuts, peanuts, or pine nuts for almonds, if you prefer.

1 cup sugar
¹⁄₂ cup light-colored corn syrup
³⁄₄ cup coarsely chopped almonds, toasted
1 tablespoon butter
¹⁄₂ teaspoon vanilla extract
¹⁄₈ teaspoon salt
1 teaspoon baking soda

1. Line a jelly-roll pan with parchment paper. Combine sugar and syrup in a 2-quart glass bowl. Microwave at HIGH 3 minutes (sugar mixture will be clear and bubbly). Stir in almonds. Microwave at HIGH 3 minutes or until mixture is a light caramel color, stirring every minute. Stir in butter, vanilla, and salt. Microwave at HIGH 1½ minutes or until mixture is the color of peanut butter. Add baking soda, and stir until texture is foamy. Quickly pour mixture onto prepared pan. Spread to ¼-inch thickness. Let stand 30 minutes. Break brittle into pieces, and store in an airtight container for up to a week. Serves 13

CALORIES 142; FAT 4g (sat 0.8g, mono 2.2g, poly 0.8g); PROTEIN 1.3g; CARB 27.3g; FIBER 0.8g; CHOL 2mg; IRON 0.2mg; SODIUM 136mg; CALC 19mg

WHAT'S WITH ALL THOSE BUTTONS?

Microwave control pads aren't as confounding as the average TV remote, but they have lots of buttons whose purposes aren't immediately clear. If you don't know where the owner's manual is, here's a primer on some key features.

POWER: DO I REALLY NEED 10 POWER LEVELS?
In most cases, probably not. But it's worth knowing that power setting 10 cooks at 100% power, and settings 1 through 9 logically cook at 10% to 90% power. At lower power settings, the microwave pulses its energy source—the fantastically named magnetron—at varying rates. Manufacturers suggest lower settings for slow-cooking stews and larger cuts of meat.

DEFROST: WHAT DISTINGUISHES DEFROST FROM AUTO DEFROST?
Standard defrost, or time defrost, lets you choose how long to defrost a food. The setting usually defaults to about 30% power (which aids even thawing and keeps the exterior from cooking). The auto defrost option is recommended for frozen meats and fish. It allows you to specify how many pounds of a specific food you're defrosting, and then automatically adjusts the power and time. The defrost setting is designed just to defrost, not to heat up foods or cook them.

SENSOR: I'VE NEVER USED THE SENSOR. WHAT EXACTLY DOES IT SENSE?
Built-in sensors measure humidity emitted from food as a signal of doneness. How fast foods get to the steam point depends on their weight and water content. Most microwaves allow you to choose foods by type, like vegetables, potatoes (a vegetable, of course, but starchy), and chicken or fish. Depending on the model of microwave, the display readout may ask you to enter an estimate of how much your food weighs.

REHEAT: WHAT'S THE DIFFERENCE BETWEEN REHEAT AND PLAIN OLD HEAT?
The reheat button is an automatic setting that uses the microwave's sensors to determine when the food starts steaming. It also helps prevent overcooking, which can dry out food and lead to overdone edges.

Quick & Easy

Cod with Fennel and Orange

Hands-on: 4 min. Total: 11 min. This entrée cooks in 7 minutes, with very little cleanup. The bags we used (Ziploc) are dioxin-free and food-safe in the microwave.

2 (6-ounce) cod fillets
½ teaspoon kosher salt
1 cup thinly sliced fennel bulb
2 tablespoons dry white wine
1 teaspoon unsalted butter
¼ teaspoon crushed red pepper
4 thyme sprigs
4 orange rind strips
2 garlic cloves, thinly sliced
⅓ cup orange sections
2 teaspoons finely chopped fennel
  fronds
1 teaspoon extra-virgin olive oil

1. Sprinkle fish evenly with salt; place 1 fillet in each of 2 quart-sized microwavable zip-top plastic bags. Divide fennel and next 6 ingredients evenly between the 2 bags. Gently press out as much air as possible from bags; seal tightly.
2. Place bags on a microwave-safe plate. Microwave at POWER LEVEL 7 for 5 minutes or until desired degree of doneness. Cool 2 minutes. Remove fish and vegetable mixture from each bag onto each of 2 plates. Top fillets evenly with orange sections and fennel fronds; drizzle with oil. Serves 2 (serving size: 1 fish fillet and about ½ cup fennel mixture)

CALORIES 222; FAT 5.5g (sat 1.8g, mono 2.3g, poly 0.8g); PROTEIN 31.4g; CARB 8.4g; FIBER 2.3g; CHOL 78mg; IRON 1.2mg; SODIUM 596mg; CALC 71mg

A WORD ON WATTS

We developed our recipes using 1,100-watt ovens. If your microwave is 1,800 watts, it will cook the dishes nearly twice as fast. A 2,900-watt machine will cook them three times faster. If your microwave is 900 or 700 watts, these dishes will take about 20% or 50% more time, respectively. There's a handy website that does the math for you: foodserviceequipment.com/prolink-web/microwaveconversion.htm.
If you're unsure how many watts your microwave actually has—and the owner's manual is nowhere to be found—look inside the oven. There may be a sticker that lists the model's wattage (or kilowattage) output.

Kid Friendly • Quick & Easy

Asparagus and Lemon Risotto

Hands-on: 15 min. Total: 32 min. This risotto is not covered while it microwaves. Be sure you use at least a 2-quart bowl to allow plenty of room for the liquid to boil.

¾ cup chopped onion
2 tablespoons butter
1 tablespoon olive oil
2 garlic cloves, minced
1 cup uncooked Arborio rice or other
  medium-grain rice
3 cups unsalted chicken stock
⅓ cup dry white wine
1 pound asparagus, trimmed and cut
  into ½-inch pieces
½ teaspoon grated lemon rind
1½ tablespoons fresh lemon juice
½ teaspoon salt
¼ teaspoon freshly ground black pepper
1½ ounces shaved Parmigiano-
  Reggiano cheese (⅓ cup), divided

1. Combine first 4 ingredients in a 2-quart microwave-safe glass bowl. Microwave at HIGH 3 minutes. Stir in rice; microwave at HIGH 3 minutes. Stir in stock and wine; microwave at HIGH 16 minutes, stirring for 30 seconds every 4 minutes. Add

asparagus; microwave at HIGH 2 minutes. Stir in rind, juice, salt, pepper, and half of cheese. Top with remaining cheese. Serves 4 (serving size: 1 cup)

CALORIES 349; FAT 11.7g (sat 5.3g, mono 4.5g, poly 0.7g); PROTEIN 13.4g; CARB 47.6g; FIBER 4.9g; CHOL 21mg; IRON 3.1mg; SODIUM 550mg; CALC 130mg

Kid Friendly • Quick & Easy
Make Ahead • Vegetarian

Microwave Sweet Potato Chips

Hands-on: 5 min. Total: 15 min. You'll need a mandoline to slice the potato thin enough to crisp.

Cooking spray
1 (14-ounce) sweet potato, very thinly
  sliced, divided
1 teaspoon finely chopped fresh
  rosemary, divided
½ teaspoon salt, divided
¼ teaspoon freshly ground black
  pepper, divided

1. Cut a circle of parchment paper to fit a microwave-safe plate; coat parchment lightly with cooking spray. Arrange one-fourth of potato slices in a single layer on parchment. Sprinkle evenly with ¼ teaspoon rosemary, ⅛ teaspoon salt, and dash of pepper. Microwave at POWER LEVEL 9 for 4 minutes. Check for crispness. Continue to cook at 30-second intervals until done. Repeat procedure with remaining potato, rosemary, salt, and pepper. Serves 8 (serving size: ½ cup)

CALORIES 43; FAT 0.1g (sat 0g, mono 0.1g, poly 0g); PROTEIN 0.8g; CARB 10.1g; FIBER 1.5g; CHOL 0mg; IRON 0.3mg; SODIUM 175mg; CALC 15mg

Kid Friendly • Quick & Easy

Everyday Meat Loaf

Hands-on: 13 min. Total: 21 min. *The meat loaf cooks in the microwave for just 8 minutes, a fraction of the time it takes for traditionally baked meat loaf. Broiling the cheese on top of the cooked meat loaf lends the dish a pleasing, oven-baked look.*

⅓ cup reduced-sodium marinara sauce
⅓ cup panko (Japanese breadcrumbs)
2 tablespoons grated onion
1 teaspoon chopped fresh thyme
½ teaspoon kosher salt
½ teaspoon freshly ground black pepper
1 pound ground sirloin
1 large egg
Cooking spray
2 ounces part-skim mozzarella cheese, shredded (about ½ cup)

1. Combine first 8 ingredients in a large bowl; stir gently to combine. Spread beef mixture evenly in a 9½-inch microwave-safe loaf dish coated with cooking spray; do not pack beef mixture into dish. Loosely cover with a paper towel. Microwave at HIGH 8 minutes.
2. Preheat broiler.
3. Sprinkle meat loaf with cheese; broil 3 minutes or until browned. Serves 4

CALORIES 232; FAT 10.2g (sat 3.9g, mono 3.2g, poly 0.8g); PROTEIN 28.5g; CARB 7.2g; FIBER 0.9g; CHOL 114mg; IRON 2.1mg; SODIUM 492mg; CALC 114mg

TOTALLY TACOS!

A 10-recipe gallop deep into taco territory, including classic combos and some fun, new ideas for great, easy hand food.

Tacos rival burgers for sheer fun packaging. First there's the wrap. Corn and flour tortillas are very different characters: A fresh corn tortilla is full of heady masa aroma and a pleasantly springy texture, while the best flour tortillas are soft but chewy. Then come the fillings. Almost anything goes, including eggs, Mexican sausage, spicy shrimp, beer-braised chicken, crunchy pan-fried tofu, and even ice cream. It's all fun and healthy, and it's all right here.

Kid Friendly • Freezable

Chocolate Tacos with Ice Cream and Peanuts

(pictured on page 219)

Hands-on: 40 min. Total: 1 hr. 10 min. *When shaping the shells, balance the wooden spoons between objects that are about 6 inches apart. Allow plenty of room so you can work quickly.*

½ cup powdered sugar
1.1 ounces all-purpose flour (about ¼ cup)
3 tablespoons unsweetened cocoa
1 teaspoon cornstarch
¼ teaspoon salt
3 tablespoons egg whites
1 teaspoon 2% reduced-fat milk
¼ teaspoon vanilla extract
Cooking spray
½ cup semisweet chocolate chips
1 teaspoon canola oil
½ cup finely chopped unsalted, dry-roasted peanuts, divided
2⅔ cups vanilla low-fat ice cream

1. Preheat oven to 400°.
2. Combine first 5 ingredients, stirring well. Stir in egg whites, milk, and vanilla.
3. Coat a baking sheet with cooking spray. Using your finger, draw 4 (5-inch) circles on baking sheet. Spoon 1 tablespoon batter onto each circle, spreading to edges of circle using the back of a spoon. Bake at 400° for 6 minutes or until edges begin to brown. Loosen edges with a spatula; remove from baking sheet. Working quickly, gently drape each taco over suspended wooden spoons, gently shaping into a shell; cool completely. (Shells are delicate and should be handled carefully when shaped.) Repeat procedure to form a total of 8 shells.
4. Combine chocolate chips and oil in a microwave-safe bowl. Microwave at HIGH 1 minute or until chocolate melts, stirring after 30 seconds; stir until smooth. Gently spread about 1 teaspoon chocolate mixture on the top third of the outside of both sides of cooled shells, and sprinkle with about 1 teaspoon chopped peanuts. Spoon ⅓ cup ice cream into each shell. Drizzle remaining chocolate mixture evenly over ice cream; sprinkle evenly with remaining peanuts. Freeze for at least 30 minutes before serving. Serves 8 (serving size: 1 taco)

CALORIES 233; FAT 11.8g (sat 4g, mono 2.6g, poly 1.6g); PROTEIN 6.5g; CARB 32.8g; FIBER 4.5g; CHOL 3mg; IRON 0.9mg; SODIUM 121mg; CALC 73mg

BREAKFAST, LUNCH, OR DINNER—THERE'S EVEN A RIFF ON THE FAST-FOOD DOUBLE TACO. OUR VERSION OFFERS A BIGGER PORTION WITH FEWER CALORIES AND LESS FAT.

Quick & Easy
Potato, Poblano, and Chorizo Tacos

Hands-on: 30 min. Total: 30 min.
Mexican chorizo is a raw pork sausage flavored with cumin and garlic. If you can't find it, you can substitute regular American breakfast sausage.

2 poblano chiles
1 tablespoon canola oil
2 cups diced white potato
1 cup chopped onion
1 cup fresh corn kernels
1/8 teaspoon ground red pepper
5 garlic cloves, minced
3 ounces Mexican raw chorizo, casings removed
3/4 cup unsalted chicken stock
3/8 teaspoon kosher salt
8 (6-inch) corn tortillas
1/4 cup sliced green onions
1 ounce Manchego cheese, shredded (about 1/4 cup)
8 lime wedges

1. Preheat broiler to high.
2. Cut poblanos in half lengthwise; discard seeds and membranes. Place poblano halves, skin sides up, on a foil-lined baking sheet; flatten with hand. Broil 8 minutes or until blackened. Place in a paper bag; fold to close tightly. Let stand 5 minutes. Peel; coarsely chop.
3. Heat a large nonstick skillet over medium-high heat. Add oil to pan; swirl to coat. Add potato; cook 5 minutes, stirring occasionally. Remove potato; place in a large bowl. Add onion to pan; cook 3 minutes. Add poblano, corn, red pepper, and garlic; cook 2 minutes, stirring frequently. Add onion mixture to potato. Add chorizo to pan; cook 1½ minutes, stirring to crumble. Return potato mixture to pan. Stir in stock and salt; bring to a boil. Partially cover, reduce heat, and simmer 6 minutes or until potato is tender, chorizo is done, and liquid almost evaporates.
4. Working with 1 tortilla at a time, heat tortillas over medium-high heat directly on the eye of a burner for about 15 seconds on each side or until lightly charred. Arrange about 1/3 cup potato mixture in center of each tortilla; top with 1½ teaspoons onions and 1½ teaspoons cheese. Serve with lime wedges. Serves 4 (serving size: 2 tacos and 2 lime wedges)

CALORIES 348; FAT 14.9g (sat 5.8g, mono 6.5g, poly 2.6g); PROTEIN 11.4g; CARB 46.6g; FIBER 6.1g; CHOL 38mg; IRON 1mg; SODIUM 447mg; CALC 146mg

TILAPIA IS A GREAT FISH FOR A TACO WHEN YOU ADD THE TANG OF TOMATILLO AND THE HEAT OF JALAPEÑO.

Quick & Easy
Fish Tacos with Tomatillo Sauce

Hands-on: 26 min. Total: 26 min. *Tilapia is a sustainable freshwater fish that's widely available and offers mild flavor. You can use a more assertively flavored fish, such as mackerel, if you prefer.*

3 garlic cloves
2 medium tomatillos, husked and rinsed
1/2 medium jalapeño pepper
1/2 cup cilantro stems
3 tablespoons canola mayonnaise (such as Hellmann's)
1/2 teaspoon sugar
3/8 teaspoon salt, divided
2 cups very thinly sliced red cabbage
1 tablespoon fresh lime juice
1 tablespoon extra-virgin olive oil
4 (6-ounce) tilapia fillets
1/4 teaspoon freshly ground black pepper
Cooking spray
8 (6-inch) corn tortillas
1/4 cup cilantro leaves

1. Preheat broiler to high.
2. Arrange garlic, tomatillos, and jalapeño in a single layer on a foil-lined jelly-roll pan. Broil 3 minutes on each side or until blackened. Place tomatillo mixture, cilantro stems, mayonnaise, sugar, and 1/8 teaspoon salt in a mini food processor or blender; blend until smooth.
3. Combine cabbage, juice, and oil in a medium bowl; toss to coat.
4. Heat a large skillet over medium-high heat. Sprinkle fish evenly with 1/4 teaspoon salt and black pepper. Coat pan with cooking spray. Add fish to pan; cook 2 minutes. Turn fish over; cook 1 minute.
5. Working with 1 tortilla at a time, heat tortillas over medium-high heat directly on the eye of a burner for about 15 seconds on each side or until lightly charred. Arrange half of a tilapia fillet in center of each tortilla;

top each with ¼ cup cabbage mixture, about 1½ tablespoons tomatillo mixture, and about 1½ teaspoons cilantro leaves. Serves 4 (serving size: 2 tacos)

CALORIES 291; FAT 10.3g (sat 1.3g, mono 5g, poly 2.6g); PROTEIN 28.5g; CARB 23.4g; FIBER 3.2g; CHOL 64mg; IRON 1.2mg; SODIUM 375mg; CALC 55mg

Kid Friendly • Quick & Easy
Steak Tacos with Lime Mayo

Hands-on: 31 min. Total: 31 min. Look for bagged baby peppers at most supermarkets—no need to peel the skins after roasting. Use fresh salsa found in the produce section or your favorite jarred salsa.

20 baby sweet peppers
Cooking spray
1 teaspoon ground chipotle chile pepper
1 teaspoon paprika
½ teaspoon kosher salt
1 (1-pound) flank steak, trimmed
3 tablespoons canola mayonnaise (such as Hellmann's)
1 teaspoon grated lime rind
1 tablespoon fresh lime juice
1 teaspoon minced garlic
1 teaspoon water
8 (6-inch) corn tortillas
½ cup refrigerated fresh salsa
2 ounces queso fresco, crumbled (about ½ cup)

1. Preheat broiler to high.
2. Arrange bell peppers in a single layer on a foil-lined jelly-roll pan; lightly coat peppers with cooking spray. Broil peppers 4 minutes on each side or until blackened. Cool slightly; discard stems. Cut peppers into strips.
3. Combine chipotle, paprika, and salt; rub spice mixture evenly over steak. Place steak on a broiler pan coated with cooking spray; broil 5 minutes on each side or until desired degree of doneness. Let steak stand 10 minutes; thinly slice steak across the grain.

Combine mayonnaise and next 4 ingredients; stir well.
4. Working with 1 tortilla at a time, heat tortillas over medium-high heat, directly on the eye of a burner, for about 15 seconds on each side or until lightly charred. Place 2 tortillas on each of 4 plates. Divide steak evenly among tortillas; top each taco with ¼ cup sweet peppers, 1 tablespoon salsa, 1 tablespoon cheese, and 1½ teaspoons mayonnaise mixture. Serves 4 (serving size: 2 tacos)

CALORIES 324; FAT 12.8g (sat 3.6g, mono 4.9g, poly 2.1g); PROTEIN 26.9g; CARB 23.8g; FIBER 3.5g; CHOL 69mg; IRON 2mg; SODIUM 460mg; CALC 82mg

Quick & Easy
Blackened Shrimp Tacos

Hands-on: 32 min. Total: 32 min.

2 tablespoons buttermilk
2 tablespoons canola mayonnaise
½ teaspoon minced garlic
½ teaspoon white vinegar
2 ounces queso fresco, crumbled (about ½ cup)
2 teaspoons paprika
1½ teaspoons ground cumin
¾ teaspoon garlic powder
½ teaspoon dried oregano
¼ teaspoon salt
¼ teaspoon dried thyme
¼ teaspoon ground red pepper
1 pound medium shrimp, peeled and deveined
Cooking spray
8 (6-inch) corn tortillas
½ cup diced plum tomato
1 ripe avocado, peeled and roughly mashed

1. Combine first 5 ingredients in a small bowl; set aside.
2. Combine paprika and next 6 ingredients in a large zip-top plastic bag. Add shrimp to bag; seal and shake well to coat. Remove shrimp.

3. Heat a grill pan over high heat. Coat pan with cooking spray. Add shrimp; cook 2 minutes per side or until done.
4. Working with 1 tortilla at a time, heat tortillas over medium-high heat directly on the eye of a burner for about 15 seconds on each side or until lightly charred. Divide shrimp evenly among tortillas; divide tomato, avocado, and sauce evenly among tacos. Serves 4 (serving size: 2 tacos)

CALORIES 287; FAT 13.5g (sat 2.1g, mono 6.6g, poly 2.4g); PROTEIN 17.9g; CARB 26.7g; FIBER 6.4g; CHOL 120mg; IRON 1.2mg; SODIUM 372mg; CALC 130mg

Kid Friendly • Quick & Easy
Vegetarian
Huevos Rancheros Tacos

Hands-on: 15 min. Total: 20 min. This is more of a knife-and-fork taco. The soft egg yolk oozes and coats the filling.

4 (6-inch) corn tortillas
Cooking spray
½ cup shredded reduced-fat 4-cheese Mexican blend cheese
½ cup black beans, rinsed and drained
2 teaspoons olive oil
4 large eggs
¼ teaspoon black pepper
¼ cup fresh pico de gallo
2 tablespoons Mexican crema
½ ripe peeled avocado, chopped
¼ cup cilantro leaves
4 lime wedges

1. Preheat broiler to high.
2. Arrange tortillas on a baking sheet; lightly coat tortillas with cooking spray. Broil 2 minutes; remove pan from oven. Turn tortillas over. Top each tortilla with 2 tablespoons cheese and 2 tablespoons beans. Broil 1 minute or until cheese melts. Remove from oven.
3. Heat a large nonstick skillet over medium-high heat. Add oil to pan;

continued

swirl to coat. Crack eggs into pan; cook 2 minutes. Cover and cook 2 minutes or until whites are set. Place 1 egg in center of each tortilla; sprinkle with pepper. Top tacos evenly with pico de gallo, crema, avocado, and cilantro. Serve with lime. Serves 4

CALORIES 278; FAT 17.3g (sat 5.5g, mono 7.2g, poly 1.9g); PROTEIN 12.6g; CARB 19.6g; FIBER 4.5g; CHOL 203mg; IRON 1.6mg; SODIUM 407mg; CALC 153mg

Quick & Easy

Cobb Salad Tacos

Hands-on: 30 min. Total: 40 min.
Adding a tortilla transforms this American salad into a fun, portable meal. Choose a pungent blue cheese, like Roquefort, for a strong hit of flavor, or go with milder Gorgonzola for just a touch.

2 large eggs
2 center-cut bacon slices
2 tablespoons minced shallots
2 garlic cloves, minced
2 tablespoons red wine vinegar
1½ tablespoons extra-virgin olive oil
¼ teaspoon Dijon mustard
2 cups shredded skinless, boneless rotisserie chicken breast
2 tablespoons canola mayonnaise (such as Hellmann's)
2 tablespoons low-fat buttermilk
1 ounce blue cheese, crumbled (about ¼ cup)
8 (6-inch) corn tortillas
2 cups thinly sliced iceberg lettuce
½ cup diced tomato
½ ripe peeled avocado, chopped

1. Place eggs in a large saucepan. Cover with water to 1 inch above eggs. Bring just to a boil. Remove from heat; cover and let stand 13 minutes. Drain; cool in ice water 5 minutes. Peel and dice.
2. Cook bacon in a medium nonstick skillet over medium heat until crisp (about 8 minutes). Remove bacon from pan, reserving drippings in pan. Drain bacon on paper towels; crumble bacon, and set aside. Add shallots and garlic to drippings in pan; cook 1 minute, stirring frequently. Remove from heat; add vinegar, oil, and mustard, stirring until combined. Add chicken to pan; toss to coat. Combine mayonnaise and buttermilk in a small bowl, stirring until smooth. Stir in cheese.
3. Working with 1 tortilla at a time, heat tortillas over medium-high heat directly on the eye of a burner for about 15 seconds on each side or until lightly charred. Arrange about ¼ cup chicken mixture in center of each tortilla; top tacos evenly with lettuce, tomato, and chopped avocado. Divide egg and bacon evenly among tacos, and drizzle evenly with dressing. Serves 4 (serving size: 2 tacos)

CALORIES 365; FAT 19.7g (sat 4.4g, mono 9.8g, poly 3.1g); PROTEIN 25.7g; CARB 24.2g; FIBER 4.6g; CHOL 154mg; IRON 1.3mg; SODIUM 503mg; CALC 115mg

Quick & Easy

Double-Layer Beef Tacos

Hands-on: 28 min. Total: 32 min.

1½ teaspoons canola oil
½ cup diced onion
1 tablespoon minced garlic
1 tablespoon minced jalapeño pepper
1½ teaspoons chili powder
¾ teaspoon ground cumin
¾ teaspoon ground coriander
⅛ teaspoon kosher salt
¼ teaspoon black pepper
6 ounces 90% lean ground beef
2 tablespoons unsalted tomato sauce
½ cup fat-free refried beans
4 (6-inch) flour tortillas
2 ounces preshredded reduced-fat Mexican-blend cheese or cheddar cheese (about ½ cup)
4 hard taco shells
½ cup thinly sliced iceberg lettuce
½ cup diced tomato
¼ cup reduced-fat sour cream

1. Preheat broiler to high.
2. Heat a large skillet over medium-high heat. Add oil; swirl to coat. Add onion; sauté 4 minutes, stirring occasionally. Add garlic and next 6 ingredients (through black pepper); sauté 1 minute, stirring constantly. Add beef; cook 3 minutes or until browned, stirring to crumble. Remove beef mixture from pan using a slotted spoon; drain on paper towels. Return beef mixture to pan; stir in tomato sauce. Cover, reduce heat, and simmer 10 minutes, stirring occasionally.
3. Spread 2 tablespoons beans evenly over 1 side of each flour tortilla; sprinkle each with about 2 tablespoons cheese. Place tortillas on a baking sheet; broil 2 minutes or until cheese melts. Carefully wrap 1 tortilla around 1 hard taco shell, pressing gently until cheese sticks to shell. Repeat procedure with remaining tortillas and shells. Spoon about ¼ cup beef mixture into each shell; top each with 2 tablespoons lettuce, 2 tablespoons tomato, and 1 tablespoon sour cream. Serves 4 (serving size: 1 taco)

CALORIES 327; FAT 13.9g (sat 4.9g, mono 4.9g, poly 0.7g); PROTEIN 18.7g; CARB 33.9g; FIBER 5.3g; CHOL 38mg; IRON 3mg; SODIUM 551mg; CALC 233mg

WITH THESE RECIPES, POUR A FRESH SELTZER WITH LIME AND AGAVE SYRUP, OR A BEER, OR, OF COURSE, A PERFECT MARGARITA.

Vegetarian

Super Crunch Tofu Tacos

Hands-on: 16 min. Total: 42 min. Pickled daikon radishes and carrots plus a spicy Sriracha sauce set these Asian-inspired tacos apart. Pan-sautéed cashews lend meaty crunch to this vegetarian dish.

1 (14-ounce) package extra-firm tofu, drained
1/2 teaspoon salt
1/4 teaspoon freshly ground black pepper
2 tablespoons canola oil
2 tablespoons unsalted cashews
1/4 cup rice wine vinegar
3 tablespoons water
1 1/2 tablespoons sugar
1 1/2 cups (2-inch) julienne-cut carrots
1 1/2 cups (2-inch) julienne-cut peeled daikon radish
2 tablespoons canola mayonnaise
1 1/2 teaspoons Sriracha (hot chile sauce, such as Huy Fong)
1 teaspoon rice wine vinegar
8 (6-inch) corn tortillas
1/4 cup diagonally sliced green onions

1. Cut tofu lengthwise into 2 (1-inch-thick) slices. Cut each slice lengthwise into 4 (1-inch-thick) strips. Place tofu on several layers of heavy-duty paper towels. Cover tofu with additional paper towels; top with a cast-iron skillet or other heavy pan. Let stand 15 minutes.
2. Heat a large skillet over medium-high heat. Sprinkle tofu with salt and pepper. Add canola oil to pan, and swirl to coat. Add tofu to pan; cook 10 minutes or until browned, turning to brown all sides. Remove tofu from pan, and drain on paper towels. Add cashews to pan; cook 30 seconds or until nuts are just beginning to brown. Remove nuts with a slotted spoon, and coarsely chop. Cut tofu strips crosswise into 1-inch cubes. Combine 1/4 cup vinegar, 3 tablespoons water, and sugar in a small saucepan; bring to a boil. Remove from heat; add carrots and radish. Let stand 15 minutes; drain. Combine mayonnaise, Sriracha, and 1 teaspoon vinegar in a small bowl, stirring with a whisk.
3. Working with 1 tortilla at a time, heat tortillas over medium-high heat directly on the eye of a burner for about 15 seconds on each side or until lightly charred. Arrange about 1/4 cup carrot mixture in center of each tortilla; top with 4 tofu pieces, about 1/2 teaspoon cashews, about 1 teaspoon mayonnaise mixture, and 1 1/2 teaspoons green onions. Serves 4 (serving size: 2 tacos)

CALORIES 397; FAT 18.6g (sat 1.6g, mono 10.9g, poly 3.2g); PROTEIN 13g; CARB 45.7g; FIBER 6.6g; CHOL 0mg; IRON 2.5mg; SODIUM 516mg; CALC 256mg

Quick & Easy

Beer-Braised Chicken Tacos with Cabbage Slaw

Hands-on: 35 min. Total: 35 min. Cabbage and apple slaw adds a nice crunch. When you pair the slaw with beer-braised chicken, the tacos take on a German flair.

4 bone-in chicken thighs, skinned
1/2 teaspoon kosher salt
1/2 teaspoon black pepper
1 tablespoon extra-virgin olive oil, divided
1 1/2 cups brown ale
1 teaspoon all-purpose flour
1/4 teaspoon sugar
4 center-cut bacon slices
2 tablespoons cider vinegar
1 teaspoon Dijon mustard
2 cups thinly sliced red cabbage
1 cup julienne-cut Granny Smith apple
8 (6-inch) corn tortillas

1. Heat a medium skillet over medium-high heat. Sprinkle chicken evenly with salt and pepper. Add 2 teaspoons oil to pan; swirl to coat. Add chicken to pan, flesh side down; cook 5 minutes or until browned. Turn chicken over; cook 2 minutes. Combine beer, flour, and sugar in a medium bowl, stirring with a whisk until smooth. Slowly add beer mixture to pan; bring to a boil. Reduce heat to medium-low; cook 15 minutes or until chicken is done, turning once. Remove chicken from pan; let stand 5 minutes. Remove chicken from bones; shred. Discard bones. Bring cooking liquid to a boil, scraping pan to loosen browned bits; cook 2 minutes or until reduced to 1/3 cup. Return chicken to pan; toss to coat.
2. Cook bacon in a large skillet over medium heat until crisp (about 8 minutes). Remove bacon from pan, reserving drippings. Drain bacon on paper towels; crumble. Add 1 tablespoon drippings to a medium bowl. Add 1 teaspoon oil, vinegar, and mustard to drippings in bowl, stirring with a whisk. Add bacon, cabbage, and apple; toss to coat.
3. Working with 1 tortilla at a time, heat tortillas over medium-high heat directly on the eye of a burner for about 15 seconds on each side or until lightly charred. Arrange about 1/4 cup chicken mixture in center of each tortilla, and top with about 1/4 cup cabbage mixture. Serves 4 (serving size: 2 tacos)

CALORIES 386; FAT 13.5g (sat 3.2g, mono 5.8g, poly 2.6g); PROTEIN 37.5g; CARB 26.5g; FIBER 3.4g; CHOL 169mg; IRON 1.7mg; SODIUM 576mg; CALC 55mg

TODAY'S LESSON: POUND CAKE

The original recipe for this classic cake had a 1-to-1-to-1-to-1 ratio of eggs, butter, sugar, and flour—often calling for a full pound of butter. The result was confection perfection: compact, moist little crumbs surrounded by a browned sugar crust. Here, we reveal our best tricks for producing the same delightful dessert with less than a quarter of the traditional quantity of butter.

Kid Friendly • Make Ahead

Pound Cake with Strawberry Glaze
(pictured on page 218)

Hands-on: 26 min. Total: 1 hr. 26 min.
Look for whole-wheat pastry flour in the baking aisle at major supermarkets. Garnish with additional strawberries and fresh mint leaves.

Cake:
2 cups sugar
⅓ cup canola oil
6 tablespoons butter, softened
2 large eggs
½ teaspoon vanilla extract
2 teaspoons grated lemon rind
2 tablespoons fresh lemon juice
9 ounces all-purpose flour (about 2 cups)
3.4 ounces whole-wheat pastry flour (about ¾ cup)
1 teaspoon baking powder
¼ teaspoon baking soda
¼ teaspoon salt
1 cup light sour cream
¼ cup 2% reduced-fat milk
Baking spray with flour
Glaze:
2 cups chopped strawberries
⅓ cup sugar
1 tablespoon cornstarch
1 tablespoon fresh lemon juice
Dash of salt

1. Preheat oven to 350°.
2. To prepare cake, combine first 3 ingredients in a large bowl; beat with a mixer at medium speed until light and fluffy. Add eggs, beating until incorporated. Stir in vanilla, lemon rind, and 2 tablespoons lemon juice.
3. Weigh or lightly spoon flours into dry measuring cups; level. Combine flours, powder, soda, and salt. Combine sour cream and milk. Add flour mixture and sour cream mixture alternately to butter mixture, beginning and ending with flour mixture.
4. Spoon batter into a 10-cup Bundt pan coated with baking spray. Bake at 350° for 55 minutes or until a wooden pick inserted in center comes out clean. Cool cake in pan on a wire rack 15 minutes. Remove from pan; cool on wire rack.
5. To prepare glaze, combine strawberries and remaining ingredients in a saucepan; bring to a boil. Reduce heat; cook 3 minutes or until thick. Strain through a sieve over a bowl; discard solids. Drizzle glaze over cake. Serves 16 (serving size: 1 slice)

CALORIES 318; **FAT** 11.7g (sat 4.4g, mono 4.8g, poly 1.8g); **PROTEIN** 4g; **CARB** 50.4g; **FIBER** 1.8g; **CHOL** 40mg; **IRON** 1.3mg; **SODIUM** 119mg; **CALC** 60mg

Variation: Double-Chocolate Swirl
1. Prepare base recipe through step 3, decreasing granulated sugar to 1¾ cups and omitting rind and juice. Combine 1 teaspoon canola oil and 1 ounce chopped bittersweet chocolate in a microwave-safe dish. Microwave at HIGH 1 minute, stirring every 20 seconds until smooth. Stir in 2 tablespoons unsweetened cocoa. Remove 2½ cups vanilla batter; add to chocolate mixture, and stir.
2. Using 2 ice-cream scoops, add batters alternately to a 10-cup Bundt pan coated with baking spray; swirl with a pick.
3. Bake at 350° for 50 minutes or until a wooden pick inserted in center comes out clean. Cool in pan 15 minutes on a wire rack. Remove from pan; cool on wire rack.
4. Combine ⅔ cup powdered sugar, 2 tablespoons 2% reduced-fat milk, 1 tablespoon unsweetened cocoa, ¼ teaspoon vanilla extract, and ⅛ teaspoon salt; stir until smooth. Drizzle glaze over cake. Serves 16 (serving size: 1 slice)

CALORIES 311; **FAT** 12.7g (sat 4.8g); **SODIUM** 124mg

SWIRL IN TWO STEPS

1.

2.

Alternate batters using two ice-cream scoops; then swirl with a pick.

OUR FRESH CROP OF CARROTS

This month from the *Cooking Light* Garden: a lovely assortment of the root veggie our gardening gurus like to call "soil candy."

I f you're only familiar with standard supermarket carrots—that is, bagged, topless, and uniformly orange—then venturing into the world of heirloom varieties will bring real delight. The visual change-ups constitute the first striking difference: Some are round like baby beets, others long and digit-slender. And the stunning sunset colors—deep purple, flaming orange, saffron yellow—sometimes appear within one carrot. (Centuries ago, purple carrots were the norm, until farmers cultivated wild carrots into the orange varieties that dominate today.) Although the three types of carrots that Mary Beth and David Shaddix grew for us didn't taste significantly different from each other, all were profoundly sweet and much more carroty than supermarket vegetables—hence their "soil-candy" nickname, describing a sweetness that gets even sweeter when you roast and caramelize these treats.

Kid Friendly • Quick & Easy
Vegetarian

Newfangled Peas and Carrots

Hands-on: 30 min. Total: 30 min. The peas here come in the form of tendrils—wispy, tender sprouts of the pea plant. Substitute watercress if tendrils aren't available.

6 cups water
12 ounces baby carrots
1 tablespoon butter
2 cups vertically sliced spring onion,
    white parts only (about 9 ounces)
1 teaspoon sugar
2 teaspoons rice vinegar
1/4 teaspoon kosher salt
1/4 teaspoon freshly ground black
    pepper
1 teaspoon chopped fresh tarragon
2 cups pea tendrils or watercress

1. Bring 6 cups water to a boil in a large saucepan. Add carrots; reduce heat, and simmer 5 minutes or until crisp-tender. Drain; rinse under cold water. Rub carrot peels off with a clean, dry kitchen towel.
2. Melt butter in a large skillet over medium-high heat; swirl to coat. Add onion; sauté 3 minutes or until slightly tender. Add carrots, sugar, vinegar, salt, and pepper; cook 2 minutes or until sugar dissolves and carrots are thoroughly heated. Stir in tarragon. Top with pea tendrils. Serves 4 (serving size: about 3/4 cup)

CALORIES 85; FAT 3.1g (sat 1.9g, mono 0.8g, poly 0.2g); PROTEIN 2.1g; CARB 14.2g; FIBER 4.8g; CHOL 8mg; IRON 2mg; SODIUM 232mg; CALC 75mg

Quick & Easy • Vegetarian

Moroccan-Spiced Baby Carrots

Hands-on: 7 min. Total: 22 min. Warm spices like cumin and cinnamon play deliciously off the sweetness of the carrots.

2 tablespoons extra-virgin olive oil
12 ounces peeled baby carrots
1 lemon, cut into 8 wedges
1 teaspoon ground cumin
1/2 teaspoon ground cinnamon
1/4 teaspoon kosher salt
1/4 teaspoon ground red pepper
1 tablespoon chopped fresh cilantro

1. Preheat oven to 450°.
2. Combine first 3 ingredients in a medium bowl; sprinkle with cumin, cinnamon, salt, and pepper, tossing to coat carrots. Arrange carrot mixture in a single layer on a jelly-roll pan. Bake at 450° for 13 minutes, turning once. Sprinkle with cilantro. Serves 4 (serving size: about 2/3 cup)

CALORIES 96; FAT 7g (sat 1g, mono 4.9g, poly 0.8g); PROTEIN 0.7g; CARB 8.7g; FIBER 3.3g; CHOL 0mg; IRON 1mg; SODIUM 187mg; CALC 39mg

TYPES OF CARROTS

Paris Market
The squat, round shape of Paris Market carrots makes these French imports ideal for planting in shallow soil—perfect for container or window box gardeners.

Dragon
Striking colors inside and out set Dragon carrots apart. Serve them halved lengthwise and roasted. For an even more dramatic presentation, shave raw into thin strips and toss in a salad.

Little Finger
Finger-thin but considerably longer—averaging about 6 inches—these are great all-purpose carrots. Their uniform size ensures even cooking, whether roasted, steamed, or sautéed.

5 EASY DISHES FOR 5 SPRING JEWELS

From the markets and out of the gardens come the first sweet offerings of the season. Dig in.

1 BABY BEETS

Buy firm, smooth-skinned beets without nicks and cuts. Green tops should be vibrant. Refrigerate in a plastic bag up to two weeks (the greens last only a few days; trim them and store in a separate bag). To prep, wash whole, trimmed beets. Cook with skin on to preserve color. Wear latex gloves while peeling to avoid dyeing your skin with beet juice.

Vegetarian

Roasted Baby Beets and Blood Orange Salad with Blue Cheese

Hands-on: 20 min. Total: 1 hr. 15 min. If blood oranges aren't available, substitute 3 large navel oranges.

12 multicolored baby beets
4 medium blood oranges
1½ tablespoons balsamic vinegar
4 teaspoons extra-virgin olive oil
1 teaspoon Dijon mustard
¼ teaspoon salt
⅛ teaspoon freshly ground black pepper
1 (5-ounce) package mixed baby greens
2 ounces blue cheese, crumbled (about ½ cup)
¼ cup chopped walnuts, toasted

1. Preheat oven to 400°.
2. Leave root and 1 inch stem on beets; scrub with a brush. Cut an 18 x 12–inch sheet of foil. Place beets in center of foil. Gather edges of foil to form a pouch; tightly seal edges. Place pouch on a baking sheet. Bake at 400° for 45 minutes or until tender. Cool 20 minutes. Trim off beet roots; rub off skins. Cut beets into quarters.
3. Grate 1 teaspoon orange rind. Peel and section oranges over a large bowl; squeeze membranes to extract juice. Set sections aside; reserve 3 tablespoons juice. Discard membranes. Combine rind, juice, vinegar, and next 4 ingredients (through pepper) in a small bowl; stir with a whisk.
4. Divide greens evenly among 8 plates. Arrange beets and orange sections on top of greens. Sprinkle each serving with 1 tablespoon cheese and 1½ teaspoons nuts. Drizzle each serving with about 2 teaspoons dressing. Serves 8

CALORIES 163; **FAT** 6.9g (sat 1.9g, mono 2.6g, poly 2.1g); **PROTEIN** 4.8g; **CARB** 21.9g; **FIBER** 5.6g; **CHOL** 5mg; **IRON** 1.3mg; **SODIUM** 291mg; **CALC** 92mg

2 BABY ARTICHOKES

Look for bright green artichokes with firm, tightly layered leaves with no discoloration. Refrigerate, unwashed, in a plastic bag up to seven days. Cut about ½ inch from the top. Rinse, and then snap off outer leaves until you reach pale, yellow-green leaves. Cut the stem, leaving about 1 inch. Unlike big artichokes, baby ones don't have an inedible, thistly "choke" that needs to be scooped from the center.

Roasted Baby Artichokes with Lemon Aioli

Hands-on: 16 min. Total: 31 min.

6 cups water
5 tablespoons fresh lemon juice, divided
12 baby artichokes
5 teaspoons extra-virgin olive oil, divided
¼ teaspoon kosher salt
⅛ teaspoon freshly ground black pepper
¼ cup light mayonnaise
1 teaspoon minced garlic
½ teaspoon grated lemon rind

1. Preheat oven to 425°.
2. Combine 6 cups water and 4 tablespoons juice in a large bowl. Cut off top ½ inch of each artichoke. Cut off stem of each artichoke to within 1 inch of base; peel stem. Remove bottom leaves and tough outer leaves, leaving tender heart and bottom. Cut each artichoke in half lengthwise. Place artichokes in juice mixture.
3. Drain artichokes; pat dry with paper towels. Combine artichokes, 1 tablespoon oil, salt, and pepper; toss well. Arrange in a single layer on a baking sheet. Bake at 425° for 15 minutes or until tender, turning after 10 minutes.
4. Combine 1 tablespoon juice, 2 teaspoons oil, mayonnaise, garlic, and lemon rind in a small bowl. Serve aioli with artichokes. Serves 4 (serving size: 6 artichoke halves and about 1 tablespoon aioli)

CALORIES 116; **FAT** 10.7g (sat 1.5g, mono 4.1g, poly 3.6g); **PROTEIN** 0.7g; **CARB** 5g; **FIBER** 1.4g; **CHOL** 5mg; **IRON** 0.2mg; **SODIUM** 254mg; **CALC** 14mg

3 ASPARAGUS

Choose firm asparagus with closed tips. Green asparagus should have bright green stalks and violet tips. Wrap the bottoms of the stalks in a wet paper towel. Refrigerate in a plastic bag for up to four days. To prep, cut or snap off woody bottoms. For stalks ¾ inch wide or bigger, peel bottom half of remaining stalk to remove fibrous layers and ensure tenderness. After steaming or boiling green asparagus, plunge into an ice bath to set the bright color.

Quick & Easy • Vegetarian

Roasted Asparagus and Arugula Salad with Poached Egg

Hands-on: 13 min. Total: 38 min. Pair this light entrée with some roasted new potatoes.

1 pound green asparagus, trimmed
3 tablespoons extra-virgin olive oil, divided
½ teaspoon freshly ground black pepper, divided
¼ teaspoon kosher salt, divided
3 tablespoons minced shallots
2 tablespoons fresh lemon juice
2 teaspoons chopped fresh tarragon
1 (5-ounce) package baby arugula
1 tablespoon white wine vinegar
4 large eggs
4 (¾-ounce) slices Italian bread, toasted and cut in half diagonally

1. Preheat oven to 450°.
2. Place asparagus on a jelly-roll pan. Drizzle with 2 teaspoons oil; sprinkle with ¼ teaspoon pepper and ⅛ teaspoon salt. Toss gently to coat; arrange in a single layer. Bake at 450° for 5 minutes or until crisp-tender.
3. Place 7 teaspoons oil, ⅛ teaspoon pepper, ⅛ teaspoon salt, shallots, juice, and tarragon in a large bowl; stir well with a whisk. Add arugula; toss gently to coat. Place about 1½ cups arugula mixture on each of 4 plates. Top each serving with

one-fourth of the asparagus.
4. Add water to a large skillet, filling two-thirds full; bring to a boil. Reduce heat; simmer. Add vinegar. Break each egg into a custard cup, and pour each gently into pan; cook 3 minutes or until desired degree of doneness. Carefully remove eggs from pan using a slotted spoon; place 1 poached egg on each salad. Sprinkle with ⅛ teaspoon pepper. Arrange 2 bread halves on each serving. Serves 4

CALORIES 261; FAT 15.3g (sat 2.8g, mono 9.5g, poly 2.3g); PROTEIN 11.9g; CARB 19.8g; FIBER 3.6g; CHOL 180mg; IRON 4.7mg; SODIUM 327mg; CALC 133mg

4 FAVA BEANS

Choose firm, bright pods free of black marks—avoid pods on which the outline of the beans inside is pronounced, indicating older favas. Refrigerate pods in a plastic bag for up to seven days. Pods stay fresh longer than shelled, peeled beans. To shell, split the pod open and remove beans. To make the skinlike shells easier to remove, boil beans briefly, and rinse under cold water. When cool enough to handle, squeeze beans from their shells.

Kid Friendly

Spring Pasta with Fava Beans and Peas

Hands-on: 41 min. Total: 41 min.

1½ cups shelled fava beans (about 1¾ pounds unshelled)
6 ounces uncooked campanelle or farfalle (bow tie pasta)
2 tablespoons extra-virgin olive oil, divided
6 center-cut bacon slices, cut into ½-inch pieces
1½ cups sliced red onion
8 garlic cloves, sliced
3 ounces thinly sliced mushrooms
1 cup fresh shelled or frozen green peas, thawed
2 teaspoons fresh lemon juice

¼ teaspoon kosher salt
1½ ounces fresh pecorino Romano cheese (about 6 tablespoons), grated and divided
½ cup torn basil leaves

1. Place fava beans in a large pot of boiling water; cook 1 minute. Drain; rinse with cold water. Drain well. Remove tough outer skins from beans.
2. Cook pasta according to package directions, omitting salt and fat; drain.
3. Heat a large nonstick skillet over medium-high heat. Add 1 tablespoon oil to pan; swirl to coat. Add bacon; sauté 3 minutes or until bacon begins to brown. Add onion and garlic; sauté 3 minutes or until vegetables are tender. Add mushrooms; sauté 3 minutes or until mushrooms begin to brown. Add fava beans and peas; sauté 2 minutes. Stir in 1 tablespoon oil, pasta, juice, and salt; cook 2 minutes or until thoroughly heated. Remove pan from heat. Stir in 3 tablespoons cheese. Divide pasta mixture evenly among 4 bowls, and top evenly with 3 tablespoons cheese and basil. Serve immediately. Serves 4 (serving size: about 1¾ cups)

CALORIES 371; FAT 13.2g (sat 4.2g, mono 5g, poly 1g); PROTEIN 16.2g; CARB 48.3g; FIBER 5.8g; CHOL 19mg; IRON 3.2mg; SODIUM 521mg; CALC 127mg

5 MORELS

Buy firm, unshriveled morels that are dry, not slimy, and free of excessive dirt. Refrigerate, either in a bowl with a slightly damp towel on top or in a paper bag. Avoid plastic bags—the mushrooms need to breathe. Don't wash before storing; they'll deteriorate faster. Remove dirt with a vegetable brush. For stubborn dirt, swish morels in a bowl of cold water for several seconds; pat dry thoroughly.

continued

Morel Mushroom and Asparagus Sauté

Hands-on: 20 min. Total: 31 min.
Blanching the asparagus first helps set its color and texture.

3 quarts water
12 ounces white asparagus, trimmed
12 ounces green asparagus, trimmed
1 tablespoon butter
1 shallot, thinly sliced
4 cups fresh morel mushrooms, halved
    lengthwise (about 8 ounces)
½ teaspoon kosher salt, divided
1 tablespoon extra-virgin olive oil
¼ teaspoon freshly ground black
    pepper

1. Bring 3 quarts water to a boil in a large saucepan. Peel bottom 2 inches of white and green asparagus. Cook white asparagus in boiling water 5 minutes or until crisp-tender; remove with a slotted spoon to a colander. Rinse under cold water; drain well. Cook green asparagus in boiling water 2 minutes or until crisp-tender; remove with a slotted spoon to a colander. Rinse under cold water; drain well. Cut asparagus diagonally into 1½-inch pieces.
2. Melt butter in a large nonstick skillet over medium-high heat; swirl to coat. Add shallots; sauté 1 minute, stirring constantly. Add morels and ¼ teaspoon salt; sauté 5 minutes or until mushrooms are lightly browned. Add asparagus, ¼ teaspoon salt, oil, and pepper; toss gently to coat. Cook 2 minutes or until asparagus is thoroughly heated. Serves 4 (serving size: about 1 cup)

CALORIES 115; **FAT** 6.6g (sat 1.4g, mono 3.2g, poly 0.6g); **PROTEIN** 6g; **CARB** 11.5g; **FIBER** 4.3g; **CHOL** 8mg; **IRON** 3mg; **SODIUM** 267mg; **CALC** 28mg

RECIPE MAKEOVER

20-MINUTE BISCUITS

Made from scratch with whole grains and less fat: A new method makes biscuits an everyday option.

The bliss of a freshly baked biscuit is worth the effort—all that measuring of flour, cutting in of butter, rolling out of dough.

These are treats to serve with love and pride. Problem is, a traditional biscuit may set you back 300 calories or more. Add fruity preserves and a smear of butter—or, in the South, a piece of salty country ham—and you have quite a rich breakfast. It's true that canned biscuits aren't as caloric, but they can deliver sodium and trans fats. We set out with two goals: lighter biscuits and less prep time.

Getting that fluffy texture while using less butter is a trick, and speeding up the recipe is also a challenge because it's the cutting in of cold butter that takes a lot of the time. Here is the breakthrough: We stir melted butter into cold, nonfat buttermilk and let everything get lumpy as the butter congeals, at which point those little pockets of butter disperse evenly throughout the batter, allowing us to use half the amount of the original.

White whole-wheat flour adds nutty, whole-grain goodness, and a touch of canola oil keeps the biscuits nice and tender. No pastry blender or rolling pin is required—just mix, scoop, and bake until puffy and golden. Our lighter, made-from-scratch drop biscuits come together as fast as you can pop a can—and leave a little wiggle room for all those tasty toppers.

Fluffy Buttermilk Drop Biscuits

Hands-on: 7 min. Total: 21 min. *When the warm butter meets the cold buttermilk, it will begin to form clumps—little droplets of fat throughout the liquid—a sign of success.*

5.6 ounces unbleached all-purpose
    flour (about 1¼ cups)
3.6 ounces white whole-wheat flour
    (about ¾ cup)
2 teaspoons baking powder
1 teaspoon sugar
¾ teaspoon salt
½ teaspoon baking soda
¼ cup unsalted butter
1¼ cups very cold nonfat buttermilk
1 tablespoon canola oil

1. Preheat oven to 450°.
2. Weigh or lightly spoon flours into dry measuring cups; level with a knife. Combine flours, baking powder, sugar, salt, and baking soda in a large bowl, stirring with a whisk to combine.
3. Place butter in a microwave-safe bowl. Microwave at HIGH 1 minute or until completely melted. Add cold buttermilk, stirring until butter forms small clumps. Add oil, stirring to combine.
4. Add buttermilk mixture to flour mixture; stir with a rubber spatula until just incorporated (do not overmix) and

	CLASSIC	MAKEOVER
	312 calories per serving	133 calories per serving
	502 milligrams sodium	305 milligrams sodium
	10 grams saturated fat	2.6 grams saturated fat

batter pulls away from sides of bowl. (Batter will be very wet.)

5. Drop batter in mounds of 2 heaping tablespoonfuls onto a baking sheet lined with parchment paper. Bake at 450° for 11 minutes or until golden. Cool 3 minutes; serve warm. Serves 12 (serving size: 1 biscuit)

CALORIES 133; FAT 5.4g (sat 2.6g, mono 1.8g, poly 0.6g); PROTEIN 3.5g; CARB 18.3g; FIBER 1.3g; CHOL 10mg; IRON 1mg; SODIUM 305mg; CALC 82mg

EVERYDAY VEGETARIAN

MEATLESS MONDAYS

Quick & Easy • Vegetarian

Fried Chickpea and Arugula Pita Sandwiches with Lime Tzatziki

Hands-on: 23 min. Total: 23 min.

1 cup plain 2% reduced-fat Greek yogurt
3 tablespoons chopped fresh mint
2 teaspoons fresh lime juice
⅝ teaspoon kosher salt, divided
2 garlic cloves, minced
1 cucumber (about 8 ounces), peeled, seeded, and shredded
6 (6-inch) whole-wheat pitas, halved
2 (15-ounce) cans organic chickpeas (garbanzo beans), rinsed and drained
3 tablespoons extra-virgin olive oil, divided
2 teaspoons ground cumin
2 teaspoons Spanish smoked paprika
¼ teaspoon ground red pepper
1 tablespoon fresh lemon juice
¼ teaspoon freshly ground black pepper
8 cups loosely packed arugula
12 (¼-inch-thick) slices tomato

1. Preheat oven to 350°.
2. Combine yogurt, mint, lime juice, ⅛ teaspoon salt, garlic, and cucumber in a small bowl.
3. Wrap pitas in foil; bake at 350° for 10 minutes or until warm.
4. Place chickpeas in a single layer on paper towels. Cover with additional paper towels; pat dry. Heat a large skillet over medium-high heat. Add 2 tablespoons oil to pan; swirl to coat. Add chickpeas to pan; sauté 10 minutes or until lightly browned and crispy, stirring frequently. Remove chickpeas from pan using a slotted spoon; drain on paper towels. Combine ½ teaspoon salt, chickpeas, cumin, paprika, and red pepper in a medium bowl; toss well to coat.
5. Combine 1 tablespoon olive oil, lemon juice, and black pepper in a small bowl, stirring well with a whisk. Add arugula; toss gently to coat. Add chickpea mixture; toss to coat.
6. Fill each pita half with about ⅔ cup chickpea mixture, 1 tomato slice, and 2 tablespoons sauce. Serve immediately. Serves 6 (serving size: 2 pita halves)

CALORIES 370; FAT 10.4g (sat 1.8g, mono 5.2g, poly 2g); PROTEIN 15.8g; CARB 57g; FIBER 9.9g; CHOL 3mg; IRON 3.9mg; SODIUM 586mg; CALC 131mg

Quick & Easy • Vegetarian

Soba Noodles with Miso-Glazed Tofu and Vegetables

Hands-on: 22 min. Total: 22 min. Soba noodles lose about 80% of their sodium when cooked in unsalted water. Rinse and drain the soba thoroughly after cooking to remove any lingering salt.

2½ tablespoons canola oil, divided
3 tablespoons rice vinegar
2 tablespoons white miso
1 tablespoon minced peeled fresh ginger
1 tablespoon minced garlic
1 tablespoon lower-sodium soy sauce
1½ teaspoons sugar
1 teaspoon dark sesame oil
4 ounces uncooked organic soba noodles
1 (14-ounce) package extra-firm tofu, drained
6 ounces shiitake mushrooms, stems discarded
1 pound asparagus spears, trimmed and cut into 1-inch pieces
¼ cup thinly sliced green onions

1. Combine 1 tablespoon canola oil and next 7 ingredients in a medium bowl, stirring with a whisk.
2. Cook noodles according to package directions; drain and rinse. Combine noodles and ¼ cup miso mixture in a bowl; toss to coat.
3. Heat a large nonstick skillet over medium-high heat. Add 1 tablespoon canola oil to pan; swirl to coat. Cut tofu crosswise into 4 (1-inch-thick) slices. Add tofu to pan; cook 3 minutes on each side or until browned. Add 1 tablespoon miso mixture to pan; toss to coat. Remove tofu from pan; keep warm. Add 1½ teaspoons canola oil to pan; swirl to coat. Add mushrooms and asparagus to pan; sauté 4 minutes or until tender. Add remaining 2 tablespoons miso mixture to pan; toss to coat. Sprinkle with green onions. Arrange ½ cup noodle mixture in each of 4 bowls; top each serving with ½ cup vegetable mixture and 1 tofu steak. Serves 4

CALORIES 346; FAT 16.3g (sat 1.4g, mono 10.4g, poly 4g); PROTEIN 20.1g; CARB 36.8g; FIBER 3.5g; CHOL 0mg; IRON 5.2mg; SODIUM 446mg; CALC 217mg

SIBLING-PLEASING SCHNITZEL

"Today, I made the best pork schnitzel for my brothers and me. It is hard to find something both my 14- and 8-year-old brothers will eat. I think this recipe solved our problem because they both loved it! All the flavors blended really well together, and I added fresh vegetables to complete the meal. If you do not have a meat mallet, you can pound the pork by putting the chops in a zip-top plastic bag and carefully using a regular hammer. I also enjoyed using parsley in this dish, as it adds a fresh flavor and helps with garlic breath. The dill in the ranch sauce added a nice earthy flavor that I enjoyed. My brothers, however, were not too keen on the dill, so I made a couple of options, including replacing the dill with mint and adding lemon wedges to squeeze on the meat. It all tasted good to me!"

IF YOU DON'T HAVE SOUR CREAM, YOU CAN USE GREEK YOGURT FOR THE SAUCE.

Kid Friendly • Quick & Easy

Pork Schnitzel

with Buttermilk Ranch Sauce

Hands-on: 14 min. Total: 24 min.

¼ cup fat-free sour cream
1 tablespoon chopped fresh dill
2 tablespoons low-fat buttermilk
⅝ teaspoon kosher salt, divided
¾ teaspoon freshly ground black pepper, divided
¼ cup fat-free milk
1 large egg, lightly beaten
¾ cup dry breadcrumbs
2 tablespoons chopped fresh flat-leaf parsley
½ teaspoon garlic powder
4 (4-ounce) boneless center-cut loin pork chops, trimmed and pounded to ⅛-inch thickness
2 tablespoons olive oil

1. Combine sour cream, dill, buttermilk, ⅛ teaspoon salt, and ¼ teaspoon pepper in a bowl; set aside.
2. Combine milk and egg in a dish; stir with a whisk. Combine breadcrumbs, parsley, garlic powder, and ½ teaspoon pepper in another dish. Dip pork in milk mixture; sprinkle with ½ teaspoon salt. Dredge pork in breadcrumb mixture.
3. Heat a large nonstick skillet over medium-high heat. Add 1 tablespoon oil to pan; swirl to coat. Place 2 pork chops in pan. Cook 3 minutes on each side or until done. Remove from pan. Repeat procedure with 1 tablespoon olive oil and 2 pork chops. Serve with sauce. Serves 4 (serving size: 1 schnitzel and 1½ tablespoons sauce)

CALORIES 329; **FAT** 15.2g (sat 3.6g, mono 7.5g, poly 1.6g); **PROTEIN** 27.4g; **CARB** 19.3g; **FIBER** 1g; **CHOL** 115mg; **IRON** 1.1mg; **SODIUM** 540mg; **CALC** 80mg

RADICALLY SIMPLE

MOTHER'S DAY

By Rozanne Gold

I got my love of cooking from my beautiful mother, Marion, who had a special love for foods from her homeland, Hungary. But she appreciated all cuisines—really anything well prepared. As a result of her influence, I like to combine a jumble of flavors for a harmonious end. This halibut dish, a cultural mash-up of refined French fish stew and rustic Thai curry, shows my affinity for lusty food. I know the sophistication and intriguing flavors of green curry and fresh mint paired with succulent halibut and shrimp certainly would have pleased my mom, especially on Mother's Day.

SERVE THIS SUCCULENT SEAFOOD FEST WITH RICE FOR A SPECIAL MOTHER'S DAY TREAT.

Quick & Easy
Halibut and Shrimp with Minted Broth

Hands-on: 20 min. Total: 38 min. The fish fillets should fit rather snugly in the pot with enough room for some shrimp to slip between the crevices.

1¹/₂ tablespoons olive oil
1¹/₂ tablespoons unsalted butter
2 large leeks, trimmed, thinly sliced, and thoroughly rinsed
1 tablespoon minced garlic
2 medium carrots, peeled and thinly sliced
¹/₄ teaspoon kosher salt
4 (4-ounce) halibut fillets
12 medium peeled and deveined shrimp, tails on
1 cup fat-free, lower-sodium chicken broth
¹/₄ cup dry white wine
1 tablespoon green curry paste
2 tablespoons finely chopped fresh mint

1. Heat a large skillet over medium-high heat. Add oil and butter to pan; swirl until butter melts. Add leeks; sauté 3 minutes, stirring occasionally. Add garlic and carrots; sauté 3 minutes, stirring constantly. Remove from heat. Sprinkle salt evenly over both sides of fillets; arrange fillets and shrimp in a single layer on top of carrot mixture.
2. Combine broth, wine, and curry paste in a small bowl, stirring with a whisk. Add curry mixture to pan with fish; bring to a boil. Cover, reduce heat, and simmer 10 minutes or until desired degree of doneness. Place 1 fillet in each of 4 shallow soup bowls; divide shrimp, vegetables, and broth evenly among servings. Sprinkle each serving with 1½ teaspoons mint. Serves 4

CALORIES 307; **FAT** 12g (sat 3.9g, mono 5.4g, poly 1.3g); **PROTEIN** 34.5g; **CARB** 11.7g; **FIBER** 1.8g; **CHOL** 174mg; **IRON** 1.5mg; **SODIUM** 564mg; **CALC** 96mg

QUICK TRICKS
RICE STIR-INS

Start with 2 cups unseasoned hot cooked long-grain white rice simmered in water. Choose your favorite flavor, and proceed.

Curry Carrot
Stir ¾ cup grated carrot, 2 tablespoons golden raisins, 1 teaspoon Madras curry powder, and ¼ teaspoon kosher salt into rice. Serves 4 (serving size: about ⅔ cup)

CALORIES 127; **FAT** 0.4g (sat 0.1g); **SODIUM** 136mg

Golden Saffron
Combine 1 tablespoon hot water and ⅛ teaspoon saffron threads, and let stand 5 minutes; stir into rice. Heat 1 tablespoon extra-virgin olive oil in a saucepan over medium heat. Add ¼ cup minced onion; cook 5 minutes, stirring occasionally. Combine rice mixture, onion mixture, and ¼ teaspoon kosher salt. Serves 4 (serving size: ½ cup)

CALORIES 137; **FAT** 3.6g (sat 0.5g); **SODIUM** 121mg

Thai Cilantro & Serrano
Heat a small skillet over medium-high heat. Add 1 tablespoon canola oil; swirl. Add 1 tablespoon grated peeled fresh ginger, 1 tablespoon sliced garlic, and 2 serrano chiles, seeded and thinly sliced; sauté 1 minute. Stir ginger mixture, ¾ cup chopped fresh cilantro, and ¼ teaspoon kosher salt into rice. Serves 4 (serving size: ½ cup)

CALORIES 139; **FAT** 3.8g (sat 0.3g); **SODIUM** 122mg

Double Sesame
Stir 2 teaspoons dark sesame oil, 1 teaspoon toasted sesame seeds, ¼ teaspoon kosher salt, ¼ teaspoon freshly ground black pepper, and 2 diagonally sliced green onions into rice. Serves 4 (serving size: ½ cup)

CALORIES 130; **FAT** 2.9g (sat 0.5g); **SODIUM** 122mg

Pine Nut, Butter, & Parsley
Stir 2 tablespoons toasted pine nuts, 2 tablespoons minced fresh flat-leaf parsley, 1 tablespoon melted butter, and ¼ teaspoon kosher salt into rice. Serves 4 (serving size: ½ cup)

CALORIES 157; **FAT** 6g (sat 2g); **SODIUM** 147mg

Chile-Spiked
Combine 1 tablespoon sambal oelek (ground fresh chile paste), 1 tablespoon extra-virgin olive oil, ½ teaspoon ground cumin, ¼ teaspoon ground coriander, ¼ teaspoon kosher salt, and 3 minced garlic cloves; stir mixture into rice. Serves 4 (serving size: ½ cup)

CALORIES 140; **FAT** 3.7g (sat 0.5g); **SODIUM** 122mg

Rum-Raisin Pudding
Combine ½ cup raisins and ¼ cup rum in a microwave-safe bowl. Microwave at HIGH 2 minutes; let stand 5 minutes. Stir raisin mixture, 2 (3.5-ounce) vanilla pudding snack cups, ⅓ cup toasted sliced almonds, ¼ teaspoon ground cinnamon, and a dash of ground nutmeg into rice. Serves 4 (serving size: ¾ cup)

CALORIES 289; **FAT** 5.9g (sat 0.9g); **SODIUM** 78mg

Browned Butter & Sage
Heat 1 tablespoon butter in a skillet over medium-high heat; cook 1 minute or until butter begins to brown. Stir butter, 1½ teaspoons chopped fresh sage, ¼ teaspoon kosher salt, and ⅛ teaspoon black pepper into rice. Serves 4 (serving size: ½ cup)

CALORIES 129; **FAT** 3.1g (sat 1.9g); **SODIUM** 121mg

FEED 4 FOR LESS THAN $10

Kid Friendly

$2.49/serving
$9.96 total

Chicken Noodle Bowl

Hands-on: 40 min. Total: 56 min.

4 ounces uncooked linguine
2 teaspoons canola oil, divided
2 skinless, boneless chicken thighs
1 cup chopped onion
2 tablespoons minced peeled fresh ginger, divided
2 tablespoons minced garlic, divided
¼ teaspoon crushed red pepper
3¼ cups unsalted chicken stock
1¾ cups water
2 teaspoons dark sesame oil
1¼ cups sliced mushrooms
1 tablespoon lower-sodium soy sauce
1 teaspoon sugar
¾ cup sugar snap peas, cut diagonally into 1-inch pieces (about 4 ounces)
6 green onions, cut diagonally into 1-inch pieces
½ teaspoon kosher salt

1. Cook pasta according to package directions, omitting salt and fat; drain. Rinse under cold water; drain.
2. Heat a large saucepan over medium heat. Add 1 teaspoon canola oil; swirl to coat. Add chicken; cook 4 minutes on each side or until done. Let stand 5 minutes. Shred.
3. Return pan to medium-high heat. Add 1 teaspoon canola oil; swirl to coat. Add onion, 1 tablespoon ginger, 1 tablespoon garlic, and red pepper; cook 4 minutes. Add stock and 1¾ cups water; bring to a boil, scraping pan to loosen browned bits. Cover and simmer 15 minutes. Pour stock mixture through a sieve over a bowl;

discard solids. Return stock mixture to pan; keep warm.
4. Heat a large skillet over medium-high heat. Add sesame oil; swirl to coat. Add mushrooms; cook 6 minutes. Add 1 tablespoon ginger and 1 tablespoon garlic; cook 1 minute, stirring constantly. Add mushroom mixture, chicken, soy sauce, and sugar to stock mixture; bring to a simmer.
5. Stir in sugar snap peas; cook 1 minute. Remove from heat; stir in green onions and salt. Divide pasta evenly among 4 bowls; ladle stock mixture over pasta. Serves 4 (serving size: about 1⅔ cups)

CALORIES 262; **FAT** 6.7g (sat 1g, mono 2.9g, poly 2g); **PROTEIN** 17.7g; **CARB** 33.9g; **FIBER** 3.4g; **CHOL** 33mg; **IRON** 2.8mg; **SODIUM** 484mg; **CALC** 71mg

Kid Friendly

$2.32/serving
$9.28 total

Pork and Sweet Pepper Kebabs

Hands-on: 23 min. Total: 1 hr. 23 min.
Substitute 1-inch red or yellow bell pepper squares if you can't find the mini bells. Wooden skewers need to soak at least 30 minutes before they go on the grill, so plan ahead, if using them.

¼ cup lower-sodium soy sauce
1 tablespoon fresh lemon juice
1 tablespoon ketchup
2 teaspoons brown sugar
1 teaspoon Worcestershire sauce
¼ teaspoon crushed red pepper
4 garlic cloves, minced
1 (1-pound) pork tenderloin, trimmed and cut into ½-inch cubes
¼ teaspoon kosher salt
16 mini bell peppers
Cooking spray

1. Place first 7 ingredients in a large zip-top bag, stirring well. Add pork; seal bag. Refrigerate 1 hour, turning after 30 minutes.

2. Preheat grill to medium-high heat.
3. Remove pork from bag, and discard marinade. Thread pork evenly onto 4 (6-inch) skewers; sprinkle evenly with salt. Thread 4 mini bell peppers onto each of 4 (6-inch) skewers. Arrange skewers in a single layer on grill rack coated with cooking spray; grill 3 minutes on each side or until desired degree of doneness. Serves 4 (serving size: 1 pork skewer and 1 pepper skewer)

CALORIES 175; **FAT** 3g (sat 0.8g, mono 0.9g, poly 0.5g); **PROTEIN** 25.5g; **CARB** 10.3g; **FIBER** 2.4g; **CHOL** 74mg; **IRON** 1.9mg; **SODIUM** 408mg; **CALC** 19mg

Kid Friendly • Vegetarian

$2.42/serving
$9.68 total

Individual Mushroom, Onion, and Arugula Pizzas

Hands-on: 14 min. Total: 55 min.

12 ounces refrigerated pizza dough
5 teaspoons extra-virgin olive oil, divided
1 (8-ounce) package presliced mushrooms
1 medium onion, thinly sliced
2 garlic cloves, minced
1 tablespoon cornmeal
¾ cup part-skim ricotta cheese
1½ ounces fresh pecorino Romano cheese, grated (about ⅓ cup)
2 cups baby arugula
1 teaspoon fresh lemon juice

1. Remove dough from refrigerator; let stand at room temperature, covered, 30 minutes.
2. Place a pizza stone or heavy baking sheet in oven. Preheat oven to 500° (keep pizza stone or baking sheet in oven as it preheats).
3. Heat a large nonstick skillet over medium-high heat. Add 4 teaspoons oil to pan; swirl to coat. Add mushrooms and onion; sauté 5 minutes or until slightly tender and mushrooms

start to release liquid, stirring occasionally. Stir in garlic; cook 3 minutes or until lightly browned, stirring occasionally. Remove from heat.
4. Divide dough into 4 equal portions. Roll each portion into a 6-inch circle on a lightly floured surface; pierce entire surface of dough circles liberally with a fork. Carefully remove pizza stone from oven; sprinkle with cornmeal. Arrange dough circles on pizza stone. Combine cheeses in a small bowl. Divide cheese mixture into 4 equal portions; spread each portion evenly over 1 dough circle, leaving a ½-inch border. Divide mushroom mixture evenly among pizzas. Bake at 500° for 12 minutes or until crust is browned and crisp. Combine 1 teaspoon oil, arugula, and lemon juice in a bowl. Divide arugula mixture evenly among pizzas. Cut each pizza into 4 wedges. Serves 4 (serving size: 1 pizza)

CALORIES 405; **FAT** 14g (sat 4.9g, mono 6.9g, poly 1.3g); **PROTEIN** 18.9g; **CARB** 49.6g; **FIBER** 7.4g; **CHOL** 3mg; **IRON** 2mg; **SODIUM** 557mg; **CALC** 267mg

JUICING CITRUS

Cut citrus lengthwise (end to end) to get 10%–15% more juice.
—Robert Schueller,
Cooking Light produce guru

DINNER TONIGHT

Fast weeknight menus from the *Cooking Light* Test Kitchen

READY IN
40
MINUTES

The
SHOPPING LIST

Quick Seafood Stew
Small red potatoes
Leeks
Garlic
Fresh thyme
Bay leaf
Fresh flat-leaf parsley
Extra-virgin olive oil
Dry white wine
Unsalted chicken stock
Clam juice
Crushed red pepper
Striped bass fillets
Mussels
French Bread

Basil Green Beans
Shallots
Green beans
Fresh basil
Olive oil

The
GAME PLAN

While potatoes cook:
 ▪ Prepare broiler.
 ▪ Cook fish.
While stock mixture comes to a boil:
 ▪ Toast bread.
 ▪ Start green beans.

Quick Seafood Stew

with Basil Green Beans

Shopping Tip: Try a pinot grigio to complement the seafood.
Prep Pointer: Searing the fish speeds up cooking and deepens flavor.
Simple Sub: Use littleneck clams or shrimp instead of mussels.

1½ cups small red potatoes, quartered (about 10 ounces)
1½ tablespoons extra-virgin olive oil
¾ pound striped bass fillets
1½ cups thinly sliced leek
4 garlic cloves, thinly sliced
½ cup dry white wine
1 cup water
1 cup unsalted chicken stock (such as Swanson)
½ cup clam juice
½ teaspoon crushed red pepper
⅛ teaspoon kosher salt
2 thyme sprigs
1 bay leaf
24 medium mussels, scrubbed and debearded
2 tablespoons chopped fresh flat-leaf parsley
4 (1-ounce) slices diagonally cut French bread
1 garlic clove, halved

1. Place potatoes in a saucepan. Add water to cover potatoes; bring to a boil. Reduce heat to medium. Simmer 10 minutes; drain potatoes. Set aside.
2. Preheat broiler to high.
3. Heat a large Dutch oven over high heat. Add oil to pan; swirl to coat. Add fish, skin side down; cook 2 minutes or until skin is crisp. Remove from pan; break into 2-inch pieces.
4. Reduce heat to medium-high. Add leek and sliced garlic; sauté 5 minutes or until lightly browned, stirring occasionally. Add wine; bring to a boil,
continued

scraping pan to loosen browned bits. Add 1 cup water and next 6 ingredients; bring to a boil. Add potatoes, fish, and mussels; cover and cook 4 minutes or until shells open and fish is done. Discard any unopened shells, thyme, and bay leaf. Sprinkle with parsley.

5. Arrange bread in a single layer on a baking sheet. Broil 1½ minutes or until toasted. Rub bread generously with cut side of garlic. Serve with stew.

Sustainable Choice | Serves 4 (serving size: about 2½ cups stew and 1 toast slice) | *Look for farmed U.S. striped bass.*

CALORIES 378; FAT 10g (sat 1.7g, mono 4.9g, poly 2.1g); PROTEIN 33.1g; CARB 35.5g; FIBER 2.5g; CHOL 96mg; IRON 7.2mg; SODIUM 655mg; CALC 97mg

For the Basil Green Beans:

Heat a large skillet over medium-high heat. Add 2 teaspoons olive oil to pan; swirl to coat. Add ¼ cup thinly sliced shallots; sauté 2 minutes. Add 2 cups 2-inch-cut trimmed green beans and ¼ cup water. Cover and cook 4 minutes. Stir in 3 tablespoons thinly sliced fresh basil, ¼ teaspoon salt, and ¼ teaspoon freshly ground black pepper. Serves 4 (serving size: about ½ cup)

CALORIES 44; FAT 2.4g (sat 0.3g); SODIUM 152mg

READY IN 40 MINUTES

The
SHOPPING LIST

Grilled Asian Flank Steak with Mango Salad
Fresh cilantro
Ginger
Garlic
Lime (1)
Romaine lettuce
Green cabbage
Fresh mint
Green onions
Mango
Sugar
Fish sauce
Lower-sodium soy sauce
Reduced-fat peanut butter
Crushed red pepper
1 (1-pound) flank steak

Sesame Wonton Crisps
Wonton wrappers
Dark sesame oil
Sesame seeds

The
GAME PLAN

While grill preheats:
- Marinate beef.
- Preheat oven.

While steak grills:
- Make salad.
- Bake crisps.

Quick & Easy
Grilled Asian Flank Steak with Mango Salad
with Sesame Wonton Crisps

Flavor Hit: Ginger and garlic add aromatic depth to the marinade.
Time-Saver: Ask your butcher to trim your flank steak at the store.
Simple Sub: If you can't find mango, pineapple works equally well in the salad.

¼ **cup chopped fresh cilantro**
5 **teaspoons sugar, divided**
1 **tablespoon grated peeled fresh ginger**
1 **tablespoon minced fresh garlic**
1 **tablespoon fish sauce**
1 **tablespoon lower-sodium soy sauce**
1 **(1-pound) flank steak, trimmed**
Cooking spray
3 **tablespoons fresh lime juice**
2 **tablespoons water**
1 **tablespoon reduced-fat peanut butter**
½ **teaspoon crushed red pepper**
3 **cups shredded romaine lettuce**
2 **cups shredded green cabbage**
½ **cup mint leaves**
½ **cup cilantro leaves**
¼ **cup thinly sliced green onions**
1 **mango, peeled and diced**

1. Preheat grill to medium-high heat.
2. Combine chopped cilantro, 1 tablespoon sugar, and next 4 ingredients in a large zip-top plastic bag. Add beef; let stand 15 minutes. Remove beef from marinade; reserve marinade.
3. Place beef on grill rack coated with cooking spray. Drizzle with reserved marinade. Grill 5 minutes on each side or until desired degree of doneness. Remove from grill; cover with foil. Let stand 5 minutes; cut across the grain into thin slices.
4. Combine lime juice, 2 tablespoons water, peanut butter, 2 teaspoons sugar, and pepper in a large bowl; stir with a whisk. Add lettuce and next

4 ingredients; toss to coat. Divide salad evenly among 4 plates; top evenly with mango. Serve with beef. Serves 4 (serving size: about 1 cup salad and 3½ ounces beef)

CALORIES 285; FAT 8.4g (sat 2.8g, mono 2.4g, poly 0.4g); PROTEIN 28g; CARB 26.4g; FIBER 3.8g; CHOL 70mg; IRON 2.9mg; SODIUM 489mg; CALC 81mg

For the Sesame Wonton Crisps:

Preheat oven to 425°. Cut 6 wonton wrappers in half diagonally. Arrange triangles in a single layer on a baking sheet coated with cooking spray. Brush evenly with 1½ teaspoons dark sesame oil. Sprinkle evenly with 2 teaspoons sesame seeds and ⅛ teaspoon salt. Bake at 425° for 4 minutes or until browned. Serves 4 (serving size: 3 crisps)

CALORIES 60; FAT 2.8g (sat 0.4g); SODIUM 143mg

Kid Friendly • Quick & Easy

Grilled Chicken and Vegetable Quesadillas

with Avocado-Tomato Salad

Kid Tweak: Omit the ground red pepper.
Prep Pointer: The chicken and vegetables can be grilled indoors on a grill pan.
Simple Sub: For a spicier quesadilla, add a grilled jalapeño to the vegetable mix.

1½ teaspoons paprika
½ teaspoon garlic powder
½ teaspoon dried oregano
½ teaspoon ground cumin
¼ teaspoon kosher salt
¼ teaspoon black pepper
2 (6-ounce) skinless, boneless chicken breast halves
1 small onion, cut into ½-inch-thick slices
1 small orange bell pepper, cut into ½-inch-thick wedges
Cooking spray
3 ounces Monterey Jack cheese, shredded (about ¾ cup)

4 (6-inch) flour tortillas
¼ cup reduced-fat sour cream

1. Preheat grill to medium-high heat.
2. Combine paprika, garlic powder, oregano, cumin, salt, and black pepper in a small bowl. Rub paprika mixture evenly over chicken; let stand 10 minutes.
3. Arrange chicken, onion, and bell pepper on grill rack coated with cooking spray. Cook vegetables 4 minutes on each side or until tender. Cook chicken 6 minutes on each side or until done. Remove chicken and vegetables from grill; coarsely chop vegetables. Let chicken stand 5 minutes; thinly slice.
4. Sprinkle about 3 tablespoons cheese over half of each tortilla; divide vegetables and chicken evenly over cheese. Fold each tortilla in half over filling; lightly coat tortillas with cooking spray.
5. Heat a large nonstick skillet over medium heat. Place 2 quesadillas in pan; cook 2 to 3 minutes on each side or until cheese melts and tortillas are lightly browned. Repeat procedure with remaining 2 quesadillas. Cut each quesadilla into 2 wedges; serve with sour cream. Serves 4 (serving size: 2 quesadilla wedges and 1 tablespoon sour cream)

CALORIES 310; FAT 13g (sat 6.1g, mono 4.1g, poly 1.1g); PROTEIN 26.8g; CARB 20.4g; FIBER 1.9g; CHOL 79mg; IRON 1.9mg; SODIUM 552mg; CALC 228mg

For the Avocado-Tomato Salad:

Combine 2 tablespoons fresh lime juice, 1 teaspoon ground cumin, ¼ teaspoon freshly ground black pepper, ¼ teaspoon ground red pepper, and ⅛ teaspoon kosher salt; stir with a whisk. Add 2 cups halved grape tomatoes, ½ cup vertically sliced white onion, ¼ cup chopped fresh cilantro, and ½ ripe peeled avocado, coarsely chopped; toss gently to combine. Serves 4 (serving size: about ⅔ cup)

CALORIES 69; FAT 4g (sat 0.6g); SODIUM 68mg

READY IN 40 MINUTES

The
SHOPPING LIST

Grilled Chicken and Vegetable Quesadillas
Onion (1)
Orange bell pepper
Paprika
Garlic powder
Dried oregano
Ground cumin
4 (6-inch) flour tortillas
2 (6-ounce) skinless, boneless chicken breast halves
Monterey Jack cheese
Reduced-fat sour cream

Avocado-Tomato Salad
Lime (1)
Grape tomatoes
Onion (1)
Fresh cilantro
Avocado
Ground cumin
Ground red pepper

The
GAME PLAN

While grill preheats:
■ Rub spice mixture on chicken.
■ Slice onion and bell pepper.
While chicken cooks:
■ Prepare salad.

Lemon-Tarragon Crab Cakes with Arugula-Parsley Salad

Flavor Hit: The anise flavor of tarragon pairs well with seafood.
Time-Saver: Find bagged baby arugula in the produce section.
Prep Pointer: Wet your hands to make shaping the patties easier.

1¼ cups fresh breadcrumbs, toasted
¼ cup minced shallots
¼ cup chopped green onions
2 tablespoons unsalted butter, melted
1½ teaspoons grated lemon rind
2 tablespoons fresh lemon juice
1 teaspoon chopped fresh tarragon
¼ teaspoon kosher salt
¼ teaspoon freshly ground black pepper
⅛ teaspoon ground red pepper
1 pound lump crabmeat, shell pieces removed
1 large egg, lightly beaten
1 large egg white, lightly beaten
1 teaspoon olive oil

1. Combine all ingredients except olive oil in a bowl. Toss gently. Divide crab mixture into 6 equal portions (about ⅔ cup each), shaping each into a ½-inch-thick patty.
2. Heat a nonstick skillet over medium-high heat. Add oil to pan; swirl to coat. Add 3 crab cakes to pan; cook 4 minutes on each side or until lightly browned and heated through. Remove crab cakes from pan; keep warm. Repeat procedure with remaining 3 crab cakes. Serves 6 (serving size: 1 crab cake)

CALORIES 218; FAT 7.2g (sat 3.3g, mono 2g, poly 0.6g); PROTEIN 18.8g; CARB 18.7g; FIBER 1.3g; CHOL 113mg; IRON 0.7mg; SODIUM 567mg; CALC 82mg

For the Arugula-Parsley Salad:
Combine 2 tablespoons extra-virgin olive oil, 2 tablespoons fresh lemon juice, 2 teaspoons whole-grain Dijon mustard, 1 teaspoon agave syrup, ¼ teaspoon salt, and ¼ teaspoon freshly ground black pepper in a large bowl; stir with a whisk. Add 5 cups baby arugula, 1 cup flat-leaf parsley leaves, and ½ cup vertically sliced red onion to bowl; toss well to coat. Serves 6 (serving size: about 1 cup)

CALORIES 60; FAT 4.8g (sat 0.7g); SODIUM 151mg

READY IN 40 MINUTES

The SHOPPING LIST

Lemon-Tarragon Crab Cakes
Shallots
Green onions
Lemon
Fresh tarragon
Ground red pepper
Olive oil
Lump crabmeat
Unsalted butter
Eggs
Fresh breadcrumbs

Arugula-Parsley Salad
Lemon
Baby arugula
Fresh flat-leaf parsley
Red onion
Extra-virgin olive oil
Whole-grain Dijon mustard
Agave syrup

The GAME PLAN

While crab cakes cook:
■ Prepare salad.

SUPERFAST 20-MINUTE COOKING

Springy pastas, a twist on meat loaf, quick muffins, and more fast and easy weeknight favorites your family will love.

Spring Vegetable Penne with Lemon-Cream Sauce

If you can find them, use shelled fresh English peas instead of frozen.

1 tablespoon extra-virgin olive oil
¾ cup chopped Vidalia or other sweet onion
1 (4-ounce) package presliced mushrooms
1 teaspoon chopped fresh thyme
1 garlic clove, minced
1 tablespoon all-purpose flour
½ cup fat-free, lower-sodium chicken broth
½ cup half-and-half
¾ cup frozen green peas
3 tablespoons shaved fresh Parmesan cheese, divided
½ teaspoon grated lemon rind
1 tablespoon fresh lemon juice
½ teaspoon salt
½ teaspoon freshly ground black pepper
8 ounces uncooked penne
1 pound (1-inch) diagonally cut asparagus

1. Heat a large skillet over medium-high heat. Add oil; swirl to coat. Add onion and mushrooms; sauté 5 minutes or until tender. Add thyme and garlic; sauté 1 minute. Sprinkle mushroom mixture evenly with flour; cook 30 seconds, stirring constantly. Stir in broth and half-and-half; cook 2 minutes or until slightly thickened. Add peas, 2 tablespoons cheese, rind, and next 3 ingredients (through pepper); cook 1 minute or until peas are thoroughly heated.

2. Cook pasta according to package directions, omitting salt and fat. During the last 3 minutes of cooking, add asparagus to pan; drain. Add pasta mixture to mushroom mixture; toss gently to coat. Sprinkle with 1 tablespoon cheese. Serves 4 (serving size: about 1¾ cups)

CALORIES 363; **FAT** 9.2g (sat 3.6g, mono 3.8g, poly 0.7g); **PROTEIN** 15.5g; **CARB** 57.6g; **FIBER** 6.3g; **CHOL** 14mg; **IRON** 5.1mg; **SODIUM** 507mg; **CALC** 130mg

---

Kid Friendly • Quick & Easy

Mini Greek-Style Meat Loaves with Arugula Salad

10 ounces ground sirloin
5 ounces lean ground lamb
⅓ cup dry breadcrumbs
⅓ cup grated red onion
4 teaspoons chopped fresh mint
4 teaspoons chopped fresh thyme
⅜ teaspoon salt, divided
¼ teaspoon ground allspice
¼ teaspoon crushed red pepper
3 garlic cloves, minced
1 large egg, lightly beaten
Cooking spray
½ cup plain fat-free Greek yogurt
2 ounces reduced-fat feta, crumbled
2 tablespoons fresh lemon juice, divided
1 tablespoon extra-virgin olive oil
¼ teaspoon freshly ground black pepper
4 cups baby arugula leaves
1½ cups (¼-inch-thick) diagonally sliced seeded peeled cucumber

1. Preheat oven to 450°.
2. Combine first 4 ingredients in a large bowl. Stir in 1 tablespoon mint, 1 tablespoon thyme, ¼ teaspoon salt, allspice, and next 3 ingredients

Press meat mixture into 8 muffin cups coated with cooking spray. Bake at 450° for 7 minutes. Turn broiler to high; broil 3 minutes.
3. Place yogurt, feta, 1 tablespoon juice, 1 teaspoon mint, and 1 teaspoon thyme in a mini food processor; pulse 10 times to combine.
4. Combine 1 tablespoon juice, oil, ⅛ teaspoon salt, and pepper in a bowl; stir. Add arugula and cucumber; toss. Serves 4 (serving size: 2 meat loaves, 2 tablespoons feta sauce, and 1 cup salad)

CALORIES 347; **FAT** 17.3g (sat 6.3g, mono 7.5g, poly 1.4g); **PROTEIN** 33.9g; **CARB** 13.5g; **FIBER** 1.6g; **CHOL** 123mg; **IRON** 2.7mg; **SODIUM** 588mg; **CALC** 145mg

---

Quick & Easy

Raspberry-Chipotle Chicken Breasts with Cucumber Salad

2 tablespoons seedless raspberry jam
1½ tablespoons fresh lime juice
1 tablespoon minced chipotle chile, canned in adobo sauce
1 teaspoon minced fresh garlic
½ teaspoon grated lime rind
Cooking spray
4 (6-ounce) skinless, boneless chicken breast halves
⅜ teaspoon kosher salt, divided
¼ teaspoon freshly ground black pepper
3 cups shaved English cucumber
½ cup vertically sliced red onion
1 tablespoon red wine vinegar
½ teaspoon sugar

1. Combine first 5 ingredients in a small saucepan, stirring with a whisk until smooth. Cook over medium heat 4 minutes or until slightly syrupy.
2. Heat a large grill pan over medium-high heat. Coat pan with cooking spray. Sprinkle chicken evenly with ¼ teaspoon salt and pepper. Grill chicken

6 minutes on each side or until done. Spoon raspberry mixture over chicken.
3. Combine ⅛ teaspoon salt, cucumber, and remaining ingredients in a medium bowl; toss to combine. Serves 4 (serving size: 1 chicken breast half and ½ cup salad)

CALORIES 243; **FAT** 4.7g (sat 1g, mono 1.3g, poly 0.7g); **PROTEIN** 36.9g; **CARB** 11.3g; **FIBER** 1.1g; **CHOL** 109mg; **IRON** 0.9mg; **SODIUM** 401mg; **CALC** 27mg

---

Quick & Easy

Seared Tuna with Avocado Salsa

Before you sear the tuna, be sure to get the pan screaming hot—this gives you a deep crust without overcooking the interior. Look for yellowfin tuna caught using the troll or pole-and-line technique.

1 cup halved grape tomatoes
½ cup vertically sliced red onion
3 tablespoons chopped fresh cilantro
2 tablespoons fresh lime juice
⅜ teaspoon salt
½ teaspoon freshly ground black pepper
2 avocados, peeled and diced
2 garlic cloves, minced
1 jalapeño pepper, seeded and finely chopped
2 tablespoons lower-sodium soy sauce
2 teaspoons dark brown sugar
Cooking spray
4 (6-ounce) tuna steaks

1. Combine first 9 ingredients in a medium bowl.
2. Combine soy sauce and brown sugar in a small bowl, stirring until brown sugar dissolves. Reserve 1 tablespoon soy sauce mixture. Heat a grill pan over high heat. Coat pan evenly with cooking spray. Add steaks to pan; cook 2 minutes on each side or until desired degree of doneness, basting steaks frequently with soy mixture. Remove
continued

Sustainable Choice

steaks from grill pan; drizzle with reserved 1 tablespoon soy mixture. Serve fish with salsa. Serves 4 (serving size: 1 tuna steak and about ⅓ cup salsa)

CALORIES 384; FAT 15.9g (sat 2.5g, mono 10.1g, poly 2.1g); PROTEIN 44.8g; CARB 17g; FIBER 7.8g; CHOL 66mg; IRON 2.3mg; SODIUM 504mg; CALC 35mg

Kid Friendly • Quick & Easy
Freezable • Make Ahead • Vegetarian

Zucchini Mini Muffins

These are tasty for breakfast or as a snack. For even portions, use a small ice-cream scoop to spoon the batter into the muffin cups.

**6 ounces all-purpose flour
   (about 1⅓ cups)**
½ cup packed dark brown sugar
1 teaspoon baking powder
1 teaspoon ground cinnamon
½ teaspoon salt
¼ teaspoon ground allspice
**⅔ cup shredded zucchini (about 1
   medium zucchini)**
3 tablespoons canola oil
2 tablespoons butter, melted
2 tablespoons 1% low-fat milk
1 teaspoon vanilla extract
1 large egg, lightly beaten
Cooking spray

1. Preheat oven to 400°.
2. Weigh or lightly spoon flour into dry measuring cups; level with a knife. Combine flour and next 5 ingredients (through allspice) in a large bowl. Combine zucchini and next 5 ingredients (through egg) in a small bowl; stir with a whisk. Add zucchini mixture to flour mixture, stirring batter just until combined. Divide batter evenly among 24 miniature muffin cups coated with cooking spray.

Bake at 400° for 10 minutes or until a wooden pick inserted in center of muffins comes out clean. Serves 12 (serving size: 2 muffins)

CALORIES 146; FAT 6.1g (sat 1.7g, mono 2.9g, poly 1.2g); PROTEIN 2.3g; CARB 20.8g; FIBER 0.7g; CHOL 21mg; IRON 0.9mg; SODIUM 160mg; CALC 41mg

Kid Friendly • Quick & Easy

Shrimp Fettuccine with Spinach and Parmesan

8 ounces uncooked fettuccine
2 tablespoons butter
1 tablespoon extra-virgin olive oil
2 garlic cloves, thinly sliced
**10 ounces medium shrimp, peeled and
   deveined**
⅜ teaspoon salt
**¼ teaspoon freshly ground black
   pepper**
6 ounces fresh baby spinach
**1¼ ounces fresh Parmesan cheese,
   shaved**

1. Cook pasta according to package directions, omitting salt and fat.
2. Heat a large skillet over medium heat. Add butter and oil; swirling until butter melts. Add garlic to pan; cook 1 minute. Remove garlic from pan with a slotted spoon; place in a small bowl. Increase heat to medium-high. Add shrimp, salt, and pepper to pan; cook 4 minutes or until shrimp are done, stirring occasionally. Add pasta, spinach, and garlic to pan; cook 1 minute or until spinach wilts, tossing to coat. Sprinkle with cheese. Serves 4 (serving size: about 1⅔ cups)

CALORIES 388; FAT 13.4g (sat 6g, mono 4.8g, poly 0.8g); PROTEIN 22.2g; CARB 45.4g; FIBER 2.8g; CHOL 112mg; IRON 3.3mg; SODIUM 549mg; CALC 194mg

Quick & Easy

Open-Faced Chicken Sandwiches with Artichoke Pesto

**3 (8-ounce) skinless, boneless chicken
   breast halves**
½ teaspoon salt, divided
½ teaspoon black pepper, divided
Cooking spray
**6 ounces drained canned artichoke
   hearts**
**2 ounces fresh Parmigiano-Reggiano
   cheese, shaved and divided (about
   ½ cup)**
2 tablespoons pine nuts
2 tablespoons canola mayonnaise
2 teaspoons olive oil
3 garlic cloves
6 (1-ounce) slices multigrain bread
**3 tablespoons chopped fresh flat-leaf
   parsley**

1. Preheat broiler to high.
2. Cut each chicken breast half in half lengthwise to form 2 cutlets. Sprinkle with ¼ teaspoon salt and ¼ teaspoon pepper. Heat a grill pan over medium-high heat. Coat pan with cooking spray. Add chicken to pan; cook 4 minutes on each side or until done.
3. Place artichokes, 3 tablespoons cheese, nuts, mayonnaise, oil, ¼ teaspoon salt, ¼ teaspoon pepper, and garlic in a mini food processor; pulse until coarsely ground.
4. Place bread slices on a baking sheet; broil 1 minute on each side. Spread 2½ tablespoons pesto on each slice. Slice chicken; place 3 ounces on each bread slice. Top evenly with 5 tablespoons cheese and parsley. Serves 6

CALORIES 284; FAT 11.6g (sat 1.9g, mono 5g, poly 2.7g); PROTEIN 29.4g; CARB 14.2g; FIBER 3.1g; CHOL 76mg; IRON 2mg; SODIUM 601mg; CALC 74mg

Orzo with Pecorino and Mushrooms

3/4 cup uncooked orzo
1 1/2 tablespoons butter
3 cups sliced cremini mushrooms
1/2 teaspoon black pepper
3/8 teaspoon salt
1/4 cup fat-free, lower-sodium chicken broth
1 tablespoon white balsamic vinegar
1/4 cup minced fresh chives
1 ounce fresh pecorino Romano cheese, shaved (about 1/4 cup)

1. Cook pasta according to package directions, omitting salt and fat.
2. Melt butter in a large skillet over medium heat; cook 1 minute or until lightly browned. Add mushrooms, pepper, and salt. Cook 4 minutes or until mushrooms release their liquid, stirring frequently. Add broth and vinegar; stir in orzo and chives. Top with cheese. Serves 6 (serving size: 1/2 cup)

CALORIES 156; FAT 5.1g (sat 3g, mono 0.8g, poly 0.2g); PROTEIN 5.9g; CARB 22.4g; FIBER 1.5g; CHOL 13mg; IRON 1.2mg; SODIUM 304mg; CALC 48mg

Garlicky Spinach

Prepare base recipe through step 1. Melt 1 tablespoon butter in skillet over medium heat; cook 1 minute or until browned. Add 4 cups spinach and 2 teaspoons minced garlic; cook 1 minute. Stir in orzo; 1 ounce grated fresh Parmesan cheese; 1/4 cup fat-free, lower-sodium chicken broth; 1 tablespoon white balsamic vinegar; 3/8 teaspoon salt; and 1/4 teaspoon crushed red pepper. Serves 6 (serving size: about 1/3 cup)

CALORIES 149; FAT 3.8g (sat 2g); SODIUM 299mg

Tarragon and Peas

Prepare base recipe through step 1. Melt 1 tablespoon butter in skillet over medium heat; cook 1 minute or until lightly browned. Add 2 1/2 cups frozen peas; cook 1 minute or until thoroughly heated. Stir in orzo; 1/4 cup fat-free, lower-sodium chicken broth; 2 tablespoons minced tarragon leaves; 1 tablespoon fresh lemon juice; 1/2 teaspoon black pepper; and 3/8 teaspoon salt. Serves 6 (serving size: 1/2 cup)

CALORIES 171; FAT 3.7g (sat 1.9g); SODIUM 269mg

Sun-Dried Tomato and Basil

Prepare base recipe through step 1. Heat a skillet over medium heat. Add 1 1/2 tablespoons olive oil to pan. Add 1/4 cup finely chopped sun-dried tomatoes, 1/4 cup pine nuts, and 1 teaspoon minced garlic; cook 2 minutes. Stir in orzo, 1/2 cup minced fresh basil, 1 tablespoon white balsamic vinegar, 1/2 teaspoon pepper, and 3/8 teaspoon salt. Serves 6 (serving size: 1/2 cup)

CALORIES 178; FAT 7.8g (sat 0.8g); SODIUM 154mg

IF SALMON TURNS WHITE, THEN IT'S OVERCOOKING.

TODAY'S SPECIAL

BROILED SALMON CROSTINI FROM SPUR RESTAURANT IN SEATTLE

May in the Pacific Northwest means one thing above all: fantastically fresh salmon. In particular, the region's sockeye salmon—robustly flavored, brilliantly ruby-colored, loaded with healthy fats—is beginning to be offered fresh and wild-caught nationwide this time of year. We turned to Brian McCracken and Dana Tough, the chef-owners of the wildly popular gastropub Spur in Seattle, for a quick and easy dish that highlights this superb fish. They gently oil-poach the salmon and pair it with creamy mascarpone, tangy pickled shallots, and briny fried capers in a delicious twist on bagels and lox. (Those out West can find this version on the Spur menu this month.)

Inspired by the Spur dish, we developed a streamlined version for the home cook, one that still showcases the velvety texture and bold flavor of sockeye salmon. Our version broils the fish, keeping the tang with capers, lemon rind, and crème fraîche. If you can't find sockeye, any variety of salmon will work, though Tough and McCracken favor sockeye above all. "We like the fat content—it's fatty, but not too much," Tough says. "And it's less metallic-flavored than king salmon. It tastes more like the ocean."

McCracken cautions cooks not to overcook the fish. "We like to keep it pink throughout," he explains. "Watch the fish closely—if salmon turns white, then it's overcooking." —Tim Cebula

continued

Sockeye Salmon Crostini

Hands-on: 10 min. Total: 10 min.

1 (6-ounce) fresh or frozen sustainable
  sockeye salmon fillet (such as
  Alaskan)
¼ teaspoon freshly ground black
  pepper
2 tablespoons finely chopped shallots
1 tablespoon chopped drained capers
3 tablespoons crème fraîche
¼ teaspoon grated lemon rind
1 teaspoon fresh lemon juice
12 (½-ounce) slices diagonally cut
  French bread baguette, toasted
12 small dill sprigs

1. Preheat broiler to high.
2. Place fillet on a foil-lined baking
sheet; sprinkle fillet evenly with pepper. Broil 6 minutes or until desired
degree of doneness. Cool 2 minutes;
flake fillet.
3. Combine shallots and next 4
ingredients in a small bowl, stirring
well. Place 2 toasted baguette slices on
each of 6 small plates. Divide salmon
evenly among baguette slices; top each
crostini with 1 teaspoon crème fraîche
mixture and 1 dill sprig. Serves 6
(serving size: 2 crostini)

CALORIES 142; **FAT** 4.3g (sat 2g, mono 0.5g, poly 0.6g);
PROTEIN 8.2g; **CARB** 16.7g; **FIBER** 0.8g; **CHOL** 18mg;
IRON 1.2mg; **SODIUM** 228mg; **CALC** 17mg

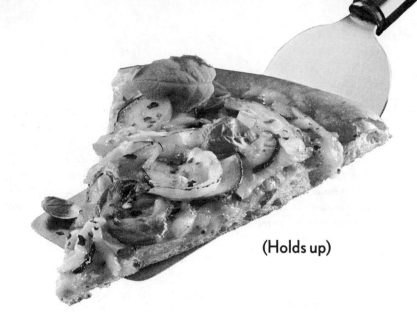

(Holds up)

OOPS!

YOUR PIZZA CRUST IS SOGGY

Here are several tricks to turning out a
firm, crisp crust.

Perfect pizza crust—crisp yet chewy,
not soggy or saggy—can be tricky.
Pizza geography presents a challenge:
The bare coastal edges cook faster
than the topped center. What's more,
the natural tendency to pile on toppings
leads to overloaded, soggy crusts.

The solution: Sear the crust first to
firm it up. Put your pan or pizza stone
in the oven as it preheats, and arrange
the dough on the hot pan before you
top; this sets the crust. For veggie pizzas, sauté toppings to keep ingredients
like zucchini and mushrooms from
watering out as they bake, and use
restraint with those toppings. Spread
a scant layer of sauce (about ¼ cup), so
the dough is still visible underneath,
and finely chop or thinly slice vegetables (big chunks cook unevenly). If
you have very fresh mozzarella, drain
off any excess milk before adding.

(Gives up)

SUMMER COOKBOOK

Summer 2012...It was 95° in the shade, and our Alabama garden was bursting with amazing heirloom produce. At last we could go fully home-grown with our annual ode to the season, developing recipes exclusively from local heirloom bounty. A year later, as the garden promises another bumper crop (the voles have mostly been vanquished), we're sharing our first batch of simple, delicious vegetarian dishes—along with some growing trips from our Gardener in Chief, Mary Beth Burner Shaddix.

TOMATOES

These are the stars of the garden for so many reasons: spectacularly colored fruit, bursting with juices both sugary and acidic, underscored by meaty texture that delivers real depth of flavor. Our garden's selection ran the gamut: superabundant cherries, dense paste tomatoes, and beefy slicers--in a glorious rainbow of colors. Chopped up for an herby salad or veggie pasta, or mixed into ultramoist cupcakes (no kidding), our tomatoes show how one perfect ingredient makes simple fare sublime.

Kid Friendly • Quick & Easy
Vegetarian

Penne with Herbs, Tomatoes, and Peas

Hands-on: 20 min. Total: 20 min.

8 ounces uncooked penne pasta
1 cup frozen green peas, thawed
3 tablespoons extra-virgin olive oil
6 garlic cloves, thinly sliced
3 cups cherry tomatoes, halved
½ teaspoon kosher salt
¼ teaspoon freshly ground black pepper
⅓ cup thinly sliced basil leaves
3 tablespoons chopped fresh flat-leaf parsley
1 ounce fresh Parmesan cheese, shaved (about ¼ cup)

1. Cook pasta according to package directions, omitting salt and fat. Add peas during last 2 minutes of cooking. Drain.
2. Heat a large nonstick skillet over medium-low heat. Add oil; swirl to coat. Add garlic; cook 4 minutes or until garlic begins to brown, stirring occasionally. Increase heat to medium-high. Add tomatoes to pan; cook 1 minute. Add pasta mixture, salt, and pepper to pan; cook 3 minutes or until thoroughly heated, stirring occasionally. Stir in basil and parsley. Sprinkle with cheese. Serves 4 (serving size: 1½ cups)

CALORIES 381; FAT 13.4g (sat 2.9g, mono 8g, poly 1.3g); PROTEIN 13.7g; CARB 53.3g; FIBER 4.9g; CHOL 6mg; IRON 3.1mg; SODIUM 396mg; CALC 126mg

STORAGE TIP

Chilling gorgeously ripe tomatoes turns their texture mushy and mealy, and their flavor insipid. Store them instead at room temperature, in a dry spot away from direct sunlight, which will ripen them unevenly.

Vegetarian

Heirloom Tomato and Beet Salad
(pictured on page 223)

Hands-on: 15 min. Total: 1 hr. 30 min.

2 medium-sized red beets
2 medium-sized golden beets
3 tablespoons chopped fresh chives
2 tablespoons chopped fresh tarragon
2 tablespoons chopped shallots
1 tablespoon capers
3 tablespoons extra-virgin olive oil
2 tablespoons balsamic vinegar
1 teaspoon Dijon mustard
3 cups heirloom cherry tomatoes, halved
2 pounds heirloom tomatoes, sliced
½ teaspoon kosher salt
¼ teaspoon freshly ground black pepper

continued

1. Preheat oven to 400°.
2. Trim roots and stems from beets. Pierce beets with a fork, and wrap in foil. Bake at 400° for 1 hour or until tender. Cool; peel beets and cut into ¼-inch-thick slices.
3. Combine chives and next 6 ingredients in a small bowl, stirring with a whisk. Combine cherry tomatoes and about 5 teaspoons mustard mixture; toss to coat. Place sliced beets and sliced tomatoes on each of 6 plates. Drizzle each serving with about 3 teaspoons remaining mustard mixture. Top each serving evenly with cherry tomatoes. Sprinkle with salt and pepper. Serves 6 (serving size: about 3 beet slices, about 4 tomato slices, and ½ cup cherry tomatoes)

CALORIES 127; FAT 7.3g (sat 1g, mono 5g, poly 0.9g); PROTEIN 2.8g; CARB 14.9g; FIBER 4g; CHOL 0mg; IRON 1.1mg; SODIUM 275mg; CALC 35mg

Kid Friendly • Make Ahead Vegetarian

Green Tomato and Fig Cupcakes

Hands-on: 20 min. Total: 65 min.

8 ounces green tomato, cored and quartered
7.6 ounces cake flour, sifted (2 cups)
1 teaspoon baking powder
½ teaspoon baking soda
½ teaspoon ground cinnamon
¼ teaspoon salt
1 cup granulated sugar
½ cup canola oil
2 large eggs
2 teaspoons grated orange rind
4 ounces fresh Black Mission figs, stemmed and chopped
3 ounces chopped pecans (²/₃ cup)
Cooking spray
4 ounces ⅓-less-fat cream cheese
1¼ cups powdered sugar
½ teaspoon vanilla extract
Dash of salt
Sliced fresh figs (optional)

1. Preheat oven to 350°.
2. Place tomato in a blender; blend until smooth.
3. Weigh or lightly spoon flour into dry measuring cups; level with a knife. Combine flour, baking powder, baking soda, cinnamon, and ¼ teaspoon salt in a bowl. Place sugar, oil, and eggs in a large bowl; beat with a mixer at high speed until blended. Stir in tomato puree and orange rind. Add flour mixture to egg mixture; beat at low speed just until combined. Stir in chopped figs and pecans.
4. Place 18 muffin cup liners in muffin cups; coat liners with cooking spray. Spoon batter into cups. Bake at 350° for 17 minutes or until a wooden pick inserted in center comes out with moist crumbs clinging. Cool in pans 5 minutes. Remove from pans; cool completely on wire racks.
5. Place cream cheese in a large bowl; beat with a mixer at high speed until smooth. Add powdered sugar, vanilla, and dash of salt; beat until smooth. Spread frosting over the top of each cupcake. Garnish with sliced figs, if desired. Serves 18 (serving size: 1 cupcake)

CALORIES 245; FAT 12.3g (sat 2.3g, mono 6.3g, poly 3g); PROTEIN 2.8g; CARB 32g; FIBER 1g; CHOL 27mg; IRON 1.2mg; SODIUM 139mg; CALC 31mg

GROWING TIP

Plant your backyard crop with variety in mind: Choose a slicer (one that grows big enough to yield hearty slices for salads and sandwiches), a paste tomato for long, slow cooking, and snackable cherry tomatoes. Remember, cherries can be very prolific, so you really only need one or two plants.

FROM OUR GARDEN

STRIPED ROMAN
This paste tomato, with pretty yellow splotches, is at its best when cooked down. It has meatier flesh and less seedy liquid than other types.

GREEN ZEBRA
Has vibrant green and yellow stripes when mature, with lime-green, juicy, tart flesh. The bold color makes it perfect for mixed tomato salads and platters.

CHOCOLATE CHERRY
As close to candy as tomatoes get. Kids love them: The chocolate color adds a fun factor. Highly prolific: One plant yields loads.

CHEROKEE PURPLE
One of the most widely available heirlooms, these huge fruits—up to a pound or so each—have deep, winey flavor.

SPEAR'S TENNESSEE GREEN
This big slicing variety—about 8–10 ounces—is sweet but well balanced, with acid and citrus notes. An all-time favorite for heirloom tomato fans.

GERMAN PINK
These rich, sweet, full-flavored slicers boast some heft, weighing over a pound each.

ROMA
The ultimate paste tomato, a fantastic all-purpose cooking fruit. Make batches of marinara for the cold months ahead with this meaty-fleshed classic.

GARDEN PEACH
Distinctive for its fuzzy skin that turns gold with touches of rosy blush as it ripens. Soft flesh makes it a great candidate for blended dishes like gazpacho.

COSTOLUTO GENOVESE
The striking, deep red color matches the flavor: meaty, almost savory. This sturdy slicer can be served raw and minimally dressed, or stuffed and baked.

GREEN DOCTORS
Our staff favorite: candy-sweet and so juicy and perfectly acid-balanced they dress themselves. They make a striking salad with Chocolate Cherries.

BEETS

Even if you already love beets, you'll enjoy them even more when you grow your own. When you pluck them fresh from the soil, they give you three gifts: first, the beetroot itself, with flesh that's earthy yet sweet, dense yet tender, colorful as jewelry. Then the beet greens, which, when just-picked, are wonderfully vibrant, crisp-tender, bitter-sweet, and a little peppery. And third, the gardener's reward for time spent thinning the crop: baby greens from seedlings (sold as "microgreens" for fancy prices).

Vegetarian

Roasted Beets with Jalapeño Cream

Hands-on: 9 min. Total: 60 min. A creamy jalapeño dressing livens up earthy roasted beets. Seed the pepper for less heat.

1 pound medium-sized red beets
1 pound medium-sized golden beets
1/3 cup reduced-fat sour cream
1/4 cup finely chopped green onions
1/4 teaspoon salt
1 jalapeño pepper, finely chopped
16 Bibb or Boston lettuce leaves

1. Preheat oven to 450°.
2. Remove stems and roots from beets; wrap beets in foil. Bake at 450° for 45 minutes or until tender. Cool beets slightly; peel and cut into 1-inch wedges.
3. Combine sour cream, onions, salt, and jalapeño in a small bowl. Place lettuce leaves on each of 8 plates; top evenly with beets and jalapeño mixture. Serves 8 (serving size: 2 lettuce leaves, ½ cup beets, and about 1 tablespoon jalapeño cream)

CALORIES 68; **FAT** 1.5g (sat 0.8g, mono 0g, poly 0.1g); **PROTEIN** 2.6g; **CARB** 12.2g; **FIBER** 3.5g; **CHOL** 5mg; **IRON** 1.2mg; **SODIUM** 170mg; **CALC** 43mg

Make Ahead • Vegetarian

Rosé and Raspberry Pickled Beets

Hands-on: 12 min. Total: 9 hr. 12 min.

1 pound Chioggia beets or red beets (about 2)
1 tablespoon whole black peppercorns
4 thyme sprigs
1½ cups fresh raspberries
1½ cups dry rosé wine
3/4 cup sugar
1/3 cup red wine vinegar
2 teaspoons kosher salt

1. Preheat oven to 425°.
2. Leave root and 1 inch stem on beets; scrub with a brush. Place beets in an 8-inch square glass or ceramic baking dish; add water to a depth of 2 inches. Cover with foil; bake at 425° for 50 minutes or until just tender. Drain and cool. Peel beets; cut into 1-inch wedges. Place beets in a large heatproof glass jar or bowl with peppercorns and thyme.
3. Combine raspberries and remaining ingredients in a medium saucepan. Bring to a simmer; cook 4 minutes, stirring occasionally, until sugar dissolves and raspberries begin to break down. Strain raspberry mixture through a fine sieve over a bowl; discard solids. Pour hot raspberry liquid over beet mixture; cover and chill at least 8 hours or overnight. Serves 8 (serving size: about 1/3 cup)

CALORIES 37; **FAT** 0.1g (sat 0g, mono 0g, poly 0.1g); **PROTEIN** 1g; **CARB** 7.8g; **FIBER** 1.8g; **CHOL** 0mg; **IRON** 0.5mg; **SODIUM** 92mg; **CALC** 11mg

FROM OUR GARDEN

GOLDEN
Not a beet fan? This one might win you over. A little sweeter than darker varieties, is still has an alluring earthiness. Also, it doesn't stain everything purple-red.

BULL'S BLOOD
With its deep crimson color, this beet is often grown for its tender, sweet-spicy leaves. But the tasty flesh is intense red, often beautifully ringed with pink.

CHIOGGIA
Stunning red-and-white-striped flesh sets these apart and makes them great for shaving thin and serving raw in salads (the flesh turns uniformly red when cooked).

GROWING TIP

The beet seed boasts a special construction: What appears like one single seed is actually a tight cluster of several seeds. So one planted beet "seed" can yield multiple plants. Thin the seedlings (young plants 2–3 inches high) to about 2–3 inches apart so they have ample room to mature.

STORAGE TIP

Beet greens are a great indicator of the root's freshness: If the greens are vibrant and healthy enough to serve in a raw salad, you know the beet has been freshly picked. But it's best to cut the greens off after buying or harvesting and refrigerate them separately, since the greens pull moisture from the roots. The greens will also wilt within a few days, so use them quickly.

BEANS

It's hard for us to pick a favorite bean from our garden's crop. We love the pole beans, picked young and tender, that give just the right amount of snap and crunch to a picnic-perfect bean salad. But then there are the bush beans, with their striking striations of color, that we shell for the seeds that cook up meaty and creamy, great for that very same salad or pureed into a velvety summer soup. And shell beans have this advantage: They can be dried, and then cooked all year long.

FROM OUR GARDEN

CHEROKEE TRAIL OF TEARS
Multipurpose pole beans that can be eaten fresh when picked young. Or leave them to dry; then shell: The beans inside turn glossy black and are great in stew and chili.

DRAGON TONGUE
This bush bean starts out light green, and then grows splotchy as it ripens. Can be eaten as snaps when young or shelled for hearty beans when mature.

ITALIAN ROSE
The beautiful shell on these tends to be thick and fibrous: They're best for shelling fresh or dried. Very similar to the popular cranberry beans.

GOLDEN WAX
Best when picked fresh and young so they stay tender. Pluck them from the vine before you see the bean seed bumps forming, which means they've toughened.

Make Ahead • Vegetarian

Chilled Butter Bean Soup with Basil-Corn Relish

(pictured on page 224)

Hands-on: 10 min. Total: 2 hr. 45 min. *You'll need about 1½ pounds of butter bean pods to get 2 cups shelled beans. You can substitute fresh lima beans.*

2½ cups organic vegetable broth
2 cups shelled fresh butter beans
¾ cup chopped onion
¼ teaspoon salt
⅛ teaspoon black pepper
1 basil sprig
1 garlic clove, crushed
1 tablespoon fresh lemon juice
¼ cup fresh corn kernels
¼ cup chopped red bell pepper
¼ cup chopped basil leaves
1 tablespoon extra-virgin olive oil

1. Combine first 7 ingredients in a medium saucepan over medium heat; bring to a simmer. Cover and cook 40 minutes or until beans are tender. Discard basil sprig. Reserve ¼ cup beans; set aside.
2. Place remaining bean mixture in a blender; add juice. Remove center piece of blender lid (to allow steam to escape); secure blender lid on blender. Place a clean towel over opening in blender lid (to avoid splatters). Blend until smooth. Cool slightly; refrigerate 2 hours or until chilled.
3. Heat a small nonstick skillet over medium-high heat. Add corn; sauté 2 minutes or until browned. Combine reserved ¼ cup beans, corn, red pepper, chopped basil, and oil in a small bowl. Ladle soup evenly into each of 8 bowls; top with corn mixture. Serves 8 (serving size: ½ cup soup and 3 tablespoons corn mixture)

CALORIES 202; FAT 2.3g (sat 0.4g, mono 1.3g, poly 0.4g); PROTEIN 10.9g; CARB 35.5g; FIBER 10.9g; CHOL 0mg; IRON 3.3mg; SODIUM 254mg; CALC 48mg

---

PREPARATION TIP

Remove the stem end from pole or string beans before cooking: Line up the beans with the stems facing the same direction, and use a chef's knife to slice the tips off cleanly. The tail end can remain on young pole beans. For dried beans, thrash them. It's stress relief and shelling all in one. Place dried bean pods in a bag, and beat them against something until the beans release.

Quick & Easy • Make Ahead
Vegetarian

Italian Three-Bean Salad

Hands-on: 25 min. Total: 30 min. *Prepare the salad up to 1 day ahead, and store in the refrigerator. If you can't find fresh cranberry beans, substitute rinsed and drained canned cannellini beans, and add them to the snap beans for the last 2 minutes of cooking.*

2 cups quartered cherry tomatoes
½ cup chopped green onions
¼ cup chopped pitted kalamata olives
1 tablespoon chopped fresh oregano
2 teaspoons grated lemon rind
2 tablespoons fresh lemon juice
2 teaspoons olive oil
½ teaspoon freshly ground black pepper
¼ teaspoon kosher salt
8 cups water
½ pound shelled fresh cranberry beans
2 cups (2-inch) cut green beans
2 cups (2-inch) cut yellow wax beans
2 ounces fresh Parmigiano-Reggiano cheese, shaved (about ½ cup)

1. Combine cherry tomatoes and next 8 ingredients in a large bowl.
2. Combine 8 cups water and cranberry beans in a large saucepan; bring to a boil. Reduce heat, and simmer 15 minutes or until tender. Add green and yellow beans; cook 5 minutes or until crisp-tender. Drain and rinse with cold water; drain well.
3. Add bean mixture to tomato mixture, and toss gently to coat. Sprinkle

with shaved cheese. Serves 12 (serving size: about ⅔ cup)

CALORIES 117; **FAT** 3.4g (sat 1.1g, mono 1.7g, poly 0.4g); **PROTEIN** 7g; **CARB** 15.7g; **FIBER** 6.5g; **CHOL** 4mg; **IRON** 1.3mg; **SODIUM** 177mg; **CALC** 104mg

STORAGE TIP

Leave shell beans in their pods to store in a paper bag in the refrigerator. They'll last 3 or 4 days longer than when shelled. After shelling, store them refrigerated in an air-tight container. For longer-term storage, shell and blanch the beans; then freeze for up to 6 months.

CUCUMBERS

Cucumber offerings in the supermarket are so limited that until the boom in farmers' markets it was easy to suppose that there were only two or three varieties. In fact, there are dozens of dozens, wonderfully different in shape, color, and flavor. We planted a couple of varieties for fresh eating—few summer vegetables are as refreshing as a crispy cuke—and some little ones for pickling. When choosing a pickling cuke, go for one that's small enough to fit whole in a jar; gherkins are ideal.

GROWING TIP

We had a challenge making our cuke plants bountiful because bees weren't pollinating the plants enough. The simple solution: hand-pollination. When the plant begins to sprout yellow flowers, go from one flower to the next with a cotton swab or tiny paintbrush, gently rubbing the inside to distribute the pollen.

Quick & Easy • Vegetarian

Cucumber Salad

Hands-on: 10 min. Total: 10 min.

2 tablespoons extra-virgin olive oil
1 tablespoon white wine
1 tablespoon fresh lemon juice
¼ teaspoon kosher salt
¼ teaspoon freshly ground black pepper
⅛ teaspoon sugar
½ cup (1-inch) slices red bell pepper
½ cup (1-inch) slices green bell pepper
3 tablespoons chopped fresh chives
1 tablespoon chopped fresh flat-leaf parsley
1 English cucumber, sliced

1. Combine first 6 ingredients in a medium bowl, stirring with a whisk.
2. Add bell peppers and remaining ingredients to wine mixture; toss gently to coat. Serves 4 (serving size: ¾ cup)

CALORIES 83; **FAT** 7g (sat 1g, mono 4.9g, poly 0.8g); **PROTEIN** 0.8g; **CARB** 4.1g; **FIBER** 1.2g; **CHOL** 0mg; **IRON** 0.4mg; **SODIUM** 124mg; **CALC** 14mg

FROM OUR GARDEN

WHITE WONDER
Also known as Albino, Ivory King, and Jack Frost, this cucumber is distinguished by its pale skin. Harvest young for thinner skin and crisp flesh.

GOLD STANDARD
The yellow flesh offers as much as 5 times the beta-carotene of other cuke varieties. It's an excellent choice for both pickling and eating fresh.

GHERKIN
The unique shape lends itself to dramatic presentations as a pickle on charcuterie boards. Pick young, as gherkins grown spinier as they mature.

STRAIGHT EIGHT
The quintessential cuke. The variety is foolproof for novice gardeners; true to their name, they grow straight. Classic dill pickle material.

PREP TIP

While garden-fresh cukes won't sport the tough, waxy skin of traditional supermarket types, some may have thicker skins than English cucumbers, for instance. But peeling the entire thing robs much of its visual pizzazz. Instead, peel skin in alternating rows, leaving the cuke handsomely striped and more tender by half.

Make Ahead • Vegetarian

Cucumber Pimm's Cup

(pictured on page 220)

Hands-on: 7 min. Total: 8 hr. 7 min.
A traditional Pimm's Cup may include slices of lemon and orange, mint, and sometimes rosemary or thyme, along with cucumber spears. We steeped the cucumber slices in lemonade overnight to bring out their flavor.

2 cups prepared lemonade
1 large cucumber, cut into ½-inch-thick slices
1 cup Pimm's No. 1, chilled
1 cup ginger ale, chilled
6 cucumber spears (optional)
Mint leaves (optional)

1. Combine prepared lemonade and cucumber slices in a large pitcher. Refrigerate for 8 hours or overnight.
2. Add Pimm's and ginger ale to pitcher. Pour 1 cup mixture into each of 6 ice-filled glasses. Garnish with cucumber spears and mint leaves, if desired. Serves 6 (servings size: 1 cup)

CALORIES 152; **FAT** 0.2g (sat 0g, mono 0g, poly 0g); **PROTEIN** 0.6g; **CARB** 15.6g; **FIBER** 0.7g; **CHOL** 0mg; **IRON** 0.3mg; **SODIUM** 10mg; **CALC** 15mg

EGGPLANT

From a simple kitchen standpoint, what sets eggplants apart from other summer garden produce is that they require cooking. Raw, the flesh is spongy and plain. But once roasted, grilled, sautéed, or stir-fried, the eggplant comes into its full glory: tender, creamy flesh with a satisfying meatiness that makes it ideal for something like a Vietnamese-style veggie sandwich. Or you can serve it as a sort of warm side salad with tangy-sweet pepper sauce, a perfect flavor pairing.

Vegetarian

Grilled Eggplant Banh Mi Sandwich

Hands-on: 25 min. Total: 25 min.

¹⁄₂ cup rice wine vinegar
1¹⁄₂ tablespoons sugar
¹⁄₄ teaspoon salt
2 cups julienne-cut peeled carrot (about 4 medium)
1¹⁄₄ pounds eggplant
1¹⁄₂ tablespoons canola oil
¹⁄₃ cup creamy peanut butter
¹⁄₄ cup minced green onions
1 tablespoon minced peeled fresh ginger
2 teaspoons yellow miso (soybean paste)
1¹⁄₂ teaspoons fresh lime juice
1 (16-ounce) French bread baguette, cut in half horizontally
1 cup thinly sliced cucumber
1 cup fresh cilantro leaves
Thinly sliced jalapeño pepper (optional)

1. Preheat oven to 375°.
2. Combine vinegar, sugar, and salt in a bowl, stirring until sugar dissolves. Add carrot; let stand 15 minutes, stirring occasionally. Drain.
3. Heat a grill pan over medium-high heat. Cut eggplant stem off. Cut eggplant lengthwise into ¼-inch-thick slices; brush with oil. Grill 7 minutes or until tender, turning once.
4. Combine peanut butter, onions, ginger, miso, and juice in a bowl; stir well.
5. Hollow out top and bottom halves of bread, leaving a 1-inch-thick shell; reserve torn bread for another use. Place bread on a baking sheet, cut sides up. Bake at 375° for 5 minutes or until golden brown. Spread bottom half of bread with peanut butter mixture. Arrange eggplant evenly over peanut butter mixture. Arrange carrot mixture and cucumber evenly over eggplant; top with cilantro and jalapeño, if desired. Place top half of bread on sandwich. Cut into 5 equal pieces. Serves 5 (serving size: 1 piece)

CALORIES 392; FAT 14.6g (sat 2.5g, mono 7.1g, poly 4.4g); PROTEIN 14.4g; CARB 54.7g; FIBER 8.2g; CHOL 0mg; IRON 3.3mg; SODIUM 575mg; CALC 70mg

Vegetarian

Grilled Eggplant with Roasted Red Pepper Sauce

Hands-on: 20 min. Total: 60 min.
If you're working on a charcoal grill set up for indirect heat, mound the coals to one side of the grill.

1 whole garlic head
2 large red bell peppers
Cooking spray
1 teaspoon cumin seeds, toasted
1 tablespoon red wine vinegar
¹⁄₂ teaspoon kosher salt, divided
³⁄₄ teaspoon freshly ground black pepper, divided
2 pounds eggplant, cut lengthwise into ¹⁄₂-inch-thick slices (about 2 large)

1. Preheat grill to medium-high heat using both burners. After preheating, turn the left burner off (leave the right burner on).
2. Remove white papery skin from garlic head (do not peel or separate the cloves). Wrap garlic in foil. Place garlic over left burner; grill 40 minutes. Remove from heat; let stand 10 minutes. Separate garlic cloves; squeeze to extract garlic pulp. Discard garlic skins.
3. Cut bell peppers in half lengthwise; discard seeds and membranes. Flatten bell peppers with hand. Lightly coat grill rack with cooking spray. Arrange bell peppers, skin sides down, over right burner, and grill 15 minutes or until bell peppers begin to blacken. Place bell peppers in a paper bag; fold

to close tightly. Let stand 5 minutes, and peel.

4. Place toasted cumin seeds in a mini food processor, and process until finely ground. Add garlic pulp, grilled bell peppers, vinegar, ¼ teaspoon salt, and ¼ teaspoon black pepper; process until smooth.

5. Lightly coat eggplant slices with cooking spray; sprinkle with ¼ teaspoon salt and ½ teaspoon black pepper. Arrange eggplant slices over right burner; grill 5 minutes on each side or until tender. Serve eggplant with pepper sauce. Serves 8 (serving size: 3 tablespoons sauce and about 2 slices eggplant)

CALORIES 63; FAT 0.6g (sat 0.1g, mono 0.1g, poly 0.2g); PROTEIN 2.5g; CARB 13.9g; FIBER 6.7g; CHOL 0mg; IRON 0.9mg; SODIUM 126mg; CALC 30mg

PEPPERS

Whatever a peck of peppers amounts to, it's safe to say we picked way more than that from our hugely bountiful crop, plenty for pickling, roasting, grilling, and slicing fresh. The eye-popping thing about home-grown peppers—beyond the sheer volume—is the vast spectrum of heat and flavor they span. Some of ours delivered lemony tang along with searing heat, while others were sweet and apple-crisp. We mix them up in a tasty relish, though fiery ones alone make a great homemade condiment.

GROWING TIP

A healthy hot-pepper plant will give you dozens—even hundreds—of spicy chiles. In our experience, one or two plants per variety more than suffice. Frequently harvesting peppers will further boost the yield. But for the best flavor, let them fully mature and ripen before picking. Like egg-plants, peppers are a heat-loving crop and do very well in the heart of the summer. Ours absolutely thrived from July through September in Alabama.

PREPARATION TIP

All peppers have ribs and seeds inside. With sweet peppers, you'll remove them before cooking. With hot peppers, it's a matter of taste: The seeds contain much of a chile's heat, and the ribs have even more. So for milder taste, remove both ribs and seeds. When handling hot peppers, it's a good idea to wear rubber gloves to protect your skin from the fiery oils. Remember not to touch your eyes before washing your hands thoroughly.

Make Ahead • Vegetarian

Hot Pepper Vinegar

Hands-on: 10 min. Total: 1 week Chop and sprinkle these pickled peppers over salads or on sandwiches. Use the vinegar mixture to kick up salad dressing.

12 ounces hot chile peppers, such as jalapeño or serrano (about 4 cups)
2 garlic cloves, halved
1½ cups white wine vinegar
2 teaspoons sugar
½ teaspoon salt

1. Slice 6 peppers in half lengthwise. Arrange halved peppers, remaining peppers, and garlic in a 1-quart glass jar, or divide among 4 (8-ounce) jars.
2. Combine vinegar, sugar, and salt in a small saucepan over medium-high heat. Cook 4 minutes, stirring occasionally, until sugar dissolves. Pour vinegar mixture over peppers. Cool to room temperature. Cover; refrigerate at least 1 week. Serves 12 (serving size: 4 small peppers and about 1 tablespoon vinegar mixture)

CALORIES 15; FAT 0.1g (sat 0g, mono 0g, poly 0.1g); PROTEIN 0.6g; CARB 3.4g; FIBER 0.4g; CHOL 0mg; IRON 0.3mg; SODIUM 101mg; CALC 5mg

FROM OUR GARDEN

LEMON DROP
These dazzling hot peppers have fantastically complex citrus notes that aren't clobbered by their moderately high heat (between jalapeño and cayenne). Great for fruit salsas.

FISH
Perhaps slightly hotter than a serrano and about 3 inches long, they're an African-American heirloom popularly used in the 19th century for fish and shellfish cooking.

KOREAN DARK GREEN
Not quite as hot as Thai chiles, these are still spicier than serranos. One plant will yield hundreds of peppers, so think in terms of preservation: Pickle, or roast and freeze.

THAI LONG SWEET
Don't let the name fool you—these are very hot! Thai Longs grow to about 6 inches. They're ideal for grilling or roasting until charred, and then chopping up into spicy salsa.

RED CHEESE
Glossy, brilliant red skin with sweet flesh that's thicker than bell peppers. They're small—about 3 inches—and flat, but gorgeous and worth the effort to stuff and roast.

CHOCOLATE BEAUTY
This sweet bell pepper starts out green, and then turns purple-brown as it ripens. Intensely sweet when ripe, it's versatile enough to eat raw, grill, roast, or sauté into pasta sauce.

GOLDEN TREASURE
A 9-inch-long sweet pepper that's a snap to prep: It has relatively few seeds, all located by the top stem and easy to slice right off. This Italian heirloom has thick flesh and tender skin.

MELROSE
When young and green, it tastes like a green bell pepper; when red and fully ripe, it's sweet and richer. Hugely popular in Chicago among Italian-Americans.

Vegetarian

Sweet and Spicy Pepperonata

Hands-on: 20 min. Total: 55 min. *Use a variety of hot and sweet peppers in red, orange, and yellow for superior flavor and color in this dish. Serve as a side with grilled meat or fish, or as an appetizer spooned over grilled bread.*

2 tablespoons olive oil
1/2 teaspoon kosher salt
2 pounds assorted peppers, such as mini sweet, bell, and hot long peppers, seeded and cut into strips
6 shallots, peeled and halved (about 1/2 pound)
3 tablespoons red wine vinegar
2 teaspoons sugar
1 teaspoon chopped fresh thyme

1. Heat a Dutch oven over medium-high heat. Add oil to pan; swirl to coat. Add salt, peppers, and shallots; cook 3 minutes or until shallots begin to brown. Reduce heat to medium-low; cook, covered, 20 minutes or until peppers are tender.
2. Increase heat to medium-high. Add vinegar, sugar, and thyme; cook 15 minutes or until peppers are tender and shallots are golden brown, stirring occasionally. Serve warm or at room temperature. Serves 6 (serving size: about 1/2 cup)

CALORIES 119; FAT 5g (sat 0.7g, mono 3.3g, poly 0.6g); PROTEIN 2.8g; CARB 16.9g; FIBER 3.1g; CHOL 0mg; IRON 1.2mg; SODIUM 167mg; CALC 12mg

MELONS

Here we come to the sweetest, juiciest fruit our garden yielded: musky, fragrant cantaloupes, with their velvety flesh, and crisp, sugary watermelons in spectacular colors. Fresh slices make a perfect—and perfectly simple—summertime dessert, but we found that with a little extra effort you can put together a creamy sherbet that's the absolute essence of melon. And they shine with savory elements, too: A little salty cheese, pungent onion, and lightly bitter greens bring out their best.

GROWING TIP

Melon patches tend to sprawl as the vines creep across the ground, sometimes spanning 20 feet or more. Gardeners should be prepared to devote ample space to these plants. For the acreage-challenged, stick to dwarf melon varieties, with vines that grow only about 3–4 feet long.

Quick & Easy • Vegetarian

Watermelon-Cucumber Salad

Hands-on: 20 min. Total: 20 min. *Briny feta cheese and tangy lime juice make great partners for sweet watermelon.*

6 cups watermelon, cut into 1-inch pieces
1 cup coarsely chopped watercress
3/4 cup thinly sliced Vidalia onion
1 medium English cucumber, sliced (about 3 cups)
2 tablespoons chopped fresh mint
2 tablespoons chopped fresh cilantro
2 tablespoons fresh lime juice
2 teaspoons extra-virgin olive oil
1/4 teaspoon kosher salt
2 ounces reduced-fat feta cheese, crumbled (about 1/2 cup)
Mint sprigs (optional)

1. Combine first 4 ingredients in a large bowl. Combine mint and next 3 ingredients in a small bowl, stirring with a whisk. Add juice mixture and salt to watermelon mixture; toss gently to coat. Sprinkle with feta; garnish with mint sprigs, if desired. Serves 6 (serving size: 1 1/2 cups)

CALORIES 93; FAT 3.1g (sat 1.1g, mono 1.2g, poly 0.2g); PROTEIN 3.5g; CARB 15.1g; FIBER 1.3g; CHOL 3mg; IRON 0.6mg; SODIUM 218mg; CALC 58mg

STORAGE TIP

Melons store well at room temperature for a week or longer, depending on ripeness. Uncut, they can handle about 5–7 days in the fridge. Once cut, they deteriorate quickly; watermelon gets mealy after a couple of days.

Kid Friendly • Make Ahead Vegetarian • Freezable

Cantaloupe Sherbet

Hands-on: 25 min. Total: 2 hr.

3/4 cup water
1/2 cup sugar
1/4 cup light-colored corn syrup
1/8 teaspoon salt
4 cups chopped cantaloupe (about 3 pounds)
2 tablespoons vodka
1 tablespoon fresh lime juice
2 tablespoons heavy cream

1. Bring first 4 ingredients to a boil in a saucepan; cook 1 minute or until sugar dissolves. Remove from heat. Place pan in a large ice-filled bowl for 15 minutes or until sugar mixture cools completely, stirring occasionally.
2. Place cantaloupe, vodka, and juice in a food processor; process until smooth. Strain cantaloupe mixture through a

sieve over a bowl; discard solids. Add sugar mixture and cream to cantaloupe mixture; stir well.

3. Pour cantaloupe mixture into the freezer can of an ice-cream freezer; freeze according to manufacturer's instructions. Spoon sherbet into a freezer-safe container; cover and freeze 1 hour or until firm. Serves 10 (serving size: ½ cup)

CALORIES 120; **FAT** 3.1g (sat 1.9g, mono 0.9g, poly 0.2g); **PROTEIN** 0.7g; **CARB** 22.4g; **FIBER** 0.5g; **CHOL** 11mg; **IRON** 0.1mg; **SODIUM** 48mg; **CALC** 12mg

FROM OUR GARDEN

MOON AND STARS
An heirloom brought back from the edge of extinction some 30 years ago, this hefty melon has sweet, meaty flesh.

WHITE WONDER
It shares a name with one of our cuke varieties but stands alone among melons: Its fragrant, crisp, sugary flesh boasts a hint of lemon. The best melon we've had.

OLD-TIME TENNESSEE
A watermelon-sized cantaloupe (8–10 pounds) with classic muskmelon aroma. The soft flesh bruises easily, so handle with care.

FIVE WAYS WITH 'WICHES

Here's a mighty handful of supersatisfying sandwiches to kick off the casual start of summer: great portable food, loaded with flavor, healthy but still hearty.

Quick & Easy

Grilled Chicken Sandwiches with Pickled Squash and Romesco Mayonnaise

Hands-on: 20 min. Total: 40 min.
What makes it great: The satisfying snap of quick-pickled squash plays well with creamy-smoky red bell pepper mayo, peppery arugula, and savory chicken. Use a mandoline to get perfectly uniform, thin slices of squash. Or for delicate squash ribbons, shave the squash lengthwise with a vegetable peeler.

¼ cup cider vinegar
¼ cup water
1¼ teaspoons salt, divided
1 teaspoon sugar
1 thyme sprig
1 (5-ounce) yellow summer squash, very thinly sliced
¼ cup canola mayonnaise
½ teaspoon smoked paprika
⅛ teaspoon ground red pepper
3 ounces bottled roasted red bell peppers, rinsed and drained
1 ounce blanched almonds, toasted
4 (4-ounce) chicken cutlets
¼ teaspoon freshly ground black pepper
Cooking spray
4 (2-ounce) focaccia rolls, halved and toasted
2 cups arugula

1. Combine vinegar, ¼ cup water, 1 teaspoon salt, sugar, and thyme in a saucepan. Bring to a boil, stirring until salt and sugar dissolve. Pour hot mixture over squash in a bowl. Let stand 30 minutes, tossing occasionally. Drain.
2. Place mayonnaise and next 4 ingredients in a mini food processor; process until smooth. Set sauce aside.
3. Heat a grill pan over medium-high heat. Sprinkle chicken evenly with ¼ teaspoon salt and black pepper. Coat pan with cooking spray. Add chicken to pan; cook 4 minutes on each side or until done.
4. Spread about 2 tablespoons sauce on bottom half of each roll. Top each with 1 chicken cutlet, about ⅓ cup squash, ½ cup arugula, and top half of roll. Serves 4 (serving size: 1 sandwich)

CALORIES 349; **FAT** 12.2g (sat 1g, mono 6.6g, poly 3g); **PROTEIN** 25.3g; **CARB** 34g; **FIBER** 2.4g; **CHOL** 54mg; **IRON** 2.7mg; **SODIUM** 758mg; **CALC** 44mg

Sautéed Greens, Smoked Turkey, and Provolone Panini

Kid Friendly • Quick & Easy

Hands-on: 15 min. Total: 15 min.
What makes it great: The crusty grilled exterior gives way to a cheesy, savory interior loaded with earthy kale. Even finicky eaters will find this a delicious way to get their greens.

1 tablespoon olive oil
1/4 teaspoon crushed red pepper
2 large garlic cloves, minced
5 ounces chopped kale
2 tablespoons water
4 ounces thinly sliced reduced-fat provolone cheese
8 (3/4-ounce) slices ciabatta bread
4 ounces thinly sliced smoked turkey breast (such as Applegate Farms)
Cooking spray

1. Heat a large cast-iron skillet over medium heat. Add oil to pan; swirl to coat. Add red pepper and garlic, and cook 1 minute, stirring frequently. Add kale and 2 tablespoons water; cook 4 minutes or until kale wilts, stirring occasionally.
2. Divide half of cheese evenly among 4 bread slices. Top evenly with smoked turkey and kale mixture. Top evenly with remaining half of cheese and remaining bread slices.
3. Heat a grill pan over medium-high heat. Lightly coat both sides of sandwiches with cooking spray. Arrange sandwiches in pan. Place cast-iron skillet on top of sandwiches; press gently to flatten. Cook sandwiches 2 minutes on each side or until cheese melts and bread is toasted (leave skillet on sandwiches while they cook). Cut each sandwich in half. Serves 4 (serving size: 1 sandwich)

CALORIES 276; **FAT** 11.4g (sat 3.7g, mono 5.4g, poly 0.9g); **PROTEIN** 17.5g; **CARB** 28.3g; **FIBER** 1.5g; **CHOL** 25mg; **IRON** 2mg; **SODIUM** 779mg; **CALC** 275mg

Open-Faced Pastrami Omelet on Pumpernickel

Quick & Easy

Hands-on: 15 min. Total: 15 min.
What makes it great: The old-school deli-shop flavors of pumpernickel, pastrami, horseradish, and whole-grain mustard are irresistible—in a package much lighter than a full deli pileup.

1 1/2 cups thinly sliced peeled English cucumber
1 tablespoon whole-grain Dijon mustard
1 tablespoon cider vinegar
1/2 teaspoon prepared horseradish
1/4 teaspoon salt, divided
3/8 teaspoon freshly ground black pepper, divided
2 tablespoons chopped fresh dill
6 large eggs, lightly beaten
3 ounces chopped pastrami
3 green onions, thinly sliced
2 teaspoons olive oil
4 large Bibb lettuce leaves
4 (1-ounce) slices pumpernickel bread, toasted

1. Combine cucumber, mustard, vinegar, horseradish, 1/8 teaspoon salt, and 1/8 teaspoon pepper in a bowl. Let stand 10 minutes, tossing occasionally.
2. Combine 1/8 teaspoon salt, 1/4 teaspoon pepper, dill, eggs, pastrami, and onions in a bowl, stirring with a whisk.
3. Heat a medium nonstick skillet over medium heat. Add oil to pan; swirl to coat. Add egg mixture to pan; cook 2 minutes. Cover, reduce heat to low, and cook 8 minutes or until set. Cut into 4 wedges. Place 1 lettuce leaf on each bread slice; top with 1 omelet wedge and 1/4 cup cucumber mixture. Serves 4 (serving size: 1 sandwich)

CALORIES 246; **FAT** 11.7g (sat 3g, mono 5.2g, poly 2.1g); **PROTEIN** 17.3g; **CARB** 18.3g; **FIBER** 2.7g; **CHOL** 290mg; **IRON** 3.3mg; **SODIUM** 766mg; **CALC** 86mg

Breaded Fish Sandwiches with Mint-Caper Tartar Sauce

Kid Friendly • Quick & Easy

Hands-on: 21 min. Total: 28 min.
What makes it great: Spiking tartar sauce with mint and capers improves the classic fish sandwich deliciously. Cutting the fish into a square shape helps it fit the roll better.

2 tablespoons canola mayonnaise
2 tablespoons low-fat sour cream
1 tablespoon capers, chopped
1 tablespoon finely chopped fresh mint
2 teaspoons finely chopped fresh flat-leaf parsley
1/2 teaspoon red wine vinegar
3/8 teaspoon freshly ground black pepper, divided
1 medium Vidalia onion, thinly sliced
3 cups ice water
1/4 teaspoon salt
4 (6-ounce) square-cut mahimahi fillets
1/4 cup all-purpose flour
2 large egg whites, lightly beaten
1 cup panko (Japanese breadcrumbs)
1 1/2 tablespoons olive oil
4 (1 1/2-ounce) Kaiser rolls, halved and toasted
8 thin tomato slices

1. Preheat oven to 350°.
2. Combine first 6 ingredients in a small bowl; stir in 1/8 teaspoon pepper. Set tartar sauce aside.
3. Combine onion and ice water; soak 20 minutes. Drain on paper towels.
4. Sprinkle 1/4 teaspoon pepper and 1/4 teaspoon salt evenly over fish. Place flour in a shallow dish; place egg whites in another dish. Place panko in another. Dredge both sides of fish in flour; dip in egg white, and dredge in panko. Heat a large nonstick skillet over medium-high heat. Add oil to pan; swirl to coat. Add fish to pan;

cook 2 minutes on each side or until browned. Place fish on a baking sheet. Bake at 350° for 6 minutes or until fish flakes easily when tested with a fork.
5. Spread about 4 teaspoons mint mixture on bottom half of each roll. Top each with 1 fish fillet. Arrange onion evenly over fish; top with 2 tomato slices and top half of roll. Serves 4 (serving size: 1 sandwich)

CALORIES 413; FAT 11.4g (sat 1.8g, mono 5.9g, poly 2.4g); PROTEIN 39.3g; CARB 35.7g; FIBER 2.1g; CHOL 127mg; IRON 4.1mg; SODIUM 678mg; CALC 99mg

Kid Friendly • Quick & Easy

Short Rib Cheesesteak Sandwiches

Hands-on: 18 min. Total: 18 min.
What makes it great: Pure hearty goodness: the richness of beefy short ribs napped in Dijon-spiked cheese sauce. You can find thinly cut boneless short ribs in many supermarkets, but especially in Asian markets.

1 (12-ounce) French bread baguette
1/2 cup 1% low-fat milk
1 teaspoon all-purpose flour
1 teaspoon Dijon mustard
3/8 teaspoon salt, divided
2 ounces 50%-less-fat sharp cheddar cheese, shredded (about 1/2 cup)
2 teaspoons olive oil, divided
1 cup vertically sliced onion
4 garlic cloves, thinly sliced
1 large orange bell pepper, cut into strips
12 ounces lean boneless beef short ribs, trimmed and very thinly sliced
1/4 teaspoon freshly ground black pepper

1. Preheat broiler to high.
2. Cut bread in half lengthwise and again crosswise. Hollow out tops and bottoms of bread, leaving a 1/2-inch-thick shell. Place bread halves on a baking sheet, cut sides up. Broil 1 1/2 minutes or until toasted.

3. Combine milk, flour, and mustard in a medium microwave-safe bowl, stirring with a whisk. Microwave at HIGH 1 1/2 minutes or until thickened, stirring every 30 seconds. Remove from microwave; add 1/8 teaspoon salt and cheese, stirring until cheese melts.
4. Heat a large cast-iron skillet over medium-high heat. Add 1 teaspoon oil to pan; swirl to coat. Add onion, garlic, bell pepper, and 1/8 teaspoon salt; sauté 5 minutes or until tender. Remove onion mixture from pan; keep warm. Add 1 teaspoon oil to pan; swirl to coat. Add beef, 1/8 teaspoon salt, and black pepper to pan; sauté 3 minutes or until tender.
5. Divide beef mixture evenly among bottom halves of bread; top with onion mixture. Drizzle cheese sauce evenly over sandwiches. Top with top halves of bread; cut each sandwich in half. Serves 4 (serving size: 1 sandwich)

CALORIES 356; FAT 11.7g (sat 4.9g, mono 4.7g, poly 0.5g); PROTEIN 22.3g; CARB 42.2g; FIBER 2.2g; CHOL 44mg; IRON 3.3mg; SODIUM 743mg; CALC 158mg

EVERYDAY VEGETARIAN

MEATLESS MONDAYS

—Recipe by Joanne Weir

Quick & Easy • Vegetarian

Asparagus Salad with Poached Eggs and Tapenade Toasts

Hands-on: 34 min. Total: 34 min.

1 1/2 pounds asparagus spears, trimmed
1/2 teaspoon grated orange rind
3 tablespoons fresh orange juice, divided

2 1/2 tablespoons olive oil, divided
4 teaspoons white wine vinegar, divided
1 tablespoon capers, chopped
1/2 teaspoon ground fennel seeds
1 1/2 ounces kalamata olives, pitted and coarsely chopped (about 1/3 cup)
1 garlic clove, minced
12 (1/2-ounce) slices whole-wheat baguette
6 large eggs
1/4 teaspoon black pepper
1/8 teaspoon kosher salt

1. Preheat broiler to high.
2. Bring a large saucepan of water to a boil. Add asparagus; cook 3 minutes or until crisp-tender. Drain; keep warm.
3. Combine rind, 2 tablespoons orange juice, 2 tablespoons oil, and 2 teaspoons vinegar in a bowl, stirring well with a whisk.
4. Place 1 tablespoon orange juice, 1 1/2 teaspoons oil, capers, fennel seeds, olives, and garlic in a food processor; process until finely chopped.
5. Place baguette slices on a baking sheet. Broil 2 minutes or until golden, turning after 1 minute.
6. Add water to a large skillet, filling two-thirds full; bring to a boil. Reduce heat; simmer. Stir in 2 teaspoons vinegar. Break each egg into a custard cup. Gently pour eggs into pan; cook 3 minutes or until desired degree of doneness. Carefully remove eggs from pan using a slotted spoon.
7. Spread tapenade evenly onto toasts; place 2 toasts on each of 6 plates. Drizzle asparagus with dressing, tossing gently to coat. Divide asparagus evenly among plates. Top asparagus with 1 poached egg; sprinkle eggs evenly with pepper and salt. Serve immediately. Serves 6

CALORIES 236; FAT 12.7g (sat 2.6g, mono 7.4g, poly 1.8g); PROTEIN 11.4g; CARB 19.4g; FIBER 3g; CHOL 186mg; IRON 4.2mg; SODIUM 418mg; CALC 63mg

A NICE LIGHT SUMMER DINNER FROM THE SOUTH

Field pea salad, squash blossoms stuffed with pimiento cheese: it's good, y'all.

Story by John Kessler

Southerners may find that the current vogue for Southern cooking in New York City and elsewhere brings to mind that Barbara Mandrell song from the '80s, "I Was Country When Country Wasn't Cool."

But this attention is real and deserved: Regional heritage, flavors, and ingredients are all being celebrated in the passion for country ham, grits, fried chicken, and chowchow.

Cooking Light's Test Kitchen and editorial offices are in the heart of the South, down in Birmingham, Alabama, where agrarian roots run as deep as any. We wanted this menu to reflect the exciting culinary developments of the new South, characterized by reverence for the past and spiked with lots of inventive ideas. We wanted a menu perfect for cooks with overactive vegetable gardens and healthy mind-sets. The recipes abide by Southern kitchen principles: Keep it simple, get creative in combining native Southern ingredients, and find some use for all that fragrant garden mint that will take over everything if given half a chance.

Sweet Tea Mint Juleps

***Hands-on: 20 min. Total: 50 min.** Chill your glasses while the tea mixture chills. You can also shake the cocktail with ice before serving, but strain the ice before you pour.*

1/2 cup sugar
1/2 cup water
4 Earl Grey tea bags
1 (1-ounce) package fresh mint (about 1 cup)
1 1/4 cups bourbon
1/3 cup fresh lime juice
1 3/4 cups chilled sparkling wine
Mint sprigs (optional)

1. Combine sugar and 1/2 cup water in a microwave-safe bowl; microwave at HIGH 3 minutes, stirring until sugar dissolves. Add tea bags and mint to sugar syrup; steep 20 minutes. Discard tea bags and mint. Stir in bourbon and juice; chill. Pour tea mixture into a pitcher; stir in sparkling wine. Garnish with mint sprigs, if desired; serve immediately. Serves 8 (serving size: 1/2 cup)

CALORIES 169; **FAT** 0g; **PROTEIN** 0g; **CARB** 14.3g; **FIBER** 0.1g; **CHOL** 0mg; **IRON** 0mg; **SODIUM** 1mg; **CALC** 2mg

Quick & Easy
Pimiento Cheese-Stuffed Squash Blossoms

***Hands-on: 16 min. Total: 25 min.** Fresh squash blossoms are a lovely seasonal treat. Enjoy the contrast of crisp, fresh flowers with rich, creamy cheese spread. Be sure to use the best bacon you can find—brands that smoke with real wood offer the best flavor. And roast your own pepper; jarred versions may taste tinny. Use plain cheddar cheese for a mild flavor, or choose extra-sharp for more tang.*

1 small red bell pepper, halved and seeded
1/2 cup fat-free cream cheese, softened
3 tablespoons minced green onions
1 tablespoon canola mayonnaise
1/2 teaspoon hot sauce (such as Texas Pete)
Dash of ground red pepper
2.5 ounces cheddar cheese, shredded (about 3/4 cup)
1 applewood-smoked bacon slice, cooked and crumbled
8 fresh squash blossoms

1. Preheat broiler to high.
2. Place bell pepper halves, skin sides up, on a foil-lined baking sheet, and flatten with hand. Broil 8 minutes or until blackened. Place roasted pepper in a paper bag, and fold to close bag tightly. Let stand 5 minutes. Peel and chop bell pepper.
3. Place 3 tablespoons bell pepper in a medium bowl; reserve remaining pepper for another use. Add cream cheese and next 6 ingredients to pepper in bowl, and stir until well blended. Carefully make a slit in each squash blossom; open and spoon 2 tablespoons cheese mixture into each blossom. Press to close. Serves 8 (serving size: 1 stuffed blossom)

CALORIES 72; **FAT** 3.8g (sat 1.8g, mono 0.4g, poly 0.2g); **PROTEIN** 5.7g; **CARB** 2.9g; **FIBER** 0.5g; **CHOL** 12mg; **IRON** 0.2mg; **SODIUM** 207mg; **CALC** 142mg

Mini Cornmeal Cakes with Heirloom Tomato Relish

(pictured on page 221)

Hands-on: 25 min. Total: 25 min.

Relish:
2 small heirloom tomatoes, seeded and finely chopped (about 1 pound)
¼ cup chopped fresh basil
1 teaspoon extra-virgin olive oil
½ teaspoon kosher salt
½ teaspoon freshly ground black pepper
3 garlic cloves, minced
Pancakes:
1.75 ounces all-purpose flour (about ⅓ cup)
2 tablespoons yellow cornmeal
¼ teaspoon kosher salt
¼ teaspoon freshly ground black pepper
4½ tablespoons whole buttermilk
1 large egg, separated
Cooking spray
Remaining ingredient:
4 teaspoons crème fraîche or reduced-fat sour cream

1. To prepare relish, combine first 6 ingredients.
2. To prepare pancakes, weigh or lightly spoon flour into a dry measuring cup; level. Combine flour and next 3 ingredients in a medium bowl. Combine buttermilk and egg yolk; add buttermilk mixture to flour mixture, stirring with a whisk just until moist.
3. Place egg white in a bowl; beat with a mixer at high speed until medium peaks form. Fold one-fourth of egg white into buttermilk mixture. Gently fold in remaining egg white.
4. Heat a large skillet over medium-high heat. Lightly coat pan with cooking spray. Spoon about 1 tablespoon batter per pancake into pan, spreading slightly. Cook 1 minute or until tops are covered with bubbles and edges begin to set. Turn and cook 1 minute. Repeat with remaining batter for a total of 16 pancakes. Top each pancake with ¼ teaspoon crème fraîche and 1½ teaspoons tomato relish. Serve immediately. Serves 8 (serving size: 2 topped pancakes)

CALORIES 69; FAT 2.5g (sat 1g, mono 0.7g, poly 0.3g); PROTEIN 2.5g; CARB 9.2g; FIBER 1g; CHOL 26mg; IRON 0.7mg; SODIUM 201mg; CALC 24mg

Freezable • Make Ahead

Peach Cobbler Ice Cream with Bourbon-Caramel Sauce

Hands-on: 12 min. Total: 8 hr. 40 min.
Here's a delicious ice-cream recipe that doesn't require an ice-cream maker: Just stir the ingredients together, and freeze. Fold the whipped topping in with as few strokes as possible while making sure everything is well blended.

Ice cream:
4 ounces refrigerated pie dough
Cooking spray
1 tablespoon sugar
¼ teaspoon ground cinnamon
1 cup chopped peeled peaches, divided (about 2 medium peaches)
½ cup fat-free sweetened condensed milk
2 tablespoons peach schnapps
1 tablespoon fresh lemon juice
Dash of salt
2 cups frozen reduced-fat whipped topping, thawed
Sauce:
½ cup sugar
2 tablespoons water
1 tablespoon light-colored corn syrup
Dash of salt
¼ cup half-and-half
1 tablespoon butter, softened
1 tablespoon bourbon

1. Preheat oven to 425°.
2. To prepare ice cream, place pie dough on a baking sheet lined with parchment paper; lightly coat with cooking spray. Combine 1 tablespoon sugar and cinnamon in a small bowl. Sprinkle sugar mixture evenly over pie dough. Using a knife or pizza cutter, score dough at 1-inch intervals. Bake at 425° for 10 minutes or until browned. Cool completely; break into ½-inch pieces.
3. Place ½ cup peaches in a medium bowl, and mash with a fork until almost smooth. Add ½ cup peaches and next 4 ingredients; stir well. Gently fold in crumbled piecrust and whipped topping. Scoop mixture into a freezer-safe container; cover and freeze overnight.
4. To prepare sauce, combine ½ cup sugar, 2 tablespoons water, corn syrup, and dash of salt in a small saucepan over medium heat, stirring just until sugar melts; bring to a boil. Cook 12 minutes or until amber; remove from heat. Drizzle in half-and-half, stirring constantly with a whisk. Add butter and bourbon; whisk until smooth. Serves 8 (serving size: about ½ cup ice cream and 1½ tablespoons sauce)

CALORIES 264; FAT 8.1g (sat 5g, mono 0.4g, poly 0.1g); PROTEIN 2.5g; CARB 44.2g; FIBER 0.3g; CHOL 11mg; IRON 0.1mg; SODIUM 136mg; CALC 61mg

WE WANTED A MENU PERFECT FOR COOKS WITH OVER-ACTIVE VEGETABLE GARDENS AND HEALTHY MIND-SETS.

Roasted Cider-Brined Pork Loin with Green Tomato Chutney

Hands-on: 35 min. Total: 19 hr. 30 min.
For the deepest flavor, use unfiltered cider.

2 quarts water, divided
1 cup granulated sugar
1/2 cup kosher salt
2 quarts apple cider
1 (2½-pound) pork loin roast, trimmed
Cooking spray
1/2 cup packed brown sugar
1/3 cup diced red onion
1/3 cup apple cider vinegar
1/3 cup golden raisins
1 tablespoon minced fresh garlic
3/4 teaspoon minced peeled fresh ginger
1/4 teaspoon ground red pepper
1/4 teaspoon ground cinnamon
1/8 teaspoon kosher salt
1 pound green tomatoes, diced

1. Combine 1 quart water, granulated sugar, and ½ cup salt in a large stock-pot; bring to a boil, stirring until sugar and salt dissolve. Add 1 quart water and cider; cool to room temperature. Add pork; refrigerate 12 to 18 hours, turning occasionally.
2. Preheat oven to 375°.
3. Remove pork from brine; pat dry with paper towels. Place pork on a broiler pan coated with cooking spray. Bake at 375° for 55 minutes or until a thermometer inserted into thickest part of pork registers 140°. Remove pork from pan; let stand 15 minutes. Cut crosswise into thin slices.
4. Combine brown sugar and remaining ingredients in a medium saucepan over medium heat; bring to a boil.

Reduce heat to low; cook 1 hour and 45 minutes, stirring occasionally. Serves 10 (serving size: 3 ounces pork and about 3 tablespoons chutney)

CALORIES 237; **FAT** 5.9g (sat 1.7g, mono 2.1g, poly 0.7g); **PROTEIN** 22.1g; **CARB** 23.8g; **FIBER** 0.9g; **CHOL** 66mg; **IRON** 1.1mg; **SODIUM** 540mg; **CALC** 33mg

Vegetarian
Lady Pea Salad

Hands-on: 15 min. Total: 1 hr. 15 min.
Delicate green lady peas are perfect in this summer side. If you can't find them, sub any field pea, such as pink-eye or crowder.

4 cups fresh lady peas
4 cups water
1/2 teaspoon kosher salt
2 thyme sprigs
1 small onion, trimmed and quartered
1 teaspoon fennel seeds
3 tablespoons extra-virgin olive oil
2 tablespoons white balsamic vinegar
2 tablespoons whole-grain Dijon mustard
1/4 teaspoon freshly ground black pepper
1/4 cup chopped fresh chives

1. Combine first 5 ingredients in a medium saucepan; bring to a boil. Partially cover, reduce heat, and simmer 30 minutes. Drain. Discard onion and thyme. Place peas on a jelly-roll pan; let cool 30 minutes.
2. Heat a small skillet over medium heat. Add fennel seeds; cook 3 minutes or until toasted, stirring occasionally. Combine fennel seeds, oil, vinegar, mustard, and pepper in a medium bowl, stirring with a whisk. Add peas; toss to coat. Stir in chives. Serves 8 (serving size: about 2/3 cup)

CALORIES 58; **FAT** 5.2g (sat 0.7g, mono 3.7g, poly 0.6g); **PROTEIN** 0.7g; **CARB** 2.5g; **FIBER** 0.4g; **CHOL** 0mg; **IRON** 0.5mg; **SODIUM** 237mg; **CALC** 17mg

NUTRITION MADE EASY
A LIGHTER CHURN

Summer becomes a lot more summery when there's a batch of homemade ice cream in the freezer. For us, it gets even brighter if we don't have to stop at one scoop. We believe in maintaining a healthy attitude about occasional splurges, but the fact is a scoop from a traditional recipe made with cream, eggs, and sugar yields 300 calories, with loads of saturated fat. If there's a way to get ice-cream pleasure with less of all that, bring it on. The quest to lighten can start—as many light ice-cream recipes do—by swapping out heavy cream in favor of reduced-fat milk. That churns up a tasty dessert, but it's also an icy one—a milk ice, basically—thanks to the higher water content in reduced-fat dairy. Our trick: Trade the heavy cream for evaporated low-fat milk, which has 60% less water than regular milk. When combined with half-and-half, sugar, and the essential egg yolks, the canned milk fosters a rich custard that stays creamy instead of icy. A touch of light-colored corn syrup adds a velvety-smooth mouthfeel, and a real vanilla bean is worth the splurge for its vibrant flavor. This smarter scoop has almost half the calories, a fraction of the fat, and the lion's share of the texture and taste of full-fat ice cream.

Kid Friendly • Make Ahead
Freezable

Vanilla Bean Ice Cream

Hands-on: 23 min. Total: 4 hr. 30 min.

1 cup half-and-half
½ cup sugar, divided
2 tablespoons light-colored corn syrup
⅛ teaspoon salt
1 (12-ounce) can evaporated low-fat milk
1 vanilla bean, split lengthwise
3 large egg yolks

1. Combine half-and-half, ¼ cup sugar, corn syrup, salt, and evaporated milk in a medium heavy saucepan. Scrape seeds from vanilla bean; add seeds and bean to milk mixture. Heat milk mixture to 180° or until tiny bubbles form around edge (do not boil). Remove pan from heat; cover and let stand 10 minutes. Combine ¼ cup sugar and egg yolks in a medium bowl, stirring well with a whisk. Gradually add hot milk mixture to egg mixture, stirring constantly with a whisk. Return milk mixture to pan. Cook over medium heat until a thermometer registers 160°, stirring constantly. Remove from heat. Place pan in a large ice-filled bowl for 20 minutes or until egg mixture is cool, stirring occasionally. Pour milk mixture through a fine sieve into the freezer can of an ice-cream freezer; discard solids. Freeze according to manufacturer's instructions. Spoon ice cream into a freezer-safe container; cover and freeze 3 hours or until firm. Serves 8 (serving size: about ½ cup)

CALORIES 161; FAT 5.9g (sat 3.1g, mono 1.9g, poly 0.4g); PROTEIN 4.9g; CARB 23.1g; FIBER 0g; CHOL 88mg; IRON 0.2mg; SODIUM 108mg; CALC 161mg

CLASSIC	MAKEOVER
303 calories per scoop	161 calories per scoop
23.6 grams total fat	5.9 grams total fat
13.9 grams saturated fat	3.1 grams saturated fat

OUR CLASSIC VANILLA ICE CREAM HAS 75% LESS FAT–BUT IT'S STILL CREAMY AND RICH, THANKS TO ONE SECRET INGREDIENT.

SECRETS TO A CREAMIER CHURN

Making ice cream that's silky and light isn't such an easy task. We nailed it, though, thanks to these key ingredients.

EVAPORATED LOW-FAT MILK
With 60% of the water removed, it yields fewer ice crystals and a creamier texture. Save 12g sat fat per serving over heavy cream.

VANILLA BEAN
They're a little pricey, but real vanilla beans make all the difference. Steeped in milk, they lend a creamier texture and maximum vanilla goodness.

CORN SYRUP
It's more viscous than sugar, producing a smoother mouthfeel in the final churned product that's especially noticeable the day after.

TODAY'S LESSON: POACHED FISH

Three reasons why you should turn to this underused technique: speed, ease, and success.

If cooking delicate fish fillets makes you anxious, poaching is your ticket to healthy perfection. It's simple and foolproof, provided you maintain a constant, moderate temperature as the fish cooks. Our recipes take the method into weeknight territory by skipping the time-consuming steps of simmering, skimming, and straining the cooking liquid. Instead, the fish cooks in vibrant broths that go straight from pan to plate for an elegant, fast dinner.

1. Build Flavor
Sauté aromatics, and add wine or stock for flavor-filled poaching liquid.

2. Control the Temp
Heat liquid to 155°, add fish, and maintain temp at 150° to cook fish.

Quick & Easy

Poached Cod with Shiitakes

Hands-on: 28 min. Total: 28 min.

1 tablespoon dark sesame oil
1 tablespoon minced peeled fresh ginger
8 ounces sliced shiitake mushroom caps
3 garlic cloves, sliced
½ cup unsalted chicken stock (such as Swanson)
¼ cup sake (rice wine)
2½ tablespoons lower-sodium soy sauce
2½ teaspoons white miso (soybean paste)
1 tablespoon sherry vinegar
½ teaspoon sugar
4 (6-ounce) cod fillets
4 (1-inch) sliced green onions
3 tablespoons fresh cilantro
¼ teaspoon black pepper

1. Heat a large skillet over medium-high heat. Add oil; swirl to coat. Add ginger, mushrooms, and garlic; sauté 5 minutes, stirring frequently. Add stock and next 5 ingredients; heat to 155°. Reduce heat to medium-low; arrange fish on top of mushroom mixture. Cover and simmer 10 minutes or until desired degree of doneness, maintaining a constant temperature of 150°.
2. Gently remove fish from pan; keep warm. Increase heat to medium-high; add onions. Cook, uncovered, 1 minute or until stock is slightly thickened. Ladle ⅔ cup stock mixture into each of 4 shallow bowls; top each serving with 1 fillet. Sprinkle evenly with cilantro and pepper. Serves 4

CALORIES 234; **FAT** 4.6g (sat 0.7g, mono 1.6g, poly 1.9g); **PROTEIN** 31.3g; **CARB** 12.4g; **FIBER** 3.6g; **CHOL** 80mg; **IRON** 1.7mg; **SODIUM** 616mg; **CALC** 61mg

Kid Friendly • Quick & Easy

Mediterranean Striped Bass

Hands-on: 16 min. Total: 16 min.

2 tablespoons extra-virgin olive oil, divided
¾ cup chopped onion
1 tablespoon chopped fresh oregano
½ teaspoon crushed red pepper
5 garlic cloves, sliced
¾ cup dry white wine
½ cup torn basil leaves, divided
1 tablespoon drained capers
⅜ teaspoon salt, divided
4 (6-ounce) striped sea bass fillets
3 plum tomatoes, sliced
2 teaspoons chopped fresh flat-leaf parsley
¼ teaspoon black pepper
8 pitted Castelvetrano olives, halved

1. Heat a large skillet over medium-high heat. Add 1 tablespoon oil; swirl. Add onion and next 3 ingredients; sauté 2 minutes. Stir in wine, ¼ cup basil, capers, and ⅛ teaspoon salt; heat to 155°. Reduce heat to medium-low; sprinkle fish with ¼ teaspoon salt. Nestle fish and tomatoes in broth. Cover and simmer 6 minutes or until desired degree of doneness, maintaining a constant temperature of 150°. Sprinkle with ¼ cup basil, parsley, black pepper, and olives. Drizzle each serving with ¾ teaspoon oil. Serves 4 (serving size: 1 fillet, 3 tomato slices, and about ¼ cup broth mixture)

CALORIES 315; FAT 12.3g (sat 2g, mono 6.9g, poly 2.3g); PROTEIN 32.2g; CARB 10.9g; FIBER 2.6g; CHOL 136mg; IRON 2.6mg; SODIUM 491mg; CALC 81mg

TRAVELIN' CHEF

A SOUTHERN CHEF IN ISRAEL

One of the country's hottest chefs returns from a food fling with fresh ideas and recipes for culinary mash-ups.

By Hugh Acheson

I knew Jewish food before I went to Israel—at least I thought I did. Growing up in Ottawa and living in Montreal gives you a kinship with the latkes, the smoked fish, the matzo meal. I was a brash, young, secular Anglican, but Lord did I love latkes smothered with sour cream, smoked meats on piping hot rye, and lox with a schmear of cream cheese. But Ottawa is also a town with a huge Lebanese population, and we ate it all, reveling in shawarma, hummus, lamb, eggplant, and warm flatbread. Good food at bargain prices, fueling youthful beer-soaked shenanigans. Sometimes

I ate meze and braised lamb with my dad and his friends at the fancy spots, where Dad would become enamored with the belly dancer.

Two food cultures, proximate but essentially separate—that's how it seemed. Then, last year, I went to Israel. What I found stirred up questions of geography and culture that have interested me since, as a chef, I found my adopted home in the South. The flow of peoples and flavors, locals and immigrants, is profound in a region as stirred up as the Middle East. Does food emanate from the population, or is it more a reflection of a region's bounty? Here was a country rich with food lore, whose cuisine abounds with Middle Eastern flavors of pomegranate, peppers, tomatoes, parsley, mint, olive oil, and citrus, all under the influence of people—Jews and Arabs—who have been there for thousands of years and others who arrived just recently. I found it a stunning cuisine and quickly lost interest in seeking anything close to a definition of "Israeli" food.

The cooking is an intense product of Arab, Kurdish, Christian, and Jewish origins, influenced by waves of Jews who have come from Brazil, Brooklyn, Italy, Spain, Yemen, and beyond. It's a mosaic, enhanced by a splendid array of chefs, young and old, now pushing the boundaries of what can be done with local bounty.

We spanned much of the country and saw complex fine dining; young, independent community restaurants; wonderfully stocked grocers; rural markets; quaint agriturismi; stellar bakeries; an amazing truck stop Lebanese restaurant; shawarma stands; and festive, busy bars in alleyways. Amid all the news and conflict, you seldom hear this: Israel is a country with a rich, dynamic culinary soul.

The food just sings with acid from citrus; bright herbaceous hits from parsley, mint, and purslane; pleasant bitterness from sumac; and richness from local olive oil. It's food that is constantly fresh and nourishing,

something that, to me, Southern food can also be.

Back home in Athens, Georgia, immersed again in the cooking traditions I know and adore, I realized that the South can easily borrow from the excitement I had seen. Inspired, I added some of the light zest and full flavors that connect the Israeli mosaic to my own familiar traditions. Here are a couple of recipes made in a Middle Eastern style with staples from my own backyard.

Quick & Easy • Vegetarian
Southern Fattoush

Hands-on: 24 min. Total: 24 min. The ubiquitous Israeli bread salad makes a fine gathering place for black-eyed peas and sweet Georgia onions. Whisk the salad dressing together in a bowl, or do as I do—shake all the ingredients together in (what else?) a mason jar.

Dressing:
4 teaspoons cider vinegar
2 teaspoons whole-grain mustard
2 teaspoons fresh lemon juice
⅜ teaspoon ground sumac
2 small garlic cloves, minced
½ teaspoon kosher salt
¼ teaspoon freshly ground black pepper
6 tablespoons extra-virgin olive oil
Salad:
2 (6-inch) pitas, torn into bite-sized pieces
1 cup chopped tomato
1 cup sliced English cucumber
½ cup diced red bell pepper
½ cup chopped fresh flat-leaf parsley
¼ cup chopped fresh mint
¼ cup chopped arugula
¼ cup minced Vidalia onion
1 (15-ounce) can unsalted black-eyed peas, rinsed and drained

1. Preheat oven to 400°.
2. To prepare dressing, combine first 7 ingredients in a medium bowl;
continued

stir with a whisk. Gradually drizzle in oil, stirring constantly with a whisk.
3. To prepare salad, arrange torn pita in a single layer on a baking sheet. Bake at 400° for 7 minutes, stirring after 4 minutes. Cool completely. Reserve ½ cup toasted pita.
4. Combine tomato and remaining ingredients in a large bowl. Add remaining toasted pita and dressing to bowl; toss well to coat. Top evenly with reserved ½ cup toasted pita. Serve immediately. Serves 6 (serving size: 1 rounded cup)

CALORIES 224; **FAT** 14g (sat 1.9g, mono 9.9g, poly 1.5g); **PROTEIN** 5.2g; **CARB** 20.8g; **FIBER** 2.8g; **CHOL** 0mg; **IRON** 2.1mg; **SODIUM** 268mg; **CALC** 45mg

Vegetarian

Roasted Eggplant with Pomegranate, Pickled Chiles, and Pecans

Hands-on: 20 min. Total: 50 min.
Eggplant is a staple in the Middle East, and they sure do know how to cook it. It's stellar: smoky and light and not at all bitter. The trick is to cook it whole over a gas stovetop burner or on a hot grill. The outside gets all charred as the inside steams, gathering a nice smoky overtone and becoming perfectly cooked. Toasted pecans and pickled jalapeños infuse some Southern accents into the traditional dish. If you can't find pomegranate arils (they come already "shucked" in the produce section), just omit them, or drizzle on a wee bit of pomegranate molasses.

¼ cup white wine vinegar
¼ cup water
2 teaspoons sugar
20 thin jalapeño pepper slices
2 medium globe eggplants (about 2 pounds)
¼ cup plain whole-milk yogurt
2 teaspoons tahini (roasted sesame seed paste)
½ teaspoon kosher salt, divided
2 garlic cloves, minced
2 tablespoons extra-virgin olive oil, divided
2 teaspoons fresh lemon juice
2 cups arugula or watercress
¼ cup pomegranate arils
¼ cup pecans, toasted and crushed

1. Combine first 3 ingredients in a small saucepan; bring to a boil. Remove from heat, and add jalapeño; let stand 15 minutes. Drain.
2. Preheat grill to medium-high heat.
3. Place whole eggplants on grill rack; grill 15 minutes or until charred on all sides and tender when pierced with a thin knife, turning frequently. Remove from heat; gently scrape off charred skin, if desired. Cool eggplants slightly; halve lengthwise. Lightly score flesh.
4. Combine yogurt, tahini, ¼ teaspoon salt, and garlic, stirring well. Drizzle 4 teaspoons oil and lemon juice over eggplant flesh; top with yogurt mixture.
5. Combine arugula, 2 teaspoons olive oil, and ¼ teaspoon salt in a medium bowl; toss gently. Top each eggplant half with about ½ cup arugula, 5 jalapeño slices, 1 tablespoon pomegranate arils, and 1 tablespoon pecans. Serves 4 (serving size: 1 topped eggplant half)

CALORIES 205; **FAT** 14.2g (sat 2g, mono 8.4g, poly 3g); **PROTEIN** 4.5g; **CARB** 19.5g; **FIBER** 9.3g; **CHOL** 2mg; **IRON** 1.1mg; **SODIUM** 256mg; **CALC** 69mg

KID IN THE KITCHEN

OUR KID COOKS QUINOA— AND IT'S A HIT

"I was excited to make this recipe, especially since it includes one of my most favorite ingredients—quinoa. I've used quinoa in place of rice before but have never used it in a breakfast dish. This recipe was really easy to make and smelled amazing while cooking. I am not a huge fan of coconut so I was not sure I would like it, but I was surprised—this dish tasted really good. However, you can also try it with almond milk and top it with toasted slivered almonds. I would also recommend using any seasonal fruit and switching it up often. The quinoa is sweet and creamy, so you can use a tart fruit as a flavor contrast."

Kid Friendly • **Quick & Easy**
Vegetarian

Breakfast Quinoa

Hands-on: 10 min. Total: 22 min. *Like most whole grains, quinoa is surprisingly filling, but if you need more for breakfast, serve with an egg on the side.*

½ cup uncooked quinoa
¾ cup light coconut milk
2 tablespoons water
1 tablespoon light brown sugar
⅛ teaspoon salt
¼ cup flaked unsweetened coconut
1 cup sliced strawberries
1 cup sliced banana

> "REMEMBER TO KEEP YOUR EYE ON THE COCONUT AS IT TOASTS SO THAT IT DOESN'T BURN."

1. Preheat oven to 400°.

2. Place quinoa in a fine sieve, and place sieve in a large bowl. Cover quinoa with water. Using your hands, rub the grains together for 30 seconds; rinse and drain quinoa. Repeat the procedure twice. Drain well. Combine quinoa, coconut milk, 2 tablespoons water, brown sugar, and salt in a medium saucepan, and bring to a boil. Reduce heat, and simmer 15 minutes or until liquid is absorbed, stirring occasionally. Stir mixture constantly during the last 2 minutes of cooking.

3. While quinoa cooks, spread flaked coconut in a single layer on a baking sheet. Bake at 400° for 5 minutes or until golden brown. Cool slightly.

4. Place about ½ cup quinoa mixture in each of 4 bowls. Top each serving with ¼ cup strawberry slices, ¼ cup banana slices, and 1 tablespoon toasted coconut. Serve warm. Serves 4

CALORIES 178; FAT 5.5g (sat 3.8g, mono 0.4g, poly 0.8g); PROTEIN 4.4g; CARB 30.4g; FIBER 3.7g; CHOL 0mg; IRON 1.6mg; SODIUM 89mg; CALC 22mg

THE VERDICT

KAHLO (AGE 6):
He liked the smooth and creamy texture of the quinoa (and also that I made it!). **10/10**

JASPER (AGE 8):
He said that he liked that the dish was sweet, like dessert. **10/10**

MATISSE (AGE 12):
I usually eat oatmeal for breakfast, but I think this is going to be my new go-to hot cereal every morning! **10/10**

GLOBAL PANTRY

TAMARIND

By Naomi Duguid

I use tamarind in all kinds of dishes, but many American cooks aren't familiar with this ingredient, which is mostly associated with Indian and Southeast Asian cooking. The fruits look like long, brown pods; inside is the pulp, dark brown and sticky, with seeds and some membrane embedded within. Luckily, you can buy convenient blocks of the pulp, separated from the pods, in Asian markets. You will need to mash the pulp with some warm water, working it with a fork or your fingers, to make tamarind liquid for use in recipes.

Make the effort to find some, and get to know tamarind. It's a flavor gift to any cook, giving a delicious tart note to many dishes. It's good for sauces where hot-sour is the goal, such as barbecue; balance it with a hint of sugar and suddenly you have great complexity. Try a dash in salad dressings, or make a simple and delectable relish for burgers or grilled meat by cooking up caramelized onions, salting them generously, and then balancing the sweetness with a little tamarind liquid. The final touch is a generous quantity of cilantro or mint. Or for an easy summer quencher, try the refreshing drink at right.

THE FLAVOR OF TAMARIND IS TART AND SEDUCTIVE.

Kid Friendly • Quick & Easy
Make Ahead

Tart-Sweet Tamarind Drink

Hands-on: 5 min. Total: 27 min. We call for tamarind pulp here, but it is sometimes deceptively labeled as tamarind paste. When shopping, make sure what you are getting contains the fiber and seeds—see box below. For an extra-special touch, sugar the rim of the glass.

7½ cups cold water, divided
4 ounces tamarind pulp, coarsely chopped
½ cup brown sugar
Lime slices (optional)

1. Bring 1 cup water to a boil. Combine boiling water and tamarind pulp in a bowl; mash with a fork. Let stand 10 minutes. Mash tamarind again. Press through a sieve into a bowl, pressing pulp firmly against the sieve to extract all liquid. Discard solids.

2. Combine tamarind liquid and ½ cup water in a small saucepan over medium heat. Add sugar; bring to a boil, stirring until sugar dissolves. Reduce heat, and simmer 5 minutes or until liquid thickens slightly. Remove from heat; cool 5 minutes.

3. Combine tamarind syrup with 6 cups water in a large pitcher. Serve over ice. Garnish with lime slices, if desired. Serves 8 (serving size: about 1 cup)

CALORIES 86; FAT 0.1g (sat 0.1g, mono 0g, poly 0g); PROTEIN 0.4g; CARB 22.4g; FIBER 0.4g; CHOL 0mg; IRON 0.5mg; SODIUM 8mg; CALC 2mg

TAMARIND PULP

Look for blocks of tamarind pulp in Asian markets; it keeps a long time in the fridge when well sealed. Avoid tamarind paste that's sold in tins or jars; it often has a metallic taste.

GRILLED VIDALIA ONION SALAD

The world of sweet onions is full of regional pride—Washington's Walla Wallas and Hawaii's Maui onions certainly have their share of devoted fans—but there's no touching the fierce loyalty inspired by the Vidalia. It's Georgia's official state vegetable, taking its name from the town where it was first harvested. The sugary-sweet allium's season runs from April through September, peaking right about now. And though it's versatile enough to be a kitchen staple—and typically is, down in Dixie—Georgia-based chefs like Ford Fry, whose highly lauded restaurants include JCT. Kitchen & Bar and The Optimist, find brilliant ways to let the Southern superstar shine. "Whenever they're in season, that's the only onion we use in my restaurants," says Fry.

To showcase Vidalia onions in a dish, keep the approach simple, he explains. A drizzle of olive oil and a sprinkle of salt and pepper are all it takes to bring out their best nature, whether they're roasted, sautéed, or grilled. At The Optimist, Fry grills them over a wood fire, and then glazes them with chicken jus. Or he might roast them with a splash of sherry for a straightforward yet incredibly satisfying side dish. "They're even great just shaved raw into a salad because their flavor is not too sharp," he says.

In the fast and easy summer salad featured here, Fry grills the baby bulbs to caramelize their sugars and lend a whiff of smoke to complement the natural sweetness. Then he pairs them with juicy heirloom tomatoes and a tangy vinaigrette with some mustardy bite to lend the right balance. "It's a play on the classic French dish—leeks vinaigrette."

If you're in the Atlanta area this month, you can sample this salad at Fry's newest restaurant, King + Duke, located in Buckhead.

Quick & Easy • Vegetarian

Grilled Vidalia Onion Salad

Hands-on: 22 min. Total: 22 min.

3 tablespoons extra-virgin olive oil, divided
8 Vidalia onion bulbs (about 1 pound)
½ teaspoon kosher salt, divided
½ teaspoon freshly ground black pepper, divided
1 tablespoon whole-grain Dijon mustard
1 tablespoon red wine vinegar
2 teaspoons chopped fresh flat-leaf parsley
2 teaspoons chopped fresh tarragon
12 heirloom cherry tomatoes, halved
2 hard-cooked eggs, sliced
2 tablespoons minced fresh chives

1. Preheat charcoal or gas grill to medium heat.
2. Rub 1 tablespoon olive oil evenly over onions. Sprinkle evenly with ¼ teaspoon salt and ¼ teaspoon pepper. Grill 6 minutes or until well marked and greens are tender, turning occasionally. Cool completely.
3. Combine Dijon mustard and vinegar in a small bowl, stirring with a whisk. Gradually add 2 tablespoons olive oil, stirring with a whisk. Stir in parsley, tarragon, ¼ teaspoon salt, and ¼ teaspoon pepper.
4. Arrange 2 onions on each of 4 plates, and top evenly with tomatoes. Drizzle 1 tablespoon vinaigrette over each salad; top evenly with sliced eggs and minced chives. Serves 4 (serving size: 1 salad)

CALORIES 177; **FAT** 12.7g (sat 2.2g, mono 8.3g, poly 1.6g); **PROTEIN** 4.6g; **CARB** 11.9g; **FIBER** 1.8g; **CHOL** 93mg; **IRON** 1mg; **SODIUM** 378mg; **CALC** 47mg

---

FIRST BITES

Make Ahead • Vegetarian

Pickled Baby Pattypan Squash

Hands-on: 14 min. Total: 48 hr. 14 min.
Find these mini summer veggies in markets this month. The toy-top shape makes them great for pickling whole. The spicy brine pairs perfectly with the mild squash flavor.

1½ cups white vinegar
1½ cups water
⅓ cup sliced shallots
1 tablespoon kosher salt
1 tablespoon sugar
1 tablespoon black peppercorns
1 teaspoon white peppercorns
1 teaspoon coriander seeds
1 teaspoon mustard seeds
½ teaspoon crushed red pepper
3 garlic cloves, crushed
1 bay leaf
2½ cups baby pattypan squash, divided
4 tarragon sprigs
4 green onions (green parts only), halved lengthwise
1 lemon wedge

1. Combine first 12 ingredients in a medium saucepan; bring to a boil, stirring until sugar dissolves. Place 1¼ cups squash in a 1-quart canning jar; add tarragon, onions, and lemon. Add remaining squash to jar; top with hot vinegar mixture. Cover and seal. Refrigerate 2 days. Serves 8 (serving size: about ⅓ cup)

CALORIES 16; **FAT** 0.1g (sat 0g, mono 0g, poly 0.1g); **PROTEIN** 0.8g; **CARB** 3.5g; **FIBER** 0.8g; **CHOL** 0mg; **IRON** 0.3mg; **SODIUM** 75mg; **CALC** 17mg

BRIGHT AND SUNNY SUMMER SMOOTHIES

Place 1 cup plan 2% reduced-fat Greek yogurt in a blender; choose your favorite flavor combination, and proceed.

Watermelon, Cucumber & Mint:

Add 3 cups chopped English cucumber, ⅓ cup mint leaves, and ¼ cup fresh lemon juice to blender; process until smooth. Strain cucumber mixture through a fine sieve over a bowl; discard solids. Add cucumber mixture, 6 cups chopped frozen watermelon, and 3 tablespoons agave nectar to blender; process until smooth. Serves 4 (serving size: 1½ cups)

CALORIES 173; FAT 1.8g (sat 1.1g) SODIUM 26mg

Spinach:

Add 6 cups fresh baby spinach, 1½ cups plain sweetened almond milk, 1 tablespoon agave nectar, 2 medium sliced peeled frozen ripe bananas, and 2 chopped peeled kiwifruit to blender; process until smooth. Serves 4 (serving size: 1½ cups)

CALORIES 164; FAT 2.4g (sat 0.8g) SODIUM 134mg

Tropical:

Add 1 cup cubed peeled fresh pineapple, 1 cup diced peeled mango, ¼ cup fresh orange juice, 3 tablespoons agave nectar, 2 teaspoons fresh lime juice, and a dash of salt to blender; process until smooth. Add 1 cup crushed ice; process until smooth. Serves 4 (serving size: about 1 cup)

CALORIES 135; FAT 1.4g (sat 0.8g) SODIUM 57mg

Gingered Carrot:

Place 2 cups chopped peeled carrot, ½ cup carrot juice, and 1 tablespoon grated peeled fresh ginger in a food processor. Process until smooth. Strain carrot mixture through a fine sieve; discard solids. Add carrot mixture, 1½ cups crushed ice, and ¼ cup honey to blender; process until smooth. Serves 4 (serving size: 1 cup)

CALORIES 143; FAT 1.5g (sat 1g); SODIUM 86mg

Horseradish-Tomato:

Add ½ cup crushed ice, ¼ cup vegetable juice (such as V8), 2½ tablespoons grated fresh horseradish, 1 tablespoon fresh lemon juice, ¼ teaspoon kosher salt, ⅛ teaspoon freshly ground black pepper, 3 trimmed green onions, 2 cored seeded ripe red globe tomatoes, and 1 crushed garlic clove to blender; process until smooth. Serves 4 (serving size: ¾ cup)

CALORIES 71; FAT 1.5g (sat 0.8g); SODIUM 172mg

Orange Cream:

Add 1 cup orange sherbet, 1 teaspoon grated orange rind, ¾ cup fresh orange sections (about 1 large orange), and ½ teaspoon vanilla extract to blender; process until smooth. Add 1 cup ice; process until smooth. Pour into glasses; top evenly with 2 tablespoons coarsely chopped cinnamon-roasted almonds. Serve immediately. Serves 3 (serving size: 1 cup)

CALORIES 167; FAT 4.4g (sat 1.7g); SODIUM 48mg

FEED 4 FOR LESS THAN $10

Quick & Easy

Mussels Fra Diavolo with Linguine

$2.49/serving, $9.96 total

Hands-on: 20 min. Total: 20 min.
Fra diavolo means "brother devil" in Italian and refers to a spicy, tomato-based sauce. Here we use store-bought marinara that's jazzed up with fresh fennel, crushed red pepper, and garlic.

8 ounces uncooked linguine
1 tablespoon olive oil
1 cup chopped fennel bulb
½ cup chopped onion
2 tablespoons minced fresh garlic
¾ teaspoon crushed red pepper
¼ teaspoon kosher salt
1 cup lower-sodium marinara sauce
1½ pounds mussels, scrubbed and debearded (about 40)
¼ cup chopped fresh flat-leaf parsley

1. Cook pasta according to package directions, omitting salt and fat. Drain pasta in a colander over a bowl, reserving ¾ cup pasta water.
2. Heat a large nonstick skillet over medium-high heat. Add oil to pan; swirl to coat. Add fennel and onion to pan; sauté 3 minutes. Add garlic, pepper, and salt; sauté 2 minutes, stirring constantly. Add reserved pasta water and marinara to pan; cook 1 minute. Add mussels; cover and cook 3 minutes or until shells open. Discard any unopened shells. Place 1 cup pasta in each of 4 shallow bowls. Top each serving with about 1½ cups mussels mixture. Sprinkle evenly with parsley. Serves 4

CALORIES 423; FAT 8.5g (sat 1.4g, mono 3.3g, poly 1.4g); PROTEIN 28.4g; CARB 58.2g; FIBER 4.2g; CHOL 45mg; IRON 9.5mg; SODIUM 654mg; CALC 99mg

Kid Friendly • Quick & Easy

Shrimp and Broccoli Stir-Fry

$2.29/serving, $9.16 total

Hands-on: 30 min. Total: 30 min. Just a touch of honey adds a slight sweetness that rounds out the flavor in this quick stir-fry. Pat the shrimp dry with paper towels before adding them to the wok so they brown nicely. Serve with hot cooked brown rice.

1 pound medium shrimp, peeled and deveined
1 tablespoon cornstarch
2½ tablespoons canola oil, divided
¼ cup (1-inch) diagonally cut green onions
2 teaspoons minced peeled fresh ginger
3 garlic cloves, thinly sliced
2 cups broccoli florets
¼ cup lower-sodium soy sauce
2 tablespoons rice vinegar
1 teaspoon honey
⅛ teaspoon crushed red pepper

1. Combine shrimp and cornstarch in a medium bowl, tossing to coat. Heat a large wok or skillet over high heat. Add 1 tablespoon oil to pan; swirl to coat. Add shrimp; stir-fry 4 minutes. Remove shrimp from pan; place in a medium bowl. Add 1½ teaspoons oil to pan; swirl to coat. Add green onions, ginger, and garlic to pan; stir-fry 45 seconds. Add onion mixture to shrimp.
2. Add 1 tablespoon oil to pan; swirl to coat. Add broccoli; stir-fry 1½ minutes. Stir in shrimp mixture, soy sauce, and remaining ingredients; bring to a boil. Cook 1 minute or until shrimp are done and broccoli is crisp-tender. Serves 4 (serving size: about 1 cup)

CALORIES 201; **FAT** 10.1g (sat 0.8g, mono 5.6g, poly 2.7g); **PROTEIN** 18g; **CARB** 10.5g; **FIBER** 1.7g; **CHOL** 143mg; **IRON** 1.3mg; **SODIUM** 571mg; **CALC** 96mg

---

DINNER TONIGHT

Fast weeknight menus from the Cooking Light Test Kitchen

READY IN **30** MINUTES

The SHOPPING LIST

Grilled Pork Chops with Nectarines
Fresh thyme
Garlic
Nectarines (2)
Extra-virgin olive oil
Sugar
Ground cumin
Ground red pepper
4 (6-ounce) bone-in center-cut pork chops
Mascarpone cheese

Bacon-Herb Salad
1 (6-ounce) package herb salad mix
Sherry vinegar
Dijon mustard
Honey
Center-cut bacon (2 slices)

The GAME PLAN

While grill preheats:
- Rub oil mixture on pork.
- Make sugar mixture for nectarines.

While pork rests:
- Grill nectarines.
- Prepare salad.

Kid Friendly • Quick & Easy

Grilled Pork Chops with Nectarines

With Bacon-Herb Salad

Simple Sub: Substitute plums or peaches.
Flavor Swap: For a fruitier vinaigrette, use balsamic vinegar.
Kid Tweak: Omit the ground red pepper.

1 tablespoon chopped fresh thyme
3½ teaspoons extra-virgin olive oil, divided
2 teaspoons minced fresh garlic
4 (6-ounce) bone-in center-cut pork chops (about ½ inch thick)
¼ teaspoon kosher salt
¼ teaspoon freshly ground black pepper
Cooking spray
2 ripe nectarines
½ teaspoon sugar
¼ teaspoon ground cumin
⅛ teaspoon ground red pepper
4 teaspoons mascarpone cheese

1. Preheat grill to medium-high heat.
2. Combine thyme, 1 tablespoon oil, and garlic in a small bowl. Rub oil mixture evenly over pork chops; sprinkle with salt and black pepper. Place pork on grill rack coated with cooking spray; grill 3 minutes on each side or until desired degree of doneness. Let stand 10 minutes.
3. While pork stands, cut nectarines in half; discard pits. Combine sugar, ½ teaspoon oil, cumin, and red pepper in a small bowl. Sprinkle sugar mixture evenly over cut sides of nectarines. Place nectarines on grill rack coated with cooking spray; grill 5 minutes on each side or until tender. Cut nectarines into wedges; top evenly with mascarpone cheese. Serve with pork. Serves 4 (serving size: 1 pork chop, 1 nectarine half, and 1 teaspoon cheese)

CALORIES 330; **FAT** 17.3g (sat 5.5g, mono 6.1g, poly 1.5g); **PROTEIN** 33.4g; **CARB** 9.7g; **FIBER** 1.5g; **CHOL** 111mg; **IRON** 1.4mg; **SODIUM** 192mg; **CALC** 52mg

For the Bacon-Herb Salad:

Cook 2 center-cut bacon slices in a small nonstick skillet over medium heat until crisp. Remove bacon from pan; crumble. Pour drippings into a medium bowl. Add 2 tablespoons sherry vinegar, 2 teaspoons Dijon mustard, 1 teaspoon honey, ¼ teaspoon freshly ground black pepper, and ⅛ teaspoon kosher salt to bowl; stir with a whisk. Add 1 (6-ounce) package herb salad mix; toss to coat. Sprinkle with bacon. Serves 4 (serving size: about 1 cup)

CALORIES 30; FAT 1g (sat 0.5g); SODIUM 203mg

Kid Friendly • Quick & Easy

Garden Alfredo with Chicken

With Arugula-Tomato Salad

Simple Sub: You can use linguine instead of pappardelle.
Kid Tweak: Broccoli or carrots can sub in for any of the vegetables.
Time-Saver: Look for bagged baby arugula.

1 pound skinless, boneless chicken breast halves
⅝ teaspoon kosher salt, divided
½ teaspoon black pepper, divided
Cooking spray
6 ounces uncooked pappardelle pasta
2 medium zucchini
2 medium yellow squash
2 teaspoons olive oil
5 ounces thin asparagus spears, trimmed
1 red bell pepper, cut into thin strips
6 garlic cloves, thinly sliced
¾ cup fat-free, lower-sodium chicken broth
½ cup half-and-half
2 teaspoons all-purpose flour
2 ounces fresh Parmesan cheese, grated
2 tablespoons flat-leaf parsley leaves

1. Heat a large skillet over medium-high heat. Sprinkle chicken with ¼ teaspoon salt and ¼ teaspoon pepper. Coat pan with cooking spray. Add chicken; cook 4 minutes on each side or until done. Remove from pan; let stand 5 minutes. Cut chicken across the grain into thin slices; keep warm. Reserve drippings in pan.
2. While chicken cooks, cook pasta according to package directions. Drain; keep warm.
3. Cut each zucchini and squash in half crosswise. Cut ½-inch slices from outer "walls" of zucchini and squash; discard cores. Slice pieces lengthwise into thin strips.
4. Heat a nonstick skillet over medium-high heat. Add oil; swirl. Add zucchini, squash, asparagus, and bell pepper; sauté 3 minutes. Sprinkle with ⅜ teaspoon salt. Add garlic; sauté 2 minutes. Remove pan from heat.
5. Combine broth, half-and-half, and flour; stir with a whisk. Add broth mixture to reserved drippings in skillet. Bring to a boil; cook 2 minutes or until slightly thickened, stirring constantly. Remove from heat. Add cheese; stir until cheese melts. Add pasta, vegetables, and chicken; toss. Sprinkle with ¼ teaspoon black pepper and parsley. Serves 4 (serving size: 2 cups)

CALORIES 456; FAT 13.6g (sat 5.6g, mono 4.7g, poly 1.2g); PROTEIN 38.7g; CARB 43.2g; FIBER 4.4g; CHOL 106mg; IRON 4mg; SODIUM 718mg; CALC 270mg

---

For the Arugula-Tomato Salad:

Combine 2 tablespoons champagne vinegar, 1 tablespoon extra-virgin olive oil, ½ teaspoon Dijon mustard, ¼ teaspoon black pepper, and ⅛ teaspoon salt in a medium bowl; stir with a whisk. Add 6 ounces baby arugula, 1 pint halved grape tomatoes, and ⅓ cup vertically sliced red onion; toss to coat. Serves 4 (serving size: about 1¼ cups)

CALORIES 61; FAT 3.7g (sat 0.5g); SODIUM 104mg

READY IN 40 MINUTES

The
SHOPPING LIST

Garden Alfredo with Chicken
Zucchini (2)
Yellow squash (2)
Asparagus (5 ounces)
Red bell pepper (1)
Garlic
Fresh flat-leaf parsley
Pappardelle pasta (6 ounces)
Olive oil
Fat-free, lower-sodium chicken broth
All-purpose flour
Skinless, boneless chicken breast halves (1 pound)
Half-and-half
Parmesan cheese (2 ounces)

Arugula-Tomato Salad
Baby arugula (6 ounces)
Grape tomatoes (1 pint)
Red onion (1)
Champagne vinegar
Extra-virgin olive oil
Dijon mustard

The
GAME PLAN

While chicken cooks:
 ▪ Cook pasta.
 ▪ Cut vegetables.

While sauce cooks:
 ▪ Prepare vinaigrette for salad.

The SHOPPING LIST

Grilled Chicken with Tomato-Avocado Salad
Fresh flat-leaf parsley
Shallots (1)
Fresh thyme
Garlic
Yellow corn (2 ears)
Red onion (1)
Yellow tomatoes (2)
Red tomatoes (2)
Cherry tomatoes (1 cup)
Avocado (1)
Canola mayonnaise
Cider vinegar
Olive oil
Onion powder
Ground cumin
Chipotle chile powder
4 (6-ounce) skinless, boneless chicken breast halves
Nonfat buttermilk

Grilled French Bread
Garlic
Olive oil
French bread loaf

The GAME PLAN

While grill preheats:
- Make dressing.
- Rub spice mixture on chicken.

While chicken grills:
- Grill bread.

While chicken rests:
- Prepare salad.

Kid Friendly • Quick & Easy

Grilled Chicken with Tomato-Avocado Salad

With Grilled French Bread

Flavor Hit: While the bread is warm, rub it with a halved garlic clove.
Simple Sub: For less heat, use regular chili powder in place of chipotle chile powder.
Shop Smart: Buy corn with tight husks to ensure fresh, juicy kernels.

¼ cup nonfat buttermilk
3 tablespoons canola mayonnaise
2 tablespoons minced fresh flat-leaf parsley
1 tablespoon minced shallots
1 teaspoon minced fresh thyme
1 teaspoon cider vinegar
¼ teaspoon freshly ground black pepper
⅛ teaspoon kosher salt
1 garlic clove, minced
4 (6-ounce) skinless, boneless chicken breast halves
Cooking spray
1½ tablespoons olive oil
1 teaspoon onion powder
¾ teaspoon ground cumin
¾ teaspoon kosher salt, divided
¼ teaspoon chipotle chile powder
2 ears yellow corn, shucked
1 small red onion, cut into ½-inch slices
2 yellow tomatoes, each cut into 4 slices
2 red tomatoes, each cut into 4 slices
1 cup cherry tomatoes, halved
1 sliced peeled ripe avocado

1. Preheat grill to high heat.
2. Combine first 9 ingredients in a small bowl; stir with a whisk. Chill buttermilk mixture until ready to serve.
3. Lightly coat chicken with cooking spray. Combine oil, onion powder, cumin, ½ teaspoon salt, and chipotle; rub evenly over chicken. Coat corn and onion with cooking spray. Arrange chicken, corn, and onion on grill rack; grill 8 minutes or until done, turning chicken and onion once and corn occasionally. Remove from grill; let stand 5 minutes. Cut corn kernels from cobs.
4. Slice chicken. Arrange 1 breast on each of 4 plates. Arrange 2 yellow and 2 red tomato slices on each plate. Top each serving with ¼ cup cherry tomatoes. Divide corn, onion, and avocado evenly among plates. Sprinkle ¼ teaspoon salt over salads. Drizzle about 1½ tablespoons dressing over each salad. Serves 4

CALORIES 448; FAT 23.9g (sat 3.6g, mono 13.5g, poly 4.7g); PROTEIN 39g; CARB 21.4g; FIBER 5.9g; CHOL 98mg; IRON 2.4mg; SODIUM 618mg; CALC 68mg

For the Grilled French Bread:
Preheat grill to high heat. Place 4 (1-ounce) slices French bread on grill; grill 1 minute on each side or until grill marks appear. Brush each slice with ½ teaspoon olive oil; rub slices with cut side of a halved garlic clove. Serves 4 (serving size: 1 bread slice)

CALORIES 102; FAT 2.8g (sat 0.5g); SODIUM 146mg

Quick & Easy

Creole Shrimp and Rice

With Garlic and Red Pepper Asparagus

Time-Saver: Have your fishmonger peel and devein the shrimp.
Flavor Hit: Creole seasoning adds a kick of spice to the dish.
Prep Pointer: Before roasting, snap the tough ends off the asparagus.

1 (3½-ounce) bag boil-in-bag long-grain rice
4 teaspoons canola oil, divided
¾ pound medium shrimp, peeled and deveined
1½ teaspoons Creole seasoning (such as Tony Chachere's)
⅛ teaspoon ground red pepper

1 cup chopped onion
½ cup chopped green bell pepper
½ cup chopped celery
1 tablespoon chopped fresh thyme
4 garlic cloves, minced
1 cup 1% low-fat milk
1 tablespoon all-purpose flour
2 cups cherry tomatoes, quartered
¼ teaspoon freshly ground black
  pepper
2 tablespoons minced fresh chives

1. Cook rice according to package directions, omitting salt and fat.
2. Heat a large skillet over medium heat. Add 2 teaspoons oil to pan; swirl to coat. Sprinkle shrimp evenly with Creole seasoning and red pepper. Add shrimp to pan; sauté 3 minutes or until browned, stirring occasionally. Remove from pan.
3. Add 2 teaspoons oil to pan; swirl to coat. Add onion and next 4 ingredients to pan; sauté 5 minutes. Combine milk and flour in a small bowl, stirring with a whisk. Add milk mixture to pan; bring to a simmer. Reduce heat to medium; cook 3 minutes or until slightly thickened. Add tomatoes and black pepper to pan; cook 2 minutes or until tomatoes are tender. Stir in shrimp; sprinkle with chives. Serve with rice. Serves 4 (serving size: 1¾ cups shrimp mixture and ½ cup rice)

CALORIES 283; FAT 7.3g (sat 1.2g, mono 3.6g, poly 1.9g); PROTEIN 17.9g; CARB 36.7g; FIBER 4.1g; CHOL 110mg; IRON 1.3mg; SODIUM 699mg; CALC 164mg

For the Garlic and Red Pepper Asparagus:
Preheat oven to 425°. Combine 1 pound trimmed asparagus, 2 tablespoons extra-virgin olive oil, ¼ teaspoon kosher salt, ¼ teaspoon crushed red pepper, ¼ teaspoon freshly ground black pepper, and 2 thinly sliced garlic cloves on a jelly-roll pan; toss to coat. Bake at 425° for 8 minutes or until asparagus is crisp-tender. Serves 4 (serving size: about 6 asparagus spears)

CALORIES 85; FAT 6.9g (sat 1g); SODIUM 123mg

READY IN
40
MINUTES

The
SHOPPING LIST

Creole Shrimp and Rice
Onion (1)
Green bell pepper (1)
Celery
Fresh thyme
Garlic
Cherry tomatoes (1 pint)
Fresh chives
Creole seasoning
Canola oil
Ground red pepper
All-purpose flour
Boil-in-bag long-grain rice
Medium shrimp (¾ pound)
1% low-fat milk

Garlic and Red Pepper Asparagus
Asparagus (1 pound)
Garlic
Extra-virgin olive oil
Crushed red pepper

The
GAME PLAN

While oven preheats:
  ▪ Cook rice.
  ▪ Trim asparagus.
While asparagus cooks:
  ▪ Cook shrimp mixture.

SUPERFAST 20-MINUTE COOKING

Kick off summer with quick breaded catfish, kid-friendly chicken skewers, seared scallops, easy wraps, and more fast, fresh, seasonal dishes.

Quick & Easy
Seared Scallop Salad with Prosciutto Crisps
(pictured on page 222)

5 teaspoons extra-virgin olive
  oil, divided
1 tablespoon cider vinegar
1 tablespoon minced shallots
2 teaspoons Dijon mustard
4 cups mixed salad greens
2 cups cherry tomatoes, halved
½ cup sliced English cucumber
1 ounce prosciutto, thinly sliced
16 sea scallops (about 1 pound)
½ teaspoon freshly ground
  black pepper
¼ teaspoon kosher salt

1. Combine 1 tablespoon oil, cider vinegar, minced shallots, and Dijon mustard in a large bowl, stirring with a whisk. Add salad greens, halved cherry tomatoes, and cucumber to bowl; toss gently to coat.
2. Heat a large nonstick skillet over medium-high heat. Add sliced prosciutto to pan; cook 3 minutes or until prosciutto is crisp; coarsely chop. Pat scallops dry with paper towels; sprinkle with freshly ground black pepper and kosher salt. Add 2 teaspoons olive oil to pan; swirl to coat pan. Add scallops to pan; cook 3 minutes on each side or until desired degree of doneness. Place
continued

4 scallops and ⅔ cup salad mixture on each of 4 plates; sprinkle with prosciutto. Serves 4

CALORIES 171; FAT 7.1g (sat 1.2g, mono 4.5g, poly 0.9g); PROTEIN 16.7g; CARB 10.3g; FIBER 2.3g; CHOL 31mg; IRON 1.3mg; SODIUM 493mg; CALC 18mg

Quick & Easy

Chicken, Arugula, and Radish Pizza

If you don't have white wine vinegar on hand, substitute red wine vinegar or champagne vinegar.

1 (12-inch) thin pizza crust
  (such as Boboli)
2 tablespoons extra-virgin olive oil,
  divided
1½ cups skinless, boneless rotisserie
  chicken breast, shredded
⅓ cup part-skim ricotta cheese
1.5 ounces goat cheese, crumbled
  (about ⅓ cup)
½ teaspoon freshly ground black pepper
¼ teaspoon crushed red pepper
2 tablespoons white wine vinegar
1 teaspoon Dijon mustard
1½ cups baby arugula
½ cup thinly sliced radishes

1. Place a baking sheet in the oven. Preheat oven to 475° (keep baking sheet in oven as it preheats).
2. Brush crust with 1 tablespoon olive oil; top pizza evenly with shredded chicken and ricotta cheese. Sprinkle with goat cheese, black pepper, and red pepper. Carefully place pizza on preheated baking sheet; bake at 475° for 10 minutes.
3. Combine white wine vinegar, 1 tablespoon olive oil, and Dijon mustard in a medium bowl, stirring with a whisk. Add arugula and radish slices; toss to coat. Top pizza with arugula mixture. Cut pizza into 8 wedges. Serves 4 (serving size: 2 wedges)

CALORIES 407; FAT 16.9g (sat 6g, mono 6.7g, poly 1.1g); PROTEIN 24.9g; CARB 37.1g; FIBER 0.5g; CHOL 53mg; IRON 0.7mg; SODIUM 668mg; CALC 111mg

Quick & Easy

Peanut Chicken Noodle Soup

If you can't find udon, substitute 6 ounces uncooked spaghetti.

14 ounces uncooked fresh udon noodles
½ cup unsalted chicken stock
3 tablespoons reduced-fat creamy
  peanut butter
½ teaspoon kosher salt
½ teaspoon freshly ground black
  pepper
1 (13.5-ounce) can light coconut milk
3 cups shredded skinless, boneless
  rotisserie chicken breast (about 15
  ounces)
3 cups thinly sliced napa cabbage
¼ cup cilantro leaves
1 small serrano chile, thinly sliced
2 tablespoons Sriracha (hot chile
  sauce)

1. Cook noodles according to package directions, omitting salt and fat. Drain in a colander over a bowl, reserving 2 cups cooking liquid.
2. Heat stock and next 4 ingredients in a saucepan over medium-low heat.
3. Add cooking liquid and chicken to milk mixture; cook 3 minutes or until chicken is heated. Add noodles and cabbage; cook 2 minutes or until cabbage wilts. Sprinkle with cilantro and serrano; serve with Sriracha. Serves 6 (serving size: about 1¼ cups soup and 1 teaspoon Sriracha)

CALORIES 293; FAT 10.9g (sat 4.6g, mono 3.3g, poly 1.5g); PROTEIN 25.1g; CARB 25.6g; FIBER 2.1g; CHOL 73mg; IRON 1.7mg; SODIUM 656mg; CALC 43mg

Kid Friendly • Quick & Easy

Honey-Lime Chicken Kebabs

with Mango Slices

For a colorful accompaniment, add mini bell peppers to the broiler pan with the skewers.

1 pound skinless, boneless chicken
  breast, cut into 1-inch cubes
2 teaspoons grated lime rind
2 teaspoons minced fresh garlic
1 teaspoon chili powder
¼ teaspoon kosher salt
Cooking spray
2 tablespoons fresh lime juice
1 tablespoon honey
2 sliced peeled mangoes
Chili powder (optional)

1. Preheat broiler to high.
2. Combine first 5 ingredients; toss to coat. Thread chicken onto 8 (6-inch) skewers. Place kebabs on a broiler pan coated with cooking spray; broil 4 minutes on each side or until done.
3. Combine juice and honey in a small bowl; stir with a whisk. Arrange kebabs and mango slices on a platter; drizzle with honey mixture, and sprinkle with chili powder, if desired. Serves 4 (serving size: 2 kebabs and 1 sliced mango half)

CALORIES 254; FAT 3.8g (sat 0.8g, mono 1.1g, poly 0.6g); PROTEIN 25.7g; CARB 30.9g; FIBER 2.9g; CHOL 73mg; IRON 0.9mg; SODIUM 265mg; CALC 30mg

Kid Friendly • Quick & Easy
Vegetarian

Sunflower Granola Breakfast Parfaits

To make this portable breakfast a snap, prepare the granola in advance and store it in an airtight container. Be sure to keep a close eye on the broiler so the granola doesn't burn. You can also sub pitted fresh cherries or any ripe berry for the raspberries.

1 cup old-fashioned rolled oats
¼ cup raw sunflower seed kernels
¼ cup shredded sweetened coconut
¼ cup chopped walnuts
¼ cup flaxseed meal
½ teaspoon ground cinnamon
¼ teaspoon salt
2 tablespoons butter, melted
2 tablespoons honey
½ teaspoon vanilla extract
4 cups plain fat-free Greek yogurt
2 cups raspberries

1. Place oven rack on middle shelf, about 10 inches below broiler. Preheat broiler to high.
2. Combine first 7 ingredients on a baking sheet; toss well. Broil 3 minutes or until lightly toasted, stirring every 1 minute. Combine butter, honey, and vanilla in a small bowl. Drizzle butter mixture over oat mixture; toss to coat. Broil granola an additional 2 minutes or until well toasted, stirring after 1 minute. Remove granola from oven; cool on pan 8 minutes, stirring occasionally.
3. Spoon ½ cup yogurt into each of 8 bowls. Top with about ⅓ cup granola and about ¼ cup berries. Serves 8

CALORIES 235; FAT 10.6g (sat 3.3g, mono 2.5g, poly 4.1g); PROTEIN 14g; CARB 23.2g; FIBER 4.9g; CHOL 8mg; IRON 1.3mg; SODIUM 150mg; CALC 98mg

Kid Friendly • Quick & Easy

Baby Potatoes

with Tomato-Corn Sauté

12 ounces small baby potatoes, halved
1 tablespoon olive oil
1 cup fresh corn kernels (about 2 ears)
1½ teaspoons thinly sliced garlic
¼ teaspoon salt
¼ teaspoon crushed red pepper
1 cup halved grape tomatoes
⅓ cup chopped fresh cilantro
1 ounce fresh Parmesan cheese, shaved (about ¼ cup)

1. Place potatoes in a medium saucepan; cover with water. Bring to a boil. Cook 10 minutes or until tender; drain.
2. Heat a large nonstick skillet over medium-high heat. Add oil to pan; swirl to coat. Add corn and next 3 ingredients to pan; sauté 2 minutes. Add potatoes and tomatoes to pan; cook 1 minute. Top with cilantro and cheese. Serves 4 (serving size: ¾ cup)

CALORIES 160; FAT 6g (sat 1.8g, mono 3.2g, poly 0.7g); PROTEIN 5.9g; CARB 22.5g; FIBER 2.7g; CHOL 6.2mg; IRON 0.9mg; SODIUM 279mg; CALC 96mg

Variation 1: Arugula Pesto
Place 1 pound baby potatoes in a saucepan; cover with water. Bring to a boil. Cook 11 minutes; drain. Pulse 1 cup arugula, ½ cup fresh basil, 2 tablespoons grated fresh Parmesan, 2 tablespoons unsalted chicken stock, 1 tablespoon olive oil, 1 tablespoon fresh lemon juice, ⅜ teaspoon salt, and ¼ teaspoon pepper in a mini food processor. Combine potatoes and arugula mixture in a medium bowl; toss. Serves 4 (serving size: ¾ cup)

CALORIES 125; FAT 4.3g (sat 1g); SODIUM 286mg

Variation 2: Warm Bacon Vinaigrette
Place 1 pound quartered baby potatoes in a saucepan; cover with water. Bring to a boil. Cook 8 minutes; drain. Cook 2 center-cut bacon slices in a skillet until crisp; crumble. Combine drippings, 2 tablespoons cider vinegar, 1 tablespoon olive oil, 1 tablespoon Dijon, 1 teaspoon brown sugar, and ¼ teaspoon salt in a bowl. Add potatoes and 2 cups spinach. Top with ¼ cup green onions and bacon. Serves 4 (serving size: ¾ cup)

CALORIES 134; FAT 4.6g (sat 1g); SODIUM 304mg

Variation 3: Kale and Garlic
Place 1 pound sliced baby potatoes in a saucepan; cover with water. Bring to a boil. Cook 8 minutes; drain. Heat a large skillet over medium-high heat. Add 1½ tablespoons canola oil, swirl to coat. Add potatoes and 2 tablespoons sliced garlic; cook 3 minutes. Add 3 cups chopped kale and 1 tablespoon water. Cover and cook 3 minutes. Add 1 teaspoon sesame oil, ½ teaspoon salt, and ¼ teaspoon pepper; toss. Serves 4 (serving size: ¾ cup)

CALORIES 168; FAT 6.9g (sat 0.6g); SODIUM 338mg

Cornmeal-Dusted Catfish

with Quinoa Sauté

1/3 cup uncooked quinoa
1/2 cup hot water
1/4 cup cornmeal
4 (6-ounce) catfish fillets
1/2 teaspoon salt, divided
1/2 teaspoon freshly ground black pepper, divided
2 1/2 tablespoons olive oil, divided
1 cup chopped green bell pepper
1 tablespoon minced jalapeño pepper
2 teaspoons thinly sliced garlic
1 cup fresh corn kernels (about 2 ears)
1 cup chopped tomato
1/4 cup chopped green onions
1 tablespoon fresh lime juice
4 lemon wedges

1. Place quinoa in a fine sieve; place sieve in a large bowl. Cover quinoa with water. Using your hands, rub grains together for 30 seconds; rinse and drain. Repeat procedure twice. Drain well. Combine 1/2 cup hot water and quinoa in a small saucepan; bring to a boil. Cover, reduce heat, and simmer 13 minutes or until liquid is absorbed and quinoa is tender.
2. Heat a large nonstick skillet over medium-high heat. Place cornmeal in a shallow dish. Sprinkle fish with 1/4 teaspoon salt and 1/4 teaspoon black pepper. Dredge fish in cornmeal. Add 1 tablespoon oil to pan; swirl to coat. Add fish to pan; cook 4 minutes on each side or until desired degree of doneness. Remove fish from pan; keep warm.
3. Return pan to medium-high heat. Add remaining 1 1/2 tablespoons oil to pan. Add bell pepper, jalapeño, garlic, 1/4 teaspoon salt, and 1/4 teaspoon black pepper to pan; sauté 3 minutes. Add corn; sauté 2 minutes. Stir in quinoa, tomato, onions, and juice. Serve fish with quinoa mixture and lemon wedges. Serves 4 (serving size: 1 fillet, about 2/3 cup quinoa mixture, and 1 lemon wedge)

CALORIES 363; FAT 14.9g (sat 2.7g, mono 8g, poly 3.1g); PROTEIN 32.4g; CARB 26g; FIBER 3.9g; CHOL 99mg; IRON 2mg; SODIUM 380mg; CALC 54mg

FOR A KID-FRIENDLY DISH, OMIT THE JALAPEÑO IN THE QUINOA.

Curried Pork Salad Wraps

If you can't find lavash, try lower-sodium flatbreads or sandwich wraps.

2 teaspoons olive oil
1 (1-pound) pork tenderloin, trimmed and cut into bite-sized pieces
2 teaspoons curry powder
1/2 teaspoon kosher salt
1/4 cup chopped celery
1/4 cup chopped unsalted, shelled, dry-roasted pistachios
1/4 cup raisins
3 tablespoons plain fat-free yogurt
3 tablespoons canola mayonnaise
4 lavash flatbreads
8 butter lettuce leaves
12 (1/8-inch-thick) slices tomato

1. Heat a large skillet over medium-high heat. Add olive oil to pan; swirl to coat. Add pork, curry, powder, and salt to pan; sauté 4 minutes or until pork is done. Let pork mixture cool slightly. Combine pork mixture, celery, pistachios, raisins, yogurt, and canola mayonnaise in a medium bowl.
2. Top each lavash with 2 lettuce leaves, 3 tomato slices, and about 3/4 cup pork mixture, leaving a 1/2-inch border around edges. Roll up wraps, and cut in half diagonally. Serves 4

CALORIES 446; FAT 16.7g (sat 2.3g, mono 8.9g, poly 4g); PROTEIN 32.8g; CARB 42.6g; FIBER 8.1g; CHOL 78mg; IRON 4mg; SODIUM 521mg; CALC 88mg

OOPS!
YOUR BREADING FALLS OFF

How to keep it on the chicken, not on the pan

A golden, crunchy-crisp coating adds oodles of eating pleasure to chicken breasts, fish fillets, pork chops, and the like. But then a breading failure happens—a kitchen tragedy. The problem is often a pan that's too cool. A cool pan grabs breading and won't let go, causing whole slabs to peel off. Uneven coating will also chip and tear. Yes, lots of frying oil would make the job easier, but that's not the way we do things. Technique is the key.

The solution: Flour first, and keep your pan nice and hot. Breading works best as a three-step process: Dredge in flour, dip in liquid (usually egg or buttermilk), and coat with breadcrumbs. Flour helps the liquid cling, which in turn holds the breading in place. Shake off excess at every stage to keep coating uniform. Heat oil over medium-high heat (a drop of water should sizzle when it hits the pan), and cook a few minutes without touching; hands-off cooking helps form a crust that adheres. Turn the food gently with a spatula; tongs will pinch and tear the breading. Cook until done.

(Gold star!)

(Sad. Just Sad.)

TOTAL BURGER AWESOMENESS

Seven magnificent regional versions of the great American sandwich.

Mom's apple pie is the first dessert of hungry patriots, but no culinary canvas is as broad and American as the good old burger. Coast to coast, north to south, the burger is us, the essential food of the people of the Fourth. Burger definitions are broad, and variations run deep—kind of like American culture itself. In honor of the Fourth of July, here's a virtual road trip across the American burger landscape, seven regional expressions of the essential bun-and-patty satisfier. This holiday, fly your burger flag high—and then keep it flying all summer, because these recipes are healthy as well as delicious.

Vegetarian

Berkeley Veggie Burger

Hands-on: 42 min. Total: 42 min.

6 (1½-ounce) artisanal sandwich rolls
Cooking spray
3 cups grated cooked golden beet
  (about 3 medium)
⅓ cup chopped walnuts, toasted
⅓ cup panko (Japanese breadcrumbs)
3 tablespoons grated fresh horseradish
3 tablespoons minced fresh chives
¼ teaspoon freshly ground black
  pepper
1 (8.8-ounce) package precooked
  brown rice
2 teaspoons Dijon mustard
2 large eggs
1 large egg white
⅜ teaspoon kosher salt, divided
2 tablespoons canola oil, divided
¼ cup canola mayonnaise
1 teaspoon fresh lemon juice
2 ounces blue cheese, crumbled (½ cup)
1½ cups arugula

1. Preheat broiler to high.
2. Place rolls, cut sides up, on a baking sheet; coat with cooking spray. Broil 2 minutes or until toasted. Set aside.
3. Reduce oven temperature to 400°; place a baking sheet in oven.
4. Combine beet and next 6 ingredients (through rice). Combine mustard, eggs, and egg white. Add ¼ teaspoon salt and mustard mixture to beet mixture; stir well. Spoon about ⅔ cup rice mixture into a (4-inch) round biscuit cutter; pack mixture down. Remove mold; repeat 5 times to form 6 patties.
5. Heat a large skillet over medium-high heat. Add 1 tablespoon oil; swirl to coat. Carefully add 3 patties to pan; cook 3 minutes. Carefully transfer patties to preheated baking sheet coated with cooking spray, turning patties over. Repeat procedure with 1 tablespoon oil and 3 patties. Return baking sheet to oven; bake patties at 400° for 12 minutes.
6. Combine mayonnaise, juice, cheese, and ⅛ teaspoon salt. Place bottom half of each roll on a plate. Divide mayonnaise mixture among roll bottoms; top each with 1 patty. Arrange ¼ cup arugula on each patty; top with roll tops. Serves 6 (serving size: 1 burger)

CALORIES 384; FAT 17.8g (sat 3.4g, mono 6.9g, poly 6.3g); PROTEIN 13.3g; CARB 43.1g; FIBER 4.1g; CHOL 69mg; IRON 2.7mg; SODIUM 649mg; CALC 111mg

Pacific Northwest Burger

Hands-on: 47 min. Total: 47 min.

½ cup water
¼ cup rice vinegar
1 tablespoon sugar
1 teaspoon salt
1½ cups very thinly sliced radish
⅓ cup canola mayonnaise
1½ tablespoons grated fresh ginger
2 teaspoons rice vinegar
½ teaspoon sugar
1 tablespoon lower-sodium soy sauce
1 tablespoon Thai sweet chili sauce
4 (6-ounce) salmon fillets, skinned
½ teaspoon freshly ground black
  pepper
¼ teaspoon kosher salt
Cooking spray
4 (1½-ounce) hamburger buns
1½ cups watercress

1. Combine first 4 ingredients in a saucepan; bring to a boil, stirring until sugar dissolves. Pour hot liquid over radish. Chill 30 minutes; drain well.
2. Combine mayonnaise and next 3 ingredients. Cover and refrigerate.
3. Preheat grill to high heat.
4. Combine soy sauce and chili sauce, stirring with a whisk. Sprinkle fillets

with pepper and ¼ teaspoon kosher salt. Place fillets on grill rack coated with cooking spray; grill 4 minutes, brushing with half of soy mixture. Carefully turn fillets; grill 4 minutes or until desired degree of doneness, brushing with remaining soy mixture.
5. Spread 2 tablespoons mayo mixture on bottom half of each bun; top each with 1 fillet. Top evenly with radishes. Arrange about ⅓ cup watercress on each fillet; top with top halves of buns. Serves 4 (serving size: 1 burger)

CALORIES 397; **FAT** 14.9g (sat 1.6g, mono 4.7g, poly 4.1g); **PROTEIN** 37.5g; **CARB** 24.9g; **FIBER** 1.8g; **CHOL** 80mg; **IRON** 2.4mg; **SODIUM** 567mg; **CALC** 117mg

---

PACIFIC NORTH-WEST BURGER

Salmon is sacred in the region, but don't grind it, please. No fish cake beats a fillet hot off the grill, nicely charred and glazed outside, almost sushi-tender within. Watercress—the peppery green I was eating way before arugula vogued in local markets—is quintessentially Pacific Northwest. Asian flavors are beloved, so the mayo is ginger-tinged. For crunch and tang, there's a quick pickle of fresh, thin-sliced radish. This luscious treat takes me right back home.
—*Scott Mowbray, Editor*

Quick & Easy
Southwest Burger

Hands-on: 20 min. Total: 35 min.

1½ cups water
2 ancho chiles
1 tablespoon olive oil, divided
2 garlic cloves
1 teaspoon sugar
½ teaspoon dried oregano
½ teaspoon ground cumin
¼ teaspoon freshly ground black
   pepper
1 pound 90% lean ground sirloin
⅜ teaspoon kosher salt, divided
2 medium nopales (cactus paddles)
⅓ cup shredded peeled jicama
3 tablespoons cilantro leaves

3 tablespoons fresh lime juice
Cooking spray
4 (1½-ounce) hamburger buns, toasted

1. Combine 1½ cups water and chiles in a microwave-safe bowl; microwave at HIGH 2 minutes. Let stand 15 minutes. Remove chiles; discard liquid. Stem and seed chiles. Place chiles, 1 teaspoon oil, and garlic in a mini food processor; process until smooth. Combine chile mixture, sugar, and next 4 ingredients (through beef) in a medium bowl. Stir in ¼ teaspoon salt. Divide beef mixture into 4 equal portions. Gently shape each into a ½-inch-thick patty.
2. Using a knife, remove needles from nopales; peel nopales, and chop to measure 1 cup. Heat a medium skillet over medium-high heat. Add 2 teaspoons oil; swirl to coat. Add nopales; sauté 3 minutes or until tender.
3. Preheat grill to medium-high heat.
4. Combine nopales, jicama, cilantro, and juice in a small bowl; sprinkle with ⅛ teaspoon salt.
5. Place patties on grill rack coated with cooking spray; grill 3 minutes. Carefully turn patties; grill 3 minutes or until desired degree of doneness. Place 1 patty on bottom half of each bun; top each serving with ¼ cup jicama mixture and top half of bun. Serves 4 (serving size: 1 burger)

CALORIES 375; **FAT** 15.9g (sat 4.9g, mono 7.1g, poly 1.8g); **PROTEIN** 27.9g; **CARB** 29.9g; **FIBER** 3.8g; **CHOL** 72mg; **IRON** 5mg; **SODIUM** 459mg; **CALC** 123mg

---

SOUTHWEST BURGER

Chile peppers and cacti are staple ingredients in Southwestern cooking. Here I mixed a sweet-smoky ancho chile paste with bottom notes of earthy cumin into the beef patty. For a condiment, I started with nopales (cactus paddles) to give deep green veggie flavor. Jicama adds hearty crunch, while lime juice and cilantro brighten it all up.
—*Tiffany Vickers Davis, Test Kitchen Manager*

Tennessee Burger with Bourbon and BBQ Sauce

Hands-on: 44 min. Total: 44 min.

3 bacon slices
1 teaspoon extra-virgin olive oil
3 cups vertically sliced red onion
5 tablespoons bourbon, divided
1 tablespoon balsamic vinegar
½ teaspoon kosher salt, divided
½ cup lower-sodium ketchup
1 tablespoon Dijon mustard
2 teaspoons honey
2 teaspoons hot pepper sauce
2 teaspoons Worcestershire sauce
¼ teaspoon smoked paprika
¼ teaspoon garlic powder
¼ teaspoon onion powder
1½ pounds 90% lean ground sirloin
Cooking spray
6 (1½-ounce) French bread hamburger
   buns
6 (¼-inch-thick) slices tomato

1. Cook bacon in a large skillet over medium heat until crisp. Remove bacon from pan. Add oil and onion to drippings in pan; cook 15 minutes or until onion is browned and very tender, stirring occasionally. Add 3 tablespoons bourbon, vinegar, and ¼ teaspoon salt. Cook 2 minutes or until liquid almost evaporates, stirring constantly. Remove mixture from pan. Cool 5 minutes.
2. Combine 2 tablespoons bourbon, ketchup, and next 7 ingredients in a small saucepan. Bring to a boil, stirring frequently. Reduce heat; simmer 5 minutes or until sauce thickens. Remove from heat.
3. Preheat grill to medium-high heat.
4. Coarsely chop ¾ cup onion mixture; stir into beef. Divide beef mixture into 6 equal portions, gently shaping each portion into a ½-inch-thick patty. Press a nickel-sized indentation in center of
continued

each patty. Sprinkle evenly with ¼ teaspoon salt. Place patties on grill rack coated with cooking spray; grill 4 minutes on each side or until desired degree of doneness.

5. Spread each top and bottom bun half with 1 tablespoon sauce. Place patties on bottom halves; top each patty with 1 tomato slice. Divide remaining onion mixture evenly among servings. Top each serving with ½ bacon slice and top half of bun. Serves 6 (serving size: 1 burger)

CALORIES 358; FAT 11.4g (sat 3.8g, mono 4.7g, poly 1.5g); PROTEIN 22.1g; CARB 36.7g; FIBER 4.6g; CHOL 55mg; IRON 3.2mg; SODIUM 544mg; CALC 76mg

TENNESSEE BURGER

You can play with tradition in the South, but best not mess with it. There's no quinoa or fish sauce in this burger. It starts with caramelized onions, cooked low and slow. Some of the onions then get folded into the beef, keeping the patty moist and juicy. Next come salutes to barbecue and bourbon. Bacon adds savory crunch, while a shot of bourbon keeps the made-from-scratch sauce smoky and sweet. Then we bless it all with a fat, juicy, heirloom tomato slice. —*Sidney Fry, Nutrition Editor*

New England Turkey Burger

Hands-on: 13 min. Total: 45 min.

1 tablespoon olive oil
2 cups thinly sliced onion
¾ cup Samuel Adams Summer Ale
1 pound ground turkey
¼ teaspoon kosher salt
¼ teaspoon freshly ground black pepper
Cooking spray
1.5 ounces reduced-fat Vermont white cheddar cheese, shaved
4 teaspoons canola mayonnaise
2 teaspoons whole-grain mustard
4 (1½-ounce) hamburger buns, toasted
4 small green leaf lettuce leaves
4 (¼-inch-thick) slices tomato

1. Heat a large skillet over medium heat. Add oil; swirl to coat. Add onion; cook 7 minutes or until tender, stirring occasionally. Add beer; bring to a boil over medium-high heat. Reduce heat. Simmer 20 minutes or until onion is golden and liquid almost evaporates; stir occasionally. Cool.
2. Preheat grill to medium-high heat.
3. Remove ¼ cup onion mixture from pan; finely chop. Combine chopped onion mixture and turkey. Divide mixture into 4 equal portions; gently shape each into a ½-inch-thick patty. Press a nickel-sized indentation in center of each patty. Sprinkle with salt and pepper. Place patties on grill rack coated with cooking spray; grill 5 minutes. Turn patties; grill 3 minutes. Top with cheese; grill 1 minute or until cheese melts and turkey is done.
4. Combine mayonnaise and mustard. Spread 1½ teaspoons mayonnaise mixture on bottom half of each bun; top each with 1 lettuce leaf, 1 tomato slice, and 1 patty. Divide onion mixture evenly among servings; top with top halves of buns. Serves 4 (serving size: 1 burger)

CALORIES 407; FAT 18.3g (sat 4.9g, mono 6.9g, poly 4.4g); PROTEIN 28.9g; CARB 28.5g; FIBER 2g; CHOL 92mg; IRON 3mg; SODIUM 597mg; CALC 191mg

NEW ENGLAND TURKEY BURGER

Surf-and-turf sings a New England tune: Stick a few hunks of Maine lobstah on a beef patty and call it a day. But beef and lobster don't really belong together in a bun. I wanted something simpler, more basic and true to the region where I spent my college years. Turkey is a healthy choice and the essence of New England tradition. Caramelized onions simmer in hoppy Sam Adams beer, while shaved Vermont cheddar adds tang and richness to the meat.
—*Hannah Klinger, Editorial Contributor*

Quick & Easy

SoCal Guacamole Burger

Hands-on: 15 min. Total: 15 min.

1 ripe peeled avocado, divided
1 tablespoon light sour cream
1 tablespoon canola mayonnaise (such as Hellmann's)
2 teaspoons fresh lime juice
¼ teaspoon ground cumin
⅓ cup chopped seeded tomato
1 jalapeño pepper, seeded and chopped
½ teaspoon kosher salt, divided
1 pound 90% lean ground sirloin
¼ teaspoon freshly ground black pepper
Cooking spray
4 (1½-ounce) whole-grain hamburger buns
1 cup alfalfa sprouts

1. Preheat grill to medium-high heat.
2. Place half of avocado in a bowl; mash with a fork until almost smooth. Add sour cream and next 3 ingredients to bowl; stir to combine. Dice remaining half of avocado. Add diced avocado, tomato, jalapeño, and ⅛ teaspoon salt to bowl; stir gently to combine.
3. Divide beef into 4 equal portions. Gently shape each portion into a (½-inch-thick) patty. Press a nickel-sized indentation in center of each patty. Sprinkle evenly with ⅜ teaspoon salt and pepper. Place burgers on grill rack coated with cooking spray. Grill 3 minutes on each side or until desired degree of doneness. Lightly coat cut sides of buns with cooking spray. Place buns, cut sides down, on grill rack; grill 1 minute or until toasted.
4. Place ¼ cup sprouts on bottom half of each bun; top each with 1 patty, about 3 tablespoons guacamole, and top half of bun. Serves 4 (serving size: 1 burger)

CALORIES 403; FAT 21.1g (sat 5.6g, mono 10.4g, poly 2.6g); PROTEIN 27.6g; CARB 27.5g; FIBER 7g; CHOL 74mg; IRON 3.8mg; SODIUM 499mg; CALC 74mg

SOCAL GUACAMOLE BURGER

This Southern California special blends the region's produce-forward approach with Latin flair on a lean sirloin patty. Buttery avocado is the base for a guacamole that's flecked with jalapeño. For crunch, I chose alfalfa sprouts, which continue to proliferate in California stores and are prized for their bright taste and springy, crisp texture. Some locals might have gone bunless, but grains are so of-the-moment. I used a whole-grain bun, natch.
—Deb Wise, Recipe Tester and Developer

Kid Friendly • Quick & Easy

Great Plains Burger

Hands-on: 23 min. Total: 27 min.

1 ear shucked corn
1 small red onion, cut into ³/₄-inch slices
Cooking spray
2 tablespoons canola mayonnaise
1 teaspoon mustard seeds
1 teaspoon cider vinegar
³/₈ teaspoon salt, divided
1 tablespoon adobo sauce from canned chipotle chiles in adobo sauce
1¹/₂ ounces corn chips (such as Fritos)
1 tablespoon chopped fresh sage
¹/₂ teaspoon garlic powder
¹/₂ teaspoon freshly ground black pepper
1 pound lean ground bison
4 (1¹/₂-ounce) onion rolls, toasted

1. Preheat grill to high heat.
2. Place corn and onion on grill rack coated with cooking spray. Grill 9 minutes or until charred, turning corn occasionally and turning onion once. Cut kernels from corn. Place corn, mayonnaise, mustard seeds, vinegar, and ¹/₈ teaspoon salt in a mini food processor; process until smooth.
3. Combine onion and adobo sauce.

continued

10 EASY ZINGY BURGER SAUCES

Start with 2 tablespoons canola mayonnaise, and add these simple stir-ins to make flavor-packed condiments for burgers.

AVOCADO SAUCE
Add ¹/₄ cup ripe peeled mashed avocado, ¹/₄ teaspoon fresh lime juice, and ¹/₈ teaspoon kosher salt to mayo; stir until blended. Serves 6 (serving size: about 1 tablespoon)

CALORIES 30; FAT 2.9g (sat 0.2g); SODIUM 71mg

CURRY MAYO
Add ¹/₄ teaspoon Madras curry powder, ¹/₄ teaspoon fresh lemon juice, and a dash of kosher salt to mayo; stir until blended. Serves 4 (serving size: about 1¹/₂ teaspoons)

CALORIES 23; FAT 2.3g (sat 0g); SODIUM 75mg

SPICY REMOULADE
Add 2 teaspoons unsalted ketchup, 2 teaspoons chopped drained capers, 1 teaspoon chopped fresh chives, 1 teaspoon fresh lemon juice, 1 teaspoon Creole mustard, and ¹/₄ teaspoon ground red pepper to mayo; stir until blended. Serves 4 (serving size: 1 tablespoon)

CALORIES 30; FAT 2.4g (sat 0g); SODIUM 125mg

ROASTED GARLIC BALSAMIC AIOLI
Remove papery skin from 1 garlic head (do not peel cloves). Drizzle 1 teaspoon oil over garlic; wrap in foil. Bake at 375° for 45 minutes. Cool 10 minutes. Separate cloves; squeeze into a bowl. Discard skins. Mash garlic. Add garlic, 1 teaspoon balsamic vinegar, and a dash of kosher salt to mayo, stir until blended. Serves 4 (serving size: 1 tablespoon)

CALORIES 38; FAT 2.8g (sat 0.1g); SODIUM 76mg

HERBED MAYO
Add 1¹/₂ tablespoons light sour cream, 1 tablespoon chopped fresh basil, 1 teaspoon chopped fresh chives, ¹/₂ teaspoon chopped fresh thyme, and ¹/₈ teaspoon black pepper to mayo; stir until blended. Serves 4 (serving size: 1 tablespoon)

CALORIES 31; FAT 2.9g (sat 0.4g); SODIUM 49mg

SRIRACHA SAUCE
Add 2 teaspoons Sriracha (hot chile sauce, such as Huy Fong), 2 teaspoons chopped fresh cilantro, and 2 teaspoons cider vinegar to mayo; stir until blended. Serves 4 (serving size: about 1¹/₂ teaspoons)

CALORIES 26; FAT 2.3g (sat 0g); SODIUM 95mg

ROASTED BELL PEPPER SAUCE
Preheat broiler. Cut 1 orange bell pepper in half lengthwise; discard seeds and membranes. Place 1 pepper half, skin side up, on a foil-lined baking sheet (reserve remaining half); flatten with hand. Broil 8 minutes or until blackened. Wrap bell pepper in foil; let stand 5 minutes. Peel and finely chop. Add 2 tablespoons chopped bell pepper and 1 teaspoon minced fresh chives to mayo; stir until blended. Serves 4 (serving size: 1 tablespoon)

CALORIES 27; FAT 2.3g (sat 0g); SODIUM 46mg

CHIPOTLE AND LIME MAYO
Add 1¹/₂ teaspoons fresh lime juice, 1 teaspoon minced chipotle chile in adobo sauce, and 1 teaspoon adobo sauce to mayo; stir. Serves 4 (serving size: 1¹/₂ teaspoons)

CALORIES 24; FAT 2.3g (sat 0g); SODIUM 72mg

GARLICKY MAYO
Combine mayo, 1 tablespoon minced shallots, ¹/₂ teaspoon fresh lemon juice, a dash of salt, and 3 minced garlic cloves in a mortar; pound with a pestle until blended. Serves 4 (serving size: 2 teaspoons)

CALORIES 28; FAT 2.3g (sat 0g); SODIUM 76mg

TOASTED SESAME AND SOY MAYO
Add 1 teaspoon toasted sesame oil and 1 teaspoon lower-sodium soy sauce to mayo; stir until blended. Let stand 1 hour to let flavors meld, if desired. Serves 4 (serving size: about 2 teaspoons)

CALORIES 33; FAT 3.4g (sat 0.2g); SODIUM 78mg

4. Place chips in a food processor; pulse 15 times or until coarsely chopped. Combine chips, ¼ teaspoon salt, sage, garlic powder, pepper, and bison; mix well. Divide into 4 equal portions, gently shaping each into a ½-inch-thick patty. Press a nickel-sized indentation in center of each patty. Place patties on grill rack coated with cooking spray; grill 3 minutes. Carefully turn patties; grill 3 minutes or until desired degree of doneness.
5. Place 1 patty on bottom half of each roll. Spread 1 tablespoon corn mixture over each patty. Top with onion mixture and top halves of buns. Serves 4 (serving size: 1 burger)

CALORIES 420; **FAT** 17.8g (sat 4.6g, mono 5.3g, poly 2.3g); **PROTEIN** 29.5g; **CARB** 35.6g; **FIBER** 2.6g; **CHOL** 64mg; **IRON** 5.1mg; **SODIUM** 684mg; **CALC** 110mg

GREAT PLAINS BURGER

King Corn governs the Great Plains and probably always will. This burger delivers deep corn essence two ways. The first puts a happy soul-of-corn flavor right in the patty: Corn chips are crumbled into lean, free-range bison meat. Then there's a sweet, creamy fresh-corn mayo that brightens the whole thing up. Charred onion bolstered by smoky chile pepper heats and a wild whiff of sage completes the roundup of prairie gusto. —*Robin Bashinsky, Recipe Tester and Developer*

SUMMER SIDES

We sped up six classic dishes to cover all your hot-weather eating needs: backyard grilling, Fourth of July picnicking, family reunioning, and potluck partying.

Make Ahead • Quick & Easy Vegetarian

Roasted Potato Salad with Creamy Dijon Vinaigrette

Hands-on: 10 min. Total: 40 min. Here's a new twist on potato salad—a warm dish of golden-brown potato wedges with a creamy-tangy dressing drizzled on top. You can also serve it at room temperature.

2 pounds Yukon gold potatoes, cut into wedges
3 tablespoons extra-virgin olive oil, divided
2 tablespoons sliced garlic
1 teaspoon minced fresh thyme
³/₄ teaspoon kosher salt, divided
³/₄ teaspoon freshly ground black pepper, divided
1¹/₂ tablespoons white wine vinegar
2 tablespoons minced shallots
2 teaspoons Dijon mustard
1¹/₂ teaspoons chopped fresh tarragon

1. Place a large heavy baking sheet in oven. Preheat oven to 400° (keep baking sheet in oven as it preheats).
2. Combine potatoes, 1½ tablespoons oil, garlic, and thyme in a medium bowl; toss to coat. Arrange potato mixture on preheated baking sheet, and sprinkle with ½ teaspoon salt and ½ teaspoon black pepper. Bake at 400° for 30 minutes or until browned and tender, turning after 20 minutes.

3. Combine 1½ tablespoons oil, ¼ teaspoon salt, ¼ teaspoon pepper, vinegar, shallots, Dijon mustard, and tarragon in a small bowl, stirring well with a whisk. Drizzle dressing over potatoes. Serves 8 (serving size: about ¾ cup potatoes and about 2 teaspoons dressing)

CALORIES 145; **FAT** 5.1g (sat 0.7g, mono 3.7g, poly 0.5g); **PROTEIN** 2.9g; **CARB** 21.6g; **FIBER** 1.5g; **CHOL** 0mg; **IRON** 1.1mg; **SODIUM** 218mg; **CALC** 7mg

Kid Friendly • Quick & Easy Vegetarian

Mardi Gras Slaw

Hands-on: 8 min. Total: 8 min. The traditional colors of Fat Tuesday celebrations are purple, green, and yellow, and this vibrant slaw mimics that combo.

¹/₃ cup canola mayonnaise
2 tablespoons cider vinegar
1 teaspoon mustard seeds
¹/₂ teaspoon kosher salt
¹/₈ teaspoon ground red pepper
4 cups very thinly sliced green cabbage
1 cup very thinly sliced red cabbage
¹/₂ cup shredded carrot (1 medium)
3 thinly sliced green onions

1. Combine first 5 ingredients in a large bowl, stirring with a whisk. Add remaining ingredients, and toss to coat. Serves 8 (serving size: about ½ cup)

CALORIES 49; **FAT** 3.2g (sat 0g, mono 1.7g, poly 1g); **PROTEIN** 0.6g; **CARB** 3.9g; **FIBER** 1.6g; **CHOL** 0mg; **IRON** 0.4mg; **SODIUM** 195mg; **CALC** 28mg

Quick Classic Baked Beans

Hands-on: 21 min. Total: 31 min. Our baked beans are cooked mostly on the stovetop, and then briefly broiled for crusty edges. If you want extra herby flavor, garnish with fresh thyme leaves.

6 center-cut bacon slices, chopped
1 cup finely chopped onion
3 thyme sprigs
4 garlic cloves, minced
1/2 cup fat-free, lower-sodium chicken broth
1/3 cup packed dark brown sugar
1 tablespoon prepared mustard
1/2 teaspoon kosher salt
1/2 teaspoon smoked paprika
1/8 teaspoon ground red pepper
3 (15-ounce) cans organic navy beans, drained
1 (8-ounce) can unsalted tomato sauce

1. Preheat broiler to high.
2. Cook bacon in a 10-inch cast-iron skillet over medium-high heat until crisp. Remove bacon with a slotted spoon, reserving drippings. Add onion and thyme sprigs to drippings in pan; sauté 3 minutes. Add garlic; sauté 1 minute. Stir in broth and remaining ingredients; reduce heat to medium and cook, uncovered, 10 minutes or until slightly thick, stirring occasionally. Discard thyme.
3. Remove from heat; stir in bacon. Broil 4 minutes or until bubbly and edges are crusty. Serves 8 (serving size: about 1/2 cup)

CALORIES 158; **FAT** 2.1g (sat 0.8g, mono 0.6g, poly 0.4g); **PROTEIN** 7.8g; **CARB** 28.7g; **FIBER** 6.2g; **CHOL** 6mg; **IRON** 2.5mg; **SODIUM** 296mg; **CALC** 81mg

Summer Bean Salad

Hands-on: 35 min. Total: 45 min. If you purchase whole fava bean pods, you'll need to shell them, and then peel the beans: Blanch shelled beans in boiling water for a few seconds, remove to a bowl of ice water, drain, and slip off the opaque skins. You can also substitute shelled edamame.

3 tablespoons extra-virgin olive oil
1 teaspoon grated lemon rind
3 1/2 tablespoons fresh lemon juice, divided
1 tablespoon chopped fresh thyme
3/4 teaspoon freshly ground black pepper, divided
3/8 teaspoon kosher salt
8 cups water
8 ounces fresh yellow wax beans, cut into 1 1/2-inch pieces (about 3 cups)
2 cups shelled and peeled fava beans (about 3 pounds unshelled beans)
2 cups quartered cherry tomatoes
1 cup very thinly vertically sliced red onion
1 (15 1/2-ounce) can unsalted chickpeas (garbanzo beans), rinsed and drained
1/4 cup canola mayonnaise
1 tablespoon minced fresh chives

1. Combine oil, rind, 2 tablespoons lemon juice, thyme, 1/2 teaspoon pepper, and salt in a large bowl, stirring with a whisk.
2. Bring 8 cups water to a boil in a large saucepan. Add wax beans; cook 2 minutes. Add fava beans to wax beans in pan; cook an additional 2 minutes or until beans are tender. Drain and rinse with cold water. Drain. Add bean mixture, cherry tomatoes, onion, and chickpeas to dressing; toss well.

3. Combine 1 1/2 tablespoons lemon juice, 1/4 teaspoon pepper, mayonnaise, and chives in a small bowl, stirring with a whisk. Let stand 10 minutes. Drizzle mayonnaise mixture over bean mixture. Serves 8 (serving size: about 1 cup)

CALORIES 147; **FAT** 7.9g (sat 0.8g, mono 5g, poly 1.4g); **PROTEIN** 4.3g; **CARB** 15g; **FIBER** 4g; **CHOL** 0mg; **IRON** 1.4mg; **SODIUM** 160mg; **CALC** 43mg

Marinated English Cucumber and Onions

Hands-on: 8 min. Total: 3 hr. 8 min. If marinating overnight, slice the cucumber a bit thicker so it retains some crunch.

1/3 cup rice vinegar
2 tablespoons chopped fresh mint
1 1/2 tablespoons sugar
1 1/2 teaspoons honey
1/4 teaspoon salt
1/8 teaspoon freshly ground black pepper
3 cups (1/4-inch-thick) slices English cucumber
1 cup vertically sliced Vidalia or other sweet onion

1. Combine first 6 ingredients in a large bowl, stirring until sugar dissolves. Add sliced cucumber and onion, and toss well. Cover and refrigerate at least 3 hours, tossing occasionally. Serves 4 (serving size: about 3/4 cup)

CALORIES 51; **FAT** 0.1g (sat 0.1g, mono 0g, poly 0g); **PROTEIN** 0.9g; **CARB** 12.7g; **FIBER** 1.1g; **CHOL** 0mg; **IRON** 0.6mg; **SODIUM** 151mg; **CALC** 25mg

Tomato Salad with Goat Cheese and Basil

Hands-on: 5 min. Total: 65 min. Choose a variety of tomato colors to make the salad more beautiful without any additional work.

3 tablespoons extra-virgin olive oil
1½ tablespoons white wine vinegar
½ teaspoon kosher salt
¼ teaspoon freshly ground black pepper
1 garlic clove, minced
2 tablespoons chopped fresh basil
4 medium heirloom tomatoes, cored and cut into ½-inch-thick wedges (about 2 pounds)
⅓ cup small basil leaves
1.5 ounces goat cheese, crumbled (about ⅓ cup)

1. Combine first 5 ingredients in a large bowl, stirring with a whisk. Add chopped basil and tomato wedges; toss to coat. Cover and let stand 1 hour, tossing occasionally. Top with basil leaves and goat cheese. Serves 6 (serving size: about ⅔ cup)

CALORIES 108; FAT 8.6g (sat 2g, mono 5.3g, poly 0.9g); PROTEIN 2.8g; CARB 6.3g; FIBER 1.9g; CHOL 3mg; IRON 0.7mg; SODIUM 194mg; CALC 32mg

BERRY WILD

The juice, the seedy bits, the heady perfume, and the indigo stains: Bring on all the sweet and tart stuff that summer berries give!

Make Ahead

Lemony Blackberry-Vodka Gelées

Hands-on: 12 min. Total: 6 hr. Timing is important here, as you want to get the drama of two separate layers with gradation between. Let the first layer set partially but not completely—if you add the blackberry layer too soon, it will muddle your color; a bit too late, and it will slide right off the bottom layer.

1½ cups vodka, divided
4 envelopes unflavored gelatin, divided
1½ cups sugar, divided
1 cup fresh lemon juice
1 cup water, divided
Cooking spray
8 cups blackberries
Blackberries (optional)
Lemon rind strips (optional)

1. Place 1 cup vodka in a medium bowl. Sprinkle 2 envelopes gelatin evenly over vodka; let stand 3 minutes. Combine 1 cup sugar, lemon juice, and ½ cup water in a medium saucepan over medium-high heat. Bring just to a boil, stirring until sugar dissolves. Add hot lemon juice mixture to vodka mixture, stirring until gelatin dissolves. Pour lemon-vodka mixture into an 8-inch square glass or ceramic baking dish coated with cooking spray; chill 1 hour and 45 minutes.
2. Place ½ cup vodka in a medium bowl. Sprinkle 2 envelopes gelatin evenly over vodka; let stand 3 minutes. Combine ½ cup sugar, ½ cup water, and 8 cups blackberries in a large saucepan; bring to a boil. Reduce heat; simmer 10 minutes, stirring mixture occasionally. Strain blackberry mixture through a fine sieve over a 4-cup glass measuring cup; discard solids. Add 2 cups hot blackberry mixture to vodka mixture, stirring until gelatin dissolves (reserve remaining blackberry mixture for another use). Gradually pour blackberry-vodka mixture evenly over partially set lemon-vodka mixture. Chill 3 hours or until set. Cut into 36 cubes. Garnish with blackberries and lemon rind strips, if desired. Serves 18 (serving size: 2 cubes)

CALORIES 144; FAT 0.4g (sat 0g, mono 0g, poly 0.2g); PROTEIN 2.2g; CARB 23.8g; FIBER 3.2g; CHOL 0mg; IRON 0.4mg; SODIUM 4mg; CALC 20mg

THINK OF THESE SLIGHTLY BOOZY GELÉES AS JELL-O BITES, ALL GROWN UP.

Rustic Huckleberry-Blackberry Tart

Hands-on: 22 min. Total: 2 hr. 15 min. If you can't find huckleberries, use blueberries.

8 ounces cake flour (about 2 cups)
1/3 cup powdered sugar
1/3 cup chopped pecans, toasted
1/4 cup packed brown sugar
1/2 teaspoon salt, divided
1/2 cup cold butter, cut into small pieces
1 large egg yolk
Cooking spray
1 tablespoon ice water
4 cups blackberries
3 cups huckleberries
1/2 cup granulated sugar
3 tablespoons cornstarch
2 teaspoons fresh lemon juice
1 tablespoon turbinado sugar

1. Weigh or lightly spoon flour into dry measuring cups; level with a knife. Place flour, powdered sugar, pecans, brown sugar, and 1/4 teaspoon salt in a food processor; pulse 3 to 4 times to combine. Add butter to food processor; pulse 10 times or until mixture resembles coarse meal. Add egg yolk; pulse to combine. Lightly spoon 2 cups of flour mixture into a 9-inch spring-form pan coated with cooking spray; press mixture in a thin layer into bottom and up sides of pan. Cover pan with plastic wrap; chill 1 hour.
2. Add 1 tablespoon water to remaining flour mixture in food processor; pulse 3 to 4 times or until dough just comes together, adding additional ice water, 1 teaspoon at a time, as needed. Shape dough into a ball, and wrap in plastic wrap. Chill 1 hour.
3. Preheat oven to 400°.
4. Remove springform pan from refrigerator; discard plastic wrap. Line bottom of dough with parchment paper; arrange pie weights or dried beans on parchment paper. Bake at 400° for 10 minutes. Remove pie weights and parchment paper; cool on a wire rack 10 minutes (do not remove or loosen sides of springform pan).
5. Combine 1/4 teaspoon salt, berries, granulated sugar, cornstarch, and lemon juice; toss gently. Spoon mixture evenly over prepared crust.
6. Remove remaining dough from refrigerator. Working quickly, roll dough to an 11-inch circle. Cut dough lengthwise into 3/4-inch-wide strips; arrange strips in a lattice design over filling. Sprinkle strips with turbinado sugar. Bake at 400° for 40 minutes or until top is browned. Cool 15 minutes before removing sides from pan. Serves 12 (serving size: 1 wedge)

CALORIES 270; **FAT** 10.7g (sat 5.2g, mono 3.4g, poly 1.2g); **PROTEIN** 3g; **CARB** 42g; **FIBER** 3g; **CHOL** 36mg; **IRON** 2mg; **SODIUM** 173mg; **CALC** 33mg

No-Bake Chocolate Cheesecake with Mixed Berries

Hands-on: 25 min. Total: 7 hr. 25 min.

4 ounces chocolate wafers (such as Nabisco Famous Chocolate Wafers)
1 tablespoon honey
2 teaspoons unsalted butter, melted
3 tablespoons 2% reduced-fat milk
1 1/2 teaspoons unflavored gelatin
10 ounces 1/3-less-fat cream cheese, softened
1 1/4 cups powdered sugar
1 cup plain fat-free Greek yogurt
1/2 cup dark unsweetened cocoa powder (such as Hershey's Special Dark)
1/2 teaspoon vanilla extract
1 ounce bittersweet chocolate, melted and cooled
1/4 cup whipping cream
1 1/2 cups raspberries
1 1/2 cups strawberries, quartered
1 cup blueberries

1. Place chocolate wafers in a food processor; process until finely ground. Place ground wafers in a bowl; stir in honey and butter. Press mixture into bottom and up sides of a 9-inch round removable-bottom tart pan. Cover and freeze 1 hour or until firm. Wipe food processor with a paper towel.
2. Combine milk and gelatin in a microwave-safe bowl; let stand 3 minutes. Microwave at HIGH 15 seconds; stir until gelatin dissolves. Cool slightly.
3. Place cream cheese and next 4 ingredients in food processor; process until smooth. Add milk mixture and cooled melted chocolate; process until smooth. Place whipping cream in a clean bowl; beat with a mixer at high speed until stiff peaks form. Gently fold one-fourth of chocolate mixture into whipped cream. Fold whipped cream mixture into remaining chocolate mixture. Spoon chocolate mixture into prepared crust. Chill 6 hours or until set.
4. Combine berries in a bowl. Top cheesecake with berry mixture. Serves 14 (serving size: 1 slice)

CALORIES 207; **FAT** 9g (sat 5.3g, mono 1.2g, poly 0.3g); **PROTEIN** 4.9g; CARB 30g; **FIBER** 2.8g; **CHOL** 23mg; **IRON** 1mg; **SODIUM** 146mg; **CALC** 43mg

FIND NEW VARIETIES OF BERRIES AT THE MARKET. TASTE FOR TARTNESS, AND ADJUST WITH SUGAR OR LEMON.

Kid Friendly • Freezable
Make Ahead

Raspberry-Mint Ice Pops

Hands-on: 15 min. Total: 8 hr. 15 min.

⅓ cup sugar
¼ cup water
¼ cup mint leaves
4 cups raspberries
1 tablespoon fresh lemon juice

1. Combine sugar, ¼ cup water, and mint in a small saucepan over medium heat; cook 4 minutes or until sugar dissolves, stirring frequently. Let stand 30 minutes. Strain through a sieve over a bowl; discard solids.
2. Place mint syrup, berries, and juice in a blender; process until smooth.
3. Divide mixture evenly among 9 (4-ounce) ice-pop molds. Top with lid; insert craft sticks. Freeze pops overnight or until set. Serves 9 (serving size: 1 pop)

CALORIES 58; FAT 0.4g (sat 0g, mono 0g, poly 0.2g); PROTEIN 0.7g; CARB 14.1g; FIBER 3.6g; CHOL 0mg; IRON 0.4mg; SODIUM 1mg; CALC 14mg

Quick & Easy

Gooseberry Margaritas

Hands-on: 14 min. Total: 17 min. *Tart, fragrant gooseberries come in red, green, or Cape varieties (a gold berry in a papery husk). Red and green are most common—look for them at farmers' markets. If you can't find them, use raspberries instead.*

2 cups gooseberries, divided
⅓ cup granulated sugar
¼ cup water
½ cup fresh lime juice (about 4 limes)
1 cup tequila
1 cup club soda
2 tablespoons Grand Marnier
2 tablespoons white sparkling sugar
½ teaspoon kosher salt
⅛ teaspoon ground red pepper
9 lime wedges, divided

1. Place 1½ cups gooseberries in a mortar or other small bowl; gently crush with a pestle or fork.
2. Combine crushed gooseberries, granulated sugar, and ¼ cup water in a small saucepan; bring to a boil. Cook until sugar dissolves, stirring occasionally. Remove from heat; cool completely. Strain through a sieve over a bowl; discard solids. Stir in lime juice; chill.
3. Combine gooseberry mixture, tequila, soda, and Grand Marnier in a large pitcher; stir gently.
4. Combine sparkling sugar, salt, and red pepper in a saucer. Rub the rims of 8 glasses with 1 lime wedge; spin rim of each glass in salt mixture to coat. Fill each prepared glass with ice. Divide margarita mixture evenly among glasses. Garnish with remaining gooseberries and lime wedges. Serves 8 (serving size: about ½ cup)

CALORIES 178; FAT 0.4g (sat 0g, mono 0g, poly 0g); PROTEIN 1g; CARB 21.3g; FIBER 1.7g; CHOL 0mg; IRON 0.5mg; SODIUM 170mg; CALC 9mg

A BERRY GLOSSARY

YEL·LOW RASP·BER·RY /YEL-OH RAZ-BER-EE, -BUH-REE, RAHZ-/ **NOUN**
A pale cousin of the red raspberry, with the same flavor; adds great color to salads.

HUCK·LE·BER·RY /HUHK-UHL-BER-EE/ **NOUN**
Inky-black berry with thicker skin and more pucker than a blueberry. Makes a great tart jam, or a great tart tart.

RED RASP·BER·RY /RED RAZ-BER-EE, -BUH-REE, RAHZ-/ **NOUN**
Perfect raspberries are soft, small, and amazingly perfumed. They spoil quickly. Balance the sweet, floral flavor with just a dollop of tangy crème fraîche.

BLACK·BER·RY /BLAK-BER-EE, -BUH-REE/ **NOUN**
Glossy black, caviar-like beads burst on the tongue. Jammy and often tart, reminiscent of full-bodied red wines. Lots of crunchy seeds.

GOOSE·BER·RY /GOOS-BER-EE, -BUH-REE, GOOZ-/ **NOUN**
Fruit that looks like Thompson grape's offbeat cousin, with funky stripes and stubby stems. The tart flavor is unique, with notes of apricot and plum. Perfect for the late-summer cocktail.

BLUE·BER·RY /BLOO-BER-EE, -BUH-REE/ **NOUN**
Sweet, plump, and juicy, with tons of tiny seeds within. Look for firm but not under-ripe berries. If you can find the tiny wild ones, dig in. Loaded with natural thickening pectin.

BEAN SALAD WITH SHRIMP

From Talula's Garden in Philadelphia

Pound for pound, fresh-picked beans remain a relative bargain at farmers' markets, where bargains sometimes seem few and far between. This time of year, Aimee Olexy, whose Philadelphia restaurant, Talula's Garden, is a celebrated showcase for seasonal produce, likes to show some love for the humble, sometimes underappreciated bean.

"These are very versatile vegetables and great at carrying flavor," she says. "Beans provide crunch and moisture all in one, and they have a density that can pair well with steak or shrimp." They can also be served hot, at room temp, or cold, making them great for summer alfresco dining.

Although blanching or steaming is often the restaurant approach, "there's absolutely nothing wrong with boiling green beans," Olexy says. Just don't overboil. "Then just dress them with a little knob of butter or a splash of olive oil." If you plan to hold them before serving, shock the beans with ice water, and quickly reheat later.

Olexy designed the bean salad here to be simple and flavorful, with summer convenience in mind. You can serve it warm, or let it cool and serve at room temperature. Visitors to Philadelphia can try her version this month at Talula's Garden in Washington Square. —Tim Cebula

---

AIMEE OLEXY'S BEAN TIP

When buying beans, make sure the seed pods aren't bulging—a sign they're tough—or faded. "They should be brightly colored, like when they're just picked," she says.

Quick & Easy • Make Ahead

Bean Salad with Shrimp and Curry Yogurt

Hands-on: 25 min. Total: 25 min. *Pair this easy salad with seasoned whole-wheat couscous or grilled bread brushed with olive oil. The flavors marry as the dish stands, so it's a particularly good choice for a picnic or party platter.*

¼ cup finely chopped shallots
1 tablespoon chopped fresh flat-leaf parsley
1 tablespoon chopped fresh tarragon
2 tablespoons extra-virgin olive oil
1½ tablespoons white wine vinegar
1 teaspoon Dijon mustard
½ teaspoon kosher salt, divided
½ teaspoon freshly ground black pepper, divided
½ cup plain 2% reduced-fat Greek yogurt
1 teaspoon Madras curry powder
1½ teaspoons honey
½ teaspoon fresh lime juice
9 ounces fresh green beans, trimmed
1 tablespoon extra-virgin olive oil
1 pound large shrimp, peeled and deveined
1 tablespoon chopped fresh thyme

1. Combine first 6 ingredients, ¼ teaspoon salt, and ¼ teaspoon pepper in a large bowl, stirring with a whisk. Combine yogurt, curry, honey, and juice in a small bowl.
2. Cook beans in boiling water 3 minutes or until crisp-tender; drain.

Add beans to shallot mixture; toss to coat.
3. Heat a large skillet over medium-high heat. Add 1 tablespoon oil to pan; swirl to coat. Add shrimp, ¼ teaspoon salt, ¼ teaspoon pepper, and thyme to pan; sauté 3 minutes or until done. Add shrimp to green bean mixture; toss to coat. Serve with yogurt mixture. Serves 4 (serving size: about 1 cup shrimp mixture and about 2 tablespoons yogurt mixture)

CALORIES 234; **FAT** 12.3g (sat 2.1g, mono 7.5g, poly 1.3g); **PROTEIN** 19.9g; **CARB** 11.8g; **FIBER** 2.4g; **CHOL** 145mg; **IRON** 1.4mg; **SODIUM** 455mg; **CALC** 129mg

---

EASY SUMMER MENU

SIMPLE BACKYARD ENTERTAINING

Pick your favorite flavor, rub or brush it onto 4 (6-ounce) skinless, boneless chicken breast halves, and grill until done.

MENU

Grilled Chicken with Honey-Chipotle BBQ Sauce
+
Garlic-Lime Grilled Corn
+
Watermelon-Cucumber Salad
+
Sliced Peaches and Vanilla Ice Cream

---

continued

Grilled Chicken with Honey-Chipotle BBQ Sauce

Hands-on: 18 min. Total: 43 min. You can also use 8 thighs or 8 drumsticks or 4 pieces of each; cook about 10 minutes per side.

2 teaspoons olive oil
¼ cup minced shallots
½ cup lower-sodium ketchup
2 tablespoons water
1½ tablespoons honey
2 teaspoons cider vinegar
½ teaspoon dry mustard
½ teaspoon chipotle chile powder
½ teaspoon kosher salt, divided
½ teaspoon garlic powder
½ teaspoon ground cumin
¼ teaspoon black pepper
4 bone-in chicken leg-thigh quarters, skinned
Cooking spray

1. Preheat grill to medium-high heat.
2. Heat a small saucepan over medium-high heat. Add oil; swirl to coat. Add shallots; sauté 2 minutes or until tender. Stir in ketchup, next 5 ingredients (through chile powder), and ¼ teaspoon salt. Reduce heat to low, and cook 5 minutes, stirring occasionally.
3. Combine ¼ teaspoon salt, garlic powder, cumin, and black pepper; sprinkle over chicken. Place chicken on grill rack coated with cooking spray; grill 15 minutes on each side or until done. Baste chicken generously with sauce; turn over, and grill 1 minute. Baste again; turn over, and grill 1 minute. Serve with remaining sauce. Serves 4 (serving size: 1 leg quarter)

CALORIES 256; FAT 9.8g (sat 2.3g, mono 4.5g, poly 1.7g); PROTEIN 25.9g; CARB 16.3g; FIBER 0.6g; CHOL 139mg; IRON 1.5mg; SODIUM 366mg; CALC 25mg

Garlic-Lime Grilled Corn

Hands-on: 10 min. Total: 20 min.

1 tablespoon olive oil
2 teaspoons butter
1 garlic clove, minced
4 ears shucked yellow corn
Cooking spray
1 teaspoon grated lime rind
¼ teaspoon kosher salt

1. Preheat grill to medium-high heat.
2. Place oil, butter, and garlic in a small microwave-safe bowl. Microwave at HIGH 30 seconds or until butter melts; set aside.
3. Coat corn with cooking spray. Arrange corn on grill rack; grill 10 minutes or until done and lightly browned, turning occasionally. Remove from grill; brush with butter mixture. Sprinkle with rind and salt. Serves 4 (serving size: 1 ear)

CALORIES 136; FAT 6.7g (sat 2g, mono 3.4g, poly 0.9g); PROTEIN 3.4g; CARB 19.4g; FIBER 2.1g; CHOL 5mg; IRON 0.6mg; SODIUM 152mg; CALC 5mg

Watermelon-Cucumber Salad

Hands-on: 12 min. Total: 12 min.

1 tablespoon olive oil
2 teaspoons fresh lemon juice
¼ teaspoon salt
2 cups cubed seedless watermelon
1 cup thinly sliced English cucumber
¼ cup thinly vertically sliced red onion
1 tablespoon thinly sliced fresh basil

1. Combine oil, juice, and salt in a large bowl, stirring well. Add watermelon, cucumber, and onion; toss well to coat. Sprinkle salad evenly with basil. Serves 4 (serving size: about ¾ cup)

CALORIES 60; FAT 3.5g (sat 0.5g, mono 2.5g, poly 0.4g); PROTEIN 0.8g; CARB 7.6g; FIBER 0.6g; CHOL 0mg; IRON 0.3mg; SODIUM 149mg; CALC 13mg

FROM OUR GARDEN

BUNCHES OF FRAGRANT BASIL

This month from our garden: the most versatile herb to complement fresh, light food in the heat and heart of the summer

Our most perfumed summer crop bloomed like crazy for our gardeners. "Basil is a cinch for us in this Alabama heat," says Mary Beth Shaddix, master tender of the Cooking Light Garden. "If you've got the right environment for tomatoes, then it's pretty easy to grow basil." Italian sweet basil is what you'll find in most supermarkets. But there's so much more, and a home garden—even a window box or two—lets you explore basil's wider range. Some kinds offer bright citrus on top of the familiar peppery anise flavors; the deep purple colors of others make a striking garnish for simple picnic dishes. These varieties are perfect partners for summery foods such as ripe, meaty tomatoes, field peas and beans, and even sweet stone fruit and cocktails.

Field Pea and Purple Basil Succotash

Kid Friendly • Quick & Easy

Hands-on: 45 min. Total: 60 min.
Substitute lima beans if field peas aren't available. We love the contrast of deep purple basil, but you can use any fresh basil with delicious results.

1 1/2 ounces sliced pancetta, finely
  chopped
1 cup chopped onion
3 garlic cloves, minced
1 1/2 cups shelled fresh purple-hull peas
1/4 teaspoon freshly ground black
  pepper
Dash of kosher salt
1/2 cup water
1 cup fresh corn kernels
1/3 cup Castelvetrano olives, pitted and
  quartered
1/4 cup torn Round Midnight basil
  leaves

1. Heat a medium saucepan over medium-high heat. Add pancetta; cook 3 minutes or until crisp, stirring frequently. Remove pancetta from pan with a slotted spoon; set aside. Add onion to drippings in pan; cook 5 minutes or until tender. Stir in garlic; cook 1 minute. Add peas, pepper, and salt; cook 30 seconds. Add 1/2 cup water to pan; bring to a simmer. Cover and simmer 25 minutes or until peas are tender. Add corn and olives; simmer, covered, 2 minutes. Sprinkle evenly with reserved pancetta and basil. Serves 4 (serving size: 3/4 cup)

CALORIES 147; FAT 5.4g (sat 1.9g, mono 1.1g, poly 0.4g); PROTEIN 6.4g; CARB 20g; FIBER 4.7g; CHOL 8mg; IRON 1.6mg; SODIUM 297mg; CALC 43mg

Apricot, Cucumber, Pluot, and Lime Basil Salad

Quick & Easy • Vegetarian

Hands-on: 10 min. Total: 10 min. *If you don't have lime basil, substitute any fresh basil plus 1/2 teaspoon grated lime rind. Plums will also work in place of pluots.*

3 tablespoons fresh lime basil, thinly
  sliced
1 teaspoon champagne vinegar
Dash of kosher salt
Dash of freshly ground black pepper
2 apricots, pitted and cut into thin
  wedges
2 pluots, pitted and cut into thin
  wedges
1/2 English cucumber, thinly sliced

1. Combine all ingredients in a medium bowl; toss to coat well. Serves 4 (serving size: 1/2 cup)

CALORIES 31; FAT 0.1g (sat 0g, mono 0g, poly 0g); PROTEIN 0.8g; CARB 7.6g; FIBER 1.1g; CHOL 0mg; IRON 0.3mg; SODIUM 31mg; CALC 11mg

Cherry-Grapefruit Basil Sorbet

Freezeable • Make Ahead

Hands-on: 20 min. Total: 2 hrs. 50 min.
Fresh basil pairs wonderfully with the sweet-tart citrus and deep cherry flavors in this elegant sorbet. Garnish the scoops with small basil leaves, if you like.

1 cup water
1/2 cup sugar
Dash of kosher salt
1/2 cup basil leaves
3 cups pitted cherries
1/2 cup fresh ruby red grapefruit juice
  (about 1 grapefruit)
1 1/2 teaspoons fresh lime juice

1. Combine first 3 ingredients in a small saucepan; bring to a boil, stirring until sugar dissolves. Stir in basil; remove from heat. Cover and let stand 30 minutes.
2. Place cherries in a food processor; process until smooth. Add sugar mixture, grapefruit juice, and lime juice; process until well blended. Strain cherry mixture through a fine sieve over a bowl; discard solids. Pour cherry mixture into the freezer can of an ice-cream freezer; freeze according to manufacturer's instructions. Spoon sorbet into a freezer-safe container; cover and freeze 1 hour or until firm. Serves 7 (serving size: 1/2 cup)

CALORIES 105; FAT 0.2g (sat 0g, mono 0g, poly 0.1g); PROTEIN 0.9g; CARB 27g; FIBER 1.4g; CHOL 0mg; IRON 0.4mg; SODIUM 18mg; CALC 16mg

BASIL VARIETIES

CARDINAL
This plant sports gorgeous, glossy green leaves and thick purple stems. It has a heavy, strong licorice flavor—a little goes a long way.

LEMON
Strong lemon-pine scent and flavor distinguish this one. It's a good choice for fish, curries, and summery vodka cocktails.

SIAM QUEEN
Extremely fragrant and more intensely flavored than sweet Italian basil, this Thai basil is great for Southeast Asian salads and stir-fries.

ROUND MIDNIGHT
This variety's drama comes from its striking purple color. It offers mild anise flavor and can be mixed with stronger-flavored green varieties or used alone as a garnish for light-hued dishes.

LIME
A hint of lime tops the traditional anise flavor. The plant blooms often, so to ensure the best flavor and avoid bitterness, pinch it back regularly to keep it from flowering.

EAT MORE HEALTHY FATS

Taste buds, rejoice! This month is all about fat: good-for-you, delicious, heart-healthy fat.

Fat lives a double life. It can be your friend, adding flavor, pleasing texture, and satisfying richness to foods. And some fats, chiefly the poly- or monounsaturated kinds—found in plant-based foods, fish, nuts, and most oils—help your body absorb nutrients and actually lower cholesterol. But fats can also be a problem. All varieties contain more than double the calories per gram of protein or carbohydrates. Too much of the saturated stuff also clogs arteries. The less said about artificial trans fats, the better.

Fat phobia is over; fat nuance is in. The goal these days is to incorporate more of the good fats and less of the bad into all meal planning, cooking, and snacking. Here, you'll find easy opportunities to swap in good fats while lowering your sat fat intake.

USING HEART-HEALTHY-FAT-FILLED HAZELNUT FLOUR AND CANOLA OIL INSTEAD OF BUTTER SAVES 1 GRAM OF SATURATED FAT PER MINI MUFFIN.

Kid Friendly • Quick & Easy
Freezable • Make Ahead • Vegetarian

Orange-Hazelnut Snack Muffins

Hands-on: 10 min. Total: 22 min.
Hazelnut flour (often called meal) is full of heart-healthy fats, fiber, and protein.

1.5 ounces hazelnut flour (about 6 tablespoons; such as Bob's Red Mill)
2.5 ounces cake flour (about ½ cup)
1 teaspoon baking powder
¼ teaspoon salt
2 tablespoons canola oil
2 tablespoons 2% reduced-fat milk
1½ tablespoons agave nectar
1½ teaspoons grated orange rind
1 tablespoon fresh orange juice
1 large egg, lightly beaten
Cooking spray

1. Preheat oven to 350°.
2. Weigh or lightly spoon flours into dry measuring cups; level with a knife. Combine flours, baking powder, and salt in a small bowl. Combine oil, milk, agave, rind, juice, and egg in a large bowl, stirring with a whisk. Add flour mixture to oil mixture, stirring just until moist.
3. Spoon batter evenly into 12 miniature muffin cups coated with cooking spray. Bake at 350° for 12 minutes or until a wooden pick inserted in center of muffins comes out clean. Remove muffins from pan; cool on a wire rack. Serves 12 (serving size: 1 muffin)

CALORIES 81; FAT 5g (sat 0.5g, mono 1.7g, poly 0.8g); PROTEIN 1.6g; CARB 7.6g; FIBER 0.5g; CHOL 16mg; IRON 0.7mg; SODIUM 89mg; CALC 32mg

FAQS ABOUT FATS

Fear not! Healthy Habits Coach **Allison Fishman Task** is here with answers to three top questions about fats.

1. IF SOMETHING IS HIGH IN UNSATURATED FAT (LIKE AVOCADO), DOES THAT MEAN IT'S OK TO EAT MORE?
Too much of a good thing can be a calorie problem, and this includes avocado. Unsaturated fats do have health benefits, but regardless of the type of fat, if you eat a lot of it, you're taking in a lot of calories. Moderation is key—aim to work in plenty of healthy fats without busting your calorie budget. And don't replace unhealthy fats with refined carbs (white bread, sugar); reach for veggies and fruit instead.

2. DOES HEATING OLIVE OIL DESTROY ITS BENEFICIAL PROPERTIES?
Olive oils can take the heat—at least up to about 405° (slightly lower for extra-virgin)—and still retain all their nutrients. It's when they reach their smoke point that the oils begin breaking down. Olive oil can handle most stovetop applications, but for roasting or higher-temp cooking, try something with a higher smoke point, like canola oil, that still provides the same benefits. Canola oil also has the lowest saturated fat content and is a good substitute for butter in baking (try replacing half the butter called for in a recipe with canola oil).

3. ARE FOODS LABELED TRANS FAT-FREE OK TO EAT?
Zero trans fats on the nutrition panel doesn't mean there are none. If partially hydrogenated oil is in the ingredient list, the product has trans fats. Food makers can list zero grams of trans fats if one serving has less than half a gram. If you eat several servings in a day, you could quickly reach your daily limit of 2 grams. Find better-for-you snacks that deliver on convenience and flavor at CookingLight.com/HealthyHabits.

TODAY'S LESSON: CHICKEN WINGS

Our no-fry method makes it a breeze to serve these plump-crispy-sticky-saucy drumettes.

You may think of chicken wings as bar food, but these saucy babies are great for, say, watching Monday Night Football. We ditched the standard deep-frying procedure in favor of a two-step steam-and-sauté method that maintains the plump, juicy goodness of the wings while curtailing the messy effects of oil in the kitchen and on the waistline. These crowd-pleasers are a breeze to prepare, and we offer three bold flavor variations for lots of weeknight wing fun.

Quick & Easy

Garlic-Buffalo Drumettes

Hands-on: 35 min. Total: 35 min. *If the skillet gets crowded, brown the chicken in batches.*

20 chicken drumettes, skinned
¼ cup canola oil
3 tablespoons minced fresh garlic
2 tablespoons minced fresh chives
3 tablespoons hot pepper sauce (such as Frank's)
⅛ teaspoon ground red pepper
1.5 ounces blue cheese, crumbled (⅓ cup)

1. Add water to a Dutch oven to a depth of 1 inch; bring to a simmer. Place chicken in a vegetable steamer. Place steamer in pan over water; cover. Reduce heat to medium-low. Steam, covered, 10 minutes. Remove chicken from steamer; cool. Pat dry.
2. Heat a large skillet over medium-high heat. Add oil; swirl to coat. Add chicken to pan; sauté 5 minutes, turning to brown on all sides. Add garlic and chives to pan; sauté 30 seconds, stirring constantly. Remove pan from heat; transfer chicken mixture to a large bowl using a slotted spoon.
3. Combine pepper sauce and ground red pepper. Drizzle pepper mixture over chicken; toss to coat. Sprinkle with cheese. Serves 4 (serving size: 5 drumettes and about ⅓ ounce blue cheese)

CALORIES 310; FAT 16.3g (sat 4.4g, mono 7.1g, poly 3.2g); PROTEIN 36.5g; CARB 2.6g; FIBER 0.2g; CHOL 196mg; IRON 1.6mg; SODIUM 599mg; CALC 87mg

Quick & Easy
Sticky Chile Drumettes
Prepare Garlic-Buffalo Drumettes through step 2, omitting garlic and chives and adding ⅓ cup chopped green onions and 1 tablespoon minced peeled fresh ginger instead. Combine 3 tablespoons Thai sweet chili sauce (such as Mae Ploy), 1½ tablespoons Sriracha (hot chile sauce, such as Huy Fong), 2 teaspoons rice vinegar, and 2 teaspoons fish sauce, stir well. Drizzle chili mixture over chicken; toss. Serves 4 (serving size: 5 drumettes)

CALORIES 272; FAT 13.2g (sat 2.4g); SODIUM 520mg

NO-FRY CHICKEN WINGS

1. STEAM Keep heat moderately low. If overcooked, the chicken will dry out.

2. CRISP Sauté the wings in a bit of oil in a hot pan. This crisps up the exterior.

3. COAT Transfer the wings from the pan to a bowl, and douse with yummy sauce.

continued

Quick & Easy
Mango-Serrano Drumettes

Prepare Garlic-Buffalo Drumettes through step 2, omitting garlic and chives and adding ⅓ cup chopped fresh cilantro and 2 thinly sliced serrano chiles instead. Bring 1 (9.6-ounce) can mango nectar to a boil in a small saucepan over medium heat. Simmer 15 minutes or until reduced to ¼ cup, stirring occasionally. Stir in 2 tablespoons fresh lime juice and ½ teaspoon kosher salt. Drizzle mango mixture over chicken mixture; toss. Serves 4 (serving size: 5 drumettes)

CALORIES 297; FAT 13.2g (sat 2.4g); SODIUM 415mg

OUR NO-FRY METHOD MAKES IT A BREEZE TO SERVE THESE PLUMP-CRISP-STICKY-SAUCY DRUMETTES.

RECIPE MAKEOVER

KEY LIME LIGHTENS UP

It may have seemed like a light, ethereal pie all along, but it wasn't—until now. We kept the tang and the graham goodness.

There's an addictive quality to Key lime pie's finely tuned balance of the sweet and the tart, the creamy and the crunchy, all crowned with fluffy cream. It seems so airy, but it's 500 calories of airy. Time for a makeover, indeed.

This one threw us a curveball, though, as we found the graham cracker crust to be tricky. It needs fat to help bind the crumbs and to maintain a crisp texture when baked, filled, and chilled. Too little fat delivers a crumbly mess that grows soggy after sitting—as we discovered to our chagrin in our first few tests. Nor did canola oil, in place of butter, yield the crisp goodness we were looking for. The breakthrough discovery, oddly, was white chocolate. It melts to bind the crumbs in the oven, and then hardens when cooled to form a perfectly crisp crust. Fat-free condensed milk, 2% Greek yogurt, and lots of zesty, fresh-squeezed lime juice combine for a light, tangy, creamy filling. Fat-free whipped topping adds a fluffy finish with a lot less fat, of course, than cream. This pie boasts 75% less fat than the original and makes this Key lime treat a dessert you can enjoy all year long.

Kid Friendly • Make Ahead
Key Lime Pie

Hands-on: 25 min. Total: 3 hr. 4 min.

Crust:
1 cup graham cracker crumbs
1 tablespoon brown sugar
⅛ teaspoon salt
1 ounce premium white chocolate, grated or finely chopped
2 tablespoons butter, melted and cooled
1 tablespoon canola oil
Cooking spray
Filling:
½ cup plain 2% reduced-fat Greek yogurt
½ cup fresh Key lime juice or fresh lime juice
½ teaspoon grated lime rind
3 large egg yolks
1 (14-ounce) can fat-free sweetened condensed milk
¾ cup frozen fat-free whipped topping, thawed

1. Preheat oven to 350°.
2. To prepare crust, combine crumbs, sugar, salt, and chocolate in a bowl, stirring well to combine. Add butter and oil; toss with a fork until moist. Press crumb mixture into bottom and up sides of a 9-inch pie plate coated with cooking spray. Bake at 350° for 8 to 10 minutes or until beginning to brown; cool completely on a wire rack.
3. To prepare filling, place yogurt and next 4 ingredients (through milk) in a bowl; beat with a mixer at medium speed 2 minutes. Pour mixture into prepared crust. Bake at 350° for 14

CLASSIC	MAKEOVER
519 calories per slice	280 calories per slice
33.5 grams total fat	8.9 grams total fat
19.6 grams saturated fat	3.6 grams saturated fat

minutes or until set. Cool pie completely on wire rack. Cover loosely, and chill at least 2 hours. Serve with whipped topping. Serves 8 (serving size: 1 pie slice and 1½ tablespoons whipped topping)

CALORIES 280; **FAT** 8.9g (sat 3.6g, mono 3.4g, poly 1.3g); **PROTEIN** 6.6g; **CARB** 43.2g; **FIBER** 0.4g; **CHOL** 84mg; **IRON** 0.6mg; **SODIUM** 147mg; **CALC** 144mg

A LIGHTER KEY LIME PIE

START WITH WHITE CHOCOLATE IN THE CRUST
It'll melt to bind the crumbs when baked, and then keep them crisp when cooled. Save 9g sat fat per ounce over butter.

THEN ADD 2% GREEK YOGURT TO THE FILLING
It lends a creamy tang that balances the sugary fat-free condensed milk, saving 2.5g sat fat over regular condensed milk.

FINISH WITH A DOLLOP OF FAT-FREE WHIPPED TOPPING
This cool, fluffy treat will save 140 calories and 10g sat fat per slice over whipped heavy cream.

BY THE NUMBERS

This may be your biggest cookout of the year. Here are ways to keep the meal bursting with patriotic flavor—with way fewer calories.

BREW A FRESH FRUIT SANGRIA
Skip the sugar-packed margarita mixes, and stir up this sparkling 140-calorie treat. It's sweetened with real fruit and saves 30g sugar. Combine 1 cup pitted and halved cherries, 1 cup blueberries, 1 cup quartered strawberries, ½ cup chopped peaches, and ⅓ cup brandy in a large pitcher; chill 2 hours. Stir in 1 cup pineapple juice and 1 (750-milliliter) bottle chilled prosecco. Garnish with fresh mint Serves 8. Savings: 160 calories

LAY ON LOTS OF CRUNCHY CRUDITÉS
Give the chips and onion dip a day off. Nosh instead on a platter of fresh vegetables, and serve with our simple, creamy herb dip: Combine 4 ounces ⅓-less-fat cream cheese, ¼ cup nonfat buttermilk, 2 tablespoons chopped fresh chives, 1 tablespoon chopped fresh parsley, 1 tablespoon lemon juice, ¼ teaspoon salt, and 2 minced garlic cloves; beat with a mixer until smooth. Savings: 150 calories

TRIM THE TRIFLE
Billowing clouds of whipped cream send a traditional patriotic trifle into 500-plus calorie territory. Keep the berry goodness and light texture with angel food cake, but swap the cream for 12 ounces reduced-calorie whipped topping spiked with 2 tablespoons Grand Marnier. You'll save 15g sat fat with this lighter layer. Savings: 250 calories

BUILD A LEANER BURGER
Start with a 90% lean ground beef base to save 100 calories and 4g sat fat (per raw 4-ounce patty) over the 80/20 grind. A thin slice of cheese adds melty goodness for just 45 calories. Guacamole lends creamy zip with only 25 calories per tablespoon and 120mg less sodium than ketchup. Finish with farm-fresh tomatoes, red onion, and crisp greens for super-low-calorie flavor and crunch. Savings: 230 calories

SLIM THE SLAW
A little heart-healthy canola mayo goes a long way to keep our slaw creamy, while mustard seeds and a pinch of ground red pepper boost

flavor (recipe on page 162). You'll also cut out 14g fat and 300mg sodium. Savings: 166 calories

YES. MAYO, NO.
Shave calories and sodium with our version, which tosses crisp-tender taters in a tangy herb-infused olive oil sauce (recipe on page 162). Savings: 115 calories

MAKE BAKED BEANS BETTER
Dress up organic navy beans with fresh thyme and center-cut bacon. Our recipe (page 163) also saves 600mg sodium over canned pork 'n' beans. Savings: 192 calories

HOW SALTY IS YOUR PICKLE?

As we reported in the March issue, nutrition labels on supermarket foods are at best a general indicator of sodium levels. (We had to abandon our favorite low-in-sodium marinara sauce when the lab showed it wasn't low in sodium at all.) But we were curious if this applied to foods that are suspended in salty brines, which, presumably, are made from fairly precise recipes. Answer: Here, too, the numbers were all over the map.

A few supermarket pickles contained more sodium than their labels claimed—18% more in one example. Most, however, came in under. One brand was 23% lower than stated. This didn't make them low sodium, mind you: The pickles averaged 313mg per spear—14% of the daily allowance. Keep in mind that not all serving sizes are an entire spear. Some brands list a serving as two-thirds or three-quarters of a spear. (They should come with rulers.)

continued

Kid Friendly • Make Ahead
Vegetarian

Easy Dill Pickle Spears

Combine 2 cups water, 1½ cups white
wine vinegar, 1½ teaspoons sugar, 1¼
teaspoons kosher salt, 1 teaspoon black
peppercorns, 1 teaspoon dill seed, 1
teaspoon mustard seeds, and 4 thinly
sliced garlic cloves in a medium
saucepan. Bring to a boil; stir. Quarter
6 pickling cucumbers lengthwise, and
place in a bowl or jar; add ¾ ounce
fresh dill. Top with hot vinegar
mixture. Cover and refrigerate overnight. Serves 24 (serving size: 1 spear)

CALORIES 5; **FAT** 0.1g (sat 0g); **SODIUM** 49mg

EVERYDAY VEGETARIAN

MEATLESS MONDAYS

Vegetarian

Grilled Tempeh Kabobs

Hands-on: 22 min. Total: 2 hr. 10 min.
The salty-sweet glaze complements the nutty,
slightly tangy flavor of the tempeh. If you've
never experimented with this soybean cake
before, this is a good recipe to start with.

5 teaspoons rice vinegar, divided
1 tablespoon lower-sodium soy sauce
2 teaspoons dark sesame oil
2 teaspoons sambal oelek (ground
**   fresh chile paste)**
¼ teaspoon black pepper
1 (8-ounce) package organic soy
**   tempeh, cut into 16 pieces**
2 tablespoons honey
2 tablespoons fresh lime juice
1 tablespoon canola oil
½ teaspoon kosher salt
⅛ teaspoon ground red pepper
16 cherry tomatoes
16 button mushrooms
1 large yellow bell pepper, cut
**   into 16 pieces**
2 tablespoons diagonally sliced
**   green onions**

1. Combine 1 tablespoon vinegar and
next 4 ingredients (through black
pepper) in a small zip-top plastic bag;
add tempeh. Marinate in refrigerator 2
hours, turning occasionally.
2. Combine 2 teaspoons vinegar,
honey, juice, canola oil, salt, and red
pepper in a small saucepan. Bring to
a boil over medium-high heat; cook
2 minutes or until honey mixture is
slightly thickened.
3. Preheat grill to high heat.
4. Thread tempeh, tomatoes, mushrooms, and bell pepper alternately

onto each of 8 (6-inch) skewers. Place
skewers on grill; grill 10 minutes or
until browned, turning after 5 minutes
and basting occasionally with half
of honey mixture. Drizzle with
remaining honey mixture; sprinkle
with onions. Serves 4 (serving size: 2
skewers)

CALORIES 250; **FAT** 10.1g (sat 1.4g, mono 4.3g, poly 3.4g);
PROTEIN 14.5g; **CARB** 27.6g; **FIBER** 8g; **CHOL** 0mg;
IRON 2.7mg; **SODIUM** 444mg; **CALC** 108mg

RADICALLY SIMPLE

JULY FIREWORKS

By Rozanne Gold

It's easy to create exciting, brilliant
flavors while avoiding megawatt spice
and chile fire. Let fresh garlic lend its
trademark warmth, and let lemons add
mouth-tingling acidity. These tastes are
perfect for Fourth of July celebrations,
when we're slaking our thirst with
lemonade or salty margaritas, either
of which would be a great accompaniment for my colorful Shrimp, Chorizo,
and Corn Salad.

This dish sizzles with global influ-
ences coalescing into a meal that tastes
surprisingly American. Cooked in only
four minutes in a superhot pan, the
salad can be prepared several hours
ahead and served at room temperature—ideal for outdoor entertaining.
Enjoy the fireworks!

Quick & Easy • Make Ahead

Shrimp, Chorizo, and Corn Salad

Hands-on: 16 min. Total: 16 min. *Prepping the ingredients takes less than 10 minutes, and dinner is on the table in less than 20.*

12 ounces large shrimp, peeled
2 cups fresh corn kernels
1/3 cup chopped green onions
1 1/2 tablespoons Sriracha (hot chile sauce, such as Huy Fong)
2 teaspoons minced fresh garlic
1/2 teaspoon kosher salt
1 3/4 ounces thinly sliced Spanish chorizo sausage
1/2 cup chopped basil leaves, divided
12 red grape tomatoes, halved and divided
12 yellow teardrop tomatoes, halved and divided
1 1/2 tablespoons olive oil
2 teaspoons grated lemon rind
2 tablespoons fresh lemon juice

1. Combine first 7 ingredients in a large bowl. Add ¼ cup chopped basil, 12 red tomato halves, and 12 yellow tomato halves; toss shrimp mixture gently to combine.
2. Heat a large skillet over high heat. Add olive oil to pan; swirl to coat. Add shrimp mixture to pan, and cook 4 minutes or until shrimp turn pink, stirring frequently. Place about 1½ cups shrimp mixture in each of 4 shallow bowls, and sprinkle each serving with ½ teaspoon grated lemon rind, 1½ teaspoons lemon juice, 6 tomato halves, and 1 tablespoon chopped basil. Serves 4

CALORIES 256; FAT 12.2g (sat 2.9g, mono 6.6g, poly 1.8g); PROTEIN 18.2g; CARB 21.1g; FIBER 3g; CHOL 118mg; IRON 1.5mg; SODIUM 583mg; CALC 87mg

QUICK TRICKS

6 RUBS TO SPICE UP CHICKEN

Pick your favorite flavor, rub or brush onto 4 (6-ounce) skinless, boneless chicken breast halves, and grill until done.

mexican mole
Combine 1 tablespoon water and 2 teaspoons instant espresso powder in a small bowl, stirring until espresso dissolves. Stir in 2 teaspoons smoked paprika, 1 teaspoon unsweetened cocoa, 1 teaspoon ground cumin, 1 teaspoon olive oil, and ¼ teaspoon salt. Serves 4 (serving size: about 1 teaspoon)

CALORIES 18; FAT 1.5g (sat 0.1g); SODIUM 149mg

moroccan
Combine 1 teaspoon Hungarian sweet paprika, ½ teaspoon ground cumin, ½ teaspoon ground cinnamon, ¼ teaspoon salt, ¼ teaspoon ground ginger, ¼ teaspoon ground red pepper, and ¼ teaspoon freshly ground black pepper. Serves 4 (serving size: ¾ teaspoon)

CALORIES 5; FAT 0.2g (sat 0.2g); SODIUM 148mg

malaysian curry
Combine 1 tablespoon canola oil, 1 teaspoon ground turmeric, 1 teaspoon Madras curry powder, 2 teaspoons finely chopped fresh cilantro, 1 teaspoon grated lemon rind, 1 teaspoon minced fresh garlic, and ¼ teaspoon kosher salt. Serves 4 (serving size: about 2 teaspoons)

CALORIES 36; FAT 3.7g (sat 0.3g); SODIUM 120mg

juniper
Place 2 teaspoons juniper berries, 1 teaspoon black peppercorns, ½ teaspoon kosher salt, ½ teaspoon crushed red pepper, and 1 bay leaf in a coffee or spice grinder; process until finely ground. Combine juniper mixture, 2 tablespoons extra-virgin olive oil, 6 minced sage leaves, and 1 minced garlic clove. Serves 4 (serving size: about 2 teaspoons)

CALORIES 77; FAT 7.1g (sat 1.2g); SODIUM 240mg

southwestern
Combine 1 teaspoon ground cumin, 1 teaspoon Hungarian sweet paprika, ½ teaspoon garlic powder, ½ teaspoon chipotle chile powder, ¼ teaspoon salt, and ¼ teaspoon ground cinnamon in a small bowl, stirring well. Serves 4 (serving size: 1 teaspoon)

CALORIES 6; FAT 0.2g (sat 0g); SODIUM 131mg

black peppercorn
Place 1 tablespoon whole black peppercorns, 1 tablespoon oregano leaves, ¼ teaspoon salt, and 1 crushed garlic clove in a mini food processor or mini chopper; pulse 8 to 12 times or until mixture is coarsely to finely ground, as desired. Serves 4 (serving size: 1½ teaspoons)

CALORIES 3; FAT 0.1g (sat 0g); SODIUM 147mg

DRESS UP BASIC CHICKEN BREASTS WITH ONE OF THESE SIX ENTICING FLAVOR BOOSTERS

FEED 4 FOR LESS THAN $10

Kid Friendly

Panko-Crusted Chicken with Roasted Corn Hash and Buttermilk Dressing

$2.49/serving, $9.96 total

Hands-on: 20 min. Total: 50 min.
Chicken breast halves have ballooned beyond reasonable portion size, so just use 2 (8-ouncers), and cut each in half lengthwise to form 4 uniform cutlets. Bread all your cutlets and get them in the pan in rapid succession so that they soak up fairly equal amounts of bacon flavor.

1¼ cups low-fat buttermilk, divided
½ teaspoon paprika, divided
½ teaspoon ground red pepper, divided
2 (8-ounce) skinless, boneless chicken breast halves, each cut in half lengthwise
4 ears yellow corn with husks
1 tablespoon chopped fresh flat-leaf parsley
1 teaspoon fresh lemon juice
1 cup panko (Japanese breadcrumbs)
³/₈ teaspoon kosher salt, divided
3 center-cut bacon slices, chopped
1 tablespoon olive oil
3 thinly sliced green onions
2 bottled roasted red bell peppers, chopped (about 4 ounces)
1 tablespoon bottled roasted red bell pepper liquid

1. Preheat oven to 400°.
2. Combine 1 cup buttermilk, ¼ teaspoon paprika, and ¼ teaspoon ground red pepper in a large zip-top plastic bag. Add chicken; seal bag, and marinate in refrigerator 30 minutes, turning bag occasionally.
3. Place corn directly on oven rack. Bake at 400° for 30 minutes. Cool slightly; remove husks and silks. Cut kernels from ears of corn, and place in a large bowl; discard corn cobs.
4. Combine ¼ cup buttermilk, parsley, and lemon juice in a bowl.
5. Combine ¼ teaspoon paprika, ¼ teaspoon ground red pepper, and panko in a shallow dish. Remove chicken from marinade; discard marinade. Sprinkle chicken evenly with ¼ teaspoon salt. Dredge chicken in panko mixture.
6. Place bacon in a large nonstick skillet over medium heat; cook 8 minutes or until crisp. Remove bacon from pan with a slotted spoon; set aside. Add oil to drippings in pan. Add chicken; cook 4 minutes on each side or until golden brown and done.
7. Combine ⅛ teaspoon salt, corn, bacon, green onions, roasted red peppers, and red pepper liquid in a large bowl. Divide corn mixture evenly among 4 plates; top each with 1 chicken cutlet. Drizzle with buttermilk dressing. Serves 4 (serving size: ¾ cup corn mixture, 1 chicken cutlet, and 1 tablespoon dressing)

CALORIES 375; FAT 11.8g (sat 3.4g, mono 4.2g, poly 2.5g); PROTEIN 33.7g; CARB 35.2g; FIBER 3g; CHOL 87mg; IRON 1.3mg; SODIUM 558mg; CALC 18mg

Salmon and Potato Casserole

$2.49/serving, $9.96 total

Hands-on: 12 min. Total: 1 hr. 10 min.

6 cups grated peeled baking potato
½ cup thinly vertically sliced onion
¼ teaspoon kosher salt
¼ teaspoon freshly ground black pepper
5 ounces ⅓-less-fat cream cheese (about ⅔ cup), softened
2 large eggs
Cooking spray
1 (3.5-ounce) package smoked salmon
Dill sprigs

1. Place an 8-inch round metal cake pan in oven. Preheat oven to 425° (leave pan in oven).
2. Combine potato and onion in a large bowl. Combine salt, pepper, cheese, and eggs in a bowl, stirring well. Stir egg mixture into potato mixture. Remove preheated pan from oven; carefully coat pan with cooking spray. Place potato mixture in pan; pack down slightly. Bake at 425° for 50 minutes or until golden. Let stand in pan 10 minutes. Invert potato mixture onto a plate. Cut into 8 wedges; top evenly with salmon and dill. Serves 4 (serving size: 2 wedges)

CALORIES 391; FAT 12.2g (sat 5.9g, mono 1.5g, poly 0.9g); PROTEIN 17.2g; CARB 54.4g; FIBER 3.9g; CHOL 127mg; IRON 3.1mg; SODIUM 584mg; CALC 112mg

DINNER TONIGHT

Fast weeknight menus from the *Cooking Light* Test Kitchen

READY IN 30 MINUTES

······· *The* ·······
SHOPPING LIST

Shrimp and Herb Salad
Lemon (1)
1 (5-ounce) package mixed salad greens
Yellow squash (about 2 medium)
Fresh basil
Fresh oregano
Olive oil
Medium shrimp, peeled and deveined
  (1 pound)

Garlic-Parmesan Toasts
Garlic
Olive oil
Parmigiano-Reggiano cheese
French bread

······· *The* ·······
GAME PLAN

While broiler preheats:
- Prepare vinaigrette.
- Cook shrimp.
While shrimp cooks:
- Toast bread.

Quick & Easy
Shrimp and Herb Salad

With Garlic-Parmesan Toasts

Flavor Hit: Use fresh herbs to perk up ordinary mixed greens.
Prep Pointer: Have your fishmonger peel and devein the shrimp.
Simple Sub: Use zucchini or cucumber instead of yellow squash.

Cooking spray
1 pound medium shrimp, peeled and deveined
³/₈ teaspoon salt, divided
3 tablespoons olive oil
2 tablespoons fresh lemon juice
¹/₄ teaspoon freshly ground black pepper
1 (5-ounce) package mixed salad greens (about 5 cups)
1 cup shaved yellow squash (about 2 medium)
¹/₄ cup coarsely chopped basil leaves
2 tablespoons coarsely chopped oregano leaves

1. Heat a large skillet over medium-high heat. Coat pan with cooking spray. Sprinkle shrimp evenly with ⅛ teaspoon salt. Add shrimp to pan; cook 2 minutes on each side or until done.
2. Combine oil, juice, ¼ teaspoon salt, and pepper in a medium bowl; stir with a whisk. Combine greens, squash, basil, and oregano in a large bowl. Add oil mixture; toss gently to coat. Divide salad mixture evenly among 4 plates; top with shrimp. Serves 4 (serving size: 1¼ cups salad and about 3 ounces shrimp)

CALORIES 194; **FAT** 11.7g (sat 1.6g, mono 7.5g, poly 1.3g); **PROTEIN** 16.8g; **CARB** 6.2g; **FIBER** 2g; **CHOL** 143mg; **IRON** 1.1mg; **SODIUM** 417mg; **CALC** 81mg

For the Garlic-Parmesan Toasts:
Preheat broiler to high. Place 4 (1-ounce) slices French bread on a baking sheet. Broil 1 minute or until lightly toasted. Brush each slice with ½ teaspoon olive oil; rub slices with cut side of a halved garlic clove. Top each slice evenly with 1½ teaspoons grated fresh Parmigiano-Reggiano cheese. Broil 1 minute or until cheese melts. Serves 4 (serving size: 1 toast)

CALORIES 118; **FAT** 3.8g (sat 1.1g); **SODIUM** 200mg

READY IN 40 MINUTES

······· *The* ·······
SHOPPING LIST

Spiced Chicken Thighs with Garlicky Rice
Garlic
Fresh flat-leaf parsley
Basmati rice
Brown sugar
Chili powder
Paprika
Cumin
Garlic powder
Ground red pepper
Bone-in chicken thighs, skinned (8)
Butter

Raspberry and Blue Cheese Salad
Mixed baby greens (5 cups)
Raspberries
Olive oil
Red wine vinegar
Dijon mustard
Pecans
Blue cheese (1 ounce)

······· *The* ·······
GAME PLAN

While rice cooks:
- Preheat boiler.
- Prepare chicken.
While chicken broils:
- Prepare salad.

continued

Quick & Easy

Spiced Chicken Thighs with Garlicky Rice

With Raspberry and Blue Cheese Salad

Time-Saver: Look for preskinned chicken thighs at your meat counter.
Kid Tweak: Swap the blue cheese for shaved Parmesan cheese.
Prep Pointer: Lining the jelly-roll pan with foil makes for easy cleanup.

1 tablespoon butter
1 tablespoon minced fresh garlic
1 cup uncooked basmati rice
1¹/₂ cups water
³/₄ teaspoon salt, divided
3 tablespoons chopped fresh flat-leaf
    parsley
¹/₂ teaspoon freshly ground black
    pepper
2 tablespoons brown sugar
2 teaspoons chili powder
¹/₂ teaspoon paprika
¹/₂ teaspoon ground cumin
¹/₂ teaspoon garlic powder
¹/₄ teaspoon ground red pepper
8 bone-in chicken thighs (about 2¹/₂
    pounds), skinned
Cooking spray

1. Melt butter in a saucepan over medium-high heat. Add garlic; sauté 1 minute. Add rice; cook 30 seconds, stirring constantly. Add 1½ cups water and ⅜ teaspoon salt; bring to a boil. Cover, reduce heat, and simmer 12 minutes or until rice is tender and liquid is absorbed; let stand 5 minutes. Fluff rice. Stir in parsley and black pepper.

2. Preheat broiler to high.
3. Combine sugar and next 5 ingredients; stir in ⅜ teaspoon salt. Sprinkle half of spice mixture over chicken. Place chicken on a foil-lined jelly-roll pan coated with cooking spray. Broil 6 minutes. Turn chicken over; sprinkle with remaining spice mixture, and broil 6 minutes or until done. Remove chicken; reserve pan drippings. Let chicken stand 5 minutes. Spoon drippings over chicken; serve with rice. Serves 4 (serving size: 2 thighs and about ⅔ cup rice)

CALORIES 406; FAT 8.9g (sat 3.3g, mono 2.7g, poly 1.4g); PROTEIN 29.7g; CARB 53.8g; FIBER 1.8g; CHOL 139mg; IRON 3mg; SODIUM 635mg; CALC 31mg

For the Raspberry and Blue Cheese Salad:

Combine 1½ tablespoons olive oil, 1½ teaspoons red wine vinegar, ¼ teaspoon Dijon mustard, ⅛ teaspoon salt, and ⅛ teaspoon pepper. Add 5 cups mixed baby greens; toss. Top with ½ cup raspberries, ¼ cup chopped toasted pecans, and 1 ounce blue cheese. Serves 4 (serving size: about 1½ cups)

CALORIES 133; FAT 12.2g (sat 2.5g); SODIUM 193mg

READY IN
40
MINUTES

The

SHOPPING LIST

Grilled Turkey-Plum Sandwiches
Garlic
Fresh basil
Black plums (2)
Canola mayonnaise
Turkey cutlets (12 ounces)
Country-style whole-grain bread

Shaved Carrot Salad
Carrots (about 2)
Fresh dill
White balsamic vinegar
Sugar

The

GAME PLAN

While bread grills:
■ Season cutlets.
While cutlets cook:
■ Prepare salad.

Kid Friendly • Quick & Easy

Grilled Turkey-Plum Sandwiches

With Shaved Carrot Salad

Kid Tweak: Omit the raw garlic in the mayonnaise.
Flavor Swap: Try the anise notes of shaved fennel in the salad.
Simple Sub: Use chicken cutlets instead of turkey.

2½ tablespoons canola mayonnaise (such as Hellmann's)
1 teaspoon minced fresh garlic
¼ teaspoon freshly ground black pepper
8 (1-ounce) slices country-style whole-grain bread
Cooking spray
12 ounces turkey cutlets (about ¼ inch thick)
½ teaspoon salt
2 medium ripe black plums, pitted and thinly sliced
16 basil leaves

1. Combine first 3 ingredients in a small bowl; stir well. Set mixture aside.
2. Heat a grill pan over medium-high heat. Place 4 bread slices in a single layer on grill pan; grill 3 minutes on one side or until grill marks appear. Remove bread from grill pan. Repeat procedure with remaining bread.
3. Coat grill pan with cooking spray. Sprinkle turkey evenly with salt. Add turkey to pan; grill 3 minutes or until done, turning after 1½ minutes.
4. Spread 2 teaspoons mayonnaise mixture over untoasted side of each of 4 bread slices; top each serving with about 2¼ ounces turkey. Divide plum slices evenly among sandwiches; top each serving with 4 basil leaves. Top sandwiches with remaining 4 bread slices. Serves 4 (serving size: 1 sandwich)

CALORIES 292; FAT 6.1g (sat 0.7g, mono 2.1g, poly 2.2g); PROTEIN 28.9g; CARB 28.7g; FIBER 4.7g; CHOL 53mg; IRON 2.6mg; SODIUM 631mg; CALC 74mg

For the Shaved Carrot Salad:
Combine 2 cups shaved carrot, 2 teaspoons white balsamic vinegar, ½ teaspoon sugar, 1 teaspoon chopped fresh dill, and ¼ teaspoon salt in a medium bowl; toss to coat. Serves 4 (serving size: about ⅓ cup)

CALORIES 29; FAT 0.2g (sat 0g); SODIUM 190mg

READY IN
30
MINUTES

The SHOPPING LIST

Hoisin-Grilled Chicken with Soba Noodles
Sugar snap peas (1½ cups)
Green onions
Hoisin sauce
Balsamic vinegar
Worcestershire sauce
Five-spice powder
Soba noodles
Rice vinegar
Dark sesame oil
Lower-sodium soy sauce
Sambal oelek (ground fresh chile paste)
Toasted sesame seeds
3 (6-ounce) skinless, boneless chicken breast halves

Cucumber-Peanut Salad
English cucumbers (about 2)
Red onion (1)
Lime (1)
Brown sugar
Unsalted, dry-roasted peanuts

The GAME PLAN

While chicken cooks:
■ Boil noodles.
While chicken stands:
■ Prepare salad.

Quick & Easy
Hoisin-Grilled Chicken with Soba Noodles

With Cucumber-Peanut Salad

Global Sub: Use Asian black vinegar instead of balsamic and Worcestershire sauce.
Time-Saver: Purchase bagged pretrimmed sugar snap peas.
Flavor Hit: Five-spice powder adds a hint of earthiness to the chicken.

2 tablespoons hoisin sauce
1½ teaspoons balsamic vinegar
1½ teaspoons Worcestershire sauce
½ teaspoon five-spice powder
3 (6-ounce) skinless, boneless chicken breast halves
Cooking spray
6 ounces uncooked soba noodles
1½ cups sugar snap peas, trimmed and halved diagonally
2 tablespoons rice vinegar
1 tablespoon dark sesame oil
2 teaspoons lower-sodium soy sauce
1 teaspoon sambal oelek (ground fresh chile paste)
2 teaspoons toasted sesame seeds
2 green onions, thinly sliced

1. Combine first 4 ingredients in a large bowl. Add chicken; toss to coat. Heat a grill pan over medium-high heat. Coat pan with cooking spray. Add chicken; cook 10 minutes or until done, turning after 5 minutes. Let stand 5 minutes. Thinly slice across the grain.
2. Bring a large saucepan of water to a boil. Add noodles; cook 2 minutes. Add peas; cook 1 minute or until noodles are tender. Drain. Combine rice vinegar and next 3 ingredients in a bowl. Add noodle mixture; toss to coat. Arrange about 1 cup noodle mixture in each of 4 shallow bowls. Top each serving with about 3½ ounces chicken.
continued

Sprinkle with sesame seeds and onions. Serves 4

CALORIES 371; **FAT** 8.7g (sat 1.4g, mono 2.7g, poly 2.4g); **PROTEIN** 34.5g; **CARB** 36.8g; **FIBER** 3.5g; **CHOL** 82mg; **IRON** 3mg; **SODIUM** 635mg; **CALC** 32mg

For the Cucumber-Peanut Salad:

Combine 2 cups thinly sliced English cucumber, ½ cup vertically sliced red onion, 3 tablespoons fresh lime juice, 2 teaspoons light brown sugar, and ¼ teaspoon salt in a medium bowl; toss to coat. Sprinkle evenly with 2 table-spoons chopped unsalted, dry-roasted peanuts. Serves 4 (serving size: ½ cup)

CALORIES 52; **FAT** 2.4g (sat 0.3g); **SODIUM** 150mg

Quick & Easy

Seared Steaks with Red Wine–Cherry Sauce

With Almond Green Beans and Dijon Smashed Potatoes

Simple Sub: Try hazelnuts instead of almonds.
Shopping Tip: Pick up a merlot or pinot noir for the pan sauce.
Prep Pointer: Get the skillet screaming hot to ensure an even sear.

4 (4-ounce) beef tenderloin steaks
1/2 teaspoon salt
1/2 teaspoon freshly ground black pepper
1 tablespoon olive oil
1/2 cup finely chopped shallots
1 cup sweet cherries (such as Bing), pitted and halved
1 star anise
3/4 cup dry red wine
1 tablespoon butter

1. Preheat oven to 425°.
2. Heat a large cast-iron skillet over high heat. Sprinkle steaks evenly with salt and pepper. Add oil to pan; swirl to coat. Add steaks; cook 4 minutes.

Turn steaks over; bake at 425° for 5 minutes or until desired degree of doneness. Remove steaks from pan.
3. Heat skillet over medium-high heat. Add shallots; sauté 2 minutes or until just tender, stirring frequently. Add cherries and star anise; cook 1 minute. Add wine, bring to a boil, and cook 3 minutes or until slightly thickened. Discard star anise. Stir in butter. Spoon sauce over steaks. Serves 4 (serving size: 1 steak and ¼ cup sauce)

CALORIES 289; **FAT** 13.8g (sat 5.1g, mono 6.3g, poly 0.8g); **PROTEIN** 26.2g; **CARB** 10.6g; **FIBER** 1.6g; **CHOL** 81mg; **IRON** 2.5mg; **SODIUM** 387mg; **CALC** 47mg

For the Almond Green Beans:

Melt 1 tablespoon butter in a large skillet over medium heat. Add ¼ cup slivered almonds; cook 2 minutes or until lightly browned, stirring con-stantly. Remove from pan with a slotted spoon. Add 2 teaspoons minced fresh garlic to pan; cook 30 seconds, stirring constantly. Add 12 ounces trimmed green beans, 3 tablespoons water, ¼ teaspoon salt, and ¼ teaspoon freshly ground black pepper. Cover and cook 4 minutes or until beans are tender and liquid evaporates. Sprinkle with almonds. Serves 4 (serving size: about 1 cup)

CALORIES 93; **FAT** 6.4g (sat 2.1g); **SODIUM** 178mg

For the Dijon Smashed Potatoes:

Steam 1½ pounds quartered Yukon gold potatoes, covered, 20 minutes or until potatoes are very tender. Place potatoes in a large bowl; add ¾ cup whole milk, 2 tablespoons minced fresh chives, 1 tablespoon Dijon mus-tard, 1 tablespoon butter, ¼ teaspoon salt, and ½ teaspoon freshly ground black pepper. Mash potato mixture with a potato masher until desired consistency. Serves 4 (serving size: about 1 cup)

CALORIES 178; **FAT** 4.6g (sat 2.7g); **SODIUM** 313mg

READY IN
40
MINUTES

The
SHOPPING LIST

Seared Steaks with Red Wine–Cherry Sauce
Shallots
Cherries (1 cup)
Olive oil
Star anise pod
Dry red wine
4 (4-ounce) beef tenderloin steaks
Butter

Almond Green Beans
Garlic
Green beans (12 ounces)
Slivered almonds
Butter

Dijon Smashed Potatoes
Yukon gold potatoes (1½ pounds)
Fresh chives
Dijon mustard
Whole milk
Butter

The
GAME PLAN

While oven preheats:
■ Steam potatoes.
■ Sear steaks.
While steaks cook:
■ Mash potatoes.
■ Prepare green beans.

SUPERFAST 20-MINUTE COOKING

In-a-jiffy family cooking for summer includes shrimp sliders, green bean sides, 20-minute enchiladas, and more.

Quick & Easy • Vegetarian

Fettuccine with Pistachio-Mint Pesto and Tomatoes

We love this dish with pistachios, but for a less-expensive alternative, try walnuts.

1/2 cup mint leaves
1/2 cup flat-leaf parsley leaves
1/4 cup plus 4 teaspoons unsalted, shelled dry-roasted pistachios, divided
3 tablespoons extra-virgin olive oil
5/8 teaspoon kosher salt
1/4 teaspoon freshly ground black pepper
1 large garlic clove
1 (9-ounce) package refrigerated fettuccine
12 cherry tomatoes, halved
1 ounce fresh pecorino Romano cheese, shaved (about 1/4 cup)

1. Place mint leaves, parsley leaves, 1/4 cup pistachios, olive oil, kosher salt, ground black pepper, and garlic in a mini food processor; pulse mixture until coarsely chopped.
2. Cook fettuccine according to the package directions, omitting salt and fat. Drain fettuccine over a bowl, reserving 1/4 cup of the cooking liquid. Combine pesto mixture and reserved cooking liquid in a large bowl, stirring with a whisk. Add pasta to bowl; toss well to coat. Gently fold

in cherry tomatoes. Coarsely chop 4 teaspoons pistachios. Top pasta evenly with pecorino Romano cheese and chopped pistachios. Serves 4 (serving size: 1 cup)

CALORIES 371; FAT 19.1g (sat 4.5g, mono 9.9g, poly 2.5g); PROTEIN 12.3g; CARB 40.1g; FIBER 3.7g; CHOL 45mg; IRON 2.6mg; SODIUM 463mg; CALC 115mg

Quick & Easy

Spicy Shrimp Sliders with Celery Mayonnaise

If you prefer a milder sandwich, omit the ground red pepper.

2 teaspoons dark sesame oil
1 tablespoon minced peeled fresh ginger
24 medium shrimp, peeled and deveined (about 12 ounces)
1/2 teaspoon kosher salt, divided
8 (1 1/4-ounce) wheat slider buns
2 tablespoons finely chopped celery
3 tablespoons canola mayonnaise
1 tablespoon plain 2% reduced-fat Greek yogurt
2 teaspoons finely chopped shallots
1 teaspoon fresh lemon juice
1/8 teaspoon ground red pepper
8 small Bibb lettuce leaves

1. Preheat broiler.
2. Heat a large skillet over medium-high heat. Add oil to pan; swirl to coat. Add ginger; cook 1 minute. Sprinkle shrimp with 1/4 teaspoon salt. Add shrimp to pan; cook 3 minutes or until done. Keep warm.
3. Arrange buns in a single layer on a baking sheet, cut sides up. Broil 45 seconds or until toasted. Combine celery and next 4 ingredients (through juice) in a medium bowl; stir in 1/4 teaspoon salt and pepper. Place 1 lettuce leaf on bottom half of each bun. Top with 1 tablespoon mayonnaise mixture and 3 shrimp. Cover with top halves of buns.

Serves 4 (serving size: 2 sliders)

 Sustainable Choice | *For a "best choice" purchase, look for U.S. Pacific white shrimp farmed in recirculating systems or inland ponds.*

CALORIES 324; FAT 10.6g (sat 0.5g, mono 4.9g, poly 4.2g); PROTEIN 22.3g; CARB 36.4g; FIBER 2.5g; CHOL 107mg; IRON 2.2mg; SODIUM 704mg; CALC 139mg

Quick & Easy • Vegetarian

Tomato and Feta Toasts with Mixed Greens Salad

3 tablespoons extra-virgin olive oil
1 teaspoon finely chopped fresh thyme
1 teaspoon finely grated lemon rind
3/4 teaspoon freshly ground black pepper
1/4 teaspoon dried oregano
12 large basil leaves, finely chopped
4 ounces feta cheese, diced
4 (1-ounce) slices country wheat bread
1 large garlic clove, halved
12 (1/4-inch-thick) slices tomato
1 tablespoon fresh lemon juice
1/8 teaspoon sugar
1/8 teaspoon kosher salt
7 ounces spinach and arugula salad mix
1 cup sliced English cucumber
1/2 cup vertically sliced red onion

1. Preheat broiler to high.
2. Combine first 6 ingredients. Add feta; toss to coat. Let stand 10 minutes.
3. Place bread on a baking sheet; broil 45 seconds on each side. Rub with garlic. Divide tomato slices over bread. Remove feta from oil with a slotted spoon; crumble 1 ounce over each toast. Add juice, sugar, and salt to oil; stir. Add remaining ingredients; toss. Serves 4 (serving size: 1 toast and about 2 cups salad)

CALORIES 267; FAT 16.3g (sat 5.1g, mono 7.4g, poly 1.2g); PROTEIN 9.1g; CARB 23.8g; FIBER 3.5g; CHOL 12mg; IRON 3.4mg; SODIUM 605mg; CALC 375mg

A TRADITIONAL CHICKEN ENCHILADA RECIPE CAN HAVE MORE THAN 1,000 CALORIES PER SERVING!

Kid Friendly • Quick & Easy

20-Minute Chicken Enchiladas

Quick tip: While the sauce cooks, shred the chicken. For a spicy kick, top with chopped jalapeños.

1 cup prechopped onion
1 cup unsalted chicken stock
   (such as Swanson)
1 tablespoon all-purpose flour
1½ tablespoons chili powder
2 teaspoons ground cumin
¾ teaspoon garlic powder
½ teaspoon crushed red pepper
¼ teaspoon salt
1 (15-ounce) can unsalted tomato sauce
3 cups shredded skinless, boneless
   rotisserie chicken breast
   (about 15 ounces)
1 (15-ounce) can unsalted black beans,
   rinsed and drained
12 (6-inch) corn tortillas
Cooking spray
3 ounces preshredded 4-cheese
   Mexican blend cheese (about ¾ cup)
1 cup chopped tomato
¼ cup chopped fresh cilantro
6 tablespoons sour cream

1. Preheat broiler to high.
2. Combine first 9 ingredients in a medium saucepan; stir with a whisk. Bring to a boil over high heat; cook 2 minutes or until thickened. Reserve 1½ cups sauce mixture. Add chicken and beans to pan; cook 2 minutes or until chicken is thoroughly heated.
3. Stack tortillas; wrap stack in damp paper towels and microwave at HIGH for 25 seconds. Spoon about ⅓ cup chicken mixture in center of each tortilla; roll up. Arrange tortillas, seam sides down, in bottom of a 13 x 9–inch glass or ceramic baking dish coated with cooking spray. Top with reserved sauce and cheese. Broil 3 minutes or until cheese is lightly browned and sauce is bubbly. Top with tomato and cilantro. Serve with sour cream. Serves 6 (serving size: 2 enchiladas and 1 tablespoon sour cream)

CALORIES 374; FAT 13.2g (sat 6g, mono 3.3g, poly 1.4g); PROTEIN 31.2g; CARB 35.2g; FIBER 6.2g; CHOL 100mg; IRON 2.3mg; SODIUM 569mg; CALC 189mg

Kid Friendly • Quick & Easy

Grilled Peaches with Honey Cream

You can use apricots or nectarines instead of peaches. Garnish with mint, if desired.

2 tablespoons unsalted butter, melted
2 tablespoons honey, divided
¼ teaspoon ground cardamom
Dash of kosher salt
4 medium peaches, pitted and halved
Cooking spray
⅓ cup plain fat-free Greek yogurt
2½ tablespoons half-and-half
¼ teaspoon vanilla extract
1 cup raspberries

1. Combine melted butter, 1 tablespoon honey, cardamom, and salt in a medium bowl. Add peaches, and toss to coat. Let stand 5 minutes.
2. Heat a grill pan over medium heat. Coat pan with cooking spray. Arrange peaches on grill pan; grill 2 minutes on each side or until grill marks appear.
3. Combine yogurt, half-and-half, 1 tablespoon honey, and vanilla in a small bowl; stir with a whisk. Serve with peaches and raspberries. Serves 4 (serving size: ¼ cup raspberries, 2 tablespoons yogurt mixture, and 2 peach halves)

CALORIES 182; FAT 7.6g (sat 4.4g, mono 1.6g, poly 0.5g); PROTEIN 3.8g; CARB 27.9g; FIBER 4.2g; CHOL 19mg; IRON 0.7mg; SODIUM 43mg; CALC 42mg

**Kid Friendly • Quick & Easy
Vegetarian**

Steamed Green Beans with Lemon-Mint Dressing

1 pound green beans, trimmed
2 tablespoons finely chopped mint
   leaves
1 tablespoon minced shallots
2 tablespoons fresh lemon juice
1½ tablespoons extra-virgin olive oil
¼ teaspoon salt
¼ teaspoon freshly ground black
   pepper

1. Steam green beans 4 minutes or until crisp-tender; drain.
2. Combine mint and remaining ingredients in a large bowl, and stir with a whisk. Add green beans to bowl, and toss to coat. Serves 4 (serving size: about 1 cup)

CALORIES 84; FAT 5.3g (sat 0.8g, mono 3.7g, poly 0.7g); PROTEIN 2.2g; CARB 9.1g; FIBER 3.3g; CHOL 0mg; IRON 1.3mg; SODIUM 155mg; CALC 46mg

Variation 1: Red Pepper & Pesto
Place jelly-roll pan on bottom rack of oven. Preheat oven to 450°. Toss 1 pound green beans, 1 sliced red bell pepper, 1 tablespoon olive oil, and ¼ teaspoon salt; spread on pan. Bake 8 minutes, stirring after 4 minutes. Pulse ½ cup parsley, ¼ cup unsalted pistachios, 1 tablespoon water, 1 tablespoon olive oil, 2 teaspoons lemon juice, ⅛ teaspoon salt, and 1 garlic clove in food processor. Toss with bean mixture. Serves 4 (serving size: 1¼ cups)

CALORIES 153; FAT 10.6g (sat 1.4g); SODIUM 234mg

Variation 2: Ginger Sesame

Heat a skillet over medium-high heat. Add 1 tablespoon sesame oil. Add 1 pound green beans; cook 7 minutes or until beans begin to brown. Combine 1 tablespoon toasted sesame seeds, 1 tablespoon minced peeled fresh ginger, 1 tablespoon tahini, 5 teaspoons lower-sodium soy sauce, 1 tablespoon water, and 1 tablespoon fresh lime juice in a bowl. Add mixture to pan. Cook 1 minute; toss to coat. Serves 4 (serving size: about 1 cup)

CALORIES 104; FAT 6.6g (sat 1g); SODIUM 231mg

Variation 3: Stewed Tomatoes & Spices

Heat a skillet over medium-high heat. Add 1 tablespoon olive oil. Add 1 cup chopped onion and 1 pound green beans; cook 5 minutes. Stir in 1½ teaspoons ground cumin, 1 teaspoon dried marjoram, ½ teaspoon ground allspice, and 4 sliced garlic cloves. Add 2 cups chopped tomato and ⅓ cup water; cook 9 minutes. Stir in ½ teaspoon kosher salt and ¼ teaspoon black pepper. Serves 4 (serving size: 1 cup)

CALORIES 92; FAT 4g (sat 0.6g); SODIUM 253mg

Kid Friendly • Quick & Easy

Chicken and Vegetable Stir-Fry

Vary the veggies to your family's tastes—sliced carrots or snow peas would be good substitutions.

- **1 (3½-ounce) bag boil-in-bag long-grain rice**
- **2 teaspoons dark sesame oil**
- **12 ounces skinless, boneless chicken breast, cut into ¼-inch-thick strips**
- **3 cups thinly sliced napa (Chinese) cabbage**
- **1 cup sugar snap peas, trimmed and halved diagonally**
- **1 large red bell pepper, thinly sliced**
- **3 tablespoons lower-sodium soy sauce**
- **2 tablespoons hoisin sauce**
- **1 teaspoon cornstarch**
- **1 teaspoon rice vinegar**
- **2 green onions, cut diagonally into ½-inch pieces**

1. Prepare rice according to package directions, omitting salt and fat.
2. Heat a large skillet over medium-high heat. Add oil; swirl to coat. Add chicken; cook 2 minutes on each side or until done. Add cabbage, peas, and bell pepper. Cook 2 minutes or until crisp-tender, stirring occasionally. Combine soy sauce and next 3 ingredients in a small bowl; stir with a whisk. Add soy sauce mixture to pan; cook 1 minute, stirring gently to coat. Sprinkle with onions. Serve with rice. Serves 4 (serving size: 1 cup stir-fry and ½ cup rice)

CALORIES 299; FAT 5.2g (sat 0.9g, mono 1.7g, poly 1.5g); PROTEIN 22.8g; CARB 39g; FIBER 3.4g; CHOL 55mg; IRON 2.9mg; SODIUM 641mg; CALC 48mg

FIRST BITES

Kid Friendly • Freezable Make Ahead

Avocado Ice Pops

Hands-on: 10 min. Total: 4 hr. 30 min.
They're a fruit and creamy-rich—perfect for freezing on a stick.

Combine ¾ cup water and 6 tablespoons sugar in a saucepan over medium heat. Cook 4 minutes, stirring to dissolve sugar. Remove from heat; cool to room temperature. Place sugar mixture, 2 cups chopped peeled avocado, ½ teaspoon grated lime rind, 2 tablespoons fresh lime juice, and ⅛ teaspoon kosher salt in a food processor; process until smooth. Divide mixture evenly among 6 (4-ounce) ice-pop molds. Top with lid. Freeze 4 hours or until thoroughly frozen. Serves 6 (serving size: 1 ice pop)

CALORIES 130; FAT 7.3g (sat 1.1g); SODIUM 44mg

GLOBAL FINDS

NAMA SHOYU

A cut above standard soy sauces, Ohsawa's nama shoyu lends a meaty umami hit to food without overwhelming soy sauce flavor. It blends amazingly well into dishes, and it's versatile enough to use in non-Asian cooking when you want a deep savory note, like in a pot of chili.

Kid Friendly • Quick & Easy Vegetarian

Grilled Summer Squash with Shoyu

Hands-on: 8 min. Total: 15 min.

Preheat grill to medium-high heat. Combine 2 tablespoons canola oil; 2 yellow squash, cut lengthwise into ½-inch slices; and 1 large zucchini, cut lengthwise into ½-inch slices, in a large bowl. Toss well to coat. Sprinkle with ½ teaspoon freshly ground black pepper and ¼ teaspoon kosher salt. Place vegetables on grill rack coated with cooking spray; grill 7 minutes or until well marked and tender, turning once. Remove from grill; drizzle 2 teaspoons nama shoyu evenly over vegetables. Sprinkle with 2 tablespoons chopped fresh cilantro. Serves 4 (serving size: about ½ cup)

CALORIES 104; FAT 7.6g (sat 0.7g); SODIUM 219mg

(Perfect patty!)

OOPS!

YOUR BURGER "MEATBALLS" ON THE GRILL

How to make sure your patties stay flat and don't ball up

(Beef ball)

It's a classic backyard snafu: You flip the patties on the grill, and suddenly what seemed like perfectly bun-wide servings of meat contract into domed pucks. This is the dreaded meatball effect, which is the result of too much shrinkage: Proteins in the ground beef coil up during cooking, squeezing out moisture as the patty tightens into a ball. Adding more beef isn't an option for health-minded cooks, and it won't work anyway. And flattening the patties with a spatula as they grill—a technique we've witnessed many times—simply pushes out delicious juices, causing flare-ups and sooty, dry burgers.

The solution: Make the raw, 4-ounce patties a bit larger in circumference than the hamburger buns. Press the mixture together gently; overworking it increases contraction and makes the cooked meat dense and dry. Use your thumb to make a nickel-sized indentation, a little more than ¼ inch deep, in the center of each patty. This prevents the burger from doming into a ball, keeping it flat and even as it cooks. Voilà: no meatballs in sight.

THE AMAZING FIVE INGREDIENT ENTRÉE

So simple, and simply fantastic

Kid Friendly • Vegetarian

Fresh Mozzarella, Heirloom Tomato, and Basil Pizza

Hands-on: 22 min. Total: 55 min. *Allow the dough to rest at room temperature before rolling it out. If it still shrinks back when you start to work with it, let it rest for another 10 minutes, and then try again. For a pretty finishing touch, save a few small basil leaves to sprinkle over the top of the pizza after it cooks.*

12 ounces refrigerated fresh pizza dough
1 cup basil leaves
6 garlic cloves
3 tablespoons extra-virgin olive oil, divided
4 ounces fresh mozzarella cheese, thinly sliced
2 (6-ounce) heirloom tomatoes, cut into ¼-inch-thick slices
¼ teaspoon freshly ground black pepper
½ teaspoon kosher salt

1. Place a pizza stone or heavy baking sheet in oven. Preheat oven to 500° (keep pizza stone or baking sheet in oven as it preheats).
2. Let dough stand at room temperature for 30 minutes.

3. Place basil, garlic, and 2 tablespoons oil in a mini food processor; pulse 3 times to form a paste. Add 1 tablespoon oil; pulse until smooth.
4. Roll dough into a 14-inch circle on a floured surface; pierce entire surface liberally with a fork. Carefully remove pizza stone from oven. Arrange dough on pizza stone. Spread about 2½ tablespoons basil mixture over dough. Top evenly with cheese, tomatoes, and pepper. Bake at 500° for 12 minutes or until crust is browned and crisp. Top with remaining 1½ tablespoons basil mixture; sprinkle evenly with salt. Cut into 12 slices. Serves 4 (serving size: 3 slices)

CALORIES 406; **FAT** 18.5g (sat 5.4g, mono 8.3g, poly 1.6g); **PROTEIN** 13.6g; **CARB** 44.7g; **FIBER** 7.4g; **CHOL** 23mg; **IRON** 1.8mg; **SODIUM** 627mg; **CALC** 36mg

THIS IS HOW THE SIMPLE COOK ROLLS: STORE-MADE DOUGH, THIN, WITH SWEET TOMATOES AND CHEWY-MELTY MOZZARELLA...

Quick & Easy

Halibut with Bacony Corn Sauté

(pictured on page 230)

Hands-on: 20 min. Total: 20 min. *Be sure to buy fresh, never-frozen fish, summer corn on the cob and in the husks, and your favorite bacon. Applewood-smoked bacon is more subtle than hickory or mesquite and won't clobber all the other ingredients. Just a spritz of fresh lime juice brings the flavors into perfect balance.*

1 tablespoon extra-virgin olive oil
4 (6-ounce) skinless halibut fillets
¼ teaspoon salt
¼ teaspoon freshly ground black pepper
1 center-cut applewood-smoked bacon slice
2¼ cups fresh corn kernels (about 4 ears)
1½ tablespoons butter
¾ cup (1-inch) sliced green onions
4 lime wedges

1. Heat a large nonstick skillet over medium-high heat. Add oil to pan; swirl to coat. Sprinkle fish evenly with salt and freshly ground black pepper. Add fish to pan; sauté 4 minutes on each side or until golden and cooked to desired degree of doneness. Remove fish from pan; keep warm.
2. Reduce heat to medium. Add bacon to pan; cook 4 minutes or until crisp. Remove bacon from pan; crumble. Add corn to drippings in pan; cook 3 minutes or until beginning to brown, stirring occasionally. Stir in butter; cook 1 minute or until butter melts. Stir in crumbled bacon and green onions. Serve with lime wedges. Serves 4 (serving size: 1 fillet, about ½ cup corn mixture, and 1 lime wedge)

CALORIES 309; **FAT** 11.4g (sat 4.1g, mono 4.7g, poly 1.4g); **PROTEIN** 34.9g; **CARB** 17.8g; **FIBER** 2.5g; **CHOL** 96mg; **IRON** 1mg; **SODIUM** 343mg; **CALC** 32mg

Tomato Ravioli

Hands-on: 15 min. Total: 55 min.

1 pound cherry tomatoes
2 shallots, cut into wedges
Cooking spray
3 tablespoons extra-virgin olive oil, divided
2 tablespoons balsamic vinegar
¼ teaspoon kosher salt
¼ teaspoon black pepper
12 ounces cheese ravioli
2 tablespoons chopped fresh basil

1. Preheat oven to 425°.
2. Halve half of tomatoes. Arrange cut tomatoes, whole tomatoes, and shallots on a jelly-roll pan coated with cooking spray. Drizzle with 1 tablespoon oil; toss. Bake at 425° for 35 minutes.
3. Add 2 tablespoons oil, vinegar, salt, and pepper to pan. Bake 10 minutes. Place tomato mixture in a large bowl.
4. Cook ravioli according to package directions, omitting salt and fat. Drain ravioli, reserving ¼ cup cooking liquid. Add ravioli to tomato mixture; toss. Add cooking liquid, if needed. Garnish with chopped basil. Serves 4 (serving size: about 6 ravioli and ½ cup tomato mixture)

CALORIES 406; FAT 18.7g (sat 6.3g, mono 9.7g, poly 1.7g); PROTEIN 13.4g; CARB 47.8g; FIBER 3.9g; CHOL 49mg; IRON 2.3mg; SODIUM 572mg; CALC 138mg

Spaghetti with Parsley Pesto and Sausage

Hands-on: 25 min. Total: 25 min. A sprinkling of crumbled spicy sausage makes a salty-savory finishing touch to herb-drenched pasta. Some pestos tend to go drab, but this one stays a brilliant emerald green.

8 ounces uncooked spaghetti
3 ounces spicy pork Italian sausage, casings removed
4 garlic cloves, crushed and coarsely chopped
¼ cup extra-virgin olive oil, divided
1 ounce fresh Parmigiano-Reggiano cheese, grated and divided (about ¼ cup)
5 cups flat-leaf parsley leaves, divided
½ teaspoon kosher salt

1. Bring 4 quarts of water to a boil in a large saucepan or Dutch oven. Add pasta to pan, and cook 8 minutes or until almost al dente. Drain pasta in a colander over a bowl, reserving ¾ cup cooking liquid. Discard remaining cooking liquid.
2. Heat a large heavy skillet over medium-high heat. Add Italian sausage to pan; sauté 6 minutes or until browned, stirring to crumble. Remove sausage from pan, reserving drippings; drain on paper towels. Add garlic to drippings in pan; sauté 1 minute, stirring constantly. Add ½ cup reserved cooking liquid to pan; bring to a boil, scraping pan to loosen browned bits. Stir in 2 tablespoons olive oil; cook 30 seconds, stirring constantly with a whisk. Add pasta to pan; cook 1 minute, tossing to combine. Remove from heat.
3. Place about 2 tablespoons cheese and 4¾ cups parsley leaves in a food processor; process until finely ground. With motor running, add remaining ¼ cup cooking liquid and 2 tablespoons olive oil; process until smooth. Add parsley mixture and salt to pasta; toss well to coat. Divide pasta mixture evenly among 4 shallow bowls; top evenly with sausage, 2 tablespoons cheese, and ¼ cup parsley leaves. Serve immediately. Serves 4 (serving size: about 1¼ cups)

CALORIES 342; FAT 24.5g (sat 5.9g, mono 13.7g, poly 2.5g); PROTEIN 10.9g; CARB 21.6g; FIBER 3.2g; CHOL 22mg; IRON 5.2mg; SODIUM 607mg; CALC 193mg

Hickory Pulled Pork

Hands-on: 3 hr. Total: 10 hr. 30 min.

3 cups hickory wood chips
2 tablespoons dark brown sugar
2 teaspoons salt
1 teaspoon garlic powder
2 teaspoons chili powder
1 teaspoon freshly ground black pepper
1 (5-pound) bone-in pork shoulder (Boston butt), trimmed
Cooking spray

1. Submerge wood chips in water; weight with a board or plate. Soak chips for 30 minutes. Drain. Combine brown sugar, salt, garlic powder, chili powder, and black pepper, stirring well. Rub spice mixture evenly over both sides of pork shoulder. Cover loosely with foil; let pork stand at room temperature for 1 hour.
2. Set aside grill rack. Prepare grill for indirect grilling, heating one side to high and leaving one side with no heat. Pierce bottom of a disposable aluminum foil pan several times with the tip of a knife. Place pan on heat element or over coals; add 1 cup soaked wood chips to pan. Place another disposable aluminum foil pan (do not pierce pan) on unheated side of grill. Pour 2 cups water into unpierced pan. Let chips stand for 5 minutes or until smoking; reduce heat to medium-low.
3. Coat grill rack with cooking spray. Set grill rack in place. Place pork on grill rack over indirect heat. Close lid, and grill 3 hours, maintaining a constant temperature of 275°; add ½ cup soaked wood chips every 45 minutes. Grill pork an additional 3½ hours or until a thermometer inserted in pork registers 170°. Wrap pork in heavy-duty aluminum foil, and cook an additional 1½ hours or until pork reaches 190°. Remove pork from grill; let stand 30 minutes. Shred. Serves 12 (serving size: 3 ounces pork)

CALORIES 260; FAT 10.8g (sat 3.8g, mono 4.7g, poly 1.2g); PROTEIN 35.5g; CARB 2.6g; FIBER 0.1g; CHOL 113mg; IRON 2.3mg; SODIUM 530mg; CALC 29mg

FIVE RADICAL GRILLING TRICKS

Grilling, like any cooking method, can become a matter of habit. Tried-and-true methods yield tried-and-true food. But there are new truths out there, and Adam Perry Lang has really shaken up the grilling world. Here he offers five fantastic techniques. Unorthodox? Certainly. A little more time-consuming? Yes. But they're simple at heart, and they produce some of the best grilled meat recipes we've ever tasted. Trust us: These tricks pay off big time.

Double Thick-Cut Pork Chops

Hands-on: 1 hr. 20 min. Total: 17 hr. 50 min.

Pork:
2 (1-pound) bone-in center-cut pork chops (about 2½ inches thick)
Basic Brine (page 188)
Glaze:
⅔ cup sugar
⅓ cup water
2 tablespoons minced seeded jalapeño pepper
2 garlic cloves, crushed
2 tablespoons finely chopped green onions
2 teaspoons fresh lime juice
Remaining ingredients:
1 bunch thyme sprigs
1 bunch rosemary sprigs
1 bunch sage sprigs
2 tablespoons extra-virgin olive oil
2 tablespoons finely chopped fresh flat-leaf parsley
½ teaspoon freshly ground black pepper
¼ teaspoon kosher salt

1. To prepare pork, add pork chops to Basic Brine; refrigerate 16 hours, turning occasionally.
2. To prepare glaze, combine ⅔ cup sugar, ⅓ cup water, jalapeño pepper, and garlic in a small saucepan; bring to a simmer, stirring just until sugar dissolves. Stir in green onions and lime juice. Remove from heat, and let stand 1 hour.
3. Prepare charcoal grill to high heat. Set up an elevated grill rack 18 inches above surface of coals, using a second grill rack that is set atop 2 stacks of 2 bricks each (see illustration on page 190).
4. Tie herb sprig bunches tightly to the handle of a long wooden spoon.
5. Remove pork from brine. Pat pork dry with paper towels; discard brine. Place pork on elevated grill rack; grill 1 minute on each side. Grill 8 minutes, turning every 2 minutes. Grill 1 minute on each edge of pork. Continue grilling until a thermometer registers 115°, turning and basting with herb brush and jalapeño glaze every 2 minutes (about 26 minutes total). Remove pork to a platter; lightly baste. Let stand 15 minutes. Maintain grill at medium-high heat.
6. Carefully remove the elevated grill rack and bricks. Place pork on the lower grill rack; grill 7 minutes or until thermometer registers 140°, turning and basting every 1 minute. Singe herbs for 5 seconds after final basting. Finely chop herbs; reserve.
7. Combine olive oil, parsley, black pepper, salt, and reserved chopped herbs on a cutting board. Add pork to oil mixture; turn to coat. Let stand 10 minutes. Cut pork into thin slices. Turn slices on board dressing to coat. Serve pork with dressing. Serves 8 (serving size: about 3 ounces and 2 teaspoons dressing)

CALORIES 286; **FAT** 10.5g (sat 3g, mono 5.7g, poly 0.8g); **PROTEIN** 21.1g; **CARB** 26.4g; **FIBER** 0.3g; **CHOL** 57mg; **IRON** 0.8mg; **SODIUM** 396mg; **CALC** 30mg

Clinched Double-Cut Loin Lamb Chops

Hands-on: 1 hr. 25 min. Total: 1 hr. 25 min. *The chops cook directly on the coals, a technique Perry Lang calls clinching. The direct contact serves to temper the heat and cook the meat more evenly.*

Basting liquid:
¼ cup extra-virgin olive oil
1 tablespoon chopped fresh thyme
1 teaspoon unsalted butter
½ teaspoon dried oregano
½ teaspoon freshly ground black pepper
¼ teaspoon kosher salt
¼ teaspoon crushed red pepper
3 garlic cloves, peeled and crushed
1 tablespoon lemon juice
Remaining ingredients:
1 bunch thyme sprigs
1 bunch rosemary sprigs
1 bunch sage sprigs
1½ teaspoons freshly ground black pepper, divided
¾ teaspoon kosher salt, divided
½ teaspoon garlic salt
¼ teaspoon ground red pepper
4 (1-pound) double-cut lamb chops, 2½ inches thick, trimmed
2 tablespoons chopped fresh flat-leaf parsley
2 tablespoons extra-virgin olive oil

1. To prepare basting liquid, combine first 8 ingredients in a saucepan. Bring to a simmer over medium heat.

continued

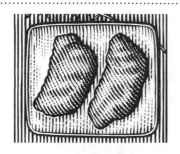

PAUSE BREAK

We all know the importance of letting cooked meat rest for a few minutes before slicing so the juices can redistribute. But Perry Lang also gives his meat a rest during the grilling process. He pulls meats from the grill when they've hit a certain temp, then bastes generously as they rest for 15 minutes or so. The oil baste helps keep the meat warm and seals in moisture. In conjunction with his frequent flipping, Perry Lang's pause break helps meat cook more evenly and serves a handy logistical purpose: It helps the chef better control the pace of cooking when grilling several steaks or chops at once.

SCRUFFING

Scruffing is all about increasing meat's surface area so there's more yummy stuff in the end. Perry Lang doesn't call for oiling the grill rack before grilling—he wants the meat to stick a little. The surface tears when you flip the meat, making nooks and crannies for delicious browning. For nonstick grill racks, Perry Lang advises lightly scoring the surface of the meat to create more surface area from the start.

Remove from heat; stir in juice. Let stand 1 hour.

2. Preheat a charcoal fire to high heat. Let burn 30 minutes or until flames subside and the coals are glowing. Spread coals to an even 4-inch thickness; fan excess ash from coals with a piece of cardboard.

3. Tie herb sprig bunches tightly to the handle of a long wooden spoon. Combine 1 teaspoon black pepper, ½ teaspoon salt, garlic salt, and red pepper in a small bowl. Rub lamb chops with spice mixture. Let stand 10 minutes.

4. Place lamb chops directly on coals, and grill 3 minutes, without moving, basting occasionally with basting liquid using herb brush. Turn lamb, baste, and cook 3 minutes. Repeat process twice; cook until a thermometer registers 120° or until desired degree of doneness. Singe herbs for 5 seconds after final basting. Finely chop herbs; reserve.

5. Combine parsley, 2 tablespoons oil, ¼ teaspoon salt, ½ teaspoon black pepper, and reserved chopped herbs on a cutting board. Add lamb to oil mixture; turn to coat. Let stand 5 minutes. Remove lamb from bones; discard bones. Cut lamb across grain into thin slices. Turn slices on board dressing to coat. Serve lamb with dressing. Serves 8 (serving size: about 3 ounces meat and 2 teaspoons dressing)

CALORIES 251; **FAT** 17g (sat 4g, mono 10.1g, poly 1.7g); **PROTEIN** 22g; **CARB** 1.2g; **FIBER** 0.3g; **CHOL** 71mg; **IRON** 2.3mg; **SODIUM** 374mg; **CALC** 22mg

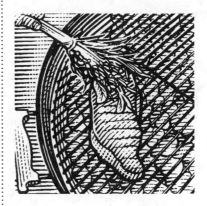

BASTING

Basting meat as it grills is critical to keep it from drying out over the intense heat of the flame. But exactly when to baste for best results is something that most backyard chefs don't consider. Perry Lang starts basting food only when it's partly cooked. "There's no point in basting raw meats," he explains. "You're not basting there; you're rinsing."

Once the meat develops an exterior crust, Perry Lang bastes immediately after turning it, on the "sizzling" side. This approach allows the basting liquid to interact with the meat's bubbling-hot surface, which better melds the flavors. And because Perry Lang bastes his grilled items with a brush made from fresh herb sprigs, heat from the meat draws essential oils out of the herbs, flavoring it even more. He turns the meat frequently so that it cooks evenly, and he bastes with every turn to thoroughly flavor it with the herbs and the oil-based basting liquid.

BASIC BRINE

Combine 5 cups water, ¼ cup kosher salt, 1 tablespoon black peppercorns, 1 tablespoon chopped fresh thyme, 1 tablespoon sugar, 8 garlic cloves, 3 bay leaves, and 1 halved lemon in a medium saucepan; bring to a boil. Remove from heat; cool. Refrigerate brine overnight.

Clinched and Planked Shrimp

Hands-on: 48 min. Total: 2 hr. 48 min.
The cedar plank lends the shrimp smoky flavor and amazing deep golden color. It makes a genuinely impressive dish for company.

Basic Brine (recipe page 188)
2 pounds large shrimp, unpeeled
2 (15 x 6¹⁄₂ x ³⁄₈-inch) cedar grilling planks
¹⁄₄ cup extra-virgin olive oil
1 tablespoon grated garlic
1 tablespoon thyme leaves
1 teaspoon sugar
1 teaspoon unsalted butter, melted
1 teaspoon lower-sodium soy sauce
¹⁄₂ teaspoon freshly ground black pepper
¹⁄₄ teaspoon kosher salt
¹⁄₄ teaspoon crushed red pepper
¹⁄₄ cup (¹⁄₂-inch) pieces chives
1 teaspoon fresh lemon juice

1. Prepare Basic Brine, increasing water to 8 cups, thyme and sugar to 2 tablespoons each, and halved lemons to 2.
2. Split shrimp shells down the back, and devein shrimp, leaving shells intact. Place shrimp in a large bowl; add brine. Cover bowl; refrigerate 1 hour.
3. Immerse and soak the cedar planks in water for 1 hour; drain.
4. Preheat a charcoal fire to high heat. Let burn 30 minutes or until flames subside and coals are glowing. Spread coals to an even 4-inch thickness; fan excess ash from coals with a piece of cardboard.
5. Drain shrimp; discard brine. Pat shrimp dry with paper towels. Combine oil and next 8 ingredients (through red pepper) in a large bowl, stirring with a whisk. Add shrimp; toss to coat. Arrange shrimp in 2 tight rows on each plank, with shrimp curled against each other.
6. Place plank on the coal bed with some coals on the exposed corners of the plank. Cover with grill lid; grill

6 minutes or until shrimp are done. Place shrimp on a platter; top with chives and juice. Serves 8 (serving size: about 4 shrimp)

CALORIES 151; FAT 8.4g (sat 1.4g, mono 5.1g, poly 0.9g); PROTEIN 15.6g; CARB 2.4g; FIBER 0.2g; CHOL 144mg; IRON 0.4mg; SODIUM 539mg; CALC 67mg

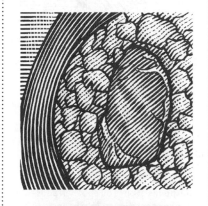

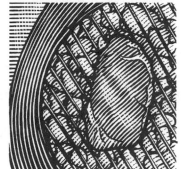

CLINCHING

Perry Lang named this technique after a boxing strategy in which a smaller fighter hangs on to his longer-armed opponent to lessen the punch threat. In grilling terms, clinched meat cooks directly on the coals (or on a rack placed in contact with the coals). Counterintuitive as it may seem, "it's actually cooler on the coals," Perry Lang explains. "They're transmitting heat in a tempered way." It also prevents flare-ups that overchar the meat.

Use hardwood lump charcoal, not briquettes: Lump coal is a natural material that keeps its structural integrity much better as it burns.

High-Low Strip Steak

Hands-on: 60 min. Total: 9 hr. The first grilling, at a cooler temperature, helps cook the steaks evenly. The second, after they rest, gives the beef delectable coal-fire flavor. Don't oil the grill rack before cooking—you want some of the meat to stick to the rack and tear, exposing more surface area to the fire in a process Perry Lang calls scruffing. You can use a foil-wrapped brick on the grill rack to hold the steak steady while it cooks and browns on its edges.

Basting liquid:
¹⁄₄ cup extra-virgin olive oil
2 tablespoons grated fresh onion
1 tablespoon chopped fresh thyme
1 tablespoon sugar
1 tablespoon grated garlic
1 teaspoon unsalted butter
1 teaspoon Worcestershire sauce
¹⁄₂ teaspoon freshly ground black pepper
¹⁄₄ teaspoon kosher salt
¹⁄₄ teaspoon crushed red pepper
Remaining ingredients:
1 bunch thyme sprigs
1 bunch rosemary sprigs
1 bunch sage sprigs
1¹⁄₂ teaspoons freshly ground black pepper, divided
³⁄₄ teaspoon kosher salt, divided
¹⁄₂ teaspoon garlic salt
¹⁄₄ teaspoon ground red pepper
2 (1-pound) New York strip steaks, trimmed
2 tablespoons chopped fresh flat-leaf parsley
2 tablespoons extra-virgin olive oil

1. To prepare basting liquid, combine first 10 ingredients in a saucepan; bring to a simmer over medium heat. Remove from heat; refrigerate in an airtight container overnight or up to 2 days.
2. Preheat charcoal grill to high heat.
continued

Set up an elevated grill rack 18 inches above surface of coals, using a second grill rack set atop 2 stacks of 2 bricks each (see illustration at right). Tie herb sprig bunches tightly to the handle of a long wooden spoon.

3. Combine 1 teaspoon black pepper, ½ teaspoon salt, garlic salt, and red pepper in a small bowl. Rub steaks with spice mixture; let stand 10 minutes. Place steaks on elevated grill rack; grill 3 minutes. Turn steaks; grill 3 minutes. Turn onto long edge; grill 3 minutes. Turn onto second long edge; grill 3 minutes or until thermometer registers 95°. Remove steaks to a platter; baste with basting liquid using herb brush. Let stand 15 minutes. Maintain grill at medium-high heat.

4. Carefully remove elevated grill rack and bricks. Place steaks on lower grill rack. Grill steaks 6 minutes or until desired degree of doneness, turning and basting every minute. Singe herbs on herb brush for 5 seconds after final basting. Finely chop herbs; reserve.

5. Combine parsley, 2 tablespoons oil, ½ teaspoon black pepper, ¼ teaspoon salt, and reserved chopped herbs on a cutting board. Add steaks to oil mixture; turn to coat. Let stand 5 minutes. Cut steaks across grain into thin slices. Turn slices in board dressing to coat. Serve steaks with dressing. Serves 8 (serving size: about 3 ounces steak and 2 teaspoons dressing)

CALORIES 265; FAT 17.2g (sat 4.2g, mono 10.2g, poly 1.3g); PROTEIN 24.6g; CARB 1.9g; FIBER 0.3g; CHOL 70mg; IRON 1.9mg; SODIUM 359mg; CALC 27mg

BOARD DRESSING

Perry Lang's four tricks guarantee juicy meat with an ultra-tasty exterior, and this step makes every bite sing with flavor. He first drizzles the cutting board with a few tablespoons of olive oil and then adds some chopped aromatics and herbs, including some from the herb brush used for basting. The meat has its final rest on this mixture. When it's sliced, meat juices mix with the dressing. Because of the oil coating, the juices float rather than seep into the board, where, sadly, they'd be lost. Perry Lang coats the meat slices in the board dressing, the simplest yet most perfect à la minute sauce for grilled meats.

ELEVATED RACK

Use 4–6 bricks to prop up a second grill rack and make two temperature zones.

Clinched and Planked Chicken Thighs
(pictured on page 228)

Hands-on: 65 min. Total: 9 hr. 5 min. You can improvise on the board dressing, adding grated garlic or shallots (use a Microplane grater), finely chopped chiles, chopped green onions, or chopped herbs such as thyme, rosemary, and sage.

Basting liquid:
¼ cup extra-virgin olive oil
2 tablespoons grated fresh onion
1 tablespoon chopped fresh thyme
1 tablespoon sugar
1 tablespoon grated garlic
1 teaspoon unsalted butter
1 teaspoon Worcestershire sauce
½ teaspoon freshly ground black pepper
¼ teaspoon kosher salt
¼ teaspoon crushed red pepper
Remaining ingredients:
Basic Brine (page 188)
8 bone-in chicken thighs, each sliced to the bone in a few places
2 (15 x 6½ x ⅜-inch) cedar grilling planks
1 bunch thyme sprigs
1 bunch rosemary sprigs
1 bunch sage sprigs
2 tablespoons white wine vinegar
1 tablespoon fresh lemon juice
2 tablespoons finely chopped fresh flat-leaf parsley
2 tablespoons extra-virgin olive oil
½ teaspoon freshly ground black pepper
¼ teaspoon kosher salt
1 tablespoon chopped fresh tarragon

1. To prepare basting liquid, combine first 10 ingredients in a saucepan. Bring to a simmer over medium heat. Remove from heat; refrigerate in an airtight container overnight or up to 2 days.

2. Combine Basic Brine and chicken thighs in a large bowl; refrigerate 3 hours. Drain; discard brine and solids. Pat chicken thighs dry with paper towels. Let stand at room temperature 30 minutes.

3. Immerse and soak the cedar planks in water for 1 hour; drain.

4. Preheat a charcoal fire to high heat. Let burn 30 minutes or until flames subside and coals are glowing. Spread coals to an even 4-inch thickness; fan excess ash from coals with a piece of cardboard.

5. Tie herb sprig bunches tightly to the handle of a long wooden spoon.

6. Arrange thighs, skin sides down, directly on the coals; grill 2 minutes, without moving. Turn, baste with basting liquid using herb brush, and grill 2 minutes. Repeat procedure twice. Remove thighs to a platter, skin sides up, and baste. Let stand 5 minutes. Add vinegar and juice to remaining basting liquid.

7. Arrange 4 thighs, skin sides up, on each plank. Baste thighs. Place planks directly on the coal bed; cover grill. Grill 11 minutes or until juices run clear when thigh is pierced with a fork. Singe herbs for 5 seconds after final basting. Finely chop herbs; reserve.

8. Combine parsley, 2 tablespoons oil, ½ teaspoon pepper, ¼ teaspoon salt, and reserved chopped herbs on a cutting board. Add thighs to oil mixture; turn to coat. Sprinkle with tarragon; let stand 3 minutes. Serve thighs with dressing. Serves 8 (serving size: 1 thigh and 2 teaspoons dressing)

CALORIES 335; **FAT** 25g (sat 5.8g, mono 13.8g, poly 4g); **PROTEIN** 22.8g; **CARB** 3.1g; **FIBER** 0.3g; **CHOL** 136mg; **IRON** 1.3mg; **SODIUM** 502mg; **CALC** 20mg

SIDES IN FIVE

That's right. No cheating! Bold, interesting, real flavors in just five minutes

Quick & Easy • Vegetarian
Beet-Citrus Salad with Pistachios

Hands-on: 5 min. Total: 5 min. This is a fresh, bright, zero-effort side, thanks to pre-cooked beets and precut fresh citrus. It makes a fine accompaniment to grilled salmon, pork, or chicken. Leave the nuts whole so they add significant crunch.

½ **teaspoon grated orange rind**
2 **tablespoons fresh orange juice**
1 **tablespoon extra-virgin olive oil**
½ **teaspoon ground cumin**
¼ **teaspoon kosher salt**
¼ **teaspoon freshly ground black pepper**
1 **(20-ounce) jar refrigerated citrus salad (such as Del Monte), drained**
1 **(8-ounce) package steamed, ready-to-eat beets, rinsed, drained, and cut into wedges**
¼ **cup shelled dry-roasted, unsalted pistachios**

1. Combine first 6 ingredients; stir with a whisk. Add citrus and beets; toss gently. Sprinkle with pistachios. Serves 4 (serving size: ¾ cup)

CALORIES 156; **FAT** 6.9g (sat 0.9g, mono 4.3g, poly 1.4g); **PROTEIN** 2.4g; **CARB** 20.3g; **FIBER** 2.8g; **CHOL** 0mg; **IRON** 0.9mg; **SODIUM** 141mg; **CALC** 40mg

Kid Friendly • Quick & Easy
Vegetarian
Greek Salad Cucumbers

Hands-on: 4 min. Total: 4 min. The vinegar is quite pumped-up because there's not much time for the cukes to pick up much flavor otherwise. Serve with grilled steak or chicken or beef kebabs.

1 **English cucumber, cut into quarters lengthwise and then crosswise**
2 **tablespoons red wine vinegar**
2 **teaspoons extra-virgin olive oil**
¼ **teaspoon sugar**
¼ **teaspoon kosher salt**
¼ **teaspoon black pepper**
1 **ounce feta cheese, crumbled (about ¼ cup)**
1 **tablespoon finely chopped fresh dill**

1. Place cucumber in a shallow dish. Combine vinegar and next 4 ingredients in a small bowl, stirring with a whisk. Drizzle vinegar mixture over cucumbers; sprinkle with cheese and dill. Serves 4 (serving size: 4 cucumber pieces)

CALORIES 49; **FAT** 3.8g (sat 1.4g, mono 2g, poly 0.3g); **PROTEIN** 1.8g; **CARB** 2.1g; **FIBER** 0.8g; **CHOL** 6mg; **IRON** 0.4mg; **SODIUM** 200mg; **CALC** 51mg

Yogurt Rice with Cumin and Chile

Hands-on: 5 min. Total: 5 min. *Using whole containers of rice and yogurt saves the time of measuring. Be sure to use standard yogurt here; Greek is a bit too thick.*

2 (8.5-ounce) pouches precooked white basmati rice (such as Uncle Ben's)
1 tablespoon canola oil
1 tablespoon bottled minced fresh ginger
1 teaspoon cumin seeds
1 serrano chile, thinly sliced
2 tablespoons chopped fresh cilantro
3/4 teaspoon kosher salt
1 (6-ounce) container plain low-fat yogurt

1. Heat rice according to package directions.
2. Heat a large skillet over medium-high heat. Add oil; swirl. Add ginger, cumin, and chile; sauté 30 seconds. Stir in rice, cilantro, salt, and yogurt; cook 1 minute. Serves 6 (serving size: ½ cup)

CALORIES 173; **FAT** 4.6g (sat 0.8g, mono 2.1g, poly 1.4g); **PROTEIN** 4.9g; **CARB** 29g; **FIBER** 0.7g; **CHOL** 2mg; **IRON** 1.2mg; **SODIUM** 265mg; **CALC** 56mg

SERVE WITH GRILLED LAMB CHOPS, ROASTED CHICKEN, OR GRILLED SALMON.

SO COLORFUL, SO DELICIOUS, SO RIDICULOUSLY EASY!

Tequila Slaw with Lime and Cilantro

Hands-on: 5 min. Total: 5 min. *Grab a bag of packaged coleslaw mix, and you've saved yourself the time of slicing cabbage and shredding carrots. A splash of tequila adds spirit and complexity (we urge you not to leave it out), while lime juice's zing perks up earthy cabbage. Serve on tacos, alongside barbecue chicken, with grilled flank or skirt steak, or with (or on) burgers.*

1/4 cup canola mayonnaise (such as Hellmann's)
3 tablespoons fresh lime juice
1 tablespoon silver tequila
2 teaspoons sugar
1/4 teaspoon kosher salt
1/3 cup thinly sliced green onions
1/4 cup chopped fresh cilantro
1 (14-ounce) package coleslaw

1. Combine first 5 ingredients in a large bowl. Add remaining ingredients; toss. Serves 6 (serving size: about 2/3 cup)

CALORIES 64; **FAT** 3g (sat 0g, mono 1.7g, poly 1g); **PROTEIN** 0.8g; **CARB** 6.4g; **FIBER** 1.8g; **CHOL** 0mg; **IRON** 0.1mg; **SODIUM** 162mg; **CALC** 37mg

Sautéed Snap Peas with Ricotta Salata and Mint

Hands-on: 5 min. Total: 5 min. *Floral lemon zest (but no tart juice) allows the sweet pea flavor to shine. Chop mint, grate lemon rind, and crumble cheese while the peas cook. Serve with panini or other sandwiches, grilled chicken, or pork chops.*

1 tablespoon olive oil
2 (8-ounce) packages trimmed sugar snap peas
3 tablespoons chopped fresh mint
1 1/2 teaspoons grated lemon rind
3/8 teaspoon freshly ground black pepper
1/4 teaspoon kosher salt
1.5 ounces ricotta salata or goat cheese, crumbled (about 1/3 cup)

1. Heat a large skillet over medium-high heat. Add oil to pan; swirl. Add peas; sauté 3 minutes or until crisp-tender. Stir in mint, rind, pepper, and salt. Sprinkle with cheese. Serves 6 (serving size: about 1 cup)

CALORIES 75; **FAT** 4.3g (sat 1.5g, mono 1.6g, poly 0.2g); **PROTEIN** 3.1g; **CARB** 6.1g; **FIBER** 1.9g; **CHOL** 8mg; **IRON** 1.7mg; **SODIUM** 197mg; **CALC** 39mg

THE FRESHEST FIVE

Easy recipes for August's sweetest, most delicious market and garden produce

Quick & Easy
BLT Panzanella Salad
(pictured on page 229)

Hands-on: 25 min. Total: 25 min. *Use the showiest farmers' market or garden tomatoes in a dish that deliciously combines a favorite sandwich and a classic Italian salad, with a touch of corn and basil thrown in for extra summery flair.*

1 tablespoon unsalted butter
3 ounces Italian bread, crusts trimmed, torn into ¼-inch pieces
¾ cup fresh corn kernels
4 large ripe heirloom tomatoes, cored and cut crosswise into ¼-inch-thick slices
1 cup small multicolored cherry tomatoes, halved
⅛ teaspoon plus dash of kosher salt, divided
¾ teaspoon freshly ground black pepper, divided
2 teaspoons balsamic vinegar
2 teaspoons extra-virgin olive oil
1 cup baby arugula
3 tablespoons canola mayonnaise (such as Hellmann's)
1 tablespoon fresh lemon juice
2 teaspoons minced fresh chives
¼ cup thinly sliced basil leaves
3 applewood-smoked bacon slices, cooked and crumbled

1. Melt butter in a large skillet over medium-high heat. Add bread; sauté 5 minutes or until bread is toasted, stirring occasionally. Remove from heat; stir in corn.
2. Sprinkle tomatoes with dash of salt and ½ teaspoon pepper; let tomatoes stand 5 minutes.
3. Combine ⅛ teaspoon salt, ¼ teaspoon pepper, vinegar, and oil in a large bowl. Add bread mixture and arugula; toss to coat. Combine mayonnaise, lemon juice, and chives in a small bowl.
4. Arrange tomatoes and bread mixture on a large platter. Drizzle with mayonnaise mixture; sprinkle evenly with basil and bacon. Serves 6

CALORIES 150; FAT 8.5g (sat 2.5g, mono 3g, poly 1.3g); PROTEIN 4.7g; CARB 15.1g; FIBER 2.3g; CHOL 10mg; IRON 0.9mg; SODIUM 299mg; CALC 33mg

TOMATOES

If you're growing tomatoes, you'll need to pick them at the right time: Heirlooms should be picked before they're fully ripe; most others should be picked when the color has evened out (i.e., a red tomato turns fully red). In the market, choose tomatoes with bright, shiny skins that feel firm but give slightly to gentle pressure. Never store in the refrigerator—the flesh will go mealy. If you need to ripen, as with those early harvested heirlooms, do so at room temperature, out of direct sunlight.

WATERMELON

There are all kinds of folksy tricks for choosing a good watermelon, from thumping the rind to shaking them. The most reliable method we know is to pick up the fruit and gauge its relative heft; you want it to seem almost surprisingly heavy for its size, a good indication that it's juicy with firm flesh. Also, look for a pale yellow spot on the bottom of the melon, which indicates where it sat on the ground and ripened on the vine.

Kid Friendly • Make Ahead
Vegetarian
Watermelon with Tangy Granita

Hands-on: 20 min. Total: 3 hr. 20 min. *Juicy-crisp watermelon chunks turn extra-refreshing with a cold topping of slushy cucumber-lime granita. If you have access to both, use red and yellow watermelon.*

1 cup water
¾ cup sugar
½ cup fresh lime juice
⅓ cup packed mint leaves
⅓ cup packed cilantro leaves
¼ teaspoon kosher salt
¼ teaspoon crushed red pepper
1 tablespoon grated lime rind
1 cucumber, peeled and seeded
8 cups (¾-inch) cubed watermelon
½ teaspoon kosher salt

1. Combine 1 cup water and sugar in a microwave-safe dish. Microwave at HIGH 2 minutes; cool completely. Place syrup, juice, and next 6 ingredients (through cucumber) in a blender; blend until smooth. Pour mixture into an 11 x 7–inch glass baking dish; cover and freeze 3 hours or until firm, stirring with a fork every 45 minutes. Remove mixture from freezer; scrape entire mixture with a fork until fluffy.

continued

2. Place watermelon cubes in a large bowl. Sprinkle with salt; toss to combine. Let stand 10 minutes. Spoon about 1½ cups watermelon mixture into each of 6 bowls; top each serving with about ½ cup granita. Serves 6

CALORIES 170; FAT 0.4g (sat 0g, mono 0.1g, poly 0.1g); PROTEIN 1.6g; CARB 43.4g; FIBER 1.3g; CHOL 0mg; IRON 0.6mg; SODIUM 244mg; CALC 25mg

PEACHES

Locally grown peaches are best. Since they haven't traveled far, it's more likely they were allowed to ripen on the tree and were plucked just a day or two before you bought them. Once harvested, peaches soften but don't continue to ripen. When they're as soft as you want them, move them to the refrigerator, but bring them to room temperature before eating for the best flavor. The best sign of a sublime peach is its sweet fragrance.

Kid Friendly • Make Ahead
Vegetarian

Peachy Almond Shortcakes

Hands-on: 25 min. Total: 50 min.

2.25 ounces almond flour (about ½ cup)
4.5 ounces all-purpose flour (about 1 cup)
¼ cup granulated sugar
1 teaspoon baking powder
⅛ teaspoon salt
¼ cup chilled butter
¼ cup reduced-fat buttermilk
2 tablespoons canola oil
1 tablespoon amaretto
Cooking spray
2 cups sliced peaches
1 tablespoon powdered sugar
1 teaspoon fresh lime juice
½ cup frozen reduced-fat whipped topping, thawed

1. Preheat oven to 350°.
2. Place almond flour in a dry skillet over medium heat. Cook 4 minutes or until lightly browned, stirring occasionally. Remove from pan. Cool.
3. Weigh or lightly spoon all-purpose flour into a dry measuring cup; level with a knife. Combine flours, sugar, baking powder, and salt in a medium bowl, stirring with a whisk; cut in butter with a pastry blender until mixture resembles coarse meal. Combine buttermilk, oil, and amaretto; add to flour mixture, stirring just until moist. Turn dough out onto a lightly floured surface; knead lightly 5 to 7 times with floured hands. Divide dough into 2 equal pieces. Pat each piece into a 4-inch circle on a baking sheet coated with cooking spray. Cut each circle into 4 wedges, cutting into but not through dough. Bake at 350° for 27 minutes or until golden. Cut rounds into wedges.
4. Combine peaches, powdered sugar, and lime juice. Split each shortcake wedge in half horizontally. Place 1 wedge on each of 8 dessert plates; fill each with ¼ cup peach mixture and 1 tablespoon whipped topping. Serves 8

CALORIES 246; FAT 13.9g (sat 4.8g, mono 6g, poly 2.2g); PROTEIN 4g; CARB 27.4g; FIBER 1.7g; CHOL 16mg; IRON 1.2mg; SODIUM 97mg; CALC 78mg

BASIL

For the sweetest flavor, choose basil whose leaves are free of bruising. Often, a plant is your best option—and as a bonus, you can keep the pot on your windowsill and snip from it whenever you need a little licorice-flavored hit. Thai basil has purple stems and a more peppery flavor; look for it in Asian markets, and seek out pristine leaves. If either type of basil is flowering, it might be bitter.

Quick & Easy
Grilled Chicken Thighs with Thai Basil Salad

Hands-on: 26 min. Total: 40 min. *A mix of Thai basil and sweet basil makes for a satisfying aromatic salad with no lettuce "filler." Cucumber and shallots offer a bit of crunch. If you can't find Thai basil, use whichever variety you can find. Look for explosively hot Thai chiles at Asian markets, or use serranos.*

1 tablespoon fish sauce, divided
1 tablespoon lower-sodium soy sauce
2 teaspoons sugar, divided
1 pound skinless, boneless chicken thighs
1 large garlic clove, minced
2 tablespoons fresh lime juice
1 tablespoon dark sesame oil
1½ Thai chiles, very thinly sliced
Cooking spray
2 cups lightly packed Thai basil leaves
1 English cucumber, halved crosswise and shaved lengthwise (about 2 cups)
1 cup lightly packed sweet basil leaves, large leaves torn in half
⅓ cup lightly packed cilantro leaves
⅓ cup very thinly sliced shallots

1. Preheat grill to high heat.
2. Combine 1 teaspoon fish sauce, soy sauce, and 1 teaspoon sugar in a large zip-top plastic bag. Add chicken; seal bag, and shake to coat. Let stand at room temperature 15 minutes.
3. While chicken marinates, mash garlic with flat side of a knife to form a paste; place in a bowl. Add 2 teaspoons fish sauce, 1 teaspoon sugar, lime juice, oil, and chiles to garlic, stirring well; let stand at room temperature 15 minutes.

4. Remove chicken from bag. Place chicken on grill rack coated with cooking spray; grill 3 minutes on each side or until chicken is done. Remove chicken from grill. Let stand 5 minutes. Cut chicken into slices.

5. Place Thai basil leaves, cucumber, sweet basil leaves, cilantro leaves, and shallots in a large bowl; toss gently to combine. Divide salad and chicken evenly among 4 plates; drizzle evenly with dressing. Serves 4 (serving size: about 3 ounces chicken and about 1 cup salad)

CALORIES 205; FAT 8.6g (sat 1.7g, mono 3.2g, poly 2.7g); PROTEIN 24.1g; CARB 8.6g; FIBER 1.3g; CHOL 108mg; IRON 2.4mg; SODIUM 489mg; CALC 83mg

Wine Note

German riesling, like the Mosel River Valley's Clean Slate Riesling, 2011 ($10), is a perfect pairing for many Asian dishes, especially spicy ones like Grilled Chicken Thighs with Thai Basil Salad. Its low alcohol and subtle sweetness soothe any heat, while brisk citrus and peach flavors beautifully complement assertive herbs like the basil and cilantro used here. —Jordan Mackay

Creamy Corn Risotto

Hands-on: 54 min. Total: 54 min.

1 large red bell pepper
4 cups fresh corn kernels (about 6 ears)
1³⁄₄ cups 1% low-fat milk
2 tablespoons butter, divided
2¹⁄₂ cups unsalted chicken stock
¹⁄₂ cup chopped onion
2 teaspoons minced fresh garlic
1 cup uncooked Arborio rice or other medium-grain rice
1 teaspoon salt
1 teaspoon freshly ground black pepper
¹⁄₄ cup dry white wine
¹⁄₂ cup sliced green onions

1. Preheat broiler to high.

2. Cut bell pepper in half lengthwise; discard seeds and membranes. Place pepper halves, skin sides up, on a foil-lined baking sheet; flatten with hand. Broil 8 minutes or until blackened. Wrap peppers in foil; let stand 5 minutes. Peel and chop.

3. Combine corn, milk, and 1 tablespoon butter in a saucepan. Bring to a simmer; cook 10 minutes. Stir in stock; keep warm over low heat.

4. Melt 1 tablespoon butter in a large saucepan over medium-high heat; swirl to coat. Add onion and garlic to pan; sauté 3 minutes. Stir in rice, salt, and black pepper; sauté 2 minutes, stirring constantly. Stir in wine; cook 30 seconds or until liquid almost evaporates, scraping pan to loosen browned bits. Reduce heat to medium. Stir in 1½ cups corn mixture; cook 3 minutes or until liquid is nearly absorbed, stirring constantly. Reserve ½ cup corn mixture. Add remaining corn mixture, 1 cup at a time, stirring frequently until each portion of corn mixture is absorbed before adding the next (about 20 minutes total). Remove pan from heat; stir in ½ cup corn mixture, bell pepper, and green onions. Serves 6 (serving size: 1 cup)

CALORIES 298; FAT 6.3g (sat 3.2g, mono 1.6g, poly 0.7g); PROTEIN 11g; CARB 51.7g; FIBER 4.4g; CHOL 14mg; IRON 1.1mg; SODIUM 531mg; CALC 115mg

CORN

For best flavor, choose the freshest ears you can find. Moist silks with lightly browned ends indicate corn that's ripe and ready to eat. (Pass over preshucked corn because it's often past its prime.) If the silks look good, peek inside the husk and check for plump kernels all the way to the tip. Pierce a kernel with your fingernail; if it's milky, you've struck gold. Store unshucked ears in the fridge for a day or two; shuck just before cooking.

TODAY'S SPECIAL

WARM SALAD OF SUMMER SQUASH

From MP Taverna in New York

Bumper crops of summer squash roll into farmers' markets and restaurants this time of year. New York chef Michael Psilakis, whose restaurants Fishtag, Kefi, and three locations of MP Taverna set the standard for modern Greek cuisine, has a deep appreciation for these mild, unassuming veggies and knows how to make the most of them.

The trick to cooking both zucchini and yellow squash, according to Psilakis, is to realize that they are like sponges, taking on flavors from the rest of the dish. They need a very hot pan or grill to put a flavorful sear on the exterior. "Don't cook it until it gets soggy. Leave some texture," he cautions. Season simply with salt and pepper, and then add an acidic touch: "A drop of lemon juice on a piece of zucchini really makes it sing."

In the pasta salad featured here, Psilakis adds raw squash blossoms as a grace note. "They're so delicate and yet more intensely flavored than the vegetable itself," he says. "This dish is the kind of thing you become known for and everybody asks about." Sample it this month at MP Taverna in Astoria.

continued

Warm Salad of Summer Squash with Swordfish and Feta

Hands-on: 15 min. Total: 30 min.

8 ounces uncooked penne pasta
3 tablespoons extra-virgin olive oil, divided
1 (10-ounce) swordfish steak
³/₄ teaspoon kosher salt, divided
³/₄ teaspoon freshly ground black pepper, divided
1 medium yellow squash, quartered lengthwise
1 medium zucchini, quartered lengthwise
8 squash blossoms, divided
¹/₄ cup mint leaves
¹/₄ cup basil leaves
¹/₄ cup dill fronds
3 tablespoons fresh lemon juice
2 ounces feta cheese, crumbled (about ¹/₂ cup)

1. Preheat grill to high heat.
2. Cook pasta according to package directions, omitting salt and fat. Drain pasta.
3. Drizzle 1 tablespoon oil evenly over fish; sprinkle with ¼ teaspoon salt and ¼ teaspoon pepper. Grill fish 5 minutes on each side or until desired degree of doneness. Remove from grill; let stand 5 minutes. Break into ¾-inch pieces.
4. Combine 1 tablespoon oil, squash, and zucchini in a large bowl; toss to coat. Sprinkle evenly with ¼ teaspoon salt and ¼ teaspoon pepper. Place vegetables, cut sides down, on grill rack; grill 3 minutes or until lightly charred and just tender. Cool slightly. Cut into 1-inch lengths.
5. Cut 4 squash blossoms into ¼-inch-wide strips. Combine blossom strips, pasta, fish, squash, zucchini, 1 table-spoon oil, ¼ teaspoon salt, ¼ teaspoon

pepper, herbs, and juice in a large bowl; toss to coat. Top with feta; garnish with remaining squash blossoms.
Serves 4 (serving size: about 2 cups)

CALORIES 458; FAT 19.1g (sat 5g, mono 10.2g, poly 2.1g); PROTEIN 25.2g; CARB 47.3g; FIBER 3g; CHOL 59mg; IRON 2.9mg; SODIUM 587mg; CALC 117mg

RECIPE MAKEOVER

SMOKIN' COBB SALAD

Our light version handily beats the classic loaded salad—in both flavor and nutrition.

The traditional Cobb is chock-full of so many good things: bacon, chicken, blue cheese, avocado, and hard-boiled egg—too much of those good things, in fact. What might seem at first like a virtuous dish blows up nutritionally. The classic recipe boasts 62 grams of fat and more than half a day's worth of sodium per serving.

Reducing the amount of bacon and blue cheese was a good reminder of how far a small amount of these intense ingredients goes. But the real calorie culprits were the oil-based dressing and the avocado. Yes, they offered heart-healthy fats, but they weighed the classic version down with more than 400 calories. We cut back on both, favoring the avocado because of its rich flavor. The result is a bright, creamy dressing with 65% less fat.

Our next trick involved rigging up

an easy stovetop smoker, which transformed ordinary chicken breast into a lower-sodium, flavor-packed star. Spinach and basil spruce up the romaine in our crisp, green base, and a sprinkle of crumbled blue cheese adds plenty of sharp, savory goodness.

Smoked Chicken Cobb Salad with Avocado Dressing

Hands-on: 30 min. Total: 48 min.

Avocado dressing:
¹/₂ cup diced peeled avocado
2 tablespoons extra-virgin olive oil
1 tablespoon fresh lemon juice
¹/₄ teaspoon kosher salt
¹/₄ teaspoon freshly ground black pepper
1 garlic clove, minced
3 tablespoons water
Salad:
3 center-cut bacon slices
1 teaspoon canola oil
2 (6-ounce) skinless, boneless chicken breast halves
1 cup hickory wood chips
¹/₃ cup unsalted chicken stock (such as Swanson)
4 cups baby spinach
4 cups romaine lettuce, coarsely chopped
¹/₂ cup chopped fresh basil leaves
¹/₃ cup diced peeled avocado
2 heirloom tomatoes, cut into ¹/₄-inch-thick slices
2 hard-cooked large eggs, chilled and quartered lengthwise
1.5 ounces blue cheese, crumbled

CLASSIC	MAKEOVER
717 calories per serving	333 calories per serving
62 grams total fat	21.7 grams total fat
1,244 milligrams sodium	487 milligrams sodium

1. To prepare dressing, place first 7 ingredients in a mini food processor; process until smooth.

2. To prepare salad, cook bacon in a nonstick skillet over medium heat until crisp. Remove bacon from pan; crumble. Add canola oil to pan; swirl to coat. Add chicken to pan; sauté 6 minutes on each side or until done. Cool slightly; shred with 2 forks.

3. Pierce 10 holes on one side of the bottom of a 13 x 9–inch disposable aluminum foil pan. Place holes over element on cooktop; place wood chips over holes inside pan. Place a shallow ovenproof bowl on opposite end of pan. Add chicken and stock to bowl. Heat element under holes to medium-high; let stand 1 minute or until chips begin to smoke. Carefully cover pan with foil. Reduce heat to low; smoke chicken 10 minutes. Remove from heat. Drain.

4. Combine spinach, romaine, and basil in a large bowl; toss. Arrange 2 cups spinach mixture on each of 4 plates. Divide bacon, chicken, ⅓ cup avocado, tomatoes, eggs, and cheese evenly among plates. Drizzle about 3 tablespoons dressing over each salad. Serves 4

CALORIES 333; FAT 21.7g (sat 5.8g, mono 11.1g, poly 2.8g); PROTEIN 27.2g; CARB 8.9g; FIBER 4.6g; CHOL 154mg; IRON 2.9mg; SODIUM 487mg; CALC 146mg

AVOCADOS' HEALTHY FATS ARE KEY TO OUR DRESSING, WHICH HAS 242 FEWER CALORIES THAN THE USUAL VINAIGRETTE

PICKED FRESH FOR AUGUST: TOMATOES

This month from the *Cooking Light* Garden: the iconic summer produce hero at its ripest, sweetest, and juiciest

For most people, the tomato would be the first plant they'd choose to grow in their own gardens," says Mary Beth Shaddix, who tends the *Cooking Light* Garden with her husband, David. "It's sort of the all-American garden hero." While strikingly colored, plump, juicy heirloom tomatoes have become much easier to find at farmers' markets and even supermarkets, there are so many varieties that you have to grow your own to really delve into the possibilities. Shaddix grew 14 types of heirloom tomatoes for us. The three featured here are wonderful, unusual tomatoes that stand in readily for round red hybrids and basic grape tomatoes yet offer much deeper tomato flavor. (You can find the other 11 types in our online collection of garden recipes at CookingLight.com/Garden.)

Make Ahead • Vegetarian
Pickled Tomatoes

Hands-on: 15 min. Total: 1 week 15 min.
Toast the spice seeds in a small skillet over medium heat, stirring constantly, until they become fragrant and start to release their flavorful oils.

1½ pounds grape or cherry tomatoes
2¾ cups water
3 tablespoons sugar
1¾ cups cider vinegar
¼ cup cilantro sprigs
¼ cup parsley sprigs
1 tablespoon kosher salt
1 teaspoon black peppercorns
1 teaspoon mustard seeds, toasted
1 teaspoon cumin seeds, toasted
1 teaspoon coriander seeds, toasted

1. Bring a large pot of water to boil. Cut an X in the base of each tomato. Add tomatoes to pot; boil 45 seconds. Rinse tomatoes under cold water until cool; peel. Discard skins. Place tomatoes in glass jars or a large glass bowl.
2. Combine 2¾ cups water and sugar in a small saucepan. Bring to a boil; cook 2 minutes or until sugar dissolves, stirring constantly. Remove from heat. Add vinegar and remaining ingredients to water mixture; cool to room temperature. Pour vinegar mixture over tomatoes. Cover and let stand in refrigerator 1 week. Serves 8 (serving size: about ½ cup)

CALORIES 29; FAT 0g; PROTEIN 1g; CARB 6.5g; FIBER 2g; CHOL 0mg; IRON 0mg; SODIUM 79mg; CALC 25mg

Bacon Endive Tomato Bites

Quick & Easy

Hands-on: 10 min. Total: 10 min.

1 cup sliced multicolored grape
 tomatoes
1 teaspoon thyme leaves
1 teaspoon chopped fresh chives
2 teaspoons champagne vinegar
1 teaspoon olive oil
$\frac{1}{4}$ teaspoon freshly ground black
 pepper
$\frac{1}{8}$ teaspoon salt
16 Belgian endive leaves (about 2
 heads)
2 center-cut bacon slices, cooked and
 crumbled

1. Combine first 7 ingredients in a
medium bowl. Spoon 1 tablespoon tomato mixture in center of each endive
leaf; sprinkle evenly with bacon. Serves
4 (serving size: 4 stuffed endive leaves)

CALORIES 38; FAT 2.2g (sat 0.7g, mono 0.8g, poly 0.1g);
PROTEIN 1.7g; CARB 3.6g; FIBER 2g; CHOL 4mg;
IRON 0.2mg; SODIUM 144mg; CALC 16mg

USE MULTICOLORED TOMATOES FOR THE PRETTIEST TERRINE.

Heirloom Tomato and Eggplant Terrine

Make Ahead • Vegetarian

Hands-on: 33 min. Total: 10 hr. 33 min.

4 medium heirloom tomatoes, cut into
 $\frac{1}{4}$-inch-thick slices
1 cup water
2 garlic cloves, crushed
1 medium leek, chopped
1 medium tomato, quartered
$\frac{3}{4}$ teaspoon salt, divided
$\frac{1}{2}$ teaspoon freshly ground black
 pepper, divided
1 tablespoon unflavored gelatin
6 ($\frac{1}{4}$-inch-thick) slices medium
 eggplant
1$\frac{1}{2}$ tablespoons extra-virgin olive oil
Cooking spray
4 ounces fresh mozzarella cheese, cut
 into $\frac{1}{8}$-inch-thick slices
1 tablespoon chopped thyme leaves,
 divided
1 tablespoon finely chopped fresh chives,
 divided

1. Preheat oven to 450°.
2. Place heirloom tomato slices on
several layers of paper towels. Top
with a single layer of paper towels. Let
stand 15 minutes.
3. Combine 1 cup water, garlic, leek,
and quartered tomato in a medium
saucepan; bring to a boil. Reduce heat;
simmer 10 minutes. Strain through a
sieve over a bowl, pressing to extract
liquid; discard solids. Pour liquid into
pan; stir in $\frac{1}{2}$ teaspoon salt and $\frac{1}{4}$ teaspoon pepper. Cool to room tempera-
ture. Sprinkle with gelatin; let stand 5
minutes. Bring gelatin mixture to a boil;
boil 3 minutes. Remove mixture from
heat.

4. Lightly brush eggplant slices with
oil; arrange in a single layer on a
baking sheet coated with parchment
paper. Bake at 450° for 10 minutes;
turn and bake an additional 5 minutes
or until tender.
5. Lightly coat a 9 x 5–inch loaf pan
with cooking spray. Line pan with
plastic wrap. Arrange tomato slices
in a double layer on bottom of pan;
sprinkle with $\frac{1}{4}$ teaspoon salt and
$\frac{1}{4}$ teaspoon pepper. Top tomatoes with
a thin layer of cheese; sprinkle with
1$\frac{1}{2}$ teaspoons thyme and 1$\frac{1}{2}$ teaspoons
chives. Arrange 3 eggplant slices over
cheese. Repeat layers, ending with
tomatoes. Pour gelatin mixture over
terrine. Cover with plastic wrap. Chill
8 hours or overnight.
6. Turn terrine out onto a platter. Let
stand 1 hour (or until room temperature). Serves 12 (serving size: 1 slice)

CALORIES 78; FAT 4.7g (sat 2g, mono 1.3g, poly 0.3g);
PROTEIN 3.2g; CARB 6.9g; FIBER 2.7g; CHOL 7mg;
IRON 0.5mg; SODIUM 182mg; CALC 19mg

TOMATO VARIETIES

RED FIG
These fig/pear-shaped cherry tomatoes
are most delicious when dried in a
dehydrator or super-low oven (200° or
less). The process turns them intensely
sweet.

BONNIE BEST
This substantial slicer usually weighs about
half a pound. Solid and meaty, it has enough
acid to can well. Great raw or cooked, too.

FLAME
When sliced open, the flesh of this
gorgeous tomato—also known as Hillbilly—
matches the variegated skin color.

NO-COOK ICE CREAM

I t's tricky enough to pull off no-cook ice cream when you have loads of sat fat–laden cream to take the place of silky stovetop custard. But when you lighten this frozen treat, it's an even bigger challenge to get smooth, creamy results. Without a lot of fat, the ice cream wants to turn into an icy, grainy mess. After many failed attempts, we finally found success with a mix of whole milk, marshmallow creme, and crème fraîche. A little corn syrup helps prevent ice crystals from forming so the texture stays creamy. Use an old-fashioned churn for best results; tabletop models simply don't whip in enough air to keep the ice cream fluffy. Our base recipe is best straight from the churn; the longer it "ripens," the harder it will freeze.

Kid Friendly • Freezable
Make Ahead • Vegetarian

No-Cook Vanilla Ice Cream

Hands-on: 15 min. Total: 2 hr. 15 min.

²/₃ cup sugar
2 teaspoons vanilla bean paste
¹/₄ teaspoon salt
1 (7.5-ounce) jar marshmallow creme
¹/₂ cup crème fraîche
4 cups whole milk, divided
2 tablespoons light-colored corn syrup

1. Combine first 4 ingredients; beat with a mixer until smooth. Beat in crème fraîche and 1 cup milk. Stir in 3 cups milk and corn syrup. Pour into the freezer can of an ice-cream freezer; freeze according to manufacturer's instructions. Serves 8 (serving size: about ¾ cup)

CALORIES 247; FAT 9.2g (sat 5.5g, mono 2.5g, poly 0.5g); PROTEIN 4.3g; CARB 49.7g; FIBER 0g; CHOL 26mg; IRON 0.1mg; SODIUM 150mg; CALC 139mg

Variation 1: Blackberry Swirl Ice Cream
Prepare No-Cook Vanilla Ice Cream. Place 1 cup blackberries and 1 tablespoon fresh lemon juice in a food processor; process until smooth. Strain the berry mixture through a fine sieve over a bowl; discard solids. Scrape ice cream into a freezer-safe container. Drizzle berry mixture over top of ice cream; swirl gently. Cover and freeze 1 hour. Serves 8 (serving size: about ¾ cup)

CALORIES 255; FAT 9.2g (sat 5.5g); SODIUM 150mg

Variation 2: Chocolate-Almond Ice Cream with Coconut
Prepare No-Cook Vanilla Ice Cream, increasing sugar to 1 cup and adding ½ cup unsweetened dark cocoa to sugar. Stir ⅓ cup chopped salted roasted almonds into ice cream; scrape ice cream into a freezer-safe container. Cover and freeze 2 hours or until firm. Scoop about ¾ cup ice cream into each of 9 bowls; sprinkle ⅓ cup toasted unsweetened shaved coconut evenly over ice cream. Serves 9

CALORIES 289; FAT 11.1g (sat 5.5g); SODIUM 150mg

1. ADD SOME AIR
Fluffy marshmallow creme lends an ethereal quality to the texture.

2. SMOOTH IT OUT
Use a hand mixer to work out any lumps and incorporate more air.

3. GO LOW-TECH
The end result is much better if you use an old-fashioned churn.

4. ENJOY SOFT-SERVE
Freeze until the motor labors and stops; enjoy right out of the churn.

MEATLESS MONDAYS

Vegetarian

Tomato Ricotta Tart

Hands-on: 20 min. Total: 55 min. This crust, made tender and flaky with heart-healthy olive oil, makes the perfect base for farm-fresh tomatoes and earthy-sweet basil.

Crust:
5.6 ounces unbleached all-purpose flour (about 1¼ cups)
2 tablespoons pine nuts, toasted and coarsely chopped
¼ teaspoon kosher salt
¼ teaspoon baking powder
¼ teaspoon freshly ground black pepper
¼ cup extra-virgin olive oil
3 tablespoons ice water
Cooking spray
Filling:
¾ cup part-skim ricotta cheese
1 large egg, lightly beaten
2 garlic cloves, minced
½ teaspoon kosher salt
½ cup chopped fresh basil, divided
1.5 ounces aged Gruyère cheese, shredded and divided (about 6 tablespoons)
1 pound heirloom tomatoes, seeded and cut into ¼-inch-thick slices

1. Preheat oven to 450°.
2. To prepare crust, weigh or lightly spoon flour into dry measuring cups; level with a knife. Place flour and next 4 ingredients in a food processor; pulse 3 times or until combined. Combine oil and 3 tablespoons ice water in a small bowl. With processor on, slowly add oil mixture through food chute, and process until dough is crumbly. Sprinkle dough into a 9-inch glass or ceramic pie plate coated with cooking spray. Press dough into an even layer in bottom and up sides of dish. Bake at 450° for 10 minutes. Remove from oven.
3. Combine ricotta, egg, garlic, and ½ teaspoon salt, stirring with a whisk. Add ¼ cup basil and ¼ cup Gruyère cheese, stirring to combine. Spread ricotta mixture evenly over crust. Arrange tomato slices in a circular pattern over ricotta mixture, slightly overlapping. Sprinkle tomatoes with 2 tablespoons Gruyère cheese. Bake at 450° for 25 minutes or until filling is set. Let stand 10 minutes. Sprinkle with ¼ cup basil. Serves 6 (serving size: 1 wedge)

CALORIES 296; FAT 17g (sat 4.6g, mono 8.9g, poly 2.5g); PROTEIN 10.7g; CARB 25.7g; FIBER 1.8g; CHOL 48mg; IRON 2.1mg; SODIUM 340mg; CALC 192mg

Quick & Easy • Vegetarian

Poblano Sopes with Avocado Salad

Hands-on: 20 min. Total: 25 min. We lighten up these traditionally deep-fried Spanish tortilla cakes with a quick pan-sear to ensure a good, crispy edge, and then finish them off in the oven for even cooking.

1 poblano chile
¼ cup uncooked quinoa
5 ounces masa harina (about 1 cup)
1 cup warm water
½ teaspoon salt, divided
½ teaspoon freshly ground black pepper, divided
2 tablespoons canola oil
1½ teaspoons extra-virgin olive oil
1½ teaspoons fresh lime juice
¼ teaspoon sugar
2 cups baby arugula
1½ cups halved cherry tomatoes
2 tablespoons cilantro leaves
2 ounces queso fresco, crumbled (about ½ cup)
1 medium avocado, peeled and coarsely chopped (about 1 cup)

1. Preheat broiler.
2. Cut chile in half lengthwise; discard seeds and membranes. Place chile halves, skin sides up, on a foil-lined baking sheet; flatten with hand. Broil 6 minutes or until blackened. Place in a paper bag; fold to close tightly. Let stand 5 minutes. Peel and chop chile.
3. Preheat oven to 350°.
4. Combine chile, uncooked quinoa, masa harina, 1 cup water, ¼ teaspoon salt, and ¼ teaspoon pepper in a medium bowl; stir until a soft dough forms. Divide mixture into 4 equal pieces; shape each piece into a 4-inch patty. Heat a large ovenproof skillet over medium-high heat. Add canola oil to pan; swirl to coat. Add sopes to pan; cook 3 minutes or until browned. Turn sopes over; place pan in oven. Bake at 350° for 10 minutes or until browned and heated through.
5. Combine ¼ teaspoon salt, ¼ teaspoon pepper, olive oil, juice, and sugar in a medium bowl, stirring with a whisk. Add arugula and remaining ingredients; toss gently to coat. Serve over sopes. Serves 4 (serving size: 1 sope and ¾ cup salad)

CALORIES 317; FAT 17.3g (sat 2.4g, mono 9.9g, poly 3.3g); PROTEIN 8g; CARB 36.3g; FIBER 6.7g; CHOL 5mg; IRON 3mg; SODIUM 319mg; CALC 116mg

GET TO KNOW MASA HARINA

Masa harina (corn flour) lays a rich corn flavor foundation while absorbing and helping to carry other flavors (here, poblano). You'll find it with the Latin foods. You can also use it to thicken stews or to dredge fish or chicken before pan-frying.

SERIOUSLY GOOD SNACK BARS

"I loved these Chewy Oat Squares. They were so simple to make and are nice to snack on. If you make these ahead of time, they would be good for breakfast on the run or with a bowl of yogurt on the side. I am usually late getting up in the morning, so these squares were an easy breakfast solution. I usually like more savory foods, so in the future, I think I could cut down on the cane syrup a little bit. I also tried this recipe with raisins instead of cherries, and it was just as delicious. You could also add some almonds or walnuts if you wanted."

Kid Friendly • Make Ahead
Vegetarian

Chewy Oat Squares

Hands-on: 18 min. Total: 1 hr. 20 min.
These hearty squares are simple to make and wonderfully portable—they are perfect for packing in lunch boxes or for snacking in the car.

Cooking spray
¼ cup apple juice
6 whole pitted dates, coarsely chopped
5 tablespoons unsalted butter
½ cup golden cane syrup (such as Lyle's Golden Syrup)
⅛ teaspoon kosher salt
2 cups old-fashioned rolled oats
½ cup dried cherries, chopped
½ cup semisweet chocolate chips
¼ cup sesame seeds, toasted

1. Preheat oven to 325°.
2. Line a 9-inch square metal baking pan with parchment paper; coat with cooking spray. Place juice and dates in a food processor; pulse until dates are finely chopped.
3. Melt butter in a medium saucepan over medium heat. Stir in date mixture, syrup, and salt. Remove date mixture from heat. Cool 5 minutes. Stir in oats, cherries, chocolate, and sesame seeds. Spoon oat mixture into prepared pan. Using wet hands, carefully press the mixture into the corners of the pan.
4. Bake at 325° for 30 minutes or until golden brown. Cool 10 minutes. Place pan in refrigerator; cool 20 minutes. Invert oat mixture onto cutting board; cut into 16 squares. Serves 16 (serving size: 1 square)

CALORIES 159; **FAT** 7.1g (sat 3.5g, mono 2.1g, poly 0.9g); **PROTEIN** 2.1g; **CARB** 26.6g; **FIBER** 2.3g; **CHOL** 10mg; **IRON** 1.1mg; **SODIUM** 52mg; **CALC** 32mg

LET THE MIXTURE COOL BEFORE ADDING THE CHOCOLATE.

THE VERDICT

KAHLO (AGE 6)
It took some convincing, but once she tried them, she came back for more. She said they were better than store-bought snack bars!
10 out of 10

JASPER (AGE 8)
They were a little sweet for him, too, but he enjoyed the raisins.
9 out of 10

MATISSE (AGE 12)
This is a nice treat—one slice is just enough to satisfy a sweet tooth.
9 out of 10

6 LEMONADE TWISTS

To make these quenchers, start with ½ cup fresh lemon juice in a pitcher. Choose a variation, and serve over ice.

Kid Friendly • Quick & Easy
Make Ahead • Vegetarian

Blueberry & Basil:
Combine 2 cups fresh blueberries, ¼ cup torn basil leaves, and 6 tablespoons granulated sugar in pitcher with lemon juice; muddle. Add 4 cups water; let stand 30 minutes. Press through a fine sieve into a medium bowl; discard solids. Return mixture to pitcher. Serves 5 (serving size: 1 cup)

CALORIES 72; **FAT** 0.1g (sat 0g); **SODIUM** 1mg

Kid Friendly • Quick & Easy
Make Ahead • Vegetarian

Honeydew:
Combine ½ cup water and 6 tablespoons sugar in a bowl; microwave at HIGH 2 minutes. Stir until sugar dissolves; cool. Place sugar mixture, 3½ cups water, and 2 cups diced peeled honeydew melon in a blender; process until smooth. Press through a fine sieve over pitcher with lemon juice. Stir to combine. Serves 4 (serving size: 1 cup)

CALORIES 88; **FAT** 0.1g (sat 0g); **SODIUM** 4mg

HONEYDEW MELON MAKES THIS SIPPER JUST A LITTLE SWEETER THAN THE REST.

TANGY RHUBARB ENHANCES THE PUCKERY PUNCH OF THIS COOL CUP.

Kid Friendly • Quick & Easy
Make Ahead • Vegetarian
Strawberry & Rhubarb:
Place 4 cups water, 2 cups frozen rhubarb, 1 cup quartered strawberries, and 6 tablespoons sugar in a sauce-pan. Bring to a boil; reduce heat, and simmer 5 minutes. Place in freezer 30 minutes. Press mixture through a fine sieve into pitcher with lemon juice; discard solids. Stir to combine. Serves 4 (serving size: about 1 cup)

CALORIES 78; **FAT** 0.1g (sat 0g); **SODIUM** 1mg

Quick & Easy • Make Ahead
Vegetarian
Blackberry-Vanilla Vodka:
Place 3 cups fresh blackberries and 6 tablespoons sugar in a food processor; process until blended. Press mixture through a fine sieve into pitcher with lemon juice, and discard solids. Scrape seeds from ½ vanilla bean, halved lengthwise, into pitcher. Stir in 1½ cups vodka. Serves 8 (serving size: about ¾ cup)

CALORIES 142; **FAT** 0.1g (sat 0g); **SODIUM** 1mg

Quick & Easy • Make Ahead
Vegetarian
Peachy Bourbon:
Combine 4 cups water, 2 cups chopped peeled peaches, ¼ cup mint leaves, and 6 tablespoons sugar in a saucepan. Bring to a boil. Reduce heat; simmer 5 minutes. Place in freezer 30 minutes. Press through a fine sieve into pitcher with lemon juice; discard solids. Stir in 1 cup bourbon. Serves 7 (serving size: ¾ cup)

CALORIES 124; **FAT** 0.1g (sat 0g); **SODIUM** 1mg

Quick & Easy • Make Ahead
Vegetarian
Cilantro-Lime-Jalapeño:
Combine 6 tablespoons sugar and ½ cup cilantro sprigs in a mortar; grind leaves with pestle. Add cilantro mixture and 4 cups water to pitcher with lemon juice, stirring until sugar dissolves. Add 1 sliced lime and 1 thinly sliced jalapeño pepper. Let stand 30 minutes before serving. Serves 4 (serving size: 1 cup)

CALORIES 86; **FAT** 0.1g (sat 0g); **SODIUM** 1mg

GLOBAL PANTRY

SESAME OIL

For people who are cutting back on sodium, roasted sesame oil is a great ingredient to keep on hand. It's used primarily in Asian cooking, but the deep, toasty flavor is friendly to many other dishes, where it adds intense flavor in place of salt. Rather than sprinkling extra salt on a salad, drizzle on a little dark sesame oil (and perhaps slightly increase the amount of lemon juice or vinegar you use in your dressing). This works best with a salad made from vegetables—raw or cooked—that have a more robust fla-vor, such as arugula, carrots, or beets. Once you have sesame oil in your cupboard (it keeps well if stored in a cool, dark place), you'll find that it has all kinds of flexible uses. I use it not for cooking but as a top dressing or final flavoring: It's great drizzled on meat, stirred into rice, or dribbled onto soup. Combine it with a few more ingredi-ents, as in the recipe below, for a dipping/drizzling sauce for which you'll find myriad uses.

Quick & Easy • Make Ahead
Vegetarian

Sesame Dipping Sauce

Hands-on time: 6 min. Total time: 6 min.
Serve this simple, versatile sauce as a zippy condiment for roast beef or pork, or drizzle it onto a platter of sliced grilled meat (especially lamb) or sliced grilled vegetables, such as egg-plant or zucchini. Omit the onions and ginger, and it's delicious on cooked greens such as bok choy, mustard greens, or kale.

Combine ¼ cup fresh lime juice, 2 tablespoons water, 1 tablespoon lower-sodium soy sauce, 2 teaspoons dark sesame oil, a dash of salt, and a dash of ground red pepper (optional) in a medium bowl; stir with a whisk. Stir in 2 tablespoons finely chopped green onions and 1 teaspoon minced peeled fresh ginger. Serves 8 (serving size: 1 tablespoon)

CALORIES 14; **FAT** 1.2g (sat 0.2g); **SODIUM** 91mg

DINNER TONIGHT

Fast weeknight menus from the *Cooking Light* Test Kitchen

READY IN
30
MINUTES

········· *The* ·········
SHOPPING LIST

Grilled Sirloin Steak with Mango and Chile Salad
Fresh cilantro
Lime (1)
Mango (1 medium)
Red jalapeño pepper (1)
Unsalted, dry-roasted peanuts
Sirloin steak (1 pound)

Coconut-Ginger Rice
Ginger
Fresh cilantro
Bay leaf
Jasmine rice
Light coconut milk

········· *The* ·········
GAME PLAN

While grill preheats:
- Season steak.
- Prepare rice.

While steak stands:
- Prepare salad.

Quick & Easy

Grilled Sirloin Steak with Mango and Chile Salad

With Coconut-Ginger Rice

Kid Tweak: Substitute red bell pepper for the jalapeño in the salad.
Shopping Tip: Look for golden Champagne (aka Ataulfo) mangoes at the store.
Simple Sub: Use basmati rice instead of jasmine for a fluffier texture.

1 (1-pound) sirloin steak, trimmed
½ teaspoon salt, divided
¼ teaspoon freshly ground black pepper
Cooking spray
2 tablespoons chopped fresh cilantro
1 tablespoon fresh lime juice
1 medium ripe mango, peeled and diced
1 red jalapeño pepper, thinly sliced
2 tablespoons chopped unsalted, dry-roasted peanuts

1. Preheat grill to medium-high heat.
2. Sprinkle steak evenly with ⅜ teaspoon salt and pepper. Place steak on grill rack coated with cooking spray; grill 4 minutes on each side or until desired degree of doneness. Let steak stand 5 minutes. Cut steak diagonally across the grain into thin slices.
3. Combine ⅛ teaspoon salt, cilantro, and next 3 ingredients (through jalapeño) in a medium bowl; toss. Top with peanuts. Serve salad with steak. Serves 4 (serving size: about 3 ounces steak and about ⅓ cup salad)

CALORIES 230; **FAT** 7.4g (sat 2.1g, mono 3.1g, poly 1g); **PROTEIN** 26.9g; **CARB** 14.4g; **FIBER** 1.9g; **CHOL** 68mg; **IRON** 2.1mg; **SODIUM** 360mg; **CALC** 42mg

For the Coconut-Ginger Rice:
Bring 1 cup water, ½ teaspoon minced peeled fresh ginger, ¼ teaspoon salt, and 1 bay leaf to a boil in a small saucepan. Add 1 cup uncooked jasmine rice and ¼ cup light coconut milk to pan; bring to a boil. Reduce heat to low, cover, and cook

---

until liquid is absorbed and rice is done (about 15 minutes). Discard bay leaf; fluff rice. Stir in 2 tablespoons chopped fresh cilantro. Serves 4 (serving size: about ½ cup)

CALORIES 194; **FAT** 1.2g (sat 0.8g); **SODIUM** 153mg

READY IN
40
MINUTES

········· *The* ·········
SHOPPING LIST

Gazpacho with Lemon-Garlic Shrimp
1 (10-ounce) container grape tomatoes
English cucumbers (2)
Red bell pepper (1)
Vidalia or other sweet onion (1)
Garlic
Lemon (1)
Sherry vinegar
1 (28-ounce) can San Marzano tomatoes
20 medium shrimp, peeled and deveined (about 8 ounces)
Extra-virgin olive oil

Manchego Toasts
Manchego cheese
Baguette

········· *The* ·········
GAME PLAN

While soup chills:
- Cook shrimp.
- Broil toasts.

continued

Gazpacho with Lemon-Garlic Shrimp

With Manchego Toasts

Prep Pointer: Using a regular cucumber? Peel the thick skin.
Time-Saver: Have the fishmonger peel and devein the shrimp.
Simple Sub: Instead of Manchego cheese, try pecorino Romano.

1 (10-ounce) container grape tomatoes, divided
1¹⁄₂ cups sliced English cucumber, divided
1 cup diced red bell pepper, divided
³⁄₄ cup diced Vidalia or other sweet onion, divided
3 tablespoons extra-virgin olive oil, divided
2 tablespoons sherry vinegar
⁵⁄₈ teaspoon kosher salt, divided
¹⁄₂ teaspoon freshly ground black pepper, divided
3 garlic cloves
1 (28-ounce) can San Marzano tomatoes, drained
1 tablespoon fresh lemon juice
1 teaspoon minced fresh garlic
20 medium shrimp, peeled and deveined (about 8 ounces)

1. Cut 8 grape tomatoes into quarters. Combine quartered tomatoes, ¼ cup cucumber, ¼ cup bell pepper, and ¼ cup onion in a small bowl; set aside.
2. Place remaining grape tomatoes, 1¼ cups cucumber, ¾ cup bell pepper, ½ cup onion, 2 tablespoons oil, vinegar, ½ teaspoon salt, ¼ teaspoon pepper, garlic cloves, and canned tomatoes in a food processor; pulse until almost smooth or until desired consistency. Refrigerate 25 minutes.
3. Combine 1 tablespoon oil, juice, minced garlic, ¼ teaspoon pepper, ⅛ teaspoon salt, and shrimp in a medium bowl. Heat a large nonstick skillet over medium-high heat. Add shrimp mixture to pan; cook 3 minutes or until done, stirring occasionally.
4. Place about 1 cup soup into each of 4 bowls. Top each serving with 5 shrimp and ¼ cup cucumber mixture. Serves 4

CALORIES 215; **FAT** 11.1g (sat 1.5g, mono 7.8g, poly 1.3g); **PROTEIN** 10.9g; **CARB** 18.7g; **FIBER** 4.8g; **CHOL** 71mg; **IRON** 1.9mg; **SODIUM** 587mg; **CALC** 111mg

For the Manchego Toasts:
Preheat broiler to high. Place 8 (½-ounce) slices baguette on a baking sheet. Broil 2 minutes or until toasted. Sprinkle about 2 teaspoons Manchego cheese on each toast slice; broil 1 minute or until cheese melts and begins to brown. Serves 4 (serving size: 2 toasts)

CALORIES 112; **FAT** 3.1g (sat 1.9g); **SODIUM** 188mg

Ground Lamb and Hummus Pita "Pizzas"

With Tomato, Sweet Onion, and Parsley Salad

Simple Sub: Try ground sirloin in place of the lamb.
Flavor Hit: Cumin and cinnamon add an earthy warmth to the lamb mixture.
Time-Saver: Purchase pretoasted pine nuts at the store.

6 ounces ground lamb
1 teaspoon extra-virgin olive oil
1¹⁄₂ cups chopped yellow onion
1 tablespoon minced fresh garlic
1¹⁄₂ teaspoons ground cumin
¹⁄₂ teaspoon dried oregano
³⁄₈ teaspoon salt
¹⁄₄ teaspoon ground cinnamon
¹⁄₂ cup water
¹⁄₂ cup chopped seeded tomato
1¹⁄₂ tablespoons fresh lemon juice
2 (6-inch) pitas
¹⁄₂ cup plain hummus
¹⁄₄ cup chopped fresh cilantro
1 tablespoon pine nuts, toasted

1. Preheat broiler to high.
2. Heat a large nonstick skillet over medium-high heat. Add lamb to pan; cook 3 minutes or until browned, stirring to crumble lamb. Remove lamb from pan. Add oil to pan; swirl to coat. Add onion to pan; sauté 4 minutes. Stir in garlic and next 4 ingredients; sauté 1 minute. Stir in ½ cup water and tomato; bring to a simmer. Cook 4 minutes or until tomatoes begin to soften. Stir in cooked lamb. Cover, reduce heat, and simmer 4 minutes. Stir in lemon juice.
3. Split each pita into 2 rounds. Place pita rounds on a baking sheet. Broil 1 minute on each side or until crisp. Spread 2 tablespoons hummus on each round. Top each serving with about ⅓ cup lamb mixture. Sprinkle evenly with cilantro and nuts. Serves 4 (serving size: 1 "pizza")

CALORIES 313; **FAT** 14.4g (sat 4.2g, mono 6g, poly 2.7g); **PROTEIN** 17.1g; **CARB** 29.3g; **FIBER** 4.3g; **CHOL** 41mg; **IRON** 2.9mg; **SODIUM** 535mg; **CALC** 76mg

For the Tomato, Sweet Onion, and Parsley Salad:
Combine 1½ teaspoons extra-virgin olive oil, 1 teaspoon red wine vinegar, ⅛ teaspoon salt, and ⅛ teaspoon freshly ground black pepper in a medium bowl; stir with a whisk. Add 1½ cups halved grape tomatoes, ½ cup thinly sliced Vidalia or other sweet onion, and ½ cup chopped fresh flat-leaf parsley to bowl; toss to coat. Sprinkle salad with 2 tablespoons crumbled feta cheese. Serves 4 (serving size: about ½ cup)

CALORIES 49; **FAT** 2.8g (sat 1g); **SODIUM** 134mg

The
SHOPPING LIST

Ground Lamb and Hummus Pita "Pizzas"

Yellow onion (1)
Garlic
Tomato (1 medium)
Lemon (1)
Fresh cilantro
Pine nuts
Ground cumin
Dried oregano
Ground cinnamon
Plain hummus
Ground lamb (6 ounces)
6-inch pitas
Extra-virgin olive oil

Tomato, Sweet Onion, and Parsley Salad

Grape tomatoes (1 pint)
Vidalia or other sweet onion (1)
Fresh flat-leaf parsley
Red wine vinegar
Feta cheese
Extra-virgin olive oil

The
GAME PLAN

While broiler preheats:
■ Cook lamb.
■ Start preparing salad.
While lamb mixture simmers:
■ Toast pita rounds.
■ Finish salad.

Quick & Easy

Clams with Israeli Couscous

With Wilted Swiss Chard and Mushrooms

Flavor Hit: If you have saffron, add ½ teaspoon with the wine for extra flavor. Simple Sub: Try mussels instead of clams. Time-Saver: Look for presliced mushrooms in the produce section.

2 teaspoons olive oil
1 cup finely chopped yellow onion
1 cup finely chopped fennel bulb
1 cup uncooked Israeli couscous
1 garlic clove, thinly sliced
⅓ cup dry white wine
1½ cups fat-free, lower-sodium chicken broth
1 cup unsalted tomato sauce
½ teaspoon kosher salt
¼ teaspoon crushed red pepper
24 littleneck clams (about 1½ pounds)
3 tablespoons chopped fresh flat-leaf parsley
4 lemon wedges

1. Heat a large nonstick skillet over medium-high heat. Add oil to pan; swirl to coat. Add onion and fennel; sauté 3 minutes. Add couscous and garlic to pan; sauté 1 minute. Add wine to pan; cook 1 minute or until liquid almost evaporates. Stir in broth, tomato sauce, salt, and pepper; bring to a boil. Cover, reduce heat, and simmer 7 minutes. Nestle clams in couscous mixture. Cover and cook 8 minutes or until clams open. Discard any unopened shells. Sprinkle with parsley; serve with lemon wedges. Serves 4 (serving size: about 1¼ cups)

CALORIES 415; **FAT** 4.6g (sat 0.7g, mono 1.9g, poly 0.6g); **PROTEIN** 33.8g; **CARB** 57.2g; **FIBER** 4.7g; **CHOL** 51mg; **IRON** 3.9mg; **SODIUM** 571mg; **CALC** 103mg

For the Wilted Swiss Chard and Mushrooms:

Remove stems from 10 ounces Swiss chard. Thinly slice stems to measure 1 cup; coarsely chop leaves to measure 3 cups. Heat a large skillet over medium heat. Add 1 tablespoon olive oil to pan; swirl to coat. Add 1 thinly sliced shallot; cook 1 minute. Add 6 ounces sliced cremini mushrooms, chard stems, and ¼ teaspoon black pepper to pan; cook 5 minutes, stirring occasionally. Add chard leaves, 2 teaspoons lower-sodium soy sauce, and 1 tablespoon water to pan. Cover and cook 2 minutes or until chard wilts. Serves 4 (serving size: ½ cup)

CALORIES 59; **FAT** 3.7g (sat 0.5g); **SODIUM** 242mg

The
SHOPPING LIST

Clams with Israeli Couscous

Yellow onion (1)
Fennel (1)
Garlic
Fresh flat-leaf parsley
Lemon (1)
Israeli couscous
Dry white wine
Fat-free, lower-sodium chicken broth
Unsalted tomato sauce
Crushed red pepper
24 littleneck clams (about 1½ pounds)
Olive oil

Wilted Swiss Chard and Mushrooms

Swiss chard (10 ounces)
Shallot (1)
Cremini mushrooms (6 ounces)
Lower-sodium soy sauce
Olive oil

The
GAME PLAN

While couscous cooks:
■ Slice Swiss chard.
While clams cook:
■ Cook chard and mushroom mixture.

READY IN
40
MINUTES

The SHOPPING LIST

Open-Faced Crab Cake Sandwiches with Tzatziki

English cucumber (1)
Garlic
Red bell pepper (1)
Green onions
Fresh dill
Lemon (1)
Red leaf lettuce
Panko (Japanese breadcrumbs)
Lump crabmeat (12 ounces)
Plain 2% reduced-fat Greek yogurt
Egg
Sourdough bread
Olive oil

Sweet Pepper and Almond Salad

Mixed baby greens (4 cups)
Baby red bell peppers
Sherry vinegar
Unsalted, dry-roasted almonds
Extra-virgin olive oil

The GAME PLAN

While patties cook:
- Toast bread.
- Prepare salad.

Quick & Easy

Open-Faced Crab Cake Sandwiches with Tzatziki

With Sweet Pepper and Almond Salad

Prep Pointer: Wet your hands to make shaping the patties easier.
Flavor Hit: Fresh dill and lemon brighten up the crabby patties.
Simple Sub: Have Marcona almonds on hand? Try them in the salad.

6 tablespoons plain 2% reduced-fat Greek yogurt, divided
3 tablespoons finely chopped English cucumber
2 teaspoons minced fresh garlic
1/2 teaspoon freshly ground black pepper, divided
2/3 cup panko (Japanese breadcrumbs), divided
1/4 cup finely diced red bell pepper
2 tablespoons thinly sliced green onions
1 tablespoon finely chopped fresh dill
1 teaspoon grated lemon rind
2 teaspoons fresh lemon juice
3/8 teaspoon salt
1 large egg white
12 ounces lump crabmeat, shell pieces removed
2 tablespoons olive oil
4 (1 1/2-ounce) slices sourdough bread, toasted
4 red leaf lettuce leaves

1. Combine 1/4 cup yogurt, cucumber, garlic, and 1/4 teaspoon pepper in a small bowl; set yogurt mixture aside.
2. Combine 2 tablespoons yogurt, 1/4 teaspoon black pepper, 1/3 cup panko, bell pepper, onions, dill, rind, juice, salt, and egg white in a medium bowl. Gently stir in crab. Divide crab mixture into 4 equal portions (about 1/2 cup each), shaping each into a 3/4-inch-thick patty. Place 1/3 cup panko in a shallow dish. Dredge patties in panko.
3. Heat a large skillet over medium heat. Add oil to pan; swirl to coat. Add patties; cook 3 minutes on each side or until golden. Top each bread slice with 1 lettuce leaf, 1 patty, and about 2 tablespoons reserved yogurt mixture. Serves 4 (serving size: 1 sandwich)

CALORIES 323; **FAT** 9.2g (sat 1.6g, mono 5.2g, poly 1.4g); **PROTEIN** 24.5g; **CARB** 34.8g; **FIBER** 2.2g; **CHOL** 52mg; **IRON** 2.3mg; **SODIUM** 748mg; **CALC** 90mg

For the Sweet Pepper and Almond Salad:

Combine 1 tablespoon extra-virgin olive oil, 1 tablespoon sherry vinegar, and 1/8 teaspoon kosher salt in a medium bowl, stirring with a whisk. Add 4 cups mixed baby greens and 1 cup thinly sliced baby red bell peppers; toss to coat. Sprinkle with 2 tablespoons chopped unsalted, dry-roasted almonds. Serves 4 (serving size: 1 cup)

CALORIES 78; **FAT** 5.7g (sat 0.6g); **SODIUM** 82mg

FEED 4 FOR LESS THAN $10

Greek-Seasoned Steak Sandwiches

$2.28/serving, $9.12 total

Hands-on: 15 min. Total: 45 min. Serve these hearty sandwiches with a side of crisp carrot and celery sticks and light ranch dressing for dipping. Make breadcrumbs with the parts of pita you cut off by pulsing in a food processor; freeze for a couple of months.

3 tablespoons red wine vinegar, divided
4 teaspoons extra-virgin olive oil, divided
1 tablespoon minced fresh garlic
1 teaspoon dried oregano
12 ounces flank steak, trimmed
1/2 teaspoon kosher salt, divided
3/8 teaspoon freshly ground black pepper, divided
Cooking spray
2 tablespoons plain fat-free Greek yogurt
1/4 teaspoon Dijon mustard
4 (6-inch) whole-wheat pitas
4 romaine lettuce leaves
4 thin red onion slices
1 cucumber, peeled and thinly sliced
1 tomato, cut into 8 slices

1. Combine 2 tablespoons vinegar, 1 teaspoon oil, garlic, and oregano in a large zip-top plastic bag. Add steak to bag; seal. Let stand at room temperature 20 minutes, turning once. **2.** Heat a grill pan over medium-high heat. Remove steak from bag; discard marinade. Sprinkle 3/8 teaspoon salt and 1/4 teaspoon pepper evenly over both sides of steak. Coat pan with cooking spray. Place steak in pan; grill 5 minutes on each side or until desired degree of doneness. Remove steak from pan; let stand 10 minutes. Cut steak across the grain into thin slices. **3.** Combine 1 tablespoon vinegar, 1 tablespoon oil, 1/8 teaspoon salt, 1/8 teaspoon pepper, yogurt, and mustard in a bowl, stirring with a whisk. **4.** Cut off one-third of each pita; discard or reserve for another use. Arrange 1 lettuce leaf, 1 onion slice, one-fourth of cucumber slices, 2 tomato slices, and one-fourth of steak in each pita; top each sandwich with 1 tablespoon yogurt mixture. Serves 4 (serving size: 1 sandwich)

CALORIES 313; FAT 11.9g (sat 3.3g, mono 5.8g, poly 1.2g); PROTEIN 23.3g; CARB 29g; FIBER 4.5g; CHOL 51mg; IRON 3mg; SODIUM 517mg; CALC 48mg

SUPERFAST 20-MINUTE COOKING

Quick & Easy

Egg Salad Sandwiches with Bacon and Sriracha

Look for precooked eggs, such as Eggland's Best, in the dairy section of the supermarket.

2 center-cut bacon slices
1/3 cup thinly sliced green onions
2 tablespoons canola mayonnaise
1 tablespoon plain fat-free yogurt
1 1/2 teaspoons Sriracha (hot chile sauce, such as Huy Fong)
1/4 teaspoon freshly ground black pepper
1/8 teaspoon kosher salt
6 hard-cooked large eggs, chopped
2 cups arugula
8 whole-grain bread slices

1. Cook bacon in a medium saucepan over medium-high heat 3 minutes or until crisp. Remove bacon from pan; crumble. Place bacon in a large bowl. Stir in onions and next 5 ingredients. Gently stir in eggs. **2.** Arrange 1/2 cup arugula on each of 4 bread slices. Top each serving with 1/3 cup egg mixture and 1 bread slice. Serves 4 (serving size: 1 sandwich)

CALORIES 326; FAT 16.6g (sat 3.9g, mono 6.9g, poly 4.1g); PROTEIN 18.4g; CARB 24.9g; FIBER 4.3g; CHOL 286mg; IRON 3mg; SODIUM 571mg; CALC 123mg

Quick & Easy

Chicken Salad with Orange-Pistachio Vinaigrette

1 (8.5-ounce) package precooked quinoa and brown rice (such as Seeds of Change)
2 tablespoons extra-virgin olive oil
1 tablespoon white wine vinegar
1 tablespoon fresh orange juice
3/8 teaspoon salt
1/4 teaspoon freshly ground black pepper
2 cups shredded skinless, boneless rotisserie chicken breast (about 10 ounces)
1/2 cup chopped fresh basil
1/4 cup chopped unsalted, dry-roasted pistachios
4 ounces fresh mozzarella cheese, torn into bite-sized pieces
2 medium heirloom tomatoes, each cut into 6 wedges

1. Heat grains according to package directions; set aside. **2.** Combine oil and next 4 ingredients in a medium bowl, stirring with a whisk. Add chicken, basil, pistachios, and cheese; toss to coat. Place about 3/4 cup chicken mixture, 1/2 cup quinoa mixture, and 3 tomato wedges on each of 4 plates. Serves 4

CALORIES 404; FAT 20.9g (sat 6.1g, mono 9.7g, poly 2.4g); PROTEIN 30.1g; CARB 25.2g; FIBER 2.9g; CHOL 86mg; IRON 1.7mg; SODIUM 653mg; CALC 43mg

Beef Noodle Soup

Quick & Easy

If you have the time, freeze the steak for 20 minutes prior to preparation for easier slicing.

3 cups fat-free, lower-sodium beef broth
2 cups hot water
1 tablespoon hoisin sauce
1 1/2 teaspoons five-spice powder
1/8 teaspoon salt
1 (1-inch) piece fresh ginger, thinly sliced
3 ounces uncooked rice noodles
4 cups chopped baby bok choy (about 2)
12 ounces boneless sirloin steak, thinly sliced
1 cup fresh bean sprouts
2 teaspoons Sriracha (hot chile sauce)
12 basil leaves
8 jalapeño pepper slices
8 lime wedges

1. Combine first 6 ingredients in a large saucepan over high heat; bring to a boil. Remove ginger with a slotted spoon; discard. Add noodles to pan; cook 2 minutes. Stir in bok choy and beef; cook 2 minutes or until noodles are done and bok choy wilts. Place about 1 1/2 cups soup in each of 4 bowls. Top each serving with 1/4 cup bean sprouts, 1/2 teaspoon Sriracha, 3 basil leaves, 2 jalapeño slices, and 2 lime wedges. Serves 4

CALORIES 227; FAT 4.4g (sat 1.4g, mono 1.4g, poly 0.2g); PROTEIN 20.5g; CARB 26.3g; FIBER 2g; CHOL 31mg; IRON 3.2mg; SODIUM 572mg; CALC 102mg

Grilled Pork with Mango and Rum Sauce

Quick & Easy

Serve with a simple side salad of mixed baby greens and cherry tomatoes.

1 tablespoon Jamaican jerk seasoning (such as Spice Islands)
2 tablespoons fresh lime juice, divided
1 1/2 teaspoons canola oil, divided
1 (1-pound) pork tenderloin, trimmed
2 ripe mangoes
Cooking spray
1/4 cup packed dark brown sugar
1/4 cup golden rum (such as Bacardi)
2 teaspoons unsalted butter
1/4 teaspoon kosher salt

1. Combine jerk seasoning, 1 tablespoon lime juice, and 1 teaspoon oil in a medium bowl.
2. Cut pork crosswise into 8 pieces. Using your hand, flatten each piece to 1/2-inch thickness. Add pork to spice mixture; toss well to coat.
3. Cut mangoes in half lengthwise; discard pits. Cut each mango half into 1-inch cubes, cutting to, but not through, the skin. Brush cut sides of mangoes with 1/2 teaspoon oil.
4. Heat a grill pan over high heat. Coat pan with cooking spray. Add pork to pan; cook 4 minutes on each side or until desired degree of doneness. Add mango halves, skin sides up, to pan; cook 3 minutes. Remove from heat.
5. Combine sugar and next 3 ingredients in a small saucepan. Bring to a boil. Reduce heat, and simmer 4 minutes or until thickened. Stir in 1 tablespoon lime juice. Drizzle sauce over pork and mangoes. Serves 4 (serving size: 2 pork medallions, 1 mango half, and about 1 tablespoon sauce)

CALORIES 295; FAT 6.6g (sat 2.2g, mono 2.6g, poly 1g); PROTEIN 24.4g; CARB 31.8g; FIBER 1.9g; CHOL 79mg; IRON 1.4mg; SODIUM 397mg; CALC 29mg

Sour Cream and Onion Dip

Kid Friendly • Quick & Easy
Make Ahead • Vegetarian

Serve this creamy dip with carrot and celery batons, sliced bell pepper, or pita chips.

1 teaspoon canola oil
2 cups finely chopped sweet yellow onion (about 1 onion)
1 tablespoon minced fresh garlic
1/4 teaspoon salt, divided
1 cup reduced-fat sour cream
1/2 cup canola mayonnaise
2 tablespoons minced fresh chives, divided
1/4 teaspoon ground white pepper

1. Heat a small skillet over medium-high heat. Add oil to pan; swirl to coat. Add onion, garlic, and 1/8 teaspoon salt; cook 4 minutes, stirring frequently. Reduce heat to medium-low; cook 6 minutes, stirring frequently. Cool onion mixture slightly.
2. Combine sour cream, mayonnaise, 1 1/2 tablespoons chives, pepper, and 1/8 teaspoon salt in a large bowl. Add onion mixture; stir well. Top with 1 1/2 teaspoons chives. Serves 12 (serving size: about 2 tablespoons)

CALORIES 67; FAT 5.3g (sat 1.5g, mono 2.5g, poly 1.1g); PROTEIN 1g; CARB 3.6g; FIBER 0.5g; CHOL 8mg; IRON 0.1mg; SODIUM 139mg; CALC 29mg

Classic Chicken Noodle Soup,
page 27

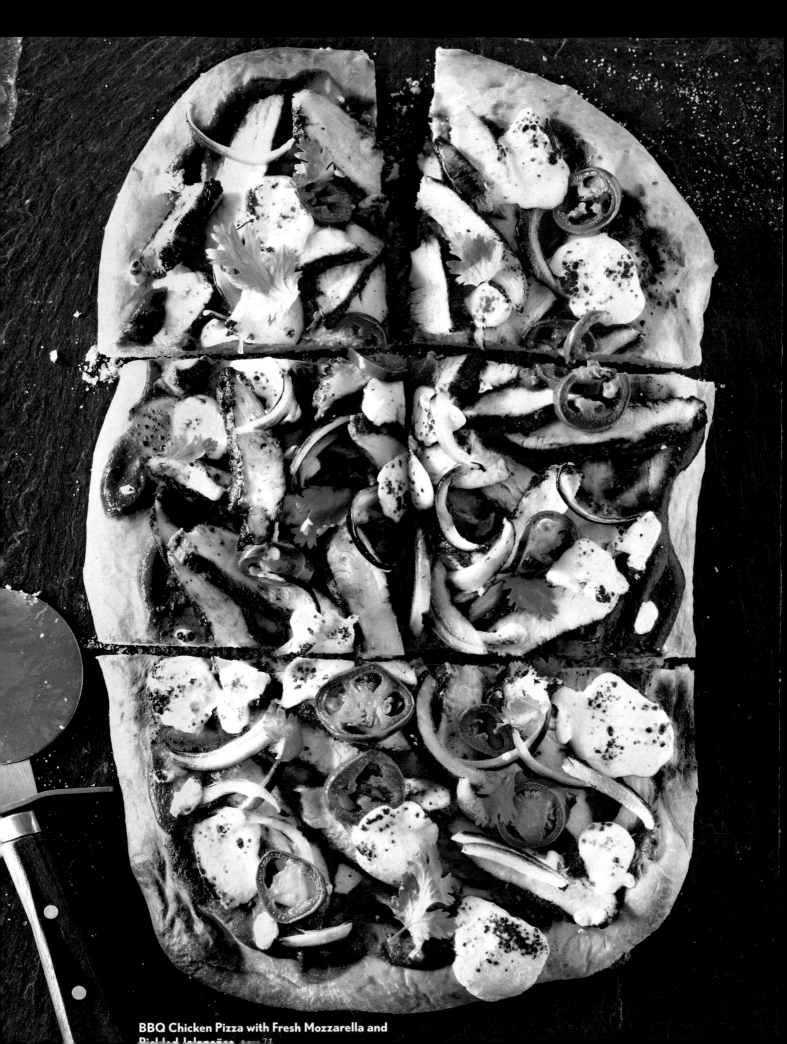

BBQ Chicken Pizza with Fresh Mozzarella and
Pickled Jalapeños page 31

Chicken BLT Salad,
page 34

Spicy Shrimp Noodle Soup with Pickled Vegetables,
page 43

Western Omelet
page 23

Apple-Toffee Hand Pies,
page 39

Spaghetti with Clams and Slow-Roasted Cherry Tomatoes, *page 52*

Classic Pad Thai,
page 59

213

Pappardelle with Salmon and Leeks,
page 52

Sparkling Raspberry Parfaits,
page 94

Butternut Soup with Coconut Milk,
page 102

Warm Potato and Steak Salad,
page 86

Portobello Sandwiches with Red Pepper Sauce,
page 88

Herbed Corn Muffins,
page 92

Glazed Baby Carrots,
page 89

**Smoky Haricots Verts
and Mushrooms,** *page 93*

**Rosemary-Garlic
Roasted Potatoes,** *page 92*

**Grapefruit, Walnut, and Feta
Salad,** *page 90*

**Quick Chilled Pea
Soup,** *page 90*

217

Pound Cake with Strawberry Glaze,
page 112

Chocolate Tacos with Ice Cream and Peanuts, *page 107*

Cucumber Pimm's Cup,
page 133

Mini Cornmeal Cakes with
Heirloom Tomato Relish,
page 141

Seared Scallop Salad with Prosciutto Crisps,
page 153

Heirloom Tomato and Beet Salad, *page 129*

Chilled Butter Bean Soup with
Basil-Corn Relish, *page 132*

Garlic-Lime Grilled Corn, *page 168*

Grilled Chicken with Honey-Chipotle BBQ Sauce, *page 168*

Watermelon-Cucumber Salad, *page 168*

Bean Salad with Shrimp and Curry Yogurt,
page 167

New England Turkey Burger,
page 160

227

Clinched and Planked
Chicken Thighs,
page 190

228

BLT Panzanella Salad,
page 193

Halibut with Bacony Corn Sauté,
page 185

Spaghetti and Meatballs, *page 252*

Couscous Salad with Chicken, Dates, and Walnuts, *page 261*

Kale and Caramelized Onion Grilled Cheese, *page 263*

Two-Cheese Mac and Cheese, *page 266*

Tsukune (Japanese Chicken Meatballs),
page 252

Banana Bread with Chocolate Glaze,
page 278

Whole-Wheat, Buttermilk, and Orange Pancakes,
page 279

Cream Cheese Danish Braid,
page 329

Pepita Pesto-Stuffed Mushrooms, *page 310*

Melted Manchego Tortas with Romesco and Chorizo, *page 309*

Polenta Toasts with Balsamic Onions, Roasted Peppers, Feta, and Thyme, *page 310*

Smoked Trout, Arugula, and Granny Smith Stacks, *page 311*

Citrusy Gin and Blood Orange Punch, *page 312*

Mashed Potato Soufflé, *page 302*

Speedy Apple-Beet Salad, *page 307*

Corn Bread Stuffing Muffins, *page 305*

Cranberry-Orange Relish, *page 300*

Oil-Basted Parmesan Turkey with Walnut Gravy, *page 300*

Green Beans with Sherried Mushroom Sauce, *page 306*

Quick Traditional Sweet Potato
Casserole, *page 303*

239

**No-Bake Cheesecake with
Pecan Caramel,**
page 304

Shrimp Tacos with Corn Salsa

Tossing the shrimp in a little honey before cooking helps to create tasty grill marks.

1 cup fresh corn kernels (about 2 ears)
1 teaspoon olive oil
2 tablespoons chopped green onions
2 tablespoons chopped fresh cilantro
3 tablespoons fresh lime juice, divided
1/4 teaspoon salt
1/4 teaspoon freshly ground black pepper
1 diced peeled avocado
Cooking spray
1 pound medium shrimp, peeled and deveined
2 teaspoons honey
1/4 cup light sour cream
8 (6-inch) corn tortillas

1. Preheat broiler to high.
2. Combine corn and oil in small bowl; toss gently to coat. Arrange corn in an even layer on a jelly-roll pan; broil 6 minutes or until lightly browned. Combine corn, onions, cilantro, 1 tablespoon juice, salt, pepper, and avocado in a medium bowl; toss gently.
3. Heat a large grill pan over medium-high heat. Coat pan with cooking spray. Combine shrimp, 1 tablespoon juice, and honey in a medium bowl; toss to coat. Add shrimp to pan; cook 2 minutes on each side or until done.
4. Combine sour cream and remaining 1 tablespoon juice in a small bowl.
5. Warm tortillas according to package directions. Place 2 tortillas on each of 4 plates. Top each tortilla with about 1/4 cup corn mixture, about 4 shrimp, and 1 1/2 teaspoons sour cream mixture. Serves 4 (serving size: 2 tacos)

CALORIES 318; **FAT** 12.9g (sat 2.5g, mono 6.4g, poly 1.9g); **PROTEIN** 20g; **CARB** 35.2g; **FIBER** 6.3g; **CHOL** 149mg; **IRON** 0.8mg; **SODIUM** 345mg; **CALC** 109mg

Bulgur with Peaches and Mint

2 cups water
1 cup uncooked bulgur
2 tablespoons champagne vinegar
2 tablespoons extra-virgin olive oil
2 teaspoons brown sugar
1/4 teaspoon salt
1/4 teaspoon freshly ground black pepper
1 cup diced peaches
2 1/2 ounces chopped hazelnuts, toasted
1/4 cup small fresh mint leaves

1. Bring 2 cups water and bulgur to a boil in a small saucepan. Cover, reduce heat, and cook 12 minutes. Drain; rinse with cold water. Drain.
2. Combine vinegar and next 4 ingredients in a large bowl, stirring with a whisk until sugar dissolves. Add bulgur, peaches, nuts, and mint; toss. Serves 6 (serving size: 2/3 cup)

CALORIES 212; **FAT** 12.1g (sat 1.2g, mono 8.7g, poly 1.6g); **PROTEIN** 4.9g; **CARB** 24.2g; **FIBER** 5.9g; **CHOL** 0mg; **IRON** 1.3mg; **SODIUM** 103mg; **CALC** 27mg

Variation 1: Grits-Style with Corn-Basil Relish

Bring 2 1/4 cups water and 1 cup uncooked bulgur to a boil in a small saucepan. Cover, reduce heat, and cook 8 minutes. Stir in 2 ounces shredded extra-sharp cheddar cheese and 1/4 teaspoon salt. Combine 1 cup fresh corn kernels, 1/4 cup finely chopped fresh basil, 1 tablespoon minced shallots, 1 tablespoon white wine vinegar, and 1/8 teaspoon salt in a small bowl. Top bulgur mixture with corn mixture. Serves 4 (serving size: 2/3 cup bulgur and 1/4 cup corn relish)

CALORIES 209; **FAT** 5.5g (sat 3.2g); **SODIUM** 324mg

Variation 2: Tabbouleh-Style

Bring 1 1/2 cups water and 3/4 cup uncooked bulgur to a boil in a small saucepan. Cover, reduce heat, and cook 12 minutes. Drain; rinse with cold water. Drain. Combine bulgur, 3/4 cup chopped fresh flat-leaf parsley, 3/4 cup chopped tomato, 3/4 cup chopped seeded peeled cucumber, 2 tablespoons fresh lemon juice, 1 tablespoon olive oil, 1 teaspoon ground cumin, 1/2 teaspoon salt, and 2 thinly sliced green onions in a large bowl; stir to combine. Serves 6 (serving size: 2/3 cup)

CALORIES 92; **FAT** 2.7g (sat 0.4g); **SODIUM** 207mg

Variation 3: Grilled Zucchini Pilaf

Heat a saucepan over medium-high heat. Add 1 tablespoon olive oil, 3/4 cup chopped onion, and 1/3 cup chopped celery; sauté 3 minutes. Add 2 cups water and 1 cup bulgur; bring to a boil. Cover, reduce heat, and simmer 11 minutes. Heat a grill pan over medium-high heat; coat with cooking spray. Quarter 1 zucchini. Grill zucchini 5 minutes; dice. Combine bulgur, zucchini, 1/4 cup chopped fresh parsley, 1/2 teaspoon salt, and 1/4 teaspoon pepper. Serve with lemon wedges. Serves 6 (serving size: 2/3 cup)

CALORIES 116; **FAT** 2.8g (sat 0.4g); **SODIUM** 210mg

Michael Symon's Grilled Salmon and Zucchini Salad

If you prepare this on a grill pan, it takes only 10 minutes from start to finish. On an outdoor grill, total prep plus cook time still clocks in at around 20 minutes.

4 (6-ounce) salmon fillets
3 tablespoons extra-virgin olive
oil, divided
³/₄ teaspoon kosher salt, divided
¹/₂ teaspoon freshly ground black
pepper, divided
1 lemon
3 cups thinly sliced zucchini
(about 2 small)
¹/₄ cup chopped fresh dill
¹/₄ cup sliced almonds, toasted

1. Preheat grill or grill pan to high heat.
2. Drizzle fillets with 1 tablespoon oil. Sprinkle fillets evenly with ⅜ teaspoon salt and ¼ teaspoon pepper. Arrange fillets on grill rack or grill pan; grill 5 minutes or until desired degree of doneness, turning once.
3. Grate lemon rind to equal 1½ teaspoons; squeeze juice to equal 2 tablespoons. Combine rind, juice, 2 tablespoons oil, ⅜ teaspoon salt, ¼ teaspoon pepper, zucchini, and dill in a bowl; toss gently to coat. Place 1 fillet on each of 4 plates. Top each serving with about ⅔ cup salad; sprinkle each serving with 1 tablespoon almonds. Serves 4

CALORIES 379; **FAT** 22.7g (sat 3g, mono 11.2g, poly 4g); **PROTEIN** 38.2g; **CARB** 4.8g; **FIBER** 1.6g; **CHOL** 89mg; **IRON** 1.4mg; **SODIUM** 461mg; **CALC** 50mg

OOPS!
YOUR PESTO GETS DARK & MURKY

But it should be bright green!

Pesto is the perfect answer to a bumper crop of basil, but if you're not careful, the herb mélange can discolor faster than a batch of guacamole, dulling as soon as it hits hot pasta—or even before, in the food processor. There are two causes: Chopping basil produces ethylene, the gas that turns vibrant leafy vegetables a dull, dark color. Also, overworking the basil in the processor heats the mixture, breaking down the chlorophyll, which is the source of the green. Some chopping is necessary for the herb's essential oils to release their flavor. But a prolonged puree turns things muddy.

The solution: Pulse; don't puree. Place whole basil leaves, garlic, cheese, nuts, and about 2 tablespoons oil in the bowl of a food processor, and pulse 2 to 3 times or until a rough paste forms. Repeat with more oil, pulsing after each addition, just until smooth. You can also add a couple tablespoons of parsley or spinach to help preserve that bright green color. When it's time to serve, top hot foods with pesto in the serving bowl at the last minute, rather than in the skillet. To store, place in an airtight container, and place plastic wrap directly on the surface of the pesto. You can also drizzle on a top layer of oil to help prevent oxidation.

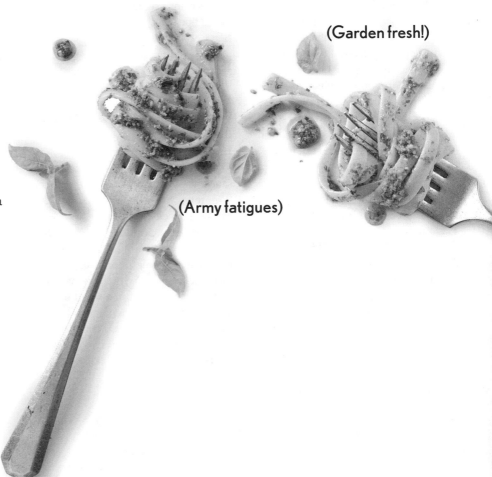

(Garden fresh!)

(Army fatigues)

COOKING LIGHT'S BIG GUIDE TO FOOD ON THE MOVE!

Back to work, back to school: Here's a breakfast, lunch, dinner, and snacking guide to healthy eating for fast-paced families. On your mark, get set...

GET A JUMP ON BREAKFAST

Before you go to bed, spend 10 minutes prepping tomorrow's morning meal. It will save time, and the food will be a perfect start to your day.

Kid Friendly • Quick & Easy
Vegetarian

Huevos Rancheros Wraps

Hands-on: 15 min. Total: 15 min.
The night before: Make salsa.
In the morning: Cook eggs. Make wraps.

⅓ cup frozen whole-kernel corn
⅓ cup lower-sodium canned black beans, rinsed and drained
¼ cup chopped seeded tomato
3 tablespoons chopped green onions
1 tablespoon chopped fresh cilantro
1 teaspoon minced seeded jalapeño pepper
½ teaspoon freshly ground black pepper, divided
⅜ teaspoon salt, divided
4 large eggs, lightly beaten
1 teaspoon olive oil
1 ounce cheddar cheese, shredded (about ¼ cup)
2 (8-inch) whole-wheat flour tortillas

1. Place corn in a medium microwave-safe bowl. Microwave at HIGH 1 minute. Stir in beans, tomato, onions, cilantro, jalapeño, ¼ teaspoon black pepper, and ⅛ teaspoon salt.
2. Combine ¼ teaspoon salt, ¼ teaspoon black pepper, and eggs in a medium bowl; stir with a whisk. Heat a small nonstick skillet over medium-high heat. Add oil; swirl to coat. Add egg mixture to pan; cook 1 minute, stirring frequently. Add cheese; cook 1 minute, stirring frequently.
3. Heat tortillas according to package directions. Divide egg mixture evenly between tortillas; top evenly with corn mixture. Roll up each burrito, jelly-roll fashion. Cut each burrito in half. Serves 4 (serving size: ½ burrito)

CALORIES 182; **FAT** 8.8g (sat 3.2g, mono 3.4g, poly 1.2g); **PROTEIN** 10.8g; **CARB** 15.1g; **FIBER** 1.8g; **CHOL** 193mg; **IRON** 1.7mg; **SODIUM** 453mg; **CALC** 115mg

MOVING PREP DUTIES TO THE NIGHT BEFORE MEANS YOU CAN ENJOY WEEKEND-STYLE FOODS ON ANY WEEKDAY MORN.

Kid Friendly • Quick & Easy
Vegetarian

Strawberry Cream Cheese Waffle Sandwiches

Hands-on: 10 min. Total: 20 min.
The night before: Make filling.
In the morning: Toast waffles. Assemble sandwiches.

4 ounces ⅓-less-fat cream cheese (about ½ cup)
4 teaspoons brown sugar
¼ teaspoon ground cinnamon
¾ cup sliced strawberries
8 frozen multigrain waffles (such as Kashi), toasted

1. Place first 3 ingredients in a medium bowl; beat with a mixer at medium speed until well blended. Gently fold in strawberries. Spread about 3 tablespoons cream cheese mixture over each of 4 waffles; top sandwiches with remaining 4 waffles. Serves 4 (serving size: 1 sandwich)

CALORIES 269; **FAT** 9.2g (sat 4.1g, mono 3g, poly 1.3g); **PROTEIN** 10.3g; **CARB** 42.1g; **FIBER** 6.7g; **CHOL** 20mg; **IRON** 1.6mg; **SODIUM** 443mg; **CALC** 91mg

Quick & Easy • Vegetarian

Herby Frittata with Vegetables and Goat Cheese

Hands-on: 15 min. Total: 15 min.
The night before: Blanch asparagus. Stir together egg mixture.
In the morning: Cook frittata.

6 ounces asparagus, trimmed and cut into 2-inch pieces
1/4 cup water
3 tablespoons chopped fresh chives
2 tablespoons chopped fresh dill
3/8 teaspoon salt
1/4 teaspoon freshly ground black pepper
7 large eggs, lightly beaten
1 teaspoon olive oil
2 ounces soft goat cheese (about 1/4 cup)

1. Combine asparagus and 1/4 cup water in a small microwave-safe bowl; cover and microwave at HIGH 2 minutes or until tender. Rinse with cold water; drain. Combine chives, dill, salt, pepper, and eggs in a medium bowl; stir with a whisk.
2. Preheat broiler to high.
3. Heat a small ovenproof nonstick skillet over medium heat. Add oil; swirl to coat. Add asparagus and egg mixture to pan; cook 3 minutes or until eggs are partially set, stirring occasionally. Sprinkle with cheese. Place pan under broiler. Broil 2 minutes or until eggs are set and top is lightly browned. Remove pan from oven. Run a spatula around edge and under frittata to loosen from pan; slide frittata onto a plate or cutting board. Cut into 4 wedges. Serves 4 (serving size: 1 wedge)

CALORIES 196; **FAT** 13.8g (sat 5.8g, mono 5g, poly 1.9g); **PROTEIN** 15.1g; **CARB** 2.9g; **FIBER** 1g; **CHOL** 337mg; **IRON** 2.7mg; **SODIUM** 420mg; **CALC** 105mg

THE NIGHT BEFORE PARBOIL STEEL-CUT OATS FOR A HEARTY, QUICK BOWL THE NEXT MORNING.

Kid Friendly • Vegetarian

Steel-Cut Oats with Cinnamon-Blueberry Compote

Hands-on: 15 min. Total: 8 hr. 20 min.
The night before: Prepare blueberry mixture through step 1. Prepare oats through step 2.
In the morning: Cook blueberry compote. Finish oatmeal.

2 cups frozen blueberries
1/4 cup sugar
1 teaspoon grated lemon rind
1 tablespoon fresh lemon juice
1/2 teaspoon ground cinnamon, divided
4 cups water
1 cup steel-cut oats
1/4 teaspoon salt
1 tablespoon butter

1. Combine blueberries, sugar, rind, juice, and 1/4 teaspoon cinnamon in a medium bowl; toss to coat. Refrigerate.
2. Bring 4 cups water to a boil in a medium saucepan. Stir in 1/4 teaspoon cinnamon, oats, and salt; cook 1 minute. Remove oat mixture from heat, cover, and refrigerate in pan overnight.
3. Bring blueberry mixture to a boil in a small saucepan over high heat. Cook 6 minutes or until slightly thickened, stirring frequently. Bring oat mixture to a boil over medium-high heat; cook 5 minutes or until thoroughly heated, stirring frequently. Add butter to oat mixture. Spoon 3/4 cup oatmeal into each of 4 bowls; top each serving with 1/4 cup blueberry compote. Serves 4

CALORIES 256; **FAT** 5.9g (sat 2.4g, mono 0.8g, poly 0.3g); **PROTEIN** 6.4g; **CARB** 49.6g; **FIBER** 6.3g; **CHOL** 8mg; **IRON** 2mg; **SODIUM** 174mg; **CALC** 31mg

Kid Friendly • Quick & Easy Vegetarian

Mango Lassi Smoothie

Hands-on: 8 min. Total: 8 min.
The night before: Cut and freeze mango.
In the morning: Blend ingredients.

1 1/2 cups 1% low-fat milk
1 cup plain low-fat yogurt
1 tablespoon honey
Dash of ground cardamom
2 cups chopped peeled ripe mango, frozen (about 2 medium)

1. Place first 4 ingredients in a blender; pulse to combine. Add mango to blender; process until smooth. Serves 4 (serving size: about 1 cup)

CALORIES 143; **FAT** 2.2g (sat 1.3g, mono 0.6g, poly 0.1g); **PROTEIN** 7g; **CARB** 25.6g; **FIBER** 1.3g; **CHOL** 8mg; **IRON** 0.2mg; **SODIUM** 84mg; **CALC** 236mg

THE NIGHT BEFORE CHOP AND FREEZE THE MANGO FOR THIS BREAKFAST SMOOTHIE.

MAKE LUNCH A LOT MORE FUN

Inspired by the bento box craze, we fashioned healthy lunches for kids, teens, foodies, and more.

Bento box culture from Japan has lately been inspiring lunch box creativity on this side of the Pacific. There are bento blogs, cookbooks, and all kinds of bento-inspired food containers. We love bentos because the compartments help with portion control and naturally lead to a healthy variety of foods. Each lunch is a little puzzle, an elegant surprise—so much more fun than a sandwich-and-chips brown bag. A bento lunch doesn't have to be Japanese, of course, and it doesn't have to take a long time to prepare. Here are five make-ahead lunches we concocted to delight different types of eaters, from little kids to teenagers to cubicle-dwellers.

Kid Friendly • Quick & Easy Make Ahead

Quick Chicken-Sesame Rice Balls

***Hands-on: 20 min. Total: 20 min.** Rice balls (onigiri) are a classic Japanese bento box dish. You can decorate them with nori to make pandas, kittens, rabbits, or your kids' favorite characters. For even more fun, cut the kiwi slices with a cookie cutter.*

1 (7.4-ounce) package precooked sticky rice (such as Annie Chun's)
2 teaspoons rice vinegar, divided
1/4 teaspoon sugar
1/4 teaspoon kosher salt
2 tablespoons thinly sliced green onion tops
1 teaspoon lower-sodium soy sauce
1/2 teaspoon dark sesame oil
2 ounces skinless, boneless rotisserie chicken breast, finely shredded
Nori sheets for decoration (optional)

1. Heat rice according to package directions; spread on a plate. Sprinkle with 1½ teaspoons vinegar, sugar, and salt; cool completely.
2. Combine ½ teaspoon vinegar, onions, soy sauce, oil, and chicken in a small bowl.
3. Arrange 4 (6-inch) squares of plastic wrap on a work surface. Divide rice mixture into 4 equal portions, shaping each into a ball. Lightly press each rice ball into a disc between palms; place 1 disc on each plastic wrap square. Make an indentation in each. Top each indentation with one-fourth of chicken mixture. Working with one rice ball at a time, lightly press the rice over the filling. Gather up ends of plastic wrap, and twist tightly to form a ball. Gently remove plastic wrap; decorate with nori, if desired. Serves 2 (serving size: 2 rice balls)

CALORIES 208; FAT 2.2g (sat 0.4g, mono 0.9g, poly 0.6g); PROTEIN 11.4g; CARB 35.2g; FIBER 0.3g; CHOL 25mg; IRON 0.6mg; SODIUM 435mg; CALC 9mg

Kid Friendly • Quick & Easy Make Ahead

Succotash with Shrimp

Hands-on: 19 min. Total: 19 min.

2/3 cup frozen baby lima beans, thawed
2/3 cup fresh corn kernels
2/3 cup quartered cherry tomatoes
1/4 cup diced Vidalia onion
1/4 cup diced red bell pepper
1/4 cup torn basil leaves
1 teaspoon minced jalapeño pepper
2 teaspoons red wine vinegar
1½ tablespoons extra-virgin olive oil, divided
1/2 teaspoon freshly ground black pepper, divided
3/8 teaspoon kosher salt, divided
12 peeled and deveined large shrimp
1/8 teaspoon ground red pepper

1. Combine first 8 ingredients in a medium bowl. Stir in 1 tablespoon oil, ¼ teaspoon black pepper, and ¼ teaspoon salt.
2. Toss shrimp with ¼ teaspoon black pepper, ⅛ teaspoon salt, and ground red pepper. Heat a medium skillet over

continued

medium-high heat. Add remaining 1½ teaspoons oil to pan; swirl to coat. Add shrimp; sauté 5 minutes or until done. Serves 2 (serving size: 1 cup succotash and 6 shrimp)

CALORIES 260; FAT 11.4g (sat 1.6g, mono 7.7g, poly 1.4g); PROTEIN 12.4g; CARB 28.2g; FIBER 5.8g; CHOL 53mg; IRON 1.9mg; SODIUM 594mg; CALC 73mg

Kid Friendly • Quick & Easy Make Ahead

Crispy Pan-Fried Chicken with Ranch Dipping Sauce

***Hands-on: 18 min. Total: 18 min.** The panko breading holds up and stays crisp when these chicken fingers are made ahead.*

1 (6-ounce) skinless, boneless chicken breast
1 tablespoon cornstarch
½ teaspoon garlic powder
Dash of ground red pepper
2 tablespoons 1% low-fat milk
1 large egg white, lightly beaten
½ cup panko (Japanese breadcrumbs)
1 tablespoon canola oil
¼ cup reduced-fat ranch dressing

1. Cut chicken breast into 6 strips. Combine cornstarch, garlic powder, and pepper in a shallow bowl. Combine milk and egg white in another shallow bowl. Place panko in a third shallow bowl. Dredge chicken in cornstarch mixture; dip in milk mixture. Place chicken in panko, turning to coat.
2. Heat a medium nonstick skillet over medium-high heat. Add oil to pan; swirl to coat. Add chicken; sauté 3 minutes on each side or until browned and done. Serve with ranch dressing. Serves 2 (serving size: 3 chicken strips and 2 tablespoons ranch dressing)

CALORIES 292; FAT 12.9g (sat 1.7g, mono 5.3g, poly 3.2g); PROTEIN 23.4g; CARB 21.1g; FIBER 1g; CHOL 62mg; IRON 1.7mg; SODIUM 453mg; CALC 23mg

THE FAST-FOOD LOVER'S BENTO

For the teen who needs to break a bad food habit, this box contains healthier options and a big dose of protein to help keep all engines firing through after-school activities.

MAKE OUR RECIPE
Crispy Pan-Fried Chicken with Ranch Dipping Sauce

THEN ADD
1 cup carrot sticks
1 cup celery sticks
1 cup cucumber sticks
2 high-protein chewy granola bars (such as Kellogg's FiberPlus Protein Mixed Nut Chewy Bars)

Serves 2
Each lunch has 504 calories, 21.2g fat, (5.3g sat fat), 34.7g protein, 48.5g carbs, 10.7g fiber, and 742mg sodium.

Make Ahead • Vegetarian

Wheat Berry, Kale, and Cranberry Salad

***Hands-on: 15 min. Total: 65 min.** If your supermarket carries frozen or shelf-stable pre-cooked wheat berries, you'll save 50 minutes; use 1 cup of cooked grains.*

½ cup uncooked wheat berries
2 cups shredded baby kale
½ cup diced celery
¼ cup minced red onion
¼ cup dried cranberries
1 tablespoon cider vinegar
1½ teaspoons olive oil
⅜ teaspoon kosher salt
¼ teaspoon freshly ground black pepper

1. Place wheat berries in a medium saucepan. Cover with water to 2 inches above wheat berries; bring to a boil. Cover, reduce heat to medium, and cook 50 minutes or until chewy-tender. Drain and rinse with cold water; drain.

2. Place wheat berries and remaining ingredients in a large bowl; toss gently. Serves 2 (serving size: about 2 cups)

CALORIES 284; FAT 4.8g (sat 0.8g, mono 2.6g, poly 0.9g); PROTEIN 8.7g; CARB 55.9g; FIBER 8.5g; CHOL 0mg; IRON 1.3mg; SODIUM 415mg; CALC 107mg

THE WHOLE-GRAINS BENTO

Holy whole grains! For crunchy-granola types, there's good-for-you nutrition all over this lunch, which gives you about two-thirds of the daily whole-grain recommendation.

MAKE OUR RECIPE
Wheat Berry, Kale, and Cranberry Salad

THEN ADD
12 100% whole-grain crackers (such as Wheat Thins)
1 ounce Manchego cheese, thinly sliced
2 whole-grain oatmeal cookies with chocolate (such as Kashi Oatmeal Dark Chocolate Cookies)

Serves 2
Each lunch contains 527 calories, 17.1g fat (6.2g sat fat), 15g protein, 83.8g carbs, 13.3g fiber, and 671mg sodium.

Quick & Easy • Make Ahead

Herby Potato, Green Bean, and Tuna Salad

Hands-on: 25 min. Total: 25 min.

6 ounces baby potatoes
6 ounces haricots verts or green beans
¼ cup fresh lemon juice
2½ tablespoons minced fresh flat-leaf parsley
1 tablespoon thyme leaves
2 tablespoons minced shallots
2 tablespoons unsalted chicken stock (such as Swanson)
1½ teaspoons minced fresh rosemary

4 teaspoons olive oil
1 teaspoon Dijon mustard
1/4 teaspoon kosher salt
1/4 teaspoon freshly ground black pepper
4 niçoise olives, pitted and chopped
1 (4.5-ounce) jar sustainable albacore tuna in oil (such as Wild Planet), drained and chunked

1. Place potatoes in a medium saucepan; cover with water. Bring to a boil; cook 7 minutes or until almost tender. Add beans; cook 3 minutes or until tender. Drain and rinse with cold water. Drain and place in a medium bowl.
2. Combine juice and next 10 ingredients (through olives) stirring with a whisk. Drizzle half of dressing over potato mixture; toss to coat. Top with tuna. Reserve remaining dressing to drizzle on greens before serving. Serves 2 (serving size: 1½ cups)

CALORIES 348; FAT 24g (sat 3.6g, mono 16g, poly 2.6g); PROTEIN 12.4g; CARB 25.1g; FIBER 4.6g; CHOL 15mg; IRON 2.4mg; SODIUM 604mg; CALC 69mg

THE FOODIE BENTO

She'd rather be at a sidewalk table at the new French bistro, but a looming deadline has the die-hard foodie eating at her desk. With this deconstructed salade niçoise, a girl can daydream.

MAKE OUR RECIPE
Herby Potato, Green Bean, and Tuna Salad

THE ADD
2 cups gourmet salad greens
1/2 cup grape tomatoes
2 multigrain, seeded flatbread crackers (such as Back to Nature)
1 hard-cooked large egg, quartered
2 tablespoons dark chocolate–covered espresso beans

Serves 2
Each lunch contains 493 calories, 30.4g fat (6.2g sat fat), 17.9g protein, 42g carbs, 7.6g fiber, and 696mg sodium.

JAZZ UP SNACK TIME

Portable sweet and savory bites to please all tastes

Kid Friendly • Make Ahead Vegetarian

Parmesan-Rosemary Flatbread Crackers

Hands-on: 1 hr. 20 min. Total: 1 hr. 20 min. These crackers can be stored in an airtight container for up to three days.

6.75 ounces all-purpose flour (about 1½ cups)
3 tablespoons finely ground flaxseed meal
1½ tablespoons chopped fresh rosemary
1 teaspoon baking powder
1/4 teaspoon freshly ground black pepper
1.5 ounces Parmigiano-Reggiano cheese, grated (about 1/3 cup)
1/2 cup water
1/3 cup butter, softened
1½ teaspoons kosher salt

1. Place a baking sheet on the middle rack in oven. Preheat oven to 425° (keep pan in oven as it preheats).
2. Weigh or lightly spoon flour into dry measuring cups; level with a knife. Combine flour and next 5 ingredients (through cheese) in a large bowl. Make a well in center of mixture; add ½ cup water and butter. Stir with a wooden spoon until dough pulls together in a shaggy mass. Turn dough out onto a lightly floured work surface; knead gently 6 to 8 times or until the dough is smooth and soft.
3. Divide dough into 8 equal portions. Working with 1 portion at a time

(keep remaining portions covered with a damp towel to prevent drying), divide into 3 equal pieces. Place the 3 dough pieces 3 inches apart in the center of a baking sheet–sized piece of parchment paper. Top with another piece of parchment paper. Roll dough pieces into long oval shapes, about 6 x 3 inches (dough will be very thin). Carefully remove the top piece of parchment. Sprinkle dough lightly with salt, pressing to adhere. Place parchment with rolled dough on the preheated baking sheet. Bake at 425° for 5 minutes or until crackers are browned in spots. Remove parchment and crackers from oven, and place on a wire rack to cool. Repeat procedure with the remaining dough and salt. Serves 24 (serving size: 1 cracker)

CALORIES 60; FAT 3.2g (sat 1.8g, mono 0.8g, poly 0.4g); PROTEIN 1.5g; CARB 6.4g; FIBER 0.5g; CHOL 8mg; IRON 0.5mg; SODIUM 180mg; CALC 27mg

Make Ahead • Vegetarian

Peppery Pepita Brittle

Hands-on: 24 min. Total: 24 min.

1/4 cup butter
1 cup unsalted pumpkinseed kernels
1/2 teaspoon kosher salt
1/4 teaspoon freshly ground black pepper
1/8 teaspoon ground cumin
1/8 teaspoon ground red pepper
2/3 cup sugar
1/3 cup light-colored corn syrup
1/4 cup water
3/4 teaspoon baking soda

1. Melt butter in a small saucepan over medium heat. Add pumpkinseed kernels and next 4 ingredients; cook 3 minutes, stirring frequently. Set aside.
2. Combine sugar, corn syrup, and ¼ cup water in a medium, heavy saucepan over medium-high heat; bring to a boil,

continued

stirring just until sugar dissolves. Cook until a candy thermometer registers 335°. Remove pan from heat; add pumpkinseed mixture and baking soda. Working quickly, spread mixture in a thin, even layer on a baking sheet lined with parchment paper; let stand until set. Break into pieces. Serves 24

CALORIES 83; FAT 4.6g (sat 1.7g, mono 1.4g, poly 1.2g); PROTEIN 1.7g; CARB 9.9g; FIBER 0.3g; CHOL 5mg; IRON 0.5mg; SODIUM 100mg; CALC 4mg

spray. Repeat procedure with remaining 6 phyllo sheets, pepper mixture, oil, and tomato mixture.
3. Bake at 375° for 10 minutes or until phyllo is golden. Serve warm or at room temperature. Serves 12 (serving size: 1 turnover)

CALORIES 101; FAT 6.7g (sat 1.6g, mono 4.1g, poly 0.7g); PROTEIN 2.4g; CARB 8g; FIBER 0.6g; CHOL 5mg; IRON 0.6mg; SODIUM 143mg; CALC 34mg

3. Divide dough into 24 equal portions (4 teaspoons each). Roll portions into small balls; arrange balls 2 inches apart on baking sheets lined with parchment paper. Flatten balls slightly. Bake at 350° for 15 minutes or until bottoms of cookies just begin to brown. Serves 24 (serving size: 1 cookie)

CALORIES 133; FAT 5.9g (sat 1.5g, mono 2.8g, poly 1.2g); PROTEIN 1.6g; CARB 19g; FIBER 0.8g; CHOL 11mg; IRON 0.6mg; SODIUM 87mg; CALC 20mg

Kid Friendly • Make Ahead
Vegetarian
Tomato Turnovers

Hands-on: 25 min. Total: 35 min.

8 (14 x 9-inch) sheets frozen phyllo
  dough, thawed
1/4 cup olive oil, divided
2 tablespoons grated fresh
  Parmigiano-Reggiano cheese
1 teaspoon freshly ground black pepper
1 cup multicolored grape tomatoes,
  quartered lengthwise
1/4 cup thinly sliced shallots
2 tablespoons chopped fresh basil
1 teaspoon chopped fresh thyme
1/4 teaspoon kosher salt
1.5 ounces aged fontina cheese, grated
Cooking spray

1. Preheat oven to 375°.
2. Place 1 phyllo sheet on a work surface (cover remaining phyllo to prevent drying); lightly brush phyllo sheet with 1½ teaspoons oil. Combine Parmigiano-Reggiano cheese and pepper, stirring well. Sprinkle about 1 teaspoon pepper mixture evenly over phyllo; top with another phyllo sheet. Combine tomatoes and next 5 ingredients in a bowl. Arrange about 1/3 cup tomato mixture along short side of phyllo; roll up phyllo, jelly-roll fashion, starting with short side. Lightly brush outside of roll with oil. Cut into thirds. Place on a baking sheet coated with cooking

Kid Friendly • Make Ahead
Vegetarian
Quinoa-Granola Chocolate Chip Cookies

Hands-on: 25 min. Total: 1 hr. 25 min.

4.5 ounces all-purpose flour (about
  1 cup)
2.25 ounces quinoa flour (about 1/2 cup)
1 teaspoon baking powder
1/2 teaspoon salt
1/2 cup granulated sugar
1/2 cup packed brown sugar
1/3 cup canola oil
2 tablespoons butter, softened
1½ teaspoons vanilla extract
1 large egg
1 3/4 cups Nutty Whole-Grain Granola
  (recipe at right)
1/3 cup semisweet chocolate minichips

1. Weigh or lightly spoon flours into dry measuring cups; level with a knife. Combine flours, baking powder, and salt, stirring with a whisk. Place sugars, oil, and butter in a large bowl; beat with a mixer at medium speed until combined. Add vanilla and egg; beat until well blended. Add flour mixture, beating at low speed just until combined. Stir in Nutty Whole-Grain Granola and chocolate chips. Cover and chill dough 45 minutes.
2. Preheat oven to 350°.

Kid Friendly • Make Ahead
Vegetarian
Nutty Whole-Grain Granola

Hands-on: 10 min. Total: 38 min.

2 cups old-fashioned rolled oats
1 cup packed brown sugar
2/3 cup uncooked millet
2/3 cup dried cherries
1/4 cup walnut halves
1/4 cup roasted, salted whole almonds
1/4 cup hazelnuts
3/4 teaspoon kosher salt
3 tablespoons butter, melted
2 tablespoons light-colored corn syrup
1 large egg white
Cooking spray

1. Preheat oven to 400°.
2. Combine first 8 ingredients, tossing to combine. Combine butter, syrup, and egg white, stirring well. Drizzle butter mixture over oat mixture; toss well to coat. Spread mixture in a single layer on a baking sheet lined with parchment paper coated with cooking spray. Bake at 400° for 27 minutes or until golden, stirring twice. Serves 20 (serving size: 1/3 cup)

CALORIES 162; FAT 5.3g (sat 1.5g, mono 2g, poly 1.4g); PROTEIN 2.8g; CARB 27g; FIBER 1.8g; CHOL 5mg; IRON 0.8mg; SODIUM 95mg; CALC 18mg

Salty-Sweet Pine Nut Bars

Hands-on: 14 min. Total: 55 min. Lightly pat the flour mixture into the bottom of the pan so the crust bakes evenly. Pine nuts can be expensive; pecans are a less pricey but equally delicious alternative.

2.7 ounces cake flour (about ²/₃ cup)
¹/₂ cup powdered sugar
¹/₄ cup cornstarch
⁵/₈ teaspoon salt, divided
3 ounces fat-free cream cheese
2 tablespoons butter
Cooking spray
³/₄ cup maple syrup
¹/₃ cup granulated sugar
1 teaspoon vanilla extract
2 large eggs
¹/₂ cup pine nuts

1. Preheat oven to 400°.
2. Weigh or lightly spoon flour into a dry measuring cup, and level with a knife. Combine flour, powdered sugar, cornstarch, and ⅛ teaspoon salt, stirring with a whisk. Cut in cream cheese and butter with a pastry blender or 2 knives until mixture resembles coarse meal. Transfer mixture to a 9-inch square metal baking pan coated with cooking spray; pat mixture evenly into pan. Bake at 400° for 18 minutes or until lightly browned.
3. Reduce oven temperature to 350°.
4. Combine maple syrup and next 3 ingredients, stirring with a whisk. Stir in pine nuts. Pour syrup mixture over crust, spreading nuts evenly over top. Sprinkle with ½ teaspoon salt. Bake at 350° for 25 minutes or until set. Cool. Cut into 25 squares. Serves 25 (serving size: 1 bar)

CALORIES 99; **FAT** 3.2g (sat 0.9g, mono 0.9g, poly 1.1g);
PROTEIN 1.7g; **CARB** 16.2g; **FIBER** 0.2g; **CHOL** 18mg;
IRON 0.5mg; **SODIUM** 87mg; **CALC** 25mg

Peanut-Almond Snack Bars

Hands-on: 12 min. Total: 1 hr. 12 min.

2¹/₂ tablespoons butter
3 cups miniature marshmallows
¹/₂ cup chunky peanut butter
2¹/₄ cups chocolate toasted oat cereal (such as Cheerios)
1¹/₄ cups old-fashioned rolled oats
1 cup crushed hard pretzel twists
¹/₃ cup roasted, salted almonds
¹/₄ teaspoon kosher salt
Cooking spray

1. Melt butter in a large saucepan over medium heat. Add marshmallows and peanut butter; cook 3 minutes or until smooth, stirring constantly. Remove mixture from heat; stir in cereal and next 4 ingredients.
2. Working quickly, spread mixture in an 8-inch square metal baking pan coated with cooking spray. Using a wet spoon, spread mixture into an even 1-inch layer; let stand 1 hour or until set. Cut into 16 squares. Serves 16 (serving size: 1 bar)

CALORIES 162; **FAT** 8.1g (sat 1.9g, mono 3.6g, poly 2g);
PROTEIN 3.7g; **CARB** 19.9g; **FIBER** 1.8g; **CHOL** 5mg;
IRON 1.5mg; **SODIUM** 162mg; **CALC** 27mg

WE'VE COVERED THE BASES: CRUNCHY-SALTY, FUDGY-CHEWY, BUTTERY-NUTTY.

HYPERSPEED YOUR SUPPERS

6 prepared supermarket foods cleverly transformed into 6 fast, satisfying meals

Fish Stick Tacos

Hands-on: 20 min. Total: 35 min. To get an extra-crispy crust on the fish, we bake the sticks at a higher temperature than called for on the box.

3 tablespoons light sour cream, divided
2 tablespoons canola mayonnaise (such as Hellmann's)
2 tablespoons fresh lime juice, divided
1 tablespoon chopped chipotle chile, canned in adobo sauce
1 teaspoon sugar
1 teaspoon red wine vinegar
¹/₂ teaspoon grated lime rind
³/₈ teaspoon kosher salt, divided
¹/₄ teaspoon freshly ground black pepper
3 cups packaged cabbage-and-carrot coleslaw
2 tablespoons 1% low-fat milk
¹/₂ ripe peeled avocado, diced (about ¹/₂ cup)
1 garlic clove, chopped
16 sustainable frozen fish sticks (such as Ian's; about 8 ounces)
Cooking spray
8 (6-inch) corn tortillas
8 lime wedges

1. Preheat oven to 425°.
2. Combine 1 tablespoon sour cream, mayonnaise, 1 tablespoon lime juice, chipotle, sugar, vinegar, rind, ¼ teaspoon salt, and pepper in a medium bowl, stirring with a whisk. Add coleslaw; toss to coat.

continued

3. Place 2 tablespoons sour cream, 1 tablespoon lime juice, ⅛ teaspoon salt, milk, avocado, and garlic in a mini food processor; process until smooth.
4. Arrange frozen fish sticks in a single layer on a baking sheet coated with cooking spray. Bake at 425° for 27 minutes or until browned and crisp, turning once.
5. Heat tortillas according to package directions. Top each tortilla with about 1 tablespoon avocado mixture, 2 fish sticks, and ⅓ cup slaw mixture. Serve with lime wedges. Serves 4 (serving size: 2 tacos and 2 lime wedges)

CALORIES 374; **FAT** 16.6g (sat 2.3g, mono 7.4g, poly 4.1g); **PROTEIN** 12.5g; **CARB** 46.3g; **FIBER** 6.8g; **CHOL** 28mg; **IRON** 1.1mg; **SODIUM** 470mg; **CALC** 90mg

Kid Friendly • Quick & Easy
Spinach-Artichoke Pasta with Vegetables

Hands-on: 22 min. Total: 22 min. An appetizer favorite becomes a silky, creamy sauce for this quick weeknight pasta dinner full of cheesy, veggie, nutty goodness.

8 ounces uncooked rotini pasta
2 cups (2-inch) cut asparagus
1 cup (2 x ½-inch) cut yellow bell pepper
⅔ cup 1% low-fat milk
1 (8-ounce) package frozen spinach-and-artichoke cheese dip (such as T.G.I. Friday's), thawed
½ teaspoon kosher salt
12 grape tomatoes, halved
¼ cup basil leaves, torn
3 tablespoons pine nuts, toasted
1 ounce Parmigiano-Reggiano cheese, shaved (about ¼ cup)

1. Cook pasta according to package directions, omitting salt and fat. During the last 3 minutes of cooking, add asparagus and bell pepper to pan; drain.
2. Combine milk and spinach dip in a medium saucepan over medium heat; bring to a simmer. Reduce heat, and cook 5 minutes or until slightly thickened. Combine pasta mixture, spinach mixture, salt, and tomatoes in a large bowl; toss to coat. Sprinkle with basil, pine nuts, and cheese. Serves 4 (serving size: about 1¾ cups)

CALORIES 388; **FAT** 10.9g (sat 4.1g, mono 1.9g, poly 2.4g); **PROTEIN** 19g; **CARB** 55.5g; **FIBER** 5.3g; **CHOL** 16mg; **IRON** 4mg; **SODIUM** 577mg; **CALC** 290mg

Kid Friendly • Quick & Easy
Chicken and Pierogi Dumplings

Hands-on: 36 min. Total: 36 min. The browned veggies lend color and flavor to the sauce; be sure to keep them moving in the pan so they don't get too brown.

¾ pound skinless, boneless chicken breast, cut into bite-sized pieces
¾ teaspoon freshly ground black pepper
⅛ teaspoon kosher salt
Cooking spray
¾ cup diced onion
½ cup diced carrot
½ cup diced celery
1 tablespoon chopped fresh thyme
2 cups unsalted chicken stock (such as Swanson)
1 cup 2% reduced-fat milk
5 tablespoons all-purpose flour
20 frozen potato and cheddar mini pierogies (such as Mrs. T's)
2 tablespoons chopped fresh flat-leaf parsley

1. Heat a large skillet over medium-high heat. Sprinkle chicken with pepper and salt. Coat pan with cooking spray. Add chicken to pan; cook 4 minutes, browning on all sides. Remove chicken from pan; keep warm.
2. Return pan to medium-high heat. Add onion, carrot, celery, and chopped thyme to pan. Cook 6 minutes or until vegetables are tender and lightly browned, stirring frequently. Combine stock, milk, and flour in a bowl, stirring with a whisk until well blended. Gradually add stock mixture to pan, stirring constantly; bring to a boil. Cook 2 minutes or until thickened. Stir in chicken and pierogies; cook 4 minutes or until chicken is done and pierogies are warm. Sprinkle with chopped parsley. Serves 4 (serving size: about 1¼ cups)

CALORIES 298; **FAT** 5.1g (sat 1.7g, mono 1g, poly 0.5g); **PROTEIN** 27.1g; **CARB** 35.4g; **FIBER** 2.4g; **CHOL** 63mg; **IRON** 2.4mg; **SODIUM** 555mg; **CALC** 127mg

Kid Friendly • Quick & Easy
Make Ahead
Herbed Parmesan Potato Soup

Hands-on: 24 min. Total: 24 min. Prepared mashed potatoes tend to come packed with a lot of sodium—too much for a side dish. Here we stretch them out into an entrée-sized soup that's creamy, cheesy, and brightened with fresh herbs.

1 teaspoon olive oil
3 shallots, chopped
3 garlic cloves, chopped
3 cups unsalted chicken stock (such as Swanson)
1 (24-ounce) container prepared traditional mashed potatoes (such as Simply Potatoes)
½ cup torn basil leaves, divided
6 thyme sprigs
2 tablespoons coarsely chopped fresh chives, divided
¼ cup half-and-half
2 ounces Parmigiano-Reggiano cheese, grated (about ½ cup)
¼ teaspoon freshly ground black pepper

1. Heat a medium saucepan over medium heat. Add oil to pan; swirl to coat. Add shallots; cook 5 minutes or until shallots begin to brown, stirring frequently. Add garlic; cook 1 minute

or until fragrant. Stir in stock; cook 30 seconds. Transfer stock mixture to a blender; process until smooth.
2. Return stock mixture to pan; add potatoes, stirring with a whisk until combined. Stir in ¼ cup basil, thyme, and 1 tablespoon chives; bring to a boil. Cook 1 minute. Remove from heat; discard thyme. Stir in half-and-half, cheese, and pepper. Sprinkle with ¼ cup basil and 1 tablespoon chives. Serves 6 (serving size: 1 cup)

CALORIES 198; FAT 9g (sat 5.4g, mono 2.4g, poly 0.7g); PROTEIN 9.7g; CARB 19.9g; FIBER 2.8g; CHOL 27mg; IRON 1.2mg; SODIUM 597mg; CALC 174mg

Kid Friendly • Make Ahead Vegetarian

Easy Ravioli Lasagna

***Hands-on: 12 min. Total: 53 min.** With ricotta cheese and spinach already tucked inside each ravioli, this is a shortcut way to a well-rounded lasagna. Classic meat sauce makes it über family friendly.*

Cooking spray
4 ounces hot pork Italian sausage
4 ounces 90% lean ground sirloin
4 garlic cloves, minced
2 cups lower-sodium marinara sauce (such as Dell'Amore)
⅛ teaspoon kosher salt
¼ teaspoon crushed red pepper
1 (22-ounce) bag frozen whole-wheat spinach and cheese ravioli (such as Whole Foods 365 Everyday Value)
3 ounces part-skim mozzarella cheese, shredded (about ¾ cup)
1 ounce Parmigiano-Reggiano cheese, grated (about ¼ cup)

1. Preheat oven to 375°.
2. Heat a large skillet over medium-high heat. Coat pan with cooking spray. Add sausage, beef, and garlic; cook 4 minutes or until meat is browned, stirring frequently to crumble. Stir in marinara sauce, salt,

and pepper; bring just to a simmer. Remove from heat. Stir in frozen ravioli; toss to combine.
3. Coat an 8-inch square broiler-safe glass or ceramic baking dish with cooking spray. Spoon ravioli mixture into pan; top evenly with mozzarella cheese. Cover dish tightly with foil coated with cooking spray. Bake at 375° for 40 minutes. Uncover and sprinkle evenly with Parmigiano-Reggiano cheese.
4. Preheat broiler (leave dish in oven). Broil 3 minutes or until cheese is bubbly and lightly browned. Serves 6

CALORIES 397; FAT 14.7g (sat 5.7g, mono 4g, poly 0.9g); PROTEIN 22g; CARB 42.6g; FIBER 7.4g; CHOL 46mg; IRON 2.7mg; SODIUM 666mg; CALC 390mg

THE FUN PART IS MAKING THE LEAP FROM THE USUAL TO THE INGENIOUS: CAN RAVIOLI BE USED TO RIFF OFF A LASAGNA THEME? YES, IT TURNS OUT.

Quick & Easy • Vegetarian

Hummus-and-Rice Fritters with Mediterranean Salad

***Hands-on: 25 min. Total: 25 min.** When using flour as a binder for things that are not baked, such as these pan-seared fritters, the finer grade of cake flour yields a creamier texture in the cooked product. If you don't have it, don't sweat it: You can just use all-purpose.*

1½ cups precooked packaged brown rice (such as Uncle Ben's)
1 cup prepared traditional hummus (such as Sabra Classic Hummus)
3 tablespoons cake flour
⅛ teaspoon ground red pepper
1 large egg white
7 teaspoons extra-virgin olive oil, divided
½ teaspoon kosher salt, divided
1 tablespoon fresh lemon juice
¼ teaspoon freshly ground black pepper
2 cups baby arugula
1 cup halved cherry tomatoes
1 cup diagonally cut slices seeded peeled cucumber
½ cup thinly sliced red onion
1 ounce goat cheese, crumbled (about ¼ cup)

1. Place first 5 ingredients in a food processor; process until smooth. Heat a large nonstick skillet over medium heat. Add 2 teaspoons oil to pan; swirl to coat. Add 4 (¼-cup) batter mounds to pan, pressing each with the back of a spatula to flatten slightly. Cook 4 minutes on each side or until golden and thoroughly cooked. Remove from pan; keep warm. Repeat procedure with 2 teaspoons oil and remaining batter. Sprinkle fritters with ¼ teaspoon salt.
2. Combine 1 tablespoon oil, ¼ teaspoon salt, lemon juice, and black pepper in a large bowl, stirring with a whisk. Add arugula, cherry tomatoes, cucumber, and onion; toss gently to coat. Arrange about 1 cup salad, 2 fritters, and 1 tablespoon goat cheese on each of 4 plates. Serve immediately. Serves 4

CALORIES 348; FAT 20.8g (sat 4.2g, mono 10.1g, poly 4g); PROTEIN 9.6g; CARB 32.3g; FIBER 6.3g; CHOL 3mg; IRON 2.2mg; SODIUM 551mg; CALC 40mg

WE LOVE MEATBALLS

We love 'em with noodles, we love 'em in soups, we love 'em on skewers, too...

Tsukune (Japanese Chicken Meatballs)
(pictured on page 232)

Hands-on: 45 min. Total: 1 hr. 15 min.
These meatballs make a terrific party snack. Look for flat skewers at Asian markets, or use two skewers for each group of meatballs so they'll turn easier.

Meatballs:
1 tablespoon dark sesame oil
4 ounces sliced shiitake mushroom caps
1½ tablespoons minced peeled fresh ginger, divided
1½ tablespoons minced fresh garlic, divided
2 tablespoons dry sherry
2 teaspoons red miso (soybean paste)
1½ pounds ground chicken
½ cup panko (Japanese breadcrumbs)
2 teaspoons cornstarch
½ teaspoon freshly ground black pepper
¼ teaspoon kosher salt
2 green onions, thinly sliced
1 large egg white
Sauce:
3 tablespoons mirin (sweet rice wine)
3 tablespoons lower-sodium soy sauce
1 tablespoon dark brown sugar
2 teaspoons sherry vinegar
1 tablespoon fresh lime juice
2 teaspoons grated peeled fresh ginger
1 serrano chile, thinly sliced
Remaining ingredients:
Cooking spray
1 tablespoon toasted sesame seeds

1. To prepare meatballs, heat a small skillet over medium-high heat. Add oil to pan; swirl to coat. Add mushrooms, 1 tablespoon minced ginger, and 1 tablespoon garlic; sauté 2 minutes. Add sherry; cook 3 minutes or until liquid evaporates and mushrooms are tender. Remove from heat; cool. Place mushroom mixture and miso in a mini chopper; pulse 10 times or until very finely chopped.
2. Combine mushroom mixture, 1½ teaspoons minced ginger, 1½ teaspoons garlic, chicken, and next 6 ingredients in a bowl. Shape mixture into 36 (1-inch) meatballs. Thread 3 meatballs onto each of 12 (6-inch) flat bamboo skewers. Chill for 30 minutes.

MEATBALLS ARE A GLOBAL FAVE. THIS JAPANESE VERSION HAS A SWEET GLAZE OF MIRIN, SOY SAUCE, AND GINGER.

3. To prepare sauce, combine mirin, soy sauce, sugar, and vinegar in a small saucepan. Bring to a boil; cook 3 minutes or until slightly thickened. Remove from heat; cool slightly. Stir in juice, 2 teaspoons grated ginger, and serrano. Reserve 2 tablespoons sauce.
4. Heat a grill pan over medium heat. Coat pan with cooking spray. Place 6 skewers in pan; cook 9 minutes, turning to brown on all sides. Remove from pan; brush half of sauce over meatballs. Repeat procedure with remaining 6 skewers and sauce. Sprinkle with sesame seeds; serve with reserved 2 tablespoons sauce. Serves 6 (serving size: 6 meatballs and 1 teaspoon sauce)

CALORIES 265; **FAT** 12.7g (sat 3.1g, mono 5.4g, poly 3.2g); **PROTEIN** 22.9g; **CARB** 12.8g; **FIBER** 1g; **CHOL** 98mg; **IRON** 1.6mg; **SODIUM** 524mg; **CALC** 35mg

Kid Friendly
Spaghetti and Meatballs
(pictured on page 231)

Hands-on: 38 min. Total: 48 min. *You can't go wrong with this classic family favorite. We amp up jarred marinara with charred onion, garlic, and plum tomatoes.*

¾ cup chopped onion
2 teaspoons canola oil
6 garlic cloves, divided
1 pound plum tomatoes, halved lengthwise
1⅓ cups lower-sodium marinara sauce
½ teaspoon salt, divided
⅓ cup panko (Japanese breadcrumbs)
¼ teaspoon crushed red pepper
12 ounces 90% lean ground sirloin
1 large egg
Cooking spray
6 ounces uncooked spaghetti
1.5 ounces fresh Parmesan cheese, grated (about 6 tablespoons)

1. Preheat broiler to high.
2. Combine onion, oil, 3 garlic cloves, and tomatoes in a bowl; toss to coat

vegetables. Arrange tomato mixture on a foil-lined baking sheet. Broil 10 minutes or until vegetables char slightly, stirring after 5 minutes. Spoon tomato mixture into food processor; pulse 6 times or until mixture is coarsely chopped. Combine tomato mixture, marinara, and ⅜ teaspoon salt in a medium saucepan; bring to a simmer.
3. Mince 3 garlic cloves. Combine minced garlic, ⅛ teaspoon salt, panko, red pepper, beef, and egg in a large bowl; mix gently just until combined. Working quickly with damp hands, gently shape beef mixture into 12 meatballs (do not pack). Arrange meatballs in a single layer on a baking sheet coated with cooking spray. Broil 6 inches from heat 6 minutes, turning meatballs once. Remove pan from oven. Add meatballs to tomato mixture; simmer 4 minutes or until meatballs are done.
4. Cook pasta according to package directions, omitting salt and fat. Serve meatballs and sauce over pasta; sprinkle with cheese. Serves 4 (serving size: ¾ cup pasta, 3 meatballs, about ¾ cup sauce, and about 1½ tablespoons cheese)

CALORIES 476; FAT 16.8g (sat 6g, mono 6.6g, poly 1.7g); PROTEIN 31.2g; CARB 48.9g; FIBER 4.2g; CHOL 111mg; IRON 5mg; SODIUM 621mg; CALC 184mg

Kid Friendly • Quick & Easy
Meatball Subs

Hands-on: 29 min. Total: 29 min. These meaty, saucy, two-napkin sandwiches are destined for heavy dinnertime rotation.

⅓ cup panko (Japanese breadcrumbs)
¼ teaspoon salt
¼ teaspoon crushed red pepper
12 ounces 90% lean ground sirloin
3 garlic cloves, minced
1 large egg
Cooking spray
2 yellow bell peppers, halved and seeded
1⅓ cups lower-sodium marinara sauce
¾ cup sliced onion
4 (2-ounce) hoagie sandwich buns
2 ounces fresh mozzarella cheese, thinly sliced
Thinly sliced fresh basil (optional)

1. Preheat broiler to high.
2. Combine first 6 ingredients in a bowl; mix gently. Working with damp hands, gently shape beef mixture into 16 meatballs. Arrange meatballs in a single layer on a heavy-duty baking sheet coated with cooking spray, leaving 6 inches of open space on one end. Place bell pepper halves, skin sides up, on open space on pan. Broil 6 inches from heat 7 minutes, turning meatballs once. Remove pan from oven. Place peppers in a small paper bag; fold to close tightly. Let stand 10 minutes. Remove peppers from bag. Peel and slice into ¼-inch-thick strips.
3. Bring marinara sauce to a simmer in a large skillet over medium-low heat; add meatballs, tossing to coat. Keep warm.
4. Heat a grill pan over medium-high heat; coat pan with cooking spray. Add onion slices; cook 4 minutes on each side or until charred. Remove onion from pan.
5. Coat insides of buns with cooking spray, and broil 2 minutes or until toasted. Top each bun with 4 meatballs and ⅓ cup sauce. Divide peppers, onions, and cheese evenly among sandwiches; broil sandwiches 2 minutes or until bubbly and browned. Garnish with basil, if desired. Serves 4 (serving size: 1 sandwich)

CALORIES 423; FAT 16g (sat 6.2g, mono 5.6g, poly 1.7g); PROTEIN 25.7g; CARB 44.3g; FIBER 4.8g; CHOL 100mg; IRON 4.1mg; SODIUM 708mg; CALC 107mg

LOADED UP WITH MARINARA, MOZZARELLA, AND GARLICKY MEATBALLS

IN OUR PLAY ON ITALIAN WEDDING SOUP, COOKED QUINOA SERVES AS A NUTTY, WHOLE-GRAIN BINDER FOR THE MEATBALLS.

Make Ahead
Turkey Meatball Soup with Greens

Hands-on: 40 min. Total: 60 min. We like the tenderness of lacinato kale, but you can substitute other varieties in this soup.

1 pound ground turkey breast
½ cup cooked quinoa
2 ounces Parmigiano-Reggiano cheese, grated and divided (about ½ cup)
2 tablespoons chopped fresh flat-leaf parsley
2 tablespoons chopped fresh basil
¾ teaspoon kosher salt, divided
½ teaspoon freshly ground black pepper, divided
6 garlic cloves, minced and divided
1 large egg, lightly beaten
4 teaspoons extra-virgin olive oil, divided
½ cup chopped shallots
½ cup chopped celery
8 cups trimmed chopped lacinato kale (about 1 pound)
¼ teaspoon crushed red pepper
5 cups unsalted chicken stock (such as Swanson)
Lemon wedges (optional)

1. Combine turkey, quinoa, ¼ cup cheese, parsley, basil, ¼ teaspoon salt, ¼ teaspoon black pepper, 2 garlic cloves, and egg in a large bowl; mix gently just
continued

until combined. Working with damp hands, shape turkey mixture into 24 meatballs (about 2 tablespoons each).
2. Heat a large Dutch oven over medium-high heat. Add 1 teaspoon oil to pan; swirl to coat. Add 12 meatballs; cook 8 minutes, turning to brown on all sides. Remove from pan. Repeat procedure with 1 teaspoon oil and 12 meatballs. Add 2 teaspoons oil to pan; swirl to coat. Add shallots and celery to pan; sauté 5 minutes. Add 4 garlic cloves; sauté 1 minute. Add kale, remaining ½ teaspoon salt, ¼ teaspoon black pepper, and red pepper; cook 2 minutes, stirring occasionally. Add stock; bring to a boil. Return meatballs to pan. Reduce heat; simmer 10 minutes or until kale is tender and meatballs are done. Ladle 1⅓ cups soup into each of 6 bowls; divide remaining cheese evenly among bowls. Serve with lemon, if desired. Serves 6

CALORIES 264; **FAT** 8.5g (sat 2.7g, mono 3.3g, poly 0.9g); **PROTEIN** 30.7g; **CARB** 18.1g; **FIBER** 3.3g; **CHOL** 70mg; **IRON** 3.1mg; **SODIUM** 608mg; **CALC** 271mg

BEEFY SIRLOIN DRAPED IN WINE-SPIKED, CREAMY MUSHROOM SAUCE: THE COMFORT OF STROGANOFF WITH A MEATBALL TWIST

Kid Friendly • Quick & Easy
Meatball Stroganoff

Hands-on: 40 min. Total: 40 min. *Serve sautéed Broccolini, spinach, or Brussels sprouts alongside this hearty entrée.*

6 ounces uncooked egg noodles
4 teaspoons canola oil, divided
1¼ cups diced yellow onion
12 ounces 90% lean ground sirloin
⅓ cup chopped fresh flat-leaf parsley, divided
3 tablespoons panko (Japanese breadcrumbs)
3 tablespoons 2% reduced-fat milk
½ teaspoon salt, divided
½ teaspoon freshly ground black pepper, divided
Cooking spray
12 ounces cremini mushrooms, sliced
2 teaspoons minced fresh garlic
¼ teaspoon paprika
¼ cup dry white wine
1 tablespoon all-purpose flour
1 cup unsalted beef stock (such as Swanson)
⅓ cup sour cream
1 teaspoon Dijon mustard
Dash of nutmeg

1. Place a foil-lined jelly-roll pan in oven on the middle rack. Preheat oven to 450° (keep pan in oven).
2. Cook noodles according to package directions, omitting salt and fat. Drain; keep warm.
3. Heat a large skillet over medium-high heat. Add 2 teaspoons oil to pan; swirl to coat. Add onion to pan; sauté 6 minutes or until tender. Place onion in a small bowl. Combine beef, 3 tablespoons parsley, panko, milk,

¼ teaspoon salt, and ¼ teaspoon pepper in a large bowl; stir in ⅓ cup cooked onion. Shape beef mixture into 16 (1½-inch) meatballs. Place meatballs on preheated pan coated with cooking spray. Bake at 450° for 12 minutes or until done, turning after 6 minutes.
4. Return skillet to medium-high heat. Add 2 teaspoons oil to pan; swirl to coat. Add mushrooms, garlic, and paprika to pan; sauté 8 minutes or until mushrooms are lightly browned. Add wine to pan; cook 1 minute or until liquid almost evaporates. Sprinkle flour over mushroom mixture; cook 30 seconds, stirring constantly. Add stock; bring to a boil, scraping pan to loosen browned bits. Reduce heat, and simmer 3 minutes or until sauce slightly thickens. Stir in remaining cooked onion; remove pan from heat. Stir in ¼ teaspoon salt, ¼ teaspoon pepper, sour cream, mustard, and nutmeg. Add meatballs to sauce; toss to coat. Spoon sauce and meatballs over cooked noodles. Sprinkle evenly with remaining parsley. Serves 4 (serving size: about ¾ cup noodles and 1 cup meatball mixture)

CALORIES 463; **FAT** 18.9g (sat 6.5g, mono 7.5g, poly 1.8g); **PROTEIN** 27.5g; **CARB** 44.6g; **FIBER** 3.4g; **CHOL** 113mg; **IRON** 4.3mg; **SODIUM** 459mg; **CALC** 82mg

WINE NOTE

Go for a citrusy and mildly floral white, like A to Z's Oregon Pinot Gris, 2012 ($12). This crisp, full-bodied wine has enough structure to stand up to the meatballs and plenty of racy sharpness to complement the tangy combination of sour cream, garlic, and mustard. —Jordan Mackay

GRILLED SKIRT STEAK & HONEYED SUNCHOKES

By Tim Cebula

Sunchokes are the kind of root veggie that can steal the show. Brown, knobby, and homely, they transform plates and attitudes if properly handled; people eating them for the first time resolve to make a habit of it. Chef Todd Erickson puts these tubers to delectable use at his hip gastro-lounge, Haven, in Miami Beach. (Erickson's innovative, precise cooking won Slow Food Miami's "Snail of Approval" award this spring, judged by *Cooking Light* Editor Scott Mowbray.)

"They're a great alternative to potatoes, with much more depth of flavor," the chef says of sunchokes, which are sometimes called Jerusalem artichokes, though they are neither artichokes nor from Jerusalem. He likes their versatility: They can be sliced paper-thin and served raw, or roasted until tender, and then mashed and mixed in with potatoes or roasted squash. He prefers to leave the skin on to take advantage of the extra snap it provides. The flavor is rich and nutty.

Erickson's steak and sunchoke dish is a play on classic meat and potatoes, with amped-up flavor from herby chimichurri. The sunchokes are roasted with a touch of honey until tantalizingly caramelized. Sample Erickson's version this month at Haven.

SUNCHOKE PREP

Clean: Scrub with a vegetable brush to remove dirt or grit from the exterior. Handle carefully to avoid bruising the flesh.

Trim: Cut to a uniform size so slices cook evenly. Leave the skin on to add snappy texture to the cooked choke.

Cook immediately: Once cut, roast, sauté, or steam right away; the white flesh turns brown soon after being exposed to the air.

Grilled Skirt Steak with Mint Chimichurri and Honey-Roasted Sunchokes

Hands-on: 22 min. Total: 2 hr. 7 min.

¼ cup coarsely chopped fresh mint
¼ cup chopped fresh flat-leaf parsley
3 tablespoons extra-virgin olive oil
1 tablespoon dried oregano
1 tablespoon cider vinegar
½ teaspoon grated lemon rind
1 teaspoon fresh lemon juice
½ jalapeño pepper
1 (1-pound) skirt steak, trimmed
2 tablespoons honey
1 tablespoon fresh lemon juice
4 teaspoons extra-virgin olive oil
¼ teaspoon kosher salt
1 pound sunchokes, cut into
  ½-inch-thick slices
3 large shallots, peeled and cut
  into wedges
½ teaspoon kosher salt
½ teaspoon freshly ground black
  pepper

1. Place first 8 ingredients in food processor; pulse to combine. Rub steak evenly with half of herb mixture; place in a zip-top plastic bag. Reserve remaining half of herb mixture. Let steak stand 1 hour, or refrigerate overnight.
2. Preheat oven to 425°.
3. Combine honey and next 5 ingredients in a large bowl; toss to coat. Arrange sunchoke mixture in a single layer on a jelly-roll pan. Bake at 425° for 35 minutes or until vegetables are tender and caramelized, stirring twice.
4. Preheat grill to medium-high heat.
continued

5. Remove steak from bag; discard marinade. Sprinkle steak evenly with ½ teaspoon salt and black pepper. Place steak on grill rack; grill 4 minutes on each side or until desired degree of doneness. Let stand 10 minutes. Cut steak across the grain into thin slices; top with reserved herb mixture. Serve with sunchoke mixture. Serves 4 (serving size: 3 ounces steak, 2 teaspoons herb mixture, and 1 cup sunchoke mixture)

CALORIES 447; **FAT** 25g (sat 6g, mono 15.8g, poly 1.9g); **PROTEIN** 25.6g; **CARB** 33.7g; **FIBER** 2.6g; **CHOL** 51mg; **IRON** 7.2mg; **SODIUM** 432mg; **CALC** 49mg

PEAK SEASON

Quick & Easy • Make Ahead Vegetarian

Roasted Hatch Chile Salsa

Preheat broiler to high. Place 3 Hatch chiles, 1 pound tomatoes, 4 peeled medium shallots, and 3 unpeeled garlic cloves on a baking sheet. Broil vegetable mixture 10 minutes or until charred, turning once after 5 minutes. Remove chiles from pan. Place in a paper bag; fold to close tightly. Let stand 15 minutes. Remove skins, tops, and seeds from chiles; discard. Remove skins from garlic; discard. Place chiles, garlic, tomatoes, shallots, 2 tablespoons chopped fresh cilantro, 2½ tablespoons fresh lime juice, and ¾ teaspoon kosher salt in food processor; pulse 10 times or until mixture is well combined. Serves 12 (serving size: ¼ cup)

CALORIES 34; **FAT** 0.2g (sat 0g); **SODIUM** 185mg

PICKED FRESH FOR SEPTEMBER: LETTUCES

This month from the *Cooking Light* Garden: Fall's sweet, crispy, leafy greens

When cooler weather hits the garden, lettuce starts to thrive. For master gardener Mary Beth Shaddix and our *Cooking Light* Garden in Alabama, the fall crop means a bounty of gorgeous leafy greens, something that Shaddix has recently come to relish.

"I didn't really eat fresh salads until I grew my own," Shaddix says. "I thought salad greens lacked flavor. But when you grow your own, you can really explore the varieties—some have soft, buttery texture; others are crisp-crunchy. And they all have real taste."

Shaddix grew interesting varieties of three main lettuce types: romaine, butterhead, and loose leaf. The first two are typically harvested as whole heads, while loose leaf can be harvested sporadically, from the outside of the plant inward. We put them all to use here in ways that showcase their fantastic textures and fresh, lightly mineral flavors.

Quick & Easy

Blackened Chicken Salad with Blue Cheese Vinaigrette

Hands-on: 18 min. Total: 18 min.

1 teaspoon Hungarian sweet paprika
1 teaspoon freshly ground black pepper
½ teaspoon kosher salt
½ teaspoon garlic powder
½ teaspoon dried oregano
½ teaspoon dried thyme
½ teaspoon ground red pepper
4 (6-ounce) skinless, boneless chicken breast halves
Cooking spray
2 tablespoons extra-virgin olive oil
1 tablespoon white wine vinegar
1 tablespoon minced shallots
½ teaspoon Dijon mustard
¼ teaspoon freshly ground black pepper
⅛ teaspoon kosher salt
1 ounce blue cheese, crumbled (about ¼ cup)
2 heads romaine lettuce, halved lengthwise
1 cup grape tomatoes, halved

1. Combine first 7 ingredients. Sprinkle chicken with mixture. Heat a grill pan over medium-high heat. Coat pan with cooking spray. Add chicken to pan; cook 5 minutes on each side or until done. Let stand 5 minutes; cut across the grain into thin slices.

2. Combine oil and next 5 ingredients in a small bowl, stirring with a whisk. Stir in cheese.

3. Place 1 lettuce half and ¼ cup tomatoes on each of 4 plates. Top each serving with 1 sliced chicken breast half, and drizzle each with about 1½ tablespoons vinaigrette. Serves 4

CALORIES 349; **FAT** 14.4g (sat 3.4g, mono 6.8g, poly 2g); **PROTEIN** 42.1g; **CARB** 13.9g; **FIBER** 7.7g; **CHOL** 114mg; **IRON** 4.2mg; **SODIUM** 639mg; **CALC** 165mg

Spicy Steak Lettuce Wraps

Hands-on: 18 min. Total: 65 min.

1 (12-ounce) sirloin steak
2 tablespoons dark brown sugar
3 tablespoons rice vinegar
3 tablespoons lower-sodium soy sauce
2 tablespoons grated shallots
2 tablespoons sambal oelek (chile paste)
1 tablespoon grated peeled fresh ginger
2 teaspoons sesame oil
Cooking spray
12 large Boston lettuce leaves (about 2 heads)
1 cup matchstick-cut English cucumber
1 cup thinly sliced red onion
1 cup matchstick-cut carrot
½ cup cilantro leaves

1. Place steak in freezer 15 minutes. Remove from freezer; cut across the grain into ⅛-inch-thick slices. Combine sugar and next 6 ingredients in a large zip-top plastic bag; seal bag, and shake. Remove 3 tablespoons marinade, and set aside. Add steak to marinade in bag; seal and shake. Marinate in refrigerator 1 hour. Remove steak from bag; discard marinade. Heat a large skillet over medium-high heat. Coat pan with cooking spray. Add steak to pan, and cook 1 minute on each side.
2. Divide steak evenly among lettuce leaves. Top each leaf with 4 teaspoons cucumber, 4 teaspoons onion, 4 teaspoons carrot, and 2 teaspoons cilantro; drizzle with reserved 3 tablespoons marinade. Serves 4 (serving size: 3 lettuce wraps)

CALORIES 268; **FAT** 13.5g (sat 4.7g, mono 5.6g, poly 1.5g); **PROTEIN** 19.3g; **CARB** 17.9g; **FIBER** 1.9g; **CHOL** 64mg; **IRON** 2.2mg; **SODIUM** 363mg; **CALC** 57mg

Quick & Easy • Vegetarian

Mixed Greens Salad with Hoisin-Sesame Vinaigrette

Hands-on: 15 min. Total: 15 min.

2 tablespoons extra-virgin olive oil
1 tablespoon rice vinegar
2 teaspoons finely chopped green onions
2 teaspoons fresh lemon juice
2 teaspoons hoisin sauce
1 teaspoon dark sesame oil
½ teaspoon minced fresh garlic
¼ teaspoon freshly ground white pepper
⅛ teaspoon kosher salt
6 cups torn mixed romaine lettuce leaves
1 cup trimmed snow peas, sliced diagonally
1 cup thinly sliced red bell pepper
½ cup chopped fresh cilantro
1 tablespoon toasted sesame seeds

1. Combine first 9 ingredients in a large bowl, and stir with a whisk.
2. Add lettuce, peas, bell pepper, and cilantro; toss. Top with sesame seeds. Serves 4 (serving size: about 1½ cups)

CALORIES 114; **FAT** 9.2g (sat 1.3g, mono 5.8g, poly 1.8g); **PROTEIN** 2g; **CARB** 7.4g; **FIBER** 2.8g; **CHOL** 0mg; **IRON** 1.4mg; **SODIUM** 158mg; **CALC** 36mg

LETTUCE VARITIES

WINTER DENSITY
This Bibb-romaine blend is tender yet crisp, hearty, and substantial enough to stand up to dressings like a warm bacon vinaigrette.

BLACK-SEEDED SIMPSON
Seeds for this tender, sweet leaf lettuce look like black sesame seeds. The greens hold up well to heat: a good choice for warmer climates.

RED ROSE
As a deep red-tinted romaine lettuce, it makes for great visual contrast in salads. Try mixing it with chopped romaine in a Caesar.

LOLLO ROSSA
One of the most colorful varieties we grew, this loose leaf lettuce runs from wine red to hot pink and lime green. It's hardy enough to grow late into the fall.

ROSALITA
A red-tipped leaf that's a little more tender than other varieties of romaine, it adds textural contrast in salads and works well as a wrap.

CHICKEN POTPIES

Chicken potpie lovers are split between two camps: Some love the fluffy deliciousness of a biscuit topping, while others prefer crisp, flaky pastry as a contrast to the tender chicken and veggies in silky sauce. Here, we show you how to make both, with one filling that sits just fine under either topping. Go with your favorite, or try both and let us know which you prefer. Either way, you'll have a healthy, delicious meal that's sure to be a hit with your family.

Kid Friendly

Biscuit-Topped Chicken Potpie

Hands-on: 35 min. Total: 1 hr. 15 min.

Filling:
1 tablespoon canola oil
1½ cups chopped onion
1 cup chopped carrot
½ cup chopped celery
1 garlic clove, minced
1.1 ounces all-purpose flour (about ¼ cup)
¼ teaspoon kosher salt
¼ teaspoon black pepper
4 cups unsalted chicken stock (such as Swanson)
2 cups shredded cooked chicken breast
1 cup frozen green peas, thawed

1 (¾-ounce) package fresh poultry blend herbs
Cooking spray
Biscuits:
4.5 ounces all-purpose flour (about 1 cup)
1 teaspoon baking soda
¼ cup cold butter, cubed
⅓ cup buttermilk

1. Preheat oven to 425°.
2. To prepare filling, heat oil in a large saucepan over medium-high heat. Add onion, carrot, and celery; sauté 4 minutes. Add garlic; sauté 30 seconds. Weigh or lightly spoon 1.1 ounces (¼ cup) flour into a dry measuring cup; level with a knife. Stir flour, salt, and pepper into vegetables; cook 1 minute, stirring constantly. Stir in stock; bring to a boil. Reduce heat to medium; simmer 8 minutes, stirring occasionally. Stir in chicken and peas; simmer 5 minutes. Remove from heat. Remove rosemary from herb package; reserve for another use. Strip leaves from stems of remaining herbs; chop leaves to measure 2 tablespoons. Stir herbs into filling. Pour filling in a 2-quart baking dish or cast-iron skillet coated with cooking spray.
3. To prepare biscuits, weigh or lightly spoon 4.5 ounces (1 cup) flour into a dry measuring cup; level with a knife. Combine flour and baking soda. Using a pastry blender or 2 knives, cut butter into flour mixture until it resembles coarse meal. Stir in buttermilk. Turn dough out onto a lightly floured surface; knead gently 5 to 6 times. Roll to a 9-inch circle. Cut with a 2-inch round biscuit cutter, rerolling scraps. Arrange biscuits over filling; coat with cooking spray. Bake at 425° for 35 minutes or until browned. Serves 6 (serving size: about 1½ cups)

CALORIES 334; **FAT** 12.8g (sat 5.9g, mono 4.1g, poly 1.5g); **PROTEIN** 23g; **CARB** 31g; **FIBER** 3.3g; **CHOL** 62mg; **IRON** 2.5mg; **SODIUM** 543mg; **CALC** 55mg

Pastry-Topped Chicken Potpie Variation
Prepare Biscuit-Topped Chicken Potpie through Step 2. Cut a 9-inch circle of refrigerated pie dough into ¾-inch-wide strips. Weave strips over filling; coat with cooking spray. Bake at 425° for 30 minutes. May be prepared in 6 (10-ounce) ramekins, as shown. Serves 6 (serving size: about 1¼ cups)

CALORIES 312; **FAT** 13.1g (sat 4.4g); **SODIUM** 556mg

STEPS FOR MAKING PASTRY-TOPPED CHICKEN POTPIE

1 LAY THE FOUNDATION
Arrange pastry strips over filling, leaving space between strips.

2 START WEAVING
Pull back every other strip; arrange 1 strip perpendicular to them.

3 ALTERNATE STRIPS
Pull back alternating strips, and arrange another strip across.

4 SEAL THE DEAL
Pinch ends of strips, pressing gently so that pastry adheres to dish.

BLONDIES MADE BETTER

Half the calories, 100% whole grain, and full of buttery brown sugar goodness—that's the new blondie.

Rich and chewy on the inside and golden crisp around the edges, blondies are the seductive cousins of the more aggressive chocolate brownie. Though lighter in color, they're still heavy-weights in calories—285 in one square, plus nearly 9g saturated fat. That fair complexion comes from way too much light brown sugar and melted butter.

We wanted to go beyond a calorie and fat makeover and introduce some whole-grain goodness here, too. That can get tricky because not all baked goods are successful candidates for a whole-wheat makeover. Regular whole-wheat flour can compromise a delicate texture. However, the finer texture of whole-wheat pastry flour works well with the buttery-sweet profile of these bars, yielding a tender crumb. Butter has its place here, too—just less of it, paired with canola oil and butterscotch chips, which we melt into the batter for silky texture and rich flavor. These lightened bars even had room for a few chocolate chips. With nearly half the fat and calories of the original, these whole-grain treats are easy to make and fun to eat.

CLASSIC	MAKEOVER
285 calories per square	154 calories per square
13.3 grams total fat	7.6 grams total fat
8.8 grams saturated fat	3.2 grams saturated fat

Butterscotch Blondies

Hands-on: 12 min. Total: 52 min. Whole-wheat pastry flour is more finely ground than regular whole-wheat flour, with a delicate texture that yields lighter, more tender bar cookies.

4.5 ounces whole-wheat pastry flour
   (about 1 cup)
½ teaspoon baking powder
½ teaspoon salt
¼ cup butterscotch morsels
2 tablespoons half-and-half
¾ cup packed brown sugar
3 tablespoons canola oil
3 tablespoons butter, melted
1 teaspoon vanilla extract
2 large eggs
⅓ cup semisweet chocolate chips
Cooking spray

1. Preheat oven to 350°.
2. Weigh or lightly spoon flour into a dry measuring cup; level with a knife. Combine flour, baking powder, and salt in a medium bowl; stir with a whisk until thoroughly combined.
3. Combine butterscotch morsels and half-and-half in a medium microwave-safe bowl; microwave at HIGH 45 seconds, stirring every 15 seconds. Stir until smooth. Add brown sugar, canola oil, butter, vanilla, and eggs, and beat with a mixer at high speed 2 minutes. Add flour mixture to butterscotch mixture, stirring just until combined. Stir in chocolate chips. Pour batter into an 8-inch square metal baking pan coated with cooking spray. Bake at 350° for 40 minutes or until a wooden pick inserted in center comes out with moist crumbs clinging. Cool in pan on a wire rack. Serves 16 (serving size: 1 square)

CALORIES 154; FAT 7.6g (sat 3.2g, mono 2.9g, poly 1g); PROTEIN 1.9g; CARB 20.4g; FIBER 1.3g; CHOL 30mg; IRON 0.7mg; SODIUM 101mg; CALC 30mg

BAKING BETTER BLONDIES

WHOLE-WHEAT PASTRY FLOUR
This nutrient-packed flour adds 100% whole-grain goodness, boosting fiber to 1.3g per square.

CANOLA OIL
We replaced half the butter with this heart-healthy oil to save 3g sat fat per blondie while keeping them supermoist.

A DUO OF MORSELS
Melted butterscotch subs in for some of the butter to save 2.5g sat fat and add flavor. Chocolate chips add extra yum.

MEATLESS MONDAYS

Quick & Easy • Make Ahead
Vegetarian

Farro Salad with Creamy Feta

Hands-on: 30 min. Total: 30 min. Good news, whole-grain shoppers! Precooked farro is popping up in both the grain aisle and the frozen-foods section of many supermarkets. Alternatively, you can cook up a batch of unpearled farro in about 45 minutes—it keeps, refrigerated, for up to 1 week and freezes beautifully.

2 tablespoons extra-virgin olive oil
2 tablespoons fresh lemon juice
2 tablespoons chopped green onions
2 teaspoons chopped fresh oregano
1/4 teaspoon black pepper
2 1/2 cups precooked whole-grain farro
1 cup chopped tomato
1 cup cucumber, peeled and thinly
   sliced
1 cup organic canned chickpeas, rinsed
   and drained
1 cup chopped fresh flat-leaf parsley
1/2 teaspoon kosher salt
1 (6-inch) whole-wheat pita
Cooking spray
1/8 teaspoon paprika
1/4 cup 2% reduced-fat Greek yogurt
2 tablespoons water
2 ounces 1/3-less-fat cream cheese,
   softened (about 1/4 cup)
1.5 ounces feta cheese, crumbled
   (about 1/3 cup)

1. Preheat oven to 350°.
2. Combine first 5 ingredients in a large bowl, stirring well with a whisk. Add farro; toss gently to combine.
3. Combine tomato and next 4 ingredients (through salt) in a medium bowl. Let stand 10 minutes. Add tomato mixture to farro mixture; toss gently to combine.
4. Split pita into 2 rounds; cut each round into 6 wedges. Lightly coat pita with cooking spray; sprinkle with paprika. Arrange pita wedges on a baking sheet; bake at 350° for 15 minutes or until crisp.
5. Combine yogurt, 2 tablespoons water, cream cheese, and feta, stirring with a whisk. Serve with farro salad and pita chips. Serves 4 (serving size: about 1 1/4 cups salad, 2 tablespoons yogurt mixture, and 3 pita chips)

CALORIES 377; FAT 15.6g (sat 4.7g, mono 6.5g, poly 1.5g); PROTEIN 14.5g; CARB 56.2g; FIBER 7.1g; CHOL 21mg; IRON 2.3mg; SODIUM 589mg; CALC 135mg

MATISSE DRUMS UP A CROWD-PLEASER

Matisse Reid is a kid who cooks for friends and family.

This has been one of the best recipes that I've ever made! The chicken is so flavorful and crunchy, and the buttermilk marinade made the drumsticks nice and tender. We were having a sleepover, so we made everything ahead of time: We breaded the drumsticks, put them in the fridge, and threw them in the oven when we were ready for dinner. It was a really good crowd-pleaser and great for picky kids. Younger children can help by making the dipping sauce—I got my 4-year-old cousin to help me, and he loved mixing the ingredients. All the flavors in this recipe were so good; I will definitely be making this again!

MAKE SURE YOU SPREAD THE DRUMSTICKS OUT ON YOUR PAN SO THAT EACH ONE CAN CRISP UP NICELY.

Kid Friendly

Panko-Crusted Chicken Drumsticks with Honey-Mustard Dipping Sauce

Hands-on: 19 min. Total: 1 hr. 49 min. You can also serve the drumsticks with light ranch dressing. Here's a quick tip for skinning drumsticks: Loosen the skin around the meaty part of the drumstick. Grab the loosened skin with a paper towel, and pull toward the bone end.

8 chicken drumsticks, skinned
1/2 cup whole buttermilk
2 tablespoons grated onion
1 tablespoon grated garlic
Cooking spray
1/4 teaspoon black pepper
1/8 teaspoon salt
3/4 cup panko (Japanese breadcrumbs)
1 ounce Parmesan cheese, grated
   (about 1/4 cup)
2 tablespoons minced fresh chives
2 tablespoons canola mayonnaise
2 tablespoons plain fat-free
   Greek yogurt
1 1/2 teaspoons honey
1 1/2 teaspoons yellow mustard
1/2 teaspoon Dijon mustard

1. Using a paring knife, cut 3 slits in the meatiest portion of each drumstick. Place buttermilk, onion, garlic, and drumsticks in a large zip-top plastic bag; refrigerate 1 hour.

2. Preheat oven to 425°.

3. Place a rack on a jelly-roll pan; coat rack with cooking spray. Remove drumsticks from bag; discard marinade. Sprinkle drumsticks with pepper and salt. Combine panko, cheese, and chives in a shallow dish. Dredge each drumstick in panko mixture. Arrange drumsticks in a single layer on rack; coat drumsticks lightly with cooking spray. Bake drumsticks at 425° for 30 minutes or until chicken is done.

4. Combine mayonnaise and remaining ingredients in a small bowl. Serve sauce with chicken. Serves 4 (serving size: 2 drumsticks and 1 tablespoon sauce)

CALORIES 398; FAT 14.6g (sat 3.6g, mono 5.2g, poly 3g); PROTEIN 51.2g; CARB 11.4g; FIBER 0.6g; CHOL 226mg; IRON 1.8mg; SODIUM 561mg; CALC 116mg

THE VERDICT

JADEN (AGE 4)
He loved that he could pick the drumsticks up with his fingers.
10 out of 10

SHEVAUGHAN (AGE 12)
She liked how crispy the chicken was and was really impressed with the sauce.
10 out of 10

MATISSE (AGE 12)
I loved the dipping sauce, which gave the chicken a zing before the crunch.
10 out of 10

OVEN ESSENTIAL

A wire rack is a baker's best friend, helping to cool cakes, cookies, and other treats. But it can also be useful for oven-frying meat and vegetables. In this recipe, the open grate increases air circulation so the chicken cooks evenly, elevating the drumsticks to ensure a nicely browned panko coating. It also prevents the crust from turning soggy, unlike a baking sheet, which traps moisture where the meat touches the metal. Bonus: The pan underneath catches crumbs and juice for easy cleanup.

RADICALLY SIMPLE COOKING

By Rozanne Gold

September means back to school and busy schedules, leaving little time for preparing family meals. But don't despair, and definitely don't call for takeout. Couscous Salad with Chicken, Dates, and Walnuts is fantastically simple, the type of dish you'll keep in rotation. In just 20 minutes, you can turn out a sophisticated Mediterranean-style dinner the family will love, and it's even fit for company. It'll also keep if you want to make it ahead—cover and chill, and then serve at room temperature.

PLUMP, STICKY MEDJOOL DATES

It's worth every penny to upgrade to Medjool dates, which have an exquisite, caramel-like flavor. Dried on the trees themselves, they exhibit a plumpness that screams more "fruit" than "dried." You'll find them in the produce section of most supermarkets and not with the dried fruit—a telling testament to their freshness.

Kid Friendly • Quick & Easy
Make Ahead

Couscous Salad with Chicken, Dates, and Walnuts
(pictured on page 231)

Hands-on: 20 min. Total: 20 min.
This dish is a cinch to prepare, and you can make it your own using fresh mint instead of cilantro, or almonds or hazelnuts instead of walnuts. Also try it with chicken breast or pork tenderloin in place of chicken thighs. Dates add a delicious Mediterranean touch, yielding a lovely sweet-savory flavor balance; for more tang, substitute dried apricots.

1½ cups water
1 cup uncooked couscous
½ cup low-fat buttermilk (1%)
2 teaspoons ground cumin, divided
⅜ teaspoon salt, divided
⅜ teaspoon freshly ground black pepper, divided
⅔ cup chopped walnuts
¼ cup chopped fresh cilantro
12 pitted Medjool dates, diced
1 green onion, thinly sliced
1½ teaspoons olive oil
3 skinless, boneless chicken thighs (about 12 ounces)
2 garlic cloves, mashed to a paste

1. Preheat broiler to high.

2. Bring 1½ cups water to a boil in a medium saucepan. Stir in couscous; cover pan. Remove from heat; let couscous mixture stand, covered, 5 minutes. Uncover pan; fluff couscous with a fork. Combine buttermilk, 1½ teaspoons cumin, ¼ teaspoon salt, and ¼ teaspoon black pepper in a large bowl, stirring with a whisk. Add couscous, walnuts, cilantro, dates, and green onion; stir mixture gently to combine.

3. Drizzle olive oil evenly over chicken thighs; rub both sides of chicken with ½ teaspoon cumin, ⅛ teaspoon salt,

continued

⅛ teaspoon pepper, and garlic. Arrange chicken in a single layer in a large ovenproof skillet. Broil chicken 5 minutes; turn chicken over. Broil an additional 3 minutes or until done. Remove chicken from pan; let stand 5 minutes. Pour pan juices into couscous mixture; toss gently to combine. Spoon about 1 cup couscous mixture onto each of 6 plates. Slice chicken crosswise; divide chicken evenly over couscous. Serves 6

CALORIES 323; FAT 12.5g (sat 1.7g, mono 2.9g, poly 6.9g); PROTEIN 17.7g; CARB 36.4g; FIBER 3.6g; CHOL 55mg; IRON 1.5mg; SODIUM 224mg; CALC 65mg

QUICK TRICKS

JAZZ UP YOUR BROCCOLI

Toss any of these high-flavor combos with 4 cups steamed broccoli florets. Start with 2 tablespoons canola oil, pick one of the flavor variations below, and proceed.

Orange-Sesame
Add 1 teaspoon grated orange rind, 2 tablespoons orange juice, 1 tablespoon honey, ½ teaspoon black pepper, ¼ teaspoon salt, and ¼ teaspoon crushed red pepper to oil. Add broccoli, ½ cup orange sections, 2 chopped green onions, and 1 teaspoon sesame seeds. Serves 4

CALORIES 123; FAT 7.7g (sat 0.6g); SODIUM 171mg

Pine Nut & Parmesan
Add 2 tablespoons toasted pine nuts, ¼ teaspoon grated lemon rind, ¼ teaspoon kosher salt, and ¼ teaspoon black pepper to oil. Toss with broccoli and 2 tablespoons grated fresh Parmesan cheese. Serves 4

CALORIES 124; FAT 10.9g (sat 1.2g); SODIUM 180mg

Spicy Anchovy
Heat oil, 2 teaspoons chopped fresh thyme, 2 teaspoons grated lemon rind, ¾ teaspoon crushed red pepper, ¼ teaspoon kosher salt, 3 minced garlic cloves, and 2 drained and minced anchovy fillets in a small skillet over medium heat; cook 2 minutes or until garlic begins to sizzle. Add broccoli; toss to coat. Serves 4

CALORIES 93; FAT 7.5g (sat 0.6g); SODIUM 216mg

Tahini & Lemon
Add 1½ tablespoons tahini, 1 tablespoon water, 1 tablespoon fresh lemon juice, 2 teaspoons lower-sodium soy sauce, and ¼ teaspoon black pepper to oil. Add broccoli, toss. Serve 4

CALORIES 120; FAT 10.3g (sat 1g); SODIUM 113mg

Chimichurri
Place ½ cup flat-leaf parsley leaves, ¼ cup chopped shallots, 2 teaspoons fresh oregano, and 1 garlic clove in a mini food processor; pulse until minced. Add oil, 1½ tablespoons lime juice, ¼ teaspoon salt, ¼ teaspoon ground cumin, and ¼ teaspoon crushed red pepper; process until blended. Toss with broccoli. Serves 4

CALORIES 98 FAT 7.4g (sat 0.6g) SODIUM 175mg

Lime-Soy-Sesame
Heat canola oil and 1 teaspoon toasted sesame oil in a large skillet over medium-high heat. Add broccoli; sauté 1 minute or until lightly browned. Add 1 tablespoon fresh lime juice, 1½ teaspoons fish sauce, 1 teaspoon lower-sodium soy sauce, 1 teaspoon sugar, and ¼ teaspoon crushed red pepper; cook 30 seconds or until liquid almost evaporates. Serves 4

CALORIES 101; FAT 8.5g (sat 0.7g); SODIUM 243mg

Garlic & Red Pepper
Heat oil, 3 sliced garlic cloves, and ¼ teaspoon crushed red pepper in a skillet over medium-high heat; sauté 1 minute. Toss with broccoli and ¼ teaspoon salt. Serves 4

CALORIES 88; FAT 7.3g (sat 0.6g); SODIUM 170mg

BUDGET COOKING

FEED 4 FOR LESS THAN $10

Kid Friendly • Quick & Easy Vegetarian

$2.32/serving, $9.28 total

Summer Pea Pasta

Hands-on time: 22 min. Total time: 22 min. Make sure to zest the lemon before you squeeze the juice. Serve with a quick tomato salad: Combine 3 ounces mini mozzarella cheese balls with 1 pint halved cherry tomatoes, 2 tablespoons olive oil, and 2 tablespoons balsamic vinegar; toss to coat.

4 quarts water
8 ounces uncooked linguine
3 tablespoons butter
5 garlic cloves, thinly sliced
2 cups frozen green peas, thawed
½ teaspoon sugar
3 tablespoons fresh lemon juice
¾ teaspoon kosher salt
6 tablespoons torn mint leaves
1 teaspoon grated lemon rind

1. Bring 4 quarts water to a boil in a large saucepan. Add pasta to pan; cook 8 minutes or until almost al dente. Drain pasta in a colander over a bowl, reserving ½ cup cooking liquid.
2. Melt butter in a large skillet over medium-high heat. Add garlic to pan; sauté 1 minute. Stir in peas and sugar; cook 2 minutes, stirring frequently. Stir in cooked pasta, reserved ½ cup cooking liquid, and juice; cook 2 minutes. Remove from heat. Sprinkle with salt, mint, and rind; toss to combine. Serve immediately. Serves 4 (serving size: 1¼ cups)

CALORIES 347; FAT 9.7g (sat 5.8g, mono 2.3g, poly 0.4g); PROTEIN 11.6g; CARB 55.8g; FIBER 5.8g; CHOL 23mg; IRON 3mg; SODIUM 489mg; CALC 43mg

Pork Tacos with Mango Slaw

$2.42/serving, $9.68 total

Hands-on: 23 min. Total: 28 min. *Whole tenderloin is seared and sliced for these quick pork tacos. Serve with lime wedges.*

2 tablespoons canola oil, divided
1 (12-ounce) pork tenderloin, trimmed
1/2 teaspoon kosher salt, divided
1/4 teaspoon black pepper
1 1/2 cups thinly sliced green cabbage
1 cup chopped ripe mango
1/2 cup thinly sliced radishes
1/3 cup diagonally sliced green onions
1/4 teaspoon ground red pepper
2 tablespoons fresh lime juice
1 ripe peeled avocado, chopped
8 (6-inch) corn tortillas

1. Preheat oven to 425°.
2. Heat an ovenproof skillet over medium-high heat. Add 1 tablespoon oil; swirl to coat. Sprinkle pork with 1/4 teaspoon salt and pepper. Add pork to pan; cook 4 minutes or until browned. Turn pork over; place pan in oven. Bake at 425° for 12 minutes or until a thermometer registers 145° or until desired degree of doneness. Remove pork from pan. Let stand 10 minutes; cut pork across the grain into thin slices.
3. Combine 1 tablespoon oil, cabbage, and next 4 ingredients (through red pepper) in a bowl. Combine juice and avocado in a bowl. Add avocado mixture to cabbage mixture; sprinkle with 1/4 teaspoon salt. Toss gently to combine.
4. Heat tortillas according to package directions. Place 2 tortillas on each of 4 plates; divide pork evenly among tortillas. Top tacos evenly with cabbage mixture. Serves 4 (serving size: 2 tacos)

CALORIES 354; FAT 17.4g (sat 2.2g, mono 10.1g, poly 3.7g); PROTEIN 21.7g; CARB 31.2g; FIBER 7.3g; CHOL 55mg; IRON 1.5mg; SODIUM 313mg; CALC 57mg

DINNER TONIGHT

Fast, healthy weeknight menus

READY IN
40
MINUTES

The
SHOPPING LIST

Kale and Caramelized Onion Grilled Cheese
Kale leaves
Red onions (2 medium)
Red wine vinegar
Parmesan cheese (1 ounce)
Raclette cheese (3.5 ounces)
Multigrain bread
Canola oil

Poblano-Tomato Soup
Tomatoes (2 pounds)
Garlic
Shallots (3)
Red bell pepper (1)
Poblano pepper (1)
Fresh cilantro
Lime (1)
Unsalted chicken stock (such as Swanson)
Ground cumin
Ground coriander
Canola oil

The
GAME PLAN

While vegetables for soup roast:
■ Blanch kale.
■ Cook onions.
While sandwiches bake:
■ Finish soup.

Kale and Caramelized Onion Grilled Cheese

With Poblano-Tomato Soup
(pictured on page 231)

Kid Tweak: Omit the poblano pepper from the soup.
Simple Sub: If raclette isn't available, substitute Gruyère cheese.
Flavor Hit: Broiling the tomatoes adds a smoky, fire-roasted flavor.

4 medium kale leaves, stems removed
2 teaspoons canola oil
2 medium red onions, cut into 1/2-inch-thick slices
1/4 teaspoon freshly ground black pepper
1/8 teaspoon kosher salt
1 teaspoon red wine vinegar
8 (1-ounce) slices multigrain bread
Cooking spray
1 ounce finely grated Parmesan cheese, divided (about 1/4 cup)
3.5 ounces shredded raclette cheese (about 7/8 cup)

1. Preheat oven to 300°.
2. Bring a small pot of water to a boil; add kale. Remove from heat; let stand 4 minutes or until kale is bright green. Drain; rinse kale under cold water until cool. Pat leaves dry.
3. Heat a skillet over medium-high heat. Add oil; swirl to coat. Add onion, pepper, and salt. Cook 10 minutes or until onion is tender and browned, stirring frequently. Remove from heat; stir in vinegar, tossing to coat. Coarsely chop onion.
4. Heat a large nonstick skillet over medium heat. Lightly coat 1 side of each bread slice with cooking spray. Working with 2 slices at a time,

continued

arrange bread in pan, sprayed side down. Cook 1½ minutes or until bread begins to brown. Sprinkle 1 tablespoon Parmesan on 1 bread slice in pan. Top with 1 kale leaf, one-fourth of onion mixture, and about ¼ cup raclette. Top with other toasted bread slice. Transfer sandwich to a baking sheet. Repeat procedure with remaining 6 bread slices, Parmesan, 3 kale leaves, onion mixture, and raclette. Bake sandwiches at 300° for 5 minutes or until cheese melts. Serves 4 (serving size: 1 sandwich)

CALORIES 318; FAT 15g (sat 5.9g, mono 4.2g, poly 1.1g); PROTEIN 16.6g; CARB 31.3g; FIBER 6.2g; CHOL 27mg; IRON 1.5mg; SODIUM 652mg; CALC 323mg

For the Poblano-Tomato Soup:

Place a jelly-roll pan in oven. Preheat broiler to high. Combine 2 pounds halved tomatoes, 6 garlic cloves, 3 halved shallots, 1 halved seeded red bell pepper, and 1 halved seeded poblano pepper in a bowl. Add 1 tablespoon canola oil; toss. Carefully arrange vegetables on preheated pan; broil 10 minutes or until blackened. Place roasted vegetables in a blender. Remove center piece of blender lid (to allow steam to escape); secure lid on blender. Place a clean towel over opening in lid (to avoid splatters). Blend until smooth. Stir in 1 cup unsalted chicken stock, ¼ teaspoon salt, ¼ teaspoon ground cumin, and ⅛ teaspoon ground coriander. Top with ¼ cup cilantro leaves; serve with 4 lime wedges. Serves 4 (serving size: about 1¼ cups)

CALORIES 112; FAT 4.1g (sat 0.3g); SODIUM 196mg

READY IN 40 MINUTES

············· *The* ·············
SHOPPING LIST

Lemon-Parsley Chicken with Corn and Tomato Salad
Fresh flat-leaf parsley
Lemon (1)
Garlic
Boston lettuce
Corn (2 ears)
Heirloom cherry tomatoes (1 cup)
Extra-virgin olive oil
Dijon mustard
4 (6-ounce) skinless, boneless chicken breast halves

Herbed Couscous
Fresh flat-leaf parsley
Garlic
Lemon (1)
Couscous
Butter

············· *The* ·············
GAME PLAN

While grill preheats:
■ Season chicken.
■ Start couscous.
While couscous stands:
■ Grill chicken.
■ Prepare salad.

Kid Friendly • Quick & Easy
Lemon-Parsley Chicken with Corn and Tomato Salad

With Herbed Couscous

Time-Saver: Use thawed frozen corn kernels in place of fresh.
Simple Sub: Substitute green leaf lettuce for the Boston lettuce.
Budget Buy: Use non-heirloom grape or cherry tomatoes.

¼ cup minced fresh flat-leaf parsley
2 teaspoons grated lemon rind
2 teaspoons minced fresh garlic
¾ teaspoon kosher salt, divided
¾ teaspoon ground black pepper, divided
4 (6-ounce) skinless, boneless chicken breast halves, halved lengthwise to form 8 cutlets
Cooking spray
2 tablespoons fresh lemon juice
2 tablespoons extra-virgin olive oil
1 teaspoon Dijon mustard
5 cups torn Boston lettuce
1 cup fresh corn kernels
1 cup heirloom cherry tomatoes, quartered
¼ cup flat-leaf parsley leaves

1. Preheat grill to high heat.
2. Combine minced parsley, lemon rind, garlic, ½ teaspoon salt, and ½ teaspoon pepper in a small bowl. Sprinkle chicken with parsley mixture; let stand 10 minutes. Place chicken on grill rack coated with cooking spray; grill 3 minutes on each side or until chicken is done.
3. Combine juice, oil, mustard, ¼ teaspoon salt, and ¼ teaspoon pepper in a large bowl; stir with a whisk. Add lettuce and remaining ingredients; toss to coat. Serves 4 (serving size: 2 chicken cutlets and about 1¼ cups salad)

CALORIES 311; FAT 12.1g (sat 2.1g, mono 6.4g, poly 1.7g); PROTEIN 39g; CARB 11.9g; FIBER 2.5g; CHOL 109mg; IRON 2.4mg; SODIUM 603mg; CALC 54mg

For the Herbed Couscous:
Bring 1¼ cups water to a boil in a small saucepan. Stir in 1 cup uncooked couscous; cover. Remove from heat; let stand 5 minutes. Stir in 2 tablespoons chopped fresh flat-leaf parsley, 1 tablespoon melted butter, 1 teaspoon minced garlic, 2 teaspoons fresh lemon juice, ¼ teaspoon kosher salt, and ¼ teaspoon freshly ground black pepper. Serves 4 (serving size: ¾ cup)

CALORIES 191; **FAT** 3.2g (sat 1.9g); **SODIUM** 151mg

READY IN
40
MINUTES

The
SHOPPING LIST

Pork Scaloppine with Mustard Pan Sauce and Baby Carrots
Shallots (1)
Garlic
Fresh flat-leaf parsley
Baby carrots (1 pound)
Unsalted chicken stock
   (such as Swanson)
Whole-grain Dijon mustard
Reduced-fat sour cream
Canola oil
Olive oil
1 (1-pound) pork tenderloin

Rolls with Honey-Orange Butter
Orange (1)
Honey
Frozen dinner rolls (such as
   Alexia Artisan French Rolls)
Butter

The
GAME PLAN

While oven preheats:
■ Season carrots.
While carrots roast:
■ Cook pork.
Bake rolls.

Kid Friendly • Quick & Easy
Pork Scaloppine with Mustard Pan Sauce and Baby Carrots

With Rolls with Honey-Orange Butter

Flavor Swap: Use honey mustard instead of Dijon for a sweeter sauce.
Technique Tip: Pound the pork cutlets for even browning and quick cooking.
Prep Pointer: Sour cream adds body to the pan sauce.

1 pound baby carrots, halved lengthwise
1 tablespoon olive oil
½ teaspoon salt, divided
¾ teaspoon freshly ground black pepper, divided
1 (1-pound) pork tenderloin, trimmed, cut crosswise into 12 pieces, and pounded to ¼-inch thickness
1 tablespoon canola oil, divided
¼ cup minced shallots
2 teaspoons minced fresh garlic
½ cup unsalted chicken stock (such as Swanson)
2 tablespoons whole-grain Dijon mustard
3 tablespoons reduced-fat sour cream
1 tablespoon chopped fresh flat-leaf parsley

1. Preheat oven to 450°.
2. Combine carrots and olive oil on a jelly-roll pan; toss to coat. Sprinkle with ¼ teaspoon salt and ½ teaspoon pepper. Bake at 450° for 20 minutes or until tender, stirring after 10 minutes.
3. Sprinkle pork evenly with ¼ teaspoon salt and ¼ teaspoon pepper. Heat a large skillet over medium-high heat. Add 1 teaspoon canola oil; swirl to coat. Add 6 cutlets; cook 2 minutes on each side or until done. Remove from pan; keep warm. Repeat procedure with 1 teaspoon canola oil and remaining pork.

4. Return skillet to medium-high heat. Add 1 teaspoon canola oil to pan; swirl to coat. Add shallots and garlic to pan; cook 2 minutes, stirring occasionally. Add stock and mustard; cook 1 minute, scraping pan to loosen browned bits. Stir in sour cream; cook 1 minute. Serve pork with sauce and carrots. Sprinkle with parsley. Serves 4 (serving size: 3 pieces pork, about 2 tablespoons sauce, and about 6 carrot halves)

CALORIES 261; **FAT** 10.9g (sat 2.4g, mono 6g, poly 1.9g); **PROTEIN** 25.8g; **CARB** 13.9g; **FIBER** 3.8g; **CHOL** 78mg; **IRON** 2.4mg; **SODIUM** 651mg; **CALC** 64mg

For the Rolls with Honey-Orange Butter:
Preheat oven to 450°. Combine 1½ tablespoons softened butter, ½ teaspoon grated orange rind, and ½ teaspoon honey in a small bowl. Place 4 frozen dinner rolls (such as Alexia Artisan French Rolls) on a baking sheet. Bake at 450° for 10 minutes or until heated and lightly browned. Serve rolls with butter mixture. Serves 4 (serving size: 1 roll and about 1 teaspoon butter mixture)

CALORIES 150; **FAT** 4.8g (sat 2.7g); **SODIUM** 266mg

READY IN 40 MINUTES

.... *The* ....

SHOPPING LIST

Two-Cheese Mac and Cheese
Garlic
Large elbow macaroni
Unsalted chicken stock
  (such as Swanson)
All-purpose flour
2% reduced-fat milk
1/3-less-fat cream cheese (4 ounces)
Extra-sharp cheddar cheese (3 ounces)
Canola oil

Roasted Broccoli and Red Bell Pepper
Broccoli florets (6 cups)
Red bell pepper (1)
Garlic
Olive oil

.... *The* ....

GAME PLAN

While pasta cooks:
■ Cut broccoli and bell pepper.
■ Prepare cheese sauce.
Roast broccoli.
Broil Mac and Cheese.

Quick & Easy
Two-Cheese Mac and Cheese

With Roasted Broccoli and Red Bell Pepper
(pictured on page 231)

Flavor Hit: Unsalted stock adds rich flavor without the extra sodium.
Simple Sub: If you can't find large elbow macaroni, substitute rotini.
Time-Saver: Buy precut broccoli florets in the produce section.

---

10 ounces large elbow macaroni
2 tablespoons canola oil
3 garlic cloves, crushed
2¼ cups unsalted chicken stock
  (such as Swanson), divided
½ cup 2% reduced-fat milk
8 teaspoons all-purpose flour
4 ounces ⅓-less-fat cream cheese
½ teaspoon salt
¼ teaspoon freshly ground black
  pepper
Cooking spray
3 ounces extra-sharp cheddar cheese,
  shredded (about ¾ cup)

1. Cook pasta according to package directions, omitting salt and fat; drain. Set aside.
2. Preheat broiler to high.
3. Heat a Dutch oven over medium heat. Add oil to pan; swirl to coat. Add garlic to pan; cook 3 minutes or until garlic is fragrant, stirring frequently (do not brown). Stir in 1 cup stock; bring to a boil. Cook 1 minute. Combine remaining 1¼ cups stock, milk, and flour; stir with a whisk until flour dissolves. Add milk mixture to garlic mixture, stirring with a whisk. Bring to a boil; cook 5 minutes or until mixture begins to thicken. Remove milk mixture from heat; add cream cheese, stirring until smooth. Stir in salt and pepper. Add cooked pasta to milk mixture, tossing to coat. Let stand 5 minutes. Pour pasta mixture into a 2-quart baking dish coated with cooking spray. Sprinkle cheddar evenly over pasta mixture. Broil 3 minutes or until cheese melts and begins to brown. Let stand 5 minutes. Serves 6 (serving size: about 1 cup)

CALORIES 358; **FAT** 15g (sat 6.1g, mono 5.6g, poly 1.9g); **PROTEIN** 14.4g; **CARB** 40.7g; **FIBER** 1.7g; **CHOL** 31mg; **IRON** 2mg; **SODIUM** 409mg; **CALC** 170mg

For the Roasted Broccoli and Red Bell Pepper:
Preheat oven to 400°. Place 6 cups broccoli florets, 1 sliced red bell pepper, 2 sliced garlic cloves, 2 tablespoons olive oil, ¼ teaspoon salt, and ¼ teaspoon freshly ground black pepper on a jelly-

---

roll pan; toss to coat. Bake vegetables at 400° for 10 minutes or until lightly browned, stirring after 5 minutes. Serves 4 (serving size: about 1¼ cups)

CALORIES 105; **FAT** 7.3g (sat 1g); **SODIUM** 178mg

READY IN 30 MINUTES

.... *The* ....

SHOPPING LIST

Steak with Lemon-Herb Pesto and Spinach Salad
Fresh flat-leaf parsley
Fresh cilantro
Lemon (1)
Garlic
Baby spinach (6 cups)
Red onion (1)
Extra-virgin olive oil
Dijon mustard
1 (1-pound) flank steak

Quick Mashed Potatoes
Fresh chives
Frozen mashed potatoes
  (such as Ore Ida Steam n' Mash)
2% reduced-fat milk
Butter

.... *The* ....

GAME PLAN

While steak cooks:
■ Prepare salad.
While steak rests:
■ Prepare mashed potatoes.

Steak with Lemon-Herb Pesto and Spinach Salad

With Quick Mashed Potatoes

Simple Sub: Use green onions instead of chives in the potatoes.
Prep Pointer: Milk and butter enrich prepared mashed potatoes.
Flavor Hit: This herbaceous pesto also pairs well with fish or chicken.

1/2 cup flat-leaf parsley leaves
1/2 cup cilantro leaves
3 tablespoons extra-virgin olive oil, divided
1/2 teaspoon lemon rind
5 teaspoons fresh lemon juice, divided
5/8 teaspoon salt, divided
3/4 teaspoon freshly ground black pepper, divided
5 garlic cloves, divided
Cooking spray
1 (1-pound) flank steak, trimmed
1 teaspoon Dijon mustard
6 cups fresh baby spinach
1/2 cup vertically sliced red onion

1. Place parsley, cilantro, 2 tablespoons oil, lemon rind, 1 tablespoon lemon juice, 1/4 teaspoon salt, 1/4 teaspoon pepper, and 4 garlic cloves in a mini food processor; process until finely chopped.
2. Heat a grill pan over medium-high heat. Coat pan with cooking spray. Sprinkle steak with 1/4 teaspoon salt and 1/4 teaspoon pepper. Add steak to pan; cook 5 minutes on each side or until desired degree of doneness. Let steak stand 5 minutes. Thinly slice steak across the grain.
3. Mince 1 garlic clove. Combine minced garlic, 1 tablespoon extra-virgin olive oil, 2 teaspoons lemon juice, Dijon mustard, 1/4 teaspoon freshly ground black pepper, and 1/8 teaspoon salt in a medium bowl; stir with a whisk. Add baby spinach and sliced red onion to bowl; toss gently to coat. Serve steak with salad and pesto. Serves 4 (serving size: 3 ounces beef, 3/4 cup salad, and 1 tablespoon pesto)

CALORIES 301; FAT 18.6g (sat 4.8g, mono 10.7g, poly 1.4g); PROTEIN 25.6g; CARB 8g; FIBER 2.5g; CHOL 74mg; IRON 3.6mg; SODIUM 524mg; CALC 77mg

For the Quick Mashed Potatoes:
Place 2 cups frozen mashed potatoes (such as Ore Ida Steam n' Mash) in a medium microwave-safe bowl; microwave at HIGH for 3 minutes or until hot. Stir in 1/4 cup 2% reduced-fat milk, 3 tablespoons chopped fresh chives, 1 tablespoon butter, and 1/8 teaspoon freshly ground black pepper. Serves 4 (serving size: 1/2 cup)

CALORIES 87; FAT 3.2g (sat 2g); SODIUM 206mg

SUPERFAST 20-MINUTE COOKING

White Bean and Spinach Tacos

To quickly warm tortillas, stack and wrap them in damp paper towels; microwave at HIGH for 25 seconds. Serve immediately.

1 tablespoon canola oil
1 1/2 cups vertically sliced onion
4 garlic cloves, chopped
1 (15-ounce) can cannellini beans, rinsed and drained
3/8 teaspoon kosher salt, divided
8 cups bagged prewashed spinach (about 5 1/2 ounces)
1 1/2 cups chopped tomato
1/2 cup finely chopped onion
1/4 cup chopped fresh cilantro
1 tablespoon fresh lime juice
1 sliced jalapeño pepper
12 corn tortillas
2 ounces queso fresco, crumbled (about 1/2 cup)

1. Heat a large skillet over medium-high heat. Add oil to pan; swirl to coat. Add sliced onion, and sauté 5 minutes or until lightly browned, stirring occasionally. Add garlic to pan; sauté 30 seconds. Stir in beans and 1/4 teaspoon salt; cook 1 minute. Add spinach to pan; cook 1 minute or until spinach wilts and beans are thoroughly heated.
2. Combine tomato, chopped onion, cilantro, lime juice, 1/8 teaspoon salt, and jalapeño in a small bowl. Warm tortillas according to package directions. Arrange 1/3 cup bean mixture in center of each tortilla. Top each taco with 3 tablespoons tomato mixture and about 1 tablespoon cheese. Serves 4 (serving size: 3 tacos)

CALORIES 337; FAT 7.4g (sat 1.5g, mono 3.1g, poly 2.3g); PROTEIN 13.3g; CARB 58.6g; FIBER 10.9g; CHOL 5mg; IRON 4.7mg; SODIUM 330mg; CALC 231mg

Chicken Salad Melts

2 cups shredded skinless, boneless rotisserie chicken breast
1/4 cup plain fat-free Greek yogurt
1/4 cup canola mayonnaise (such as Hellmann's)
2 teaspoons chopped fresh dill
1/4 teaspoon salt
1/4 teaspoon freshly ground black pepper
3 green onions, thinly sliced
6 whole-wheat English muffins, split and toasted
3 ounces sharp cheddar cheese, shredded (about 3/4 cup)
3/4 cup thinly sliced apple
6 Bibb lettuce leaves

continued

1. Preheat broiler to high.
2. Combine first 7 ingredients in a medium bowl; stir well. Place ⅓ cup chicken mixture on bottom half of each muffin. Top evenly with cheese. Broil 1 minute or until cheese melts. Top sandwiches evenly with apple, lettuce, and top halves of muffins. Serves 6 (serving size: 1 sandwich)

CALORIES 304; FAT 9.9g (sat 3.5g, mono 2.3g, poly 1.2g); PROTEIN 25.1g; CARB 28.8g; FIBER 3.7g; CHOL 58mg; IRON 1.9mg; SODIUM 682mg; CALC 204mg

Kid Friendly • Quick & Easy
Vegetarian

Black Forest Parfaits

Strawberries would be a good substitute for the cherries in this quick dessert. For a less sweet parfait, try using plain Greek yogurt in place of the vanilla frozen yogurt.

2 cups frozen pitted sweet cherries
½ teaspoon cornstarch
14 chocolate wafer cookies, crumbled (such as Nabisco Famous Chocolate Wafers)
2 cups vanilla fat-free frozen Greek yogurt

1. Combine cherries and cornstarch in a medium microwave-safe bowl. Microwave cherry mixture at HIGH 3 minutes or until hot. Mash cherries with a fork or potato masher until desired consistency.
2. Divide half of chocolate wafer crumbs evenly among 4 parfait glasses. Spoon 2 tablespoons cherry mixture into each glass. Top each serving with ½ cup yogurt; divide remaining cherry mixture and remaining chocolate wafer crumbs among servings. Serves 4

CALORIES 315; FAT 3g (sat 1.1g, mono 1.1g, poly 0.4g); PROTEIN 8.9g; CARB 65.1g; FIBER 3.4g; CHOL 8mg; IRON 1.2mg; SODIUM 220mg; CALC 166mg

Kid Friendly • Quick & Easy

Flank Steak with Tomato-Balsamic Sauce

This sauce is also tasty with sautéed chicken breasts or pork chops.

1 tablespoon extra-virgin olive oil
1 (1-pound) flank steak, trimmed
½ teaspoon salt
½ teaspoon freshly ground black pepper, divided
3 garlic cloves, thinly sliced
1 shallot, thinly sliced
¼ cup balsamic vinegar
2 cups cherry tomatoes, quartered
⅓ cup torn fresh basil, divided
⅓ cup green onions, thinly sliced and divided

1. Heat a large skillet over medium-high heat. Add olive oil; swirl to coat. Sprinkle steak with salt and ¼ teaspoon pepper. Add steak to pan, and cook 5 minutes on each side or until desired degree of doneness. Transfer steak to a cutting board; let stand 5 minutes. Cut across the grain into thin slices.
2. Add garlic and shallot to pan; sauté 1½ minutes or until lightly browned. Add vinegar, and cook 1½ minutes or until liquid almost evaporates. Add tomatoes, ¼ cup basil, ¼ cup green onions, and ¼ teaspoon pepper. Cook 2 minutes or until tomatoes soften and begin to release their liquid, stirring occasionally. Serve tomato mixture over sliced steak. Sprinkle with remaining basil and remaining green onions. Serves 4 (serving size: 3 ounces steak and ¼ cup sauce)

CALORIES 246; FAT 11.7g (sat 3.9g, mono 5.8g, poly 0.8g); PROTEIN 25.5g; CARB 8.5g; FIBER 1.3g; CHOL 74mg; IRON 2.5mg; SODIUM 366mg; CALC 58mg

Kid Friendly • Quick & Easy

Cheesy Chicken and Pepper Subs

Serve with crunchy vegetable sticks, a simple tossed salad, or steamed green beans.

4 (3-ounce) whole-wheat hoagie rolls, split
1 tablespoon canola oil
1 pound chicken breast tenders
½ teaspoon dried oregano
¼ teaspoon kosher salt
¼ teaspoon freshly ground black pepper
1 large julienne-cut yellow bell pepper
½ cup lower-sodium marinara sauce (such as Dell'Amore)
2 ounces part-skim mozzarella cheese, shredded (about ½ cup)

1. Preheat broiler to high.
2. Hollow out top and bottom halves of hoagie rolls, leaving a 1-inch-thick shell; reserve torn bread for another use. Place hoagie rolls, cut sides up, on a baking sheet, and broil 1 minute or until rolls are toasted.
3. Heat a large nonstick skillet over medium heat. Add oil; swirl to coat. Sprinkle chicken evenly with oregano, salt, and pepper. Add chicken to pan; cook 7 minutes, turning occasionally. Add bell pepper to pan; cook 2 minutes or until bell pepper is tender and chicken is done. Stir in marinara sauce, and cook 30 seconds or until marinara is thoroughly heated.
4. Transfer top halves of rolls to a plate. Divide chicken mixture evenly among bottom halves of rolls; top evenly with cheese. Broil 1 minute or until cheese melts. Top with top halves of rolls. Serves 4 (serving size: 1 sandwich)

CALORIES 412; FAT 13g (sat 3g, mono 4.3g, poly 3.1g); PROTEIN 37g; CARB 38.8g; FIBER 5.6g; CHOL 80mg; IRON 0.9mg; SODIUM 666mg; CALC 120mg

Wilted Kale with Bacon and Vinegar

Quick & Easy

3 center-cut bacon slices
¾ cup vertically sliced red onion
8 cups lacinato kale, stemmed
  and chopped
⅔ cup unsalted chicken stock
  (such as Swanson)
1 tablespoon sherry vinegar
1 teaspoon maple syrup

1. Cook bacon in a Dutch oven over medium-low heat until crisp. Remove from pan; crumble. Increase heat to medium. Add onion to drippings in pan; sauté 3 minutes. Add kale; cook 2 minutes or until kale begins to wilt, stirring occasionally. Add stock; cover and cook 4 minutes or until tender, stirring occasionally. Stir in vinegar and syrup. Sprinkle with crumbled bacon. Serves 4 (serving size: ⅔ cup)

CALORIES 76; FAT 2g (sat 0.8g, mono 0g, poly 0.2g); PROTEIN 5g; CARB 11.2g; FIBER 1.9g; CHOL 6mg; IRON 1.3mg; SODIUM 155mg; CALC 108mg

Variation 1: Coconut, Ginger & Lime
Heat a Dutch oven over medium-low heat. Add 1 tablespoon light coconut milk and 1 teaspoon canola oil. Add 1 seeded minced jalapeño and 2 teaspoons minced fresh ginger; cook 1 minute. Add 8 cups chopped kale; cook 2 minutes. Add ¼ cup light coconut milk, ¼ cup water, and ½ teaspoon sugar; cover and cook 4 minutes. Stir in ¼ cup light coconut milk, 2 teaspoons fresh lime juice, and ⅛ teaspoon kosher salt. Serves 4 (serving size: ½ cup)

CALORIES 69; FAT 3.4g (sat 1.8g); SODIUM 99mg

Variation 2: Farro & Walnuts
Prepare 1 cup pearled farro. Heat a Dutch oven over medium-low heat. Add 2 teaspoons walnut oil and 3½ cups chopped kale; cook 2 minutes. Add ⅓ cup unsalted chicken stock; cover and cook 4 minutes. Combine 4 teaspoons sherry vinegar and 1 teaspoon maple syrup in a bowl. Add farro, 2 teaspoons walnut oil, and ¼ teaspoon kosher salt. Add kale mixture and 2 tablespoons toasted chopped walnuts. Serves 4 (serving size: ¾ cup)

CALORIES 256; FAT 8.1g (sat 0.7g); SODIUM 143mg

Variation 3: Golden Shallots
Heat a Dutch oven over medium heat. Add 2 tablespoons olive oil; swirl to coat. Add 2 sliced shallots; cook 5 minutes or until golden, stirring frequently. Add 8 cups chopped kale, ¼ teaspoon salt, and ¼ teaspoon black pepper to pan; cook 2 minutes. Add ⅔ cup unsalted chicken stock; cover and cook 4 minutes or until tender, stirring occasionally. Serves 4 (serving size: ½ cup)

CALORIES 109; FAT 7.3g (sat 1g); SODIUM 200mg

LACINATO KALE IS ALSO CALLED TUSCAN, DINOSAUR, OR BLACK KALE. YOU CAN ALSO USE REGULAR CURLY KALE.

Broccoli-Cheese Soup

Kid Friendly • Quick & Easy
Make Ahead

Traditional broccoli-cheese soup has nearly 400 calories and more than 18g saturated fat per serving. Ours has less than half the calories and one-fourth of the saturated fat.

3 cups unsalted chicken stock
1¾ cups broccoli florets, coarsely
  chopped (about 8 ounces)
1 cup diced yellow onion
½ cup chopped carrot
⅜ teaspoon salt
¼ teaspoon freshly ground black
  pepper
2 garlic cloves, minced
¾ cup half-and-half
4 ounces shredded reduced-fat extra-
  sharp cheddar cheese, divided
¼ cup fresh flat-leaf parsley leaves

1. Combine first 7 ingredients in a large saucepan; bring to a boil. Reduce heat, and simmer 10 minutes or until broccoli is tender. Pour soup into a blender. Remove center piece of blender lid (to allow steam to escape); secure lid on blender. Place a clean towel over opening in blender lid (to avoid splatters). Blend until smooth. Return soup to pan. Stir in half-and-half and 2 ounces cheese. Top evenly with remaining cheese and parsley. Serves 4 (serving size: about 1 cup soup and 2 tablespoons cheese)

CALORIES 160; FAT 7.4g (sat 4.5g, mono 2.1g, poly 0.3g); PROTEIN 13.6g; CARB 10.7g; FIBER 2.1g; CHOL 23mg; IRON 0.9mg; SODIUM 532mg; CALC 213mg

OOPS!

YOUR PASTA CLUMPS TOGETHER

How to cook perfect noodles that hold their sauce.

(Nice noodles!)

(Rubbing elbows)

A bowl of hot pasta misses the mark catastrophically if the noodles come out of the pot sticking together or, worst of all, knotted up in gummy clumps. The problem is pot space: Noodles need room to release starch and cook evenly. Pasta absorbs nearly double its dry weight in water. If the noodles don't boil in enough water, sticking happens. A shallow boil also means very starchy water, which makes for gluey noodles. Adding some oil to the pot isn't an ideal deterrent to sticking; it makes the noodles too slippery for sauce to stick.

The Solution: Use plenty of water, about 5 quarts per pound of dry pasta. Give the pot a stir as soon as you add the pasta to help keep the noodles separated when they plunge in. Boil vigorously until al dente. Drain the pasta (never rinse), and do as chefs do: Finish the last bit of cooking in the pan in which you've made your sauce. The noodles absorb more flavor this way, and everything just marries together nicely. Add a little reserved pasta cooking water if the sauce becomes dry.

OUR 25 ALL-TIME FAVORITE RECIPES

We combed the archives, grilled readers, polled online users, and interrogated staff with one goal in mind: Find the all-time favorite *Cooking Light* dishes.

Define "favorite," you say. It turns out there is more than one definition. Some cited no-fail standbys, dishes they make over and over. Others nominated recipes that represent an ideal expression of a dish, be it casual, fast, or fancy. Eventually we had a too-long list, so we retested everything. Some fell out under hard judging; some got flavor tweaks or nutrition makeovers. A few passed with no alterations at all. The final 25 are, no matter the definition, true favorites.

Kid Friendly • Freezable
Make Ahead

1 Beef Daube Provençal

The definition of a meaty stew: great today, even better tomorrow

Hands-on: 40 min. Total: 3 hr. 15 min.
We just love this recipe, and according to the online reviews, so do many of you. It's foolproof, surefire, an absolute winner. We wouldn't change a thing.

2 teaspoons olive oil
12 garlic cloves, crushed
1 (2-pound) boneless chuck roast, trimmed and cut into 2-inch cubes
1¼ teaspoons salt, divided
½ teaspoon freshly ground black pepper, divided
1 cup red wine
2 cups chopped carrot

1½ cups chopped onion
½ cup lower-sodium beef broth
1 tablespoon tomato paste
1 teaspoon chopped fresh rosemary
1 teaspoon chopped fresh thyme
Dash of ground cloves
1 (14.5-ounce) can diced tomatoes
1 bay leaf
3 cups cooked medium egg noodles (about 4 cups uncooked noodles)

1. Preheat oven to 300°.
2. Heat a small Dutch oven over low heat. Add oil to pan; swirl to coat. Add garlic; cook 5 minutes or until garlic is fragrant, stirring occasionally. Remove garlic with a slotted spoon; set aside. Increase heat to medium-high. Add beef to pan; sprinkle with ½ teaspoon salt and ¼ teaspoon pepper. Cook 5 minutes, browning on all sides. Remove beef from pan. Add wine to pan; bring to a boil, scraping pan to loosen browned bits. Add garlic, beef, remaining ¾ teaspoon salt, remaining ¼ teaspoon pepper, carrot, and next 8 ingredients (through bay leaf); bring to a boil.

3. Cover and bake at 300° for 2½ hours or until beef is tender. Discard bay leaf. Serve over noodles.
Note: To make in a slow cooker, prepare through step 2. Place beef mixture in an electric slow cooker. Cover and cook on HIGH for 5 hours or until beef is tender. Serves 6 (serving size: about ¾ cup stew and ½ cup noodles)

CALORIES 367; FAT 12.8g (sat 4.3g, mono 5.8g, poly 0.9g); PROTEIN 29.1g; CARB 33.4g; FIBER 3.9g; CHOL 105mg; IRON 4.3mg; SODIUM 678mg; CALC 76mg

Kid Friendly • Freezable
Make Ahead • Vegetarian

2 Brioche Rolls

Best expression of pure yeasty perfection

Hands-on: 35 min. Total: 12 hr. 16 min.
When we retested these rolls (originally a recipe makeover) for this story, we were unanimous in our praise: They are perfect as is. Each roll has about 75% fewer calories and 80% less fat than classic brioche rolls, but all the flaky, buttery essence is thankfully still there. An overnight proof in the fridge builds depth and flavor; don't be tempted to skip that step.

1 package dry yeast (about 2¼ teaspoons)
⅓ cup warm 1% low-fat milk (100° to 110°)
15.75 ounces unbleached all-purpose flour (about 3½ cups)
⅓ cup sugar
½ teaspoon salt
4 large eggs, lightly beaten
8½ tablespoons unsalted butter, softened and divided
Cooking spray
1 tablespoon water
1 large egg white

1. Dissolve yeast in warm milk in the bowl of a stand mixer fitted with the paddle attachment; let stand for 5 minutes. Weigh or lightly spoon flour into dry measuring cups; level

continued

with a knife. Add flour, sugar, salt, and eggs to milk mixture; beat at low speed until smooth, scraping sides of bowl with spatula as needed. Remove paddle attachment; insert dough hook. Beat dough at low speed 5 minutes or until soft and elastic and dough just begins to pull away from sides of bowl. Cut 6½ tablespoons butter into large cubes; add half of cubed butter to dough, beating at medium speed to blend. Add remaining butter cubes to dough; beat at medium speed until incorporated. Beat dough at medium speed 4 minutes or until smooth and elastic.
2. Place dough in a large bowl coated with cooking spray, turning to coat top. Cover and let rise in a warm place (85°), free from drafts, 1 hour or until doubled in size. (Gently press two fingers into dough. If indentation remains, dough has risen enough.) Punch dough down; form into a ball. Return dough to bowl; cover with plastic wrap, and refrigerate 8 hours or overnight.
3. Uncover dough; let stand 90 minutes or until room temperature. Divide dough into 4 equal portions. Working with 1 portion at a time (cover remaining dough to prevent drying), cut dough into 6 equal pieces. Roll each piece into a 1½-inch ball. Repeat procedure with remaining 3 dough portions to make 24 rolls total. Place rolls in muffin cups coated with cooking spray. Cover and let rise 45 minutes or until almost doubled in size.
4. Preheat oven to 350°.
5. Combine 1 tablespoon water and egg white; stir with a whisk. Gently brush rolls with egg mixture. Bake at 350° for 14 minutes or until golden. Place pans on wire racks. Place 2 tablespoons butter in a microwave-safe bowl; microwave at HIGH 20 seconds or until butter melts. Brush butter onto rolls. Serves 24 (serving size: 1 roll)

CALORIES 128; **FAT** 4.9g (sat 2.8g, mono 1.4g, poly 0.4g); **PROTEIN** 3.4g; **CARB** 17.2g; **FIBER** 0.6g; **CHOL** 41mg; **IRON** 1.1mg; **SODIUM** 94mg; **CALC** 13mg

Kid Friendly • Quick & Easy

3 Crispy Fish with Lemon-Dill Sauce

Ultimate crispity, crunchity satisfaction

Hands-on: 15 min. Total: 30 min. *Crispy breaded fish is a weeknight favorite, and you can have it without reaching into the freezer case. What we love about this recipe is that you don't even need to pan-fry the fillets; they get breaded and go right under the broiler. Be sure to use a broiler pan; the air vents keep the fish from getting soggy. Our only change was to slightly decrease the amount of salt—it's still fantastic.*

2 large egg whites, lightly beaten
1 cup panko (Japanese breadcrumbs)
½ teaspoon paprika
¾ teaspoon onion powder
¾ teaspoon garlic powder
4 (6-ounce) skinless cod fillets
1 teaspoon black pepper
⅜ teaspoon salt
Cooking spray
¼ cup canola mayonnaise (such as Hellmann's)
2 tablespoons finely chopped dill pickle
1 teaspoon fresh lemon juice
1 teaspoon chopped fresh dill
4 lemon wedges

1. Preheat broiler to high.
2. Place egg whites in a shallow dish. Combine panko, paprika, onion powder, and garlic powder in a shallow dish. Sprinkle fish evenly with pepper and salt. Dip fillets in egg white, and dredge in panko mixture; place on a broiler pan coated with cooking spray. Broil 4 minutes on each side or until desired degree of doneness.
3. Combine mayonnaise, pickle, lemon juice, and dill. Serve fish with sauce and lemon wedges. Serves 4 (serving size: 1 fillet, about 2 tablespoons sauce, and 1 lemon wedge)

CALORIES 245; **FAT** 5.2g (sat 0.2g, mono 2.7g, poly 1.4g); **PROTEIN** 34.5g; **CARB** 11.5g; **FIBER** 0.8g; **CHOL** 63mg; **IRON** 0.7mg; **SODIUM** 580mg; **CALC** 18mg

Great home cooks, like chefs, know that sauces can be the critical difference between a bland dish and an exciting one: Think of what a perfect, simple pan sauce does for sautéed chicken. This version of a classic romesco makes a superb, bright, healthy dip for crudités. But it's also great as a sandwich spread or salad dressing.

Kid Friendly • Freezable
Make Ahead • Vegetarian

4 Catalonian Pepper and Nut Sauce (Salsa Romesco)

Most versatile condiment

Hands-on: 15 min. Total: 64 min.
Making this recipe is time well spent: You'll be rewarded with lots of smoky-garlicky-peppery sauce, which keeps in the fridge for up to two weeks or in the freezer for a couple of months. There are lots of delicious ways to use it: Dip veggies or steamed shrimp in it, use it to flavor omelets, thin it with a little vinegar and water for salad dressing, try it as a sandwich spread, or smear it over pizza dough for a Spanish pie.

2 dried ancho chiles
2 small red bell peppers
½ cup hazelnuts
½ cup blanched almonds, toasted
4 garlic cloves, chopped
1 (1-ounce) slice bread, toasted
¼ cup red wine vinegar
2 tablespoons tomato paste
4 teaspoons sweet smoked paprika
¼ teaspoon ground red pepper
⅔ cup extra-virgin olive oil
¼ cup hot water
½ teaspoon salt

1. Place ancho chiles in a small saucepan. Cover with water; bring to a boil. Remove from heat; cover and let stand 20 minutes. Drain well. Remove stems, seeds, and membranes from chiles; discard. Place chiles in a medium bowl.

2. Preheat broiler.

3. Cut bell peppers in half lengthwise; discard seeds and membranes. Place pepper halves, skin sides up, on a foil-lined baking sheet; flatten with hand. Broil 10 minutes or until blackened. Place in a paper bag; fold to close tightly. Let stand 15 minutes. Peel and cut into 2-inch pieces. Add bell peppers to chiles.

4. Reduce oven temperature to 350°.

5. Arrange hazelnuts in a single layer on a baking sheet. Bake at 350° for 8 minutes or until toasted. Turn nuts out onto a towel. Roll up towel; rub off skins. Place hazelnuts in a food processor. Add almonds, garlic, and bread to food processor; process 1 minute or until finely ground. Add chile mixture, vinegar, tomato paste, paprika, and ground red pepper; process 1 minute or until combined. With processor on, slowly pour oil through food chute; process until well blended. Add ¼ cup hot water and salt; process 10 seconds or until combined. Serves 40 (serving size: about 1 tablespoon)

CALORIES 59; FAT 5.7g (sat 0.7g, mono 3.9g, poly 0.9g); PROTEIN 0.9g; CARB 2.1g; FIBER 0.7g; CHOL 0mg; IRON 0.3mg; SODIUM 36mg; CALC 8mg

Kid Friendly

5 Pulled Chicken Sandwiches

Feeds the picnic instinct—outside or on the living room floor

Hands-on: 20 min. Total: 40 min. This recipe received multiple nominations for its family friendly appeal. It's lick-your-fingers good, with a sweet-spicy sauce draped over spice-rubbed chicken. We tweaked it just a bit to make it a little less sweet, and we love it even more.

Chicken:
2 tablespoons dark brown sugar
1 teaspoon paprika
¾ teaspoon ground cumin

½ teaspoon ground chipotle chile pepper
¼ teaspoon ground ginger
⅛ teaspoon salt
2 pounds skinless, boneless chicken thighs
Cooking spray
Sauce:
2 teaspoons canola oil
½ cup finely chopped onion
1 tablespoon dark brown sugar
1 teaspoon chili powder
½ teaspoon garlic powder
½ teaspoon dry mustard
¼ teaspoon ground allspice
⅛ teaspoon ground red pepper
1 cup ketchup
2 tablespoons cider vinegar
Remaining ingredients:
8 (1½-ounce) hamburger buns, toasted
16 hamburger dill chips

1. Preheat grill to medium-high heat.

2. To prepare chicken, combine first 6 ingredients; rub evenly over chicken. Place chicken on grill rack coated with cooking spray; cover and grill 15 minutes or until a thermometer registers 180°, turning occasionally. Let stand 5 minutes. Shred with 2 forks.

3. To prepare sauce, while chicken grills, heat canola oil in a medium saucepan over medium heat. Add onion; cook 5 minutes or until tender, stirring occasionally. Stir in 1 tablespoon sugar and next 5 ingredients (through ground red pepper); cook 30 seconds. Stir in ketchup and vinegar; bring to a boil. Reduce heat, and simmer 10 minutes or until slightly thickened, stirring occasionally. Stir in chicken; cook 2 minutes.

4. Place ⅓ cup chicken mixture on bottom half of each bun; top each with 2 pickle chips and top of bun. Serves 8 (serving size: 1 sandwich)

CALORIES 325; FAT 9.7g (sat 2.3g, mono 3.8g, poly 2.4g); PROTEIN 23.9g; CARB 35.4g; FIBER 1.6g; CHOL 106mg; IRON 2.7mg; SODIUM 786mg; CALC 99mg

> With its fragrant cumin base and salsa verde tang, this stew is a perfect example of the way global ingredients can enliven light cooking. The perfume of cilantro, the crunch and pepper of radish, the zing of lime top this dish that has a unique earthy depth. We're talking serious flavor in comfort-food form, from ingredients that are available to more U.S. cooks than ever before.

Freezable • Make Ahead

6 Pork Posole

Comfort food, Mexican-style

Hands-on: 25 min. Total: 1 hr. 35 min. It's amazing how much flavor there is in such a humble (and, by the way, inexpensive) dish. The star of the soup is hominy, with its chewy texture and toasty-corn character; you'll find it with the Latin foods in the supermarket. Updates were minor: We simply omitted some oil and meat drippings for a cleaner broth.

1 teaspoon olive oil
12 ounces boneless pork shoulder, trimmed and cut into ½-inch pieces
1 cup chopped onion
4 garlic cloves, minced
1½ teaspoons ground cumin
½ teaspoon ground red pepper
½ cup beer
2 cups unsalted chicken stock (such as Swanson)
½ cup salsa verde
1 (28-ounce) can hominy, drained
¼ cup cilantro leaves
4 radishes, sliced
4 lime wedges

1. Heat a Dutch oven over medium-high heat. Add oil; swirl to coat. Add pork; sauté 5 minutes, turning to brown on all sides. Remove pork from pan, reserving 1 tablespoon drippings in pan. Add onion to pan; sauté 4 minutes, stirring occasionally. Add garlic; sauté 1 minute, stirring constantly. Return pork to pan; stir in cumin and pepper. Add beer; bring to a boil. Cook until liquid almost evaporates (about 9 minutes).

continued

2. Add chicken stock, salsa, and hominy; bring to a boil. Cover, reduce heat, and simmer 1 hour and 10 minutes or until pork is very tender, stirring occasionally. Ladle about 1⅓ cups soup into each of 4 bowls. Top each serving with 1 tablespoon cilantro leaves and 1 sliced radish. Serve with lime wedges. Serves 4

CALORIES 231; **FAT** 5.5g (sat 1.3g, mono 2.3g, poly 1g); **PROTEIN** 14.2g; **CARB** 30.3g; **FIBER** 5.5g; **CHOL** 27mg; **IRON** 2.9mg; **SODIUM** 581mg; **CALC** 70mg

Make Ahead

7 Grilled Stuffed Jalapeños

Irresistible pick-me-up app

Hands-on: 30 min. Total: 40 min. *With their cheesy bacon filling, these poppers are addictive. While we didn't want to futz with this recipe, we recognize that jalapeños vary wildly in heat level—sometimes incendiary and sometimes mild. So here's a suggestion: If you'll have guests who are sensitive to heat, try doing half the batch in jalapeños (for the chile-heads) and half in mini sweet peppers. That way, everyone wins!*

2 center-cut bacon slices
4 ounces cream cheese, softened (about ½ cup)
4 ounces fat-free cream cheese, softened (about ½ cup)
1 ounce extra-sharp cheddar cheese, shredded (about ¼ cup)
¼ cup minced green onions
1 teaspoon fresh lime juice
¼ teaspoon kosher salt
1 small garlic clove, minced
14 jalapeño peppers, halved lengthwise and seeded
Cooking spray
2 tablespoons chopped fresh cilantro
2 tablespoons chopped seeded tomato

1. Preheat grill to medium-high heat.
2. Cook bacon in a skillet over medium heat until crisp. Remove bacon from pan; drain on paper towels. Crumble bacon. Combine crumbled bacon, cheeses, and next 4 ingredients (through garlic) in a bowl, stirring well to combine. Divide cheese mixture evenly to fill pepper halves. Place peppers, cheese sides up, on grill rack or grill grate coated with cooking spray. Cover and grill peppers 8 minutes or until bottoms of peppers are charred and cheese mixture is lightly browned. Place peppers on a serving platter; sprinkle with cilantro and tomato. Serves 14 (serving size: 2 pepper halves)

CALORIES 56; **FAT** 4.1g (sat 2.2g, mono 1.1g, poly 0.2g); **PROTEIN** 2.9g; **CARB** 2.1g; **FIBER** 0.5g; **CHOL** 13mg; **IRON** 0.2mg; **SODIUM** 157mg; **CALC** 55mg

8 Fresh Pear Cocktail

Fall flavors in a martini glass

Hands-on: 10 min. Total: 10 min. *We adore this drink, with fresh pear juice (easy to make!) lending its unmistakable sweet flavor and fragrance. It still makes us swoon exactly as we first published it.*

1 medium Bosc pear
2 tablespoons citrus-infused vodka
1 tablespoon pomegranate juice
1 tablespoon fresh lime juice
1 tablespoon agave syrup (or sugar syrup)
3 tablespoons hard apple cider or cidre doux
Pear slices (optional)

1. Shred pear; place shredded pear pulp on several layers of cheesecloth. Gather edges of cheesecloth together, and squeeze over a glass measuring cup to yield ⅓ cup fresh pear juice. Discard solids. Combine pear juice, vodka, pomegranate juice, lime juice, and agave syrup in a martini shaker with ice; shake. Strain about 3 tablespoons of the vodka mixture into each of 2 martini glasses. Top each serving with 1½ tablespoons cider. Garnish with pear slices, if desired. Serves 2

CALORIES 131; **FAT** 0.1g (sat 0g, mono 0g, poly 0.1g); **PROTEIN** 0.4g; **CARB** 24.4g; **FIBER** 0.3g; **CHOL** 0mg; **IRON** 0.2mg; **SODIUM** 2mg; **CALC** 10mg

9 Herbed Cheese Pizzas

A Turkish twist on classic street food

Hands-on: 50 min. Total: 2 hr. 10 min. *The recipe makes eight individual pizzas, enough for an interactive cooking party. The original recipe didn't meet our current sodium and calorie guidelines, so we adjusted a few ingredients. Great news: The pizzas are still show-stealers.*

Dough:
9.5 ounces bread flour (about 2 cups), divided
1 teaspoon sugar
2 packages dry yeast (about 4½ teaspoons)
1½ cups warm water (100° to 110°), divided
9 ounces all-purpose flour (about 2 cups), divided
¾ teaspoon salt
1 teaspoon olive oil
Cooking spray
Topping:
2 teaspoons dried oregano
2 teaspoons ground cumin
1 teaspoon hot paprika
¾ teaspoon coarsely ground black pepper, divided
1 teaspoon olive oil
1 cup finely chopped onion
½ teaspoon salt
5 garlic cloves, minced
1 bay leaf
1 (28-ounce) can unsalted diced tomatoes, undrained
8 ounces kasseri cheese, thinly sliced
3 tablespoons minced fresh flat-leaf parsley

1. To prepare dough, weigh or lightly spoon bread flour into dry measuring cups; level with a knife. Combine 4.75 ounces (about 1 cup) bread flour, sugar, yeast, and 1 cup warm water in a bowl; let stand 15 minutes.

2. Weigh or lightly spoon all-purpose flour into dry measuring cups; level with a knife. Combine 7.5 ounces (1⅔ cups) all-purpose flour, remaining 4.75 ounces (about 1 cup) bread flour, and ¾ teaspoon salt in a large bowl; make a well in center of mixture. Add yeast mixture, ½ cup warm water, and 1 teaspoon oil to flour mixture; stir well. Turn dough out onto a floured surface. Knead until smooth and elastic (about 10 minutes); add enough of remaining all-purpose flour, 1 tablespoon at a time, to prevent dough from sticking to hands (dough will feel tacky).

3. Place dough in a large bowl coated with cooking spray, turning to coat top. Cover and let rise in a warm place (85°), free from drafts, 45 minutes or until doubled in size. (Press two fingers into dough. If indentation remains, the dough has risen enough.) Punch dough down; divide dough into 8 equal portions. Cover and let rest 20 minutes.

4. To prepare topping, combine oregano, cumin, paprika, and ½ teaspoon black pepper; set aside. Heat 1 teaspoon oil in a large nonstick skillet over medium-high heat. Add onion; sauté 3 minutes. Add ½ teaspoon salt, ¼ teaspoon black pepper, garlic, bay leaf, and tomatoes; bring to a boil. Reduce heat to medium; simmer 15 minutes or until thick. Remove from heat; discard bay leaf.

5. Preheat oven to 450°.

6. Working with 1 dough portion at a time (cover remaining dough to keep from drying), roll each portion into a 6-inch circle on a lightly floured surface; place circle on a baking sheet coated with cooking spray. Repeat procedure with remaining dough portions.

7. Top each crust with ¼ cup tomato mixture, 1 ounce cheese, and ½ teaspoon oregano mixture. Bake at 450° for 12 minutes or until crusts are lightly browned. Sprinkle with minced parsley. Serves 8 (serving size: 1 pizza)

CALORIES 402; FAT 11.4g (sat 5.4g, mono 3.6g, poly 1.3g); PROTEIN 16.6g; CARB 57.9g; FIBER 4.6g; CHOL 30mg; IRON 3.7mg; SODIUM 676mg; CALC 247mg

THE CRUST IS CRISP AND TENDER, THE TOPPING DIVINE.

10 Brazilian Feijoada

A slow-cooker miracle

Hands-on: 47 min. Total: 9 hr. 47 min.
Slow-cooker recipes can be a little disappointing—flavors a bit exhausted, textures a bit too soft. Not so with this recipe, a standout in every way. It's a classic Brazilian dish (pronounced fay-ZWAH-da) that is pure porky perfection, one we'll happily enjoy whenever we get the chance. Serve over rice, and spritz with the orange wedge for a fresh, sweet finish.

2 cups dried black beans
4 applewood-smoked bacon slices
1 (1-pound) boneless pork shoulder (Boston butt), trimmed and cut into ½-inch cubes
¾ teaspoon salt, divided
½ teaspoon freshly ground black pepper, divided
3 bone-in beef short ribs, trimmed (about 2 pounds)
3 cups finely chopped onion (about 2 medium)
1¼ cups fat-free, lower-sodium chicken broth
4 garlic cloves, minced
1 (9-ounce) smoked ham hock
1 tablespoon white vinegar
8 orange wedges

1. Place black beans in a small saucepan; cover with cold water. Bring to a boil; cook beans 2 minutes. Remove from heat; cover and let stand 1 hour. Drain beans.

2. Cook bacon in a large skillet over medium heat until crisp. Remove bacon from pan; crumble. Sprinkle pork evenly with ⅛ teaspoon salt and ¼ teaspoon pepper. Increase heat to medium-high. Add pork to drippings in skillet; sauté 8 minutes, turning to brown on all sides. Transfer pork to a 6-quart electric slow cooker. Sprinkle ribs evenly with ⅛ teaspoon salt and ¼ teaspoon pepper. Add ribs to skillet; cook 3 minutes on each side or until browned. Place ribs in slow cooker. Add drained beans, ½ teaspoon salt, onion, and next 3 ingredients (through ham hock) to slow cooker, stirring to combine. Cover and cook on LOW 8 hours or until beans and meat are tender.

3. Remove ribs from slow cooker; let stand 15 minutes. Remove meat from bones; shred meat with 2 forks. Discard bones. Discard ham hock. Return beef to slow cooker. Stir in vinegar and crumbled bacon. Serve with orange wedges. Serves 8 (serving size: 1¼ cups bean mixture and 1 orange wedge)

CALORIES 458; FAT 17.4g (sat 6.8g, mono 6.7g, poly 1.1g); PROTEIN 39.5g; CARB 35.8g; FIBER 11.6g; CHOL 96mg; IRON 6.4mg; SODIUM 533mg; CALC 102mg

Americans have an insatiable appetite for chicken, so the bird is well represented in this collection: recipes for breasts, thighs, ground meat, and whole bird. This dish uses pounded and browned skinless, boneless breasts, and then develops a deeply mushroomy sauce that is classically finished with Marsala wine. Regarding those breasts, note that a *Cooking Light* portion is 6 ounces (raw), but the breasts in the store are often much larger. We suggest weighing the breasts and trimming down to size; cube the trimmings, and freeze or use the next night in a salad, soup, or tacos.

11 Saucy Chicken Marsala

"They'll never know it was so easy" dinner-party dish

Hands-on: 28 min. Total: 45 min. When we revisited David Bonom's 2010 recipe Chicken and Mushrooms with Marsala Wine Sauce, we loved it but wanted more of the earthy, wine-licked sauce. Our update keeps the soul of the original dish, but with more luscious, 'shroomy goodness. You simply must serve it over mashed potatoes, polenta, or spaghetti to catch all the sauce.

1/2 cup dried porcini mushrooms (about 1/2 ounce)
2 cups boiling water
4 (6-ounce) skinless, boneless chicken breast halves
3/4 teaspoon kosher salt, divided
1/4 teaspoon freshly ground black pepper
2 tablespoons olive oil, divided
1/2 cup finely chopped onion
5 garlic cloves, thinly sliced
1 1/2 cups thinly sliced shiitake mushroom caps (about 4 ounces)
1 1/2 cups thinly sliced button mushrooms (about 4 ounces)
1 1/2 tablespoons chopped fresh oregano
2 tablespoons all-purpose flour
2/3 cup unsalted chicken stock
1/2 cup dry Marsala wine
1/4 cup small fresh basil leaves

1. Place porcini mushrooms in a medium bowl; cover with 2 cups boiling water. Cover and let stand 30 minutes or until tender. Drain in a sieve over a bowl, reserving soaking liquid. Thinly slice mushrooms.
2. Place each chicken breast half between 2 sheets of heavy-duty plastic wrap; pound to 1/2-inch thickness using a meat mallet or small heavy skillet. Sprinkle 1/4 teaspoon salt and black pepper over chicken. Heat a large stainless steel skillet over medium-high heat. Add 1 tablespoon oil to pan; swirl to coat. Add chicken; cook 3 minutes on each side or until browned and done. Remove chicken from pan; cover and keep warm.
3. Heat 1 tablespoon oil in pan over medium-high heat. Add onion and garlic; sauté 2 minutes or until onion is lightly browned. Add 1/2 teaspoon salt; porcini, shiitake, and button mushrooms; and oregano. Sauté 6 minutes or until mushrooms release moisture and darken. Sprinkle with flour; cook 1 minute, stirring constantly. Stir in stock, wine, and porcini soaking liquid; cook 3 minutes or until thickened, stirring frequently. Add chicken; cook 2 minutes or until heated, turning chicken once. Sprinkle with basil. Serves 4 (serving size: 1 chicken breast half, about 2/3 cup sauce, and 1 tablespoon basil)

CALORIES 336; FAT 11.5g (sat 1.9g, mono 6.2g, poly 1.5g); PROTEIN 40.5g; CARB 12.1g; FIBER 2g; CHOL 109mg; IRON 2.1mg; SODIUM 585mg; CALC 39mg

12 Slow-Roasted Grape Tomatoes

Best way to get summer flavors year-round

Hands-on: 10 min. Total: 3 hr. 10 min. Though we adore the recipe these are based on (David Bonom's Aromatic Slow-Roasted Tomatoes from December 2009), we wanted a faster update. So in place of plum tomatoes we went with little grape tomatoes, which roast to concentrated sweetness in less than half the time. Serve as they are for a side dish, on crostini with ricotta for an appetizer, or tossed with pasta and oil for a main dish.

1 tablespoon extra-virgin olive oil
1 1/2 teaspoons sugar
1/2 teaspoon salt
1/2 teaspoon dried basil
1/2 teaspoon dried oregano
1/4 teaspoon freshly ground black pepper
2 pounds grape tomatoes, halved lengthwise
Cooking spray

1. Preheat oven to 200°.
2. Combine first 7 ingredients, tossing gently to coat. Arrange tomatoes, cut sides up, on a baking sheet coated with cooking spray. Roast at 200° for 3 hours. Serves 8 (serving size: about 1/2 cup)

CALORIES 55; FAT 1.7g (sat 0.2g, mono 1.2g, poly 0.2g); PROTEIN 1.4g; CARB 8.9g; FIBER 2.8g; CHOL 0mg; IRON 0.1mg; SODIUM 157mg; CALC 35mg

BEST WAY TO GET SUMMER FLAVORS YEAR-ROUND. AND WE FOUND A WAY TO SPEED THE DISH.

The key to this recipe, submitted by Catherine Lyet from Lancaster, Pennsylvania, is toasting and grinding the cumin: That practice, used widely in many cuisines to bring out the aromatic goodness of spices, lends a depth that complements the buttery richness of the fish. We did change the fish in this update to address sustainability issues. Chilean sea bass (the original choice) and sablefish (also called black cod) are similar in texture, but the latter is a greener choice.

Sustainable Choice

Kid Friendly • Quick & Easy

13 Cumin-Crusted Sablefish

Most crazy-delicious reader-submitted recipe ever

Hands-on: 5 min. Total: 20 min. We made an important update to this recipe. It originally called for Chilean sea bass—and although you can sometimes find a sustainable type of that fish (longline-caught in the McDonald and Falkland islands), sablefish (also known as black cod) and white sea bass are consistently good choices with a similarly rich, buttery texture. It's worth the tiny bit of effort to toast and grind your own cumin seeds—the flavor payoff is huge.

1 tablespoon cumin seeds
1/2 teaspoon salt
1/4 teaspoon freshly ground black pepper
4 (6-ounce) sablefish or white sea bass fillets
1/2 teaspoon olive oil
2 tablespoons chopped fresh flat-leaf parsley
4 lemon wedges

1. Preheat oven to 375°.
2. Cook cumin seeds in a large skillet over medium heat 2 minutes or until toasted. Place cumin, salt, and pepper in a spice or coffee grinder; process until finely ground. Rub cumin mixture over top and bottom sides of fillets.

3. Heat oil in pan over medium-high heat. Add fillets; cook 2 minutes on each side or until browned. Wrap handle of pan with foil. Bake at 375° for 4 minutes or until fish flakes easily when tested with a fork. Sprinkle with parsley; serve with lemon wedges. Serves 4 (serving size: 1 fillet)

CALORIES 331; FAT 26g (sat 5.3g, mono 13.8g, poly 3.5g); PROTEIN 22.3g; CARB 0.9g; FIBER 0.3g; CHOL 80mg; IRON 3.3mg; SODIUM 391mg; CALC 75mg

Kid Friendly • Make Ahead Freezable

14 Chicken, Kale, and Quinoa Soup

Best mash-up of all your favorites

Hands-on: 59 min. Total: 59 min. We took four of the top recipe search categories from our website—chicken, kale, quinoa, and soup—and combined them into one tasty dish that we think will become your new favorite. Rinse the quinoa to ensure that any bitter coating is removed.

4 center-cut bacon slices
1 1/2 cups chopped onion
3/4 cup chopped carrot
1 teaspoon kosher salt, divided
6 garlic cloves, minced
Cooking spray
1 pound skinless, boneless chicken thighs, cut into 3/4-inch pieces
1/2 teaspoon freshly ground black pepper, divided
6 cups unsalted chicken stock
2 bay leaves
2/3 cup uncooked quinoa
6 cups chopped kale
2 teaspoons thyme leaves

1. Cook bacon in a Dutch oven over medium heat until crisp. Remove bacon from pan, reserving drippings. Crumble bacon; set aside.

2. Increase heat to medium-high. Add onion, carrot, and 1/4 teaspoon salt to drippings in pan; sauté 5 minutes, stirring occasionally. Add garlic; sauté 2 minutes. Remove mixture from pan.
3. Coat pan with cooking spray. Add chicken to pan; sprinkle with 1/4 teaspoon salt and 1/4 teaspoon pepper. Sauté 6 minutes or until chicken is browned and done. Stir in onion mixture, chicken stock, bay leaves, 1/2 teaspoon salt, and 1/4 teaspoon pepper; bring to a boil.
4. Place quinoa in a fine sieve; place sieve in a large bowl. Cover quinoa with water. Using your hands, rub grains together for 30 seconds; rinse and drain. Repeat procedure twice. Drain well. Add quinoa to pan; cover and simmer 15 minutes. Add kale and thyme to pan; simmer, uncovered, 5 minutes or until kale is tender. Discard bay leaves. Ladle about 1 2/3 cup soup into bowls; sprinkle with 1 teaspoon bacon. Serves 6

CALORIES 262; FAT 6.2g (sat 1.7g, mono 1.4g, poly 1.6g); PROTEIN 26.6g; CARB 26.3g; FIBER 3.9g; CHOL 77mg; IRON 3.2mg; SODIUM 650mg; CALC 147mg

Kid Friendly • Make Ahead

15 Chicken Enchiladas

Superb casual casserole

Hands-on: 47 min. Total: 1 hr. 52 min.
For many staffers, this is the go-to make-for-company dish—a sure bet. Once you taste the mix of spicy jalapeño, tangy salsa verde, tender chicken, and luscious cream cheese, you'll be as hooked as we are.

4 cups cold water
2 cups fat-free, lower-sodium chicken broth
1 tablespoon whole black peppercorns
5 garlic cloves, crushed
2 (6-ounce) skinless, boneless chicken breast halves
1 celery stalk, coarsely chopped
1 large carrot, peeled and cut into ¹/₂-inch pieces
1 jalapeño pepper, halved
¹/₂ medium onion, cut into wedges
1 (7-ounce) can salsa verde
¹/₄ cup heavy whipping cream
1 cup chopped seeded tomato
¹/₄ cup chopped fresh cilantro
¹/₄ teaspoon kosher salt
¹/₂ teaspoon ground cumin
¹/₄ teaspoon ground red pepper
4 ounces ¹/₃-less-fat cream cheese, softened
12 (6-inch) corn tortillas
Cooking spray
1 ounce sharp cheddar cheese, shredded (about ¹/₄ cup)

1. Combine first 9 ingredients in a saucepan over medium heat; bring to a simmer. Cook 8 minutes or until chicken is done. Remove chicken from pan with a slotted spoon; let stand 10 minutes. Shred chicken; set aside. Drain cooking liquid through a sieve over a bowl; reserve liquid. Discard solids.
2. Combine reserved cooking liquid and salsa verde in a wide saucepan; bring to a boil over medium-high heat. Cook until reduced to 1¹/₂ cups (about 30 minutes). Reduce heat to low; stir in whipping cream. Place pan over low heat.
3. Preheat oven to 400°.
4. Place chicken in a medium bowl. Add tomato and next 5 ingredients (through cream cheese) to chicken; toss. Dip each tortilla in sauce mixture for 10 seconds. Fill each tortilla with about ¹/₃ cup chicken mixture; roll up. Arrange filled tortillas, seam sides down, in an 11 x 7–inch glass or ceramic baking dish coated with cooking spray. Spoon sauce over tortillas; top with cheddar cheese. Bake at 400° for 20 minutes or until lightly browned. Serves 6 (serving size: 2 enchiladas)

CALORIES 262; FAT 10.8g (sat 5.7g, mono 0.2g, poly 0.7g); PROTEIN 18.3g; CARB 22.8g; FIBER 2.5g; CHOL 65mg; IRON 0.6mg; SODIUM 715mg; CALC 79mg

Quick & Easy

16 Green Curry Fritters

Global flavors favorite

Hands-on: 25 min. Total: 25 min. *Talk about flavor! Green curry paste (found in the Asian-foods section) and chile paste impart tons of savory-spicy-fragrant hits to ground chicken. Only a tiny tweak to this recipe: Our fritters got a little too browned, so we reduced the cooking temperature from medium-high to medium and cooked them a little longer.*

²/₃ cup panko (Japanese breadcrumbs)
¹/₄ cup diagonally sliced green onions
1 pound ground chicken breast
2 tablespoons canola mayonnaise
1¹/₂ tablespoons green curry paste
1 tablespoon dark sesame oil
1 tablespoon lower-sodium soy sauce
2 teaspoons sambal oelek (ground fresh chile paste)
³/₈ teaspoon kosher salt
¹/₂ teaspoon grated peeled fresh ginger
1 large egg
2 tablespoons canola oil, divided

1. Place first 3 ingredients in a large bowl. Combine mayonnaise and next 7 ingredients (through egg). Add mayonnaise mixture to chicken mixture; mix lightly until combined. Divide into 12 equal portions; gently shape each portion into a small patty (do not pack).
2. Heat a large skillet over medium heat. Add 1 tablespoon canola oil to pan; swirl to coat. Add 6 patties to pan; cook 3¹/₂ minutes on each side or until done. Remove from pan. Repeat procedure with remaining oil and patties. Serves 6 (serving size: 2 fritters)

CALORIES 206; FAT 11.9g (sat 1.2g, mono 6.3g, poly 3.4g); PROTEIN 18.4g; CARB 6g; FIBER 0.3g; CHOL 75mg; IRON 0.2mg; SODIUM 368mg; CALC 8mg

Kid Friendly • Make Ahead
Vegetarian

17 Banana Bread with Chocolate Glaze

Most tempting of all our quick breads (*pictured on page 233*)

Hands-on: 12 min. Total: 1 hr. 52 min.
Mom's Banana Bread, a recipe dating back to 1996 when it was submitted by reader Stacey A. Johnson, has been a consistent staff and reader favorite. The new chocolate topping makes it even more irresistible.

1 cup sugar
¹/₄ cup butter, softened
1²/₃ cups mashed ripe banana (about 3 bananas)
¹/₄ cup fat-free milk
¹/₄ cup reduced-fat sour cream
2 large egg whites
9 ounces unbleached all-purpose flour (about 2 cups)
1 teaspoon baking soda
¹/₂ teaspoon salt
Cooking spray
2¹/₂ tablespoons half-and-half
2 ounces semisweet chocolate, finely chopped

1. Preheat oven to 350°.
2. Combine sugar and butter in a bowl; beat with a mixer at medium speed until well blended. Add banana, milk, sour cream, and egg whites.
3. Weigh or lightly spoon flour into dry measuring cups; level with a knife. Combine flour, baking soda, and salt, stirring with a whisk. Add flour mixture to banana mixture; beat just until blended (do not overbeat). Spoon batter into a 9 x 5–inch metal loaf pan coated with cooking spray. Bake at 350° for 1 hour or until a wooden pick inserted in center comes out clean. Cool in pan 10 minutes on a wire rack; remove from pan. Cool on rack.
4. Place half-and-half and chocolate in a microwave-safe bowl. Microwave at HIGH 1 minute or until chocolate melts, stirring every 20 seconds. Cool slightly; drizzle over bread. Serves 16 (serving size: 1 slice)

CALORIES 184; FAT 5.2g (sat 3.1g, mono 1.4g, poly 0.3g); PROTEIN 3g; CARB 32.6g; FIBER 1.3g; CHOL 11mg; IRON 1mg; SODIUM 190mg; CALC 18mg

Kid Friendly • Make Ahead
Vegetarian

18 Spinach-and-Artichoke Dip

Mob-worthy, large-batch party-pleaser

Hands-on: 13 min. Total: 46 min. This has been a staff favorite ever since we first tried it 13 years ago. It's rich, savory, and super-creamy, with a nice hit of garlic. We made a few small tweaks—increased the amount of spinach and decreased the mozzarella to lower the sat fat to an acceptable level. Serve with tortilla chips.

1/2 cup fat-free sour cream
1/4 teaspoon freshly ground black pepper
3 garlic cloves, minced
1 (14-ounce) can artichoke hearts, drained and chopped

1 (10-ounce) package frozen chopped spinach, thawed, drained, and squeezed dry
1 (8-ounce) block 1/3-less-fat cream cheese, softened
1 (8-ounce) block fat-free cream cheese, softened
6 ounces part-skim mozzarella cheese, shredded and divided (about 1 1/2 cups)
1 ounce fresh Parmesan cheese, grated and divided (about 1/4 cup)

1. Preheat oven to 350°.
2. Combine first 7 ingredients in a large bowl, stirring until well blended. Add 4 ounces (1 cup) mozzarella and 2 tablespoons Parmesan; stir well. Spoon mixture into a broiler-safe 1 1/2-quart glass or ceramic baking dish. Sprinkle with 1/2 cup mozzarella and 2 table-spoons Parmesan. Bake at 350° for 30 minutes or until bubbly.
3. Preheat broiler to high (leave dish in oven). Broil dip 3 minutes or until cheese is lightly browned. Serves 22 (serving size: about 1/4 cup)

CALORIES 75; FAT 4.2g (sat 2.4g, mono 1.1g, poly 0.2g); PROTEIN 5.9g; CARB 3.7g; FIBER 0.4g; CHOL 15mg; IRON 0.5mg; SODIUM 216mg; CALC 150mg

Kid Friendly • Vegetarian

19 Whole-Wheat, Buttermilk, and Orange Pancakes

Sunday-morning-in-your-jammies breakfast
(pictured on page 234)

Hands-on: 30 min. Total: 40 min. Here we've updated Bill and Cheryl Jamison's fantastic Whole-Wheat Buttermilk Pancakes from 2002 with a little citrus zest. Allowing the batter to sit before cooking gives the leaveners a chance to work, creating light, fluffy pancakes.

2 tablespoons butter, softened
1/4 teaspoon grated orange rind
3/4 teaspoon fresh orange juice
3.5 ounces white whole-wheat flour (about 3/4 cup)
3.4 ounces unbleached all-purpose flour (about 3/4 cup)
2 tablespoons sugar
1 1/2 teaspoons baking powder
1/2 teaspoon baking soda
3/8 teaspoon salt
1 1/2 cups low-fat buttermilk
1/4 cup fresh orange juice
1 tablespoon canola oil
1 large egg
1 large egg white
Cooking spray
3/4 cup maple syrup

1. Combine first 3 ingredients.
2. Weigh or lightly spoon flours into dry measuring cups; level with a knife. Combine flours and next 4 ingredients (through salt) in a medium bowl, stirring with a whisk. Combine buttermilk, 1/4 cup juice, oil, and 1 egg in a small bowl, stirring with a whisk. Add buttermilk mixture to flour mixture, stirring just until moist; let stand 15 minutes. Place egg white in a medium bowl; beat with a whisk until medium peaks form. Gently fold egg white into batter.
3. Preheat a griddle to medium heat. Coat pan with cooking spray. Spoon 1/4 cup batter per pancake onto griddle. Cook 3 minutes or until edges begin to bubble and bottom is browned. Turn pancakes over; cook 3 minutes or until done. Serve with orange butter and syrup. Serves 6 (serving size: 2 pancakes, 1 teaspoon butter, and 2 tablespoons syrup)

CALORIES 336; FAT 8g (sat 3.2g, mono 3g, poly 1.1g); PROTEIN 7.4g; CARB 59.1g; FIBER 2.5g; CHOL 44mg; IRON 1.5mg; SODIUM 477mg; CALC 182mg

Kid Friendly • Make Ahead

20 Fresh Lemonade Cake

Most "Pinned" dessert ever—improved

Hands-on: 35 min. Total: 1 hr. 30 min. *Lemonade Layer Cake, developed by Ann Taylor Pittman as a recipe makeover, has been loved by readers since it debuted in April 2002. When we retested it for this story, we felt we could make big improvements in the texture and flavor. Instead of using a lemonade product, we've made a concentrated fresh lemonade syrup that adds zippy citrus hits to the more-tender cake.*

Cake:
Baking spray with flour
11 ounces cake flour (about 2³/₄ cups)
1 teaspoon baking powder
¹/₂ teaspoon baking soda
¹/₂ teaspoon salt
³/₄ cup nonfat buttermilk
¹/₂ cup 1% low-fat milk
1 cup granulated sugar
5 tablespoons butter, softened
3 tablespoons canola oil
2 large egg yolks
1 tablespoon grated lemon rind
3 large egg whites
¹/₈ teaspoon cream of tartar
Lemonade syrup:
¹/₄ cup granulated sugar
2 tablespoons fresh lemon juice
2 tablespoons finely chopped lemon sections
1 tablespoon water

Frosting:
8 ounces ¹/₃-less-fat cream cheese, chilled
2 teaspoons grated lemon rind
1 teaspoon fresh lemon juice
2¹/₂ cups powdered sugar

1. Preheat oven to 350°.
2. To prepare cake, lightly coat 2 (8-inch) round metal cake pans with baking spray; line bottoms of pans with wax paper. Coat wax paper with baking spray.
3. Weigh or lightly spoon flour into dry measuring cups; level with a knife. Combine flour, baking powder, baking soda, and salt in a medium bowl, stirring well with a whisk. Combine buttermilk and low-fat milk. Combine 1 cup granulated sugar, butter, and oil in a large bowl; beat with mixer at medium speed 3 minutes or until light and fluffy. Add egg yolks, 1 at a time, beating well after each addition. Beat in 1 tablespoon rind. Add flour mixture and milk mixture alternately to butter mixture, beginning and ending with flour mixture and beating just until combined.
4. Place 3 egg whites and cream of tartar in a medium bowl; beat with a mixer at high speed until medium peaks form, using clean, dry beaters. Gently fold egg white mixture into batter. Divide batter evenly between prepared pans. Bake at 350° for 25 minutes or until a wooden pick inserted in center comes out clean. Cool in pans 10 minutes on wire racks. Loosen edges with a knife, and invert cake layers onto racks. Carefully remove wax paper, and discard.
5. To prepare lemonade syrup, while cake layers bake, combine ¼ cup granulated sugar and next 3 ingredients (through 1 tablespoon water) in a 1-cup glass measure. Microwave at HIGH 45 seconds or until mixture boils; stir until sugar dissolves. Cool slightly. Pierce warm cake layers liberally with a wooden pick. Brush syrup over warm cake layers until all of syrup is absorbed. Cool completely.
6. To prepare frosting, place chilled cream cheese, 2 teaspoons rind, and 1 teaspoon juice in a large bowl; beat with a mixer at medium speed until well combined. Gradually add powdered sugar; beat at low speed just until blended (do not overbeat). Place 1 cake layer on a plate; spread half of frosting over top. Top with remaining layer. Spread remaining frosting over top. Store, loosely covered, in refrigerator. Serves 16 (serving size: 1 slice)

CALORIES 314; **FAT** 10.3g (sat 4.6g, mono 3.7g, poly 1.2g); **PROTEIN** 4.7g; **CARB** 51.8g; **FIBER** 0.5g; **CHOL** 44mg; **IRON** 1.6mg; **SODIUM** 244mg; **CALC** 64mg

Kid Friendly • Make Ahead

21 Mexican Chocolate Cream Pie

A pie with real sass

Hands-on: 35 min. Total: 4 hr. *No changes here: We love the combo of deep, rich chocolate and the tingly pinch of cinnamon and red pepper. We also enjoy the ease and forgiving nature of a graham cracker crust, which is less fussy than pastry. If you can't find espresso granules with the coffee, look in the Latin-foods section (that's where we sometimes find them).*

Crust:
1¹/₂ cups graham cracker crumbs (about 10 cookie sheets), divided
2 tablespoons sugar
1 teaspoon ground cinnamon
¹/₈ teaspoon salt
2 tablespoons egg white
2 tablespoons butter, melted
Cooking spray
Filling:
¹/₂ cup sugar
2 tablespoons cornstarch
1 tablespoon unsweetened cocoa
¹/₄ teaspoon instant espresso granules
¹/₈ teaspoon salt

1/8 teaspoon ground red pepper
1 large egg
1 large egg yolk
1¾ cups 2% reduced-fat milk
2 ounces dark chocolate, chopped
1½ cups frozen reduced-calorie
   whipped topping, thawed

1. Preheat oven to 375°.
2. To prepare crust, reserve 1 table-spoon crumbs for topping. Combine remaining crumbs, 2 tablespoons sugar, cinnamon, and ⅛ teaspoon salt in a bowl, stirring well. Stir in egg white and butter. Press crumb mixture into bottom and up sides of a 9-inch pie plate coated with cooking spray. Bake at 375° for 9 minutes or until lightly toasted; cool completely on a wire rack.
3. To prepare filling, combine ½ cup sugar and next 7 ingredients (through egg yolk) in a bowl, stirring well with a whisk. Place milk in a medium, heavy saucepan over medium-high heat; cook until milk reaches 180° or until tiny bubbles form around edge (do not boil). Gradually add hot milk to egg mixture, stirring constantly with a whisk. Return milk mixture to pan; cook over medium heat 10 minutes or until thick and bubbly, stirring constantly. Remove from heat. Add chocolate; stir until smooth.
4. Place pan in a large ice-filled bowl for 10 minutes or until mixture cools, stirring occasionally. Spoon filling into crust; cover surface of filling with plastic wrap. Chill 3 hours or until set; remove plastic wrap. Spread whipped topping over pie; sprinkle with reserved cracker crumbs. Serves 8 (serving size: 1 slice)

CALORIES 278; **FAT** 10.3g (sat 5.8g, mono 2.8g, poly 1g); **PROTEIN** 5g; **CARB** 42.1g; **FIBER** 1.3g; **CHOL** 57mg; **IRON** 1.5mg; **SODIUM** 231mg; **CALC** 81mg

Kid Friendly • Make Ahead

22 Mocha Cake with Fluffy Meringue Topping

A luscious cake perfect for wowing a crowd

Hands-on: 23 min. Total: 1 hr. 38 min.
Since 2006, readers have professed their love for contest winner Anna Ginsberg's One-Bowl Chocolate Mocha Cream Cake, touting it as the moistest cake ever. We agree—the cake is incredible. But online reviews suggested that the topping could use some tweaking. Instead of the original "mocha cream" of whipped topping, marshmallow creme, and coffee, we now have a creamy, less-sweet meringue. We also replaced reduced-fat mayonnaise (yes, mayo—it's the secret ingredient that makes for a fantastically moist cake) with canola mayo, our current product of choice.

Cake:
9 ounces unbleached all-purpose flour
   (about 2 cups)
1 cup granulated sugar
1 cup packed dark brown sugar
¾ cup unsweetened cocoa
1½ teaspoons baking soda
1½ teaspoons baking powder
½ teaspoon salt
1 cup canola mayonnaise (such as
   Hellmann's)
3 tablespoons canola oil
1 cup hot strong brewed coffee
2 teaspoons vanilla extract
⅓ cup semisweet chocolate chips
Cooking spray
Meringue:
9 tablespoons sugar
¼ teaspoon cream of tartar
¼ teaspoon salt
6 large egg whites
⅓ cup light chocolate syrup

1. Preheat oven to 350°.
2. To prepare cake, weigh or lightly spoon flour into dry measuring cups; level with a knife. Combine flour and next 6 ingredients (through ½ teaspoon salt) in a large bowl. Add mayonnaise and oil; beat with a mixer at low speed until well blended. Slowly add brewed coffee and vanilla; beat with a mixer at low speed 1 minute or until well blended. Stir in chocolate chips; pour batter into a 13 x 9–inch metal baking pan coated with cooking spray. Bake at 350° for 30 minutes or until a wooden pick inserted in center comes out clean. Cool in pan on a wire rack.
3. To prepare meringue, combine 9 tablespoons sugar and next 3 ingredients in the top of a double boiler. Cook over simmering water 2 minutes or until candy thermometer registers 150°, stirring constantly with a whisk. Remove from heat. Beat egg mixture with a mixer at medium speed until soft peaks form; beat at high speed until stiff peaks form. Spread meringue over cake. Store cake, loosely covered, in refrigerator. Drizzle each serving with 1 teaspoon chocolate syrup. Serves 16 (serving size: 1 piece)

CALORIES 289; **FAT** 8.2g (sat 1.2g, mono 4.5g, poly 2.3g); **PROTEIN** 4g; **CARB** 52.1g; **FIBER** 1.8g; **CHOL** 0mg; **IRON** 1.6mg; **SODIUM** 412mg; **CALC** 47mg

23 Roasted Asparagus with Balsamic Browned Butter

Weekend elegance in a weeknight-easy side dish

Hands-on: 7 min. Total: 25 min. *We've adored this recipe for more than a decade. Something magical happens when asparagus picks up a little toasty flavor, and then gets tossed in nutty browned butter with a splash of sweet balsamic vinegar: The vegetable outshines the entrée.*

**40 thick asparagus spears, trimmed
   (about 2 pounds)**
Cooking spray
1/4 teaspoon kosher salt
1/8 teaspoon black pepper
2 tablespoons butter
2 teaspoons lower-sodium soy sauce
1 teaspoon balsamic vinegar

1. Preheat oven to 400°.
2. Arrange asparagus spears in a single layer on a baking sheet; coat with cooking spray. Sprinkle with salt and pepper. Bake at 400° for 12 minutes or until tender.
3. Melt butter in a small skillet over medium heat; cook 3 minutes or until lightly browned, shaking pan occasionally. Remove from heat; stir in soy sauce and vinegar. Drizzle over asparagus, tossing well to coat. Serve immediately. Serves 8 (serving size: 5 spears)

CALORIES 45; **FAT** 3g (sat 1.8g, mono 0.9g, poly 0.2g); **PROTEIN** 1.9g; **CARB** 3.9g; **FIBER** 1.7g; **CHOL** 8mg; **IRON** 0.7mg; **SODIUM** 134mg; **CALC** 18mg

24 Mashed Potato Casserole

Ultimate potato comfort

Hands-on: 25 min. Total: 49 min. *We changed the procedure from using a food mill to a ricer, but you can use either one, or a standard potato masher.*

**1 1/2 pounds Yukon gold potatoes, peeled
   and cut into 1/2-inch-thick slices**
**1 1/2 pounds baking potatoes, peeled
   and cut into 1/2-inch-thick slices**
5 garlic cloves, thinly sliced
1 1/4 teaspoons kosher salt, divided
**6 ounces 1/3-less-fat cream cheese,
   softened (about 3/4 cup)**
Cooking spray
**2 ounces Parmigiano-Reggiano cheese,
   grated (about 1/2 cup)**
1/2 cup panko (Japanese breadcrumbs)
2 tablespoons thinly sliced chives

1. Preheat oven to 350°.
2. Place potatoes, garlic, and 1/2 teaspoon salt in a large saucepan, and cover with water. Bring to a boil. Reduce heat; simmer 15 minutes or until tender. Drain in a colander over a bowl, reserving 1/2 cup cooking liquid.
3. Press mixture in batches through a ricer into a bowl. Stir in 1/2 cup cooking liquid, 3/4 teaspoon salt, and cream cheese.
4. Spoon mixture into a broiler-safe 11 x 7–inch glass or ceramic baking dish coated with cooking spray. Bake at 350° for 20 minutes or until thoroughly heated.
5. Preheat broiler.
6. Combine Parmigiano-Reggiano and panko; sprinkle evenly over top of potatoes. Broil 4 minutes or until golden brown. Sprinkle with chives. Serves 8 (serving size: about 2/3 cup)

CALORIES 243; **FAT** 6.5g (sat 3.6g, mono 1.7g, poly 0.3g); **PROTEIN** 8.3g; **CARB** 37.9g; **FIBER** 2.6g; **CHOL** 20mg; **IRON** 1.2mg; **SODIUM** 361mg; **CALC** 93mg

25 Bistro Roast Chicken

A Sunday dinner centerpiece

Hands-on: 15 min. Total: 1 hr. 55 min. *Five ingredients (not counting salt, pepper, and cooking spray), and you have an absolutely delicious, roast chicken. Fresh tarragon is crucial; don't leave it out. Our only update was to decrease the salt just a bit to bring the sodium within our current nutrition guidelines.*

2 tablespoons minced fresh tarragon
1 tablespoon minced fresh thyme
4 teaspoons butter, melted
3/4 teaspoon salt
1 teaspoon Dijon mustard
**1/2 teaspoon freshly ground black
   pepper**
1 (4 1/2-pound) roasting chicken
Cooking spray

1. Preheat oven to 375°.
2. Combine first 6 ingredients.
3. Remove giblets and neck from chicken; discard. Trim excess fat. Starting at neck cavity, loosen skin from breast and drumsticks by inserting fingers, gently pushing between skin and meat. Rub herb mixture under loosened skin and over breast and drumsticks. Tie legs together with kitchen twine. Lift wing tips up and over back; tuck under chicken. Place chicken, breast side down, on rack of a broiler pan or shallow roasting pan coated with cooking spray; place in pan.
4. Bake chicken at 375° for 40 minutes. Carefully turn chicken over (breast side up). Bake an additional 40 minutes or until a thermometer inserted in the meaty part of thigh registers 165°. Place chicken on a cutting board; let stand 10 minutes before carving. Discard skin. Serves 5 (serving size: about 4 ounces meat)

CALORIES 262; **FAT** 8.7g (sat 3.3g, mono 2.5g, poly 1.5g); **PROTEIN** 42.5g; **CARB** 0.6g; **FIBER** 0.1g; **CHOL** 143mg; **IRON** 2.2mg; **SODIUM** 556mg; **CALC** 32mg

LOCAL HEROES, DONE LIGHT

Lighten Up, America! serves up favorite regional foods and the stories behind them.

For our latest cookbook, we sent ebullient and tireless contributing editor Allison Fishman Task on a food-finding mission: to crisscross this great land in search of favorite regional treats. The result of her road-tripping culinary anthropology is an almost dizzying collection of classic dishes from the diners, county fairs, cocktail parties, and hotel dining rooms of our collective yore.

Between the Reuben sandwiches, Waldorf salads, sweet-and-sour meatballs, red flannel hash, and apple pie, there's enough comforting nostalgia here to butter all of New England's lobster rolls. But Task also had her mind on a bigger theme: lightening these American classics for a country that is starting to think hard about what it eats, even as it reaffirms what it loves from its past. Task's food journeys and recipe tinkering add up to a new sort of cultural preservation: classic flavors reimagined for a healthier generation. This is important because the recent push toward megaburgers, bacon bombs, five-cheese pizzas, and other over-the-top glop isn't doing much to honor and advance our national food culture, let alone our national health.

"I had a ball doing this," Task says. "What's powerful about American cooking and food culture is that we are a country of so many people and regions, all contributing threads to the great American culinary tapestry."

Task's approach gives lots of love to regional character and tradition but makes room for vastly lighter versions. "Love what you eat today" is her message, but with a healthy future in mind. Keep an eye out, as Task did, for the new favorites—the Mexican fish tacos, the Vietnamese bánh mì sandwiches, the shakshuka featured here—that continue the evolution of American food through the gifts of immigrant cooks.

HONOR LOCAL TASTES WITH DISHES THAT ARE UPDATED FOR TODAY'S FAMILIES.

Kid Friendly • Make Ahead

Ohio Buckeyes

Hands-on: 33 min. Total: 2 hrs. *In this classic confection from the Buckeye State, creamy peanut butter and chocolate combine to create an adorable replica of an Ohio tree nut.*

2 cups powdered sugar
6 tablespoons unsalted butter, softened
2 ounces ⅓-less-fat cream cheese, softened
½ teaspoon kosher salt
1½ cups reduced-fat creamy peanut butter
¼ cup graham cracker crumbs
8 ounces dark chocolate (60–65% cacao), chopped

1. Place first 4 ingredients (through salt) in a medium bowl; beat with a mixer at medium speed until creamy. Add peanut butter and graham cracker crumbs; beat until blended.
2. Cover a baking sheet with parchment paper. Shape peanut butter mixture by tablespoonfuls into 38 balls. Place balls on baking sheet; refrigerate 1 hour.
3. Place chocolate in the top of a double boiler; place over simmering water, stirring until almost melted. Remove from heat; stir until smooth. Let cool slightly.
4. Place each ball on a fork, and dip ball in chocolate until partially coated; return to parchment paper to harden. Serves 38 (serving size: 1 buckeye)

CALORIES 141; **FAT** 8.3g (sat 3.5g, mono 2.9g, poly 1.2g); **PROTEIN** 2.7g; **CARB** 14.7g; **FIBER** 1.1g; **CHOL** 6mg; **IRON** 0.6mg; **SODIUM** 95mg; **CALC** 6mg

Quick & Easy • Vegetarian

Shakshuka

Hands-on: 13 min. Total: 25 min. *Don't let the funny name deter you; this dish is a delicious way to get vegetables with your breakfast.*

1 tablespoon olive oil
1 cup (¼-inch-wide) strips red bell
   pepper
1 cup (¼-inch-wide) strips green bell
   pepper
2 cups (¼-inch-thick) vertically sliced
   red onion
¼ teaspoon kosher salt
2 garlic cloves, minced
2 cups lower-sodium marinara sauce
1 teaspoon smoked paprika
4 large eggs
2 cups cooked brown rice
¼ cup baby basil leaves
2 tablespoons crumbled feta cheese

1. Heat a 10-inch nonstick skillet over medium heat. Add oil to pan; swirl to coat. Add bell peppers, onion, and salt; cook 5 minutes, stirring occasionally. Add garlic; cook 30 seconds. Stir in marinara sauce and paprika. Bring to a boil; reduce heat, cover, and simmer 5 minutes.
2. Form 4 (2-inch) indentations in sauce, using the back of a spoon. Crack eggs, 1 at a time, into a small custard cup, and gently slip into each indentation. Cover and cook 6 minutes or until eggs are done.
3. Place rice into 4 shallow bowls. Spoon egg mixture over rice, and sprinkle with basil and cheese. Serves 4 (serving size: ½ cup rice, 1 cup sauce, 1 egg, 1 tablespoon basil, and 1½ teaspoons cheese)

CALORIES 305; FAT 11.3g (sat 3g, mono 5.2g, poly 2.3g); PROTEIN 11.9g; CARB 39.5g; FIBER 5.2g; CHOL 190mg; IRON 3.4mg; SODIUM 354mg; CALC 108mg

Kid Friendly • Make Ahead

Chicken and Dumplings

Hands-on: 47 min. Total: 11 hr. 21 min. *This lightened-up version of a classic—beloved in both the South and the Midwest—is satisfying enough to be a one-dish meal.*

1 (4-pound) whole chicken
10 cups water
4 cups unsalted chicken stock
1 tablespoon black peppercorns
3 celery stalks, coarsely chopped
   (about 6 ounces)
2 carrots, cut into 1-inch pieces (about
   5 ounces)
2 bay leaves
1 onion, peeled and cut into wedges
   (about 10 ounces)
½ bunch fresh flat-leaf parsley (about
   2 ounces)
3 tablespoons butter, divided
1 cup chopped onion
¼ cup sliced celery
1 carrot, halved lengthwise and sliced
1 tablespoon all-purpose flour
1 teaspoon kosher salt, divided
½ teaspoon freshly ground black
   pepper
4.5 ounces all-purpose flour (about 1
   cup)
1 teaspoon baking soda
6 tablespoons nonfat buttermilk
1 tablespoon chopped fresh thyme
3 tablespoons chopped fresh flat-leaf
   parsley

1. Remove giblets and neck from chicken; trim excess fat. Place chicken, 10 cups water, and next 7 ingredients (through parsley bunch) in an 8-quart stockpot. Bring to a boil; reduce heat and simmer, uncovered, 1 hour, skimming foam from the surface as necessary. Remove from heat, and let stand 20 minutes.
2. Remove skin from chicken; remove chicken from bones, discarding skin and bones. Shred chicken with 2 forks. Strain stock through a sieve into a large bowl; discard solids. Cool stock and chicken to room temperature. Cover and chill stock and chicken separately for 8 to 24 hours. Skim solidified fat from surface of stock; discard fat. Reserve 8 cups stock and chicken. (Refrigerate remaining stock in an airtight container for up to 1 week, or freeze for up to 3 months.)
3. Melt 1 tablespoon butter in a Dutch oven over medium heat. Add 1 cup onion, ¼ cup celery, and sliced carrot to pan; cook 8 minutes, stirring occasionally. Stir in 1 tablespoon flour, ¾ teaspoon salt, and ground pepper; cook, stirring constantly, 1 minute. Stir in 8 cups reserved stock. Bring to a boil; reduce heat and simmer 15 minutes, stirring occasionally.
4. Weigh or lightly spoon 4.5 ounces flour (about 1 cup) into a dry measuring cup; level with a knife. Combine flour, baking soda, and ¼ teaspoon salt, stirring with a whisk. Cut in 2 tablespoons butter with a pastry blender or 2 knives until mixture resembles coarse meal. Add buttermilk, stirring until moist.
5. Drop dough in 24 portions (about 1 teaspoon each) into stock mixture. Cover and cook 8 minutes. Gently stir in reserved shredded chicken and thyme. Simmer over very low heat 6 minutes or until thoroughly heated and dumplings are done. Remove from heat, and ladle into shallow bowls. Sprinkle evenly with chopped parsley. Serves 8 (serving size: 1¼ cups chicken mixture, 3 dumplings, and 1 teaspoon parsley)

CALORIES 258; FAT 7.4g (sat 3.5g, mono 2g, poly 1g); PROTEIN 26.2g; CARB 20.7g; FIBER 2.2g; CHOL 77mg; IRON 2.5mg; SODIUM 629mg; CALC 69mg

BUTTERNUT SQUASH AU GRATIN

From Benoit in Manhattan.

Butternut squash is the go-to vegetable for adding sweetness and substance to cool-weather cooking. Legendary French chef Alain Ducasse—whose restaurants around the world have earned him a staggering 17 Michelin stars—knows better than anyone how to make this everyday fall veggie shine.

But there's no big-kitchen wizardry required: Ducasse says the simplest way to showcase butternut's comfortingly tender texture is to slice the squash open lengthwise, remove the seeds, and then bake until fork-tender. "You can even toast the squash seeds and season to taste," Ducasse says. "Use them as a crunchy-textured garnish or as a snack."

Nor is his rich, hearty gratin much more complicated. Ducasse blends mashed butternut with earthy wild mushrooms and bits of bacon to balance the squash's sweetness. Our version substitutes more readily available beef stock for veal jus (which Ducasse uses), though the stock still delivers a savory umami note.

Butternut Squash au Gratin with Wild Mushrooms and Crispy Bacon

Hands-on: 50 min. Total: 1 hr. 50 min.

1 tablespoon extra-virgin olive oil
2 thinly sliced green onions
8 cups finely diced peeled butternut squash, divided (about 4 pounds)
1/2 teaspoon kosher salt, divided
2 center-cut bacon slices
4 ounces sliced chanterelle mushrooms
4 ounces sliced shiitake mushroom caps
1 1/2 tablespoons chopped fresh sage
1/4 cup unsalted beef stock (such as Swanson)
2 ounces Parmigiano-Reggiano cheese, grated and divided (about 1/2 cup)
2 tablespoons part-skim ricotta cheese
1/4 teaspoon freshly ground black pepper
Cooking spray
6 ounces oyster mushrooms, sliced

1. Preheat oven to 350°.
2. Heat a large skillet over medium-high heat. Add oil; swirl to coat. Add green onions; sauté 30 seconds. Add 6 cups squash; sauté 2 minutes. Reduce heat to medium-low, and stir in 1/4 teaspoon salt. Cook, covered, 15 minutes or until tender. Increase heat to medium-high. Cook, uncovered, 2 minutes or until liquid evaporates, stirring frequently. Place squash mixture in a large bowl; mash with a potato masher or fork until smooth.
3. Cook bacon in a large nonstick skillet over medium-high heat until crisp. Remove bacon from pan, reserving drippings in pan; crumble bacon. Add chanterelles, shiitakes, and sage to drippings; sauté 8 minutes or until mushrooms are browned. Add stock; cook 3 minutes or until liquid almost evaporates. Add mushroom mixture, 2 cups diced squash, 1/4 teaspoon salt, 1 ounce Parmigiano-Reggiano cheese, ricotta cheese, and black pepper to mashed squash mixture, stirring to combine. Spoon squash mixture into a broiler-safe 11 x 7–inch glass or ceramic baking dish coated with cooking spray. Cover with foil; bake at 350° for 1 hour. Remove pan from oven; discard foil.
4. Preheat broiler to high.
5. Combine bacon, 1 ounce Parmigiano-Reggiano, and oyster mushrooms in a bowl; sprinkle over gratin. Broil 6 minutes or until lightly browned. Let stand 5 minutes before serving. Serves 8 (serving size: about 1 cup)

CALORIES 163; FAT 5g (sat 1.9g, mono 1.9g, poly 0.4g); PROTEIN 6.9g; CARB 26.4g; FIBER 5.3g; CHOL 9mg; IRON 2.3mg; SODIUM 286mg; CALC 188mg

HOW TO PREP CHANTERELLE MUSHROMS

Clean: Use a damp cloth or paper towel to gently brush any dirt or woodland debris from the wild mushrooms.

Trim: Cut up to 1/4 inch from the bottom of any stems that appear discolored, soggy, or not completely fresh.

PICKED FRESH FOR OCTOBER: WINTER SQUASH

This month from the *Cooking Light* Garden: The sweetest, meatiest cool-weather veggies

Prized by cooks for its versatility, buttery-rich winter squash is a go-to veggie in the fall. But on the production end, it takes a little more time on the vine. Our gardener, Mary Beth Shaddix, sowed seeds this spring. By late summer, she was pushing aside enormous umbrella-like leaves to check their progress.

Unlike summer squash, winter squash needs to be harvested when the skin is too hard for a fingernail to dent. For best storage, it needs to first sit, or "cure," in a dry, sunny spot for several weeks after harvest. "One of my favorite things about squash is that it can store until we're planting lettuces again in early spring," Shaddix says. "It's a sweet reminder of our productive summer garden during the coldest months."

Kid Friendly • Make Ahead

Sugar Pumpkin Custards with Graham Crumble

Hands-on: 45 min. Total: 10 hr. 45 min.

1 small sugar pumpkin (about 2½ pounds)
⅓ cup sugar
1 tablespoon butter, melted
1½ teaspoons vanilla extract
4 large egg yolks
1 large egg
1 cup half-and-half
½ teaspoon salt
½ teaspoon ground cinnamon
¼ teaspoon ground nutmeg
1 (12-ounce) can fat-free evaporated milk
6 tablespoons graham cracker crumbs
1 tablespoon egg whites, lightly beaten
2 teaspoons butter, melted
2 teaspoons sugar
¼ teaspoon ground cinnamon
Cooking spray
½ cup frozen reduced-fat whipped topping, thawed

1. Preheat oven to 325°.
2. Pierce pumpkin 5 times with a knife; place on a baking sheet. Bake at 325° for 1 hour and 15 minutes or until tender when pierced. Let stand 10 minutes. Discard stem, skin, and seeds. Place 1 cup chopped pumpkin (8½ ounces) in a large bowl. (Save remaining pumpkin for another use.) Beat with a mixer at medium speed until smooth. Add ⅓ cup sugar and next 4 ingredients (through whole egg); beat until well blended.

3. Place half-and-half and next 4 ingredients (through milk) in a saucepan over medium heat. Heat to 180° or until tiny bubbles form around edge. Add milk mixture to pumpkin mixture. Beat at low speed 1 minute. Strain mixture through a cheesecloth-lined sieve into a bowl. Discard solids. Divide mixture evenly among 8 (4-ounce) ramekins. Place ramekins in a large roasting pan. Add hot water to pan to a depth of 1 inch; bake at 325° for 50 minutes or until center barely moves when pan is touched. Remove ramekins from pan; cool on a wire rack. Cover and chill 4 hours.

4. Combine cracker crumbs and next 4 ingredients. Spread mixture in a single layer on a baking sheet coated with cooking spray. Bake at 325° for 25 minutes. Let stand 5 minutes. Place crumb mixture in a zip-top plastic bag, and coarsely crush using a meat mallet or small heavy skillet. Top each custard with 1 tablespoon whipped topping and about 2 teaspoons graham crumble. Serves 8

CALORIES 206; **FAT** 10g (sat 5.4g, mono 2.1g, poly 0.7g); **PROTEIN** 7.2g; **CARB** 22.4g; **FIBER** 0.4g; **CHOL** 135mg; **IRON** 0.9mg; **SODIUM** 269mg; **CALC** 184mg

Quick & Easy • Vegetarian

Roasted Red Onions and Delicata Squash

Hands-on: 5 min. Total: 30 min. Thin-skinned delicata squash has an edible peel, helping this side come together quickly.

1 tablespoon unsalted butter, melted
1 tablespoon chopped fresh thyme
1 tablespoon honey
2 teaspoons olive oil
3 garlic cloves, sliced
2 (12-ounce) delicata squashes, halved lengthwise, seeded, and cut into ½-inch slices

1 (1-pound) red onion, cut into
   12 wedges
½ teaspoon salt, divided
½ teaspoon freshly ground black
   pepper, divided
Cooking spray
3 tablespoons chopped fresh flat-leaf
   parsley

1. Place a baking sheet in oven. Preheat oven to 475° (leave pan in oven). 2. Combine first 5 ingredients in a large bowl, stirring with a whisk. Add squash and onion; toss gently to coat. Sprinkle vegetable mixture with ¼ teaspoon salt and ¼ teaspoon pepper. Carefully remove preheated pan from oven; coat pan with cooking spray. Arrange vegetable mixture in a single layer on pan. Bake at 475° for 20 minutes or until tender, turning once. Sprinkle with ¼ teaspoon salt, ¼ teaspoon pepper, and chopped parsley. Serves 6 (serving size: about 1 cup)

CALORIES 120; FAT 3.6g (sat 1.5g, mono 1.6g, poly 0.3g); PROTEIN 2g; CARB 22.7g; FIBER 3.2g; CHOL 5mg; IRON 1.2mg; SODIUM 205mg; CALC 63mg

Vegetarian

Spaghetti Squash Fritters with Sriracha Mayonnaise

Hands-on: 35 min. Total: 55 min.

1 (2-pound) spaghetti squash
1 (8-ounce) package baby spinach
½ cup panko (Japanese breadcrumbs)
2 tablespoons grated fresh Parmesan
   cheese
1 tablespoon minced fresh garlic
½ teaspoon freshly ground black
   pepper
¼ teaspoon baking powder
2 large egg whites
1 tablespoon olive oil, divided
5 teaspoons canola mayonnaise

2 teaspoons 2% reduced-fat milk
1 teaspoon Sriracha (hot chile sauce,
   such as Huy Fong)
1 teaspoon cider vinegar

1. Cut squash in half lengthwise. Scoop out seeds; discard. Place squash halves, cut sides up, in a microwave-safe bowl. Cover with a damp paper towel. Microwave at HIGH 20 minutes or until tender. Let stand 10 minutes. Scrape inside of squash with a fork to remove spaghettilike strands to measure 4 cups. 2. Heat a large skillet over medium-high heat. Add spinach to pan; cook 2 minutes or until spinach wilts. Place squash and spinach on a clean dish towel; squeeze until barely moist. Coarsely chop squash mixture, and place in a large bowl. Add panko and next 4 ingredients (through baking powder), and toss well to combine. Place egg whites in a medium bowl; beat with a mixer at high speed until soft peaks form. Gently fold egg whites into squash mixture. 3. Fill a ¼-cup dry measuring cup with squash mixture. Invert onto work surface; gently pat into a ¾-inch-thick patty. Repeat procedure with remaining squash mixture, forming 10 patties total. Heat a large nonstick skillet over medium heat. Add 1½ teaspoons oil to pan, and swirl to coat. Add 5 patties to pan; cook 3 minutes on each side or until browned. Remove patties from pan; keep warm. Repeat procedure with 1½ teaspoons oil and squash patties. 4. Combine mayonnaise and remaining ingredients in a small bowl. Serve with fritters. Serves 5 (serving size: 2 patties and about 2 teaspoons sauce)

CALORIES 172; FAT 8.8g (sat 1.5g, mono 4.3g, poly 1.8g); PROTEIN 6g; CARB 19.6g; FIBER 4g; CHOL 4mg; IRON 1.9mg; SODIUM 228mg; CALC 139mg

WINTER SQUASH

ACORN
Named for its shape, this relatively small winter squash is good for individual servings: Cut in half lengthwise, fill with your favorite stuffing, and bake.

DELICATA
No need to peel this squash; its skin is much softer than that of other varieties and is completely edible.

GOLDEN NUGGET
Like miniature pumpkins, these little guys average about a pound each. They're incredibly sweet and work well in desserts.

BUTTERNUT
Because of its elongated shape and smaller seed cavity, butternut squash is easy to peel, seed, and cut into cubes.

MIRIN

By Naomi Duguid

You may have bought a bottle of mirin for a particular recipe, or perhaps because you thought it was a type of vinegar and wanted to try it. Either way, you'll have discovered that it is a sweet Japanese rice wine and a great ingredient to keep on hand. I find that in recipes that need a little sweetening to balance other flavors, mirin can be a delicious option, a substitute for sugar.

Mirin is made by fermenting rice, koji (rice starter), and glutinous rice for some months, and then filtering it. (If you are shopping for mirin, look for a traditionally made product; the ingredients listed should be only rice, glutinous rice, koji, and water.) The sweetness comes strictly from the natural sweetness of the rice, not from any added sugar. Interestingly, in earlier centuries, when sugar was in short supply in Japan, mirin was commonly used as a sweetener in cooking.

In traditional and modern Japanese cooking, mirin is used in marinades and basting sauces for meat, fish, and vegetables on the grill. It is always cooked in some way to evaporate out the "raw" alcohol taste.

I love mirin as a quick flavoring for grilled fish—just brush it on at the beginning of cooking—or as part of a marinade for grilled chicken. You can also add it to a pork marinade if you like your pork sweet.

I like to use it to dress salads and cooked vegetables that need a hit of sweetness to balance their bitterness or tartness (see recipe at right). Even in an herby potato salad—because there, too, herbs like parsley, tarragon, and mint have a touch of bitterness—I like to add a dash of mirin. I will also use

a splash when stir-frying dandelion greens to balance their bitter edge and add a zippy depth. Any way you use it, the flavor permeates the food, giving it a tart-sweet note.

Quick & Easy • Vegetarian

Bitter Greens Salad with Spiced Mirin Dressing

Hands-on: 5 min. Total: 15 min. It's common to add a touch of sweetness to salad dressings for bitter greens. Instead of sugar or honey, here I use the richness of mirin.

2 dried red Thai chiles
4 cups baby arugula
2 cups torn radicchio
1 cup sliced Belgian endive
2 tablespoons extra-virgin olive oil
2 teaspoons minced fresh garlic
1/2 teaspoon fennel seeds (optional)
6 tablespoons mirin (sweet rice wine)
1/2 teaspoon salt

1. Soak chiles in warm water 10 minutes; drain.
2. Place arugula, radicchio, and endive in a large bowl; toss gently to combine.
3. Heat a large skillet or wok over medium-high heat. Add oil; swirl to coat pan. Add garlic, fennel seeds, if desired, and chiles; stir constantly 30 seconds. Reduce heat to low; cook 1 minute. Stir in mirin and salt; increase heat to high. Bring to a boil; boil 15 seconds. Remove chiles from mixture. Drizzle hot dressing over greens; toss gently to coat. Serve salad immediately. Serves 6 (serving size: about 1 cup)

CALORIES 84; FAT 4.7g (sat 0.7g, mono 3.3g, poly 0.5g); PROTEIN 0.8g; CARB 6.8g; FIBER 0.9g; CHOL 0mg; IRON 0.4mg; SODIUM 204mg; CALC 32mg

PORTION-PERFECT CHICKEN PARM

This dish demonstrates how cooks can make it easier to take a healthy serving.

The easiest way to start the healthy portioning of food is with its preparation. Dishes that are put together piecemeal, such as fish fillets, chicken breasts, and sandwiches, lend themselves to clear portioning. But because many foods have been supersized, the cook has to step in.

For example, the average chicken breast now weighs in at 8 to 10 ounces, while the recommended serving is just 4 ounces. Unless your prep work takes that into account, a portion of Chicken Parm will be twice the size of the recommended serving—and that's before you've coated the chicken in breadcrumbs. If you bulk up the sauce and cheese proportionally, you're looking at a 600-calorie portion on the plate before adding side dishes.

The fix: Split an 8-ounce chicken breast in half lengthwise. The thinner cuts cook quickly and flatten nicely. In our recipe, we use canola mayo instead of egg wash to lock in moisture and keep the crunchy panko-and-Parm mixture on the chicken. Wire racks help avoid the soggy bottoms that can result from oven-frying. Smoky, low-sodium, oven-roasted tomatoes stand in for jarred sauce, and fresh mozzarella adds a cheesy finish. We keep it under 400 calories, with room for whole grains and crunchy greens.

Chicken Parmesan with Oven-Roasted Tomato Sauce

Hands-on: 16 min. Total: 1 hr. 12 min.

1 pound cherry tomatoes, halved
2 tablespoons olive oil,
   divided
1 shallot, sliced
4 garlic cloves, thinly sliced
¼ cup unsalted chicken stock
¼ cup dry white wine
1 teaspoon fresh thyme leaves
³⁄₈ teaspoon kosher salt
¼ teaspoon freshly ground black pepper
½ cup whole-wheat panko
2 (8-ounce) skinless, boneless
   chicken breast halves
3 tablespoons canola mayonnaise (such
   as Hellmann's)
1.5 ounces fresh Parmesan cheese,
   grated and divided (about
   6 tablespoons)
2 tablespoons fat-free milk
1 teaspoon garlic powder
Cooking spray
2 ounces fresh mozzarella cheese, very
   thinly sliced
¼ cup basil leaves

1. Preheat oven to 375°.
2. Combine tomatoes and 1 tablespoon oil; toss. Arrange tomato mixture on a jelly-roll pan. Bake at 375° for 35 minutes or until browned.
3. Increase oven temperature to 425°.
4. Heat 1 tablespoon oil in a medium skillet over medium heat. Add shallot; cook 5 minutes. Add garlic; cook 1 minute. Add tomatoes, stock, wine, thyme, salt, and pepper; cook 4 minutes or until liquid almost evaporates.
5. Place panko in a large skillet; cook over medium heat 3 minutes or until toasted, stirring frequently.
6. Cut each chicken breast in half horizontally to form 4 cutlets. Combine mayonnaise, half of Parmesan cheese, and milk in a bowl. Spread mayonnaise mixture evenly over both sides of cutlets. Combine panko, garlic powder, and remaining half of Parmesan cheese in another dish. Dredge cutlets in panko mixture.
7. Place cutlets on a wire rack coated with cooking spray. Place rack on a baking sheet. Bake at 425° for 15 minutes or until chicken is done.
8. Preheat broiler to high.
9. Top each cutlet with 2 tablespoons tomato mixture; top tomato mixture evenly with mozzarella cheese. Broil 3 minutes or until cheese is bubbly. Sprinkle with basil, and serve with remaining tomato mixture. Serves 4 (serving size: 1 cutlet and 1½ tablespoons sauce)

CALORIES 391; FAT 19.6g (sat 5.4g, mono 8.5g, poly 2.5g); PROTEIN 34.2g; CARB 16.1g; FIBER 2.9g; CHOL 94mg; IRON 1.6mg; SODIUM 594mg; CALC 162mg

CLASSIC	MAKEOVER
625 calories per serving	391 calories per serving
13.5 grams saturated fat	5.4 grams saturated fat
1,418 milligrams sodium	594 milligrams sodium

OUR PARM: LESS BIRD, MORE FLAVOR

CHICKEN CUTLETS
A 4-ounce cutlet saves 130 calories and still leaves plenty of surface area for a crunchy coating.

FRESH TOMATOES
Oven-roasting lends a sweet-smokiness and saves 325mg sodium over jarred marinara.

CANOLA MAYO
This secret ingredient locks in moisture during the baking process to save 10.5g fat over frying.

MEATLESS MONDAYS

Quick & Easy • Vegetarian

Lentil Salad with Soft-Cooked Eggs

Hands-on: 35 min. Total: 35 min. Green lentils keep a firm texture even after cooking, a desirable trait for this hearty salad.

1¼ cups dried petite green lentils
6 large eggs
3 tablespoons extra-virgin olive oil
3 tablespoons red wine vinegar
1 tablespoon Dijon mustard
2 teaspoons minced fresh garlic
¾ teaspoon kosher salt
³⁄₈ teaspoon freshly ground black
   pepper, divided
1¼ cups diced red bell pepper
½ cup chopped green onions
½ cup diced celery
8 cups baby arugula

1. Place lentils in a medium saucepan. Cover with water to 3 inches above lentils; bring to a boil. Reduce heat, and simmer 20 minutes or until lentils are tender. Drain and keep warm.
2. Add water to a large saucepan to a depth of 3 inches; bring to a boil. Add eggs; boil 5 minutes and 30 seconds. Drain. Plunge eggs into ice water; let stand 5 minutes. Drain and peel.

3. Combine oil, vinegar, mustard, garlic, salt, and ¼ teaspoon black pepper in a medium bowl, stirring with a whisk. Set aside 2 tablespoons oil mixture. Add lentils, bell pepper, onions, and celery to remaining oil mixture; toss gently to coat. Place reserved 2 tablespoons oil mixture and arugula in a large bowl; toss to coat.
4. Place about ¾ cup lentil mixture and about 1 cup arugula mixture on each of 6 plates. Cut eggs in half lengthwise; top each serving with 2 egg halves. Sprinkle evenly with ⅛ teaspoon black pepper. Serves 6

CALORIES 282; **FAT** 15.9g (sat 2.5g, mono 6.8g, poly 1.8g); **PROTEIN** 15.9g; **CARB** 27.5g; **FIBER** 7.3g; **CHOL** 186mg; **IRON** 3.9mg; **SODIUM** 393mg; **CALC** 102mg

WITH THEIR RICH, CREAMY INTERIOR, SOFT-COOKED EGGS ARE GREAT OVER SALADS, PASTAS, AND WHOLE GRAINS, AS THE RUNNY, NUTRI-ENT-RICH YOLK DOUBLES AS A SILKY DRESSING.

FIRED UP FOR FRIED RICE

Matisse Reid is a kid who cooks for friends and family.

This week, I made Quick and Easy Pork Fried Rice. I love this dish, so it was good for me to learn how to make it properly. For this recipe, I had big critics—a 6-year-old and a 16-year-old—but everyone loved it. The pork was so tender, and the sauce had a yummy sweet and sour flavor. The hoisin and soy sauces mellowed out the chili garlic, but for those who like the heat, feel free to add a little bit more hot sauce. Don't be afraid to make substitutions if you don't have ingredients on hand. For example, I used dry edamame instead of frozen, and it added a nice crunch to the dish. Overall, this dish was really good—much better than any takeout I have ever had.

THE VERDICT

KAHLO (AGE 6)
She said, "This is yummy. Can you make it again?" This is from a girl who didn't even want to try it!
9 out of 10

JASON (AGE 13)
He thought the dish was so good. He loved the pork and loved the spice.
10 out of 10

ZAVIA (AGE 16)
She loved the whole dish, especially the pork.
10 out of 10

MATISSE (AGE 12)
The pork was so tender. My favorite recipe so far!
10 out of 10

Quick and Easy Pork Fried Rice

Hands-on: 20 min. Total: 20 min.

2 (8.5-ounce) pouches precooked
  basmati rice
¼ cup lower-sodium soy sauce
1 tablespoon chili garlic sauce
1½ teaspoons hoisin sauce
2 tablespoons peanut oil, divided
1 pound boneless pork shoulder (Boston
  butt), trimmed and thinly sliced into
  1-inch pieces
1 large egg, lightly beaten
1½ cups chopped red bell pepper
1 cup frozen shelled edamame
⅔ cup thinly sliced green onions,
  divided

1. Heat rice according to package directions.
2. Combine soy sauce, chili garlic sauce, and hoisin in a bowl. Heat a wok or large skillet over high heat. Add 1 tablespoon oil; swirl to coat. Add pork to pan in a single layer; cook 2 minutes, without stirring. Stir-fry pork 4 minutes or until done. Add pork to soy sauce mixture; toss to coat.
3. Add egg to pan; cook 45 seconds or until set. Remove egg from pan; cut into bite-sized pieces.
4. Add 1 tablespoon oil to pan; swirl to coat. Add bell pepper, edamame, and ½ cup onions; stir-fry 1 minute. Add rice; stir-fry 2 minutes. Add pork and soy sauce mixture; cook 1 minute, stirring constantly. Top rice mixture with egg and remaining onions. Serves 6 (serving size: 1 cup)

CALORIES 302; FAT 10.9g (sat 2.5g, mono 4.1g, poly 2.5g); PROTEIN 16.4g; CARB 36g; FIBER 2.8g; CHOL 57mg; IRON 2.9mg; SODIUM 467mg; CALC 52mg

QUICK TRICKS

9 SWEET HALLOWEEN TREATS

Melt 2 tablespoons butter and 10 ounces marshmallows over medium-low heat. Add a flavor combo and 6 cups rice cereal. Press into a 13 x 9-inch pan coated with cooking spray.

1. Double Chocolate

Stir ¼ cup unsweetened cocoa into melted marshmallows; cook 3 minutes. Add cereal; toss well to combine. Press into prepared pan. Heat 4 ounces chopped bittersweet chocolate in microwave at HIGH 45 seconds or until melted, stirring every 15 seconds; drizzle over cereal mixture. Chill 10 minutes. Serves 20

CALORIES 117; FAT 3.9g (sat 2.1g); SODIUM 66mg

2. Maple Bacon

Stir 3 tablespoons maple syrup and 4 cooked, drained, chopped applewood-smoked bacon slices into melted marshmallows. Add cereal; toss well to combine. Press into pan. Serves 20

CALORIES 105; FAT 2.2g (sat 1.1g); SODIUM 110mg

3. Cherry Chip

Stir 1 cup finely chopped dried cherries and ¼ teaspoon vanilla extract into melted marshmallow mixture. Add cereal, and toss well to combine. Press cereal mixture into prepared pan. Sprinkle evenly with ⅓ cup semisweet chocolate minichips. Serves 20

CALORIES 125; FAT 2.1g (sat 1.3g); SODIUM 67mg

4. Espresso Toffee

Stir 1 tablespoon espresso powder into melted butter before adding marshmallows. Add 1 cup toffee bits and cereal; toss well to combine. Press into prepared pan. Serves 20

CALORIES 153; FAT 5.3g (sat 2.8g); SODIUM 82mg

5. Chocolate Butterscotch

Press cereal mixture into pan. Microwave 1 cup chocolate chips at HIGH for 1 minute, stirring every 20 seconds. Spread over cereal mixture. Microwave ½ cup butterscotch chips and 2 teaspoons fat-free milk at HIGH 30 seconds; stir once. Dollop butterscotch mixture over chocolate; swirl with a knife. Chill. Serves 20

CALORIES 149; FAT 5g (sat 3.3g); SODIUM 71mg

6. Browned Butter Pecan

Before adding marshmallows, cook melted butter 3 minutes or until browned. Add ¼ teaspoon kosher salt and ¼ teaspoon vanilla extract to melted marshmallows; stir well. Add cereal; toss well to combine. Press into prepared pan; sprinkle evenly with ½ cup chopped toasted pecans. Serves 20

CALORIES 105; FAT 3.3g (sat 0.9g); SODIUM 90mg

7. Candy Corn M&M's

Stir ⅔ cup candy corn, ½ cup M&M's, and cereal into melted marshmallows. Press into prepared pan. Serves 20

CALORIES 134; FAT 2.4g (sat 1.4g); SODIUM 70mg

8. S'mores

Char marshmallows under broiler 2 minutes before melting. Stir ½ cup graham cracker crumbs and ½ cup semisweet chocolate minichips into melted marshmallows before adding cereal; toss well to combine. Press cereal mixture into prepared pan. Serves 20

CALORIES 115; FAT 2.8g (sat 1.6g); SODIUM 76mg

9. Lemon White Chocolate

Stir 1 tablespoon grated lemon rind into melted marshmallows before adding cereal. Press cereal mixture into prepared pan. Heat 4 ounces chopped premium white chocolate in microwave at HIGH 1½ minutes or until melted, stirring every 20 seconds; drizzle over cereal mixture. Refrigerate 15 minutes before slicing. Serves 20

CALORIES 116; FAT 3.1g (sat 1.9g); SODIUM 71mg

FEED 4 FOR LESS THAN $10

Make Ahead

Smoked Salmon and Wheat Berry Salad

$2.11/serving, $8.44 total

Hands-on: 13 min. Total: 9 hr. 15 min.
This salad is all about crunch, with toasted walnuts, crisp apple, and celery. Look for wheat berries in the grain or bulk section of your supermarket.

1 cup uncooked wheat berries
1 1/2 cups diced Fuji apple
1/2 cup vertically sliced red onion
1/2 cup chopped walnuts, toasted
4 ounces smoked salmon, cut into 1-inch pieces
2 medium celery stalks, thinly sliced
2 tablespoons extra-virgin olive oil
1 teaspoon grated lemon rind
2 tablespoons fresh lemon juice
1 tablespoon Dijon mustard
1/2 teaspoon kosher salt
1/2 teaspoon ground black pepper

1. Place wheat berries in a medium bowl; cover with water to 2 inches above wheat berries. Cover and let stand 8 hours. Drain. Place wheat berries in a saucepan. Cover with water to 2 inches above wheat berries; bring to a boil. Reduce heat, and cook, uncovered, 1 hour or until tender. Drain.
2. Combine wheat berries, apple, and next 4 ingredients (through celery) in a large bowl. Combine oil and remaining ingredients in a small bowl, stirring with a whisk. Drizzle dressing over wheat berry mixture; toss to coat. Serves 4 (serving size: 1½ cups)

CALORIES 389; FAT 18.7g (sat 2.1g, mono 6.8g, poly 7.9g); PROTEIN 14.9g; CARB 45g; FIBER 8.8g; CHOL 7mg; IRON 2.7mg; SODIUM 570mg; CALC 54mg

DINNER TONIGHT

Fast, healthy weeknight menus

READY IN 40 MINUTES

The SHOPPING LIST

Pasta with Roasted-Tomato Meat Sauce
Cherry tomatoes (1 pint)
Garlic
Fresh basil
Uncooked spaghetti
Crushed red pepper
Canned anchovy fillets in oil
Dry sherry
Balsamic vinegar
80% lean ground pork (9 ounces)
Unsalted butter

Mint and Pea Pesto on Toasted Baguette
Fresh basil
Fresh mint
Lemon (1)
Garlic
Extra-virgin olive oil
Frozen green peas
Baguette

The GAME PLAN

While tomatoes roast:
■ Boil water for pasta.
While pasta cooks:
■ Make sauce.
While broiler preheats:
■ Make pesto.

Kid Friendly • Quick & Easy

Pasta with Roasted-Tomato Meat Sauce

With Mint and Pea Pesto on Toasted Baguette

Flavor Hit: Don't skip the anchovies—they add a savory, salty layer to the sauce.
Kid Tweak: Use 1/4 cup unsalted beef stock in place of the dry sherry.
Simple Sub: Substitute ground sirloin for the pork.

1 pint cherry tomatoes
8 ounces uncooked spaghetti
2 teaspoons unsalted butter
9 ounces 80% lean ground pork
1 tablespoon minced fresh garlic
1/2 teaspoon kosher salt
1/2 teaspoon crushed red pepper
3 canned anchovy fillets in oil, drained and chopped
1/4 cup dry sherry
1 1/2 tablespoons balsamic vinegar
1/4 cup basil leaves

1. Preheat oven to 400°.
2. Place cherry tomatoes on a jelly-roll pan. Bake at 400° for 12 minutes or until tomatoes are lightly browned.
3. Cook pasta according to package directions, omitting salt and fat.
4. Melt the butter in a large skillet over medium-high heat. Add pork, garlic, salt, pepper, and anchovies to pan; cook 4 minutes or until pork is browned, stirring to crumble. Add sherry to pan; cook 30 seconds, scraping pan to loosen browned bits. Add tomatoes and vinegar; cook 2 minutes or until tomatoes release their liquid and sauce is slightly thickened. Combine pasta and sauce in a large bowl; toss to coat. Sprinkle with basil. Serves 4 (serving size: 1½ cups)

CALORIES 428; FAT 15.8g (sat 6g, mono 6.4g, poly 1.7g); PROTEIN 20g; CARB 47.5g; FIBER 2.9g; CHOL 53mg; IRON 3mg; SODIUM 402mg; CALC 37mg

For the Mint and Pea Pesto on Toasted Baguette:

Preheat broiler to high. Slice 4 ounces baguette into 8 (½-inch-thick) slices. Place bread in a single layer on a baking sheet. Broil 2 minutes or until browned. Place ½ cup basil leaves, ½ cup mint leaves, ¼ cup thawed frozen green peas, 2 tablespoons extra-virgin olive oil, 1 tablespoon fresh lemon juice, ⅛ teaspoon salt, and 2 garlic cloves in a mini food processor; pulse until smooth. Spread about 1 tablespoon pesto on each bread slice. Serves 4 (serving size: 2 slices)

CALORIES 147; FAT 6.9g (sat 1g); SODIUM 268mg

Quick & Easy

Roasted Chicken with Mustard Greens

With Cumin and Chile Rice

Budget Buy: Ask the butcher to break down a 3½-pound chicken.
Simple Sub: Use spinach or kale instead of mustard greens.
Kid Tweak: Omit the crushed red pepper in the rice.

2 skin-on, bone-in chicken breast halves (about 1 pound)
2 bone-in chicken leg-thigh quarters, skinned (about 1¼ pounds)
1 teaspoon paprika
¾ teaspoon freshly ground black pepper, divided
½ teaspoon kosher salt, divided
1 teaspoon canola oil
1 tablespoon butter
1 cup sliced onion
3 garlic cloves, coarsely chopped
½ cup fat-free, lower-sodium chicken broth
1 teaspoon brown sugar
8 cups chopped mustard greens, stems removed (about 7 ounces)

1. Preheat oven to 450°.
2. Sprinkle chicken evenly with paprika, ½ teaspoon pepper, and ¼ teaspoon salt. Heat a 10-inch cast-iron skillet over high heat. Add oil to pan; swirl to coat. Add chicken, flesh sides down; cook 5 minutes. Turn chicken over; cook 2 minutes. Place pan in oven. Bake at 450° for 20 minutes or until done. Let stand 5 minutes.
3. Melt butter in a large nonstick skillet over medium-high heat. Add onion and garlic to pan; sauté 3 minutes or until lightly browned. Add broth and sugar to pan; cook 3 minutes or until broth almost evaporates. Add greens to pan; sauté 3 minutes or until tender. Sprinkle with ¼ teaspoon pepper and ¼ teaspoon salt. Serves 4 (serving size: 1 breast half or 1 leg-thigh quarter and about ⅔ cup greens)

CALORIES 305; FAT 12.4g (sat 4g, mono 4.6g, poly 2.1g); PROTEIN 37.8g; CARB 10.8g; FIBER 4.5g; CHOL 154mg; IRON 3mg; SODIUM 522mg; CALC 143mg

For the Cumin and Chile Rice:

Place 1 teaspoon cumin seeds, 1 teaspoon canola oil, ½ teaspoon crushed red pepper, and ¼ teaspoon kosher salt in a small saucepan over medium heat; cook 2 minutes, stirring occasionally. Add ¾ cup uncooked long-grain white rice to pan; cook 2 minutes, stirring occasionally. Add 1¼ cups fat-free, lower-sodium chicken broth to pan; bring to a boil. Reduce heat, cover, and simmer 15 minutes. Remove from heat; let stand 10 minutes or until liquid is absorbed. Serves 4 (serving size: ½ cup)

CALORIES 144; FAT 1.6g (sat 0.2g); SODIUM 301mg

READY IN
40
MINUTES

The
SHOPPING LIST

Roasted Chicken with Mustard Greens
Onion (1)
Garlic
Mustard greens (about 7 ounces)
Paprika
Butter
Fat-free, lower-sodium chicken broth
Brown sugar
Canola oil
Skin-on, bone-in chicken breast halves (2)
Bone-in chicken leg-thigh quarters, skinned (2)

Cumin and Chile Rice
Cumin seeds
Crushed red pepper
Long-grain white rice
Fat-free, lower-sodium chicken broth
Canola oil

The
GAME PLAN

While oven preheats:
■ Season and sear chicken.
While chicken roasts:
■ Prepare greens.
■ Cook rice.

READY IN 40 MINUTES

The SHOPPING LIST

Sweet Potato and Chickpea Cakes with Avocado Salsa

Yellow onion (1)
Garlic
Jalapeño pepper (1)
Sweet potato (8 ounces)
Lime (1)
Avocado (2 small)
Tomato (1 large)
Red onion (1)
Olive oil
Panko (Japanese breadcrumbs)
1 (15-ounce) can unsalted chickpeas (garbanzo beans)
Ground red pepper
Egg (1)

Sautéed Lemony Broccolini

Broccolini (1 pound)
Lemon (1)
Butter
Dry white wine

The GAME PLAN

While onion mixture cooks:
■ Grate potato.
While patties bake:
■ Make salsa.
■ Cook Broccolini.

Kid Friendly • Quick & Easy

Sweet Potato and Chickpea Cakes with Avocado Salsa

With Sautéed Lemony Broccolini

Budget Buy: Use regular broccoli instead of the Broccolini.
Prep Pointer: Use a long, flat spatula to carefully flip the patties.
Flavor Hit: Onion and spicy jalapeño contrast the sweet potato cakes.

2¹/₂ tablespoons olive oil, divided
¹/₂ cup chopped yellow onion
6 garlic cloves, crushed
1 jalapeño pepper, seeded and minced
1³/₄ cups grated sweet potato (about 8 ounces)
⁵/₈ teaspoon kosher salt, divided
¹/₂ teaspoon freshly ground black pepper
¹/₂ cup panko (Japanese breadcrumbs)
2¹/₂ tablespoons fresh lime juice, divided
1 (15-ounce) can unsalted chickpeas (garbanzo beans), rinsed and drained
1 large egg
1 cup chopped peeled avocado
1 cup chopped tomato
¹/₂ cup vertically sliced red onion
¹/₈ teaspoon ground red pepper

1. Preheat oven to 400°.
2. Heat a large ovenproof skillet over medium-high heat. Add 1 tablespoon oil to pan; swirl to coat. Add yellow onion, garlic, and jalapeño to pan; sauté 3 minutes. Add sweet potato, ⅜ teaspoon salt, and black pepper to pan; sauté 2 minutes. Place potato mixture, panko, 1½ tablespoons juice, chickpeas, and egg in a food processor; pulse until chickpeas are coarsely ground. Divide potato mixture into 4 equal portions, shaping each into a 4-inch patty. Return skillet to medium-high heat. Add 1½ tablespoons oil to pan; swirl to coat. Add patties to pan; cook 3 minutes or until browned. Carefully turn patties over. Place pan in oven; bake at 400° for 6 minutes or until browned.
3. Combine avocado, tomato, red onion, 1 tablespoon juice, ¼ teaspoon salt, and red pepper in a bowl; toss. Serve salsa with cakes. Serves 4 (serving size: 1 cake and about ½ cup salsa)

CALORIES 330; FAT 16.1g (sat 2.4g, mono 10.3g, poly 1.9g); PROTEIN 9g; CARB 39.6g; FIBER 8.5g; CHOL 47mg; IRON 1.9mg; SODIUM 393mg; CALC 90mg

For the Sautéed Lemony Broccolini:
Melt 2 teaspoons butter in a large skillet over medium-high heat. Add 1 pound trimmed Broccolini to pan; cook 4 minutes, stirring occasionally. Add ¼ cup dry white wine to pan. Cover, reduce heat to medium-low, and cook 6 minutes or until Broccolini is tender. Add 2 teaspoons grated lemon rind, 1 tablespoon fresh lemon juice, ¼ teaspoon salt, and ¼ teaspoon freshly ground black pepper to Broccolini; toss. Serves 4 (serving size: about 5 stalks)

CALORIES 78; FAT 1.9g (sat 1.2g); SODIUM 199mg

Kid Friendly • Quick & Easy

Herb-Rubbed New York Strip with Sautéed Peas and Carrots

With Roasted Potato Wedges

Budget Buy: Use 4 (4-ounce) boneless pork chops instead of the strip steaks.
Technique Tip: Cut the potato wedges roughly the same size to ensure even roasting.
Flavor Hit: Bacon lends the peas and carrots a hint of smoky flavor.

2 (8-ounce) New York strip steaks, trimmed
2 teaspoons chopped fresh thyme
2 teaspoons chopped fresh oregano

³/₈ teaspoon salt, divided
¹/₂ teaspoon black pepper, divided
2 teaspoons unsalted butter
1 teaspoon canola oil
³/₄ cup water
6 baby carrots, halved lengthwise
3 center-cut bacon slices
1¹/₂ cups frozen green peas
Oregano leaves (optional)

1. Sprinkle steaks with thyme, chopped oregano, ¼ teaspoon salt, and ¼ teaspoon pepper; press mixture into steaks. Melt butter in a large skillet over medium-high heat. Add oil to pan; swirl. Add steaks to pan; cook 4 minutes on each side or until desired degree of doneness. Let stand 5 minutes; cut across the grain into thin slices.
2. Combine ¾ cup water and carrots in a large skillet over medium-high heat. Cover and bring to a boil. Cook 6 minutes or until carrots are tender. Remove carrots from pan. Wipe pan with a paper towel. Return pan to medium-high heat. Add bacon to pan; cook 4 minutes or until crisp. Remove bacon from pan with a slotted spoon; crumble. Add carrots to drippings in pan; sauté 1½ minutes. Add peas; sauté 2 minutes or until heated. Sprinkle with ⅛ teaspoon salt, ¼ teaspoon pepper, and crumbled bacon. Serve vegetables with steak; garnish with oregano leaves, if desired. Serves 4 (serving size: 4 ounces steak and ¾ cup vegetable mixture)

CALORIES 306; **FAT** 17g (sat 7g, mono 6.7g, poly 0.9g); **PROTEIN** 28.7g; **CARB** 8.5g; **FIBER** 2.8g; **CHOL** 78mg; **IRON** 3mg; **SODIUM** 456mg; **CALC** 28mg

For the Roasted Potato Wedges:
Place a baking sheet in oven. Preheat oven to 450°. Cut each of 3 (8-ounce) baking potatoes lengthwise into 8 wedges. Combine potatoes, 1 tablespoon minced fresh rosemary, 1 tablespoon canola oil, ¾ teaspoon freshly ground black pepper, and ¼ teaspoon salt in a large bowl; toss to coat. Place potatoes on preheated pan. Bake at 450° for 30 minutes, stirring

after 15 minutes. Serves 4 (serving size: 6 wedges)

CALORIES 168; **FAT** 3.7g (sat 0.3g); **SODIUM** 156mg

READY IN
40
MINUTES

The
SHOPPING LIST

Herb-Rubbed New York Strip with Sautéed Peas and Carrots
Fresh thyme
Fresh oregano
Baby carrots (6)
2 (8-ounce) New York strip steaks, trimmed
Center-cut bacon (3 slices)
Frozen green peas
Unsalted butter
Canola oil

Roasted Potato Wedges
3 (8-ounce) baking potatoes
Rosemary
Canola oil

The
GAME PLAN

While baking sheet and oven preheat:
■ Cut potatoes.
■ Season steaks.
While potatoes roast:
■ Sear steaks.
■ Cook peas and carrots.

Kid Friendly • Quick & Easy
Crispy Fish Nuggets with Tartar Sauce

With Bell Pepper and Corn Sauté and Quick Parsley-Spinach Salad

Prep Pointer: Toast the panko before breading.
Simple Sub: For heat, sub 1 tablespoon minced jalapeño for the bell pepper.
Time-Saver: Prewashed bagged baby spinach cuts down on prep time.

1 cup panko (Japanese breadcrumbs)
1 tablespoon chopped fresh thyme
¹/₂ teaspoon kosher salt
¹/₂ teaspoon freshly ground black pepper
¹/₂ cup all-purpose flour
2 tablespoons water
1 large egg, lightly beaten
1¹/₂ pounds cod fillets, cut into 1-inch pieces
Cooking spray
¹/₄ cup canola mayonnaise
1 tablespoon chopped dill pickle
2 teaspoons chopped fresh flat-leaf parsley
¹/₄ teaspoon fresh lemon juice
¹/₄ teaspoon Dijon mustard

1. Preheat oven to 400°.
2. Heat a large skillet over medium-high heat. Add panko and thyme to pan; cook 2 minutes or until golden brown, shaking pan frequently. Combine panko mixture, salt, and pepper in a shallow dish. Place flour in another shallow dish. Combine 2 tablespoons water and egg in another shallow dish. Dredge fish in flour. Dip in egg mixture; dredge in panko mixture. Arrange in a single layer on a baking sheet coated with cooking spray. Bake at 400° for 12 minutes or until done.
3. Combine mayonnaise and remaining ingredients in a bowl; serve with nuggets. Serves 4 (serving size: 6 ounces nuggets and 1 tablespoon sauce)

CALORIES 287; **FAT** 6.3g (sat 0.6g, mono 2.9g, poly 2g); **PROTEIN** 31.3g; **CARB** 22.5g; **FIBER** 1.1g; **CHOL** 126mg; **IRON** 1.4mg; **SODIUM** 556mg; **CALC** 28mg

READY IN 40 MINUTES

The SHOPPING LIST

Crispy Fish Nuggets with Tartar Sauce
Fresh thyme
Fresh flat-leaf parsley
Lemon (1)
Panko (Japanese breadcrumbs)
All-purpose flour
Canola mayonnaise
Dill pickle
Dijon mustard
Cod fillets (1½ pounds)
Egg (1)

Bell Pepper and Corn Sauté
Onion (1)
Red bell pepper (1)
Garlic
Frozen corn
Butter

Quick Parsley-Spinach Salad
Lemon (1)
Baby spinach leaves (5 cups)
Fresh flat-leaf parsley
Olive oil
Dijon mustard
Pistachios

The GAME PLAN

While oven preheats:
■ Toast panko.
■ Prepare fish.
While fish bakes:
■ Make tartar sauce.
■ Cut vegetables for sauté.
While vegetables sauté:
■ Prepare salad.

For the Bell Pepper and Corn Sauté:
Melt 1½ teaspoons butter in a skillet over medium-high heat. Add ½ cup chopped onion, ⅓ cup diced red bell pepper, and 2 sliced garlic cloves; sauté 3 minutes. Add 2 cups thawed frozen corn, ¼ teaspoon salt, and ¼ teaspoon black pepper; sauté 3 minutes. Serves 4 (serving size: ½ cup)

CALORIES 87; **FAT** 2g (sat 1g); **SODIUM** 164mg

For the Quick Parsley-Spinach Salad:
Combine 1 tablespoon fresh lemon juice, 1 tablespoon olive oil, ¼ teaspoon salt, ¼ teaspoon freshly ground black pepper, and ¼ teaspoon Dijon mustard in a medium bowl. Add 5 cups baby spinach leaves and 1 cup fresh flat-leaf parsley leaves; toss to coat. Top with 3 tablespoons chopped pistachios. Serves 4 (serving size: 1 cup)

CALORIES 82; **FAT** 6.1g (sat 0.8g); **SODIUM** 212mg

SUPERFAST 20-MINUTE COOKING

This month, a special Italian edition in which simple ingredients bring big flavor: briny turkey piccata, garlicky grilled tuna, nutty pistachio cannoli, and more

Kid Friendly • Quick & Easy

Turkey Piccata

Chicken cutlets are a good substitute for turkey cutlets. Make your own by cutting 4 chicken breasts in half horizontally.

8 (3-ounce) turkey cutlets
¼ teaspoon salt
¼ teaspoon freshly ground black pepper
1 tablespoon olive oil, divided
2 tablespoons unsalted butter, divided
¼ cup chopped shallots
1 tablespoon sliced garlic
¾ cup dry white wine
½ cup unsalted chicken stock
1 teaspoon all-purpose flour
2 tablespoons fresh lemon juice
1½ tablespoons capers, drained
2 tablespoons chopped fresh flat-leaf parsley

1. Sprinkle turkey evenly with salt and pepper. Heat a large skillet over medium-high heat. Add 1½ teaspoons oil to pan; swirl to coat. Add 4 cutlets to pan, and cook 2 minutes on each side or until done. Remove cutlets from pan; keep warm. Repeat procedure with remaining oil and cutlets.
2. Add 1 tablespoon butter to pan. Add shallots and garlic; sauté 1 minute. Increase heat to high. Add wine; bring to a boil, and cook 2 minutes, scraping pan to loosen browned bits. Combine chicken stock and flour, stirring with a whisk. Add stock mixture to pan, and bring to a boil. Cook 5 minutes or until liquid is reduced by half. Remove from heat; stir in 1 tablespoon butter, juice, and capers. Pour sauce over cutlets; sprinkle with parsley. Serves 4 (serving size: 2 cutlets, 2 tablespoons sauce, and ½ tablespoon parsley)

CALORIES 298; **FAT** 10g (sat 4.1g, mono 4g, poly 0.6g); **PROTEIN** 43.3g; **CARB** 4.5g; **FIBER** 0.6g; **CHOL** 83mg; **IRON** 2.7mg; **SODIUM** 414mg; **CALC** 19mg

Quick & Easy

Grilled Tuna and Broccolini

With Garlic Drizzle

Look for Atlantic bigeye or yellowfin tuna caught using the troll or pole-and-line method.

¼ cup extra-virgin olive oil
2 tablespoons minced fresh garlic
5 canned anchovy fillets in oil, drained and chopped
½ teaspoon freshly ground black pepper, divided

4 (6-ounce) tuna steaks (about 1 inch thick)
Cooking spray
½ teaspoon kosher salt
1 pound Broccolini, trimmed
4 lemon wedges

1. Combine oil, garlic, anchovy fillets, and ¼ teaspoon pepper in a small saucepan over low heat. Cook 5 minutes or until garlic begins to sizzle; remove from heat. Set aside.
2. Heat a grill pan over high heat. Lightly coat tuna with cooking spray. Sprinkle with salt and ¼ teaspoon pepper. Add to pan; cook 2 minutes on each side or until desired degree of doneness. Remove from pan.
3. Combine 1 teaspoon oil mixture and Broccolini; toss. Add to pan; cook 6 minutes or until tender, turning occasionally. Place 1 tuna steak and 4 ounces Broccolini on each of 4 plates. Drizzle each serving with about 1½ tablespoons oil mixture. Serve with lemon wedges. Serves 4

CALORIES 363; **FAT** 15.7g (sat 2.5g, mono 10.4g, poly 2.1g); **PROTEIN** 43.2g; **CARB** 10.9g; **FIBER** 2g; **CHOL** 84mg; **IRON** 3.5mg; **SODIUM** 521mg; **CALC** 155mg

Quick & Easy • Vegetarian

Pasta with Eggplant, Pine Nuts, and Romano

1 (8.8-ounce) package uncooked pappardelle (wide ribbon pasta)
3 tablespoons olive oil, divided
5 large garlic cloves, crushed
1 pound eggplant, cut into 1-inch pieces
1 tablespoon chopped fresh oregano
1 (10-ounce) container grape tomatoes
½ teaspoon salt
¼ teaspoon freshly ground black pepper
¼ teaspoon crushed red pepper
2 ounces fresh pecorino Romano cheese, shaved (about ½ cup)
⅓ cup pine nuts, toasted
¼ cup chopped fresh flat-leaf parsley

1. Preheat broiler to high.
2. Cook pasta according to directions; omit salt and fat. Drain in a colander over a bowl, reserving ½ cup liquid.
3. Combine 1 tablespoon oil, garlic, eggplant, oregano, and tomatoes on a jelly-roll pan; toss. Broil 8 minutes or until tomatoes begin to soften.
4. Combine reserved cooking liquid, 2 tablespoons oil, salt, and peppers in a bowl, stirring with a whisk. Add pasta and eggplant mixture; toss. Sprinkle with cheese, pine nuts, and parsley. Serves 6 (serving size: 1⅓ cups)

CALORIES 335; **FAT** 15.8g (sat 3.9g, mono 6.4g, poly 3.4g); **PROTEIN** 10.7g; **CARB** 40.2g; **FIBER** 5.4g; **CHOL** 10mg; **IRON** 2.4mg; **SODIUM** 391mg; **CALC** 118mg

Kid Friendly • Quick & Easy

Chocolate-Dipped Cannoli with Pistachios

Budget Tip: You can substitute chopped peanuts or almonds for the pistachios.

⅔ cup part-skim ricotta cheese
2 tablespoons ⅓-less-fat cream cheese
1 teaspoon grated orange rind
¼ teaspoon vanilla extract
¼ cup powdered sugar
4 (5-inch-long) cannoli shells
1½ tablespoons finely chopped roasted pistachios
1 teaspoon finely chopped bittersweet chocolate

1. Place ricotta, cream cheese, orange rind, and vanilla extract in a mini food processor; process until smooth. Add powdered sugar, and pulse until well combined. Place ricotta mixture in a small heavy-duty zip-top plastic bag; seal bag. Snip a ½-inch hole in one bottom corner of the bag. Fill cannoli shells evenly with ricotta mixture. Combine pistachios and chocolate in a small bowl. Evenly dip ends of cannoli in pistachio mixture. Serves 4 (serving size: 1 cannolo)

CALORIES 240; **FAT** 13g (sat 5.2g, mono 4.4g, poly 2.4g); **PROTEIN** 7.8g; **CARB** 23g; **FIBER** 0.4g; **CHOL** 28mg; **IRON** 0.3mg; **SODIUM** 109mg; **CALC** 122mg

Kid Friendly • Quick & Easy

Steak Pizzaiola on Ciabatta

Kids—and adults—will enjoy the classic pizza flavors found in this hearty dish.

1 pound boneless sirloin steak, trimmed and cut into ¼-inch slices
4 teaspoons olive oil, divided
½ teaspoon salt, divided
½ teaspoon freshly ground black pepper, divided
2 teaspoons minced fresh garlic
1 tablespoon fresh oregano
1 (28-ounce) can unsalted whole tomatoes, undrained
4 (1-inch-thick) slices ciabatta bread (about 5 ounces)
2 ounces shredded part-skim mozzarella cheese (about ½ cup)
½ cup torn basil leaves

1. Preheat broiler to high.
2. Heat a large skillet over high heat. Combine steak and 1 teaspoon oil in a large bowl; toss to coat. Sprinkle steak with ¼ teaspoon salt and ¼ teaspoon pepper. Add steak to pan; cook 2 minutes or until browned, stirring occasionally. Remove steak from pan.
3. Reduce heat to medium-high. Add 1 tablespoon oil to pan, and swirl to coat. Add garlic, and sauté 30 seconds. Add oregano, ¼ teaspoon salt, ¼ teaspoon pepper, and tomatoes. Reduce heat, and simmer 6 minutes, mashing tomato mixture with a potato masher. Return steak to pan, and toss to coat.
4. Place bread on a baking sheet; broil 1 minute or until lightly toasted. Spoon tomato mixture evenly over bread slices; sprinkle evenly with

continued

cheese. Broil 2 minutes or until cheese begins to brown. Sprinkle with basil. Serves 4 (serving size: 1 topped bread slice)

CALORIES 379; **FAT** 15.8g (sat 4.8g, mono 8.1g, poly 1.1g); **PROTEIN** 32.9g; **CARB** 28.7g; **FIBER** 2.8g; **CHOL** 84mg; **IRON** 5.7mg; **SODIUM** 663mg; **CALC** 189mg

Quick & Easy • Vegetarian

Chickpea, Red Pepper, and Arugula Salad

If you want petite leaves, choose baby arugula.

1 tablespoon extra-virgin olive oil
1 tablespoon balsamic vinegar
½ teaspoon Dijon mustard
¼ teaspoon freshly ground black pepper
⅛ teaspoon salt
4 cups arugula
1 cup unsalted canned chickpeas, rinsed and drained
¼ cup bottled roasted red bell peppers, drained and cut into strips
7 pitted Italian olives (such as cerignola), halved

1. Combine olive oil, balsamic vinegar, mustard, pepper, and salt in a medium bowl, stirring with a whisk. Add arugula, chickpeas, and bell peppers; toss to coat. Sprinkle with olives. Serves 4 (serving size: 1 cup)

CALORIES 94; **FAT** 4.6g (sat 0.5g, mono 2.5g, poly 0.5g); **PROTEIN** 3.1g; **CARB** 10.4g; **FIBER** 2.2g; **CHOL** 0mg; **IRON** 1mg; **SODIUM** 215mg; **CALC** 67mg

Variation 1
Melon & Prosciutto
Place 1 tablespoon extra-virgin olive oil, 1 tablespoon balsamic vinegar, and ½ teaspoon Dijon mustard in a medium bowl, stirring with a whisk until well combined. Add 4 cups arugula to oil mixture; toss to coat greens. Top arugula mixture with 1 cup thinly sliced peeled cantaloupe and

2 ounces thinly sliced prosciutto. Serves 4 (serving size: about 1 cup)

CALORIES 78; **FAT** 4.9g (sat 0.9g); **SODIUM** 241mg

Variation 2
Bread Salad
Preheat broiler. Combine 2 tablespoons extra-virgin olive oil, 1 tablespoon balsamic vinegar, ½ teaspoon Dijon, and ¼ teaspoon pepper in a bowl; stir with a whisk. Place 2 cups (½-inch) cubed Italian bread on a jelly-roll pan. Broil 2 minutes or until toasted; stir after 1 minute. Add bread to bowl; toss. Add 2 cups arugula and 1½ cups quartered cherry tomatoes; toss. Serves 4 (serving size: 1 cup)

CALORIES 159; **FAT** 8g (sat 1.2g); **SODIUM** 261mg

Variation 3
Caesar Vinaigrette
Combine 2 tablespoons extra-virgin olive oil, ½ teaspoon grated lemon rind, 2 teaspoons fresh lemon juice, ⅛ teaspoon freshly ground black pepper, 2 chopped canned anchovy fillets, and 1 minced garlic clove in a medium bowl, stirring with a whisk. Add 4 cups arugula; toss to coat. Sprinkle with 2 tablespoons shaved fresh Parmesan cheese. Serves 4 (serving size: about 1 cup)

CALORIES 82; **FAT** 7.8g (sat 1.4g); **SODIUM** 117mg

Quick & Easy • Make Ahead

Green Vegetable Soup

With Lemon-Basil Pesto

Covering the pot when bringing the liquid to a simmer gets this soup ready even faster.

¾ cup uncooked orzo
4 teaspoons olive oil, divided
1½ cups thinly sliced leeks (about 2)
1 cup thinly sliced celery

1 tablespoon minced fresh garlic, divided
¼ teaspoon salt
3¼ cups unsalted chicken stock
1 cup water
3 thyme sprigs
1 cup frozen green peas
1 cup green beans, cut into 1-inch pieces (about ¼ pound)
1 (15-ounce) can cannellini beans, rinsed and drained
2 cups baby spinach leaves, divided
¼ cup basil leaves
2 tablespoons grated fresh Parmesan cheese
2 teaspoons grated lemon rind
1 tablespoon fresh lemon juice

1. Cook pasta according to package directions, omitting salt and fat.
2. While pasta cooks, heat a large Dutch oven over medium heat. Add 2 teaspoons oil; swirl to coat. Add leeks, celery, 2 teaspoons garlic, and salt; sauté 5 minutes. Add stock, 1 cup water, and thyme. Cover; bring to a boil. Add peas and beans, and simmer, uncovered, 4 minutes. Discard thyme. Stir in pasta and 1 cup spinach.
3. Place 1 cup spinach, basil, cheese, rind, juice, 1 teaspoon garlic, and 2 teaspoons oil in a food processor; process until smooth. Divide soup among 4 bowls; top with pesto. Serves 4

CALORIES 189; **FAT** 5.6g (sat 1.1g, mono 3.5g, poly 0.7g); **PROTEIN** 12g; **CARB** 24.4g; **FIBER** 6.6g; **CHOL** 2mg; **IRON** 3.2mg; **SODIUM** 522mg; **CALC** 136mg

OOPS!

YOUR SCRAMBLED EGGS TURN RUBBERY

A few tricks and techniques separate breakfast heaven from a sad sort of purgatory.

(Creamy!)

(Boing! Boing!)

The definition of perfect scrambled eggs differs from person to person and generally has to do with the size of the curd and the degree of wet creaminess, but there is one point on which we can all agree: Nobody wants dry, tough eggs. Cooked correctly, the proteins in an egg form a net, holding in moisture that later steams into light, fluffy curds. But too much heat and time cause the proteins to coil so tightly that moisture is wrung out.

The solution: Cook low and slow, moving the eggs constantly in the pan; this maintains the creamy texture. Heat butter in a pan over medium-low heat just until foaming; then add beaten eggs. (You don't need to add water to your eggs—it needlessly prolongs the process.) Use a wooden spoon to drag uncooked eggs to the center of the pan. Dragging the spoon, rather than stirring vigorously, creates medium-sized curds—perfect for light, fluffy eggs. If you like smaller curds, gently break the mixture more. Make sure to remove the pan from the heat when the eggs are still glossy, or slightly under-cooked; residual heat will finish cooking them.

THE EASIEST HOLIDAY RECIPES EVER

A collection of 20 faster, shorter, and make-ahead recipes for the ultimate stress-free and delicious Thanksgiving

The Thanksgiving meal, for a number of families, is the most important of the year. Many cooks relish the whole ritual of planning and preparing: It's an act of love, redolent with cultural and family meaning. Which isn't to say that a few shortcuts don't come in handy. The day can feel overstuffed, work-wise, for the person who toils in the kitchen. Most of us can use some help. In that spirit, we laid out a challenge to our Test Kitchen: Create the easiest Turkey Day recipes ever, ones that hold close to the flavors and traditions we cherish but take a few items off the cook's list of duties. We shortened ingredient lists, leaned on convenience products (where their supporting role would not stick out), developed make-ahead dishes, and called on every trick in our playbook to produce the 20 recipes on these pages.

Kid Friendly • Quick & Easy
Make Ahead • Vegetarian

Cranberry-Orange Relish

(pictured on page 238)

Hands-on: 10 min. Total: 10 min. *In place of traditional cranberry sauce, try a faster relish. The flavor is bright, crisp. Make up to 3 days ahead.*

1 tablespoon grated orange rind
1 cup orange sections
1/3 cup sugar
2 teaspoons honey
1/2 teaspoon ground cinnamon
1/8 teaspoon salt
1 (12-ounce) bag fresh cranberries, rinsed and drained
Cinnamon stick (optional)

1. Place all ingredients except cinnamon stick in a food processor; pulse to combine. Garnish with cinnamon stick, if desired. Serves 8 (serving size: 1/4 cup)

CALORIES 68; FAT 0.1g (sat 0g, mono 0g, poly 0.1g); PROTEIN 0.4g; CARB 17.8g; FIBER 2.5g; CHOL 0mg; IRON 0.2mg; SODIUM 38mg; CALC 14mg

---

SIDEBOARD SETUP

Remove clutter from the dining table by setting out all the dishes on a sideboard and letting people serve themselves. It's OK to put everything out together. Seeing all the offerings —even dessert — helps folks pace themselves: A small bite of Brie leaves room for cake later.

Kid Friendly

Oil-Basted Parmesan Turkey with Walnut Gravy

(pictured on page 238)

Hands-on: 35 min. Total: 3 hr. 35 min. *Nine ingredients (not counting salt, pepper, and cooking spray) come together for a grand holiday centerpiece with deep nutty essence from toasted walnut oil and chopped nuts. Let your turkey come to room temperature before it goes in the oven; it will cook more evenly and more quickly.*

1 (12- to 13-pound) fresh or frozen turkey, thawed and at room temperature
1/4 cup toasted walnut oil, divided
3 tablespoons chopped fresh thyme leaves
1 teaspoon kosher salt, divided
1 teaspoon freshly ground black pepper, divided
2 ounces Parmigiano-Reggiano cheese, finely shredded (about 1/2 cup)
4 pears, halved and divided
2 onions, halved and divided
Cooking spray
4 1/2 cups unsalted chicken stock, divided
5 tablespoons all-purpose flour
1/2 cup chopped walnuts, toasted

1. Preheat oven to 500°.
2. Remove giblets and neck from turkey; discard. Starting at neck cavity, loosen skin from breast and drumsticks by inserting fingers, gently pushing between skin and meat. Combine 1 tablespoon oil, thyme, 1/2 teaspoon salt, 1/2 teaspoon pepper, and cheese in a small bowl. Rub cheese mixture under loosened skin over flesh. Place 1 pear and 1 onion in cavity. Lift wing tips up and over back; tuck under turkey. Tie legs together with kitchen twine. Place turkey on the rack of a roasting pan coated with cooking spray. Arrange 3 pears and onion, cut sides down, in

a roasting pan coated with cooking spray; place rack with turkey in pan. Bake at 500° for 30 minutes. Pour 1½ cups stock over turkey; reduce heat to 350°. Bake at 350° for 1 hour. Pour 1½ cups stock over turkey; bake for 10 minutes. Brush 1½ tablespoons walnut oil over turkey; bake 20 minutes. Brush 1½ tablespoons walnut oil over turkey; bake 10 minutes or until a thermometer inserted in the thickest part of the thigh registers 160°. Remove from oven. Place turkey, breast side down, on a rimmed baking sheet coated with cooking spray. Let stand 30 minutes.

3. Strain pan drippings through a sieve into a bowl; discard solids. Place a zip-top plastic bag inside a 2-cup glass measure. Pour pan drippings into bag. Let stand 10 minutes (fat will rise to the top).

4. Seal bag; carefully snip off 1 bottom corner of bag. Drain drippings into a saucepan, stopping before fat layer reaches opening; discard fat. Combine 1½ cups stock and flour in a bowl, stirring with a whisk. Add stock mixture and walnuts to pan; bring to a boil. Reduce heat, and simmer 10 minutes or until mixture thickens. Remove from heat; stir in ½ teaspoon salt and ½ teaspoon pepper. Pour mixture into a blender. Remove center piece of blender lid (to allow steam to escape); secure lid on blender. Place a clean towel over opening in blender lid (to avoid splatters). Process until smooth. Serve gravy with turkey. Serves 18 (serving size: about 4 ounces meat and about 3 tablespoons gravy)

CALORIES 309; **FAT** 12.1g (sat 2.6g, mono 2.5g, poly 5.7g); **PROTEIN** 39.2g; **CARB** 9.9g; **FIBER** 1.8g; **CHOL** 95mg; **IRON** 2.7mg; **SODIUM** 260mg; **CALC** 72mg

HOW TO PLAN

There's only so much oven space. So plan your menu accordingly, knowing that the turkey will hog the space for a few hours. While it rests, another dish or two can bake—but don't plan for more than that. The muffins and soufflé bake together at the same temperature, and everything else is made ahead or cooked on the stovetop.

Quick & Easy • Make Ahead

White Bean and Pumpkin Bisque with Sage Pesto

Hands-on: 25 min. Total: 25 min. Start with canned pumpkin (for rich, smooth flavor) and canned white beans (for body), and you end up with a speedy first course that's crowned with a flavor-packed pesto. Make the soup a few days ahead, but do the pesto only shortly before serving so its color stays vibrant.

1 tablespoon butter
1 cup chopped onion
2 tablespoons chopped fresh sage, divided
5 garlic cloves, crushed
¼ teaspoon ground red pepper
¼ teaspoon ground cumin
2½ cups unsalted chicken stock (such as Swanson)
1 cup canned cannellini beans, rinsed and drained
1 (15-ounce) can pumpkin puree
1 cup 2% reduced-fat milk
¾ teaspoon kosher salt
2 tablespoons cider vinegar
1 cup baby spinach
1 cup basil leaves
2 tablespoons pine nuts, toasted
2 tablespoons grated fresh Parmesan cheese
2 tablespoons extra-virgin olive oil
2 tablespoons water

1. Melt butter in a large saucepan over medium-high heat. Add onion, 1 tablespoon sage, and garlic to pan; sauté 4 minutes or until lightly browned. Add pepper and cumin; sauté 1 minute. Stir in ½ cup stock; cook 1 minute, scraping pan to loosen browned bits. Place onion mixture, 2 cups stock, beans, and pumpkin in a blender; process until smooth. Return stock mixture to pan. Stir in milk and salt. Bring to a simmer; cook 5 minutes, stirring occasionally. Stir in vinegar.

2. Place 1 tablespoon sage, spinach, and remaining ingredients in a mini food processor; process until smooth. Ladle about ⅔ cup bisque into each of 8 bowls; top each serving with 2 teaspoons pesto. Serves 8

CALORIES 143; **FAT** 7.7g (sat 2.2g, mono 3.5g, poly 1.2g); **PROTEIN** 6.1g; **CARB** 13.7g; **FIBER** 3.5g; **CHOL** 7mg; **IRON** 1.8mg; **SODIUM** 286mg; **CALC** 104mg

MOST COOKS RELISH THE WHOLE RITUAL OF PLANNING AND PREPARING. IT'S AN ACT OF LOVE, REDOLENT WITH CULTURAL AND FAMILY MEANING.

Quick & Easy • Vegetarian

Brie with Jeweled Fruit Compote

Hands-on: 6 min. Total: 6 min. *This lovely
appetizer is about as quick and easy as it
gets—as tasty, too. You don't need to let the
cheese come to room temperature first; the
warm fruit that goes on top will soften it up.
Serve with crostini or crackers.*

¼ cup dried tart cherries
¼ cup dried apricots, sliced
¼ cup golden raisins
2 tablespoons brown sugar
3 tablespoons brandy
2 tablespoons water
1 tablespoon fresh lemon juice
1 teaspoon whole-grain mustard
¾ teaspoon chopped fresh rosemary
**⅛ teaspoon freshly ground black
   pepper**
Dash of kosher salt
6 small dried figs, quartered
1 (8-ounce) wheel Brie cheese

1. Combine all ingredients except
cheese in a medium microwave-safe
bowl. Microwave at HIGH 2 minutes.
Stir mixture; microwave at HIGH
1 minute or until bubbly. Serve warm
fruit over Brie. Serves 16 (serving size:
½ ounce Brie and 1 tablespoon
compote)

CALORIES 89; FAT 4g (sat 2.5g, mono 1.1g, poly 0.1g);
PROTEIN 3.3g; CARB 8.9g; FIBER 0.8g; CHOL 14mg;
IRON 0.3mg; SODIUM 108mg; CALC 38mg

Kid Friendly • Quick & Easy

Creamed Spinach Phyllo Cups

Hands-on: 9 min. Total: 29 min. *Turn a
beloved side dish into a cute and savory
appetizer. Frozen phyllo shells speed prep
time, as does bagged baby spinach (rather
than frozen). Toasting the phyllo cups keeps
them crisp longer after being filled.*

30 mini phyllo shells (such as Athens)
Cooking spray
1 tablespoon canola oil
2 teaspoons minced fresh garlic
2 (6-ounce) bags baby spinach
¼ teaspoon salt
2 tablespoons whipping cream
3 ounces ⅓-less-fat cream cheese
**½ ounce Parmigiano-Reggiano cheese,
   very thinly shaved**

1. Preheat oven to 425°.
2. Arrange phyllo shells in a single
layer on a foil-lined baking sheet.
Lightly coat shells with cooking spray.
Bake at 425° for 4 minutes or until
lightly browned and very crisp.
3. Heat a large skillet over medium
heat. Add oil; swirl to coat. Add garlic;
cook 1 minute or until fragrant but not
browned, stirring frequently. Coarsely
chop 1 bag of spinach. Add chopped
spinach to pan; cook 2 minutes or
until spinach wilts, tossing frequently.
Chop remaining spinach; add to wilted
spinach in pan. Cook 2 minutes or
until spinach wilts, tossing frequently.
Sprinkle spinach mixture with salt;
toss well. Stir in cream and cream
cheese; cook 1 minute or until cheese
melts and sauce is thoroughly heated.
Remove pan from heat.
4. Spoon about 1 tablespoon spinach
mixture into each shell. Top evenly
with Parmigiano-Reggiano. Serves 10
(serving size: 3 filled cups)

CALORIES 118; FAT 7.8g (sat 2g, mono 3.3g, poly 1.3g);
PROTEIN 2.2g; CARB 10.4g; FIBER 1.6g; CHOL 12mg;
IRON 1.1mg; SODIUM 201mg; CALC 51mg

Kid Friendly • Vegetarian

Mashed Potato Soufflé

(pictured on page 238)

Hands-on: 15 min. Total: 60 min. *Who
knew instant potato flakes could be the basis
of such an amazing dish? It's really something of
a faux-fflé—technically not a soufflé, but you
get the same puff-tacular results without even
having to whip egg whites.*

Baking spray with flour
1¼ cups 2% reduced-fat milk, divided
2 tablespoons all-purpose flour
2⅔ cups water
2⅔ cups instant potato flakes
¼ cup plain fat-free Greek yogurt
2 tablespoons butter, melted
1 teaspoon baking powder
⅝ teaspoon salt
3 large eggs, lightly beaten
**1 ounce pecorino Romano cheese, finely
   grated (about ¼ cup)**

1. Preheat oven to 400°.
2. Coat a 2-quart soufflé dish with
baking spray.
3. Combine ¼ cup milk and flour,
stirring with a whisk. Bring flour
mixture and 2⅔ cups water to a boil in
a medium saucepan; simmer 2 minutes. Remove from heat; stir in 1 cup
milk and potato flakes. Add yogurt and
remaining ingredients, stirring until
just combined. Spoon into prepared
dish. Bake at 400° for 45 minutes or
until puffy.
4. Turn on broiler (leave dish in
oven). Broil 2 minutes or until lightly
browned. Serve immediately. Serves 10
(serving size: about 1 cup)

CALORIES 126; FAT 5.3g (sat 3g, mono 1.3g, poly 0.4g);
PROTEIN 5.4g; CARB 13.8g; FIBER 1.1g; CHOL 67mg;
IRON 0.8mg; SODIUM 326mg; CALC 102mg

Kid Friendly

Easy, Cheesy Potato Gratin

Hands-on: 15 min. Total: 45 min.
Refrigerated presliced potatoes slash tons of prep and cook time.

2 (20-ounce) bags home-style potato slices (such as Simply Potatoes)
Cooking spray
1½ tablespoons butter
1 tablespoon chopped fresh thyme
4 garlic cloves, minced
6 tablespoons all-purpose flour
3 cups 2% reduced-fat milk, divided
½ teaspoon salt
¼ teaspoon freshly ground black pepper
1.5 ounces aged Gruyère cheese, shredded (about ⅓ cup)
1 ounce Parmigiano-Reggiano cheese, grated (about ¼ cup)
1 tablespoon chopped fresh chives

1. Preheat oven to 400°.
2. Arrange potatoes in a broiler-safe 11 x 7–inch baking dish coated with cooking spray. Cover with plastic wrap; vent. Microwave at HIGH 10 minutes; uncover carefully.
3. Melt butter in a medium saucepan over medium heat; swirl to coat. Add thyme and garlic; sauté 3 minutes. Sprinkle with flour; stir in ⅓ cup milk. Cook 1 minute, stirring constantly with a whisk. Stir in remaining 2⅔ cups milk. Bring mixture to a simmer; cook 4 minutes or until slightly thick, stirring frequently. Remove from heat.

Stir in salt, pepper, and Gruyère. Pour sauce over potatoes; sprinkle with Parmigiano-Reggiano. Bake at 400° for 20 minutes or until potatoes are tender when pierced with a knife.
4. Turn on broiler (leave dish in oven). Broil gratin 2 minutes or until browned. Sprinkle with chives. Serves 12 (serving size: about ⅔ cup)

CALORIES 125; FAT 4.5g (sat 2.8g, mono 1.3g, poly 0.2g); PROTEIN 5.4g; CARB 16g; FIBER 1.1g; CHOL 15mg; IRON 0.6mg; SODIUM 192mg; CALC 139mg

Kid Friendly • Quick & Easy
Vegetarian

Quick Traditional Sweet Potato Casserole
(pictured on page 239)

Hands-on: 10 min. Total: 40 min.

2 (29-ounce) cans yams or sweet potatoes in syrup, drained
¼ cup crème fraîche
2½ tablespoons butter, melted
1 tablespoon cake flour
¾ teaspoon salt
½ teaspoon ground cinnamon
¼ teaspoon vanilla extract
1 large egg, lightly beaten
Cooking spray
⅔ cup mini marshmallows
⅓ cup almonds, coarsely chopped

1. Preheat oven to 375°.
2. Place yams in a large bowl. Coarsely mash with a potato masher. Stir in crème fraîche and next 6 ingredients.

Spoon mixture into an 8-inch square glass or ceramic baking dish coated with cooking spray. Sprinkle with marshmallows and almonds. Bake at 375° for 30 minutes or until thoroughly heated and marshmallows are browned. Serves 10 (serving size: ½ cup)

CALORIES 242; FAT 8.3g (sat 3.5g, mono 3g, poly 1.1g); PROTEIN 3.7g; CARB 39.1g; FIBER 4.8g; CHOL 32mg; IRON 1.6mg; SODIUM 267mg; CALC 41mg

Kid Friendly • Quick & Easy
Make Ahead • Vegetarian

Pumpkin Pie Ice Cream

Hands-on: 8 min. Total: 8 min. *A few easy additions to store-bought ice cream create a custom flavor that simply tastes like Thanksgiving.*

½ cup animal crackers
3 cups vanilla low-fat ice cream
¼ cup canned pumpkin
½ teaspoon ground cinnamon
⅛ teaspoon ground ginger
6 tablespoons frozen reduced-calorie whipped topping, thawed

1. Break animal crackers into pieces. Place crackers and next 4 ingredients (through ginger) in a large bowl; gently mash with a potato masher until just combined. Spoon ½ cup ice cream mixture into each of 6 glasses or dessert bowls; top each serving with 1 tablespoon whipped topping. Serves 6

CALORIES 236; FAT 6.9g (sat 3.4g, mono 2.5g, poly 0.5g); PROTEIN 5.2g; CARB 38.5g; FIBER 0.9g; CHOL 21mg; IRON 0.8mg; SODIUM 151mg; CALC 139mg

Kid Friendly • Make Ahead

No-Bake Cheesecake with Pecan Caramel

(pictured on page 240)

Hands-on: 26 min. Total: 3 hr. 36 min.
Since we've nixed the baking (even of the crust), you save tons of time; you don't have to wait for the cheesecake to cool out of the oven. Make the cheesecake up to 3 days ahead, but prepare the caramel shortly before serving. It hardens quickly to a yummy praline-like texture.

Crust:
16 low-fat honey graham crackers (4 large cracker sheets)
1/4 cup granulated sugar
2 tablespoons butter, melted
Cooking spray
Cheesecake:
12 ounces 1/3-less-fat cream cheese, softened
12 ounces fat-free cream cheese, softened
1/2 cup granulated sugar
1/4 cup crème fraîche
2 teaspoons vanilla extract
1/4 teaspoon salt
3 tablespoons cold water
2 1/4 teaspoons unflavored gelatin
1 cup fat-free milk
Caramel:
2 tablespoons butter
2/3 cup packed brown sugar
1/3 cup maple syrup
1 tablespoon whipping cream
1/4 teaspoon salt
2 tablespoons bourbon
1/2 cup chopped pecans, toasted

1. To prepare crust, place crackers in a food processor; process until finely ground. With motor running, add 1/4 cup granulated sugar and 2 tablespoons melted butter to cracker crumbs through food chute; process until blended. Place crumb mixture in a 9-inch springform pan coated with cooking spray; press evenly into bottom of pan. Freeze 20 minutes or until firm.
2. To prepare cheesecake, combine cheeses, 1/2 cup granulated sugar, and crème fraîche in a large bowl; beat with a mixer at medium speed until smooth. Beat in vanilla and 1/4 teaspoon salt. Combine 3 tablespoons cold water and gelatin; let stand 2 minutes or until gelatin dissolves. Heat milk in a small saucepan to 180° (do not boil). Stir gelatin mixture into hot milk, stirring well. Beat gelatin mixture into cheese mixture. Pour cheese mixture into prepared crust; chill 2 hours or until set.
3. To prepare caramel, melt 2 tablespoons butter in a small saucepan over medium-high heat. Add brown sugar and next 3 ingredients (through 1/4 teaspoon salt); stir with a whisk just until sugar melts. Bring mixture to a boil; reduce heat to medium, and cook 5 minutes (do not stir). Remove pan from heat. Stir in bourbon and toasted pecans. Cool slightly.
4. Slice cheesecake into 16 wedges. Place 1 wedge on each of 16 plates; drizzle 1 tablespoon caramel over each serving. Serves 16

CALORIES 253; FAT 12g (sat 6g, mono 3.4g, poly 1g); PROTEIN 6.8g; CARB 29.4g; FIBER 0.4g; CHOL 31mg; IRON 0.4mg; SODIUM 355mg; CALC 137mg

DELIGHTFUL NEW APPROACHES TO MUCH-LOVED THANKSGIVING DISHES

Kid Friendly • Make Ahead

Carrot-Apple Spice Cake with Browned-Butter Glaze

Hands-on: 30 min. Total: 1 hr. 30 min.
We challenged ourselves to come up with a showstopping dessert that uses boxed cake mix as a starting point—and we succeeded. Fresh carrot and apple plus a splash of bourbon boost the flavor of the layers, while the browned-butter glaze is, well, the wildly delicious icing on the cake.

Cake:
1/2 cup nonfat buttermilk
1/4 cup canola oil
1/4 cup water
2 tablespoons bourbon
3 large eggs
1 (18.25-ounce) box spice cake mix (such as Duncan Hines)
1 cup grated carrot
1 cup grated peeled Honeycrisp apple (or any sweet-tart apple)
Baking spray with flour
Glaze:
1/4 cup butter
2 cups powdered sugar, divided
2 ounces 1/3-less-fat cream cheese, softened
2 tablespoons 2% reduced-fat milk
1/2 teaspoon vanilla extract
Dash of salt
1/4 cup chopped pecans, toasted

1. Preheat oven to 350°.
2. To prepare cake, combine first 5 ingredients in a large bowl; beat with a mixer at low speed 1 minute or until well combined. Add cake mix to buttermilk mixture; beat at medium speed 1 minute or until well blended. Stir in carrot and apple until just combined. Divide batter evenly among 3 (8-inch) round cake pans coated with baking spray. Bake at 350° for 20 minutes or until a wooden pick inserted in the

center comes out clean. Cool cakes in pans on a wire rack 10 minutes. Remove cakes from pans; cool completely on wire rack.

3. To prepare glaze, melt butter in a small saucepan over medium-low heat; cook 6 minutes or until lightly browned, stirring frequently. Cool slightly. Combine browned butter, 1½ cups powdered sugar, cream cheese, milk, vanilla, and salt in a medium bowl; beat with a mixer at low speed 2 minutes or until smooth.

4. To assemble cake, place 1 cake layer on a plate; spread ¼ cup glaze over cake layer. Top with second layer and spread with ¼ cup glaze. Top with third layer. Stir ½ cup powdered sugar into remaining glaze. Spread remaining glaze over top of cake. Sprinkle with chopped pecans. Serves 16 (serving size: 1 piece)

CALORIES 294; FAT 12g (sat 3.7g, mono 5g, poly 1.7g); PROTEIN 3.6g; CARB 43.7g; FIBER 0.6g; CHOL 45mg; IRON 0.8mg; SODIUM 259mg; CALC 86mg

Kid Friendly • Quick & Easy
Vegetarian

Browned-Butter Rolls

Hands-on: 10 min. Total: 30 min.

1 (13.2-ounce) package refrigerated French bread dough (such as Pillsbury Simply Rustic French Bread)
1½ tablespoons unsalted butter
2 teaspoons finely chopped fresh sage
2 garlic cloves, minced
⅛ teaspoon kosher salt

1. Preheat oven to 350°.
2. Remove dough from package. Place dough on a lightly floured surface; lightly dust dough with flour. Cut dough in half crosswise; cut each half lengthwise into 4 strips to form 8 strips total. Working with 1 strip at a time, stretch strip gently to extend length; tie in a knot, tucking the ends

under. Arrange the knots 3 inches apart on a baking sheet lined with parchment paper.
3. Bake at 350° for 20 minutes or until golden.
4. While rolls bake, melt butter in a small skillet. Cook until bubbly and lightly browned (about 2 minutes). Add sage and garlic to pan; cook 1 minute or until fragrant. Brush butter mixture over hot rolls; sprinkle evenly with salt. Serves 8 (serving size: 1 roll)

CALORIES 133; FAT 3.5g (sat 1.8g, mono 0.6g, poly 0.1g); PROTEIN 3.7g; CARB 21.9g; FIBER 0.9g; CHOL 6mg; IRON 1.3mg; SODIUM 300mg; CALC 3mg

Double-Sesame Rolls
Prepare Browned-Butter Rolls through step 3. Brush 1 tablespoon toasted sesame oil over hot rolls; sprinkle with 1 tablespoon toasted sesame seeds and ⅛ teaspoon kosher salt. Serves 8 (serving size: 1 roll)

CALORIES 134; FAT 3.6g (sat 0.8g); SODIUM 300mg

Bacon & Gruyère rolls
Prepare Browned-Butter Rolls through step 2. Sprinkle with ¼ cup shredded Gruyère cheese and 2 finely chopped uncooked bacon slices. Bake. Serves 8 (serving size: 1 roll)

CALORIES 137; FAT 3.2g (sat 1.3g); SODIUM 318mg

USE STORE-BOUGHT REFRIGERATED BREAD DOUGH TO MAKE PRETTY KNOTTED ROLLS THAT YOU CAN GUSSY UP WITH YOUR FAVORITE TOPPINGS.

Kid Friendly • Quick & Easy
Make Ahead

Corn Bread Stuffing Muffins

(pictured on page 238)

Hands-on: 15 min. Total: 30 min.

4 ounces sweet Italian turkey sausage, casings removed
¾ cup diced onion
½ cup diced celery
1 tablespoon butter
1 tablespoon chopped fresh sage
2 teaspoons chopped fresh thyme
¼ teaspoon kosher salt
¼ teaspoon freshly ground black pepper
¼ cup chopped celery leaves
⅔ cup unsalted chicken stock (such as Swanson)
3 tablespoons canola oil
2 large eggs, lightly beaten
¼ teaspoon baking powder
2 (6.5-ounce) packages corn bread and muffin mix (such as Betty Crocker)
Cooking spray
⅓ cup chopped pecans

1. Preheat oven to 400°.
2. Heat a large nonstick skillet over medium-high heat. Add sausage to pan; sauté 4 minutes, stirring to crumble. Add onion, celery, and butter to pan; sauté 5 minutes, stirring occasionally. Stir in sage, thyme, salt, and pepper; cook 1 minute. Stir in celery leaves.
3. Combine stock, oil, and eggs in a medium bowl, stirring with a whisk.
4. Combine baking powder and corn bread mix in a medium bowl. Add stock mixture and onion mixture, stirring just until moist. Spoon batter into 12 muffin cups coated with cooking spray. Sprinkle evenly with chopped pecans. Bake at 400° for 12 minutes or until lightly browned. Serves 12 (serving size: 1 muffin)

CALORIES 203; FAT 8.5g (sat 1.5g, mono 4g, poly 1.8g); PROTEIN 5.5g; CARB 24.7g; FIBER 0.6g; CHOL 40mg; IRON 0.4mg; SODIUM 328mg; CALC 21mg

Make-Ahead Layered Salad

Hands-on: 15 min. Total: 15 min.
Prechopped veggies and precooked bacon and eggs help you pull this charmingly retro dish together in a flash. You can assemble the salad, cover tightly with plastic wrap, and refrigerate for up to 1 day.

4 cups prechopped romaine lettuce
4 cups baby arugula
1/2 cup prechopped red onion
2 cups grape tomatoes, halved
4 precooked hard-cooked eggs, chopped
4 precooked bacon slices, finely chopped
2 cups frozen petite green peas, thawed
1/2 cup canola mayonnaise (such as Hellmann's)
1/2 cup plain fat-free Greek yogurt
1/4 cup nonfat buttermilk
1 teaspoon cider vinegar
1/2 teaspoon onion powder
1/2 teaspoon sugar
1/2 teaspoon dried dill
1/2 teaspoon freshly ground black pepper
1/2 teaspoon paprika
1/8 teaspoon kosher salt
1 garlic clove, finely grated
3 ounces preshredded sharp cheddar cheese (about 3/4 cup)
1 tablespoon minced fresh chives

1. Combine lettuce and arugula in a large glass serving bowl. Arrange onion over greens in an even layer; top with tomatoes. Sprinkle eggs over tomatoes; sprinkle bacon over eggs. Spread peas evenly over bacon.
2. Combine mayonnaise and next 10 ingredients (through garlic) in a medium bowl. Spread mayonnaise mixture over peas; top with cheese and chives. Serves 10 (serving size: about 3/4 cup)

CALORIES 148; FAT 8.9g (sat 2.7g, mono 3.3g, poly 1.5g); PROTEIN 8.8g; CARB 8.6g; FIBER 2.4g; CHOL 83mg; IRON 0.9mg; SODIUM 304mg; CALC 110mg

Green Beans with Sherried Mushroom Sauce

(pictured on page 238)

Hands-on: 30 min. Total: 35 min. *Here's a faster, fresher take on green bean casserole that's done all on the stovetop—one less thing to try to work into oven rotation on the big day. Although we use fresh beans and make our own creamy sauce, we've kept the French-fried onions (arguably the best part of traditional green bean casserole). To speed prep, you can purchase bags of fresh, pretrimmed green beans from the produce section.*

4 cups water
3/4 teaspoon salt, divided
2 pounds green beans, trimmed
1 1/2 tablespoons canola oil
1 1/2 cups sliced onion
1 (4-ounce) package fresh gourmet mushrooms
1/3 cup dry sherry
1 1/2 teaspoons chopped fresh thyme leaves
1 1/2 tablespoons all-purpose flour
3 tablespoons whipped cream cheese
1 1/2 cups unsalted chicken stock (such as Swanson)
1/3 cup French-fried onions, crushed (such as French's)

1. Bring 4 cups water to a boil in a large straight-sided skillet. Add 1/2 teaspoon salt and green beans. Reduce heat to medium; cook 6 minutes or until tender. Drain beans; rinse with cold water. Drain and set aside.
2. Wipe skillet clean and dry with paper towels; return skillet to medium-high heat. Add oil to pan; swirl to coat. Add sliced onion; sauté 5 minutes or until lightly browned, stirring occasionally. Add mushrooms; sauté 3 minutes or until mushrooms brown, stirring occasionally. Add sherry and thyme; sprinkle with 1/4 teaspoon salt. Bring to a boil; cook until liquid almost evaporates. Stir in flour; cook 30 seconds, stirring constantly. Add cream cheese; stir until cheese melts. Stir in stock; bring to a boil, stirring constantly. Cook 2 minutes or until slightly thick. Remove from heat. Add beans; toss to coat. Sprinkle with crushed onions. Serves 10 (serving size: about 3/4 cup)

CALORIES 100; FAT 4.3g (sat 1g, mono 1.6g, poly 0.8g); PROTEIN 3.5g; CARB 10.9g; FIBER 3g; CHOL 3mg; IRON 1.2mg; SODIUM 226mg; CALC 47mg

Sweet and Sour Brussels Sprout Salad

Hands-on: 20 min. Total: 20 min. *We love Brussels sprout salads but wanted a quicker approach than the tedium of pulling apart the leaves. The food processor slices each sprout nice and thin with lightning-fast speed.*

1 pound Brussels sprouts
7 radishes
1/4 cup fresh lemon juice
3 tablespoons extra-virgin olive oil
1 tablespoon sugar
1 tablespoon Dijon mustard
1/2 teaspoon kosher salt
1/2 teaspoon freshly ground black pepper

1. Slice Brussels sprouts and radishes in a food processor fitted with a slicing blade. Combine Brussels sprout mixture and remaining ingredients in a large bowl; toss well to coat. Serves 8 (serving size: 1 cup)

CALORIES 80; FAT 5.3g (sat 0.7g, mono 3.7g, poly 0.6g); PROTEIN 2g; CARB 7.8g; FIBER 2.3g; CHOL 0mg; IRON 0.9mg; SODIUM 181mg; CALC 26mg

Brussels Sprout Salad with Bacon Croutons

Slice 1 pound Brussels sprouts in a food processor. Cook 4 center-cut bacon slices in a skillet until crisp. Remove from pan; crumble. Add 2 teaspoons canola oil to drippings in pan. Stir in 2 ounces (½-inch) cubed country bread; sauté over medium-high 5 minutes or until crisp. Combine ¼ cup extra-virgin olive oil, ¼ cup red wine vinegar, 1 teaspoon brown sugar, ½ teaspoon pepper, and ¼ teaspoon kosher salt in a large bowl. Add Brussels sprouts; toss well. Top with croutons and bacon. Serves 8 (serving size: 1 cup)

CALORIES 129; FAT 9g (sat 1.3g); SODIUM 163mg

Waldorf Brussels Sprout Salad

Slice 1 pound Brussels sprouts in a food processor. Combine sprouts, 1¼ cups diced apple, ¾ cup chopped celery, and ¼ cup chopped toasted walnuts. Combine 5 tablespoons canola mayo, ¼ cup apple cider, 3 tablespoons light sour cream, ½ teaspoon kosher salt, and ¼ teaspoon pepper, stirring with a whisk. Drizzle over salad; toss to coat. Serves 8 (serving size: 1 cup)

CALORIES 97; FAT 5.6g (sat 0.7g); SODIUM 212mg

Quick & Easy • Vegetarian

Speedy Apple-Beet Salad

(pictured on page 238)

Hands-on: 13 min. Total: 13 min. *Hooray for the food processor, which makes this crisp, refreshing salad a snap to make. Honeycrisp apples have peel that ranges in color from bright red to golden—pick the redder ones, as they tend to be sweeter. Don't make this dish too far ahead, as it might discolor; aim for no more than 30 minutes before you plan to serve it.*

2 Honeycrisp apples, unpeeled, cored, and cut into thin wedges
¼ cup fresh lemon juice
1 tablespoon sugar
2 medium golden beets, peeled and cut into wedges
¼ small red onion, cut into two wedges
⅓ cup flat-leaf parsley leaves
½ teaspoon kosher salt
¼ teaspoon freshly ground black pepper
2 tablespoons canola oil
1½ tablespoons Dijon mustard
½ cup walnut halves, toasted
1 ounce blue cheese, crumbled (about ¼ cup)

1. Thinly slice apple wedges in a food processor fitted with a slicing blade. Combine apples, lemon juice, and sugar in a large bowl; toss to coat. Slice beet and onion wedges in food processor fitted with a slicing blade; add beet mixture and parsley to apple mixture. Sprinkle with salt and pepper. Stir in oil and mustard; toss gently to coat. Arrange about ⅔ cup salad on each of 8 plates; top each serving with 1 tablespoon walnuts and about 1½ teaspoons cheese. Serves 8

CALORIES 129; FAT 9.4g (sat 1.4g, mono 3.2g, poly 4.5g); PROTEIN 2.4g; CARB 10.4g; FIBER 1.7g; CHOL 3mg; IRON 0.4mg; SODIUM 254mg; CALC 35mg

Quick & Easy • Make Ahead

Smoky Bell Pepper Soup

Hands-on: 23 min. Total: 23 min. *Inspired by the flavors of Spanish romesco sauce, this starter soup gussies up bottled roasted bell peppers with Marcona almonds (already toasted, saving a step), lots of garlic, and sherry vinegar.*

1½ tablespoons canola oil
1½ cups chopped onion
8 garlic cloves, chopped
½ teaspoon smoked paprika
2¼ cups unsalted chicken stock (such as Swanson)
2 (12-ounce) bottles roasted red bell peppers, rinsed well and drained
¼ cup Marcona almonds
1 ounce French bread baguette, torn
¼ cup heavy whipping cream
2 teaspoons sherry vinegar
⅜ teaspoon kosher salt
Flat-leaf parsley leaves (optional)

1. Heat a medium saucepan over medium-high heat. Add oil to pan; swirl to coat. Add onion; sauté 5 minutes or until tender. Add garlic; sauté 1½ minutes. Add paprika; cook 30 seconds, stirring constantly. Add stock and bell peppers; bring to a simmer.

2. Place bell pepper mixture, almonds, and bread in a blender. Remove center piece of blender lid (to allow steam to escape); secure lid on blender. Place a towel over opening in lid. Blend until smooth. Add cream, and pulse to combine.

3. Return pureed soup to saucepan. Heat soup over medium heat 3 minutes or until thoroughly heated. Stir in vinegar and salt. Garnish with parsley, if desired. Serves 8 (serving size: about ⅔ cup)

CALORIES 116; FAT 7.7g (sat 2.2g, mono 3.9g, poly 1.4g); PROTEIN 3.3g; CARB 8.9g; FIBER 1.1g; CHOL 10mg; IRON 0.6mg; SODIUM 284mg; CALC 35mg

Slow-Cooker Blood Orange Fizzy Mulled Wine

Hands-on: 5 min. Total: 2 hr. 5 min. *The slow cooker offers great convenience here, keeping the stovetop open for meal prep. Pouring the soda into the hot wine right at the time of service brings the temperature down enough to drink immediately. Change out the orange slices for fresh when serving to punch up the look.*

10 whole black peppercorns
10 whole cardamom pods
6 whole cloves
5 whole juniper berries
2 (3-inch) cinnamon sticks
2 (750-milliliter) bottles red wine (such as zinfandel)
1 whole star anise
1 navel orange, thinly sliced
2 tablespoons sugar
1 tablespoon balsamic vinegar
1 (25.4-ounce) bottle
  blood orange Italian
  soda (such as Whole Foods)

1. Combine first 8 ingredients in an electric slow cooker. Cover and cook on HIGH 2 hours; stir in sugar and vinegar. Stir in soda just before serving. Serves 12 (serving size: ¾ cup)

CALORIES 150; FAT 0g; PROTEIN 0.2g; CARB 14.4g; FIBER 0.3g; CHOL 0mg; IRON 0.6mg; SODIUM 12mg; CALC 15mg

BRINING IS THE EASIEST PATH TO THE BEST-TASTING BIRD, ENSURING MOIST, FLAVORFUL RESULTS EVERY TIME.

Foolproof Brined Turkey

Hands-on: 50 min. Total: 28 hr. *Brining a turkey is well worth the day-ahead time investment. It removes all guesswork, producing an incredibly moist bird that's more forgiving of being slightly overcooked. If you can't find an organic turkey, look for a fresh one without "added solution."*

Brine:
1 gallon plus 2 cups water, divided
½ cup sugar
⅓ cup kosher salt
1 tablespoon black peppercorns
6 sage leaves
2 bay leaves
Turkey:
1 (12-pound) organic fresh turkey
10 flat-leaf parsley sprigs
2 sage leaves
2 celery stalks, quartered and divided
2 large carrots, quartered and divided
1 large white onion, quartered and divided
1 large Fuji apple, quartered and divided
1 lemon, quartered and divided
Cooking spray
2 cups water
2 cups unsalted chicken stock, divided
3 tablespoons unsalted butter, melted
¼ cup all-purpose flour
½ teaspoon freshly ground black pepper
¼ teaspoon kosher salt

1. To prepare brine, combine 2 cups water, ½ cup sugar, and next 4 ingredients (through bay leaves) in a saucepan over medium-high heat. Bring to a boil, stirring until salt dissolves. Remove from heat; let stand 10 minutes. Add sugar mixture and remaining 1 gallon water to a brining bag.
2. Remove giblets and neck from turkey; reserve neck. Trim excess fat; add turkey to brining bag. Seal bag; refrigerate 18 to 24 hours, turning occasionally.

3. Preheat oven to 500°.
4. Remove turkey from brine; discard brine. Pat turkey dry. Lift wing tips up and over back; tuck under turkey. Place parsley, 2 sage leaves, 3 celery pieces, 3 carrot pieces, 1 onion quarter, 2 apple quarters, and 2 lemon wedges in body cavity. Secure legs with twine. Place turkey on the rack of a roasting pan coated with cooking spray. Place turkey neck and remaining celery, carrot, onion, apple, and lemon in bottom of roasting pan; place rack with turkey in pan.
5. Bake at 500° for 45 minutes. Reduce oven temperature to 350° (do not remove turkey from oven). Place a foil tent over turkey breast. Pour 2 cups water in bottom of pan. Bake turkey at 350° for 45 minutes. Combine 1½ cups stock and butter. Rotate turkey, and baste with ½ cup stock mixture. Bake 30 minutes; rotate turkey and baste with ½ cup stock mixture. Bake an additional 30 minutes or until a thermometer inserted into thickest part of thigh registers 160°. Remove from oven; place turkey on a cutting board. Baste with remaining ½ cup stock mixture. Let stand, covered, at least 30 minutes; discard neck and skin.
6. Combine ½ cup stock and flour, stirring with a whisk. Pour pan drippings through a sieve over a bowl; discard solids. Add flour mixture to drippings, stirring with a whisk. Place mixture in a medium saucepan; bring to a boil. Cook 2 minutes or until mixture thickens. Stir in ground pepper and ¼ teaspoon salt. Serve gravy with turkey. Serves 18 (serving size: about 4 ounces turkey and ¼ cup gravy)

CALORIES 237; FAT 7.8g (sat 2.9g, mono 1.7g, poly 1.8g); PROTEIN 34.3g; CARB 5.7g; FIBER 0.8g; CHOL 91mg; IRON 2.3mg; SODIUM 307mg; CALC 45mg

YOU'RE INVITED

Cooking Light's 2013 holiday party features brilliant appetizers and dazzling cocktails with invaluable recipes and eminently useful tips.

Kid Friendly • Quick & Easy

Melted Manchego Tortas with Romesco and Chorizo

(pictured on page 236)

***Hands-on: 25 min. Total: 25 min.** Spanish flatbreads, or tortas, are a tapas staple. Make these with thin sandwich round halves and a 1 1/4-inch circular cutter. You'll only use 1/4 cup of the romesco, but the remainder makes a great sauce for meats, vegetables, or fish.*

1/2 cup sliced almonds, toasted
2 tablespoons sherry vinegar
1/2 teaspoon dried oregano
1/4 teaspoon salt
1/4 teaspoon crushed red pepper
1 tablespoon chipotle chile, canned in adobo sauce
2 large bottled roasted red bell peppers (about 4 ounces), drained
1 garlic clove
1/2 cup extra-virgin olive oil
3 whole-wheat sandwich rounds (such as Nature's Own)
2 ounces Manchego cheese, shaved (about 1 cup)
4 ounces Spanish chorizo, cut into 32 (1/16-inch) slices
32 leaves flat-leaf parsley

1. Preheat broiler.
2. Place first 8 ingredients in a food processor; pulse until blended. Slowly add oil through food chute with food processor on; process until smooth. Set aside 1/4 cup sauce; reserve remaining sauce for another use.
3. Split sandwich rounds; cut out 32 (1 1/4-inch) circles using a sharp round cookie cutter. Arrange bread in a single layer on a baking sheet; top evenly with cheese. Broil 3 minutes or until cheese melts. Remove from oven. Top each with 1 slice chorizo, 1/4 teaspoon romesco, and 1 parsley leaf. Serves 16 (serving size: 2 rounds)

CALORIES 84; **FAT** 6g (sat 2.1g, mono 2.7g, poly 0.6g); **PROTEIN** 3.5g; **CARB** 4.2g; **FIBER** 1.2g; **CHOL** 10mg; **IRON** 0.4mg; **SODIUM** 164mg; **CALC** 62mg

THESE ARE THE CRUNCHY, SAVORY, SEASONAL BITES YOUR FRIENDS WILL LOVE. OUR MAKE-AHEAD STRATEGIES MAKE IT TOTALLY DOABLE.

THE APPETIZER MENU

When it's that turkey or brisket time of year—a time of important ritual cooking—the way a cook can cut loose and entertain purely for the sake of entertaining is to throw a warm, seasonal app-and-cocktail party. A deft mix of savory bites and brilliant drinks leads to pure conviviality, real joie de vivre. The care taken with homemade food and drink makes all the difference. These appetizers will delight.

Kid Friendly • Make Ahead

Savory Crisps with Bacon and Rosemary

***Hands-on: 30 min. Total: 1 hr. 30 min.** Keeping the bacon very cold makes it much easier to cut.*

20 low-sodium saltine crackers
20 reduced-fat light buttery crackers (such as Town House)
10 center-cut bacon slices
40 fresh rosemary tips

1. Preheat oven to 250°.
2. Arrange crackers on a work surface. Cut bacon lengthwise into thirds, and then crosswise into thirds. Wrap each cracker with 1 or 2 pieces of bacon to resemble ribbon on a package. Arrange in a single layer on two parchment-lined baking sheets. Bake at 250° for 1 hour or until bacon is crisp. Tuck 1 rosemary tip under bacon on each cracker. Cool on a wire rack. Serve warm or at room temperature. Serves 20 (serving size: 2 crackers)

CALORIES 35; **FAT** 1.5g (sat 0.7g, mono 0.2g, poly 0.2g); **PROTEIN** 1.5g; **CARB** 4g; **FIBER** 0.2g; **CHOL** 4mg; **IRON** 0.2mg; **SODIUM** 100mg; **CALC** 4mg

Make Ahead • Vegetarian

Pepita Pesto-Stuffed Mushrooms

(pictured on page 236)

Hands-on: 40 min. Total: 50 min. Brown the mushrooms and make the pesto ahead, and refrigerate. To serve, bring to room temperature, and fill caps.

40 small cremini or white mushrooms, stems removed
6 tablespoons unsalted pepitas (pumpkinseeds), toasted and divided
1 cup flat-leaf parsley leaves
1 cup cilantro leaves
2 ounces cotija or fresh Parmesan cheese, grated (about 1/2 cup)
3/4 teaspoon grated orange rind
2 tablespoons fresh orange juice
1/4 teaspoon salt
1/4 teaspoon crushed red pepper
1 garlic clove, chopped
2 tablespoons olive oil

1. Heat a large nonstick skillet over medium-high heat. Arrange mushroom caps, stem sides up, in pan; cook 5 minutes, shaking pan occasionally. Turn mushrooms over; cook 5 minutes, shaking pan occasionally. Place mushrooms, stem sides down, on paper towels to drain and cool.
2. Place 4 tablespoons pepitas, parsley, and next 7 ingredients (through garlic) in a food processor; process until chopped. With processor on, slowly pour oil through food chute; process until well blended.
3. Fill each mushroom cap with about 1 teaspoon pesto; top evenly with 2 tablespoons pepitas. Serves 20 (serving size: 2 stuffed mushrooms)

CALORIES 48; FAT 3.3g (sat 0.9g, mono 1.6g, poly 0.6g); PROTEIN 2.9g; CARB 2.7g; FIBER 0.5g; CHOL 2mg; IRON 0.6mg; SODIUM 77mg; CALC 45mg

Kid Friendly • Quick & Easy Vegetarian

Crisp Persimmon with Ricotta, Honey, Pecans, and Mint

Hands-on: 15 min. Total: 15 min. Unlike soft, plum tomato–shaped Hachiya persimmons, squat, round Fuyu persimmons are crisp with an earthy sweetness.

6 Fuyu persimmons, each cut into 6 wedges
1/2 cup part-skim ricotta cheese
2 teaspoons finely grated lemon rind
3 tablespoons honey
6 mint leaves, thinly sliced
1/4 cup chopped pecans, toasted

1. Cut seeds from persimmon wedges to form a small, flat top on each wedge.
2. Combine ricotta and rind in a small bowl. Arrange 1/2 teaspoon ricotta mixture on flat top of each wedge. Drizzle each with 1/4 teaspoon honey. Sprinkle evenly with mint and pecans. Serves 18 (serving size: 2 wedges)

CALORIES 70; FAT 1.7g (sat 0.4g, mono 0.8g, poly 0.4g); PROTEIN 1.3g; CARB 14g; FIBER 2.2g; CHOL 2mg; IRON 0.2mg; SODIUM 9mg; CALC 25mg

Make Ahead • Vegetarian

Polenta Toasts with Balsamic Onions, Roasted Peppers, Feta, and Thyme

(pictured on page 236)

Hands-on: 1 hr. Total: 3 hr. The polenta and onions may be prepared a few days in advance.

3 cups water
3/4 teaspoon salt, divided
1 cup dry polenta
2 tablespoons olive oil, divided
2 tablespoons butter, divided
Cooking spray
1 teaspoon minced fresh garlic
2 cups vertically sliced onion
1 thyme sprig
1 tablespoon balsamic vinegar
1/4 cup chopped bottled roasted red bell peppers
2 ounces feta cheese, crumbled (about 1/4 cup)
2 teaspoons fresh thyme leaves

1. Bring 3 cups water and 1/2 teaspoon salt to a boil in a medium saucepan. Gradually add polenta, stirring constantly with a whisk. Reduce heat to low, and cook 20 minutes, stirring frequently. Stir in 1 tablespoon oil and 1 tablespoon butter. Spoon polenta into an 8-inch square glass or ceramic baking dish coated with cooking spray. Press plastic wrap onto surface of polenta; chill 2 hours or until firm.
2. Heat a large skillet over medium-high heat. Add 1 tablespoon oil and 1 tablespoon butter; swirl to coat. Add garlic; sauté 15 seconds. Add 1/4 teaspoon salt, onion, and thyme sprig; sauté 3 minutes or until onion begins to soften. Reduce heat to low; cook 30 minutes or until onion is very tender, stirring frequently. Add vinegar; cook 5 minutes, stirring frequently. Discard thyme sprig.
3. Invert polenta onto a cutting board; cut into 16 squares. Cut each square in half diagonally. Heat a skillet over medium heat. Lightly coat polenta triangles with cooking spray. Add 16 triangles to pan; cook 5 minutes on each side or until lightly browned. Repeat procedure with remaining triangles.
4. Divide onion mixture, bell pepper, and feta evenly among triangles. Garnish with thyme leaves. Serves 16 (serving size: 2 triangles)

CALORIES 77; FAT 4g (sat 1.7g, mono 1.8g, poly 0.3g); PROTEIN 1.5g; CARB 8.6g; FIBER 0.8g; CHOL 7mg; IRON 0.5mg; SODIUM 172mg; CALC 22mg

Smoked Salmon Salad in Cucumber Cups

Hands-on: 25 min. Total: 25 min.
Substitute gravlax or even flaked canned salmon if you prefer salmon that has not been smoked. If you want to spice things up, substitute canola mayonnaise for wasabi mayonnaise. It is available in the condiment section of most supermarkets. Of make your own by blending ½ cup mayonnaise with 1 tablespoon wasabi paste, or more wasabi to taste.

¼ cup finely chopped green onions
2 tablespoons plain 2% reduced-fat Greek yogurt
2 tablespoons canola mayonnaise
2 tablespoons drained capers
1 tablespoon chopped fresh dill, divided
1 (12-ounce) package cold-smoked salmon, coarsely chopped
3 English cucumbers
⅛ teaspoon freshly ground black pepper

1. Combine first 4 ingredients in a medium bowl. Stir in 2 teaspoons dill and chopped salmon.
2. Peel cucumbers in alternating vertical stripes. Cut cucumbers into ¾-inch-thick slices, and scoop out seeds with a small spoon or melon baller, leaving bottom intact to form a cup.
3. Spoon about 1 tablespoon salmon mixture into each cucumber cup. Sprinkle cups evenly with remaining 1 teaspoon dill and pepper. Serves 17 (serving size: 2 cucumber cups)

CALORIES 36; **FAT** 1.4g (sat 0.2g, mono 0.7g, poly 0.4g); **PROTEIN** 4g; **CARB** 1.3g; **FIBER** 0.4g; **CHOL** 5mg; **IRON** 0.3mg; **SODIUM** 201mg; **CALC** 12mg

USING CRISP APPLE AND CUCUMBER AS THE "BASE" FOR SMOKED TROUT AND SALMON MAKES FOR A HEALTHY BITE WITH LOTS OF CRUNCH AND INTERESTING, CONTRASTING FLAVORS.

Kid Friendly • Quick & Easy

Smoked Trout, Arugula, and Granny Smith Stacks

(pictured on page 236)

Hands-on: 19 min. Total: 19 min.

1 lemon
12 ounces packaged lemon-pepper smoked trout fillets (such as Ducktrap)
1½ cups baby arugula leaves
1 tablespoon fresh lemon juice
1 tablespoon extra-virgin olive oil
3 Granny Smith apples, cut into 32 thin slices

1. Slice lemon into 4 (¹⁄₁₆-inch) rounds. Cut rounds into 8 wedges.
2. Remove and discard skin from fish; flake fish.
3. Combine arugula, juice, and oil in a bowl; toss to coat.
4. Arrange apple slices in a single layer. Divide arugula mixture and fish evenly among stacks; top each with 1 lemon wedge. Serves 16 (serving size: 2 stacks)

CALORIES 62; **FAT** 3.2g (sat 0.7g, mono 1.7g, poly 0.5g); **PROTEIN** 5.4g; **CARB** 3.6g; **FIBER** 0.5g; **CHOL** 6mg; **IRON** 0mg; **SODIUM** 222mg; **CALC** 6mg

Kid Friendly • Make Ahead

Meatballs in Brussels Sprout Cups

Hands-on: 42 min. Total: 1 hr. 12 min.

2 medium shallots, divided
¼ cup red wine vinegar
½ teaspoon granulated sugar
1 pound ground pork
½ cup panko (Japanese breadcrumbs)
½ cup finely chopped shiitake mushroom caps (about 3.5 ounces)
2 tablespoons minced fresh basil
1 tablespoon brown sugar
1 tablespoon rice vinegar
1 tablespoon nama shoyu or lower-sodium soy sauce
1 teaspoon grated peeled fresh ginger
1 teaspoon dark sesame oil
½ teaspoon kosher salt
4 garlic cloves, minced
1 egg white
8 to 10 large Brussels sprouts

1. Preheat oven to 375°.
2. Thinly slice 1 shallot; separate into rings. Combine sliced shallot, red wine vinegar, and granulated sugar in a small bowl. Let stand 1 hour.
3. While shallot mixture stands, finely chop remaining shallot. Combine chopped shallot, pork and next 11 ingredients in a large bowl. With wet hands, divide mixture into 40 portions (1 scant tablespoon each). Roll each into a 1-inch ball. Arrange on a jelly-roll pan lined with parchment paper. Bake at 375° for 16 minutes.

continued

4. Preheat broiler to high. Broil meatballs on middle rack 4 minutes or until tops begin to brown.

5. While meatballs cook, bring a saucepan of water to a boil. Using a paring knife and starting from the root end, carefully remove outer leaves from Brussels sprouts, setting aside 40 large leaves. Reserve cores for another use. Add leaves to boiling water; cook 1 minute. Drain. Immediately place leaves in a bowl of ice water. Drain. Pat leaves dry with paper towels.

6. Arrange 1 meatball in each Brussels sprout "cup." Top each with 1 shallot slice. Serves 20 (serving size: 2 filled "cups")

CALORIES 81; FAT 5g (sat 1.8g, mono 2.2g, poly 0.6g); PROTEIN 4.9g; CARB 3.9g; FIBER 0.4g; CHOL 16mg; IRON 0.4mg; SODIUM 117mg; CALC 9mg

FRIENDS WILL LOVE THE INGENUITY OF THESE APPETIZERS— LITTLE MEATBALLS CRADLED IN BRUSSELS SPROUT CUPS—CLEVERLY SEASONAL.

KELLIE'S SIGNATURE COCKTAILS

Atlanta mixologist Kellie Thorn created three drinks, in three styles, for *Cooking Light* readers. Prepare to dazzle and delight your guests.

THE PUNCH

"I think of a punch as deceivingly simple," Thorn says. "Citrus, sugar, a spice element, usually a wine." In this version, there's also a base liquor, gin. The resulting drink is astonishingly delicious. The flourish is an old-fashioned ice ring, with fruit.

Punch Principles: Depth of flavor comes from the oleo saccharum, created by muddling wide strips of lemon peel with sugar, and then letting the sugar draw liquid and oils from the peel until you have a fragrant, citrus-perfumed slurry that is strained, and then mixed with lemon juice to form the base of the drink. You build the punch by adding liqueur, gin, and rosemary and letting it "hang out, chill, get integrated," Thorn says. "Right as people are showing up, pour in the bubbly, just 5 or 10 minutes beforehand, so a bit of the fruit can be released from the ice ring."

THE SPIRITS

Pür·likör { pür•likör }
The liqueur is pür•likör Spice, a German-made concoction that tastes of clove and cinnamon, with apricot notes. This ingredient is worth seeking out—have a wine store order it, or find it online (purspirits.com). You could substitute Solerno, a blood orange liqueur, but you'll lose those winter spices.

Gin { 'jin }
Thorn uses Bluecoat gin because it's "a western dry gin, not very juniper-forward, more accessible." Substitute another dry gin like New Amsterdam; steer away from those with highly perfumed botanicals.

Make Ahead

Citrusy Gin and Blood Orange Punch

(pictured on page 237)

***Hands-on: 15 min. Total: 4 hr. 45 min.** If the word "punch" makes you think of old-fashioned, too-sweet concoctions, this drink will be a revelation. Don't skip the oleo saccharum stage: The mix of oils and other citrus flavors that come from the muddling gives amazing body to the final drink.*

6 large lemons, divided
2 cups cold water
¼ cup crystallized ginger, chopped
¼ cup dried apricots, chopped
¼ cup dried cranberries
¾ cup sugar
1 cup fresh lemon juice
2 cups citrusy gin (such as Bluecoat)
¾ cup blood orange liqueur (such as pür•likör Spice)
1 (750-milliliter) bottle prosecco or other sparkling white wine, chilled
Rosemary sprigs (optional)

1. Carefully remove rind from lemons using a vegetable peeler, making sure to avoid white pith. Thinly slice rind from one lemon, and place in a Bundt pan. Add 2 cups water, ginger, apricots, and cranberries, and freeze 4½ hours or until firm.

2. While apricot mixture freezes, place rinds from remaining 5 lemons and sugar in a medium bowl. Muddle rinds and sugar together using a muddler or wooden spoon, working sugar into rinds to release their oils. Cover and let sugar mixture stand at room temperature 1½ hours.

3. Add juice to rind mixture; stir until sugar dissolves. Strain rind mixture through a sieve into a bowl; discard rinds. Stir in gin and blood orange liqueur; cover and chill at least 3 hours.

4. Unmold ice ring by dipping bottom half of Bundt pan into several inches of warm water for 5 to 10 seconds to loosen; repeat as necessary to release. Invert ice ring into a large bowl or punch bowl. Pour gin mixture over ice ring. Gradually add prosecco. Garnish with rosemary, if desired. Serves 18 (serving size: about ⅓ cup)

CALORIES 156; FAT 0g; PROTEIN 0.1g; CARB 13.2g; FIBER 0.1g; CHOL 0mg; IRON 0mg; SODIUM 0mg; CALC 1mg

Make Ahead

The Westview Cocktail

Hands-on: 5 min. Total: 5 min. (plus 1 week for infusing rye) In New York, it's common to name stirred rye cocktails after neighborhoods. This one is named for a historic neighborhood in Atlanta, the city where mixologist Kellie Thorn lives. You'll make more infused whiskey than you need for this cocktail—a good thing, as it's a delicious winter sipper.

1 cup amontillado sherry
1 cup Infused Rye Whiskey
24 dashes Angostura bitters
Sage leaves (optional)

1. Combine first 3 ingredients in a martini pitcher with ice; stir until outside of pitcher is cold. Strain into 8 small cocktail glasses. Garnish with sage, if desired. Serves 8 (serving size: a scant ½ cup)

CALORIES 107; FAT 0g; PROTEIN 0g; CARB 0.5g; FIBER 0g; CHOL 0mg; IRON 0mg; SODIUM 0.3mg; CALC 0mg

Infused Rye Whiskey:
Hands-on: 20 min. Total: 1 week

1 cup Demerara or turbinado sugar
½ cup boiling water
16 sage leaves, thinly sliced
8 ripe pears, coarsely chopped
2 vanilla beans, split
1 (750-milliliter) bottle rye whiskey
   (such as Bulleit)

1. Combine 1 cup sugar and ½ cup boiling water in a 2-cup glass measuring cup, stirring until sugar dissolves. Set aside.
2. Preheat oven to 300°.
3. Combine sage and pears in a 13 x 9–inch glass or ceramic baking dish. Scrape seeds from vanilla beans; add seeds to pear mixture. Chop beans; add to pear mixture. Add 3 tablespoons sugar syrup to pear mixture (reserve remaining sugar syrup for another use). Bake pear mixture at 300° for 20 minutes or until pears are browned and mixture is fragrant. Combine warm pear mixture and whiskey in a large bowl. Pour mixture into a container with a lid; cover and store in a cool, dark place for 1 week, shaking occasionally. Strain out solids when ready to use. Serves 18 (serving size: about 1½ ounces)

CALORIES 102; FAT 0g; PROTEIN 0g; CARB 3.1g; FIBER 0.1g; CHOL 0mg; IRON 0mg; SODIUM 0mg; CALC 0mg

THE APERITIF

With an aperitif, intended to be served before a meal, "you want something dry to stimulate appetite," Thorn says. "You don't want anything too cloying or heavy. A little bitterness is good, to get the juices flowing. And you don't want it overly spirit-heavy."

Thorn says the trend right now in Atlanta is toward lower-alcohol drinks called suppressors, in which the spirit plays a minor role and a lower-alcohol wine plays the dominant one. In this case, she uses amontillado sherry, which is dry but has rich, nutty caramel flavors. The gorgeous holiday notes come from American rye that Thorn infuses (a week before use) with roasted pears and vanilla. The vanilla "adds some softness, a sense of sweetness, without adding any more sugar."

THE SPIRIT

Rye { 'ri } is a spicier, sometimes drier whiskey than bourbon; it's currently much in fashion. Thorn likes Bulleit, which is widely available. There are plenty of others. However, don't swap in the sweeter Canadian rye whiskey.

THE SOUR

A sour is a citrus juice–based cocktail that needs to strike a perfect balance between tang and sweet (the latter usually comes from a simple syrup). Thorn's sour is, like her other drinks, rich with holiday flavors, from both her chai tea syrup (fragrant with cardamom, clove, cinnamon, and other spices) and the apple flavors of the French Calvados brandy. Pondicherry was the historic name of a French-colonized city in India.

THE SPIRIT

Calvados { kal•va•'dos } is a delicious French-made apple brandy. Ask for a good, basic Calvados from a well-informed liquor store person, or you'll overpay. You can substitute an American applejack such as Laird's, though Thorn warns the drink may turn out less complex.

Make Ahead

Pondicherry Sour

Hands-on: 10 min. Total: 2 hr. 10 min. Named for a city the French inhabited in India from 1674 to 1956, this tart, shaken cocktail spikes French apple brandy with Indian spices.

3 cups Calvados (apple brandy)
2 cups Chai Syrup (recipe on page 314)
1 cup fresh lime juice
½ cup fresh lemon juice
Star anise (optional)

1. Combine first 4 ingredients in a 2-quart container. Cover and chill 2 hours or up to overnight.
2. Pour 1 cup mixture into a 1-quart mason jar. Add ice until ice is just above the level of the liquid. Shake for at least 15 hearty shakes or until mixture is covered with white foam. Strain into glasses. Repeat procedure in batches with remaining mixture. Garnish with star anise, if desired. Serves 16 (serving size: about ½ cup)

CALORIES 152; FAT 0g; PROTEIN 0.1g; CARB 15.8g; FIBER 0.1g; CHOL 0mg; IRON 0mg; SODIUM 1mg; CALC 3mg

continued

Chai Syrup:
Hands-on: 5 min. Total: 13 min.

5 tablespoons loose-leaf chai tea (such as Rishi)
3 cups boiling water
2 cups sugar

1. Place tea in a medium bowl; stir in 3 cups boiling water. Cover and let stand 6 minutes. Strain tea through a cheesecloth-lined sieve into a bowl; discard solids. Add sugar, stirring until sugar dissolves. Serves 32 (serving size: 2 tablespoons)

CALORIES 49; FAT 0g; PROTEIN 0g; CARB 12.7g; FIBER 0g; CHOL 0mg; IRON 0mg; SODIUM 1mg; CALC 0mg

THORN MAKES A STRONG TEA—SHE PREFERS LOOSE TEA LEAVES TO TEA BAGS—AND THEN BLENDS IT WITH SUGAR TO MAKE A SYRUP. THE SYRUP IS MIXED WITH JUICE AND CALVADOS, SHAKEN—IT MUST BE SHAKEN—AND POURED INTO GLASSES.

PIES, TARTS, OH MY!

Our Test Kitchen's very own Dessert Goddess, Deb Wise, started with store-bought pie dough to create easy but oh-so-special holiday treats.

Make Ahead

Shaker-ish Lemon Pie

Hands-on: 24 min. Total: 25 hr. 14 min.
Traditional Shaker lemon pie uses the whole lemon, pith and all. This version uses only the rind and the meaty-juicy lemon part, leaving the pith for those hearty Shakers. Macerating the rinds in sugar for 24 hours tenderizes them and reduces bitterness. There's rich caramel flavor in the golden cane syrup; light-colored corn syrup will work fine, too, but the flavor won't be quite as rich.

6 large organic lemons (about 2 pounds)
1 cup golden cane syrup (such as Lyle's Golden Syrup)
3/4 cup plus 2 tablespoons sugar, divided
1/4 teaspoon salt
1 (14.1-ounce) package refrigerated pie dough (such as Pillsbury), divided
Baking spray with flour
4 large egg whites
2 large eggs
1 tablespoon unsalted butter, melted
1 tablespoon water

1. Remove rind from lemons using a vegetable peeler, avoiding white pith; thinly slice rind. Remove pith from lemons; discard. Chop lemon pulp; discard seeds. Combine rind, pulp, cane syrup, ¾ cup sugar, and salt in a bowl. Cover and refrigerate 24 hours.

2. Preheat oven to 350°.
3. Fit one pie dough circle into a 9-inch pie plate lightly coated with baking spray. Press dough against bottom and sides of pan.
4. Place egg whites and whole eggs in a bowl; lightly beat with a fork to combine. Add egg mixture and butter to lemon mixture; stir to combine. Pour filling into prepared pie plate. Place remaining dough circle over filling; fold edges under, and flute decoratively. Cut slits in top of dough to allow steam to escape. Bake at 350° for 45 minutes or until crust is golden and filling is almost set. Combine 2 tablespoons sugar and 1 tablespoon water. Remove pie from oven (leave oven on); brush sugar mixture over top of pie. Bake at 350° for an additional 5 minutes. Place pie on a wire rack; cool completely before slicing. Serves 12 (serving size: 1 wedge)

CALORIES 290; FAT 10.6g (sat 4.6g, mono 3.8g, poly 1.9g); PROTEIN 4.1g; CARB 59.2g; FIBER 2.5g; CHOL 37mg; IRON 0.5mg; SODIUM 345mg; CALC 39mg

DEB'S BAKING TIPS

"Whatever you do, don't pull or stretch the dough. It will become a rubber band: It will expand but then snap back and not hold its shape."

Kid Friendly • Make Ahead

Lattice-Topped Cranberry-Raspberry Pie

Hands-on: 30 min. Total: 2 hrs. 25 min.
Add a splash of festive color to your dessert sideboard with this tangy-fruity pie. For pretty rickrack-shaped lattice, cut the dough with a fluted pastry wheel.

1 (14.1-ounce) package refrigerated pie
   dough (such as Pillsbury), divided
Baking spray with flour
1 1/2 cups fresh or frozen, thawed
   cranberries
1 cup finely diced peeled Fuji or
   Honeycrisp apple
1 tablespoon fresh lemon juice
1/2 cup sugar
3 tablespoons cornstarch
1/4 teaspoon salt
3 (6-ounce) packages fresh
   raspberries, divided
1 teaspoon water
1 large egg white

1. Fit one pie dough circle into a 9-inch pie plate lightly coated with baking spray. Gently press dough against bottom and sides of pan. Chill dough.
2. Preheat oven to 350°.
3. Combine cranberries, apple, and lemon juice in a large bowl. Sprinkle with sugar, cornstarch, and salt; toss well to coat. Add 2 packages raspberries; toss gently to combine. Spoon mixture into prepared pie dough. Arrange remaining package of raspberries over top of cranberry mixture.
4. Gently roll remaining pie dough circle into a 10 x 5–inch rectangle. Cut dough lengthwise into 10 (½-inch) strips. Arrange in a lattice design over raspberries. Seal dough strips to edge of crust. Combine 1 teaspoon water and egg white, stirring with a whisk.

Brush lattice and dough edges with egg mixture. Bake at 350° for 55 minutes or until crust is golden and filling is bubbly, shielding edges of piecrust with foil, if necessary. Cool pie completely on a wire rack before slicing. Serves 10 (serving size: 1 wedge)

CALORIES 253; FAT 10.8g (sat 4.5g, mono 3.8g, poly 2.3g); PROTEIN 2.6g; CARB 39.5g; FIBER 4.2g; CHOL 4mg; IRON 0.4mg; SODIUM 272mg; CALC 15mg

DEB'S BAKING TIPS

"Metal and ceramic pie plates work well, but if you are a tentative baker, use glass. There's comfort in seeing what's happening with the crust."

Kid Friendly • Make Ahead

Silky Sweet Potato and Pecan Pie

Hands-on: 30 min. Total: 2 hr. 10 min.
Toasted pecans make a delicious garnish, adding crunch and adorning the pie like a necklace.

1 (1-pound) sweet potato
1/2 (14.1-ounce) package refrigerated
   pie dough (such as Pillsbury)
Baking spray with flour
1 cup 2% reduced-fat milk
1/3 cup sugar
1/2 teaspoon ground cinnamon
1/2 teaspoon ground allspice
1/4 teaspoon salt
2 large eggs
3 large egg whites, divided
1 1/2 tablespoons unsalted butter,
   melted
1/3 cup chopped pecans, toasted
1 teaspoon water

1. Preheat oven to 400°.
2. Wrap sweet potato in foil; bake at 400° for 45 minutes or until tender.

Cool completely. Peel and coarsely chop sweet potato.
3. Fit dough into a 9-inch pie plate coated with baking spray. Press dough against bottom and sides of pan. Fold edges under, and flute decoratively. Line bottom of dough with a piece of foil; arrange pie weights or dried beans on foil. Bake at 400° for 15 minutes. Remove pie weights and foil; cool crust on wire rack 5 minutes.
4. Reduce oven temperature to 350°.
5. Place sweet potato, milk, and next 5 ingredients in a food processor. Add 2 egg whites; process until smooth. Add butter; process until combined. Pour mixture into crust. Sprinkle nuts around edge of filling. Combine egg white and 1 teaspoon water in a small bowl, stirring well with a whisk. Brush egg mixture on edges of crust. Bake at 350° for 45 minutes or until almost set in the center, shielding edges of piecrust with foil, if necessary. Cool completely on a wire rack before slicing. Serves 8 (serving size: 1 wedge)

CALORIES 276; FAT 13.8g (sat 5.2g, mono 5.4g, poly 2.7g); PROTEIN 6.4g; CARB 33.7g; FIBER 2.4g; CHOL 57mg; IRON 0.8mg; SODIUM 275mg; CALC 72mg

DEB'S BAKING TIPS

"I love the ease of those $5 pie shields you can find at any kitchen store. But you can also take a 12-inch square of foil, fold it in quarters, and cut to make a circle-shaped opening in the middle: easy homemade pie shield."

Hazelnut, Pear, and Blue Cheese Tart

Hands-on: 22 min. Total: 66 min. Here's a beautiful, sophisticated, not-too-sweet dessert that captures the flavors of a great cheese course. If you don't have a rectangular tart pan, you can easily make this in a 9-inch round tart pan. For the boldest blue cheese flavor, go for Maytag or Roquefort; for a subtler effect, try Gorgonzola Dolce.

2/3 cup chopped hazelnuts, toasted and divided
1/2 cup sugar
2 tablespoons unsalted butter, softened
1/8 teaspoon salt
1 large egg
1/2 (14.1-ounce) package refrigerated pie dough (such as Pillsbury)
Baking spray with flour
2 tablespoons crumbled blue cheese
2 large Bartlett or Anjou pears, peeled, cored, and cut lengthwise into 1/8-inch-thick slices
2 teaspoons fresh lemon juice
2 tablespoons apple jelly
1 teaspoon water

1. Place oven rack in the lower third of oven. Preheat oven to 375°.
2. Place 2 tablespoons hazelnuts in a small bowl; set aside. Place remaining hazelnuts and sugar in a food processor; process until finely ground. Add butter, salt, and egg; process until a smooth paste forms.
3. Gently roll pie dough into a 16 x 12–inch rectangle, cutting dough and gently pinching seams as needed to create shape. Fit dough into a 14 x 4½–inch removable-bottom metal tart pan lightly coated with baking spray. Gently press dough against bottom and sides of pan. Spread hazelnut mixture evenly over bottom of dough. Bake in lower third of oven at 375° for 20 minutes or until lightly browned. Remove from oven. Sprinkle blue cheese evenly over top.

4. Gently toss pears with lemon juice. Arrange pear slices on top of cheese. Bake at 375° for 25 minutes or until pears are tender when pierced with the tip of a knife. Remove from oven. Place jelly and 1 teaspoon water in a small microwave-safe bowl; microwave at HIGH 1 minute or until mixture boils. Brush top of tart with jelly mixture; sprinkle with 2 tablespoons hazelnuts. Cool completely in pan on a wire rack before slicing. Serves 8 (serving size: 1 slice)

CALORIES 297; **FAT** 16.3g (sat 5.5g, mono 7.9g, poly 2.3g); **PROTEIN** 3.8g; **CARB** 37.5g; **FIBER** 2.7g; **CHOL** 35mg; **IRON** 0.7mg; **SODIUM** 200mg; **CALC** 30mg

Honey-Pecan Tart with Bittersweet Chocolate Drizzle

Hands-on: 20 min. Total: 1 hr. 30 min. Traditional pecan pie gets a delicious flavor update, with honey's sweet-tangy touch countered by bittersweet chocolate. If you'd like a more casual pie, you can make this in a 9-inch pie plate; you'll probably need to bake the filling an additional 3 to 5 minutes.

1/2 (14.1-ounce) package refrigerated pie dough
Baking spray with flour
3/4 cup light-colored corn syrup
1/2 cup packed brown sugar
1/4 cup honey
2 tablespoons unsalted butter, melted
1 teaspoon vanilla extract
1/4 teaspoon salt
3 large eggs, lightly beaten
1 cup pecan halves, toasted
1 ounce bittersweet chocolate, finely chopped

1. Place oven rack at lowest setting. Preheat oven to 350°.
2. Gently fit pie dough into a 9-inch round removable-bottom metal tart pan coated with baking spray. Gently press dough against bottom and sides of pan. Line bottom of dough with a piece of foil; arrange pie weights or dried beans on foil. Bake at 350° for 15 minutes or until edges are lightly browned. Remove pie weights and foil; cool crust on a wire rack.
3. Combine corn syrup and next 6 ingredients in a large bowl, stirring until well combined. Gently fold in pecans. Pour pecan mixture over crust. Bake in lowest part of oven at 350° for 35 minutes or until set. Cool 20 minutes in pan on a wire rack. Remove sides of tart pan; slide tart onto a serving platter.
4. Place chocolate in a microwave-safe bowl. Microwave at HIGH 1 minute or until chocolate melts, stirring every 15 seconds. Drizzle chocolate over top of tart. Serves 12 (serving size: 1 wedge)

CALORIES 291; **FAT** 14.3g (sat 4.5g, mono 5.9g, poly 3g); **PROTEIN** 3.1g; **CARB** 41.6g; **FIBER** 1g; **CHOL** 53mg; **IRON** 0.7mg; **SODIUM** 169mg; **CALC** 25mg

Spiced Apple Two-Bite Tarts

Hands-on: 40 min. Total: 60 min. The nutty pastry is absolutely delicious, like pecan shortbread. You can make the tart shells and filling the day before and assemble just before serving: Place the shells in an airtight container and chill the filling, bringing it to room temperature before adding to the shells.

Crust:
1/3 cup sugar
1/4 cup unsalted butter, softened
2 tablespoons canola oil
1 tablespoon 1% low-fat milk
1/2 teaspoon vanilla extract
1/4 teaspoon salt
4.5 ounces all-purpose flour (about 1 cup)
1/3 cup very finely chopped toasted pecans
Baking spray with flour

Filling:

2 cups finely diced peeled Granny
    Smith apple
2 teaspoons fresh lemon juice
2 tablespoons sugar
$1/2$ teaspoon ground cinnamon
$1/4$ teaspoon salt
$1/4$ teaspoon ground allspice
$1/8$ teaspoon ground ginger
1 tablespoon unsalted butter
$1/2$ teaspoon cornstarch
1 tablespoon water
$1/4$ cup crème fraîche

1. Preheat oven to 350°.
2. To prepare crust, place first 6
ingredients in a medium bowl. Beat
with a mixer at medium speed 1 minute or until well combined. Weigh or
lightly spoon flour into a dry measuring cup; level with a knife. Add flour
and nuts to butter mixture; beat until
just combined. Divide dough evenly
among 24 miniature muffin cups coated with baking spray. Press dough into
bottom and up sides of muffin cups.
Bake at 350° for 15 minutes or until
golden brown. Cool in pan on a wire
rack 5 minutes. Carefully remove from
pan; cool completely on wire rack.
3. To prepare filling, place apple and
juice in a bowl; toss to coat. Add
2 tablespoons sugar and the next 4
ingredients; toss well.
4. Melt 1 tablespoon butter in a
medium saucepan over medium heat.
Add apple mixture; cover and cook
5 minutes or until apple is tender,
stirring occasionally. Combine cornstarch and 1 tablespoon water in a
small bowl. Stir cornstarch mixture
into apple mixture; cook 1 minute
or until mixture thickens, stirring
constantly. Place apple mixture in a
bowl; cool to room temperature. Spoon
about 2 teaspoons apple mixture into
each tart shell. Top each tart with $1/2$
teaspoon crème fraîche. Serves 12
(serving size: 2 tarts)

CALORIES 180; FAT 11.2g (sat 4.5g, mono 4g, poly 1.5g);
PROTEIN 1.7g; CARB 18.8g; FIBER 0.9g; CHOL 17mg;
IRON 0.6mg; SODIUM 100mg; CALC 9mg

PURE COMFORT CASSEROLES

New-timey flavors for old-timey satisfactions

Kid Friendly • Make Ahead

Mushroom and Bacon Casserole

Hands-on: 35 min. Total: 65 min.

4 cups unsalted beef stock (such as
    Swanson)
3 cups water
8 center-cut bacon slices, chopped
1 cup chopped onion
1 tablespoon chopped fresh thyme
6 garlic cloves, minced
8 ounces sliced cremini mushrooms
8 ounces sliced shiitake mushroom caps
$1/2$ teaspoon kosher salt
2 cups uncooked pearl barley
$1/3$ cup Madeira wine
4 ounces Gruyère cheese, shredded
    (about 1 cup), divided
$1/2$ cup chopped drained oil-packed
    sun-dried tomato halves
2 teaspoons lower-sodium soy sauce
$1/4$ teaspoon black pepper
1 (10-ounce) package frozen chopped
    spinach, thawed, drained, and
    squeezed dry
Cooking spray

1. Preheat oven to 375°.
2. Bring stock and 3 cups water to a
simmer in a large saucepan (do not
boil). Keep mixture warm.

3. Cook bacon in a Dutch oven over
medium-high heat until crisp. Remove bacon from pan, reserving 1
tablespoon drippings in pan; set bacon
aside. Return pan to medium-high
heat. Add onion, thyme, and garlic to
drippings in pan; sauté 3 minutes or
until tender. Add mushrooms and salt;
cook 10 minutes or until browned, stirring occasionally. Stir in barley; cook
1 minute, stirring frequently. Add
Madeira; cook 1 minute or until liquid
is absorbed. Reduce heat to medium.
Stir in 2 cups broth mixture; cook
4 minutes or until the liquid is nearly
absorbed, stirring frequently. Add
remaining broth mixture, 1 cup at a
time, stirring frequently until each
portion of broth mixture is absorbed
before adding the next (about 30 minutes total). Stir in 2 ounces Gruyère,
tomatoes, soy sauce, pepper, spinach,
and bacon. Place barley mixture in a
2-quart glass or ceramic baking dish
coated with cooking spray; sprinkle
with cheese. Cover with aluminum
foil coated with cooking spray. Bake at
375° for 15 minutes. Remove foil, and
bake 10 minutes or until cheese melts.
Let stand 5 minutes. Serves 8 (serving
size: about 1 cup)

CALORIES 352; FAT 10.2g (sat 4.3g, mono 2.8g, poly 1g);
PROTEIN 16g; CARB 49.1g; FIBER 10.3g; CHOL 24mg;
IRON 2.7mg; SODIUM 435mg; CALC 220mg

Lamb Tagine Shepherd's Pie

Hands-on: 40 min. Total: 1 hr. 34 min.
Classic shepherd's pie gets a Moroccan up-date with heady, aromatic spices in the filling and a garlicky whipped chickpea topping in place of the usual mashed potatoes.

5 teaspoons extra-virgin olive oil, divided
1½ pounds lean boneless leg of lamb, trimmed and cut into bite-sized pieces
1 cup chopped onion
1 cup chopped carrot
1½ teaspoons kosher salt, divided
4 teaspoons minced fresh garlic
1 tablespoon tomato paste
1 teaspoon ground turmeric
¼ teaspoon ground cumin
¼ teaspoon ground cinnamon
¼ teaspoon ground red pepper
½ cup red wine
1½ cups unsalted chicken stock
¼ cup dried apricots, chopped
¼ cup golden raisins
2 tablespoons chopped fresh cilantro
2 tablespoons fresh lemon juice, divided
2 tablespoons unsalted chicken stock
2 garlic cloves
1 (15-ounce) can unsalted chickpeas, rinsed and drained
Cooking spray

1. Heat a Dutch oven over medium-high heat. Add 2 teaspoons oil to pan; swirl to coat. Add half of lamb to pan; cook 4 minutes or until browned, stirring occasionally. Remove lamb from pan. Repeat procedure with remaining lamb. Add onion and carrot to pan, and sauté 3 minutes. Stir in 1¼ teaspoons salt, 4 teaspoons garlic, and next 5 ingredients (through red pepper); sauté 30 seconds. Stir in wine; cook 1 minute, scraping pan to loosen browned bits. Stir in lamb, 1½ cups chicken stock, apricots, and raisins. Bring to a simmer; cover, reduce heat to low, and simmer 30 minutes. Stir in chopped cilantro and 1 tablespoon juice.
2. Preheat oven to 350°.
3. Place 1 tablespoon olive oil, 1 tablespoon lemon juice, ¼ teaspoon salt, 2 tablespoons chicken stock, 2 garlic cloves, and chickpeas in a mini food processor; process until smooth. Spoon ⅔ cup lamb mixture into each of 6 (7-ounce) ramekins. Top each serving with about 3 tablespoons chickpea mixture. Lightly coat chickpea mixture with cooking spray. Place ramekins on a baking sheet. Bake at 350° for 30 minutes or until tops begin to brown. Serves 6

CALORIES 373; FAT 17.5g (sat 6.1g, mono 8.1g, poly 1.5g); PROTEIN 26.6g; CARB 23.8g; FIBER 3.8g; CHOL 76mg; IRON 3.4mg; SODIUM 632mg; CALC 68mg

Kid Friendly • Make Ahead

Spanish Chicken and Rice with Saffron Cream

Hands-on: 40 min. Total: 65 min. *This rich, creamy twist on traditional chicken paella gets an alluring Spanish accent from smoky cured chorizo and the unmistakable fragrance and flavor of saffron.*

1 tablespoon extra-virgin olive oil, divided
1½ pounds skinless, boneless chicken thighs, cut into bite-sized pieces
1 cup chopped white onion
2 ounces cured Spanish chorizo sausage, diced
4 garlic cloves, minced
1 large red bell pepper, chopped
3 cups hot cooked long-grain white rice
1 cup frozen green peas, thawed
16 pimiento-stuffed green olives, chopped
1½ cups 2% reduced-fat milk
¼ cup tomato paste
2 tablespoons all-purpose flour
½ teaspoon kosher salt
¼ teaspoon saffron threads, lightly crushed
¼ teaspoon freshly ground black pepper
⅓ cup sour cream
Cooking spray

1. Preheat oven to 375°.
2. Heat a large nonstick skillet over medium-high heat. Add 1 teaspoon oil to pan; swirl to coat. Add half of chicken; cook 4 minutes, turning to brown on all sides. Remove chicken from pan; place in a large bowl. Repeat procedure with 1 teaspoon oil and remaining chicken. Add to bowl. Place 1 teaspoon oil, onion, and chorizo in pan; cook 10 minutes or until onion is tender and golden, stirring occasionally. Add garlic and bell pepper; cook 2 minutes, stirring frequently. Add chorizo mixture, cooked rice, peas, and olives to chicken; toss to combine.
3. Combine milk and next 5 ingredients (through black pepper) in a medium saucepan over medium heat; stir well with a whisk. Cook, stirring constantly, until mixture comes to a boil; cook 1 minute or until thick and bubbly. Remove pan from heat; stir in sour cream. Add sour cream mixture to chicken mixture, stirring to combine. Spoon chicken mixture into an 11 x 7–inch glass or ceramic baking dish coated with cooking spray. Cover with aluminum foil coated with cooking spray. Bake at 375° for 15 minutes. Uncover and bake an additional 10 minutes or until chicken is done. Serves 8 (serving size: about 1 cup)

CALORIES 325; FAT 12.2g (sat 3.7g, mono 5.1g, poly 2.1g); PROTEIN 23.3g; CARB 28.9g; FIBER 2.2g; CHOL 95mg; IRON 2.3mg; SODIUM 556mg; CALC 94mg

CLASSIC PAELLA FLAVORS IN A NO-FUSS, CREAMY, ONE-DISH MEAL

Make Ahead • Vegetarian

Lasagna with Grape Tomatoes and Broccoli Rabe

Hands-on: 35 min. Total: 1 hr. 25 min.
"Fresh" is a word not often associated with lasagna, yet that's exactly the sensation this one offers. Sweet-as-candy grape tomatoes burst and release their moisture and flavor, while earthy-bitter broccoli rabe and milder Broccolini balance the taste.

1 (1-pound) bunch broccoli rabe, trimmed
1 (8-ounce) bunch Broccolini, trimmed
2 1/2 tablespoons extra-virgin olive oil, divided
1 1/2 cups chopped onion, divided
10 garlic cloves, thinly sliced and divided
1/4 cup dry white wine
4 cups grape tomatoes
3/4 teaspoon kosher salt, divided
1/4 teaspoon crushed red pepper
1/2 cup chopped fresh basil, divided
1 (15-ounce) carton part-skim ricotta cheese
1 cup lower-sodium marinara sauce (such as Dell'Amore)
Cooking spray
9 cooked lasagna noodles
3 ounces part-skim mozzarella cheese, shredded (about 3/4 cup)

1. Bring a large pot of water to a boil. Add broccoli rabe and Broccolini, and cook 2 minutes. Drain and rinse vegetables under cold water; drain. Coarsely chop.
2. Preheat oven to 350°.
3. Heat a large nonstick skillet over medium-high heat. Add 1 tablespoon oil; swirl to coat. Add 3/4 cup onion and 5 garlic cloves; cook 2 minutes, stirring occasionally. Add wine; cook 1 minute. Add grape tomatoes and 1/4 teaspoon salt; cook 12 minutes or until skins split and tomatoes start to release their juices, stirring frequently. Place tomato mixture in a bowl.
4. Wipe pan dry with paper towels. Return pan to medium-high heat. Add 1 1/2 tablespoons oil; swirl to coat. Add 3/4 cup onion, remaining 5 garlic cloves, and red pepper; sauté 4 minutes. Stir in broccoli rabe mixture and 1/4 teaspoon salt; cook 3 minutes. Remove from heat.
5. Combine 1/4 cup basil, ricotta, and 1/4 teaspoon salt in a bowl. Spread 1/2 cup marinara sauce in bottom of a 13 x 9–inch glass or ceramic baking dish coated with cooking spray. Arrange 3 lasagna noodles over sauce. Spread half of ricotta mixture over noodles. Top with half of broccoli rabe mixture; spoon half of tomato mixture over broccoli rabe mixture. Repeat layers with remaining noodles, ricotta mixture, broccoli rabe mixture, and tomato mixture, ending with noodles. Top with remaining 1/2 cup marinara, and sprinkle with mozzarella. Cover with aluminum foil coated with cooking spray. Bake at 350° for 30 minutes. Uncover and bake for an additional 15 minutes or until top is lightly browned. Remove lasagna from oven, and sprinkle with 1/4 cup chopped basil. Let stand 10 minutes before serving. Serves 8

CALORIES 319; FAT 12g (sat 4.4g, mono 4.8g, poly 0.7g); PROTEIN 17.1g; CARB 35g; FIBER 3.6g; CHOL 22mg; IRON 1.5mg; SODIUM 417mg; CALC 319mg

Kid Friendly • Make Ahead

Turkey Posole Casserole with Cornmeal Biscuit Topping

Hands-on: 24 min. Total: 52 min. *The casserole is a cross between tamale pie, posole, and—somehow—chicken and dumplings. It's a great use for leftover holiday turkey, taking the flavors south of the border for a welcome break from the Thanksgiving palate. You can also use rotisserie chicken in place of turkey.*

Filling:
1 cup unsalted chicken stock
1 pound tomatillos, husks removed and quartered
1 tablespoon canola oil
2 cups chopped onion
6 garlic cloves, minced
1 large poblano pepper, seeded and chopped
1 teaspoon ground cumin
3/4 teaspoon kosher salt
2 (15-ounce) cans white hominy, rinsed and drained
2 tablespoons finely ground yellow cornmeal
3 cups shredded cooked skinless, boneless dark- and light-meat turkey
1/2 cup chopped fresh cilantro
Cooking spray
Topping:
5.63 ounces unbleached all-purpose flour (about 1 1/4 cups)
2/3 cup finely ground yellow cornmeal
1 1/2 teaspoons baking powder
1/4 teaspoon baking soda
1/4 teaspoon kosher salt
1/4 cup chilled butter, cut into small pieces
1/4 cup finely chopped green onions
3 ounces pepper-Jack cheese, shredded (about 3/4 cup)
1 1/4 cups fat-free buttermilk

continued

1. Preheat oven to 400°.
2. To prepare filling, place chicken stock and tomatillos in a blender; process until smooth. Set aside.
3. Heat a Dutch oven over medium-high heat. Add oil to pan; swirl to coat. Add onion, garlic, and poblano; sauté 5 minutes or until tender. Stir in cumin; sauté 30 seconds, stirring constantly. Add stock mixture, ¾ teaspoon salt, and hominy; bring to a simmer. Stir in 2 tablespoons cornmeal; simmer 1 minute or until thickened. Stir in turkey and cilantro. Pour into a 13 x 9–inch glass or ceramic baking dish coated with cooking spray.
4. To prepare topping, weigh or lightly spoon flour into dry measuring cups, and level with a knife. Combine flour and next 4 ingredients in a medium bowl. Cut in butter with a pastry blender or 2 knives until mixture resembles coarse meal. Stir in chopped green onions and pepper-Jack cheese. Add buttermilk; stir just until combined. Drop batter by 2 tablespoonfuls evenly over filling. Bake at 400° for 28 minutes or until topping is lightly browned. Serves 8

CALORIES 430; FAT 15g (sat 6.7g, mono 3.4g, poly 2.1g); PROTEIN 25g; CARB 47.7g; FIBER 4.6g; CHOL 67mg; IRON 3.3mg; SODIUM 699mg; CALC 196mg

A LITTLE BIT POSOLE, A LITTLE BIT CHICKEN AND DUMPLINGS, A TON OF HEARTY GOODNESS

7 SIMPLE WAYS TO BECOME A BETTER COOK

Recipes take you only so far. After that, instinct and experience must take over. We talked to some of our favorite experts to uncover easy ways to get you further down the path to kitchen fulfillment and control.

TRY ALL THE CUTS
Port-Stained Beef Medallions

Hands-on: 15 min. Total: 50 min.
In this recipe adapted from Keith Schroeder's upcoming book, Mad Delicious, *what may seem like a crazy technique for beef produces outstanding results.*

4 garlic cloves, minced
½ teaspoon kosher salt, divided
4 (4-ounce) beef tenderloin steaks, trimmed (about 1 inch thick)
2 cups port wine
1 tablespoon grated lemon rind
1 teaspoon smoked paprika
Cooking spray
½ cup canola mayonnaise (such as Hellmann's)
1 tablespoon minced seeded Fresno chile or jalapeño pepper
1 teaspoon fresh lemon juice
1 garlic clove, minced

1. Place 4 garlic cloves on a cutting board; sprinkle with ⅛ teaspoon salt. Chop until a paste forms, scraping with the flat side of a knife to mash.

Press garlic mixture into both sides of steaks. Refrigerate 30 minutes.
2. Bring wine to a boil in a saucepan over medium-high heat. Reduce heat to medium; simmer 10 minutes or until reduced to ½ cup. Stir in rind and paprika. Pour wine mixture into a pie plate or wide, shallow dish.
3. Line one tier of a 10-inch bamboo steamer with an 8-inch circle of parchment paper; lightly coat paper with cooking spray. Arrange steaks on top of paper in steamer basket. Cover with steamer lid. Add water to a large skillet to a depth of 1 inch; bring to a boil. Place steamer in pan; steam steaks 8 minutes or until desired degree of doneness. Remove steaks from steamer; place steaks in wine mixture for 10 minutes, turning after 5 minutes. Cut steaks across the grain into ½-inch-thick slices; sprinkle with ⅜ teaspoon salt.
4. Combine mayonnaise, chile, juice, and 1 garlic clove. Spread 2 tablespoons mayonnaise mixture on each of 4 plates. Top evenly with sliced steak and any remaining wine mixture. Serves 4

CALORIES 319; FAT 13.5g (sat 2.2g, mono 6.9g, poly 3.1g); PROTEIN 21.3g; CARB 9.7g; FIBER 0.5g; CHOL 59mg; IRON 1.6mg; SODIUM 503mg; CALC 27mg

SURPRISING TECHNIQUE PLAYS TO THE CUT: TENDERLOIN IS STEAMED FOR ULTRA-TENDERNESS, THEN "STAINED" TO MAKE IT LOOK ROASTED.

FIRE THINGS UP
Mexican Broiled Corn Salad

Hands-on: 45 min. Total: 45 min.

The broiler offers a fantastic way to give food the taste of fire, yet it's perhaps the most overlooked way of cooking. Here it brings alive the flavors of late-fall corn and peppers so they taste as good as at summer's peak. To help control the intense heat of a broiler, move foods closer to or farther away from the element—not just up or down the oven racks but also toward or away from the sides.

4 ears fresh corn, shucked
1 medium onion, cut into ¹/₂-inch-thick slices
2 red bell peppers
1 tablespoon chopped fresh oregano
¹/₂ teaspoon kosher salt, divided
1 cup grape tomatoes, halved
1 cup thinly sliced radishes
3¹/₂ tablespoons extra-virgin olive oil, divided
2 tablespoons chopped fresh cilantro
5 tablespoons pumpkinseed kernels, toasted and divided
1 tablespoon chopped jalapeño pepper
2 tablespoons fresh lime juice
1 tablespoon honey
1 teaspoon ground ancho chile powder
¹/₄ teaspoon ground cumin
2 garlic cloves, crushed
2.5 ounces cotija cheese, crumbled (about ²/₃ cup)

1. Preheat broiler to high.
2. Place corn and onion on a foil-lined baking sheet. Broil 4 inches from heat 15 minutes, turning occasionally. Cut bell peppers in half lengthwise; discard seeds and membranes. Place bell pepper halves, skin sides up, on baking sheet with corn and onion. Broil an additional 13 minutes or until all vegetables are charred in spots, turning corn and onion occasionally (do not turn bell peppers). Place bell peppers in a paper bag. Fold to close tightly; let stand 10 minutes. Peel and coarsely chop peppers. Cut kernels from ears of corn. Coarsely chop onion. Place bell peppers, corn, onion, oregano, and ¹/₈ teaspoon salt in a medium bowl; toss gently.
3. Combine ¹/₈ teaspoon salt, tomatoes, radishes, 1¹/₂ teaspoons oil, and cilantro in a medium bowl; toss to coat.
4. Place 2 tablespoons pumpkinseeds in a mini food processor; process until finely ground. Add ¹/₄ teaspoon salt, 3 tablespoons oil, jalapeño, and next 5 ingredients (through garlic); process until smooth.
5. Place ¹/₂ cup corn mixture in each of 8 shallow bowls, and top each serving with about 2 tablespoons tomato mixture, about 1 tablespoon dressing, about 1¹/₂ tablespoons cheese, and about 1 teaspoon pumpkinseeds. Serves 8

CALORIES 190; FAT 11.5g (sat 3g, mono 5.2g, poly 1g); PROTEIN 6g; CARB 18g; FIBER 2.8g; CHOL 9mg; IRON 0.8mg; SODIUM 333mg; CALC 144mg

USE ALL THE RIGHT METALS
Crispy Pork Stir-Fry with Baby Bok Choy

Hands-on: 30 min. Total: 30 min.

Hot! Hot! Hot! That is exactly how your wok should be before the food goes in so that you get the crispy, browned edges you want. Get the thinnest slices of meat by using a serrated knife to cut it or by freezing it for 30 minutes.

10 ounces very thinly sliced pork shoulder
1¹/₂ teaspoons dark sesame oil
¹/₂ teaspoon kosher salt
¹/₄ teaspoon white pepper
1 tablespoon canola oil
2 heads baby bok choy, quartered lengthwise
1¹/₂ cups (2-inch) pieces haricots verts (French green beans)
1 tablespoon finely chopped peeled fresh ginger
3 large garlic cloves, thinly sliced
1 red bell pepper, cut into thin strips
2 tablespoons rice vinegar
1 tablespoon lower-sodium soy sauce
2 teaspoons brown sugar
¹/₄ cup sliced green onions
2 cups hot cooked long-grain brown rice

1. Heat a large wok over high heat until very hot. Toss pork with sesame oil, salt, and pepper. Add pork to pan; let stand 2 minutes, without stirring, so that pork gets crispy and browned. Stir-fry pork 2 minutes or until well browned on all sides. Let stand 1 minute without stirring. Spoon pork into a bowl; set aside.
2. Reheat pan over high heat until very hot. Add canola oil; swirl to coat. Add bok choy; stir-fry 2 minutes. Add green beans, ginger, garlic, and bell pepper; stir-fry 3 minutes or until crisp-tender. Combine vinegar, soy sauce, and brown

continued

sugar, stirring until sugar dissolves. Remove pan from heat; stir in vinegar mixture, tossing to coat. Stir in pork. Sprinkle with green onions. Serve over rice. Serves 4 (serving size: about 1 cup stir-fry and ½ cup rice)

CALORIES 331; FAT 11.3g (sat 2.5g, mono 5.6g, poly 2.6g); PROTEIN 19.7g; CARB 39.1g; FIBER 9g; CHOL 47mg; IRON 2.3mg; SODIUM 463mg; CALC 107mg

HOW SEASONING ACTUALLY WORKS

Carbon steel pans hanging in restaurant kitchens have a black patina and worn quality that comes from thousands of uses during what food science professor and chemist Robert Wolke describes as the "wild life of a pan in the chaos of a restaurant kitchen." These are the seasoned veterans, the most beloved tools.

Seasoning is necessary because when cast iron and carbon steel are new, heated foods, especially proteins, grab on and won't let go. Seasoning involves heating oil until it breaks down into components that bond with the metal and create a nonstick surface. It's a lifetime process that creates a slick polymer coating that blackens with age.

The miracle is how slick these rough metals become, giving the cook access to the pan's full searing power with minimal added fat.

CALIBRATE YOURSELF
Pan-Seared Chicken Breast with Rich Pan Sauce

Hands-on: 17 min. Total: 35 min.
To calibrate yourself to be a better cook, learn to use all your senses throughout the process. For the richest sauce, use a stainless steel pan; the browned bits that stick to the bottom provide flavor.

4 (6-ounce) skinless, boneless chicken breast halves
$1/2$ teaspoon freshly ground black pepper, divided
$3/8$ teaspoon kosher salt, divided
4 teaspoons olive oil, divided
1 tablespoon grated onion
1 teaspoon minced fresh garlic
$1^1/2$ teaspoons all-purpose flour
$1/4$ cup dry white wine
$3/4$ cup unsalted chicken stock (such as Swanson)
1 tablespoon butter
$1/4$ teaspoon sugar
1 tablespoon chopped fresh flat-leaf parsley

1. Let chicken stand at room temperature 20 minutes. Sprinkle chicken with ¼ teaspoon pepper and ¼ teaspoon salt. Heat a large stainless steel skillet over medium-high heat. Add 1 tablespoon oil; swirl to coat. Add chicken to pan, rounded side down; cook 5 minutes. Turn chicken over; reduce heat to medium, and cook 5 minutes or until done. Remove chicken from pan; let stand 5 minutes.
2. Add 1 teaspoon oil, onion, and garlic to pan; sauté 1 minute. Add flour; sauté 30 seconds. Add wine to pan; cook 30 seconds or until liquid almost evaporates, stirring constantly. Stir in stock; bring to a boil, scraping pan to loosen browned bits. Reduce heat to medium-low; simmer 3 minutes or until reduced to ½ cup, stirring

occasionally. Remove pan from heat; stir in ¼ teaspoon pepper, ⅛ teaspoon salt, butter, and sugar. Sprinkle with parsley. Serves 4 (serving size: 1 breast half and 2 tablespoons sauce)

CALORIES 283; FAT 11.8g (sat 3.4g, mono 5.3g, poly 1.3g); PROTEIN 37.3g; CARB 2.2g; FIBER 0.2g; CHOL 116mg; IRON 0.9mg; SODIUM 428mg; CALC 18mg

A WELL CALIBRATED CHICKEN BREAST

If we had to place a bet on the food mostly likely to be overcooked in American home kitchens, it would be the humble skinless, boneless chicken breast. These are the few simple steps to producing a juicy, chickeny, tender beauty.

1 Pat breast dry and get the chill off. Heat pan to medium-hot, and add oil, which should ripple and sputter as the meat goes in.

2 Flip breast when white-pink "protein line" is halfway up. Finish cooking. Probe for 162°. Remove, and let rest 5 minutes; temp should reach 165°.

THE IMPATIENT BAKER WRECKS TEXTURE, AND TEXTURE IS EVERYTHING TO A CAKE. WHIP EGG WHITES TOO FAST, STIR INSTEAD OF FOLD, AND YOU GET A COARSE, HOLE-FILLED CRUMB.

PATIENCE, PATIENCE
Vanilla Angel Food Cake with Chocolate Sauce

Hands-on: 40 min. Total: 1 hr. 30 min.
Here's a recipe that demonstrates the need for (and rewards of) patience. When you whip egg whites slowly—first at medium-low and building up speed gradually—you end up with the softest, creamiest, fluffiest mixture, into which you need to patiently and gradually fold flour.

Cake:
4 ounces unsifted cake flour (about 1 cup)
1¹/₂ cups superfine sugar, divided
12 large egg whites, at room temperature
1 teaspoon cream of tartar
¹/₄ teaspoon salt
1¹/₂ teaspoons vanilla extract

Sauce:
³/₄ cup whole milk
¹/₄ cup half-and-half
¹/₄ cup granulated sugar, divided
Dash of salt
2 ounces bittersweet chocolate, finely chopped
1 teaspoon cornstarch
1 large egg yolk
¹/₄ teaspoon vanilla extract

1. Preheat oven to 350°.
2. To prepare cake, weigh or lightly spoon flour into a dry measuring cup; level with a knife. Sift together flour and ¾ cup superfine sugar.
3. Place egg whites in a large bowl; beat with a mixer at medium-low speed until foamy (about 1½ minutes). Add cream of tartar and salt; beat at medium speed until soft peaks form (about 2 minutes). Increase mixer speed to medium-high; add ¾ cup superfine sugar, 1 tablespoon at a time, beating until medium peaks form (about 2 minutes). Do not overbeat. Add 1½ teaspoons vanilla, and beat just until combined.
4. Sift ¼ cup flour mixture over egg white mixture; gently and gradually fold in. Repeat procedure with remaining flour mixture, ¼ cup at a time.
5. Spoon batter into an ungreased 10-inch tube pan, spreading evenly. Bake at 350° for 40 minutes or until cake springs back when lightly touched. Invert pan over the neck of a glass bottle; cool cake completely. Loosen cake from sides of pan using a narrow metal spatula. Invert cake onto plate; invert again.
6. To prepare sauce, pour milk and half-and-half into a small heavy saucepan; add 2 tablespoons granulated sugar, dash of salt, and chocolate. Heat milk mixture over medium heat to 180° or until tiny bubbles form around edge, stirring until chocolate melts and mixture is smooth (do not boil). Place 2 tablespoons granulated sugar, cornstarch, and egg yolk in a medium bowl; stir well with a whisk. Gradually add hot milk mixture to egg mixture, stirring constantly with a whisk. Return milk mixture to pan. Cook over medium-low heat until mixture boils, stirring constantly. Remove from heat. Stir in ¼ teaspoon vanilla. Serve cake with warm sauce. Serves 12 (serving size: 1 cake slice and about 1½ tablespoons sauce)

CALORIES 213; **FAT** 3.4g (sat 1.9g, mono 0.8g, poly 0.2g); **PROTEIN** 5.6g; **CARB** 41.3g; **FIBER** 0.6g; **CHOL** 19mg; **IRON** 1.2mg; **SODIUM** 125mg; **CALC** 31mg

DIG INTO PLANTS
Cauliflower Steaks with Maitake Mushrooms and Browned Butter-Caper Sauce

Hands-on: 23 min. Total: 45 min.
Nearly a full meal and absolutely satisfying—a knife-and-fork dish that highlights the vegetables.

2¹/₂ tablespoons butter, divided
1¹/₂ tablespoons canola oil
2 garlic cloves, crushed
2 cauliflower heads
2 maitake mushrooms
³/₄ teaspoon kosher salt, divided
¹/₂ teaspoon freshly ground black pepper, divided
3 cups 1% low-fat milk
¹/₂ cup water
²/₃ cup quick-cooking polenta
3 garlic cloves, thinly sliced
¹/₄ cup dry white wine
¹/₂ cup organic vegetable broth
1¹/₂ teaspoons all-purpose flour
1 tablespoon capers, chopped
1 teaspoon fresh lemon juice
2 teaspoons thyme leaves
Additional thyme leaves (optional)

continued

1. Place a jelly-roll pan in oven. Preheat oven to 450° (leave pan in oven).
2. Place 1½ teaspoons butter, oil, and crushed garlic in a small microwave-safe bowl. Microwave at MEDIUM (50% power) for 1 minute or until butter melts and garlic is fragrant. Cool slightly; discard garlic.
3. Carefully cut 2 (1-inch-thick) "steaks" vertically from center of each cauliflower head; reserve remaining cauliflower for another use. Carefully trim bottoms of maitakes, keeping the mushroom clumps intact. Carefully cut each maitake in half lengthwise. Brush tops of cauliflower steaks with oil mixture. Carefully place cauliflower steaks, oiled sides down, on preheated pan; brush tops of steaks with oil mixture.
Bake at 450° for 14 minutes or until bottoms are browned. Remove pan from oven; carefully turn cauliflower steaks over. Gently brush remaining oil mixture on both sides of maitake steaks; place on pan with cauliflower, cut sides down. Bake at 450° for 13 minutes or until cauliflower is browned and done. Remove from oven; sprinkle evenly with ¼ teaspoon salt and ¼ teaspoon pepper.

IT'S NOT ABOUT DISGUISING VEGETABLES AS MEAT. OTHER CULTURES—SUCH AS BURMA AND INDIA—GET THIS, SO LOOK TO THEIR TRADITIONS.

4. While cauliflower bakes, bring milk and ½ cup water to a simmer. Gradually add polenta, stirring constantly with a whisk. Cook 3 minutes or until thick, stirring constantly. Stir in ½ teaspoon salt. Cover and keep warm.
5. Melt remaining 2 tablespoons butter in a medium skillet over medium heat; cook 3 minutes or until browned and very fragrant. Add sliced garlic; cook 45 seconds, stirring frequently. Add wine; increase heat to medium high, and cook 1 minute or until about half of liquid evaporates. Combine broth and flour, stirring with a whisk. Add broth mixture to pan; bring to a boil. Cook 1 minute or until slightly thickened, stirring constantly; stir in capers, juice, thyme, and ¼ teaspoon pepper. Spoon about ¾ cup polenta on each of 4 plates. Top each serving with 1 cauliflower steak, 1 maitake steak, and about 2 tablespoons sauce. Garnish with thyme, if desired. Serves 4

CALORIES 372; **FAT** 14.8g (sat 6.2g, mono 5.7g, poly 1.9g); **PROTEIN** 13.4g; **CARB** 47.2g; **FIBER** 7.5g; **CHOL** 28mg; **IRON** 1.6mg; **SODIUM** 688mg; **CALC** 277mg

BE MINDFUL IN THE KITCHEN
Mushroom and Roasted Garlic Risotto

Hands-on: 60 min. Total: 1 hr. 25 min.
Risotto is a "high-mindfulness" recipe, one demanding the full attention of the cook. But here's a secret, one that restaurant cooks know: You can hit "pause" for up to a day. In step 4, after 10 to 15 minutes of adding the broth and stirring, remove the risotto from the Dutch oven; spread it out into a casserole dish or jelly-roll pan so that it cools quickly. Store risotto and stock mixture separately in the fridge. Reheat the liquid, and proceed with cooking as if you'd never stopped.

2 whole garlic heads
2 tablespoons plus 2 teaspoons extra-virgin olive oil, divided
½ cup plus 2 tablespoons Madeira, divided
5 cups unsalted chicken stock, divided
½ cup dried porcini mushrooms (½ ounce)
1¾ cups chopped onion
3 cups thinly sliced cremini mushrooms (about 8 ounces)
2½ cups thinly sliced shiitake mushroom caps (about 8 ounces)
1½ cups uncooked Arborio rice
2 ounces fresh Parmesan cheese, grated (about ½ cup)
1 teaspoon kosher salt
½ teaspoon freshly ground black pepper
2 tablespoons chopped fresh sage
Whole sage leaves (optional)

1. Preheat oven to 425°.
2. Cut the top off each garlic head; discard. Rub cut side of each garlic head with 1 teaspoon oil. Remove white papery skin from garlic heads (do not peel or separate the cloves). Wrap garlic in foil. Bake at 425° for 1 hour or until tender; cool 10 minutes. Separate cloves; squeeze to extract garlic pulp. Discard skins. Combine garlic pulp and 2 tablespoons Madeira in a bowl; mash with a fork.
3. Bring 1½ cups stock to a boil. Add porcini; let stand 30 minutes or until soft. Drain through a colander over a bowl, reserving soaking liquid; chop porcini. Combine porcini liquid and 3½ cups stock; bring to a simmer in a medium saucepan (do not boil). Keep warm.
4. Heat a Dutch oven over medium heat. Add 2 tablespoons oil; swirl to coat. Add onion to pan; sauté 5 minutes or until tender. Add cremini and shiitake mushrooms; cook 5 minutes or until browned, stirring occasionally. Stir in porcini. Add rice; sauté

1 minute, stirring constantly. Add ½ cup Madeira; cook 1 minute or until liquid is absorbed. Stir in 1½ cups stock; cook 4 minutes or until liquid is nearly absorbed, stirring constantly. Add remaining stock, ¾ cup at a time, stirring constantly until each portion of stock is absorbed before adding the next (about 25 minutes total). Reserve ⅓ cup stock from the last addition. Remove pan from heat; stir in garlic mixture, reserved stock, cheese, salt, pepper, and chopped sage. Spoon into shallow bowls. Garnish with sage leaves, if desired. Serves 6 (serving size: about 1 cup)

CALORIES 381; FAT 9.4g (sat 2.5g, mono 5.1g, poly 0.8g); PROTEIN 15.7g; CARB 54.1g; FIBER 4.4g; CHOL 6mg; IRON 1.7mg; SODIUM 589mg; CALC 169mg

EVERY DISH HAS ITS OWN STORY, ITS OWN FLAVOR ARC, AND YOU DIRECT IT. THE MINDFUL COOK KNOWS HOW TO BUY TIME, INTERRUPT THE COOKING.

TODAY'S SPECIAL

GRAPEFRUIT GRANITA

From Myers + Chang in Boston

Fresh citrus is nature's winter gift to cooks: It's a foolproof way to brighten up the heartier cooking the season demands. Even light, bold-flavored fare can benefit from a fruity spritz. Joanne Chang, the celebrated pastry chef and owner of Boston's renowned Flour Bakery + Café locations, finds that citrus—and grapefruit in particular—harmonizes especially well with Asian food at her Myers + Chang restaurant.

Grapefruit occupies the perfect middle ground between sweeter citrus, such as tangerines, and aggressively acidic fruit, like lemons.

"Our food has a lot of spicy, strong, and punchy flavors," Chang says. "I think grapefruit goes well with a lot of things because it's not an extreme flavor. I think it's an underappreciated fruit, and it's so adaptable because it's so balanced." Chang uses it in savory dishes, such as a tamarind-glazed hake with mint, jicama, and grapefruit salad, to add a burst of fresh sweet-tart juice to the mix.

Grapefruit also makes a great base for desserts that are light and refreshing, like the Grapefruit Granita featured here.

To complement the fluffy granita, Chang gently poaches pears in honey-and-vanilla-infused liquid, and then tops the dish with pomegranate arils and mint. Our version honors that flavor combo with a simpler treatment that blends fresh pear and grapefruit into a pomegranate-studded relish.

Try Chang's original dish this month at Myers + Chang in Boston's South End.

Freezable • Make Ahead

Grapefruit Granita with Pear-and-Pom Relish

Hands-on: 15 min. Total: 8 hr. 55 min.

4 cups fresh grapefruit juice (about 6 grapefruit)
6 tablespoons sugar
¼ teaspoon salt, divided
2 Bosc pears, peeled and diced
½ cup pomegranate arils
1 red grapefruit, sectioned and coarsely chopped
8 mint leaves, thinly sliced

1. Combine juice, sugar, and ⅛ teaspoon salt in a bowl; stir until sugar dissolves. Pour juice mixture into an 11 x 7–inch glass or ceramic baking dish; cover and freeze overnight.
2. Let granita stand at room temperature 30 minutes; scrape with a fork.
3. Combine ⅛ teaspoon salt, pear, and remaining ingredients in a medium bowl; let stand 10 minutes. Divide granita evenly among 8 bowls; top evenly with pear mixture. Serves 8 (serving size: about 1½ cups granita and about ⅓ cup relish)

CALORIES 136; FAT 0.2g (sat 0g, mono 0.1g, poly 0.1g); PROTEIN 1g; CARB 34g; FIBER 1.9g; CHOL 0mg; IRON 0.3mg; SODIUM 62mg; CALC 26mg

SOULFUL FLAVORS OF THE WINTER GARDEN

Let the bright colors and earthy flavors from a good produce market inspire your cooking—just as our winter harvest inspired us.

Beef Tenderloin, Swiss Chard, and Caramelized Fennel Tacos

Hands-on: 50 min. Total: 50 min. *The chard makes a wonderful peppery, lightly bitter complement to the sweet fennel. Look for crema Mexicana in the supermarket dairy section, or substitute crème fraîche.*

2 teaspoons olive oil
2 cups thinly sliced fennel
1 cup thinly sliced onion
1/2 teaspoon salt, divided
1/2 teaspoon freshly ground black pepper, divided
1/8 teaspoon ground white pepper
1/8 teaspoon ground coriander
1/8 teaspoon ground red pepper
1 (12-ounce) beef tenderloin steak
Cooking spray
2 cups thinly sliced Swiss chard
1 teaspoon fresh lemon juice
8 fresh corn tortillas (such as El Milagro)
8 teaspoons crema Mexicana

1. Heat a large skillet over medium heat. Add oil to pan; swirl to coat. Add fennel, onion, 1/4 teaspoon salt, and 1/4 teaspoon black pepper; cook 5 minutes or until tender, stirring occasionally. Cover; cook over low heat 10 minutes or until fennel mixture begins to brown, stirring occasionally. Uncover; cook 10 minutes or until mixture is golden and caramelized. Remove from pan; keep warm.
2. Combine 1/4 teaspoon salt, 1/4 teaspoon black pepper, white pepper, coriander, and red pepper in a small bowl. Rub mixture evenly over beef. Wipe skillet clean with a paper towel; return skillet to medium-high heat. Lightly coat beef with cooking spray; add to pan. Cook 4 minutes on each side or until desired degree of doneness. Let stand 5 minutes; thinly slice.
3. Combine Swiss chard and lemon juice, tossing to coat.
4. Working with 1 tortilla at a time, toast tortillas in a pan or over the flame of a gas burner until tender and blackened in spots. Arrange 1/4 cup chard mixture in center of 1 tortilla; top with about 1 ounce beef and 2 tablespoons fennel mixture. Repeat with remaining tortillas, chard mixture, beef, and fennel mixture. Top each with 1 teaspoon crema. Serves 4 (serving size: 2 tacos)

CALORIES 315; **FAT** 10.9g (sat 2.6g, mono 4.2g, poly 1.1g); **PROTEIN** 23.4g; **CARB** 31.8g; **FIBER** 5g; **CHOL** 61mg; **IRON** 2.8mg; **SODIUM** 455mg; **CALC** 150mg

Fizz Kale Salad with Roasted Garlic-Bacon Dressing and Beets

Hands-on: 20 min. Total: 1 hr. 20 min. *Fizz kale boasts delicate cabbage flavor and hearty crunch. If Fizz is unavailable, the salad will still be delicious using all Lacinato.*

1 whole garlic head
6 ounces baby yellow beets
6 ounces baby red beets
6 ounces baby striped beets (such as Chioggia)
3 tablespoons extra-virgin olive oil
1 tablespoon water
1 tablespoon heavy cream
1 1/2 teaspoons fresh lemon juice
1 teaspoon red wine vinegar
1/4 teaspoon kosher salt
1/4 teaspoon freshly ground black pepper
4 cups Fizz kale, torn
4 cups Lacinato kale, torn
1 thick applewood-smoked bacon slice, chopped

1. Preheat oven to 350°.
2. Remove white papery skin from garlic head (do not peel or separate cloves). Wrap head in foil. Arrange yellow beets on a large sheet of foil; wrap tightly. Repeat procedure with red and striped beets. Bake garlic and beets at 350° for 1 hour or until beets are tender; cool 10 minutes. Separate garlic cloves; squeeze to extract garlic pulp. Discard skins. Combine garlic pulp, oil, and next 6 ingredients (through pepper) in a small bowl, stirring with a whisk. Place kale in a large bowl.
3. Heat a medium skillet over medium heat; add bacon. Cook 5 minutes or until crisp, stirring occasionally. Increase heat to high. Stir in garlic mixture; remove from heat. Pour hot bacon mixture over kale, tossing to coat.

4. Peel beets; discard skins. Cut beets in half. Arrange over kale mixture. Serves 6 (serving size: 1 cup)

CALORIES 149; FAT 9.2g (sat 1.9g, mono 5.3g, poly 1.1g); PROTEIN 4.6g; CARB 15g; FIBER 3.1g; CHOL 5mg; IRON 2mg; SODIUM 189mg; CALC 140mg

Gardener's Pie

Hands-on: 45 min. Total: 10 hr.

8 ounces dried black-eyed peas
2 tablespoons olive oil, divided
3/4 cup chopped onion
1/2 cup chopped peeled celery root
1/3 cup chopped carrot
3 cups water
1 bay leaf
1 cup chopped peeled turnip
5 garlic cloves, minced
1 pound turnip greens, coarsely chopped
1/2 teaspoon kosher salt
1 cup unsalted chicken stock (such as Swanson)
1 teaspoon brown sugar
1 teaspoon cider vinegar
Cooking spray
1 1/2 pounds Yukon gold potatoes, peeled and thinly sliced
1/4 teaspoon salt
2 ounces Gruyère cheese, shredded (about 1/2 cup)
1/4 cup heavy cream

1. Sort and wash peas; place in a large Dutch oven. Cover with water to 2 inches above peas; cover and let stand 8 hours. Drain peas.
2. Heat a large saucepan over medium-high heat. Add 1 tablespoon oil; swirl. Add onion, celery root, and carrot; sauté 5 minutes or until onion begins to brown. Add peas, 3 cups water, and bay leaf; bring to a boil. Reduce heat, and simmer 1 hour and 15 minutes or until peas are tender. Discard bay leaf.
3. Heat a large Dutch oven over medium-high heat. Add 1 tablespoon oil; swirl to coat. Add turnip; sauté 3 minutes or until edges begin to brown.

Add garlic; sauté 1 minute. Stir in greens and 1/2 teaspoon kosher salt; sauté 1 minute. Add stock; stir until greens wilt. Cook 15 minutes or until greens are very tender. Remove from heat; stir in sugar and vinegar.
4. Preheat oven to 350°.
5. Lightly coat 6 (8-ounce) ramekins with cooking spray. Using a slotted spoon, spoon peas into prepared dishes. Top evenly with greens mixture. Layer potatoes evenly over greens; sprinkle with 1/4 teaspoon salt and cheese. Drizzle with cream. Bake at 350° for 1 hour or until potatoes are tender and cheese is golden. Serves 6 (serving size: about 1 cup)

CALORIES 389; FAT 12.3g (sat 5g, mono 5.4g, poly 1.2g); PROTEIN 17.1g; CARB 55.9g; FIBER 9.1g; CHOL 24mg; IRON 5.3mg; SODIUM 391mg; CALC 330mg

Quick & Easy

Cauliflower Soup with Shiitakes

Hands-on: 35 min. Total: 35 min. Pureed cauliflower creates a wonderfully creamy soup; meaty shiitakes add textural flair.

4 teaspoons extra-virgin olive oil, divided
3/4 cup thinly sliced leek, white and light green parts only
3/8 teaspoon kosher salt, divided
4 cups coarsely chopped cauliflower florets (about 1 medium head)
1 1/2 cups unsalted chicken stock (such as Swanson), divided
3/4 cup water
2 teaspoons chopped fresh thyme
1/4 cup 2% reduced-fat milk
1 1/2 teaspoons butter
1/4 teaspoon white pepper
1 (3.5-ounce) package shiitake mushroom caps
1 teaspoon lower-sodium Worcestershire sauce
1 teaspoon sherry vinegar
2 teaspoons chopped fresh parsley

1. Heat a large saucepan over high heat. Add 2 teaspoons oil to pan; swirl to coat. Add leek; sauté 1 minute. Add 1/8 teaspoon salt. Cover, reduce heat to low, and cook 5 minutes or until leeks are softened, stirring occasionally. Add cauliflower, 1 cup and 6 tablespoons stock, 3/4 cup water, and thyme. Bring to a boil; cover, reduce heat, and simmer 7 minutes or until cauliflower is very tender. Place cauliflower mixture in a blender. Remove center piece of blender lid (to allow steam to escape); secure blender lid on blender. Place a clean towel over opening in blender lid (to avoid splatters). Blend until smooth. Return to saucepan. Stir in 1/4 teaspoon salt, milk, butter, and pepper. Keep warm.
2. Thinly slice mushroom caps. Heat a large skillet over medium-high heat. Add remaining 2 teaspoons oil to pan, and swirl to coat. Add mushrooms; sauté 6 minutes or until browned. Add 2 tablespoons stock, Worcestershire sauce, and sherry vinegar. Cook 1 minute or until liquid is reduced and syrupy.
3. Spoon about 1 cup soup into each of 4 bowls. Top each serving with about 2 tablespoons mushroom mixture. Sprinkle evenly with parsley. Serves 4

CALORIES 113; FAT 6.7g (sat 1.8g, mono 3.8g, poly 0.6g); PROTEIN 5.5g; CARB 10.1g; FIBER 2.8g; CHOL 5mg; IRON 1.2mg; SODIUM 357mg; CALC 63mg

Quick & Easy

Roasted Broccoli with Garlic and Anchovy

Hands-on: 7 min. Total: 24 min.

6 cups broccoli florets (about 1 bunch)
2 tablespoons extra-virgin olive oil, divided
3 garlic cloves, minced
1 1/2 tablespoons butter, melted
2 teaspoons chopped fresh thyme
2 teaspoons grated lemon rind
3/4 teaspoon crushed red pepper
2 anchovy fillets, drained and minced
1/4 teaspoon kosher salt

1. Preheat oven to 450°.
2. Combine broccoli and 1 tablespoon oil in a large bowl; toss to coat. Place broccoli on a foil-lined baking sheet. Bake at 450° for 6 minutes. Remove from oven; toss with garlic. Bake at 450° for an additional 6 minutes.
3. Place 1 tablespoon oil, butter, and next 4 ingredients (through anchovy) in a large bowl; stir to combine. Add broccoli mixture; toss well to coat. Sprinkle with salt. Serves 6 (serving size: about 2/3 cup)

CALORIES 83; **FAT** 6.9g (sat 1.9g, mono 3.9g, poly 0.7g); **PROTEIN** 2.7g; **CARB** 4.5g; **FIBER** 2.3g; **CHOL** 6mg; **IRON** 0.8mg; **SODIUM** 165mg; **CALC** 43mg

Quick & Easy • Vegetarian

Cabbage with White Beans, Turnip, and Pecorino

Hands-on: 17 min. Total: 17 min. Pair this quick side with roast pork or chicken.

1 tablespoon extra-virgin olive oil
1 cup cubed peeled turnip
1 tablespoon chopped fresh thyme
1/4 cup thinly sliced shallots
3/8 teaspoon kosher salt, divided
1 (15-ounce) can unsalted white beans, rinsed and drained
4 cups thinly sliced green cabbage
1/4 cup water
1 tablespoon champagne vinegar
1/2 teaspoon freshly ground pepper
1 ounce pecorino Romano cheese, shaved (about 1/2 cup)

1. Heat a large nonstick skillet over medium-high heat. Add oil to pan; swirl to coat. Add turnip, thyme, shallots, and 1/8 teaspoon salt; sauté 2 minutes. Reduce heat to medium-low; cover and cook 6 minutes or until turnips are slightly tender, stirring occasionally. Increase heat to medium-high. Add beans; cook 2 minutes, stirring occasionally. Add 1/4 teaspoon salt, cabbage, 1/4 cup water, vinegar, and pepper; cook 1 minute or until cabbage is slightly wilted, stirring occasionally. Top evenly with cheese. Serves 4 (serving size: 1 cup)

CALORIES 136; **FAT** 6g (sat 2.3g, mono 2.5g, poly 0.4g); **PROTEIN** 6.1g; **CARB** 15.9g; **FIBER** 5.4g; **CHOL** 8mg; **IRON** 1.8mg; **SODIUM** 359mg; **CALC** 137mg

RECIPE MAKEOVER

A DANDIER DANISH

A gooey cream cheese pastry with less fat, half the sugar, and a touch of whole-grain goodness.

Nibbling away on a buttery, creamy, cheese–filled Danish is one of those delightful occasional splurges. The best are found in good pastry shops rather than supermarket cellophane, and many slices come in north of 400 calories due to the overload of butter, cream cheese, and sugar. Our goal was to enjoy Danish pleasure more often with a lighter treat that is still creamy, buttery, and good. If you're willing to invest a little time in the kitchen, you can comfortably do just that. Our pastry is fun to make and a great offering for hungry houseguests.

We start with a whole-grain-speckled yeast dough, sweetened with a touch of sugar and made tender with a little butter and light sour cream. It's more of a sweet bread than a pastry, really, which helps us cut out more than 2½ sticks of butter. Then comes the fun part: Roll out the dough, slather it with some lemon- and honey-infused low-fat ricotta and cream cheese, and weave it all together into a beautiful braid. We cut the glaze back to just a drizzle instead of a dousing, and add a sprinkle of toasted sliced almonds for a crunchy finish. This homemade 224-calorie breakfast treat will satisfy every bit of your café pastry cravings.

Cream Cheese Danish Braid

(pictured on page 235)

Hands-on: 52 min. Total: 3 hr. 37 min.
The Danish can be made the night before, through step 4. Cover, refrigerate overnight, and bring braid to room temperature before proceeding with step 5.

Sponge:
6 tablespoons very warm 1% low-fat milk (120° to 130°)
1 teaspoon sugar
1 package quick-rise yeast (about 2¼ teaspoons)
2 tablespoons unbleached all-purpose flour
Dough:
7.9 ounces unbleached all-purpose flour, divided (about 1¾ cups)
2.25 ounces whole-wheat pastry flour (about ½ cup)
¼ cup sugar
¼ cup light sour cream
3 tablespoons butter, softened
¾ teaspoon salt
1 teaspoon vanilla extract
1 large egg
Cooking spray
Filling:
4 ounces ⅓-less-fat cream cheese
⅓ cup part-skim ricotta cheese
2 tablespoons honey
2 teaspoons fresh lemon juice
Dash of salt
Remaining ingredients:
1 teaspoon water
1 large egg
⅓ cup powdered sugar
2 teaspoons 1% low-fat milk
2 tablespoons sliced almonds, toasted

1. To prepare sponge, combine first 4 ingredients in a medium bowl, stirring well with a whisk. Cover loosely with plastic wrap; let stand 15 minutes.

2. To prepare dough, weigh or lightly spoon 6.75 ounces (about 1½ cups) all-purpose flour and pastry flour into dry measuring cups; level with a knife. Combine ¼ cup sugar, sour cream, butter, salt, vanilla, 1 egg, and sponge in a large bowl; beat with a mixer at medium speed 1 minute or until well combined. Add flours; beat at low speed 3 minutes or until a soft dough forms. Turn dough out onto a lightly floured surface. Knead until smooth and elastic (about 4 minutes), adding remaining 1.15 ounces all-purpose flour, 1 tablespoon at a time, to prevent dough from sticking. Place dough in a large bowl coated with cooking spray. Cover and let rise in a warm place (85°), free from drafts, 1 hour and 15 minutes or until doubled in size. (Gently press two fingers into dough. If indention remains, dough has risen enough.)

3. To prepare filling, combine cream cheese and next 4 ingredients in a medium bowl; beat with a mixer at medium speed until smooth.

4. Punch dough down; roll dough into a 12 x 15–inch rectangle on lightly floured parchment paper. Spread cream cheese mixture down center of dough, leaving about a 5-inch border on each side and a 1-inch border at top and bottom of rectangle. Make 5-inch cuts about 1 inch apart on both sides of dough to meet filling using a sharp knife or kitchen shears. Remove 4 outer corner strips of dough from rectangle; discard. Fold top and bottom 1-inch portions of dough over filling. Fold strips over filling, alternating strips diagonally over filling. Press ends to seal. Transfer braid and parchment paper to a baking sheet. Cover and let rise 45 minutes.

5. Preheat oven to 375°. Combine 1 teaspoon water and 1 egg; stir with a whisk. Brush braid with egg mixture. Bake at 375° for 20 minutes or until golden. Cool on a wire rack 10 minutes.

6. Combine powdered sugar and 2 teaspoons milk in a bowl, stirring until smooth. Drizzle glaze over braid; sprinkle with nuts. Serves 12 (serving size: 1 slice)

CALORIES 224; FAT 7.9g (sat 4.1g, mono 2.3g, poly 0.6g); PROTEIN 6.3g; CARB 32.2g; FIBER 1.5g; CHOL 50mg; IRON 1.5mg; SODIUM 218mg; CALC 63mg

TRIM SUGAR AND FAT LIKE A PRO

HONEY
Lends a creamy, floral flavor to the filling. Its sweeter, denser consistency allows us to use less—saving 20 calories per serving over granulated sugar.

SOUR CREAM AND LESS BUTTER
We remove 2½ sticks of butter to save 10g sat fat per slice. Light sour cream adds fluffy goodness, and some butter keeps the dough tender.

POWDERED SUGAR GLAZE
Too much glaze can overpower with sweetness. Instead, we drizzle lightly and save 23 calories per slice by using nearly 1 cup less powdered sugar.

CLASSIC	MAKEOVER
415 calories per serving	224 calories per serving
24 grams total fat	7.9 grams total fat
14.3 grams saturated fat	4.1 grams saturated fat

MEATLESS MONDAYS

Quick & Easy • Vegetarian

Goat Cheese Polenta with Sautéed Kale

Hands-on: 25 min. Total: 25 min.

3¼ cups water, divided
1 thyme sprig
1 cup uncooked quick-cooking polenta
½ teaspoon kosher salt, divided
½ teaspoon black pepper, divided
2 ounces goat cheese, crumbled and divided
1 ounce ⅓-less-fat cream cheese, softened
1 large egg
Cooking spray
2 tablespoons olive oil, divided
¼ cup diced onion
½ teaspoon crushed red pepper
4 garlic cloves, thinly sliced
1 (8-ounce) package presliced cremini mushrooms
¼ cup dry white wine
6 cups chopped Lacinato kale (about 1 bunch)
2 tablespoons pine nuts, toasted

1. Bring 3 cups water and thyme to a boil in a medium saucepan. Gradually add polenta, ¼ teaspoon salt, and ¼ teaspoon black pepper. Reduce heat to medium; cook 6 minutes or until thick, stirring constantly. Discard thyme sprig. Combine 1 ounce goat cheese, cream cheese, and egg in a small bowl, stirring with a whisk until almost smooth. Add egg mixture to polenta, stirring to combine. Remove pan from heat. Line an 8-inch square glass or ceramic baking dish with plastic wrap, allowing plastic wrap to extend over edges of dish; coat plastic wrap with cooking spray. Spoon polenta into dish, spreading evenly. Cover and keep warm.
2. Heat a large skillet over medium heat. Add 1 tablespoon oil to pan; swirl to coat. Add onion, red pepper, garlic, and mushrooms; sauté 7 minutes or until tender. Add wine; cook 2 minutes or until slightly thickened. Remove mushroom mixture from pan; keep warm.
3. Return pan to medium heat. Add 1 tablespoon oil to pan; swirl to coat. Add ¼ cup water, kale, ¼ teaspoon salt, and ¼ teaspoon black pepper. Cover, reduce heat, and simmer 5 minutes or until tender.
4. Invert polenta onto a plate; remove plastic wrap. Cut into 4 squares. Cut each square into 2 triangles. Place 2 triangles on each of 4 plates; top with ½ cup mushroom mixture and ½ cup kale. Sprinkle 1 ounce goat cheese and pine nuts evenly over kale. Serves 4

CALORIES 378; FAT 17.1g (sat 4.6g, mono 7.3g, poly 3g); PROTEIN 13.9g; CARB 42.5g; FIBER 5.1g; CHOL 58mg; IRON 4.4mg; SODIUM 381mg; CALC 183mg

Vegetarian

Fall Vegetable Stew with Mint Pesto

Hands-on: 22 min. Total: 47 min. The fresh, herby pesto adds a pop of bright flavor to earthy root vegetables

8 cups water
1½ cups chopped seeded tomato
1 cup chopped onion
1 cup chopped parsnip
1 cup chopped leek
½ cup chopped carrot
½ cup chopped red potatoes (about 2 medium)
1½ teaspoons kosher salt
1 teaspoon freshly ground black pepper
4 thyme sprigs
2 (15-ounce) cans unsalted cannellini beans, rinsed and drained
2 cups (½-inch) cut green beans (about ½ pound)
¼ cup extra-virgin olive oil
4 garlic cloves, chopped
2 ounces vegetarian Parmesan cheese, grated (about ½ cup)
1½ ounces mint leaves (about 2 cups)
1 ounce basil leaves (about 2 cups)

1. Combine first 11 ingredients in a large saucepan over medium-high heat; bring to a boil. Reduce heat, and simmer 20 minutes. Stir in green beans; cook 10 minutes or until tender.
2. Place oil and remaining ingredients in a food processor; process until smooth. Ladle 1¾ cups soup into each of 8 bowls; top each serving with 1½ tablespoons pesto. Serve immediately. Serves 8

CALORIES 217; FAT 9.4g (sat 2.3g, mono 5.6g, poly 1g); PROTEIN 9.2g; CARB 26.2g; FIBER 6.4g; CHOL 6mg; IRON 3.4mg; SODIUM 489mg; CALC 193mg

Quick & Easy • Vegetarian

Comice Pear and Endive Salad

Combine 1½ tablespoons olive oil, 1 tablespoon white wine vinegar, 1 teaspoon chopped fresh thyme, ¼ teaspoon Dijon mustard, ¼ teaspoon honey, and ⅛ teaspoon salt in a bowl, stirring with a whisk. Combine 4 cups mixed salad greens, 2 cups thinly sliced Comice pear, 1 cup thinly sliced Belgian endive, and ¼ cup chopped toasted walnuts in a large bowl. Drizzle vinaigrette over salad mixture; toss to coat. Sprinkle with 1 ounce crumbled blue cheese. Serves 4 (serving size: 1½ cups)

CALORIES 144; FAT 4.7g (sat 0.7g); SODIUM 107mg

MORE PIEROGIES, PLEASE

By Matisse Reid

"This week, I made cheddar and potato pierogies. I was so excited to try this recipe because it reminded me of where I used to live in Pittsburgh. I love baseball, and the Pittsburgh Pirates always have people dressed up as giant pierogies at their games—there's even a pierogi race! These pierogies were so delicious. When you roll out the dough, put some flour on the surface that you're working on so the dough does not stick. If your dough is still too wet, add a sprinkle of flour to it. As you cook the pierogies, you can add some strips of onion and minced garlic to the pan—the onion is just the right thing to top it off. My friend Jake had never had pierogies before, and he said these were the best. I loved this dish. The potatoes were so nice and creamy."

PIEROGIES ARE BASICALLY DUMPLINGS WITH MASHED POTATO INSIDE.

Kid Friendly • Make Ahead
Vegetarian

Cheddar and Potato Pierogies

Hands-on: 50 min. Total: 65 min. *Serve with steamed broccoli florets. If you don't have a biscuit cutter, the rim of a drinking glass will work.*

1 (10-ounce) baking potato, peeled and quartered
2 ounces reduced-fat cheddar cheese, shredded (about $1/2$ cup)
2 tablespoons unsalted butter, divided
$3/4$ teaspoon kosher salt, divided
9 ounces all-purpose flour (about 2 cups)
$3/4$ cup light sour cream, divided
2 large eggs, lightly beaten
$1/2$ teaspoon extra-virgin olive oil
$3/4$ cup diced red onion
2 teaspoons minced fresh garlic
12 cups water
$1/4$ cup chopped fresh flat-leaf parsley

1. Place potato in a medium saucepan; cover with cold water. Bring to a boil. Reduce heat, and simmer 20 minutes; drain. Combine potato, cheddar cheese, 2 teaspoons butter, and ¼ teaspoon salt in a bowl; mash with a potato masher.
2. Weigh or lightly spoon flour into dry measuring cups; level with a knife. Combine flour and ½ teaspoon salt in a medium bowl. Combine ½ cup sour cream and eggs in a small bowl, stirring with a whisk. Add sour cream mixture to flour mixture, stirring just until combined. Wrap dough in plastic wrap; refrigerate 30 minutes.
3. Heat a small skillet over medium-high heat. Add oil to pan; swirl to coat. Add onion and garlic; sauté 4 minutes. Stir onion mixture into potato mixture.
4. Divide dough into 2 portions. Roll each portion to a ⅛-inch thickness on a lightly floured surface; cut with a 4-inch round cutter into 18 rounds. Working with 1 round at a time, spoon 1 tablespoon potato mixture onto each round. Fold dough over filling; press edges together to seal. Repeat with remaining dough and potato mixture.
5. Bring 12 cups water to a boil in a large saucepan. Add half of pierogies; cook 2 minutes or until pierogies float. Remove cooked pierogies with a slotted spoon. Repeat procedure with remaining pierogies.
6. Melt 2 teaspoons butter in a large nonstick skillet over medium-high heat. Add half of pierogies to pan; cook 2 minutes on each side or until golden brown. Remove from pan. Repeat procedure with 2 teaspoons butter and remaining pierogies. Place 3 pierogies on each of 6 plates; top each serving with 2 teaspoons sour cream. Sprinkle evenly with parsley. Serves 12

CALORIES 323; FAT 10.3g (sat 5.6g, mono 3.1g, poly 0.9g); PROTEIN 11.3g; CARB 45.8g; FIBER 2.2g; CHOL 85mg; IRON 3mg; SODIUM 350mg; CALC 116mg

THE VERDICT

LIZZIE (AGE 8):
She liked the texture and taste of the potato.
9 out of 10

JAKE (AGE 12):
He said, "This is the best pierogi I've had, and the only one I've had!"
8 out of 10

MATISSE (AGE 12):
It was so delicious. Loved it!
10 out of 10

RADICALLY SIMPLE COOKING

By Rozanne Gold

In this busy season of entertaining, it pays to have a fallback recipe, one you know will turn out terrifically good and that can almost go on autopilot—because don't you have enough to juggle right now? Spice-Rubbed Racks of Lamb with Yogurt Sauce is that dish: remarkably easy and delicious. A little advance prep in the form of a spice rub and overnight yogurt marinade makes the dish practically hands-free the night of your soirée and ensures the meat is deeply flavorful, perfectly tender, and moist. Serve with the suggested sides for an easy, no-fail menu.

Spice-Rubbed Racks of Lamb with Yogurt Sauce

Hands-on: 7 min. Total: 9 hr. 2 min.
Serve the lamb with a tangle of wild arugula and feta cheese dressed with good olive oil and lemon, and a side of couscous. The lamb racks we found in our markets were on the small side, so 4 little chops ended up being a reasonable portion; if your lamb is bigger, you'll need to increase both the cook time and the number of servings.

1½ teaspoons ground cumin
1½ teaspoons ground coriander
½ teaspoon freshly ground
   black pepper
¼ teaspoon ground cinnamon
½ teaspoon kosher salt, divided
2 French-cut racks of lamb
   (8 ribs each), well trimmed (about 26
   ounces trimmed)

1 cup plain low-fat yogurt, drained
2 garlic cloves, minced
1½ teaspoons extra-virgin olive oil
1 pint grape tomatoes

1. Combine first 4 ingredients in a small bowl; add ⅜ teaspoon salt. Rub spice mixture over lamb. Arrange lamb in a 13 x 9–inch glass or ceramic baking dish. Combine yogurt and garlic. Spread half of yogurt mixture over lamb. Cover and marinate lamb mixture 8 hours or overnight.
2. Combine remaining yogurt mixture, oil, and ⅛ teaspoon salt. Cover and chill.
3. Preheat oven to 425°.
4. Remove lamb from refrigerator; let stand, uncovered, 30 minutes. Remove lamb from dish, and place on a jelly-roll pan. Bake at 425° for 22 minutes or until a thermometer inserted in thickest part of lamb registers 130°. Preheat broiler to high. Add tomatoes to pan with lamb. Broil 1 minute or until lamb is browned and tomatoes start to blacken. Let stand 5 minutes. Serve with yogurt sauce. Serves 4 (serving size: about 4 ounces lamb meat, 2 tablespoons yogurt sauce, and ⅓ cup tomatoes)

CALORIES 263; FAT 13.3g (sat 5.4g, mono 5.6g, poly 0.6g); PROTEIN 26.2g; CARB 8.5g; FIBER 1.5g; CHOL 76mg; IRON 2mg; SODIUM 363mg; CALC 150mg

> HERE IS A SERIOUSLY DELICIOUS WAY TO TREAT A RACK OF LAMB THAT RESULTS IN MELTINGLY TENDER MEAT WITH AROMATIC FLAVORS.

QUICK TRICKS

8 STUFFING MIX-INS

Combine 1½ cups unsalted chicken stock and 2 eggs. Add 12 ounces toasted sourdough bread cubes. Then add a stir-in. Bake stuffing at 350° for 45 minutes in an 11 x 7–inch baking dish coated with cooking spray.

1. Tri-Pepper Chorizo
Heat a skillet over medium-high heat. Add 2 teaspoons canola oil; swirl. Add 1 cup diced poblano, 1 cup diced red bell pepper, ½ cup diced onion, 3 ounces Mexican pork chorizo, and 1 minced jalapeño; sauté 5 minutes. Stir into bread mixture before baking. Serves 12

CALORIES 148; FAT 4.7g (sat 1.7g); SODIUM 291mg

2. Simply Herby
Sauté 5 minced garlic cloves in 2 tablespoons olive oil. Stir garlic mixture, ½ cup chopped fresh parsley, 2 tablespoons chopped fresh thyme, 1 tablespoon chopped fresh sage, ½ teaspoon salt, and ½ teaspoon pepper into bread mixture. Let stand 5 minutes; bake. Serves 12

CALORIES 129; FAT 3.7g (sat 0.7g); SODIUM 332mg

3. Mushroom-Artichoke
Heat a large skillet over medium-high heat. Add 1 tablespoon olive oil. Sauté 12 ounces exotic mushroom blend and 1 tablespoon chopped fresh thyme 6 minutes. Add 1 (9-ounce) package thawed frozen artichokes, 2 teaspoons minced fresh garlic, ½ teaspoon pepper, and ¼ teaspoon salt; sauté 2 minutes. Stir into bread mixture before baking. Top with 1 ounce shaved fresh Parmesan cheese after baking. Serves 12

CALORIES 142; FAT 3.4g (sat 1g); SODIUM 329mg

4. Greek Style

Add 2 ounces coarsely chopped pitted kalamata olives, 2 ounces chopped drained sun-dried tomatoes, 3 tablespoons chopped fresh oregano, and ½ teaspoon crushed red pepper to bread mixture; toss well. Spoon into prepared dish; sprinkle with 2 ounces crumbled goat cheese before baking. Serves 12

CALORIES 151; **FAT** 4.1g (sat 1.5g); **SODIUM** 339mg

5. Ham, Gruyère & Onion

Heat a nonstick skillet over medium-high heat. Add 1 tablespoon olive oil; swirl. Sauté 2 cups finely chopped onion 2 minutes. Reduce heat to low; cook 30 minutes. Cool slightly. Add onion, 2 ounces finely chopped lower-sodium ham (about ⅔ cup), 2 ounces diced Gruyère cheese, and ¼ cup chopped fresh flat-leaf parsley to bread mixture before baking. Serves 12

CALORIES 153; **FAT** 4.4g (sat 1.6g); **SODIUM** 296mg

6. Sausage-Apple

Increase stock to 2½ cups. Brown 4 ounces reduced-fat pork breakfast sausage in a skillet. Add 1 tablespoon olive oil to pan. Add 3 cups coarsely chopped apple, ⅔ cup chopped celery, and ⅔ cup chopped onion; cook 5 minutes or until tender. Add sausage mixture, ¼ cup chopped fresh parsley, 1 tablespoon thyme leaves, ½ teaspoon pepper, and ¼ teaspoon kosher salt to bread mixture; bake. Serves 12

CALORIES 163; **FAT** 4.4g (sat 1.2g); **SODIUM** 345mg

7. Butternut-Bacon

Combine 3 cups diced peeled butternut squash, 2 tablespoons olive oil, ¼ teaspoon kosher salt, and ¼ teaspoon pepper on a baking sheet. Bake at 400° for 15 minutes. Reduce heat to 350°. Cook 3 chopped bacon slices over medium heat until crisp; remove from pan. Add 1 cup chopped onion to drippings; sauté until tender. Stir squash, onion, bacon, and 2 tablespoons chopped fresh sage into bread mixture before baking. Serves 12

CALORIES 154; **FAT** 4.3g (sat 1g); **SODIUM** 308mg

8. Chestnut, Cranberry & Leek

Bake 7.4 ounces jarred roasted chestnuts, quartered, at 350° for 20 minutes. Cover ½ cup dried cranberries with boiling water. Let stand 20 minutes; drain. Sauté 2 cups sliced leek in 1 tablespoon butter over medium heat 5 minutes. Add chestnuts, cranberries, leeks, ¼ teaspoon salt, and ¼ teaspoon pepper to bread mixture before baking. Serves 12

CALORIES 162; **FAT** 2.8g (sat 1.1g); **SODIUM** 298mg

DINNER TONIGHT

Fast weeknight menus from the *Cooking Light* Test Kitchen

Kid Friendly • Quick & Easy Make Ahead

Creamy Sweet Potato Soup

With Parmesan Cheese Toasts

Time-Saver: Microwaving the potatoes saves more than an hour over roasting.
Flavor Swap: Sub 3 tablespoons chopped sun-dried tomatoes for the bacon.
Kid Tweak: Skip the spices for a more neutral-flavored soup.

2 pounds sweet potatoes, halved lengthwise (about 2 large)
¼ cup water
2 teaspoons olive oil
1 cup chopped onion
½ teaspoon ground cumin
¼ teaspoon crushed red pepper
4 cups unsalted chicken stock (such as Swanson)
¼ teaspoon salt
6 bacon slices, cooked and crumbled
1 ounce fresh Parmesan cheese, shaved (about ¼ cup)
2 tablespoons flat-leaf parsley leaves (optional)

1. Place potatoes, cut sides down, in an 11 x 7–inch microwave-safe baking dish. Add ¼ cup water; cover with plastic wrap. Microwave at HIGH 15 minutes or until potatoes are tender. Cool slightly; discard potato skins.
2. Heat a saucepan over medium-high heat. Add oil; swirl to coat. Add onion; sauté 1 minute or until translucent. Stir in cumin and red pepper. Add stock to pan; bring to a boil. Place half of sweet potato and half of stock mixture in a blender. Remove center piece of blender lid (to allow steam to escape); secure blender lid on blender. Place a clean towel over opening in blender lid (to avoid splatters); blend until smooth. Pour pureed soup into a large bowl. Repeat procedure with remaining sweet potato and stock mixture. Stir in salt. Ladle soup into each of 6 bowls; sprinkle cooked bacon and Parmesan cheese evenly over top. Garnish with parsley, if desired. Serves 6 (serving size: about 1½ cups soup)

CALORIES 233; **FAT** 6.2g (sat 2.1g, mono 2.9g, poly 0.6g); **PROTEIN** 10.7g; **CARB** 33.9g; **FIBER** 5.1g; **CHOL** 12mg; **IRON** 1.4mg; **SODIUM** 530mg; **CALC** 123mg

For the Parmesan Cheese Toasts:
Preheat broiler. Cut 6 ounces French bread baguette in half lengthwise; cut each half into thirds. Spread cut side of each piece with 1 teaspoon butter; sprinkle evenly with 1 ounce shaved fresh Parmesan cheese and ½ teaspoon freshly ground black pepper. Arrange pieces, cut sides up, on a baking sheet. Broil 2 minutes or until cheese melts. Serves 6 (serving size: 1 piece)

CALORIES 137; **FAT** 5.7g (sat 3.4g); **SODIUM** 252mg

continued

READY IN 30 MINUTES

The
SHOPPING LIST

Creamy Sweet Potato Soup
Onion (1)
Sweet potatoes (2 large)
Ground cumin
Crushed red pepper
Parmesan cheese (1 ounce)
Olive oil
Unsalted chicken stock (such as Swanson)
Bacon (6 slices)

Parmesan French Toasts
French bread baguette (6 ounces)
Butter
Parmesan cheese (1 ounce)

The
GAME PLAN

While sweet potatoes cook:
- Preheat broiler.
- Cook bacon.

While sweet potatoes cool:
- Heat stock mixture.
- Prepare cheese toasts.

Kid Friendly • Quick & Easy
Cowboy Flank Steak with Sweet and Smoky Beans

With Garlic-Roasted Broccoli

Simple Sub: Use green beans or Brussels sprouts in place of broccoli.
Kid Tweak: Omit the chiles for milder beans.

1 tablespoon olive oil
1 cup chopped yellow onion
1 cup chopped red bell pepper
¾ cup lower-sodium tomato puree
1 tablespoon brown sugar
1 tablespoon molasses
½ teaspoon chipotle chile powder
¼ teaspoon ground cinnamon
1 (16-ounce) can pinto beans, rinsed and drained
1 (4.5-ounce) can chopped green chiles, undrained
1 tablespoon smoked paprika
1 teaspoon dried oregano
1 teaspoon freshly ground black pepper
⅜ teaspoon kosher salt
1 (1-pound) flank steak, trimmed
Cooking spray

1. Heat a large saucepan over medium heat. Add 1 tablespoon oil; swirl to coat. Add onion and red bell pepper; sauté 4 minutes or until slightly tender. Stir in tomato puree and next 6 ingredients. Cover and simmer 15 minutes, stirring occasionally.
2. Heat a grill pan over high heat. Combine paprika and next 3 ingredients in a small bowl; rub spice mixture evenly over steak. Coat pan with cooking spray. Add steak to pan; grill 6 minutes on each side or until desired degree of doneness. Let stand 5 minutes. Cut steak diagonally across grain into thin slices. Serves 4 (serving size: 3 ounces steak and ¾ cup beans)

CALORIES 350; **FAT** 12.5g (sat 4g, mono 5.9g, poly 1g); **PROTEIN** 29g; **CARB** 31g; **FIBER** 7.3g; **CHOL** 74mg; **IRON** 4.6mg; **SODIUM** 553mg; **CALC** 104mg

---

For the Garlic-Roasted Broccoli:
Preheat oven to 400°. Place 6 cups broccoli florets and 3 minced garlic cloves in a large bowl. Coat generously with cooking spray; toss to coat. Arrange mixture in a single layer on a jelly-roll pan. Roast at 400° for 12 minutes or until crisp-tender, stirring once. Serves 4 (serving size: 1¼ cups)

CALORIES 36; **FAT** 0.7g (sat 0.1g); **SODIUM** 29mg

READY IN 40 MINUTES

The
SHOPPING LIST

Cowboy Flank Steak with Sweet and Smoky Beans
Yellow onion (1)
Red bell pepper (1)
Chipotle chile powder
Ground cinnamon
Smoked paprika
Dried oregano
Olive oil
Molasses
Lower-sodium tomato puree
16-ounce can pinto beans (1)
4.5-ounce can chopped green chiles (1)
Brown sugar
Flank steak (1 pound)

Garlic-Roasted Broccoli
Broccoli florets (6 cups)
Garlic

The
GAME PLAN

While oven preheats:
- Prepare beans.

While beans simmer:
- Grill steak.
- Roast broccoli.

The SHOPPING LIST

Orange-Glazed Pork Tenderloin with Cranberry Tabbouleh

Green onions (2)
Crushed red pepper
Five-spice powder
Peanut oil
Rice vinegar
Lower-sodium soy sauce
Orange marmalade
Dried cranberries
Bulgur
Fat-free, lower-sodium chicken broth
Pork tenderloin (1 pound)

Snap Pea Sauté

Sugar snap peas (2 cups)
Snow peas (2 cups)
Ginger
Sesame seeds
Dark sesame oil
Rice vinegar
Lower-sodium soy sauce

The GAME PLAN

While oven preheats:
- Make marinade.
- Brown pork.

While pork roasts:
- Cook bulgur.
- Cook sugar snap and snow peas.

Quick & Easy

Orange-Glazed Pork Tenderloin with Cranberry Tabbouleh

With Snap Pea Sauté

Time-Saver: Heat orange marmalade for an instant, easy glaze.
Shopping Tip: Find bulgur in the specialty grains aisle of the store.
Simple Sub: Sub ground ginger and cinnamon for five-spice powder.

⅓ cup orange marmalade
2 tablespoons rice vinegar
1 tablespoon lower-sodium soy sauce
½ teaspoon crushed red pepper
1 tablespoon peanut oil
1 (1-pound) pork tenderloin, trimmed
1¼ cups fat-free, lower-sodium chicken broth
¼ cup dried cranberries
¼ teaspoon five-spice powder
¼ teaspoon salt
1 cup bulgur
2 tablespoons minced green onions

1. Preheat oven to 350°.
2. Combine first 4 ingredients in a medium bowl, stirring with a whisk. Heat a large ovenproof skillet over medium-high heat. Add oil; swirl to coat. Add pork; cook 6 minutes, turning to brown on all sides. Brush pork with half of marmalade mixture. Place pan in oven; bake at 350° for 18 minutes or until a thermometer registers 145°, turning and basting with remaining marmalade after 10 minutes. Place pork on a cutting board; reserve sauce in pan. Let pork rest 5 minutes; cut into 12 slices.

3. While pork cooks, bring broth and next 3 ingredients (through salt) to a boil in a saucepan; stir in bulgur. Remove from heat; cover and let stand 15 minutes. Fluff with a fork. Stir in green onions.
4. Place 3 pork slices on each of 4 plates; top each serving with 2 table-spoons reserved sauce. Serve each with ¾ cup bulgur mixture. Serves 4

CALORIES 371; FAT 6.5g (sat 1.5g, mono 2.5g, poly 1.8g); PROTEIN 29.4g; CARB 51.6g; FIBER 7.2g; CHOL 74mg; IRON 2.3mg; SODIUM 541mg; CALC 34mg

For the Snap Pea Sauté:
Heat a large skillet over medium-high heat. Add 1 tablespoon dark sesame oil; swirl to coat. Add 1 tablespoon minced peeled fresh ginger to pan; cook 30 seconds, stirring constantly. Add 2 cups trimmed sugar snap peas and 2 cups trimmed snow peas. Sauté 2 minutes. Add 1 tablespoon rice vinegar and 1½ teaspoons lower-sodium soy sauce to pan; cook 30 seconds. Sprinkle with 2 teaspoons toasted sesame seeds. Serves 4 (serving size: ½ cup)

CALORIES 67; FAT 4.3g (sat 0.6g); SODIUM 70mg

DON'T BE INTIMIDATED BY COOKING WITH BULGUR! IF YOU CAN MAKE RICE, THEN YOU CAN PREPARE THIS SIMPLE FALL SIDE DISH.

READY IN
40
MINUTES

The
SHOPPING LIST

Oven-Fried Tilapia with Cheesy Polenta
Lemon (1)
Fresh oregano
Parmesan cheese (1 ounce)
Dry mustard
Dried thyme
Dried rubbed sage
Celery seeds
Ground red pepper
Unsalted chicken stock (such as Swanson)
Polenta
Panko (Japanese breadcrumbs)
All-purpose flour
6-ounce tilapia fillets (4)
Egg (1)

Warm Spinach Salad
Baby spinach (6 cups)
Grape tomatoes
Garlic
Olive oil
Cider vinegar
Honey

The
GAME PLAN

While oven preheats:
■ Cook polenta.
■ Toast panko mixture.
While fish bakes:
■ Make spinach salad.

Kid Friendly • Quick & Easy
Oven-Fried Tilapia with Cheesy Polenta

With Warm Spinach Salad

Prep Pointer: Toasting the panko first adds crunch to the breading.
Budget Buy: Instead of baby spinach leaves, use chopped spinach.
Simple Sub: Instead of polenta, serve with 2 cups hot cooked rice.

2²/₃ cups unsalted chicken stock (such as Swanson)
¹/₂ teaspoon dry mustard
²/₃ cup dry polenta
1 ounce fresh Parmesan cheese, grated (about ¹/₄ cup)
2 tablespoons chopped fresh oregano
¹/₂ teaspoon salt, divided
1 cup panko (Japanese breadcrumbs)
1 teaspoon dried thyme
¹/₂ teaspoon dried rubbed sage
¹/₄ teaspoon celery seeds
¹/₄ teaspoon ground red pepper
2 tablespoons water
1 large egg, lightly beaten
2.25 ounces all-purpose flour (about ¹/₂ cup)
4 (6-ounce) tilapia fillets
Cooking spray
4 lemon wedges

1. Preheat oven to 400°.
2. Combine stock and mustard in a medium saucepan; bring to a boil. Gradually add polenta, stirring constantly with a whisk. Reduce heat to low, and cook 20 minutes, stirring frequently. Stir in Parmesan cheese, oregano, and ¹/₄ teaspoon salt.
3. Place panko and next 4 ingredients (through pepper) in a large skillet; cook over medium heat 3 minutes or until toasted, stirring frequently. Place panko mixture in a shallow dish. Combine 2 tablespoons water and egg in a shallow dish. Place flour in a shallow dish. Sprinkle fish with remaining ¹/₄ teaspoon salt. Dredge fish in flour; dip in egg mixture. Place fish in panko mixture, turning to coat.
4. Arrange fish on a baking sheet coated with cooking spray. Bake at 400° for 15 minutes or until done. Serve with lemon wedges and polenta. Serves 4 (serving size: 1 fillet, 1 lemon wedge, and about ¹/₂ cup polenta)

CALORIES 438; FAT 7.5g (sat 2.8g, mono 1.9g, poly 1g); PROTEIN 47.6g; CARB 43g; FIBER 3.1g; CHOL 138mg; IRON 3.6mg; SODIUM 640mg; CALC 137mg

For the Warm Spinach Salad:
Place 6 cups baby spinach leaves in a large bowl. Heat a small skillet over medium-high heat. Add 2 tablespoons olive oil; swirl to coat. Add 1 teaspoon minced garlic and ¹/₂ cup grape tomatoes; cook 1 minute, stirring constantly. Add 2 tablespoons cider vinegar, 1 teaspoon honey, ¹/₂ teaspoon black pepper, and ¹/₄ teaspoon salt, stirring with a whisk. Add vinegar mixture to spinach; toss to coat. Serves 4 (serving size: 1 cup)

CALORIES 87; FAT 6.8g (sat 0.9g); SODIUM 207mg

Kid Friendly • Quick & Easy
Turkey Burgers with Cranberry-Apple Relish

With Sweet Potato Wedges

Make Ahead: The cranberry-apple relish can be made a couple of days ahead.
Flavor Swap: Swiss or provolone will work in place of the cheddar.
Shopping Tip: Buy ground turkey, not turkey breast, for richest flavor.

¹/₂ cup fresh cranberries
¹/₂ cup coarsely chopped apple
1 teaspoon grated orange rind
2 tablespoons fresh orange juice
2 teaspoons sugar
³/₈ teaspoon salt, divided

2 teaspoons olive oil
½ cup finely chopped onion
¼ cup plain breadcrumbs
¼ cup chopped fresh flat-leaf parsley
1 tablespoon chopped fresh sage
¼ teaspoon freshly ground black
  pepper
1 pound ground turkey
Cooking spray
4 (½-ounce) slices reduced-fat
  white cheddar cheese
¾ cup baby arugula leaves
4 (1½-ounce) whole-wheat
  hamburger buns, toasted

1. Place first 5 ingredients in a mini food processor. Pulse 10 times or until coarsely chopped. Stir in ⅛ teaspoon salt; set aside.
2. Heat a small skillet over medium heat. Add oil; swirl to coat. Add onion to pan; sauté 3 minutes or until tender. Cool slightly. Combine onion, bread-crumbs, parsley, sage, pepper, turkey, and ¼ teaspoon salt in a large bowl, stirring just until combined. Divide mixture into 4 equal portions, shaping each into a 4-inch patty.
3. Heat a grill pan over medium-high heat; coat with cooking spray. Add patties to pan; grill 5 minutes. Turn patties; grill 3 minutes. Top each with 1 cheese slice; grill 2 minutes or until cheese melts and turkey is done.
4. Divide arugula evenly among bottom halves of buns. Top each serving with 1 patty. Divide relish evenly among servings; top with top halves of buns. Serves 4 (serving size: 1 burger)

CALORIES 415; FAT 17.4g (sat 5.3g, mono 5.4g, poly 4.1g); PROTEIN 30.2g; CARB 36.3g; FIBER 4.9g; CHOL 94mg; IRON 2.8mg; SODIUM 648mg; CALC 194mg

For the Sweet Potato Wedges:
Preheat oven to 450°. Peel 2 medium sweet potatoes (about 1½ pounds); cut in half lengthwise. Cut each half lengthwise into thirds. Place potatoes in a bowl; add 1 tablespoon olive oil, ¼ teaspoon kosher salt, and ¼ teaspoon ground red pepper, tossing to coat. Arrange potato wedges on a baking sheet coated with cooking spray; bake

at 450° for 10 minutes. Turn potatoes; bake 10 to 12 minutes or until tender. Serves 4 (serving size: 3 sweet potato wedges)

CALORIES 178; FAT 3.6g (sat 0.5g); SODIUM 214mg

READY IN
40
MINUTES

The
SHOPPING LIST

Turkey Burgers with Cranberry-Apple Relish
Apple (1)
Orange (1)
Onion (1)
Cranberries
Baby arugula
Fresh sage
Fresh flat-leaf parsley
Olive oil
Sugar
Breadcrumbs
Ground turkey (1 pound)
Reduced-fat white cheddar
  cheese slices
Whole-wheat hamburger
  buns (4)

Sweet Potato Wedges
Sweet potatoes (2)
Ground red pepper
Olive oil

The
GAME PLAN

While oven preheats:
■ Make cranberry-apple relish.
■ Prepare sweet potato wedges.
While sweet potatoes bake:
■ Cook turkey burgers.

FEED 4 FOR LESS THAN $10

Walnut and Onion Tartine

$2.10/serving, $8.40 total

Hands-on: 36 min. Total: 2 hr. 11 min. A quick, scratch-made crust forms the base for this French-inspired meal. You can substitute 2 slices of cooked, crumbled bacon for the prosciutto.

6 tablespoons warm water
  (100° to 110°)
¾ teaspoon sugar
1¾ teaspoons dry yeast
3 tablespoons olive oil, divided
5 ounces all-purpose flour
  (about 1 cup plus 2 tablespoons)
⅝ teaspoon kosher salt, divided
¼ teaspoon black pepper
Cooking spray
½ cup coarsely chopped walnuts
⅓ cup very thinly vertically sliced red
  onion
1 ounce very thin slices prosciutto,
  chopped
1 teaspoon chopped fresh thyme
2 cups arugula
1 teaspoon fresh lemon juice
1 ounce fresh Parmesan cheese, shaved
  (about ¼ cup)

1. Preheat oven to 450°.
2. Combine first 3 ingredients in a medium bowl; let stand 5 minutes or until bubbly. Stir in 4 teaspoons oil. Weigh or lightly spoon flour into a dry measuring cup and spoons; level with a knife. Add flour, ¼ teaspoon salt, and pepper to yeast mixture, stirring until a soft dough forms. Turn dough out onto a lightly floured surface; knead until smooth and elastic (dough will be soft and tacky).

continued

3. Place dough in a large bowl coated with cooking spray, turning to coat top. Cover and let rise in a warm place (85°), free from drafts, 45 minutes or until doubled in size. Punch dough down; cover and let rest 5 minutes.

4. Coat an 11 x 7–inch glass or ceramic baking dish with 2 teaspoons oil. Press dough into pan; cover and let rise 30 minutes or until puffy. Sprinkle dough with ¼ teaspoon salt, walnuts, onion, prosciutto, and thyme. Bake at 450° for 18 minutes or until crust is golden and edges are crisp.

5. Place arugula in a bowl; drizzle with 1 tablespoon oil and lemon juice, tossing to coat. Turn bread out onto a clean work surface, and slice crosswise into 4 rectangles. Top each rectangle with about ½ cup arugula mixture and 1 tablespoon shaved Parmesan cheese; sprinkle evenly with ⅛ teaspoon salt. Serves 4 (serving size: 1 tartine)

CALORIES 377; FAT 23.2g (sat 3.9g, mono 9.4g, poly 8.2g); PROTEIN 11.7g; CARB 32.6g; FIBER 2.8g; CHOL 12mg; IRON 2.5mg; SODIUM 603mg; CALC 119mg

PUMPKINS ARE FOR MORE THAN JUST CARVING. BOOST THE NUTRITION AND FLAVOR OF THIS TRADITIONAL CREAM SAUCE BY ADDING PUMPKIN PUREE.

Kid Friendly • Quick & Easy

$2.41/serving, $9.64 total

Fettuccine with Pumpkin Sauce

Hands-on: 22 min. Total: 22 min. Serve with a quick fall salad: Combine 2 tablespoons olive oil, 2 teaspoons cider vinegar, ½ teaspoon Dijon mustard, and ½ teaspoon honey in a large bowl, stirring with a whisk. Add 3 cups chopped romaine lettuce, 1 sliced apple, and 2 tablespoons pumpkinseeds; toss.

8 ounces uncooked fettuccine
2 applewood-smoked bacon slices, chopped
2 tablespoons finely chopped fresh sage, divided
2 garlic cloves, minced
¾ cup canned unsalted pumpkin puree
2 ounces fresh Parmesan cheese, grated (about ½ cup)
⅜ teaspoon salt
¼ teaspoon freshly ground black pepper
2 tablespoons heavy cream
2 tablespoons chopped fresh flat-leaf parsley

1. Cook pasta according to package directions, omitting salt and fat. Drain in a colander over a bowl, reserving ¾ cup cooking liquid.

2. Heat a large skillet over medium heat. Add bacon; cook 4 minutes or until almost crisp, stirring occasionally. Add 1 tablespoon sage and garlic, and cook 1 minute, stirring constantly. Stir in pumpkin puree, Parmesan cheese, salt, and pepper. Add pasta, reserved ¾ cup cooking liquid, and heavy cream; toss to coat. Cook 2 minutes or until thoroughly heated. Sprinkle with 1 tablespoon sage and parsley. Serves 4 (serving size: about 1 cup)

CALORIES 341; FAT 10.1g (sat 5.4g, mono 2g, poly 0.3g); PROTEIN 15.8g; CARB 479g; FIBER 3.3g; CHOL 28mg; IRON 2.7mg; SODIUM 557mg; CALC 196mg

$2.42/serving, $9.68 total

Smothered Vinegar Pork Shoulder with Apples and Kale

Hands-on: 25 min. Total: 2 hr. 55 min.

1 tablespoon olive oil, divided
1 (1½-pound) boneless pork shoulder roast (Boston butt), trimmed
½ teaspoon kosher salt
¼ teaspoon freshly ground black pepper
2½ cups sliced onion
½ cup fat-free, lower-sodium chicken broth
¼ cup rice vinegar
2 teaspoons ground cumin
½ teaspoon ground allspice
2 garlic cloves, finely chopped
5 cups chopped fresh kale
1 teaspoon canola oil
2 peeled apples, cut into ½-inch wedges
2 tablespoons cider vinegar
1 teaspoon brown sugar

1. Preheat oven to 325°.

2. Heat a Dutch oven over medium-high heat. Add 2 teaspoons olive oil to pan; swirl to coat. Sprinkle pork evenly with salt and pepper. Add pork to pan; cook 7 minutes, turning to brown on all sides. Remove pork from pan; keep warm.

3. Add 1 teaspoon olive oil to pan; swirl to coat. Add onion to pan; cook 5 minutes or until onion begins to brown, stirring occasionally. Add chicken broth and next 4 ingredients (through garlic) to pan; bring to a boil, scraping pan to loosen browned bits. Return pork to pan. Cover and bake at 325° for 1½ hours. Add kale to pan; cover and bake at 325° for 30 minutes.

4. Heat a large nonstick skillet over medium-high heat. Add canola oil; swirl to coat. Add apples; cook 3 minutes or until starting to soften. Add vinegar and brown sugar; cook 1 minute or until sugar dissolves and liquid almost evaporates. Serve apples with pork and kale mixture. Serves 4 (serving size: 3 ounces pork, about ⅓ cup kale, and about ⅓ cup apples)

CALORIES 287; FAT 11g (sat 2.6g, mono 5.7g, poly 1.6g); PROTEIN 22.8g; CARB 25.9g; FIBER 4.2g; CHOL 59mg; IRON 3.2mg; SODIUM 417mg; CALC 160mg

SUPERFAST 20 MINUTE COOKING

Quick weeknight favorites bump up the family fun factor: creamy fettuccine, veggie-packed fritters, black bean tacos, speedy apple crisps, and more.

Kid Friendly • Quick & Easy Vegetarian

Creamy Mushroom Fettuccine

The hot pasta will melt the Parmesan cheese and help the sauce cling to the noodles.

1 (9-ounce) package refrigerated fresh fettuccine
1 tablespoon extra-virgin olive oil
½ cup chopped onion
12 ounces presliced cremini mushrooms
2 garlic cloves, minced
¾ teaspoon salt, divided
¼ teaspoon freshly ground black pepper
¼ cup white wine
1 teaspoon chopped fresh thyme
½ cup half-and-half
1 ounce fresh Parmesan cheese, grated (about ¼ cup)
¼ cup chopped fresh parsley

1. Cook pasta according to package directions, omitting salt and fat. Drain.
2. Heat a large nonstick skillet over medium-high heat. Add oil; swirl to coat. Add onion, mushrooms, garlic, ¼ teaspoon salt, and pepper; sauté 10 minutes or until mushrooms are browned and have released their liquid. Add wine and thyme; cook 2 minutes or until liquid evaporates, stirring occasionally. Remove pan from heat. Add hot cooked pasta, ½ teaspoon salt, half-and-half, and Parmesan cheese to pan, tossing to combine. Sprinkle with chopped parsley. Serve immediately. Serves 4 (serving size: 1½ cups)

CALORIES 323; FAT 10.9g (sat 4.6g, mono 3.1g, poly 0.5g); PROTEIN 13.7g; CARB 42.2g; FIBER 2.6g; CHOL 55mg; IRON 2.2mg; SODIUM 587mg; CALC 156mg

Quick & Easy

Soba Noodles with Spicy Cumin Lamb

This aromatic, fiery main course may be just the thing to warm up a chilly fall evening.

7 ounces uncooked soba noodles
½ cup fat-free, lower-sodium chicken broth
2 tablespoons rice vinegar
4½ teaspoons hoisin sauce
1 teaspoon minced fresh garlic
¼ teaspoon five-spice powder
8 ounces ground lamb
1 tablespoon dark sesame oil
1 teaspoon cumin seeds
⅜ teaspoon crushed red pepper
1½ cups broccoli florets
1 cup snow peas, trimmed
½ cup thinly sliced red bell pepper
9 baby carrots, halved lengthwise

1. Cook noodles according to package directions. Drain and rinse; drain well.
2. Combine chicken broth and next 4 ingredients (through ¼ teaspoon five-spice powder) in a small bowl, stirring with a whisk.
3. Heat a large wok or skillet over medium-high heat. Add lamb; cook 2½ minutes or until browned, stirring to crumble. Remove lamb from pan with a slotted spoon; set aside.
4. Return pan to medium-high heat. Add oil to drippings in pan; swirl to coat. Add cumin and red pepper; cook 30 seconds or until seeds begin to pop, stirring frequently. Add vegetables to pan; cook 5 minutes, stirring frequently. Add lamb and broth mixture; cook 1½ minutes or until liquid is slightly reduced. Serve over noodles. Serves 4 (serving size: 1 cup noodles and 1 cup lamb mixture)

CALORIES 409; FAT 16.5g (sat 5.4g, mono 6.4g, poly 2.5g); PROTEIN 23.3g; CARB 45.4g; FIBER 2.2g; CHOL 55mg; IRON 3.6mg; SODIUM 621mg; CALC 65mg

Quick & Easy

Salmon with Polenta and Warm Tomato Vinaigrette

3½ cups water
½ teaspoon kosher salt, divided
1 cup dry polenta
1 pint grape tomatoes, halved
½ cup minced red onion
3 tablespoons olive oil, divided
1 tablespoon red wine vinegar
1 tablespoon capers, rinsed and drained
4 (6-ounce) salmon fillets
¼ teaspoon freshly ground black pepper
1 tablespoon chopped fresh parsley

1. Bring 3½ cups water and ¼ teaspoon salt to a boil in a saucepan. Gradually add polenta, stirring constantly with a whisk. Reduce heat to low; cook 12 minutes, stirring occasionally.
2. Combine tomatoes, onion, 2 tablespoons oil, vinegar, and capers.
3. Heat a large nonstick skillet over medium-high heat. Add 1 tablespoon oil; swirl to coat. Sprinkle fish with ¼ teaspoon salt and pepper. Cook, skin side down, 7 minutes; turn over, and

continued

cook 1 minute. Remove from pan. Add tomato mixture to pan, reduce heat to low, and cook 2 minutes. Spoon ¾ cup polenta into each of 4 shallow bowls. Top each serving with 1 fillet and ½ cup tomato mixture. Sprinkle with parsley. Serves 4

CALORIES 485; **FAT** 20.2g (sat 3.4g, mono 10.6g, poly 4.4g); **PROTEIN** 40.1g; **CARB** 32.1g; **FIBER** 3.5g; **CHOL** 90mg; **IRON** 2.4mg; **SODIUM** 389mg; **CALC** 37mg

Quick & Easy • Vegetarian

Black Bean Burgers with Sriracha Aioli

1 (15-ounce) can unsalted black beans, rinsed and drained
¼ cup chopped onion
¼ cup chopped fresh cilantro
1 tablespoon minced fresh garlic
2 teaspoons lower-sodium soy sauce
½ teaspoon kosher salt
¼ teaspoon freshly ground black pepper
¼ cup panko (Japanese breadcrumbs)
1 large egg, lightly beaten
Cooking spray
4 (1½-ounce) hamburger buns
¼ cup canola mayonnaise
1 teaspoon Sriracha (hot chile sauce)
1 teaspoon fresh lime juice
2 cups baby arugula

1. Preheat oven to 425°.
2. Place beans in a large bowl; lightly mash. Stir in onion and next 7 ingredients. Divide mixture into 4 portions; shape each into a ½-inch-thick patty.
3. Arrange patties on a baking sheet coated with cooking spray. Bake at 425° for 8 minutes; turn after 6 minutes. Add bun halves to pan; bake 3 minutes.
4. Combine mayonnaise, Sriracha, and juice; spread over bottom halves of buns. Top each serving with 1 patty,

½ cup arugula, and top halves of buns. Serves 4 (serving size: 1 burger)

CALORIES 250; **FAT** 6.8g (sat 0.8g, mono 3.2g, poly 2.3g); **PROTEIN** 10.4g; **CARB** 35.4g; **FIBER** 4.5g; **CHOL** 47mg; **IRON** 2.8mg; **SODIUM** 710mg; **CALC** 133mg

Kid Friendly • Quick & Easy

Black Bean Tacos with Feta Slaw

Canned beans that are already seasoned help bring these tacos together in a flash.

1 center-cut bacon slice
1 cup vertically sliced white onion
2 teaspoons minced fresh garlic
½ jalapeño pepper, seeded and chopped
1 (15-ounce) can seasoned black beans (such as Bush's), drained and divided
¾ teaspoon ground cumin
¼ teaspoon salt
1 tablespoon white wine vinegar
1 tablespoon canola mayonnaise
¼ teaspoon freshly ground black pepper
2 cups angel hair coleslaw
¼ cup cilantro leaves
2 green onions, thinly sliced
8 (6-inch) corn tortillas
1 ounce feta cheese, crumbled

1. Cook bacon in a large nonstick skillet over medium heat 2 minutes or until crisp. Remove bacon from pan; crumble. Add onion, garlic, and jalapeño to drippings in pan; cook 3 minutes or until onion is tender. Place onion mixture in a small bowl. Lightly mash 1 cup beans. Add mashed beans, cumin, salt, and remaining beans to pan; cook 2 minutes over medium heat or until thoroughly heated, stirring occasionally. Stir in bacon.
2. Combine vinegar, mayonnaise, and black pepper in a large bowl, stirring with a whisk. Add coleslaw, cilantro, and green onions; toss to coat.

3. Heat tortillas according to package directions. Divide bean mixture evenly among tortillas. Top evenly with onion mixture and coleslaw mixture. Sprinkle evenly with feta cheese. Serves 4 (serving size: 2 tacos)

CALORIES 200; **FAT** 4.4g (sat 1.3g, mono 0.9g, poly 0.9g); **PROTEIN** 8.8g; **CARB** 36.6g; **FIBER** 7.5g; **CHOL** 8mg; **IRON** 0.5mg; **SODIUM** 546mg; **CALC** 87mg

Kid Friendly • Quick & Easy Vegetarian

Crispy Broccoli- Carrot Fritters with Yogurt-Dill Sauce

These quick, crispy fritters are packed with vegetables and get supercrisp in the pan. You can omit the red pepper for a little less heat, if you wish.

4 cups water
2 cups broccoli florets
1 cup matchstick-cut carrots
2.25 ounces all-purpose flour (about ½ cup)
1.5 ounces fresh Parmesan cheese, grated (about ⅓ cup)
½ teaspoon salt
⅛ teaspoon ground red pepper
2 green onions, thinly sliced
1 large egg
2 tablespoons olive oil
1 cup plain low-fat yogurt
2 teaspoons chopped fresh dill

1. Place 4 cups water, broccoli, and carrots in a small saucepan; bring to a boil. Cook 4 minutes; drain. Pat broccoli mixture dry with paper towels; finely chop. Place broccoli mixture and flour in a large bowl; stir to coat. Add cheese, salt, pepper, onions, and egg to broccoli mixture; stir to combine.
2. Heat a large nonstick skillet over medium-high heat. Add oil to pan; swirl to coat. Spoon ¼ cup broccoli mixture into a dry measuring cup. Pour mixture into pan; flatten slightly. Re-

peat procedure 7 times to form 8 fritters. Cook 4 minutes on each side or until golden brown. Combine yogurt and dill in a small bowl. Serve yogurt mixture with fritters. Serves 4 (serving size: 2 fritters and ¼ cup yogurt mixture)

CALORIES 244; FAT 12.3g (sat 3.8g, mono 6.6g, poly 1.3g); PROTEIN 12g; CARB 22.1g; FIBER 2.6g; CHOL 60mg; IRON 1.7mg; SODIUM 551mg; CALC 272mg

Kid Friendly • Quick & Easy

Easy Individual Apple Crisps With Oatmeal Crumble

You can also peel and coarsely chop the apples, if you prefer. For more tender apples, decrease the heat to 400° and bake 5 to 10 minutes longer.

1 Granny Smith apple, halved and cored
1 Gala apple, halved and cored
¼ cup packed brown sugar
4½ teaspoons butter, melted
2 teaspoons fresh lemon juice
¼ teaspoon vanilla extract
¼ teaspoon ground cinnamon
Dash of ground nutmeg
8 small prepared oatmeal cookies, crumbled

1. Preheat oven to 425°.
2. Cut apples into thin slices using a mandoline or a sharp knife. Place apples, brown sugar, butter, lemon juice, vanilla, cinnamon, and nutmeg in a large bowl; toss to coat. Divide apple mixture evenly among 4 (6-ounce) ramekins, arranging apple slices in a fan shape. Sprinkle each ramekin evenly with crumbled oatmeal cookies. Bake at 425° for 9 minutes or until apples are crisp-tender. Serves 4 (serving size: 1 crisp)

CALORIES 259; FAT 9.8g (sat 3.8g, mono 3.4g, poly 1.9g); PROTEIN 2.3g; CARB 42.3g; FIBER 1g; CHOL 22mg; IRON 1mg; SODIUM 221mg; CALC 50mg

OOPS!
YOUR PIECRUST SHRINKS

How to avoid a slumped, sad crust.

No shortage of home bakers have witnessed the Great Piecrust Disappearing Act—dough that looks perfect in the pan but contracts in the oven. The problem: too much gluten. The gluten in dough can become like rubber bands stretched to their limit: too much strain, and the proteins snap back into a tangled heap. You need some gluten for structure, but you need to treat it gently. By the way, even packaged pie dough can shrink.

(Tall and flaky!)

The solution: Relax your dough. It's tempting to work homemade dough into a cohesive ball, but this over-develops gluten. The dough should just hold together when squeezed in the palm of your hand, with bits of fat visible throughout. Form the dough into a disk, wrap, and chill at least 20 minutes—this lets the gluten unwind. To form the pie shell, gently roll the dough into a circle larger than the pan, at least 12 inches, and then trim and flute. Stretching a too-small circle to fit the pan will stretch the gluten. Chill the pie shell before filling. (If you feel you've stretched purchased dough, chill it, too; this will relax the gluten and help prevent shrinkage.) The fat, still solid from the fridge, will melt and steam in the oven, creating delicious flaky layers.

(Uh, where's the rest?)

NO-FAIL HOLIDAY DISHES

We show you surefire tricks to make this season's most important meals guaranteed hits.

Spinach and Mushroom-Stuffed Beef Tenderloin with Truffled Wine Sauce

Hands-on: 60 min. Total: 2 hr. 15 min.
Make sure that once your tenderloin is stuffed, the grain in the roll runs the same way as before the meat was cut; otherwise you'll be slicing the beef with the grain and sacrificing tenderness.

2¹/₂ tablespoons olive oil, divided
3 applewood-smoked bacon slices, finely chopped
¹/₂ cup finely chopped shallots
2 (8-ounce) packages cremini mushrooms, finely chopped
1 tablespoon minced fresh garlic
3 cups unsalted beef stock (such as Swanson), divided
1 (6-ounce) bag baby spinach, coarsely chopped
1 (3¹/₄-pound) beef tenderloin, trimmed
1¹/₂ teaspoons salt, divided
1 teaspoon freshly ground black pepper, divided
1 cup red wine (such as pinot noir)
3 thyme sprigs
5 teaspoons all-purpose flour
3 tablespoons butter
2 teaspoons truffle oil

1. Heat a large skillet over medium heat. Add 1 tablespoon olive oil to pan; swirl to coat. Add bacon; cook 2 minutes, stirring occasionally. Add shallots; cook 2 minutes, stirring occasionally. Add mushrooms; cook 3 minutes, stirring occasionally. Increase heat to medium-high. Add garlic; sauté 30 seconds. Stir in ¹/₂ cup beef stock; cook until liquid almost evaporates, stirring occasionally (about 8 minutes). Add spinach; cook 1 minute or until spinach wilts.
2. Preheat oven to 350°.
3. Cut horizontally through center of beef, cutting to, but not through, other side using a sharp knife; open flat, as you would a book. Place beef between 2 sheets of plastic wrap; pound to an even ¹/₂-inch thickness (about 13 inches square) using a meat mallet or small heavy skillet. Brush beef with 1¹/₂ teaspoons olive oil; sprinkle with ¾ teaspoon salt and ¹/₂ teaspoon pepper. Spread mushroom mixture evenly over beef, leaving a ¹/₂-inch border around edges. Roll up beef, jelly-roll fashion. Secure at 2-inch intervals with twine. Brush all sides of beef evenly with 1 tablespoon olive oil; sprinkle with ¹/₂ teaspoon salt and ¹/₄ teaspoon pepper.
4. Place beef on a jelly-roll pan. Bake at 350° for 30 minutes. Increase oven temperature to 450° (do not remove beef); bake an additional 25 minutes or until a thermometer registers 125°. Let beef stand 15 minutes; cut across the grain into 12 slices.
5. Combine 2¹/₂ cups stock, wine, and thyme; bring to a boil. Cook until reduced to 1 cup (about 25 minutes). Discard thyme sprigs. Combine ¹/₄ cup stock mixture and flour in a small bowl, stirring with a whisk until smooth. Add flour mixture to stock mixture. Bring to a boil; cook 1 minute, stirring occasionally. Remove from heat; stir in ¹/₄ teaspoon salt, ¹/₄ teaspoon pepper, butter, and truffle oil. Serve sauce with beef. Serves 12 (serving size: 1 beef slice and about 5 teaspoons sauce)

CALORIES 306; FAT 16.5g (sat 5.7g, mono 7.6g, poly 0.9g); PROTEIN 30.2g; CARB 6.5g; FIBER 1.2g; CHOL 89mg; IRON 2.8mg; SODIUM 504mg; CALC 51mg

Make Ahead
Beer-Braised Brisket with Onion Jam

Hands-on: 37 min. Total: 13 hr. 28 min.
We like to use a mild-flavored beer like a pilsner. Budweiser works well. Highly hoppy ales and dark stouts may throw off the flavor balance in this dish.

1¹/₂ teaspoons salt, divided
1 teaspoon ground cumin
³/₄ teaspoon freshly ground black pepper
¹/₂ teaspoon smoked paprika
6 garlic cloves, minced
3 tablespoons canola oil, divided
1 (4¹/₂-pound) flat-cut brisket roast (untrimmed)
4 cups unsalted beef stock (such as Swanson)
1 (12-ounce) beer
3 medium onions, sliced
3 tablespoons cider vinegar
2 tablespoons brown sugar
1¹/₂ teaspoons cornstarch
1¹/₂ tablespoons chopped fresh thyme

1. Preheat oven to 325°.
2. Combine 1¹/₄ teaspoons salt and next 4 ingredients (through garlic) in a small bowl. Stir in 1 tablespoon oil. Rub salt mixture evenly over side

OUR NO-FAIL SECRETS

For Spinach and Mushroom-Stuffed Beef Tenderloin with Truffled Wine Sauce:
Beef tenderloin is a go-to main dish for holiday meals for good reason: When it's done right, it's velvety soft and wondrously juicy. But because it doesn't have much fat to insulate and self-baste the meat, it gets dry and livery-tasting when cooked past medium. Tenderloin cooks faster than fattier cuts, and its soft texture makes the touch test for doneness a little unreliable for all but the most experienced cooks. For the best beef tenderloin, you need to cook it quickly, keep it moist, and use a trustworthy thermometer. Pull it from the oven right when it hits 125°, and residual heat will take it to perfection.

Another thing to remember about tenderloin: Its selling point is buttery texture, not big flavor. This is why we stuff it with a mushroom-and-spinach sauté mixed with smoky bacon and plenty of garlic. And a bold sauce—like our pinot noir reduction spiked with fragrant truffle oil—is always a welcome addition.

For Beer-Braised Brisket with Onion Jam:
Brisket at its best is meltingly tender with deep, beefy flavor. But it has a reputation as a finicky cut that can end up dry and tough, especially the leaner flat end that's sold in most markets. The trick to coaxing succulent results starts with low, moist heat; a slow braise breaks down tough muscle fibers and connective tissues.

But the post-braising process is just as important: The braised brisket rests overnight in the cooking liquid. This gives the meat a chance to relax and reabsorb any juices pushed out as it cooked. The fat cap stays on the brisket while it cooks as an extra guard against dryness. It is carved off

before reheating, and the overnight chill lets any rendered fat rise to the top of the cooking liquid and solidify, so it can be removed easily. The braised brisket is tender, but that's just half the battle. Now the meat is sliced and reheated in the rich, meaty cooking liquid to guarantee that every bite is juicy. The liquid is then used in a sweet onion jam that pairs perfectly with the beefy brisket.

For Bananas Foster Breakfast Strata:
When you're looking to satisfy a brunch crowd without having to cook eggs individually for every guest, strata is just the ticket. But even though it's a casserole, strata—breakfast bread pudding—can be a tricky thing to pull off. Its success depends largely on texture: You're shooting for a toasty top layer of bread with moist, custardy goodness inside. Not too dry on top or too soggy within.

For the custard in this one, we combine eggs with a little half-and-half and some fat-free evaporated milk, which brings a little sweetness and thick, creamy texture. This thick consistency is key; it'll moisten the bread in the strata but won't oversaturate and sog it out. We add some mashed caramelized bananas for flavor and to make the custard layer even more moist and creamy. To top it all off, a walnut-studded streusel adds crisp contrast on the surface.

For Apple Brandy-Glazed Pork Tenderloin:
Holiday pork roasts often use pork loin, a tasty enough cut, but to keep it moist, you really need to brine it. Our own first tests with this dish started with a brined loin, in fact. The results were fine but not thrilling, and we remained stuck on the issue of brining: It works great to make the meat moist and seasoned throughout, but it's kind of a hassle and lengthens the cooking process by hours or even days.

So we switched to pork tenderloin, a buttery-soft cut that doesn't dry out until it's

cooked well done (and even then, sauce comes to the rescue). We cook it until pink in the middle—basting partway through to give it a flavorful crust—then pair it with sauce spiked with flavorings that formerly swished around in the brine: thyme, brandy, cider. It takes a truly discerning palate to detect those flavors in cooked brined meat, but they come through wonderfully in the sauce. We use unfiltered (cloudy) apple cider because it has pectin to thicken the sauce as it reduces, while clear apple juice does not.

For Roasted Side of Salmon with Shallot Cream:
A roasted whole side of salmon makes a mighty impressive dish for special company, but few home cooks attempt it, largely due to the fear factor. Cooking fish is daunting to many, which is understandable, to a degree: With most finfish like halibut, cod, or tilapia, it's either done perfectly or it's over- or underdone. And the difference in these three outcomes is often a matter of seconds; novice cooks can end up disappointed.

But we're cooking salmon here, and a whole side at that, which offers big advantages. Salmon doneness is a matter of taste: Some like it medium rare to medium, some like it just barely dark pink in the very middle, and others want it completely cooked through and flaky. With a whole side of fish? Done, done, and done. The thicker "head" portion of the side is necessarily going to come out more rare than the thinner "tail" portion. Our recipe gets you fish that's cooked to about medium at the thickest part and completely cooked at the thinner parts: the ultimate crowd-pleasing fish dish. And we roast it quickly at high heat; this keeps it moist throughout. The simple crème fraîche sauce amplifies salmon's natural richness.

---

of beef without fat cap; place beef, salt-mixture side down, in an enameled cast-iron Dutch oven. Combine stock and beer; pour over beef. Cover and bake at 325° for 4 hours or until tender, turning after 2 hours. Cool to room temperature; cover and refrigerate overnight.

3. Preheat oven to 350°.

4. Trim fat cap from beef; discard. Thinly slice beef. Skim fat from cooking

liquid; discard fat. Remove 1 cup liquid; set aside. Place sliced beef and remaining cooking liquid in a 13 x 9–inch glass or ceramic baking dish; cover with foil. Cook beef at 350° for 30 minutes or until thoroughly heated.

5. Heat a large skillet over medium-high heat. Add 2 tablespoons oil to pan; swirl to coat. Add onion; sauté 6 minutes. Reduce heat to medium; cook 15 minutes or until tender, stirring

occasionally. Stir in vinegar, sugar, and cornstarch; cook 30 seconds. Stir in reserved 1 cup cooking liquid; bring to a boil. Cook 1 minute, stirring frequently; remove from heat. Stir in ¼ teaspoon salt and thyme. Serve with beef. Serves 12 (serving size: 3 ounces beef and about ¼ cup onion jam)

CALORIES 287; FAT 10.6g (sat 3g, mono 6.2g, poly 1.4g); PROTEIN 38.3g; CARB 7.7g; FIBER 0.7g; CHOL 117mg; IRON 3.8mg; SODIUM 490mg; CALC 38mg

Bananas Foster Breakfast Strata

Hands-on: 15 min. Total: 1 hr. 10 min.
Take care when adding the rum to the hot pan; it flames up immediately.

Strata:
1 tablespoon canola oil
1 tablespoon butter
3 medium bananas, sliced
1/2 cup rum
1 cup packed brown sugar
1/2 teaspoon salt
1 cup half-and-half
1/2 cup granulated sugar
4 large eggs, lightly beaten
2 (12-ounce) cans fat-free evaporated milk
1 (1-pound) French bread baguette, cut into 1/2-inch cubes
Cooking spray
Streusel:
1.5 ounces all-purpose flour (about 1/3 cup)
1/4 cup chopped walnuts
1/4 cup packed brown sugar
1/4 cup old-fashioned rolled oats
1/8 teaspoon salt
1 tablespoon canola oil
2 tablespoons powdered sugar

1. Preheat oven to 350°.
2. To prepare strata, heat a large skillet over medium-high heat. Add 1 tablespoon oil and butter to pan; swirl until foamy. Stir in bananas; sauté 1 minute. Carefully add half of rum; cook rum until flames subside. Add remaining rum, brown sugar, and 1/2 teaspoon salt; cook 3 minutes or until bananas are soft. Spoon banana mixture into a large bowl; press bananas with a pastry blender or fork until chunky. Combine half-and-half, granulated sugar, eggs, and evaporated milk in a bowl, stirring well with a whisk. Add banana mixture and bread, tossing well to coat. Place bread mixture in a 13 x 9–inch metal baking pan coated with cooking spray. Bake at 350° for 20 minutes.

3. To prepare streusel, weigh or lightly spoon flour into a dry measuring cup; level with a knife. Combine flour, walnuts, and next 3 ingredients (through 1/8 teaspoon salt), stirring well with a whisk. Stir in 1 tablespoon oil. Remove strata from oven; sprinkle evenly with streusel. Bake an additional 30 minutes or until golden and set. Sprinkle with powdered sugar. Serves 14 (serving size: about 3/4 cup)

CALORIES 359; FAT 7.8g (sat 2.6g, mono 2.8g, poly 2g); PROTEIN 10.4g; CARB 63.3g; FIBER 1.6g; CHOL 34mg; IRON 1.9mg; SODIUM 440mg; CALC 205mg

Apple Brandy-Glazed Pork Tenderloin

Hands-on: 15 min. Total: 1 hr. 5 min. *A quick baste midway through cooking flavors the pork crust, promotes browning, and keeps the meat moist.*

3 cups unfiltered apple cider
1/2 cup brandy
3 thyme sprigs
1 large shallot, sliced
2 tablespoons butter
2 teaspoons Dijon mustard
1/2 teaspoon kosher salt, divided
1/2 teaspoon freshly ground black pepper, divided
2 (3/4-pound) pork tenderloins, trimmed
Cooking spray

1. Combine first 4 ingredients in a saucepan; bring to a boil. Cook until reduced to 1/2 cup (about 32 minutes). Remove from heat; discard thyme and shallot. Stir in butter, mustard, 1/8 teaspoon salt and 1/4 teaspoon pepper.
2. Preheat oven to 475°.
3. Sprinkle pork evenly with 3/8 teaspoon salt and 1/4 teaspoon pepper. Lightly coat with cooking spray. Place pork in a roasting pan; bake at 475° for 9 minutes. Turn pork over;

brush evenly with 2 tablespoons cider mixture. Bake an additional 8 minutes or until a thermometer inserted in the thickest portion registers 140°. Let stand 10 minutes. Slice pork and serve with remaining sauce. Serves 6 (serving size: 3 ounces pork and about 1 tablespoon sauce)

CALORIES 269; FAT 6.3g (sat 3.2g, mono 1.9g, poly 0.6g); PROTEIN 24.1g; CARB 16.6g; FIBER 0.4g; CHOL 84mg; IRON 1.4mg; SODIUM 308mg; CALC 11mg

Quick and Easy

Roasted Side of Salmon with Shallot Cream

Hands-on: 20 min. Total: 30 min.

1/4 cup crème fraîche
2 tablespoons finely minced shallots
1 tablespoon 2% reduced-fat milk
1 tablespoon chopped fresh dill
1 1/2 teaspoons fresh lemon juice
1 1/8 teaspoons kosher salt, divided
1 (3-pound) boneless salmon fillet
1 tablespoon olive oil
1/2 teaspoon freshly ground black pepper
1 tablespoon chopped fresh chives

1. Preheat oven to 450°.
2. Combine first 5 ingredients and 1/8 teaspoon salt in a small bowl, stirring with a whisk.
3. Place fish, skin side down, on a parchment-lined baking sheet. Rub fish with oil; sprinkle with 1 teaspoon salt and pepper. Bake at 450° for 8 minutes. Remove from oven.
4. Preheat broiler to high.
5. Broil fish 4 minutes or until desired degree of doneness. Sprinkle with chives. Cut fish crosswise into 6 equal portions. Serves 6 (serving size: about 6 ounces fish and about 1 tablespoon sauce)

CALORIES 347; FAT 15.8g (sat 4.3g, mono 4.7g, poly 2.1g); PROTEIN 47g; CARB 0.9g; FIBER 0.2g; CHOL 114mg; IRON 1mg; SODIUM 535mg; CALC 22mg

BAKE A SECOND BATCH

Kid Friendly • Make Ahead
Freezable • Quick and Easy

Triple-Chocolate Muffins

Hands-on: 15 min. Total: 35 min. To bake a second batch: If you'd like to do both batches in one fell swoop, first make sure you have enough muffin tins to accommodate 24 muffins. If you do, proceed with doubling the batter in a large bowl, and bake all the muffins at the same time in the oven. If you only have enough pans to do 12 muffins at a time, make one batch of batter, bake it, and then start over; if you double the batter, half of it will have to sit while the first batch bakes—and your baking powder will lose its efficacy.

3 tablespoons unsalted butter, diced
1 1/2 ounces 60% bittersweet chocolate, finely chopped
9 ounces all-purpose flour (about 2 cups)
1/3 cup unsweetened cocoa
2 teaspoons baking powder
1/4 teaspoon salt
1/8 teaspoon baking soda
2/3 cup granulated sugar
2/3 cup 2% reduced-fat milk
1/2 teaspoon vanilla extract
2 large eggs, lightly beaten
1/2 cup semisweet chocolate chips
3 tablespoons powdered sugar

1. Preheat oven to 425°.
2. Combine butter and bittersweet chocolate in a small microwave-safe bowl. Microwave at HIGH 45 seconds, stirring every 15 seconds. Stir until smooth. Cool to room temperature.
3. Weigh or lightly spoon flour into dry measuring cups; level with a knife.
Combine flour and next 4 ingredients in a large bowl; stir well with a whisk.
4. Combine granulated sugar, milk, vanilla, and eggs in a bowl; stir with a whisk until well combined.
5. Add butter mixture and milk mixture to flour mixture, stirring until just combined. Gently stir in chocolate chips. Divide batter evenly among 12 lined muffin cups. Bake at 425° for 5 minutes. Reduce oven temperature to 375° (do not remove muffins from oven). Bake at 375° for 10 minutes until a wooden pick inserted in the center comes out with moist crumbs clinging. Cool in pan on a wire rack 5 minutes. Remove muffins from pan; cool completely on wire rack. Sprinkle evenly with powdered sugar. Serves 12 (serving size: 1 muffin)

CALORIES 228; FAT 7.9g (sat 4.6g, mono 2g, poly 0.4g); PROTEIN 4.6g; CARB 37.6g; FIBER 2.1g; CHOL 4mg; IRON 2mg; SODIUM 163mg; CALC 77mg

Make Ahead • Freezable

Rum-Raisin Bundt Cake

*Hands-on: 35 min. Total: 2 hr. 30 min.
To bake a second batch: Double the batter in a large bowl, and bake everything at the same time. Make a standard-size Bundt for yourself, and for gift-giving, do the second batch as mini Bundts: Spoon about 6 tablespoons batter into each of 6 mini Bundt molds coated with baking spray. Spoon remaining batter into a 10-cup coated Bundt pan. Bake both pans on the same rack, located mid-oven. Rotate pans after 15 minutes; the minis will be done in about 20 minutes, and the large one should go the time indicated in the recipe.*

2/3 cup golden raisins
3 tablespoons dark rum (such as Myers's)
12 ounces cake flour (about 3 cups)
1 1/2 teaspoons baking powder
1/2 teaspoon baking soda
1/2 teaspoon salt
1/4 cup unsalted butter, softened
1/2 cup canola oil
1 1/3 cups granulated sugar, divided
1 tablespoon grated orange rind
1 tablespoon grated lemon rind
2 teaspoons vanilla extract
3 large eggs
1 cup 2% reduced-fat milk
Baking spray with flour
3 tablespoons light-colored corn syrup
2 tablespoons water
1 tablespoon powdered sugar

1. Preheat oven to 350°.
2. Combine raisins and rum in a small microwave-safe bowl; microwave at HIGH 30 seconds. Cool to room temperature.
3. Weigh or lightly spoon flour into dry measuring cups; level with a knife. Combine flour and next 3 ingredients in a bowl; stir with a whisk. Place butter in a large bowl; beat with a mixer at medium speed until smooth. Add oil, 1 cup granulated sugar, rinds, and vanilla; beat at medium speed 3 minutes or until light and fluffy. Add eggs, one at a time, beating well after each addition. Add flour mixture and milk alternately to butter mixture, beginning and ending with flour mixture. Drain raisins through a sieve over a bowl; reserve liquid. Stir raisins into batter. Pour batter into a 10-cup Bundt pan coated with baking spray. Bake at 350° for 40 minutes or until a wooden pick inserted in center comes out clean. Cool in pan 10 minutes on a wire rack. Remove from pan; place on a serving plate.
4. Combine 1/3 cup granulated sugar, corn syrup, and 2 tablespoons water in a small saucepan; bring to a boil. Cook 1 minute. Remove pan from heat; stir in reserved rum. Brush syrup over

continued

warm cake. Cool completely. Sprinkle with powdered sugar. Serves 16 (serving size: 1 slice)

CALORIES 307; FAT 11.3g (sat 2.9g, mono 5.6g, poly 2.4g); PROTEIN 4g; CARB 46.4g; FIBER 0.8g; CHOL 44mg; IRON 2.2mg; SODIUM 183mg; CALC 58mg

Make Ahead • Kid Friendly

Pineapple Shortbread Cakes

Hands-on: 1 hr. 13 min. Total: 2 hr. 18 min. To bake a second batch: Understand that these delicious cakes are a labor of love and absolutely worth the time you'll need to spend making them. The most time-consuming part is shaping the cakes; break up the process by making the filling and the dough ahead—up to a couple of days in advance, if you like.

Filling:
3 (8-ounce) cans crushed pineapple in juice, undrained
³/₄ cup granulated sugar
¹/₄ teaspoon salt
¹/₃ cup light-colored corn syrup
4 teaspoons all-purpose flour
Shortbread:
¹/₃ cup nonfat dry milk
9 ounces cake flour (about 2¹/₄ cups)
¹/₄ teaspoon salt
¹/₄ teaspoon baking powder
12 tablespoons unsalted butter, softened
¹/₂ cup powdered sugar
2 large egg yolks
1 tablespoon powdered sugar (optional)

1. To prepare filling, drain pineapple in a fine mesh sieve, pressing solids; discard or save juice for another use. Place pineapple in a medium saucepan over medium-low heat; cook 15 minutes or until all liquid has evaporated, stirring frequently. Add granulated sugar and ¼ teaspoon salt; cook 10 minutes or until liquid mostly evaporates, stirring occasionally. Add corn syrup; cook 5 minutes or until mixture is thick and sticky, stirring frequently.

Add all-purpose flour; cook 1 minute or until very thick, stirring constantly. Scrape mixture onto a baking sheet, and spread into a thin layer; cover and chill completely (about 20 minutes).
2. To prepare shortbread, sift dry milk into a bowl. Weigh or lightly spoon cake flour into dry measuring cups; level with a knife. Sift together dry milk, cake flour, ¼ teaspoon salt, and baking powder. Place butter in a large bowl; beat with a mixer at medium speed until smooth and creamy. Add ½ cup powdered sugar; beat 2 minutes or until well combined. Add egg yolks, 1 at a time, beating well after each addition. Beat 2 minutes or until fluffy. Add flour mixture; beat at low speed until just combined. Divide dough in half. Gently shape dough into 2 (10-inch) logs; cover with plastic wrap. Chill 30 minutes.
3. Arrange 1 oven rack 2 positions down from the top of oven; arrange another rack 2 positions up from the bottom of oven. Preheat oven to 325°.
4. Cut each dough log into 12 equal pieces. Working with one piece at a time, roll dough into a 3-inch circle on a lightly floured surface. Place about 1 tablespoon filling in the center; bring edges together over filling and pinch closed. Gently press into a floured 1¾-inch square mold or cookie cutter, or shape into a square shape by hand. Place cake on a parchment-lined baking sheet. Repeat procedure with remaining dough and filling, placing cakes 2 inches apart onto 2 parchment-lined baking sheets (12 cakes per sheet). Bake at 325° for 25 minutes, turning cakes over and rotating pans after 15 minutes. Remove cakes from pans; cool completely on wire racks. Sprinkle with 1 tablespoon powdered sugar, if desired. Serves 24 (serving size: 1 cake)

CALORIES 158; FAT 6.3g (sat 3.8g, mono 1.7g, poly 0.3g); PROTEIN 1.6g; CARB 24.7g; FIBER 0.4g; CHOL 31mg; IRON 0.9mg; SODIUM 64mg; CALC 23mg

Make Ahead • Kid Friendly

Chocolate-Almond Cheesecake Bars

Hands-on: 25 min. Total: 9 hr. 30 min. To bake a second batch: It's easy to double this recipe all as one process—double the crust, double the filling, divide between pans, and bake both pans together at the same time on the same oven rack. You may find that you need to add a couple extra minutes to the bake time.

3.4 ounces all-purpose flour (about ³/₄ cup)
¹/₄ cup finely ground toasted almonds
¹/₄ teaspoon salt
¹/₄ cup unsalted butter, chilled
Baking spray with flour
6 ounces ¹/₃-less-fat cream cheese, softened
4 ounces fat-free cream cheese, softened
²/₃ cup sugar
¹/₂ cup plain fat-free Greek yogurt
1 teaspoon vanilla extract
Dash of salt
1 large egg
3 ounces semisweet chocolate chips
1 tablespoon 2% reduced-fat milk
2 tablespoons almonds, chopped

1. Preheat oven to 350°.
2. Weigh or lightly spoon flour into dry measuring cups; level with a knife. Combine flour, ¼ cup ground almonds, and ¼ teaspoon salt in a medium bowl. Cut in butter with a pastry blender or 2 knives until mixture resembles coarse meal. Sprinkle flour mixture into an 8-inch square metal baking pan coated with baking spray; lightly press into bottom of pan. Bake at 350° for 30 minutes or until golden. Cool completely on a wire rack.
3. Reduce oven temperature to 325°.
4. Place cream cheeses in a medium bowl; beat with a mixer at medium speed until smooth. Add sugar, yogurt, vanilla, and dash of salt; beat at low speed until combined. Add egg; beat 1 minute or until well combined. Pour

mixture on top of cooled crust. Place chocolate chips and milk in a small microwave-safe bowl. Microwave at HIGH 30 seconds or until melted, stirring after 15 seconds; stir mixture until smooth. Dollop chocolate mixture by the spoonful over cheesecake mixture; swirl together using a knife. Sprinkle top with 2 tablespoons almonds. Bake at 325° for 30 minutes or until almost set in the middle. Cool completely on wire rack. Cover and refrigerate 8 hours or up to overnight. Serves 16 (serving size: 1 bar)

CALORIES 164; FAT 8.6g (sat 4.4g, mono 2.8g, poly 0.7g); PROTEIN 4.5g; CARB 18.1g; FIBER 0.8g; CHOL 28mg; IRON 0.6mg; SODIUM 139mg; CALC 55mg

**Make Ahead • Freezable
Kid Friendly**

Star Anise Snickerdoodles

Hands-on: 30 min. Total: 1 hr. 35 min. To bake a second batch: Make a double batch of dough in a large bowl. Bake the first batch of cookies on 2 baking sheets in the oven as directed, and keep the unused dough in the fridge as the first batch bakes. Cool baking sheets completely before proceeding with the rest of the dough.

**5³/₄ ounces all-purpose flour (about
   1¹/₄ cups)
1 teaspoon baking powder
1 teaspoon freshly ground star anise
   (about 3 pods)
¹/₄ teaspoon salt
¹/₄ teaspoon cream of tartar
6 tablespoons unsalted butter, softened
1 cup plus 2 tablespoons sugar, divided
¹/₂ teaspoon vanilla extract
1 large egg
³/₄ teaspoon ground cinnamon**

1. Weigh or lightly spoon flour into dry measuring cups; level with a knife. Combine flour and next 4 ingredients in a bowl; stir with a whisk. Place butter in a medium bowl; beat with

a mixer at medium speed 30 seconds or until smooth. Add 1 cup sugar and vanilla; beat until well combined. Add egg; beat 1 minute or until well combined. Add flour mixture; beat 30 seconds at low speed or until just combined. Shape dough into a ball; wrap in plastic wrap. Chill 1 hour.
2. Arrange 1 oven rack 2 positions down from top of oven; arrange another rack 2 positions up from bottom of oven. Preheat oven to 375°.
3. Shape dough into 24 balls. Combine 2 tablespoons sugar and cinnamon in a shallow dish. Roll dough balls in cinnamon mixture, coating completely. Place balls 3 inches apart on 2 parchment-lined baking sheets. Bake at 375° for 11 minutes or until edges are golden, rotating pans after 6 minutes. Cool on pans 5 minutes. Remove cookies from pans; cool on wire racks. Serves 24 (serving size: 1 cookie)

CALORIES 90; FAT 3.2g (sat 1.9g, mono 0.8g, poly 0.2g); PROTEIN 1g; CARB 14.6g; FIBER 0.2g; CHOL 15mg; IRON 0.4mg; SODIUM 48mg; CALC 16mg

**Kid Friendly • Make Ahead
Freezable**

Eggnog Coffee Cake

Hands-on: 15 min. Total: 60 min. To bake a second batch: Double the crumble mixture and the cake batter in large bowls. Make the round coffee cake for yourself, and do the second batch in muffin tins for gift-giving.

**Crumble:
¹/₄ cup old-fashioned rolled oats
¹/₄ cup packed brown sugar
3 tablespoons all-purpose flour
¹/₈ teaspoon salt
2 tablespoons unsalted butter, chilled
¹/₄ cup chopped pecans, toasted
Cake:
6.75 ounces all-purpose flour (about
   1¹/₂ cups)
1¹/₂ teaspoons freshly ground nutmeg
1 teaspoon baking powder**

**¹/₂ teaspoon baking soda
¹/₄ teaspoon salt
3 tablespoons unsalted butter, softened
³/₄ cup granulated sugar
1 large egg
1 large egg yolk
¹/₂ cup 2% reduced-fat milk
¹/₄ cup reduced-fat sour cream
1¹/₂ teaspoons vanilla extract
Baking spray with flour**

1. Preheat oven to 350°.
2. To prepare crumble, combine first 4 ingredients in a bowl, stirring with a whisk. Cut in 2 tablespoons butter using a pastry cutter or 2 knives until mixture resembles coarse meal. Stir in nuts.
3. To prepare cake, weigh or lightly spoon 6.75 ounces flour into dry measuring cups; level with a knife. Combine 6.75 ounces flour and next 4 ingredients; stir with a whisk. Place 3 tablespoons butter and granulated sugar in a medium bowl; beat with a mixer at medium speed until well combined. Add egg and yolk, 1 at a time, beating well after each addition. Add milk, sour cream, and vanilla; beat on low speed 1 minute or until well combined. Add flour mixture; beat on low speed 1 minute or until just combined.
4. Spoon half of batter into an 8-inch round metal cake pan coated with baking spray. Sprinkle with half of crumble. Spread remaining batter over crumble; smooth top with a spatula. Sprinkle top evenly with remaining crumble. Bake at 350° for 30 minutes or until a wooden pick inserted in center comes out clean. Cool in pan on a wire rack 15 minutes. Place a plate upside down on top of cake; invert onto plate. Serves 10 (serving size: 1 wedge)

CALORIES 266; FAT 10.1g (sat 4.9g, mono 3.1g, poly 1.1g); PROTEIN 4.4g; CARB 39.8g; FIBER 1.1g; CHOL 56mg; IRON 1.4mg; SODIUM 219mg; CALC 70mg

OUR BEST SLOW COOKER RECIPES

Recipes by the *Cooking Light* test kitchen

The slow cooker holds such promise this time of year, in the height of holiday craziness. We trust it to deliver convenience in a delicious way, expecting it to magically convert the ingredients we load in into savory, meaty stews with soul. But slow cooker dishes can sometimes disappoint, turning out food that tastes defeated, textures and flavors exhausted. Our Test Kitchen set about conquering the slow cooker, unlocking the secrets to succulent meats, tender but toothsome beans, and brilliant flavors. What follow are our learnings and our best slow cooker recipes yet.

INGREDIENTS

Meat: Prolonged exposure to heat can easily transform lovely, lean cuts of beef or pork to jerky. For the slow cooker, select meats with a reasonable layer of fat or internal marbling, such as chuck roast or brisket, to prevent drastic dry-outs. For poultry that's immersed in liquid, try to cut cook time down to about 4 hours; longer than that is likely to leave you with stringy remnants.

Veggies: Fact: Crisp is not a texture that survives 8 hours in a slow cooker. Only heartier vegetables, like root veggies cut into relatively large pieces, or vegetables that stew down nicely, like tomatoes, will maintain a pleasant consistency for the long haul. If you want to include more delicate green ingredients, such as asparagus or green beans, try tossing them in for the last 30 minutes of cooking.

Seasonings: Think you need 1 teaspoon of oregano? Use two. Slow cookers have a funny way of diluting flavor, so you'll probably need to add more flavor ingredients on the front end. When trying something new in the slow cooker, double the amount of herbs or spices that you think you need—even for intense spices like crushed red pepper.

Garnishes: As with any recipe, tossing fresh garnishes onto a completed dish from the slow cooker is an easy way to bring the meal to life. Try using fresh salsa, herbs, or ingredients with crunch to add a pop of color and vibrancy.

PRO TIPS

Get to know your cooker. Just like learning the hot spots and quirks of your oven, understanding how your slow cooker handles certain ingredients and recipes is going to take a little time and experimentation.

Go easy on liquid. By the time your timer dings, the pot will have twice as much liquid as you started with, so there's no need to completely cover the meat and veggies with stock or water from the start.

Go for size. We've found that providing the food with breathing room yields better results than attempting to pack it into a smaller cooker. A 6-quart cooker is the size we recommend. Save any mini cookers for keeping potluck queso dip warm, and break out the big guns to get dinner on the table.

FOR SUPERIOR RESULTS, SLOW COOKING ISN'T A TOTALLY HANDS-OFF PROCESS; A QUALITY RECIPE REQUIRES MORE THAN DUMPING EVERYTHING IN RAW AND TROT-TING AWAY.

Make Ahead • Kid Friendly
Classic Slow Cooker Beef Stew

Hands-on: 45 min. Total: 8 hr. A nutty dark beer adds richness and depth to the stew. Be careful not to choose a beer that's too hoppy—it will taste too bitter. To get 2 pounds of trimmed meat, you'll probably need to purchase a 2½-pound roast.

2 pounds trimmed boneless chuck roast, cut into 2-inch cubes
1½ teaspoons kosher salt, divided
1 teaspoon freshly ground black pepper, divided
2 tablespoons canola oil, divided
3 medium yellow onions, halved lengthwise and cut crosswise into ½-inch-thick slices
6 garlic cloves, thinly sliced
1 (12-ounce) nut brown ale
1¼ cups unsalted beef stock (such as Swanson), divided
1½ pounds baby Dutch potatoes, halved
1 pound carrots, peeled and cut diagonally into 2-inch pieces

4 thyme sprigs
2 bay leaves
2 tablespoons all-purpose flour
1 tablespoon Dijon mustard
1 tablespoon red wine vinegar
¼ cup flat-leaf parsley leaves

1. Heat a large skillet over medium-high heat. Sprinkle beef evenly with ¼ teaspoon salt and ¼ teaspoon pepper. Add 1½ teaspoons oil to pan; swirl to coat. Add half of beef to pan; cook 6 minutes, turning until well browned on all sides. Remove beef from pan. Repeat procedure with 1½ teaspoons oil and remaining beef; remove beef and any juices from pan.
2. Add 1 tablespoon oil to pan; swirl to coat. Add onions and garlic; sauté 4 minutes. Add beer, scraping pan to loosen browned bits. Bring to a boil; cook 2 minutes. Stir in 1 cup stock, 1¼ teaspoons salt, and ¾ teaspoon pepper. Bring to a simmer. Carefully pour mixture into a 6-quart electric slow cooker. Add beef, potatoes, carrots, thyme, and bay leaves. Cover and cook on LOW for 7 hours.
3. Combine ¼ cup stock and flour, stirring with a whisk. Stir flour mixture into stew; cook 15 minutes or until thickened. Stir in mustard and vinegar. Discard thyme sprigs and bay leaves. Sprinkle with parsley. Serves 8 (serving size: about 1¼ cups)

CALORIES 386; FAT 17.9g (sat 5.9g, mono 8.3g, poly 1.6g); PROTEIN 25.1g; CARB 28.3g; FIBER 3.5g; CHOL 86mg; IRON 3mg; SODIUM 509mg; CALC 48mg

SPEND A LITTLE (EFFORT) TO RECEIVE A LOT (OF FLAVOR).

Make Ahead

Cuban Pork Shoulder with Beans and Rice

Hands-on: 45 min. Total: 8 hr. 45 min.
Here's a hearty dinner that doesn't require presoaking of the beans—they go straight into the cooker and end up perfectly tender 8 hours later. Since you blend up a whole orange, peel and all, you should look for Florida oranges, which have a thinner skin than the thick-peeled oranges from California.

2¾ cups unsalted chicken stock (such as Swanson)
1 cup fresh orange juice (about 4 oranges)
½ cup chopped cilantro stems
1 medium orange, quartered
1¾ teaspoons kosher salt, divided
1½ teaspoons freshly ground black pepper, divided
4 center-cut bacon slices, chopped
1 (2½-pound) bone-in pork shoulder, trimmed
1 pound dried black beans
2¼ cups chopped onion, divided
10 garlic cloves, crushed and divided
¼ cup chopped fresh oregano, divided
2 teaspoons paprika
2 teaspoons ground cumin
1½ teaspoons crushed red pepper
1 bay leaf
1½ cups chopped tomato
1 jalapeño pepper, seeded and chopped
2⅔ cups hot cooked white rice
¼ cup chopped fresh cilantro

1. Place first 4 ingredients in a blender; process until smooth. Strain orange juice mixture through a fine sieve over a bowl; discard solids. Stir in ¾ teaspoon salt and ¾ teaspoon black pepper.
2. Place bacon in a large skillet over medium heat; cook 5 minutes or until crisp. Remove bacon with a slotted spoon. Place bacon in a 6-quart electric slow cooker. Sprinkle pork with ½ teaspoon salt and ½ teaspoon black pepper. Return skillet to medium-high heat. Add pork to drippings in skillet; cook 8 minutes, turning to brown on all sides. Add pork to slow cooker. Pour uncooked beans around pork.
3. Return skillet to medium-high heat. Add 2 cups onion and 6 garlic cloves; sauté 3 minutes. Add 3 tablespoons oregano, paprika, cumin, and red pepper to pan; sauté 1 minute. Add orange mixture and bay leaf to pan; bring to a boil and cook 1 minute, scraping pan to loosen browned bits. Pour onion mixture over pork. Cover and cook on LOW for 8 hours or until pork is very tender and black beans are done. Shred pork; discard bones. Discard bay leaf. Stir in ¼ teaspoon salt.
4. Combine ¼ teaspoon salt, ¼ teaspoon black pepper, ¼ cup onion, tomato, and jalapeño pepper in a bowl. Chop 4 garlic cloves; stir into tomato mixture. Spoon ⅓ cup rice onto each of 8 plates; top each serving with ½ cup bean mixture, about 3 ounces pork mixture, and 3½ tablespoons salsa. Garnish with 1 tablespoon oregano and ¼ cup cilantro. Serves 8

CALORIES 510; FAT 12.8g (sat 4.1g, mono 5.3g, poly 2.1g); PROTEIN 34.3g; CARB 62.2g; FIBER 7g; CHOL 64mg; IRON 4.9mg; SODIUM 655mg; CALC 66mg

BROWNING MEAT AND ONIONS PRIOR TO SLOW COOKING IS THE BEST WAY TO ADD DEEP, RICH FLAVOR WITHOUT A TON OF SALT OR FAT.

Creamy White Bean Soup with Smoked Ham Hocks

Hands-on: 10 min. Total: 8 hr. 10 min.
This hearty, rustic soup is the epitome of comfort: creamy, starchy, and filling. Here again, the beans go in dried—no need to soak.

2 tablespoons olive oil
1¹/₂ cups chopped onion
1 cup diced celery
1 cup diced carrot
1 tablespoon chopped fresh thyme
6 garlic cloves, chopped
2 pounds smoked ham hocks
1 pound dried Great Northern beans
2 (26-ounce) containers unsalted chicken stock (such as Swanson)
¹/₄ cup minced fresh chives
1 teaspoon freshly ground black pepper

1. Heat a skillet over medium-high heat. Add oil to pan; swirl to coat. Add onion and next 4 ingredients (through garlic); cook 10 minutes or until vegetables are soft. Scrape onion mixture into a 6-quart electric slow cooker. Add hocks, beans, and stock. Cover and cook on LOW for 8 hours or overnight.
2. Remove hocks from pan; cool slightly. Remove meat from bones; discard fat, skin, and bones. Chop meat; stir meat into beans. Cook 10 minutes to allow flavors to meld. Sprinkle with chives and black pepper. Serves 8 (serving size: about 1 cup)

CALORIES 260; FAT 5.1g (sat 1g, mono 2.5g, poly 0.7g); PROTEIN 19.1g; CARB 36.2g; FIBER 11.2g; CHOL 8mg; IRON 3.6mg; SODIUM 639mg; CALC 136mg

Chicken and Chickpea Tagine

Hands-on: 20 min. Total: 7 hr. 20 min.
Hearty canned chickpeas hold up beautifully in the slow cooker, where they're combined with lots of fragrant spices and just a little stock. Since the chicken cooks on top of the chickpea mixture and is not submerged in liquid, it retains its nice browned color. Serve with a simple green salad and a side of couscous.

1¹/₂ tablespoons canola oil
8 (5-ounce) bone-in chicken thighs, skinned
1¹/₄ teaspoons kosher salt, divided
¹/₂ teaspoon freshly ground black pepper
2¹/₂ cups chopped onion
¹/₄ cup finely chopped fresh garlic
1¹/₄ teaspoons ground cumin
1 teaspoon ground coriander
1 teaspoon paprika
³/₄ teaspoon ground turmeric
¹/₂ teaspoon ground ginger
¹/₄ teaspoon ground red pepper
1 cup unsalted chicken stock (such as Swanson)
1¹/₂ teaspoons honey
1 (3-inch) cinnamon stick
²/₃ cup chopped dried apricots
2 (15-ounce) cans organic chickpeas, rinsed and drained
¹/₄ cup chopped fresh cilantro
Lemon wedges

1. Heat a large skillet over medium-high heat. Add oil to pan; swirl to coat. Sprinkle meaty side of chicken with ½ teaspoon salt and black pepper. Add chicken to pan, meaty side down; cook 5 minutes or until well browned. Remove from pan (do not brown other side).
2. Add onion and garlic to pan; sauté 4 minutes. Add cumin and next 5 ingredients (through red pepper); cook 1 minute, stirring constantly. Add ¾ teaspoon salt, stock, honey, and cinnamon, scraping pan to loosen browned bits; bring to a simmer. Carefully pour mixture into a 6-quart electric slow cooker. Stir in apricots and chickpeas. Arrange chicken, browned side up, on top of chickpea mixture. Cover and cook on LOW for 7 hours. Discard cinnamon stick. Sprinkle with cilantro; serve with lemon wedges. Serves 8 (serving size: 1 thigh, about ⅔ cup chickpea mixture, and 1 lemon wedge)

CALORIES 255; FAT 6.9g (sat 1.1g, mono 2.9g, poly 1.6g); PROTEIN 22g; CARB 26.6g; FIBER 4.7g; CHOL 81mg; IRON 2.2mg; SODIUM 412mg; CALC 78mg

Sweet and Tangy Short Ribs

Hands-on: 28 min. Total: 8 hr. 58 min.
This saucy dish is worthy of a dinner party; just serve with a side of brown rice. Cola is the secret ingredient, yielding a luscious sauce.

2 tablespoons canola oil, divided
8 (6-ounce) bone-in beef short ribs, trimmed
³/₄ cup unsalted beef stock (such as Swanson)
¹/₃ cup lower-sodium soy sauce
¹/₄ cup rice vinegar
2 tablespoons grated peeled fresh ginger
2 tablespoons brown sugar
2 tablespoons sambal oelek
8 minced garlic cloves
1 (12-ounce) can cola
1 star anise
1 (4 x 1-inch) orange rind strip
4 cups (1-inch) diagonally cut carrot
¹/₄ cup water
1 tablespoon cornstarch
2 cups diagonally cut snow peas
¹/₄ cup chopped fresh cilantro

1. Heat a large skillet over medium-high heat. Add 1 tablespoon oil; swirl to coat. Add half of beef to pan; cook 10 minutes, turning to brown on all sides. Remove beef from pan; place in a 6-quart electric slow cooker. Repeat procedure with 1 tablespoon oil and beef. Add stock and next 9 ingredients (through rind) to slow cooker. Cover and cook on LOW for 8 hours or until beef is very tender. Carefully remove beef from pan; keep warm. Discard star anise and rind.

2. Skim fat from surface of cooking liquid; discard fat. Pour cooking liquid into a large saucepan; bring to a simmer. Add carrots to pan; cook 20 minutes or until carrots are almost done. Combine ¼ cup water and cornstarch in a small bowl, stirring with a whisk. Add cornstarch mixture to pan; bring to a boil. Stir in peas; cook 2 minutes. Place 1 short rib in each of 8 shallow bowls. Ladle ½ cup sauce and vegetables over each serving; sprinkle with 1½ teaspoons cilantro. Serves 8

CALORIES 234; **FAT** 11.6g (sat 3.7g, mono 5.7g, poly 1.3g); **PROTEIN** 15.4g; **CARB** 16.5g; **FIBER** 1.5g; **CHOL** 41mg; **IRON** 2.1mg; **SODIUM** 533mg; **CALC** 33mg

Make Ahead

Slow Cooker Chicken Verde

Hands-on: 40 min. Total: 4 hr. 40 min.
It's not hard to make your own salsa verde, with fresher flavor and way less sodium than jarred versions: Simply blacken tomatillos, chiles, and onions, and then blend.

⅓ cup garlic cloves
1 tablespoon canola oil
2 pounds tomatillos, husks removed
2 poblano chiles, stemmed and seeded
1 medium onion, quartered
½ cup chopped fresh cilantro
2 tablespoons fresh oregano
1 tablespoon cornstarch
1 teaspoon salt
¾ teaspoon freshly ground black pepper
½ cup unsalted chicken stock (such as Swanson)
Cooking spray
8 chicken leg quarters, skinned
8 lime wedges

1. Preheat broiler.
2. Combine first 5 ingredients in a large bowl, tossing to coat. Arrange on a jelly-roll pan. Broil 10 minutes or until vegetables are black in spots. Place mixture in a blender; add cilantro, oregano, cornstarch, salt, pepper, and stock. Remove center piece of blender lid (to allow steam to escape); secure blender lid on blender. Place a clean towel over opening in blender lid (to avoid splatters). Blend until smooth.
3. Heat a large heavy skillet over medium-high heat. Coat pan with cooking spray. Add 4 chicken leg quarters; cook 5 minutes or until well browned. Repeat procedure with cooking spray and remaining chicken. Arrange chicken in a 6-quart electric slow cooker; top with tomatillo mixture. Cover and cook on LOW 4 hours or until done. Serve with lime wedges. Serves 8 (serving size: 1 chicken quarter, about ¾ cup sauce, and 1 lime wedge)

CALORIES 302; **FAT** 10.6g (sat 2.2g, mono 3.9g, poly 2.7g); **PROTEIN** 38.5g; **CARB** 12.8g; **FIBER** 3g; **CHOL** 175mg; **IRON** 2.3mg; **SODIUM** 505mg; **CALC** 49mg

Freezable • Make Ahead
Kid Friendly

Slow-Cooked Ragù

Hands-on: 30 min. Total: 6 hr. 30 min.
This meaty sauce is great ladled over any kind of pasta, and leftovers freeze well.

2 ounces pancetta, chopped
1 pound ground sirloin (90% lean)
12 ounces lean ground pork
1 (4-ounce) hot turkey Italian sausage link, casing removed
1 tablespoon canola oil
1⅓ cups diced onion
⅔ cup diced carrot
⅔ cup diced celery
¼ cup unsalted tomato paste
2 tablespoons minced fresh garlic
½ cup dry white wine

2 cups unsalted chicken stock (such as Swanson)
1 (15-ounce) can unsalted crushed tomatoes
1 teaspoon salt, divided
1 teaspoon freshly ground black pepper
1 bay leaf

1. Place pancetta in a large skillet over medium-high heat; cook 4 minutes or until beginning to brown, stirring occasionally. Add beef; cook 3 minutes or until browned, stirring to crumble. Place beef mixture in a 6-quart electric slow cooker. Return skillet to medium-high heat. Add ground pork and sausage; cook 5 minutes or until browned, stirring to crumble. Add pork mixture to slow cooker.
2. Return skillet to medium-high heat. Add oil; swirl to coat. Add onion, carrot, and celery; sauté 4 minutes. Add tomato paste and garlic; cook 2 minutes, stirring frequently. Add wine; bring to a boil. Cook 2 minutes or until wine mostly evaporates, scraping pan to loosen browned bits. Add stock, tomatoes, ¾ teaspoon salt, pepper, and bay leaf; bring to a boil. Carefully pour stock mixture into slow cooker; cover and cook on LOW for 6 hours. Discard bay leaf. Stir in ¼ teaspoon salt. Serves 8 (serving size: 1 cup)

CALORIES 296; **FAT** 16.1g (sat 5.7g, mono 6.3g, poly 1.6g); **PROTEIN** 24.5g; **CARB** 10.4g; **FIBER** 2.1g; **CHOL** 78mg; **IRON** 2.8mg; **SODIUM** 589mg; **CALC** 48mg

TO CREATE A DIVERSITY OF TEXTURES, CONSIDER ADDING INGREDIENTS IN INCREMENTS THROUGHOUT THE COOKING PROCESS.

Hearty Oats and Grains

Vegetarian • Kid Friendly

Hands-on: 10 min. Total: 3 hr. 15 min.
When you have a house full of holiday guests who'd enjoy a wholesome, hearty breakfast at their own pace, the slow cooker can come to your rescue. Get it going first thing in the morning, and let folks serve themselves when they're ready to eat.

Cooking spray
3 cups water
2 cups apple cider (such as Zeigler's)
1 cup steel-cut oats
1 cup 7-grain blend (such as Laurel Hill)
1½ teaspoons ground cinnamon
½ teaspoon salt
1 cup 2% reduced-fat milk, warmed
⅓ cup maple syrup
1½ cups diced apple
½ cup chopped toasted walnuts

1. Coat the inside of a 6-quart electric slow cooker with cooking spray. Place 3 cups water and next 5 ingredients (through salt) in cooker, stirring well. Cover and cook on LOW for 3 hours. Spoon about ⅔ cup oat mixture into each of 8 bowls; top each serving with 2 tablespoons milk, 2 teaspoons syrup, 3 tablespoons apple, and 1 tablespoon nuts. Serves 8

CALORIES 292; **FAT** 7.3g (sat 1.1g, mono 0.8g, poly 3.5g); **PROTEIN** 8g; **CARB** 53.8g; **FIBER** 5.8g; **CHOL** 2.4mg; **IRON** 1.7mg; **SODIUM** 162mg; **CALC** 84mg

Tangy Italian Beef Sandwiches

Kid Friendly • Make Ahead

Hands-on: 15 min. Total: 8 hr. 15 min.
Beef slowly braises until it practically falls into shreds. We like the mixture on sandwiches, but it's also delicious served over a baked potato and topped with sour cream.

3 banana peppers
Cooking spray
½ cup white vinegar
1 tablespoon onion powder
1 tablespoon garlic powder
1½ teaspoons crushed red pepper
1 teaspoon kosher salt, divided
½ teaspoon freshly ground black pepper
7 bottled pepperoncini peppers, chopped
2¼ pounds chuck roast, trimmed and halved
8 (1½-ounce) sandwich rolls, toasted

1. Preheat broiler.
2. Arrange peppers on a baking sheet coated with cooking spray. Broil 6 minutes or until blackened in spots, turning occasionally. Place peppers in a 6-quart electric slow cooker. Add vinegar, onion powder, garlic powder, and red pepper; stir to combine. Stir in ½ teaspoon salt, black pepper, and pepperoncini peppers.
3. Heat a large skillet over medium-high heat. Coat pan with cooking spray. Add beef; cook 5 minutes, turning to brown on all sides. Place beef in slow cooker. Cover and cook on LOW for 8 hours or until beef is very tender. Remove beef from cooker; shred with 2 forks. Stir beef and ½ teaspoon salt into cooking liquid. Divide beef mixture evenly among sandwich rolls, spooning out with a slotted spoon. Serve any extra sauce for dipping. Serves 8 (serving size: 1 sandwich and about 2 tablespoons sauce)

CALORIES 356; **FAT** 15.9g (sat 6g, mono 6.4g, poly 1.3g); **PROTEIN** 26.2g; **CARB** 24.7g; **FIBER** 19g; **CHOL** 86mg; **IRON** 3.5mg; **SODIUM** 588mg; **CALC** 94mg

Slow Cooker Sausage and Squash Lasagna

Make Ahead • Kid Friendly

Hands-on: 47 min. Total: 4 hr. 57 min.
We were surprised and delighted by how well lasagna cooks up in the slow cooker. Be sure to use traditional noodles, and place them in the cooker uncooked. We tried the recipe with specially formulated no-bake noodles, and they didn't work as well.

9 ounces part-skim ricotta cheese
1 ounce Asiago cheese, grated and divided (about ¼ cup)
2 tablespoons chopped fresh flat-leaf parsley, divided
2 tablespoons chopped fresh chives, divided
¼ teaspoon freshly ground black pepper
6 garlic cloves, divided
6 cups water
½ cup red wine vinegar
1 large yellow crookneck squash, cut into ¼-inch-thick slices
1 large zucchini, cut into ¼-inch-thick slices
Cooking spray
12 ounces hot turkey Italian sausage links, casings removed
2 cups chopped onion
1 tablespoon olive oil
3 (3.5-ounce) packages shiitake mushrooms, stemmed and sliced
1 cup unsalted chicken stock (such as Swanson)
½ cup chopped basil leaves
1 (25-ounce) jar lower-sodium marinara sauce (such as Dell'Amore)
12 uncooked lasagna noodles
4 ounces fontina cheese, shredded and divided (about 1 cup)

1. Combine ricotta, 2 tablespoons Asiago cheese, 1 tablespoon parsley, 1 tablespoon chives, pepper, and 1 garlic clove, grated, in a bowl; set aside.

2. Bring 6 cups water to a boil in a large skillet; stir in vinegar. Add squash and zucchini; cook 2 minutes. Drain; set aside.

3. Heat skillet over medium-high heat. Coat pan with cooking spray. Add Italian sausage; cook 7 minutes or until browned, stirring to crumble. Stir in onion; cook 8 minutes or until onion is tender.

4. Heat oil in a large saucepan over medium-high heat. Add mushrooms; cook 10 minutes or until mushrooms begin to lose their moisture. Finely chop 5 garlic cloves; stir into mushrooms. Stir in chicken stock, basil, and marinara. Bring to a boil; remove from heat.

5. To assemble lasagna, spoon 1 cup marinara mixture into the bottom of a 6-quart electric slow cooker. Top with 4 noodles, breaking noodles to fit cooker. Layer half of squash mixture, half of Italian sausage mixture, and ¼ cup fontina cheese over noodles; top with 1 cup marinara mixture. Arrange 4 noodles over marinara mixture; top with ricotta mixture. Sprinkle with ¼ cup fontina; top with remaining half of Italian sausage mixture and remaining half of squash mixture. Arrange remaining 4 noodles over squash mixture; top with remaining 1½ cups sauce and ¼ cup fontina. Cover and cook on LOW for 4 hours.

6. Preheat broiler.

7. Uncover slow cooker; sprinkle lasagna with ¼ cup fontina and 2 tablespoons Asiago. Broil in the middle of the oven for 2 minutes or until cheese browns slightly. Sprinkle with 1 tablespoon parsley and 1 tablespoon chives. Let stand 10 minutes before serving. Serves 10 (serving size: about 1 cup)

CALORIES 342; FAT 14.1g (sat 5.5g, mono 5.5g, poly 1.6g); PROTEIN 19.8g; CARB 35.4g; FIBER 4.1g; CHOL 52mg; IRON 1.2mg; SODIUM 516mg; CALC 180mg

TODAY'S SPECIAL

COCONUT CURRIED MUSSELS WITH CAULIFLOWER

From Hinoki & the Bird in Los Angeles

Cauliflower, an unsung hero of the cruciferous family too often relegated to crudité platters and steamed vegetable medleys, has finally started to get its due. Roasty-toasty browned florets and deep-golden, thick-cut cauliflower steaks have become menu staples at the hippest restaurants. David Myers, whose Silk Road–accented Hinoki & the Bird has been a culinary sensation since its opening last January, puts cauliflower to work in Asian dishes.

"Cauliflower absorbs a lot of flavor," Myers says. That makes it great for a dish that bathes it in bold curry broth flavored with fiery chiles, fragrant lemongrass, and warm, earthy spices. His original version of this dish, inspired by a trip through Thailand, features florets simmered in the rich sauce, and raw cauliflower shaved on top at the end. This creates extra textural interest and "gives the dish a crisp, clean veggie flavor," he says.

Myers has two general preferred preparations for cauliflower. On the stovetop, he cooks it in a covered pan with a little olive oil, so it steams in its own liquid. And though home cooks don't typically think of grilling cruciferous veggies, Myers finds that a little charcoal flavor works wonders for cauliflower and enhances its natural meatiness. He starts the vegetable in foil on the grill, and then finishes it for a minute or two directly on the grill for some charring.

Try Myers' original dish this month at Hinoki & the Bird in Century City.

Quick and Easy

Coconut Curried Mussels with Cauliflower

Hands-on: 30 min. Total: 30 min.

Curry paste:
2 tablespoons thinly sliced peeled fresh lemongrass
2 tablespoons minced shallots
2 tablespoons chopped fresh cilantro
½ teaspoon ground coriander
½ teaspoon cumin seeds
½ teaspoon shrimp paste
½ teaspoon grated peeled fresh ginger
¼ teaspoon black peppercorns
¼ teaspoon crushed red pepper
2 garlic cloves, chopped
1 kaffir lime leaf
Mussels:
1 tablespoon canola oil
2 cups small cauliflower florets
1 cup unsalted chicken stock (such as Swanson)
1 cup light coconut milk
48 mussels (about 2 pounds), scrubbed and debearded
2 tablespoons fresh lime juice
2 tablespoons thinly sliced Thai basil
2 tablespoons chopped fresh cilantro
2 tablespoons chopped fresh dill

1. Combine first 11 ingredients in a mortar or bowl; grind with a pestle until mixture forms a smooth paste.

2. Heat a large Dutch oven over medium-high heat. Add oil; swirl to coat. Add cauliflower; sauté until lightly browned. Stir in curry paste, stock, and milk; bring to a boil. Add mussels; cover, and simmer 5 minutes or until mussels open. Discard any unopened shells. Stir in juice and herbs. Spoon into bowls; serve immediately. Serves 4 (serving size: 12 mussels, ½ cup broth, and ½ cup cauliflower)

CALORIES 196; FAT 6.2g (sat 3.4g, mono 0.7g, poly 0.8g); PROTEIN 18.7g; CARB 17.8g; FIBER 1.8g; CHOL 34mg; IRON 6.1mg; SODIUM 468mg; CALC 66mg

RISOTTO

Many cooks think of risotto as a restaurant dish—one to order but not to make. Maybe that's because their homemade versions are never quite as creamy, but we have the tricks to get you there every time. And if you make it yourself, you're guaranteed a healthier bowl.

Start with the right rice: We call for readily available Arborio, but you could also use Carnaroli or Vialone Nano. Certainly, stirring is important, as it agitates the grains and releases starch, which makes for that creamy texture. Using hot stock is crucial, too, for even and thorough cooking. And for the loosest, creamiest texture, our secret is to add a little liquid after the pan comes off the heat. Use a tip from contributor Kenji López-Alt of Serious Eats, and serve in warmed bowls, which will also keep things loose and luscious.

Quick and Easy • Kid Friendly

Classic Risotto Milanese

Hands-on: 29 min. Total: 29 min.

5 cups unsalted chicken stock (such as Swanson)
1¹/₂ tablespoons extra-virgin olive oil
1¹/₄ cups finely chopped onion
1¹/₂ cups Arborio rice
⁵/₈ teaspoon kosher salt
¹/₄ teaspoon saffron threads, crushed
¹/₂ cup dry white wine
1 tablespoon unsalted butter
¹/₂ teaspoon freshly ground black pepper
1.5 ounces Parmigiano-Reggiano cheese, grated (about ¹/₃ cup)
2 tablespoons chopped fresh flat-leaf parsley

1. Bring stock to a simmer in a medium saucepan (do not boil). Keep warm over low heat.
2. Heat a Dutch oven over medium heat. Add oil to pan; swirl to coat. Add onion; cook 5 minutes or until tender, stirring occasionally. Add rice, salt, and saffron; cook 1 minute, stirring frequently. Add wine; cook 2 minutes or until liquid is absorbed, stirring frequently. Stir in 1¹/₂ cups stock; cook 4 minutes or until liquid is nearly absorbed, stirring constantly. Add remaining stock, ¾ cup at a time, stirring nearly constantly until each portion of stock is absorbed before adding the next (about 22 minutes total); reserve ¹/₃ cup stock at the last addition. Remove pan from heat. Stir in reserved ¹/₃ cup stock, butter, pepper, and cheese. Garnish with parsley. Serves 4 (serving size: about 1¼ cups)

CALORIES 404; FAT 9.9g (sat 3.7g, mono 5g, poly 0.7g); PROTEIN 14g; CARB 60.9g; FIBER 2.5g; CHOL 14mg; IRON 1.3mg; SODIUM 568mg; CALC 115mg

Quick and Easy • Kid Friendly

Pancetta Risotto with Truffle Oil

Hands-on: 40 min. Total: 40 min.

5 cups unsalted chicken stock (such as Swanson)
1 tablespoon olive oil
3 ounces pancetta, chopped
¹/₂ cup minced shallots
1¹/₂ cups Arborio rice
1¹/₂ teaspoons chopped fresh rosemary
2 large garlic cloves, minced
¹/₂ cup dry white wine
1 teaspoon black pepper
1 teaspoon white truffle oil
¹/₂ teaspoon kosher salt

1. Bring stock to a simmer in a medium saucepan (do not boil). Keep warm over low heat.
2. Heat a Dutch oven over medium heat. Add olive oil; swirl to coat. Add pancetta; sauté 6 minutes or until crisp, stirring frequently. Using a slotted spoon, remove pancetta from pan; drain on a paper towel. Add shallots to drippings in pan; cook 2 minutes (do not brown), stirring frequently. Stir in rice, rosemary, and garlic; cook 1 minute, stirring constantly to coat rice. Add wine; cook 2 minutes or until liquid is absorbed, stirring frequently. Stir in 1¹/₂ cups stock; cook 4 minutes or until liquid is nearly absorbed, stirring constantly. Add remaining stock, ¾ cup at a time, stirring nearly constantly until each portion of stock is absorbed before adding the next (about 22 minutes total); reserve ¹/₃ cup stock at the last addition. Stir in pepper, truffle oil, and salt. Remove pan from heat; stir in reserved ¹/₃ cup broth. Sprinkle with pancetta. Serve immediately. Serves 5 (serving size: 1 cup)

CALORIES 365; FAT 11.6g (sat 3.2g, mono 5.7g, poly 0.8g); PROTEIN 12.8g; CARB 50.3g; FIBER 3.1g; CHOL 12mg; IRON 0.9mg; SODIUM 604mg; CALC 31mg

IF YOU MAKE RISOTTO YOURSELF, YOU'RE GUARANTEED A HEALTHIER BOWL.

EMPANADA? WE SAY YES!

Flaky, portable, chicken-and-cheese-packed hand pies with half the salt and fat of the deep-fried version

It doesn't get much better than a deep-fried pocket of tender, flaky dough that's filled with meaty, cheesy goodness—a delightfully messy delicacy that's best with a dipping sauce and a mountain of napkins. The popularity of these savory hand pies is on the rise; it's a wonder they're not yet sold on every street corner in America. The limited availability is likely for our own good, as there's a hefty 500 calories and an army of salty, fried-fatty goodness in each pie. Empanada challenge, accepted!

We're gaining confidence in our lighter-crust capabilities, and this meaty hand pie is no exception. We trade the traditional lard or butter for olive oil—a heart-healthy fat whose liquid state coats the floury dough better than a solid fat, allowing us to use less. Juicy ground chicken and mushrooms replace ground beef for a lighter filling, leaving a little calorie room for some melty Gruyère and Monterey Jack. A made-from-scratch roasted tomatillo sauce packs a tart, flavorful punch into our filling—so good, we make a little extra for dipping. A flaky, cheesy, sauce-covered experience with 309 calories per pie—now that's a trend we can get behind.

CLASSIC	MAKEOVER
495 calories per serving	309 calories per serving
32 grams total fat	16.3 grams total fat
13.2 grams saturated fat	4 grams saturated fat

Make Ahead • Freezable

Chicken-and-Mushroom Empanadas with Roasted Tomatillo Sauce

Hands-on: 30 min. Total: 1 hr. 30 min.
The empanadas can be made ahead and chilled until ready to bake. For less heat, seed the jalapeño peppers after roasting.

8 ounces unbleached all-purpose flour (about 1³/₄ cups)
1¼ teaspoons salt, divided
½ teaspoon baking powder
¹/₃ cup plus 1 teaspoon extra-virgin olive oil, divided
5 tablespoons very cold water
1 pound tomatillos, husks removed
2 jalapeño peppers, stemmed
6 garlic cloves, peeled and divided
Cooking spray
1 tablespoon fresh lime juice
½ teaspoon freshly ground black pepper, divided
½ teaspoon sugar
1 cup chopped onion
8 ounces ground chicken
4 ounces chopped mushrooms
1½ ounces shredded cave-aged Gruyère cheese (about 6 tablespoons)
1 ounce shredded Monterey Jack cheese (about ¹/₄ cup)
1 large egg, lightly beaten
1 teaspoon water

1. Weigh or lightly spoon flour into dry measuring cups; level with a knife. Place flour, ³/₄ teaspoon salt, and baking powder in a food processor; pulse to combine. Combine ¹/₃ cup oil and 5 tablespoons water. With processor on, slowly add oil mixture through food chute; process until dough is crumbly. Turn dough out onto a lightly floured surface. Knead 1 minute; add additional flour, if necessary, to prevent dough from sticking. Gently press dough into a 5-inch disk; wrap in plastic wrap, and chill at least 30 minutes.
2. Preheat oven to 450°.
3. Arrange tomatillos, jalapeños, and 4 garlic cloves in a single layer on a baking sheet coated with cooking spray; lightly coat vegetables with cooking spray. Bake at 450° for 25 minutes or until charred. Place tomatillo mixture, juice, ¼ teaspoon salt, ¼ teaspoon black pepper, and sugar in a blender; pulse until finely chopped, scraping sides.
4. Reduce oven temperature to 400°.
5. Heat a large nonstick skillet over medium heat. Add 1 teaspoon oil to pan; swirl to coat. Add onion, sauté 5 minutes. Chop 2 garlic cloves. Add garlic to pan, sauté 1 minute. Add chicken and mushrooms; cook 6 minutes or until chicken is browned, stirring to crumble. Cool slightly. Add ½ cup tomatillo sauce, ¼ teaspoon salt, ¼ teaspoon black pepper, and cheeses, stirring well to combine.
6. Combine egg and water in small bowl, stirring well with a whisk. Remove dough from refrigerator; let stand 5 minutes. Divide dough into 8 equal portions, shaping each into a ball. Roll each dough portion into a 6-inch circle on a lightly floured surface. Working with 1 portion at a time (cover remaining dough to keep from drying), spoon 3 tablespoons chicken mixture into center of each circle. Moisten edges of dough with egg mixture; fold dough over filling. Press edges together with a fork to seal. Brush remaining egg mixture evenly over empanadas. Place empanadas on

continued

a parchment-lined baking sheet coated with cooking spray. Bake at 400° for 24 minutes or until lightly browned. Serve with remaining tomatillo sauce. Serves 8 (serving size: 1 empanada and 1 tablespoon sauce)

CALORIES 309; **FAT** 16.3g (sat 4g, mono 9.2g, poly 2.1g); **PROTEIN** 12.4g; **CARB** 29g; **FIBER** 2.5g; **CHOL** 57mg; **IRON** 2.3mg; **SODIUM** 455mg; **CALC** 121mg

EXPERT EMPANADA TIPS

OLIVE OIL
This heart-healthy fat is the star in our simple, tender dough, replacing lard or butter to save 136 calories and 10g sat fat per empanada.

FRESH SALSA VERDE
Packing a tart, juicy, flavor-packed punch into our light chicken-and-mushroom filling, it doubles as a dipping sauce to save 110mg per tablespoon over store-bought.

OVEN BAKED
No need to deep-fry this olive oil–based dough. It bakes up tender and flaky on its own. Save 60 calories and 7g fat per pie over the deep fryer.

PEAK SEASON

Kid Friendly

Garlicky Turnip Fries with Pomegranate Ketchup

Hands-on: 20 min. Total: 40 min.

Place 2 baking sheets in oven. Preheat oven to 450° (keep pans in oven as it preheats). Place ¾ cup pomegranate arils, ¼ cup chopped shallots, and 2 tablespoons cider vinegar in a mini food processor; process until well blended. Strain pomegranate mixture through a fine sieve into a small saucepan; discard solids. Stir in 3 tablespoons sugar, 1 teaspoon tomato paste, and ⅛ teaspoon salt. Bring to a boil; reduce heat, and simmer 10 minutes or until thickened. Cut 4 medium peeled turnips into ½-inch matchsticks; toss with 2 tablespoons olive oil. Sprinkle with 2 tablespoons cornmeal, 2 tablespoons grated fresh Parmesan cheese, ½ teaspoon freshly ground black pepper, and ¼ teaspoon garlic salt; toss to coat. Divide turnip mixture evenly between preheated pans. Bake at 450° for 15 minutes. Turn turnips over; rotate pans. Bake an additional 8 minutes or until browned. Serves 4 (serving size: about ½ cup turnips and 1 tablespoon sauce)

CALORIES 137; **FAT** 5.3g (sat 1g); **SODIUM** 184mg

EVERYDAY VEGETARIAN

MEATLESS MONDAYS

Vegetarian • Make Ahead

Barley Risotto with Wild Mushrooms

Hands-on: 60 min. Total: 1 hr. 45 min.
The mushroom mix here is a winning combo, but use any fresh variety that's readily available in your market.

1 tablespoon extra-virgin olive oil
2 cups thinly sliced leek (about 2 large)
8 ounces oyster mushrooms, sliced
8 ounces cremini mushrooms, sliced
5 ounces shiitake mushrooms, stemmed and sliced
1 cup uncooked pearl barley
1 tablespoon minced fresh garlic
½ cup dry white wine
2 teaspoons chopped fresh thyme, divided
8 cups water
½ ounce dried porcini mushrooms, coarsely chopped
3 ounces Parmigiano-Reggiano cheese, grated (about ¾ cup)
½ teaspoon kosher salt
¼ teaspoon freshly ground black pepper

1. Heat a Dutch oven over medium heat. Add oil to pan; swirl to coat. Add leek; sauté 10 minutes or until tender. Add oyster, cremini, and shiitake mushrooms; cook 15 minutes or until tender, stirring occasionally. Add barley and garlic; cook 2 minutes or until toasted, stirring frequently. Add wine and 1 teaspoon thyme; simmer 1 minute or until liquid is nearly absorbed. Add 8 cups water and porcini mushrooms. Reduce heat, and simmer 1 hour or until barley is tender and creamy, stirring frequently. Stir in cheese, salt, and pepper. Sprinkle with 1 teaspoon thyme. Serve immediately. Serves 6 (serving size: 1½ cups)

CALORIES 273; FAT 7.1g (sat 2.9g, mono 2.9g, poly 0.7g); PROTEIN 12.6g; CARB 38.5g; FIBER 8.1g; CHOL 12mg; IRON 2.9mg; SODIUM 398mg; CALC 199mg

Vegetarian

Quinoa-Stuffed Kale Rolls with Goat Cheese

Hands-on: 60 min. Total: 2 hr. 5 min.
One of our favorite greens stuffed with one of our favorite grains—all covered with a light tomato sauce.

2 tablespoons extra-virgin olive oil, divided
2 pounds plum tomatoes, chopped
6 garlic cloves, coarsely chopped
2 teaspoons chopped fresh thyme
½ teaspoon kosher salt
12 large Lacinato kale leaves (about 1 large bunch)
¾ cup uncooked quinoa
1 medium onion, chopped
1½ cups organic vegetable broth
⅓ cup chopped walnuts, toasted and divided
Cooking spray
2 ounces goat cheese, crumbled

1. Heat a large saucepan over medium heat. Add 1 tablespoon oil to pan; swirl to coat. Add tomatoes, garlic, and thyme; cover and simmer 30 minutes or until tomatoes are very tender. Remove pan from heat. Add salt; coarsely mash with a potato masher.
2. Bring water to a boil in a large saucepan; add half of kale. Cook 1 minute. Remove kale from pan with a slotted spoon; plunge into ice water. Repeat with remaining kale. Drain and pat dry. Remove center rib from kale, leaving the leaf whole and uncut at leafy end.

3. Rinse and drain quinoa. Heat a medium saucepan over medium-high heat. Add 1 tablespoon oil to pan; swirl to coat. Add onion to pan; sauté 5 minutes or until tender. Add quinoa; cook 2 minutes, stirring constantly. Add broth; bring to a boil. Cover, reduce heat, and simmer 15 minutes or until liquid is absorbed. Remove pan from heat; stir in 3 tablespoons walnuts.
4. Preheat oven to 375°.
5. Spread about ¾ cup tomato sauce over the bottom of an 11 x 7–inch glass or ceramic baking dish coated with cooking spray. Working with 1 kale leaf at a time, place about ¼ cup quinoa mixture in center of leaf. Fold in edges of leaf; roll up, jelly-roll fashion. Repeat procedure with remaining kale leaves and quinoa mixture to form 12 rolls. Place rolls, seam sides down, in dish. Spoon remaining sauce over rolls. Cover and bake at 375° for 20 minutes. Sprinkle evenly with walnuts and cheese. Bake, uncovered, 5 minutes. Serves 4 (serving size: 3 rolls)

CALORIES 369; FAT 18.9g (sat 4g, mono 7.1g, poly 6.8g); PROTEIN 12.9g; CARB 41.2; FIBER 7.3g; CHOL 7mg; IRON 3.8mg; SODIUM 536mg; CALC 153mg

INSTEAD OF TRADITIONAL GRAPE LEAF AND RICE ROLLS, WE USED KALE AND STUFFED THE LEAVES WITH QUINOA.

KID IN THE KITCHEN

FINGER-LICKIN' CHICKEN

By Matisse Reid

I made one of the greatest chicken recipes today. Kids, you will love this dish. You can use boneless chicken thighs if you want, but chicken with the bone does not seem to dry out as quickly. I also thought this recipe would work well with a whole chicken. We doubled the recipe and put half in the freezer for a quick, easy meal another time. Make sure you cook extra, as it also makes great leftovers. We had the meat in sandwiches the next day, and it tasted even better the second time around. The first time I made this dish, I started cooking the chicken on the grill, and then put it in the oven. This added to the smoky flavor and gave the skin a nice crispy texture—yum! The second time I just cooked it in the oven and it was just as good. This dish was delish.

THE VERDICT

KALANI (AGE 15)
He liked the big piece of chicken. These flavors are usually only on bite-sized pieces.
10 out of 10

FRAANZ (AGE 9)
He said, "I loved the sticky sweet sauce. The barbecue was a nice choice."
10 out of 10

MATISSE (AGE 12)
I loved the combination of sweet and spicy flavors. I will keep this recipe on hand.
10 out of 10

continued

Sticky Asian Chicken Thighs

Kid Friendly

Hands-on: 15 min. Total: 1 hr. 10 min.
These chicken thighs are messy, but that's part of the fun. Serve with steamed sugar snap peas and hot cooked white rice.

6 bone-in chicken thighs (about 2 pounds)
¼ cup lower-sodium soy sauce
3 tablespoons fresh orange juice
2 tablespoons balsamic vinegar
1½ tablespoons honey
1 tablespoon hoisin sauce
1½ teaspoons chili garlic sauce
1 teaspoon cornstarch
Cooking spray

1. Combine first 7 ingredients in a large zip-top plastic bag; seal. Marinate 30 minutes at room temperature, turning occasionally.
2. Preheat oven to 450°.
3. Remove chicken from bag, reserving marinade. Combine reserved marinade and cornstarch in a medium saucepan, stirring with a whisk. Bring marinade mixture to a boil over medium heat; cook 3 minutes or until thickened, stirring occasionally.
4. Place chicken on a wire rack coated with cooking spray. Place rack in a baking sheet. Bake at 450° for 15 minutes. Brush ½ cup marinade mixture over chicken. Bake 15 minutes or until done. Place chicken in a large bowl. Add remaining marinade mixture; toss to coat. Serves 6 (serving size: 1 thigh)

CALORIES 240; FAT 13.3g (sat 3.6g, mono 5.6g, poly 2.7g); PROTEIN 20.8g; CARB 8.7g; FIBER 0.2g; CHOL 120mg; IRON 1.3mg; SODIUM 494mg; CALC 14mg

GLOBAL PANTRY

COUSCOUS

By Naomi Duguid

Most American cooks know that couscous is a staple in North Africa, but not many understand how versatile it can be. Couscous is a tiny pasta made of wheat or barley; wheat couscous is the most widely available version in North America, and most of it is "instant" or quick-cooking. Although couscous is traditionally hand-rolled, these days it is made by machine: Coarsely ground wheat (semolina) is moistened and tossed with fine wheat flour until it forms little round balls (think of the coarse bits as the core of a kind of wheat-flour "snowball"). In Morocco, Algeria, and Tunisia, couscous is steamed over a simmered stew, after being tossed with a little water or oil and water.

But couscous is more than just an accompaniment to stew. You can use it as a filler in beef patties (soak it in water for five minutes, and then use instead of breadcrumbs—½ cup per pound of ground beef or lamb); add leftover cooked couscous to a salad; or use it in a bread or pancake or muffin recipe (soak in an equal volume of warm water for five minutes or more before adding it—¼ cup couscous to ¾ cup wheat flour).

But to me the most appealing non-traditional couscous dish is this cross between a pilaf and a salad; it's quick to make and a great standby any time of year. (You'll find it especially useful if you are cooking for vegetarians or vegans, for whom you can omit the cheese.)

Couscous with Winter Vegetables

Vegetarian • Kid Friendly
Make Ahead

Hands-on: 20 min. Total: 1 hr. 30 min. In summer, use green beans, corn kernels, and zucchini in place of the butternut squash and chickpeas. Leftovers are delicious for breakfast with a fried egg on top.

2 tablespoons butter
1 tablespoon olive oil
½ cup chopped shallots
1 jalapeño pepper, minced
3 cups chopped peeled butternut squash
1 (15-ounce) can unsalted chickpeas (garbanzo beans), drained
1 cup uncooked couscous
1¾ cups boiling water
¾ teaspoon salt
¼ cup coarsely chopped fresh flat-leaf parsley
2 tablespoons fresh lemon juice
1 ounce vegetarian Parmesan cheese, grated (about ¼ cup)

1. Heat butter and oil in a large straight-sided skillet over medium-high heat, stirring until butter melts. Add shallots; cook 3 minutes or until soft, stirring occasionally. Add jalapeño; cook 1 minute, stirring frequently. Add squash; cook 8 minutes or until tender, stirring occasionally. Add chickpeas; cook 1 minute, stirring occasionally. Add couscous; cook 1 minute, stirring constantly. Stir in boiling water and salt; remove pan from heat. Cover and let stand 8 minutes. Fluff with a fork. Add parsley and lemon juice; toss gently to combine. Top with cheese. Serves 8 (serving size: 1 cup)

CALORIES 202; FAT 6g (sat 2.7g, mono 2.3g, poly 0.4g); PROTEIN 6.8g; CARB 31.2g; FIBER 3.9g; CHOL 10mg; IRON 1.2mg; SODIUM 318mg; CALC 93mg

7 SNACKABLE DIPS

Combine ½ cup plain fat-free Greek yogurt, ½ cup light sour cream, and your favorite flavor combination below. Serve with vegetables, fruit, or the suggested dippers.

Banana-Chocolate-Hazelnut

Mash 1 ripe banana with a fork until smooth. Combine banana, yogurt, sour cream, ⅓ cup chocolate-hazelnut spread, 2 tablespoons powdered sugar, and 1 tablespoon unsweetened cocoa. Serve with graham crackers. Serves 10 (serving size: about 2½ tablespoons)

CALORIES 91; FAT 4.4g (sat 1.8g); SODIUM 17mg

Cucumber-Dill

Combine yogurt, sour cream, 1 cup grated English cucumber, 3 tablespoons chopped fresh dill, 1 teaspoon grated garlic, ¼ teaspoon salt, and ¼ teaspoon freshly ground black pepper. Serve with sliced cucumber. Serves 8 (serving size: about 3 tablespoons)

CALORIES 32; FAT 1.7g (sat 1g); SODIUM 91mg

Smoked Salmon

Combine yogurt, sour cream, 2 ounces finely chopped cold-smoked salmon, 2 tablespoons minced red onion, 1 tablespoon chopped capers, and 1 tablespoon chopped fresh dill. Serve with seeded crackers. Serves 8 (serving size: about 2½ tablespoons)

CALORIES 39; FAT 2g (sat 1.1g); SODIUM 104mg

Blue Cheese, Bacon, and Spinach

Cook 2 center-cut bacon slices until crisp. Remove from pan; crumble. Remove all but 1 teaspoon drippings from pan. Add 4 ounces chopped fresh spinach to pan, stirring until wilted. Cool slightly. Combine bacon, spinach, yogurt, sour cream, 1 ounce crumbled blue cheese, 1 minced garlic clove, ¼ teaspoon crushed red pepper, and ⅛ teaspoon kosher salt. Serve with celery sticks. Serves 8 (serving size: about 2 tablespoons)

CALORIES 52; FAT 3.2g (sat 2g); SODIUM 141mg

Charred Red Onion

Combine 1 cup chopped grilled red onion, yogurt, sour cream, ¼ teaspoon freshly ground black pepper, ¼ teaspoon Worcestershire sauce, ⅛ teaspoon ground red pepper, and ⅛ teaspoon salt. Serve with baked sweet potato chips. Serves 8 (serving size: about 3 tablespoons)

CALORIES 37; FAT 1.7g (sat 1g); SODIUM 56mg

Caramel-Toffee

Combine yogurt, sour cream, ⅓ cup brown sugar, and ¾ teaspoon vanilla extract. Stir in 6 tablespoons toffee bits. Serve with apple wedges. Serves 12 (serving size: about 2 tablespoons)

CALORIES 83; FAT 3.6g (sat 1.9g); SODIUM 50mg

Honey-Lemon

Combine yogurt, sour cream, 3 tablespoons lemon curd, and 1½ tablespoons honey. Serve with fresh strawberries. Serves 8 (serving size: about 2 tablespoons)

CALORIES 65; FAT 2g (sat 1.2g); SODIUM 22mg

FEED 4 FOR LESS THAN $10

Quick and Easy • Kid Friendly

RIGATONI WITH MEATY MUSHROOM BOLOGNESE

$2.23/serving, $8.92 total

Hands-on: 30 min. Total: 30 min. A rich, meaty Bolognese can take hours on the stove, but this savory mushroom version is ready in just 30 minutes.

6 ounces uncooked rigatoni
8 ounces 90% lean ground sirloin
1 tablespoon olive oil
⅔ cup (¼-inch) diced carrot
1 medium red onion, chopped
1 (8-ounce) package presliced mushrooms
8 ounces zucchini, cut into ½-inch pieces
4 garlic cloves, minced
¾ teaspoon kosher salt, divided
¼ teaspoon freshly ground black pepper, divided
1 (14.5-ounce) can unsalted diced tomatoes, undrained
3 tablespoons unsalted tomato paste
¼ teaspoon crushed red pepper
2 tablespoons heavy cream
1 ounce fresh Parmesan cheese, grated and divided (about ¼ cup)

1. Cook pasta according to package directions, omitting salt and fat; drain. Keep warm.
2. Heat a large nonstick skillet over medium-high heat. Add beef; cook 2 minutes or until browned, stirring to crumble. Remove beef from pan; set aside.

continued

3. Return pan to medium-high heat. Add oil; swirl to coat. Add carrot, onion, and mushrooms; sauté 5 minutes or until just tender. Stir in zucchini, garlic, ½ teaspoon salt, and ⅛ teaspoon black pepper; cook 4 minutes or until vegetables are tender, stirring occasionally. Stir in beef; cook 1 minute. Add tomatoes, tomato paste, and crushed red pepper to pan; bring to a boil. Reduce heat to medium-low; cover and simmer 8 minutes or until slightly thickened, stirring occasionally. Stir in cream; cook 1 minute. Remove pan from heat; stir in ¼ teaspoon salt, ⅛ teaspoon black pepper, and 2 tablespoons Parmesan cheese. Divide pasta among 4 bowls. Top each serving with 1¼ cups sauce; sprinkle evenly with 2 tablespoons Parmesan cheese. Serves 4

CALORIES 414; FAT 14g (sat 5.6g, mono 5.9g, poly 0.9g); PROTEIN 23.9g; CARB 49.5g; FIBER 5.2g; CHOL 51mg; IRON 4.2mg; SODIUM 550mg; CALC 150mg

Kid Friendly • Quick and Easy

Roasted Chicken Thighs with Brussels Sprouts

$2.36/serving, $9.44 total

Hands-on: 15 min. Total: 45 min. Serve with 2 cups hot cooked brown rice.

1 tablespoon olive oil, divided
1 tablespoon minced fresh garlic
2 teaspoons chopped fresh thyme, divided
½ teaspoon kosher salt, divided
½ teaspoon freshly ground black pepper, divided
4 (6-ounce) bone-in chicken thighs
1 lemon, cut into wedges
¼ cup dry white wine
2 teaspoons butter
¼ cup thinly sliced onion
1 pound Brussels sprouts, trimmed and halved
⅓ cup fat-free, lower-sodium chicken broth

1. Preheat oven to 425°.
2. Combine 1 teaspoon oil, garlic, 1 teaspoon thyme, ¼ teaspoon salt, and ¼ teaspoon pepper in a small bowl. Loosen skin on thighs by inserting fingers, gently pushing between skin and meat. Rub garlic mixture under loosened skin. Heat a large ovenproof skillet over medium-high heat. Add 1 teaspoon oil to pan; swirl to coat. Add chicken thighs to pan, skin side down; cook 4 minutes or until skin is lightly browned. Turn thighs over; arrange lemon wedges among chicken. Place pan in oven; bake at 425° for 18 minutes or until chicken is done. Remove chicken and lemon from pan; discard lemon. Discard drippings (do not wipe out pan). Return pan to medium-high heat. Add wine; bring to a boil. Cook 2 minutes or until slightly thickened, scraping pan to loosen browned bits. Remove pan from heat; add butter, swirling until butter melts.
3. Heat a large skillet over medium-high heat. Add 1 teaspoon oil; swirl to coat. Add onion; cook 1 minute, stirring frequently. Add ¼ teaspoon salt, ¼ teaspoon pepper, and Brussels sprouts; cook 8 minutes or until Brussels sprouts are crisp-tender. Add broth to pan; cover and cook 2 minutes. Place 1 chicken thigh on each of 4 plates; serve with 1 cup Brussels sprouts and 2 tablespoons sauce. Sprinkle with 1 teaspoon thyme. Serves 4

CALORIES 343; FAT 20.4g (sat 5.8g, mono 9.2g, poly 3.5g); PROTEIN 27g; CARB 13.3g; FIBER 5.1g; CHOL 140mg; IRON 2.8mg; SODIUM 420mg; CALC 72mg

DINNER TONIGHT

Fast, Healthy Weeknight Menus

READY IN 30 MINUTES

The SHOPPING LIST

Chickpea and Sausage Minestrone
Onion (1)
Carrot (2)
Celery (2 stalks)
Garlic
Fresh parsley
Fresh thyme
Crushed red pepper
Olive oil
15-ounce can unsalted chickpeas (1)
15-ounce can fire-roasted diced tomatoes (1)
Unsalted chicken stock (such as Swanson)
Small shell pasta
Hot turkey Italian sausage

Ciabatta Parmesan Toasts
Ciabatta bread (6 ounces)
Parmesan cheese
Canola mayonnaise

The GAME PLAN

While pasta cooks:
■ Dice celery, carrots, and onion.
While vegetables cook:
■ Prepare cheese toasts.

Quick and Easy • Kid Friendly

Chickpea and Sausage Minestrone

With Ciabatta Parmesan Toasts

Make Ahead: Store the pasta and soup separately, and then reheat and combine.
Simple Sub: If you can't find ciabatta, a French bread baguette or sourdough will work.
Time-Saver: Find prechopped onion and celery in the produce section of your supermarket.

¾ cup uncooked small shell pasta
1 tablespoon olive oil
1 (4-ounce) link hot turkey Italian sausage, casing removed
1 cup diced onion
1 cup diced carrot
½ cup diced celery
2 tablespoons chopped fresh flat-leaf parsley
2 teaspoons chopped fresh thyme
5 garlic cloves, chopped
¼ teaspoon crushed red pepper
1 (15-ounce) can unsalted chickpeas, rinsed and drained
1 (15-ounce) can fire-roasted diced tomatoes, undrained
4 cups unsalted chicken stock (such as Swanson)
½ teaspoon kosher salt
¼ teaspoon freshly ground black pepper

1. Cook pasta according to package directions, omitting salt and fat; drain.
2. Heat a large saucepan over medium-high heat. Add oil to pan; swirl to coat. Add sausage; cook 3 minutes or until beginning to brown, stirring to crumble. Add onion and next 6 ingredients (through red pepper); cook 10 minutes or until vegetables are tender. Add chickpeas, tomatoes, and stock; bring to a boil. Reduce heat, and simmer 5 minutes. Stir in pasta, salt, and black pepper; cook 1 minute. Serves 6 (serving size: about 1½ cups)

CALORIES 197; FAT 4.7g (sat 0.9g, mono 2.4g, poly 0.9g); PROTEIN 12g; CARB 26.5g; FIBER 4g; CHOL 16mg; IRON 2.1mg; SODIUM 553mg; CALC 76mg

For the Ciabatta Parmesan Toasts:
Preheat broiler. Broil 6 (1-ounce) slices ciabatta bread 1 minute on each side or until toasted. Combine 1 tablespoon grated Parmesan cheese and 1 tablespoon canola mayonnaise. Spread about ½ teaspoon cheese mixture on each slice; sprinkle with a dash of freshly ground black pepper. Broil 30 seconds. Serves 6 (serving size: 1 piece)

CALORIES 89; FAT 2.1g (sat 0.3g); SODIUM 225mg

Quick and Easy

Lamb and Red Pepper Pita Sandwiches

With Mint and Pistachio Tabbouleh

Simple Sub: You can substitute almonds for the pistachios in the tabbouleh.
Flavor Hit: Folding feta into the lamb mixture adds a salty tang to the patties.
Prep Pointer: Stir the lamb mixture just until combined so the patties keep their texture.

½ cup plain dry breadcrumbs
½ cup flat-leaf parsley leaves
½ cup chopped red onion
½ cup chopped bottled roasted red bell pepper
½ teaspoon kosher salt
½ teaspoon ground cumin
½ teaspoon dried oregano
½ teaspoon freshly ground black pepper
¼ teaspoon ground red pepper
1 large egg white
6 ounces ground lamb
6 ounces 90% lean ground sirloin
2 ounces feta cheese, crumbled
6 green leaf lettuce leaves
½ cup thinly sliced cucumber
3 (6-inch) whole-wheat pitas, halved

1. Place first 10 ingredients (through egg white) in a food processor; process until smooth. Place breadcrumb mixture in a bowl; add lamb, beef, and feta, stirring gently to combine. Shape mixture into 12 (2-ounce) patties. Refrigerate 10 minutes to set.
2. Heat a large nonstick skillet over medium-high heat. Add 6 patties to pan; cook 4 minutes on each side or until desired degree of doneness. Remove from pan; repeat procedure with remaining patties.
3. Place 1 lettuce leaf, about 4 cucumber slices, and 2 lamb patties in each pita half. Serves 6 (serving size: 1 filled pita half)

CALORIES 307; FAT 12.4g (sat 5.4g, mono 4.3g, poly 1g); PROTEIN 21.6g; CARB 28g; FIBER 3.6g; CHOL 60mg; IRON 3mg; SODIUM 599mg; CALC 85mg

For the Mint and Pistachio Tabbouleh:
Combine 1 cup cooked bulgur, 1 cup chopped stemmed kale, ½ cup chopped cucumber, ½ cup halved grape tomatoes, ¼ cup chopped red onion, ¼ cup chopped fresh mint, and ¼ cup shelled pistachios in a large bowl. Combine 1 tablespoon fresh lemon juice, 2 teaspoons olive oil, ¼ teaspoon kosher salt, ¼ teaspoon black pepper, and a dash of allspice in a bowl, stirring with a whisk. Add lemon juice mixture to kale mixture; toss to coat. Serves 6 (serving size: about ⅔ cup)

CALORIES 81; FAT 4g (sat 0.5g); SODIUM 88mg

continued

The
SHOPPING LIST

Lamb and Red Pepper Pita Sandwiches

Red onion (1)

Green leaf lettuce (1 head)

Cucumber (1)

Fresh parsley

Ground cumin

Dried oregano

Ground red pepper

12-ounce jar roasted red bell peppers (1)

Plain dry breadcrumbs

Feta cheese

Egg (1)

Whole-wheat pita (3)

Ground lamb (6 ounces)

90% lean ground sirloin (6 ounces)

Mint and Pistachio Tabbouleh

Kale leaves

Cucumber (1)

Grape tomatoes

Red onion (1)

Fresh mint

Lemon (1)

Allspice

Pistachios

Olive oil

Bulgur

The
GAME PLAN

While bulgur cooks:
- Form patties.

While patties chill:
- Prepare tabbouleh.

Quick and Easy

Pepper Jelly–Glazed Chicken with Almond–Green Onion Quinoa

With Snap Pea and Bell Pepper Sauté

Shopping Tip: Red pepper jelly can be found in the jams and jellies aisle of your supermarket. Simple Sub: Green beans or slender haricots verts will work in place of the sugar snap peas. Flavor Swap: For a sweeter profile, substitute apricot jam for the red pepper jelly.

1½ cups water

1 cup uncooked quinoa

½ teaspoon salt, divided

½ teaspoon freshly ground black pepper, divided

¼ cup chopped green onions

3 tablespoons white wine vinegar, divided

2 tablespoons sliced almonds, toasted

2 tablespoons olive oil, divided

1 tablespoon fresh lemon juice

4 (6-ounce) skinless, boneless chicken breast halves

⅓ cup unsalted chicken stock (such as Swanson)

⅓ cup red pepper jelly

1. Combine 1½ cups water, quinoa, ⅛ teaspoon salt, and ⅛ teaspoon pepper in a medium saucepan; bring to a boil. Reduce heat, and simmer 15 minutes or until liquid is absorbed, stirring occasionally. Stir in green onions, 1 tablespoon vinegar, almonds, 1 tablespoon oil, and juice.

2. Sprinkle chicken with ⅜ teaspoon salt and ⅜ teaspoon pepper. Heat a large skillet over medium-high heat. Add 1 tablespoon oil; swirl to coat. Add chicken to pan; cook 6 minutes on each side or until done. Remove chicken from pan. Add stock to pan; cook 1 minute, scraping pan to loosen browned bits. Add 2 tablespoons vinegar and jelly to pan; bring to a boil. Reduce heat, and simmer 5 minutes or until slightly thickened. Place 1 chicken breast half on each of 4 plates; top with 2 tablespoons sauce. Serve with about ½ cup quinoa mixture. Serves 4

CALORIES 472; **FAT** 15.2g (sat 2.3g, mono 7.8g, poly 3.1g); **PROTEIN** 43.3g; **CARB** 39.6g; **FIBER** 3.6g; **CHOL** 109mg; **IRON** 2.9mg; **SODIUM** 527mg; **CALC** 44mg

For the Snap Pea and Bell Pepper Sauté:

Heat a large skillet over medium-high heat. Add 2 teaspoons olive oil; swirl to coat. Add 12 ounces trimmed sugar snap peas; sauté 2 minutes. Add 1 cup sliced yellow bell pepper; sauté 3 minutes or until crisp-tender. Sprinkle with ¼ teaspoon salt and ¼ teaspoon freshly ground black pepper. Serves 4 (serving size: ¾ cup)

CALORIES 63; **FAT** 2.5g (sat 0.4g); **SODIUM** 152mg

READY IN 30 MINUTES

The
SHOPPING LIST

Pepper Jelly–Glazed Chicken with Almond–Green Onion Quinoa

Green onions
Lemon (1)
Sliced almonds
Olive oil
Quinoa
White wine vinegar
Red pepper jelly
Unsalted chicken stock (such as Swanson)
6-ounce skinless, boneless chicken breast halves (4)

Snap Pea and Bell Pepper Sauté

Sugar snap peas (12 ounces)
Yellow bell pepper (1 large)
Olive oil

The
GAME PLAN

While quinoa cooks:
- Cook chicken.

While sauce reduces:
- Prepare sugar snap peas.

Quick and Easy

Seared Steak with Braised Leeks and Chard

With Mustard Mashed Potatoes

Technique Tip: Remove the root and dark green ends of the leek, halve lengthwise, and slice.
Kid Tweak: Omit the Dijon mustard from the potatoes for a simpler mash.
Budget Buy: You can use stemmed kale in place of the Swiss chard.

4 (4-ounce) beef tenderloin steaks
$3/8$ teaspoon kosher salt, divided
$1/4$ teaspoon freshly ground black pepper
Cooking spray
2 teaspoons butter
1 teaspoon mustard seeds
2 cups thinly sliced leek
$1/4$ cup dry white wine
$3/4$ cup unsalted beef stock (such as Swanson)
1 tablespoon Worcestershire sauce
4 cups chopped Swiss chard

1. Sprinkle steaks with ¼ teaspoon salt and pepper. Heat a large skillet over medium-high heat. Coat pan with cooking spray. Add steaks to pan; cook 4 minutes on each side or until desired degree of doneness. Remove steaks from pan. Add butter and mustard seeds to pan. When seeds begin to pop, add leeks; cook 2 minutes, stirring occasionally. Add wine; cook 1 minute or until liquid evaporates. Add broth and Worcestershire sauce; cook 4 minutes or until leeks are tender. Add ⅛ teaspoon salt and chard; cook 2 minutes or until wilted, stirring occasionally. Serve chard mixture with steaks. Serves 4 (serving size: 1 steak and ½ cup chard mixture)

CALORIES 243; FAT 9.9g (sat 4g, mono 3.5g, poly 0.5g); PROTEIN 26.8g; CARB 9.4g; FIBER 1.5g; CHOL 79mg; IRON 3.7mg; SODIUM 414mg; CALC 83mg

---

For the Mustard Mashed Potatoes:
Place 1 pound chopped peeled baking potatoes in a medium saucepan; cover with cold water. Bring to a boil. Reduce heat, and simmer 12 minutes or until potatoes are very tender. Drain. Return potatoes to pan; mash with a potato masher. Stir in ¼ cup 2% reduced-fat milk, ¼ cup reduced-fat sour cream, 2 teaspoons country-style Dijon mustard, ½ teaspoon freshly ground black pepper, and ¼ teaspoon salt. Serves 4 (serving size: ½ cup)

CALORIES 129; FAT 2.6g (sat 1.6g); SODIUM 231mg

READY IN 30 MINUTES

The
SHOPPING LIST

Seared Steak with Braised Leeks and Chard

Leeks (2 large)
Swiss chard
Mustard seeds
Worcestershire sauce
Dry white wine
Unsalted beef stock (such as Swanson)
Butter
4-ounce beef tenderloin steaks (4)

Mustard Mashed Potatoes

Baking potatoes (1 pound)
Country-style Dijon mustard
Reduced-fat sour cream
2% reduced-fat milk

The
GAME PLAN

While potatoes cook:
- Cook steaks.
- Slice leeks.
- Chop chard.

While leeks cook:
- Mash potatoes.

Citrus-Glazed Shrimp with Cilantro Rice

With Avocado and Radish Salad

Flavor Hit: Chipotle chile powder adds smoky heat to the shrimp.
Time-Saver: Use precooked rice, such as Uncle Ben's, in place of regular rice.
Shopping Tip: Look for canned chopped green chiles in the international aisle.

Rice:
1 cup long-grain white rice
¼ cup chopped fresh cilantro
1 tablespoon olive oil
½ teaspoon ground cumin
¼ teaspoon kosher salt
¼ teaspoon freshly ground black pepper
1 (4-ounce) can chopped green chiles, drained

Shrimp:
1 pound large shrimp, peeled and deveined
2 teaspoons minced fresh garlic
2 teaspoons grated lime rind
¼ teaspoon kosher salt
¼ teaspoon chipotle chile powder
¼ teaspoon freshly ground black pepper
Cooking spray
2 tablespoons fresh lime juice
2 tablespoons butter

1. To prepare rice, cook rice according to package directions, omitting salt and fat. Add cilantro, oil, cumin, ¼ teaspoon salt, ¼ teaspoon pepper, and green chiles, stirring to combine.
2. To prepare shrimp, combine shrimp, garlic, rind, ¼ teaspoon salt, chile powder, and ¼ teaspoon pepper in a bowl, tossing to coat.
3. Heat a large skillet over medium heat. Coat pan with cooking spray. Add shrimp mixture to pan; sauté 3 minutes. Stir in lime juice and butter; cook 1 minute, tossing to coat. Remove from pan. Serve shrimp with rice. Serves 4 (serving size: about ½ cup rice and 6 shrimp)

CALORIES 344; FAT 10.9g (sat 4.3g, mono 4.2g, poly 0.9g); PROTEIN 19.2g; CARB 40.7g; FIBER 1.3g; CHOL 158mg; IRON 2.8mg; SODIUM 579mg; CALC 93mg

For the Avocado and Radish Salad:
Combine 2 tablespoons white vinegar, 2 tablespoons extra-virgin olive oil, 1 teaspoon minced fresh garlic, ¼ teaspoon kosher salt, and ¼ teaspoon freshly ground black pepper in a large bowl. Add 1 large peeled chopped ripe avocado, ½ cup thinly sliced radishes, and 4 cups mixed baby greens; toss gently to coat. Serves 4 (serving size: 1 cup)

CALORIES 154; FAT 14.1g (sat 2g); SODIUM 149mg

READY IN 30 MINUTES

The SHOPPING LIST

Citrus-Glazed Shrimp with Cilantro Rice
Garlic
Fresh cilantro
Lime (2)
Chipotle chile powder
Ground cumin
Olive oil
4-ounce can chopped green chiles (1)
Long-grain white rice
Butter
Large shrimp, peeled and deveined (1 pound)

Avocado and Radish Salad
White vinegar
Extra-virgin olive oil
Garlic
Avocado (1)
Radishes
5-ounce container mixed baby greens (1)

The GAME PLAN

While rice cooks:
■ Cook shrimp.
■ Prepare salad.

SUPERFAST 20-MINUTE COOKING

Wrap up the year with quick, impressive meals: lemony crab cakes, grilled lamb skewers, wild mushroom pork Marsala, and more.

Quick and Easy • Kid Friendly

Red Pepper Crab Cakes with Lemony Mayo

Wet your hands with water before shaping the patties to keep the crab mixture from sticking to them.

1 tablespoon olive oil, divided
1 cup finely chopped red bell pepper
3 tablespoons finely chopped celery
1/4 cup thinly sliced green onions
1 pound lump crabmeat, shell pieces removed
2/3 cup panko (Japanese breadcrumbs)
2 tablespoons chopped fresh dill, divided
1/4 teaspoon ground red pepper
1 large egg
1 large egg white
1/4 cup canola mayonnaise
1 teaspoon grated lemon rind
2 tablespoons fresh lemon juice

1. Heat a large skillet over medium-high heat. Add 1 teaspoon oil to pan; swirl to coat. Add bell pepper, celery, and green onions to pan; sauté 4 minutes. Place vegetable mixture, crab, panko, 1 tablespoon dill, ground red pepper, egg, and egg white in a large bowl, stirring to combine. Gently shape about 1/2 cup crab mixture into a 3/4-inch-thick patty. Repeat procedure with remaining crab mixture, forming 8 patties. Wipe skillet with paper towels. Return pan to medium-high heat. Add 2 teaspoons oil to pan; swirl to coat. Add patties to pan; cook 3 minutes on each side or until golden and thoroughly heated.

2. Combine 1 tablespoon dill, mayonnaise, rind, and juice in a small bowl, stirring with a whisk. Top each crab cake with about 2 teaspoons sauce. Serves 4 (serving size: 2 cakes and about 1 1/2 tablespoons sauce)

CALORIES 277; FAT 10.3g (sat 0.9g, mono 5.3g, poly 2g); PROTEIN 31g; CARB 10.4g; FIBER 1.4g; CHOL 167mg; IRON 1.5mg; SODIUM 600mg; CALC 125mg

Quick and Easy

Turkey Schnitzel with Radicchio Slaw

Radicchio adds a bright, slightly bitter contrast to the turkey. You can also use red cabbage.

4 (4-ounce) turkey cutlets
2 tablespoons water
2 large egg whites
3/4 cup plain breadcrumbs
1 ounce Parmigiano-Reggiano cheese, finely grated (about 1/4 cup)
Cooking spray
1/2 teaspoon kosher salt, divided
2 tablespoons olive oil
1 1/2 tablespoons fresh lemon juice
1/2 teaspoon freshly ground black pepper
1/4 cup flat-leaf parsley leaves
1 small head radicchio, cored and thinly sliced (about 6 ounces)
1 Granny Smith apple, thinly sliced

1. Place each turkey cutlet between 2 sheets of heavy-duty plastic wrap; pound to 1/8-inch thickness using a meat mallet or small heavy skillet. Combine 2 tablespoons water and egg whites in a shallow dish, stirring with a whisk. Combine breadcrumbs and cheese in a shallow dish. Dip cutlets in egg mixture; dredge in breadcrumb mixture.

2. Heat a large skillet over medium-high heat. Generously coat pan with cooking spray. Add 2 cutlets to pan; cook 3 minutes on each side or until turkey is done. Remove from pan; keep warm. Wipe pan with a paper towel. Repeat procedure with cooking spray and remaining 2 cutlets. Sprinkle cooked cutlets with 1/4 teaspoon salt.

3. Combine 1/4 teaspoon salt, oil, lemon juice, and pepper in a large bowl, stirring with a whisk. Add parsley, radicchio, and apple; toss to coat. Serve with cutlets. Serves 4 (serving size: 1 cutlet and 3/4 cup salad)

CALORIES 339; FAT 11.2g (sat 2.8g, mono 5.7g, poly 1.1g); PROTEIN 36.3g; CARB 22.3g; FIBER 1.8g; CHOL 77mg; IRON 2mg; SODIUM 593mg; CALC 108mg

Quick and Easy

Sticky Korean Lamb Skewers

Lamb top round comes from the leg, a flavorful cut still tender enough for the grill.

2 green onions
2 tablespoons honey
2 tablespoons dark sesame oil
2 tablespoons lower-sodium soy sauce
1 teaspoon crushed red pepper
3 garlic cloves, minced
1 pound lamb top round, cut into 1-inch pieces
1 yellow bell pepper, cut into 1/2-inch pieces
Cooking spray
1/4 teaspoon kosher salt

1. Thinly slice green onions, reserving 2 tablespoons sliced dark green parts. Combine remaining green onions and next 5 ingredients in a large bowl. Add lamb and bell pepper; toss to coat. Thread lamb and bell pepper alternately onto each of 4 (10-inch) skewers. Heat a grill pan over medium-high heat. Coat pan with cooking spray. Add skewers to pan; grill 8 minutes

continued

or until desired degree of doneness, turning after 4 minutes. Remove skewers to a platter; sprinkle with reserved green onions and salt. Serves 4 (serving size: 1 skewer)

CALORIES 262; **FAT** 12.3g (sat 2.8g, mono 4.8g, poly 3.4g); **PROTEIN** 24.6g; **CARB** 13.8g; **FIBER** 0.9g; **CHOL** 73mg; **IRON** 2.7mg; **SODIUM** 460mg; **CALC** 24mg

Broccoli Mac and Cheese

This quick mac comes together in one pan. If you like, sprinkle an ounce of the cheese over the top, and broil 1 to 2 minutes or until melted.

8 ounces uncooked large elbow macaroni
2 cups chopped broccoli florets
1 1/2 cups 1% low-fat milk
2 tablespoons all-purpose flour
1 teaspoon chopped fresh thyme
2 teaspoons Dijon mustard
2 teaspoons Worcestershire sauce
1/8 teaspoon salt
1 center-cut bacon slice, chopped
1 1/2 teaspoons unsalted butter
4 1/2 ounces reduced-fat cheddar cheese, shredded (about 1 cup)

1. Cook pasta according to package directions, omitting salt and fat. Add broccoli during the last minute of cooking; cook 1 minute. Drain.
2. Combine milk and next 5 ingredients (through salt) in a medium bowl, stirring with a whisk.
3. Heat a large skillet over medium-high heat. Add bacon; cook 4 minutes or until crisp. Add butter to pan; swirl until butter melts. Add milk mixture to pan; bring to a boil. Cook 1 minute, stirring frequently. Add cheese; stir until smooth. Add pasta mixture to pan, stirring to coat. Serves 4 (serving size: 1 cup)

CALORIES 380; **FAT** 10.1g (sat 5.7g, mono 2.5g, poly 1.2g); **PROTEIN** 21.3g; **CARB** 52.4g; **FIBER** 3.1g; **CHOL** 28mg; **IRON** 2.4mg; **SODIUM** 480mg; **CALC** 437mg

Lemon-Parmesan Popcorn

To make sure the oil is ready for the popcorn, you can add a couple of kernels and wait for them to pop.

2 teaspoons grated lemon rind
1 teaspoon freshly ground black pepper
1/4 teaspoon kosher salt
1 1/2 ounces Parmigiano-Reggiano cheese, finely grated (about 1/3 cup)
2 tablespoons olive oil
1/2 cup unpopped popcorn kernels

1. Combine first 4 ingredients in a small bowl.
2. Heat oil in a medium, heavy saucepan over medium-high heat. Add popcorn to oil in saucepan; cover and cook 2 minutes or until kernels begin to pop, shaking pan frequently. Continue cooking 1 minute, shaking pan constantly. When popping slows down, remove pan from heat. Let stand 1 minute or until all popping stops. Pour 6 cups popcorn into a large bowl; stir in half of cheese mixture. Stir in remaining 6 cups popcorn and remaining half of cheese mixture; toss to coat. Let stand 1 minute before serving. Serves 6 (serving size: 2 cups)

CALORIES 128; **FAT** 7.2g (sat 1.9g, mono 3.9g, poly 0.6g); **PROTEIN** 4.4g; **CARB** 11.6g; **FIBER** 2.5g; **CHOL** 6mg; **IRON** 0.5mg; **SODIUM** 189mg; **CALC** 81mg

Fried Brown Rice with Snow Peas and Peanuts

1 tablespoon peanut oil
1/2 cup thinly sliced onion
1 teaspoon minced fresh garlic
1 1/2 cups snow peas, thinly sliced lengthwise
1/4 cup chopped unsalted, roasted peanuts
1 (8.8-ounce) pouch precooked brown rice (such as Uncle Ben's)
1 tablespoon rice vinegar
1 tablespoon lower-sodium soy sauce

1. Heat a large wok or skillet over medium-high heat. Add oil; swirl to coat. Add onion and garlic; stir-fry 1 minute. Add snow peas and peanuts to pan; stir-fry 2 minutes. Add rice; stir-fry 1 minute. Stir in vinegar and soy sauce; cook 1 minute. Serves 4 (serving size: 3/4 cup)

CALORIES 192; **FAT** 9.3g (sat 1.2g, mono 3.8g, poly 2.5g); **PROTEIN** 5.5g; **CARB** 24.3g; **FIBER** 3g; **CHOL** 0mg; **IRON** 1.1mg; **SODIUM** 202mg; **CALC** 20mg

Cremini Mushrooms and Pine Nuts
Heat a large wok or skillet over medium-high heat. Add 1 tablespoon peanut oil; swirl to coat. Add 1/2 cup thinly sliced onion and 1 teaspoon minced fresh garlic; stir-fry 1 minute. Add 1 1/2 cups sliced cremini mushrooms and 1/4 cup pine nuts to pan; stir-fry 2 minutes. Add 1 (8.8-ounce) pouch precooked brown rice (such as Uncle Ben's); stir-fry 1 minute. Stir in 2 tablespoons balsamic vinegar and 1/4 teaspoon salt; cook 1 minute. Serves 4 (serving size: 3/4 cup)

CALORIES 191; **FAT** 10.6g (sat 1g); **SODIUM** 158mg

Zucchini and Walnut
Heat a large wok or skillet over medium-high heat. Add 1 tablespoon peanut oil; swirl to coat. Add 1/2 cup thinly sliced onion and 1 teaspoon minced fresh garlic; sauté 1 minute. Add 1 1/2 cups sliced zucchini and 1/4 cup chopped walnuts to pan; stir-fry 2 minutes. Add 1 (8.8-ounce) pouch precooked brown rice (such as Uncle Ben's); stir-fry 1 minute. Stir in 2 tablespoons white wine vinegar, 2 teaspoons Dijon mustard, and 1/4 teaspoon salt; cook 1 minute. Serves 4 (serving size: 3/4 cup)

CALORIES 177; **FAT** 9.7g (sat 1.1g); **SODIUM** 191mg

Red Pepper and Almond
Heat a large wok or skillet over medium-high heat. Add 1 tablespoon peanut oil; swirl to coat. Add ½ cup thinly sliced onion and 1 teaspoon minced fresh garlic; stir-fry 1 minute. Add 1½ cups sliced red bell pepper and ¼ cup sliced almonds; stir-fry 2 minutes. Add 1 (8.8-ounce) pouch precooked brown rice (such as Uncle Ben's); stir-fry 1 minute. Stir in 1 tablespoon fresh lime juice and 2 teaspoons yellow curry paste; stir-fry 1 minute. Stir in ¼ cup cilantro leaves and ¼ teaspoon salt. Serves 4 (serving size: ¾ cup)

CALORIES 169; FAT 7.7g (sat 0.8g); SODIUM 221mg

Quick and Easy

Pork Cutlets and Wild Mushroom Marsala

A wild mushroom blend puts a simple spin on a restaurant classic. Serve with sautéed spinach.

1 tablespoon canola oil, divided
3 (4-ounce) packages exotic mushroom blend
1/2 teaspoon kosher salt, divided
1/4 cup Marsala wine
1/2 cup unsalted beef stock (such as Swanson)
2 tablespoons heavy whipping cream
3/8 teaspoon freshly ground black pepper, divided
4 (4-ounce) pork cutlets (1/4 inch thick)

1. Heat a large skillet over medium-high heat. Add 1 teaspoon oil to pan; swirl to coat. Add mushrooms and ¼ teaspoon salt; sauté 8 minutes or until mushrooms brown and liquid evaporates. Add Marsala; cook 1 minute or until liquid almost evaporates, scraping pan to loosen browned bits. Add stock; bring to a boil, and cook 2 minutes, stirring occasionally. Remove pan from heat; stir in cream and ⅛ teaspoon pepper.
2. Sprinkle cutlets with ¼ teaspoon salt

and ¼ teaspoon pepper. Heat a large skillet over medium-high heat. Add remaining 2 teaspoons oil to pan; swirl to coat. Add cutlets to pan; cook 2 to 3 minutes on each side or until desired degree of doneness. Place 1 cutlet on each of 4 plates; top each with about ½ cup mushroom mixture. Serves 4

CALORIES 226; FAT 9g (sat 2.8g, mono 3.9g, poly 1.6g); PROTEIN 26.9g; CARB 5.4g; FIBER 0.9g; CHOL 84mg; IRON 1.6mg; SODIUM 326mg; CALC 15mg

Quick and Easy

Spicy Tilapia and Fennel Stew

Arrabbiata, a spicy sauce of garlic, tomato, and chile pepper, forms the base for this stew.

1 large fennel bulb with stalks
Cooking spray
3 garlic cloves, minced
2 cups bottled arrabbiata sauce (such as Rao's)
1/2 cup water
1 (8-ounce) bottle clam juice
1 pound tilapia fillets, cut into 1-inch pieces

1. Trim tough outer leaves from fennel; mince feathery fronds to measure 2 tablespoons. Remove and discard stalks. Cut fennel bulb in half lengthwise; discard core. Thinly slice fennel bulb. Heat a large Dutch oven over medium-high heat. Coat pan with cooking spray. Add sliced fennel; sauté 1 minute. Reduce heat to medium; cover and cook 4 minutes or until crisp-tender. Add garlic; cook 1 minute, stirring frequently. Add arrabbiata sauce, ½ cup water, and clam juice; simmer 5 minutes. Add tilapia to pan; cover and simmer 4 minutes or until done. Divide stew among 4 bowls; sprinkle evenly with fennel fronds. Serves 4 (serving size: 1¾ cups stew)

CALORIES 213; FAT 8.2g (sat 1.7g, mono 5g, poly 1.1g); PROTEIN 24.9g; CARB 9.1g; FIBER 2.9g; CHOL 58mg; IRON 1.3mg; SODIUM 552mg; CALC 52mg

Quick and Easy • Make Ahead
Kid Friendly

Black Bean Soup with Chorizo and Lime

Smoky chorizo and bright lime add depth to a black bean soup made quick with canned beans.

2 teaspoons olive oil, divided
3 ounces Spanish chorizo, quartered lengthwise and cut into 1/2-inch pieces
1 cup chopped onion
1 cup chopped red bell pepper
2 teaspoons chopped fresh oregano
2 teaspoons minced fresh garlic
1 teaspoon ground cumin
1/2 teaspoon chipotle chile powder
1/4 teaspoon salt
2 cups unsalted chicken stock (such as Swanson)
2 (15-ounce) cans unsalted black beans, rinsed, drained, and coarsely mashed
1 tablespoon fresh lime juice
1/4 cup reduced-fat sour cream
1/4 cup chopped fresh cilantro

1. Heat a large saucepan over medium heat. Add 1 teaspoon oil to pan; swirl to coat. Add chorizo; cook 3 minutes, stirring occasionally. Remove chorizo from pan (do not wipe pan). Add 1 teaspoon oil to pan; swirl to coat. Add onion and bell pepper; cook 3 minutes, stirring occasionally. Stir in oregano and next 4 ingredients (through salt); cook 30 seconds. Stir in stock and beans. Bring to a boil; reduce heat, and simmer 3 minutes. Stir in cooked chorizo and juice. Ladle 1¼ cups soup into each of 4 bowls; top each serving with 1 tablespoon sour cream and 1 tablespoon cilantro. Serves 4

CALORIES 287; FAT 12.5g (sat 4.6g, mono 5.6g, poly 1g); PROTEIN 16.4g; CARB 27.1g; FIBER 7.7g; CHOL 27mg; IRON 2.8mg; SODIUM 514mg; CALC 119mg

CONTRIBUTORS

Hugh Acheson
Tiziana Agnello
Christine Albano
Simon Andrews
Charlotte Autry
Johnny Autry
Iain Bagwell
Andrew Bannecker
David Bonom
Katherine Brooking, R.D.
Maureen Callahan
Marian Cooper Cairns
Viviana Carballo
Mary Clayton Carl
Joanne Chang
Katherine Cobbs
Ruth Cousineau
Nigel Cox
Missie Neville Crawford
Tiffany Vickers Davis
Kathy Kitchens Downie
Mary Drennen
Alain Ducasse
Naomi Duguid
Todd Erickson
Nathan Fong
Squire Fox
Ford Fry
Shaun Garcia
Sandra Gluck
Rozanne Gold
Joyce Goldstein

Julianna Grimes
Cynthia Groseclose
Melissa Haskin
Oliver Hoffman
Christina Holmes
Raymond Hom
Lia Huber
Kenneth Hyatt
Kate Johnson
Jeanne Kelley
John Kessler
Kang Kim
Jamie Kimm
Adam Perry Lang
Frances Largeman-Roth, R.D.
Andrew Thomas Lee
Darcy Lenz
Pascaline Lepeltier
Becky Luigart-Stayner
Catherine Lyet
Jordan Mackay
Carolyn Malcoun
Ivy Manning
Domenica Marchetti
Kate Meyers
Johnny Miller
Jackie Mills
Krista Ackerbloom Montgomery
David Myers
Andrea Nguyen
Marcus Nilsson
Steven Noble

Aimee Olexy
Kate Parham
Laraine Perri
Marge Perry
Ann Taylor Pittman
Vanessa T. Pruett
Michael Psilakis
Kaityln du Ross
Christine Burns Rudalevige
Mark Scarbrough
Justin Schram
Robert Schueller
David Shaddix
Mary Beth Shaddix
Patricia Weigel Shannon
Pamela Duncan Silver
Sarah Smart
Susan Spungen
Adeena Sussman
Michael Symon
Allison Fishman Task
Kellie Thorn
Francesco Tonelli
Rori Travato
Alistair Turnbull
Justin Walker
Bruce Weinstein
Joanne Weir
Brian Woodcock
Phoebe Wu
Romulo Yanes

NUTRITION MADE EASY

Healthy Pizza Math

These two tricks really deliver calorie and sodium savings—whether you order in or bake at home.

The Delivery Trick

Downsize the diameter of your dial-in order.

16-INCH PIZZA

319 calories per slice
Eat two slices of an extra-large pepperoni pie, and that's 638 calories and 1,432mg sodium. Whoa!

14-INCH PIZZA

234 calories per slice
Eat two slices, and that's 468 calories and 1,086mg sodium.

That's a 26% decrease in calories and a 24% decrease in sodium. But you can still do better ...

12-INCH PIZZA

171 calories per slice
Eat two slices, and that's 342 calories and 796mg sodium—a reasonable entrée.

That's a 26% decrease in calories and sodium from a large and a 44% decrease from an extra-large.

The Home-Cooked Trick

Shave 4 ounces off the usual 16-ounce dough ball to make a thinner crust.

Two slices of a 14-inch pepperoni pizza made with 16 ounces of dough: **442 calories** and 910mg sodium.

Two slices of a 14-inch pizza made with 12 ounces of dough: only **370 calories** and 788mg sodium. You have room for a side salad—and leftover dough to make breadsticks for a snack tomorrow.

Tasty Dips under 125 Calories

Roasted Red Pepper Dip

Upping the pepper quantity cuts calories—160 of them.

Place 1 cup roasted red bell peppers, 2 tablespoons toasted almonds, 1 ounce whole-grain bread, 1 garlic clove, 1 table-spoon olive oil, 1 tablespoon sherry vinegar, 2 tablespoons grated fresh Parmesan, 1 tablespoon water, and ¼ teaspoon smoked paprika in a food processor; process until smooth.

SERVES 4 *(serving size: ¼ cup)*
CALORIES 122; **FAT** 8.2g (sat 2g);
SODIUM 199mg

Hot Artichoke Dip

Full-flavored Parm adds cheesy goodness. Light cream cheese and mayo save 340 calories.

Preheat oven to 400°. Place 2 garlic cloves and 1 chopped green onion in a food processor; process until chopped. Add ⅓ cup grated fresh Parme-san, ⅓ cup light mayon-naise, ¼ cup ⅓-less-fat cream cheese, 1 table-spoon fresh lemon juice, and ¼ teaspoon crushed red pepper; process until almost smooth. Stir in 12 ounces thawed frozen artichoke hearts. Spoon mixture into a 3-cup gratin dish coated with cooking spray. Bake at 400° for 15 minutes.

SERVES 6 *(serving size: ¼ cup)*
CALORIES 102; **FAT** 6.2g (sat 2.4g);
SODIUM 235mg

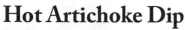

Smoked Salmon Dip

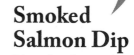

We cut the calories and sat fat in half with light cream cheese and sour cream.

Combine 4 ounces softened ⅓-less-fat cream cheese, 4 ounces light sour cream, 2 tablespoons chopped fresh dill, 1 tablespoon fresh lemon juice, 4 ounces chopped smoked salmon, and 2 tablespoons chopped red onion in a medium bowl. Garnish with additional dill.

SERVES 6 *(serving size: ¼ cup)*
CALORIES 99; **FAT** 7.1g (sat 3.8g);
SODIUM 225mg

It's dip season: New Year's Eve, Super Bowl Sunday, Oscar night. These makeovers save tons of fat and calories on ¼-cup servings.

Creamy Spinach and Feta Dip

Bright and tangy nonfat Greek yogurt helps save 100 calories and 3g sat fat.

Place 6 ounces nonfat Greek yogurt, ¾ cup crumbled feta cheese, 2 ounces softened ⅓-less-fat cream cheese, ¼ cup low-fat sour cream, and 1 crushed garlic clove in a food processor; process until smooth. Spoon yogurt mixture into a medium bowl; stir in 1½ cups finely chopped fresh spinach, 1 tablespoon chopped fresh dill, and ⅛ teaspoon black pepper. Cover and chill.

SERVES 8 *(serving size: ¼ cup)* **CALORIES** 75; **FAT** 5.1g (sat 3.3g); **SODIUM** 181mg

actual size

DIPPER CALORIE MATH

A scoop-shaped chip can easily hold a tablespoon of dip—after four, you've noshed through a ¼-cup serving. Dip lightly, in other words. But the easiest way to cut calories is to use crunchy vegetables as dippers.

DIPPER EQUIVALENTS (1 OZ.)

13 tortilla chips:
140 calories

10 baked pita chips:
132 calories

6 whole-grain crackers:
122 calories

3 crostini with olive oil:
110 calories

15 cucumber coins, carrot sticks, etc.:
10 calories

Simple Guacamole

There's no credible way to lighten guac since the main ingredient—avocado—is high in fat. But it's the heart-healthy kind.

Place 2 large ripe peeled avocados in a medium bowl, and mash roughly with a fork. Add 1 tablespoon fresh lime juice, ¼ teaspoon kosher salt, and 1 minced garlic clove; mash to desired consistency. Stir in 2 tablespoons chopped fresh cilantro.

SERVES 6 *(serving size: ¼ cup)*
CALORIES 109; **FAT** 9.8g (sat 1.4g); **SODIUM** 85mg

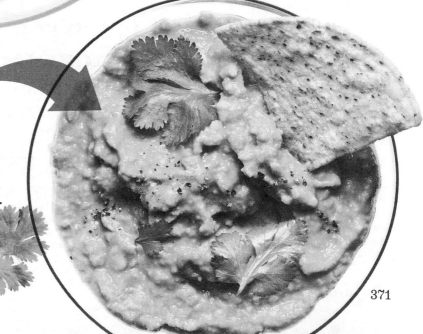

371

The Truth about Salt in the Kitchen

Does a longer brine add much salt?

Naturally lean meats, like turkey and pork, benefit from a brine. We wondered if sodium goes up with time, and if so, how much.

THE TEST

We soaked three 12-pound turkeys in a brining solution that contained ½ cup of kosher salt (that's about 46,000mg sodium!) for 12, 18, and 24 hours. For comparison, we also analyzed an unbrined bird.

THE RESULTS

(per 4 ounces roasted turkey)
No brine: white meat, 55mg; dark meat, 90mg
12-hour brine: white meat, 151mg; dark meat, 235mg
18-hour brine: white meat, 186mg; dark meat, 254mg
24-hour brine: white meat, 223mg; dark meat, 260mg

The largest sodium increase happens in the first 12 hours. It then tapers off, but the tenderizing continues. Only about 1% of the total sodium from the brine is absorbed.
Bottom line: If you like a longer brine (we prefer 24 hours), the added sodium isn't that significant. Brine for texture reasons, and put away sodium fears.

Kosher turkeys may have 200mg per 4 ounces due to the processing method. Frozen turkeys may have been washed in salt water to speed the freezing, adding 200 to 350mg per 4 ounces. And some birds are enhanced with up to 15% broth, which adds 330 to 440mg per 4 ounces. Check your labels.

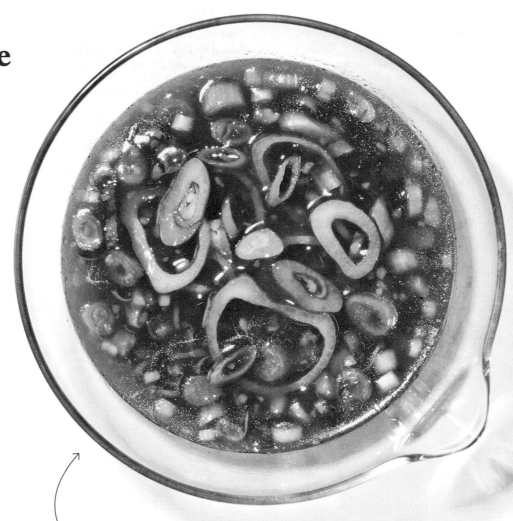

How much sodium does meat absorb from a salty marinade?

As you see with brining, sodium helps break down proteins. The acidic ingredients in a marinade do the same for connective tissues, all the while imparting flavor to the surface of the meat.

THE TEST

We marinated a pork tenderloin in a simple marinade of lower-sodium soy sauce, sesame oil, green onions, garlic, black pepper, and ginger for 1.5 hours, and then grilled the tenderloin.

Unmarinated grilled pork: 54mg sodium *per 3 ounces*

THE RESULTS

Only 6% of the salt was absorbed by the pork, but it quadrupled the sodium count in the meat.
Bottom line: Let sodium do its work; then cut back salt in any sauces or other ingredients.

Marinated grilled pork: 276mg sodium *per 3 ounces*

We put 5 common cooking techniques to the test to see just how much sodium they add to your diet.

The saltier the water, the saltier the pasta.

Many chefs implore home cooks to heavily salt pasta cooking water ("make it as salty as the ocean," says one popular TV chef). Yes, salt does enhance the pasta's flavor. But so do the sauce and other ingredients, which may be salted, too. As our tests show, sodium-wary cooks need to moderate the hand that salts the water.

THE TEST

We boiled a pound each of dry spaghetti (sodium-free) in 4 quarts of water containing varying amounts of salt.

THE RESULTS

(per 6 ounces cooked pasta)
1 teaspoon salt (2,360mg sodium): 75mg sodium
1 tablespoon salt (7,080mg sodium): 253mg sodium
2 tablespoons salt (14,160mg sodium): 446mg sodium
¼ cup salt (28,319mg sodium): 896mg sodium

Bottom line: It's not that pasta soaks up salt like a sponge: Only 3% was absorbed into each serving of pasta. But 3% of the sodium in ¼ cup is 896mg—nearly 40% of your 2,300mg daily limit. So reduce (don't eliminate) the salt in the water; save it for the sauce.

How big is your "pinch" of salt?

We asked a dozen staffers—editors and Test Kitchen folks—to give us a pinch of salt. Weights ranged from 0.06 to 1.32g, averaging 0.48g. Half a gram contains about 180mg sodium. A pinch that size per day for a year equals 65,700mg sodium!
Bottom line: Know your pinch—or measure.

Can you rinse the salt off canned beans?

Salt is used by food manufacturers to enhance flavor—we've seen more than 500mg in just ½ cup of beans. That's why we call for canned beans to be rinsed and drained before preparing.

THE TEST

We rinsed, drained, and then tested two varieties of beans and compared them with their unwashed counterparts.

THE RESULTS

Black Beans
Sodium in ½ cup: 424mg
Sodium in ½ cup, rinsed and drained: 232mg

Red Kidney Beans
Sodium in ½ cup: 260mg
Sodium in ½ cup, rinsed and drained: 148mg

Bottom line: The beans lose more than 40% of their sodium when rinsed and drained.

Salt in the Supermarket

Surprising discoveries about everyday foods. And a few takeout-food findings, too.

Why some shrimp are saltier than others.

When fresh shrimp are frozen (often just minutes after being caught), they are washed in a saline solution to help bring their temperature down faster. Quicker chilling prevents ice crystals from forming inside the shrimp, resulting in better texture when defrosted; it also helps keep them from clumping together as they freeze. "Easy-peel" shrimp are soaked in an additional sodium solution. Pro: They slip out of their shells effortlessly. Con: More salt. How much more?

THE TEST

We steamed and peeled five varieties of shrimp, and then shipped them to the lab for sodium analysis.

THE RESULTS

(per 4 ounces steamed)

Wild-caught fresh Gulf shrimp (never frozen): 97mg

Farm-raised fresh shrimp (previously frozen): 159mg

Winn-Dixie individually quick-frozen easy-to-peel wild-caught shrimp: 245mg

Whole Foods individually quick-frozen easy-to-peel shrimp: 483mg

Publix fresh frozen easy-to-peel farm-raised shrimp: 730mg

Why some salt labels don't tell the whole story.

Food labels generally tell you what's in the package, not what will be in the food after cooking. Here's a dramatic example of what that can mean for the home cook.

Soba noodle labels list as much as 900mg sodium per serving—which has limited our use of it. But when we boiled five brands of soba, they lost an average of 80% of their sodium, down to about 80mg per serving. The FDA only requires labels to list the nutritional properties of foods as packaged. Food makers may voluntarily present "as prepared" information, but that's an extra step, and calculation, for them. Most foods used in cooking are rarely consumed as packaged—like soba noodles.

Bottom line: Always consider the ingredients added and methods used in preparing foods.

One bundle of soba serves two people. About 80% of the sodium is lost in the cooking process.

Iodized Table Salt
543mg

Kosher Salt
546mg

Black Sea Salt
556mg

Coarse Sea Salt
561mg

Pink Sea Salt
587mg

Fine Sea Salt
600mg

Why coarser salt doesn't yield automatic sodium savings.

It's conventional wisdom that big-grained salt contains about 25% less sodium by volume than table salt. The idea: Coarse crystals don't pack tightly and take up more space in a measuring spoon (with lots of air between them), meaning you consume less sodium. Labels on one brand show a 110mg difference between ¼ teaspoon of their table and kosher salts; that's a 19% savings if you use kosher. But our analysis of six salts showed less variation per ¼ teaspoon than you might think. **Bottom line:** If you're watching sodium, you can't throw "gourmet" salts around with impunity.

Plus!

How salty are popular takeout foods?

Fast-food chains post data on their websites: Hardee's Monster Thickburger contains almost 3,000mg sodium. But most small, local restaurants don't post nutrition information. We got takeout from three in our town to see how entrées stacked up. They stacked up really, really high.

Trattoria pizza topped with cured meats, sausage, and olives:
3,474mg sodium

Barbecue pulled-pork sandwich with baked beans and slaw:
2,480mg sodium

Bowl of ramen with miso broth:
3,245mg sodium

Our fave sauce: a cautionary tale

We've long recommended McCutcheon's bottled marinara sauce because of its great flavor and the low sodium level on its label—only 185mg per half-cup listed. When we tested three batches, though, they came in at more than three times that number. We talked to Vanessa McCutcheon-Smith, and she attributed the difference to a change in the supplier of the canned tomatoes they use as a base (no salt is added during the cooking). It's not routine to test a batch when the tomatoes change, she explained—only to calculate nutrition based on numbers provided by suppliers.

"Knowing what I know about how things change on the supply chain, I don't put a lot of merit in the information on food panels," she added.

Nutrition label numbers are allowed 20% of wiggle room, but the FDA does few random audits. As a general rule: Trust your taste buds; if something tastes salty, it probably is, whatever the label says.

Michael's of Brooklyn and Dell' Amore are tasty and pretty low in sodium—on their labels and in our lab tests.

Navigating the *mile-long* Yogurt Aisle

Artisanal

Small producers favor **fewer preservatives, grass-fed milk.** Prices are higher. Fat runs from none to lots: "Natural" doesn't automatically mean low-fat. Some niche producers are playing up the rich, cream-on-top angle. Read your labels.

Nondairy

A hot category. **Soy, almond, and coconut milks** have less protein and require extra sugars to promote fermentation—as much as 16g. As with some dairy yogurts, plant-derived thickeners (starches, gums, etc.) are added to improve texture.

Greek

Big tang and thick texture kicked off the yogurt boom: **Strained milk,** with less water, has more protein and milk solids. Tangy doesn't mean extra-light, though. We saw 11g sat fat in one (6-ounce) version.

WHAT TO LOOK FOR

Protein: Keeps you full longer

Strained yogurts—like Greek and skyr—require three to four times more milk to produce than regular, meaning 15g to 20g more protein per 6 ounces **(equivalent to 3 ounces of meat!).**

Healthy bacteria

The FDA requires **at least two strains of bacteria in all yogurt,** *L. bulgaricus* and *S. thermophilus.* Yogurt makers can add more. Look for the National Yogurt Association seal: It ensures 100 million cultures per gram (i.e., lots).

Low-fat, for a calcium boost

When fat is removed, calcium gets concentrated. Lower-fat yogurt contains more—**30% of your recommended daily intake.** Some calcium is lost in the straining process for Greek, but it's still a great source at 20%.

Sales are way up, and shelves are sagging with choices (Greek-style almond-milk yogurt?). But some are packed with fat. Here, a tour.

Kefir

Kefir is a more liquid and naturally effervescent dairy product that uses yeast in addition to bacteria for fermentation. It's good for smoothies, and the extra probiotics—as many as 12 strains (versus the 2 required in yogurt)—aid in digestion.

Budget

Bigger containers only seem expensive. Unless there's a four-for-$5 deal on the small cups, you can get up to 32 ounces for the same price as three (6-ounce) containers. Bonus: They're usually plain with no added sugars—or calories.

OUR FAVES

Fage Total Plain 2%
"My daily breakfast companion. Add a handful of blueberries, and I'm set."
—Sidney Fry, Nutrition Editor

Atlanta Fresh
"My hometown! I love the vanilla caramel. And pretty packaging doesn't hurt."
—Rachel Lasserre, Art Director

Smari Organic Icelandic
"Nonfat, less tangy than some Greeks, creamy and light texture. Try the blueberry."
—Scott Mowbray, Editor

Limited added sugar

Six ounces of plain yogurt have about **12g of naturally occurring sugars** from the milk. Fruit and honey add more. Kid-centric yogurts come in cute 4-ounce containers, but some have more sugar (as much as 17g) than "adult" 6-ouncers.

More calories in the morning

If you're eating yogurt as breakfast, you'll need more oomph to keep you fueled until lunch—about 200 calories, but no more than 4g sat fat. Keep snacks less hefty—about half that.

100-Calorie Breakfast Swaps

One ounce of flavored syrup has about 70 calories.

INSTEAD OF A	ORDER THE	EVEN BETTER
VANILLA FRAPPUCCINO	ICED VANILLA LATTE	MAKE IT SKINNY & PLAIN

Even with 2% milk and no whipped cream, a 16-ounce Frappuccino contains 300 calories, mostly from the whopping 67g of sugar. Switch to an iced 2% vanilla latte, and save 40g. Skip the flavoring and order fat-free milk for a refreshing sip with only 11g sugar.

INSTEAD OF	POUR A BOWL OF	INSTEAD OF	FILL WITH
A BRAN MUFFIN	RAISIN BRAN	HAM & CHEDDAR	VEGGIES & CHÈVRE

Coffeehouse muffins can weigh in at 400 calories or more. Eat your bran with a spoon, using ⅔ cup 1% low-fat milk. Bonus points: 2g more fiber than the muffin and 200mg bone-building calcium.

Rebuild the three-egg omelet. Discard one of the yolks, and trade the cheddar and ham for fresh spinach, tomatoes, and an ounce of goat cheese (keep the peppers). You'll also save about 300mg sodium.

Canned cinnamon rolls have more than 650mg sodium.

INSTEAD OF	MAKE YOUR OWN	INSTEAD OF	TOAST TWO SLICES OF
A PREMADE PARFAIT	AT HOME	A CINNAMON ROLL	RAISIN BREAD

Many grab-and-go parfaits are full of syrupy, sugar-coated fruit—more dessert than breakfast. Build your own with 6 ounces fat-free yogurt, syrup-free fresh peaches, and 2 tablespoons low-fat granola.

Slather two—yes, two—slices of toasted raisin bread with 1 tablespoon ⅓-less-fat cream cheese sweetened with 1 teaspoon powdered sugar. Sprinkle with cinnamon.

Small changes can help you lose 1 pound per month. Here are 12 ways to shave 100 calories or more at breakfast. That's 12 minutes on the treadmill.

INSTEAD OF
BUTTER & SYRUP

TOP PANCAKES WITH
PECANS & YOGURT

EVEN BETTER
BEAUTIFUL BERRIES

Trade the butter for nonfat Greek yogurt, and swap 1 tablespoon maple syrup for 1 tablespoon chopped pecans. Shave off another 100 calories by making it a short stack (two 6-inch cakes instead of three), and top with 1/2 cup fresh berries.

Champagne has 40 fewer calories per ounce than vodka.

INSTEAD OF A
BLOODY MARY

SIP A
BUBBLY MIMOSA

A 12-ounce Bloody Mary contains two shots of vodka—the main source of calories—and four-digit sodium numbers. Whoa, Mary! Portion-size plus: The mimosa also comes in a sleek 8-ounce glass.

INSTEAD OF
LOX, SCHMEAR, BAGEL

CUT CARBS WITH
PUMPERNICKEL

Enjoy your lox and cream cheese open-faced on a slice of whole-grain pumpernickel instead of the 300-calorie bagel. Cut back on capers by 1/2 tablespoon, and you'll also save 125mg sodium.

INSTEAD OF
HIGH-CAL TOPPINGS

TOP OATS WITH
APPLES & HONEY

Calories from cream, brown sugar, and nuts can quickly weigh down a virtuous bowl of oats. Add crunch with apples, creaminess with nonfat Greek yogurt, and yum with a touch of honey and cinnamon.

Center-cut bacon has 33% less fat than regular.

INSTEAD OF
SAUSAGE PATTIES

FRY UP SOME
CENTER-CUT BACON

You can still be seduced by salty, fatty breakfast pork from time to time. Center-cut bacon has only 25 calories per slice. It still has nearly 200mg sodium, though, so indulge in moderation.

★★★★★
Brew a Fresh Fruit Sangria

Skip the sugar-packed margarita mixes, and stir up this sparkling 140-calorie treat. It's sweetened with real fruit and saves 30g sugar. Combine 1 cup pitted and halved cherries, 1 cup blueberries, 1 cup quartered strawberries, 1/2 cup chopped peaches, and 1/3 cup brandy in a large pitcher; chill 2 hours. Stir in 1 cup pineapple juice and 1 (750-milliliter) bottle chilled prosecco. Garnish with fresh mint. Serves 8. **Savings: 160 calories**

★★★★★
Lay on Lots of Crunchy Crudités

Give the chips and onion dip a day off. Nosh instead on a platter of fresh vegetables, and serve with our simple, creamy herb dip: Combine 4 ounces 1/3-less-fat cream cheese, 1/4 cup nonfat buttermilk, 2 tablespoons chopped fresh chives, 1 tablespoon chopped fresh parsley, 1 tablespoon fresh lemon juice, 1/4 teaspoon salt, and 2 minced garlic cloves; beat with a mixer until smooth. **Savings: 150 calories**

★
Slim the Slaw

A little heart-healthy canola mayo goes a long way to keep our slaw creamy, while mustard seeds and a pinch of ground red pepper boost flavor (recipe on page 162). You'll also cut out 14g fat and 300mg sodium. **Savings: 166 calories**

★
Potato Salad, Yes. Mayo, No.

Shave calories and sodium with our version, which tosses crisp-tender taters in a tangy herb-infused olive oil sauce (recipe on page 162). **Savings: 115 calories**

Patriotic-print muffin liners promote just-right trifle portions.

This may be your biggest cookout of the year. Here are ways to keep the meal bursting with patriotic flavor—with way fewer calories.

Light beer instead of sangria? It's about 100 calories.

★
Make Baked Beans Better
Dress up organic navy beans with fresh thyme and center-cut bacon. Our recipe (page 163) also saves 600mg sodium over canned pork 'n' beans. **Savings: 192 calories**

★★★★★
Trim the Trifle
Billowing clouds of whipped cream send a traditional patriotic trifle into 500-plus calorie territory. Keep the berry goodness and light texture with angel food cake, but swap the cream for 12 ounces reduced-calorie whipped topping spiked with 2 tablespoons Grand Marnier. You'll save 15g sat fat with this lighter layer. **Savings: 250 calories**

Pressed for time? Trade the trifle for ice-cream sandwiches— a cool, handheld, 160-calorie treat.

★★★★★
Build a Leaner Burger
Start with a 90% lean ground beef base to save 100 calories and 4g sat fat (per raw 4-ounce patty) over the 80/20 grind. A thin slice of cheese adds melty goodness for just 45 calories. Guacamole adds creamy zip with only 25 calories per tablespoon and 120mg less sodium than ketchup. Finish with farm-fresh tomatoes, red onion, and crisp greens for super-low-calorie flavor and crunch. **Savings: 230 calories**

Serve with whole-wheat buns for a 3g fiber boost over white.

100-Calorie Snack Swaps

INSTEAD OF 100% TRADITIONAL TRAIL MIX	**CUT THE MIX WITH** GOOD WHOLE GRAINS	**EVEN BETTER** NIX THE NUTS

Packed with nuts, dried fruit, and chocolate, trail mix has about 350 calories per ½ cup—great for sustaining hikers, a bit much for desk jockeys. Cut the trail mix in half, and swap in ⅓ cup whole-grain cereal. Skip the nuts, and you'll shave 100 more calories.

INSTEAD OF CHOCOLATE ALMONDS	**SPREAD CHOC & NUTS** ON A GRAHAM	**INSTEAD OF A** LEMON-LIME SODA	**STIR UP A** LEMON SPARKLER

Just two handfuls of the almonds will set you back about 240 calories. Try smearing 2 teaspoons chocolate-hazelnut spread on a graham cracker. Top with 1 teaspoon chopped nuts. You'll save 16g sugar, too.

Liquid calories are part of the snack budget, too. A 12-ounce can of soda contains 36g sugar—nearly 3 tablespoons. Instead, mix 4 ounces lemonade with 8 ounces sparkling water. Garnish with a lemon slice.

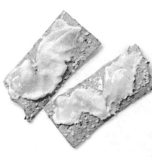

INSTEAD OF CHEESE IN A CRACKER	**SPREAD IT ON A** FLATBREAD	**INSTEAD OF** BAGGED POPCORN	**AIR-POP** YOUR OWN

Trade the cheese-filled cracker-sandwich pack for this easy sweet-salty-savory combo: Spread 1 tablespoon part-skim ricotta on each of 2 thin, crisp multigrain flatbreads. Drizzle with 1 teaspoon honey.

Buttery bagged popcorn can weigh in at 250 calories in a 3-cup serving. Pick air-popped instead, and sprinkle with 2 tablespoons grated Parmesan: 100 calories saved. Bonus sodium savings: 100mg.

Snacking powers you between meals, but it's easy to overdo it. These swaps save 100 calories or more—and often cut sugar and sodium, too.

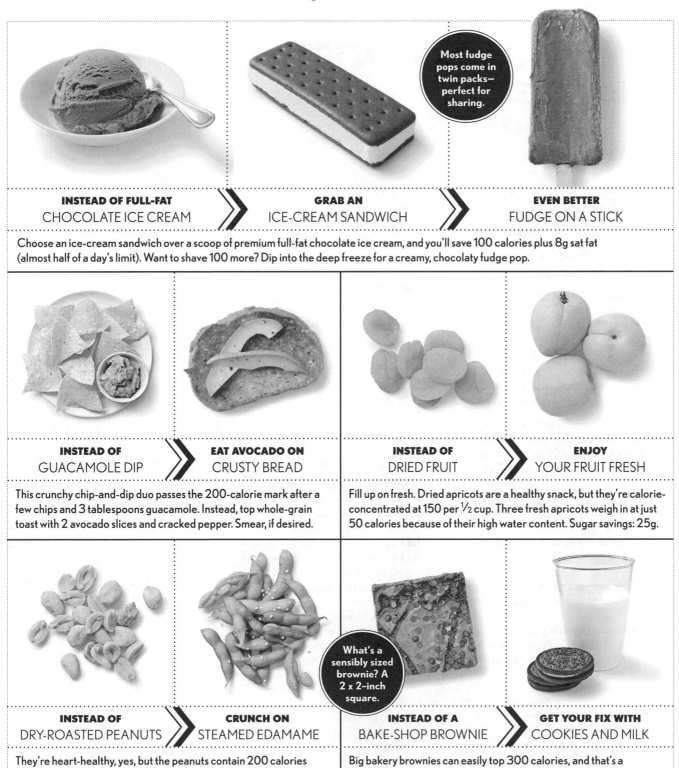

Most fudge pops come in twin packs—perfect for sharing.

INSTEAD OF FULL-FAT
CHOCOLATE ICE CREAM

GRAB AN
ICE-CREAM SANDWICH

EVEN BETTER
FUDGE ON A STICK

Choose an ice-cream sandwich over a scoop of premium full-fat chocolate ice cream, and you'll save 100 calories plus 8g sat fat (almost half of a day's limit). Want to shave 100 more? Dip into the deep freeze for a creamy, chocolaty fudge pop.

INSTEAD OF
GUACAMOLE DIP

EAT AVOCADO ON
CRUSTY BREAD

INSTEAD OF
DRIED FRUIT

ENJOY
YOUR FRUIT FRESH

This crunchy chip-and-dip duo passes the 200-calorie mark after a few chips and 3 tablespoons guacamole. Instead, top whole-grain toast with 2 avocado slices and cracked pepper. Smear, if desired.

Fill up on fresh. Dried apricots are a healthy snack, but they're calorie-concentrated at 150 per ½ cup. Three fresh apricots weigh in at just 50 calories because of their high water content. Sugar savings: 25g.

What's a sensibly sized brownie? A 2 x 2-inch square.

INSTEAD OF
DRY-ROASTED PEANUTS

CRUNCH ON
STEAMED EDAMAME

INSTEAD OF A
BAKE-SHOP BROWNIE

GET YOUR FIX WITH
COOKIES AND MILK

They're heart-healthy, yes, but the peanuts contain 200 calories per ¼ cup. Trade legume for legume with ½ cup shelled edamame, sprinkled with 1 teaspoon toasted sesame seeds.

Big bakery brownies can easily top 300 calories, and that's a conservative figure. Two chocolate cream-filled cookies have just 106, leaving room to dunk them in 8 ounces of 1% low-fat milk.

What's Your Portion Personality?

ALL-DAY SNACKER

Portion Problem

Snacks go straight from box or bag to mouth. A handful here, a handful there ... who's counting?

What to Do

It's easy to confuse thirst for hunger. **Please the palate with tea instead** of automatically reaching for food.

Make sure you **have access to healthy, low-calorie fruits and vegetables.** An apple has about 95 calories; a bag of Peanut M&M's has nearly 300.

Popcorn is a filling, healthy snack. **Opt for the mini bags,** which pop into about 5 cups, instead of the big bags, which contain up to 12 cups popped. Even better: air-popped.

100-calorie packs work, as long as you eat just one. Save money: Make your own.

Preportion tempting munchies into snack-sized bags. Read labels on big bags for recommended servings, and take only one serving with you.

A package equals 7½ snack bags.

CAVEMAN

Portion Problem

Buy meat. Cook meat. Eat meat. But the meat packages at PaleoMart are not portioned for individual servings.

14-ounce steak = **3 servings**

What to Do

Here's the beef: Cuts at supermarkets look like cuts at steak houses—too big. Even leaner tenderloins average about 8 ounces. **Grill your steak of choice, let it rest a bit, and then thinly slice.** Take a few pieces for dinner (weigh them until you can eyeball the portion), and save the leftovers for lunch.

Slice a 10-ounce supermarket chicken breast in half lengthwise into two 5-ounce cutlets (they'll cook faster, too). Or try a thigh, a smaller, juicier choice with only 1 additional gram of sat fat per ounce.

Try the smaller-plate trick. Those **smaller cuts won't look so diminutive on 8-inch lunch plates.**

Buy bone-in. Bones take up space and weight (and sometimes add flavor), so there is less meat to eat.

SWEET TOOTH

Portion Problem

Candy is never far from reach. Pans of brownies slowly disappear sliver by sliver. Ice cream travels from freezer to sofa via pint-sized container.

What to Do

Precut goodies in the pan or pie plate. An 8-inch pan divided into 16 pieces yields a brownie with 44% fewer calories than a pan divided by 9.

Hide the candy. Out of sight, out of mind. Better yet: **Put your stash where you have to walk to get a handful.**

Mini ice-cream cups are perfect ½-cup portions. If you prefer to dip from the gallon container, use a scoop (it dishes out a ½-cup serving).

If you like candy bars, buy the mini size. A big bag divides up into many calorie-reasonable snacks.

1 bar is 9 minis is 3 snacks!

Even the most careful eaters and cooks let their inner portion police take a holiday. And that's when the calories pile on. Here, some help.

SOCIAL BUTTERFLY

Portion Problem

Both work and social life involve meeting for drinks, hanging at bars, having wine before dinner ...

2 servings

What to Do

The USDA recommends no more than one drink a day for women, two for men. **That's 5 ounces of wine, 12 ounces of beer, or 1.5 ounces of liquor.** Most bars use 1.5-ounce shots, but if yours doesn't, just ask. If you're having more than one, alternate with seltzer and lime, or spiced-up tomato juice.

Another use for that shot glass: It holds one portion of mixed nuts (170 calories).

For beer, **sip an 8-ounce glass of craft-brew draft.** It's much more satisfying than two ultralight pints, with about the same amount of alcohol.

Wine with dinner? Restaurants like to pour liberally and equitably around the table. Either **order by the glass**—asking for 5 ounces—or tell the sommelier to go easy.

GRANOLA GUY

Portion Problem

Caveman's counterpart under-estimates the calorie count in carbs.

What to Do

Pour cereal into a coffee mug instead of a bowl, and you'll be less likely to overeat. It's the right vessel for a serving of cereal (which varies; check label) and ½ cup low-fat milk.

A typical hoagie or sub roll is three to four servings of bread. **Hollow out the center,** and you'll cut that almost in half.

When brown-bagging, **make sure you're using a zip-top sandwich bag.** At 5 inches square, sandwich bags are sized right for loaf bread. Quart-sized storage bags measure 7 inches—too big.

A box of pasta serves 8 to 10 people, not 4. **One cup of cooked noodles is one serving.** Load your plate with salad first, and then add the pasta.

8 cups of cooked pasta is 8 servings.

APPROXIMATOR

Portion Problem

Great cook. Adds ingredients and serves everything by sight and taste.

2 swirls around the pan = **2 tablespoons**

What to Do

Freehanding the oil can add 240 calories to a dish—a lot if it's supposed to serve only two. **Use a measuring spoon** until your eyeballing is accurate. Ditto with butter.

And ditto with salt. When we asked 12 people to freehand a pinch of salt, they added 180mg of sodium on average, 500 at worst. Work on your pinching, and **don't pour directly from the salt container**—keep a pinch bowl on the counter.

Know your sodium sources: fish sauce, sambals, pickles, etc.

Buy one of those nifty little digital scales. It's truly an eye-opener to see what an ounce of Parm, an ounce of bacon, and and an ounce of chocolate look like.

Portion carbs onto plates—rice, pasta, whole grains, mashed potatoes. Know what a serving is, and use a measuring cup.

NUTRITIONAL ANALYSIS

What the Numbers Mean For You

Glance at the end of any *Cooking Light* recipe, and you'll see how committed we are to helping you make the best of today's light cooking. With chefs, registered dietitians, home economists, and a computer system that analyzes every ingredient we use, *Cooking Light* gives you authoritative dietary detail like no other magazine. We go to such lengths so you can see how our recipes fit into your healthful eating plan. If you're trying to lose weight, the calorie and fat figures will probably help most. But if you're keeping a close eye on the sodium, cholesterol, and saturated fat in your diet, we provide those numbers, too. And because many women don't get enough iron or calcium, we can help there, as well. Finally, there's a fiber analysis for those of us who don't get enough roughage.

Here's a helpful guide to put our nutritional analysis numbers into perspective. Remember, one size doesn't fit all, so take your lifestyle, age, and circumstances into consideration when determining your nutrition needs. For example, pregnant or breast-feeding women need more protein, calories, and calcium. And women older than 50 need 1,200mg of calcium daily, 200mg more than the amount recommended for younger women.

IN OUR NUTRITIONAL ANALYSIS, WE USE THESE ABBREVIATIONS

sat	saturated fat	**CHOL**	cholesterol
mono	monounsaturated fat	**CALC**	calcium
poly	polyunsaturated fat	**g**	gram
CARB	carbohydrates	**mg**	milligram

Daily Nutrition Guide

	WOMEN ages 25 to 50	WOMEN over 50	MEN ages 25 to 50	MEN over 50
CALORIES	2,000	2,000*	2,700	2,500
PROTEIN	50g	50g	63g	60g
FAT	65g*	65g*	88g*	83g*
SATURATED FAT	20g*	20g*	27g*	25g*
CARBOHYDRATES	304g	304g	410g	375g
FIBER	25g to 35g	25g to 35g	25g to 35g	25g to 35g
CHOLESTEROL	300mg*	300mg*	300mg*	300mg*
IRON	18mg	8mg	8mg	8mg
SODIUM	2,300mg*	1,500mg*	2,300mg*	1,500mg*
CALCIUM	1,000mg	1,200mg	1,000mg	1,000mg

NUTRITIONAL VALUES USED IN OUR CALCULATIONS EITHER COME FROM THE FOOD PROCESSOR, VERSION 10.4 (ESHA RESEARCH) OR ARE PROVIDED BY FOOD MANUFACTURERS.
*Or less, for optimum health.

METRIC EQUIVALENTS

The information in the following charts is provided to help cooks outside the United States successfully use the recipes in this book. All equivalents are approximate.

Cooking/Oven Temperatures

	Fahrenheit	Celsius	Gas Mark
Freeze Water	32°F	0°C	
Room Temp.	68°F	20°C	
Boil Water	212°F	100°C	
Bake	325°F	160°C	3
	350°F	180°C	4
	375°F	190°C	5
	400°F	200°C	6
	425°F	220°C	7
	450°F	230°C	8
Broil			Grill

Liquid Ingredients by Volume

$\frac{1}{4}$ tsp	=					1 ml		
$\frac{1}{2}$ tsp	=					2 ml		
1 tsp	=					5 ml		
3 tsp	=	1 tbl	=	$\frac{1}{2}$ fl oz	=	15 ml		
2 tbls	=	$\frac{1}{8}$ cup	=	1 fl oz	=	30 ml		
4 tbls	=	$\frac{1}{4}$ cup	=	2 fl oz	=	60 ml		
5$\frac{1}{3}$ tbls	=	$\frac{1}{3}$ cup	=	3 fl oz	=	80 ml		
8 tbls	=	$\frac{1}{2}$ cup	=	4 fl oz	=	120 ml		
10$\frac{2}{3}$ tbls	=	$\frac{2}{3}$ cup	=	5 fl oz	=	160 ml		
12 tbls	=	$\frac{3}{4}$ cup	=	6 fl oz	=	180 ml		
16 tbls	=	1 cup	=	8 fl oz	=	240 ml		
1 pt	=	2 cups	=	16 fl oz	=	480 ml		
1 qt	=	4 cups	=	32 fl oz	=	960 ml		
				33 fl oz	=	1000 ml	=	1 l

Dry Ingredients by Weight

(To convert ounces to grams, multiply the number of ounces by 30.)

1 oz	=	$\frac{1}{16}$ lb	=	30 g
4 oz	=	$\frac{1}{4}$ lb	=	120 g
8 oz	=	$\frac{1}{2}$ lb	=	240 g
12 oz	=	$\frac{3}{4}$ lb	=	360 g
16 oz	=	1 lb	=	480 g

Length

(To convert inches to centimeters, multiply the number of inches by 2.5.)

1 in	=			2.5 cm		
6 in	=	$\frac{1}{2}$ ft	=	15 cm		
12 in	=	1 ft	=	30 cm		
36 in	=	3 ft	=	1 yd	=	90 cm
40 in	=			100 cm	=	1 m

Equivalents for Different Types of Ingredients

Standard Cup	Fine Powder (ex. flour)	Grain (ex. rice)	Granular (ex. sugar)	Liquid Solids (ex. butter)	Liquid (ex. milk)
1	140 g	150 g	190 g	200 g	240 ml
$\frac{3}{4}$	105 g	113 g	143 g	150 g	180 ml
$\frac{2}{3}$	93 g	100 g	125 g	133 g	160 ml
$\frac{1}{2}$	70 g	75 g	95 g	100 g	120 ml
$\frac{1}{3}$	47 g	50 g	63 g	67 g	80 ml
$\frac{1}{4}$	35 g	38 g	48 g	50 g	60 ml
$\frac{1}{8}$	18 g	19 g	24 g	25 g	30 ml

MENU INDEX

A topical guide to all the menus that appear in *Cooking Light Annual Recipes 2014.* See page 403 for the General Recipe Index.

DINNER TONIGHT

30-Minute Dinners

BEEF

(page 203) *serves 4*
Grilled Sirloin Steak with Mango and Chile Salad
Coconut-Ginger Rice

(page 267) *serves 4*
Steak with Lemon-Herb Pesto and Spinach Salad
Quick Mashed Potatoes

(page 363) *serves 4*
Seared Steak with Braised Leeks and Chard
Mustard Mashed Potatoes

FISH & SHELLFISH

(page 66) *serves 4*
Halibut with Olive and Bell Pepper Couscous
Lemon-Garlic Asparagus

(page 177) *serves 4*
Shrimp and Herb Salad
Garlic-Parmesan Toasts

(page 205) *serves 4*
Clams with Israeli Couscous
Wilted Swiss Chard and Mushrooms

(page 364) *serves 4*
Citrus-Glazed Shrimp with Cilantro Rice
Avocado and Radish Salad

LAMB

(page 204) *serves 4*
Ground Lamb and Hummus Pita "Pizzas"
Tomato, Sweet Onion, and Parsley Salad

PORK

(page 67) *serves 4*
Pork Chops with Tangy Red Currant Sauce
Mashed Potatoes
Lemon-Mint Peas

(page 150) *serves 4*
Grilled Pork Chops with Nectarines
Bacon-Herb Salad

(page 361) *serves 6*
Chickpea and Sausage Minestrone
Ciabatta Parmesan Toasts

POULTRY

(page 179) *serves 4*
Hoisin-Grilled Chicken with Soba Noodles
Cucumber-Peanut Salad

(page 333) *serves 4*
Creamy Sweet Potato Soup
Parmesan Cheese Toasts

(page 362) *serves 4*
Pepper Jelly-Glazed Chicken with Almond-Green Onion Quinoa
Snap Pea and Bell Pepper Sauté

VEGETARIAN

(page 263) *serves 4*
Kale and Caramelized Onion Grilled Cheese
Poblano-Tomato Soup

40-Minute Dinners

BEEF

(page 44) *serves 4*
Pan-Seared Steak with Chive-Horseradish Butter
Roasted Sweet Potatoes and Broccolini

(page 45) *serves 4*
Quick Beef Stroganoff
Grainy Mustard Brussels Sprouts

(page 122) *serves 4*
Grilled Asian Flank Steak with Mango Salad
Sesame Wonton Crisps

(page 180) *serves 4*
Seared Steaks with Red Wine-Cherry Sauce
Almond Green Beans
Dijon Smashed Potatoes

(page 292) *serves 4*
Pasta with Roasted-Tomato Meat Sauce
Mint and Pea Pesto on Toasted Baguette

(page 294) *serves 4*
Herb-Rubbed New York Strip with Sautéed Peas and Carrots
Roasted Potato Wedges

Meals Under 40 Minutes

CHICKEN DINNERS

RECIPE TITLE INDEX

An alphabetical listing of every recipe title that appeared in the magazine in 2013. See page 403 for the General Recipe Index.

MONTH-BY-MONTH INDEX

A month-by-month listing of every food story with recipe titles that appeared in the magazine in 2013. See page 403 for the General Recipe Index.

April

40 Meals Under 40 Minutes

May

August

September

Cooking Light's Big Guide to Food on the Move!

GENERAL RECIPE INDEX

A listing by major ingredient and food category for every recipe that appeared in the magazine in 2013.